The Big Fisherman

Books by Lloyd C. Douglas

Magnificent Obsession
Forgive Us Our Trespasses
Precious Jeopardy
Green Light
White Banners
Disputed Passage
Home for Christmas
Doctor Hudson's Secret Journal
Invitation To Live
The Robe
The Big Fisherman
Time to Remember

The Big Fisherman

BY *Lloyd C. Douglas*

ILLUSTRATED BY *Dean Cornwell*

PEOPLES BOOK CLUB

Chicago

This is a special edition published
exclusively for the members of the PEOPLES BOOK CLUB,
P.O. Box 6570A, Chicago 80, Illinois, and
228 Bloor Street West, Toronto 5,
Ontario, Canada

PRINTED IN THE U.S.A.

In appreciation of his constant kindness and encouragement in all weathers,
this book is affectionately dedicated to
JOHN WELDON ("WEARY") WILSON

The Big Fisherman

1

IT WAS a calm, early summer noon in the southern mountains of Arabia. Sheltering the King's well-guarded domain, a mile above and a dozen miles east of the Dead Sea, motionless masses of neighborly white clouds hung suspended from a remote blue ceiling.

There had been an unusually heavy snowfall in the winter, not only upon the King's land but throughout the country. It was going to be a prosperous season for everybody. Inter-tribal jangling and discontent would be reduced to a minimum. Arabia anticipated a relatively peaceful summer.

Viewed from the main entrance to the King's encampment the undulating plateau was a rich pasture on which a thousand newly shorn sheep, indifferent to the rough nuzzling of their hungry lambs, grazed greedily as if some instinct warned that there might be a famine next season.

Nor was a famine improbable, for the distribution of snow was unpredictable. Almost never were two consecutive winters partial to the same area. This accounted for the nomadic habits of the people. They held no permanent property, built no permanent homes. They lived in tents; and, with their flocks, followed the snow and the grass. All but the King, whose encampment was a fixed establishment. When the King had a dry season the tribes replenished his purse.

And few ever complained about this assessment, for the crown in Arabia was more than an ornament worn on state occasions. The King was indispensable in this country. He earned his wages and his honors. It required a strong and courageous man to deal equitably with these restless, reckless, competitive tribesmen who were distinguished throughout the East for the brevity of their tempers and the dexterity of their knives.

It had been a long time since Arabia had been governed by a ruler with the moral and physical strength of King Aretas. Everyone respected his relentless administration of justice to the rich and poor alike. There was no favoritism. They all admired his firmness, feared his frown, and—for the most part—obeyed his decrees.

Of course it would have been foolish to say that the Arabian people were sentimentally devoted to Aretas. In his difficult position he could not bid for their affection: he wanted only their obedience; prompt obedience and plenty of it. But there were a few who did sincerely love the taciturn, sober-faced, cold-blooded Aretas.

First of all there was his motherless daughter Arnon, upon whom he bestowed a tenderness that would have amazed the predatory sheiks who had often been stilled to sullen silence under his hot chastisements. And there was battle-scarred old Kedar, who had taught him to ride when he was a mere lad of ten, who had watched him draw a man's bow to full torsion when he was in his early teens, and had followed him worshipfully into all his hazardous adventures as Prince and King. And there were his twelve Counsellors who, in varying degrees, shared his confidence. Especially there was Ilderan, Chief of the King's Council. And young Zendi, Ilderan's eldest son who, everyone surmised, would presently marry the Princess Arnon with whom he was reputed to be much in love. Surely the wedding would be soon, they thought, for the Princess had recently celebrated her sixteenth birthday.

The tribesmen, who rarely agreed about anything, were unanimous in their approval of this alliance. Not only was Arnon popular for her beauty, and Zendi for his almost foolhardy courage, but—taking a long view of their marriage—there might come a day when Zendi would be their ruler; for if an Arabian King was without male issue the throne passed to the house of the Chief Counsellor. Ilderan was nearing sixty. If anything were to happen to Aretas, which was not inconceivable, considering how dangerously he lived, the gallant young Zendi might succeed him. This would be generally acceptable. All Arabia looked forward to the royal wedding. It would be a great occasion. It would last for a week. There woud be games, races and feasting.

*   *   *   *   *   *

In the shade of a clump of willows sheltering a walled spring, not far from the royal encampment, Arnon was awaiting the return of her father who had ridden early to the camp of Ilderan, seven miles east. She had joined him at breakfast, shortly after dawn, finding him moody and silent.

"Is anything amiss, my father?" Arnon had ventured to ask.

The King's reply was long delayed. Slowly lifting his eyes he had stared preoccupiedly at the tent-wall beyond her.

"Nothing you would know about," he had said, as from a distance.

Arnon had not pressed her query. Her father had made short work of his breakfast. At the tent-door he had turned to say, "I am consulting with Ilderan. I shall return by midday."

For a long time Arnon had sat alone, wondering what had happened. Perhaps it had something to do with the message her father had received yesterday. Of course there was nothing strange about the arrival of a courier with a message. It happened nearly every day. But this courier—she had seen him riding away—was apparently from afar. He was attended by a half-dozen servants with a well-laden pack-train. The donkeys had seemed cruelly overburdened. After the courier had departed, the King had retired to his own quarters. It was quite obvious that he did not want to be disturbed.

Arnon strolled restlessly about under the willows, her thoughts busily at work on the riddle. Presently her wide-set black eyes lighted as she saw her father coming up the well-worn trail, at full gallop, on his white stallion. She knew what to do. Emerging from the shade, Arnon stood beside the bridle-path with her shapely arms held high. Aretas leaned far to the left—the stallion suddenly slackening speed—and sweeping his arm about the girl's slim waist—swung her lightly over the horse's shoulder and into the saddle. Arnon laughed softly and pressed her cheek against her father's short, graying beard. No words were exchanged for a little while.

"You have something very serious on your mind, haven't you, Father?" murmured Arnon.

He drew the stallion down to an easy canter.

"I have had a strange message from Herod, the King of the Jews," said Aretas, slowing the impatient horse to a walk. "Herod wants me to meet him for a private conference, a fortnight hence, in the city of Petra."

"How fine for you, Father!" exclaimed Arnon. "You've always said you were going to visit that beautiful city!" Quickly noting her father's lack of enthusiasm, she inquired, "But—you're going; aren't you?"

"Yes—it sounds important."

"Is it not a long journey from Jerusalem to Petra? I wonder why the Jewish King wishes the conference held there?"

"Perhaps it is something that concerns Petra, too."

There was an interval of silence before Arnon spoke again.

"Is this not the first message you have ever had from the King of the Jews?"

"It is indeed! The first that has crossed our border for—" Aretas paused to reflect.

"A hundred years?" guessed Arnon.

"A thousand years!" said Aretas. "Many, many more than a thousand!"

"What do you make of it, Father? What does the Jewish King want of us?"

Aretas shook his head. They were arriving at the encampment now. Guards stepped out to meet them. Arnon was released from her father's arms and slipped lightly to the ground. Dismounting, the King beckoned to old Kedar, as his horse was led away.

"You will fit out an expedition to Petra. We are leaving on the third day of the week. The Counsellors will accompany us, and a guard of twenty riders. We may be tented at Petra for one day—or ten: it is not yet determined. The Counsellors will have had their instructions from Ilderan. You will attend to all the other arrangements."

"The festival tents?" inquired Kedar, implying that his sharp old eyes had observed the royal insignia on the accouterments of yesterday's courier.

"No," replied Aretas. "We will take only the equipment we commonly use when we visit the tribesmen."

Kedar bowed his gray head, his seamed face showing disappointment. He wanted to say that if the event was of high importance the King should make a better show of his royalty. He was turning away when Aretas spoke again, quite brusquely:

"And—Kedar—though you may have conjectured about the nature of our errand in Petra, if anyone should ask you what is afoot you will reply that you do not know. And that will be the truth."

*   *   *   *   *   *

Retiring to his private quarters, the King resumed his contemplation of the conundrum. What manner of emergency could have induced the proud and pompous Herod to ignore the age-old enmity between their nations?

For all of fifteen centuries, notwithstanding they were neighbors according to the map—their frontiers facing across an erratic little river that a boy could wade in midsummer—the Arabs and the Jews had been implacable foes. This ancient feud had not been rooted in racial incompatibility, though there was plenty of that too. The antipathy had derived from a definite incident that had occurred long ago; so very long ago that nobody knew how much of the story might be mythical. But—let the tale be half fact, half fiction—it accounted for the bitter hatred of these people.

According to the saga chanted about the Arabian campfires by wandering minstrels, a wise and wealthy migrant had ventured from Chaldea to the Plains of Mamre. It was a long story, but the minstrels never omitted their elaborate tribute to Chaldea as a land of seers and sages, oracles and astrologers. In Chaldea men dreamed prophetically and were entrusted with celestial secrets. Abraham, distinguished above them all for his learning, had received divine instructions to make a far journey southward and found a new nation.

But the prophecy was in danger of lacking fulfillment, for the years were passing and the founder of the new nation was childless. Sarah, his aging wife, was barren.

To solve this problem, the perplexed idealist had won the consent of his wife to permit his alliance with a beautiful young native in their employ. A son was born to them. They named him Ishmael. He was a handsome, headstrong, adventurous child, passionately devoted to his desert-born mother whom he closely resembled. Sarah, naturally enough, did not like him. Abraham admired the boy's vitality and courage, but Ishmael was quite a handful for the old man whose hours of pious meditation were becoming increasingly brief and confused.

To further complicate this domestic dilemma, Sarah surprised everybody by producing a son of her own. They named him Isaac. He was not a rugged child. His eyesight was defective; so defective that in his later life he had gone stone-blind. He was no match for his athletic half-brother. For a little while they all tried to be polite and conciliatory, but the inevitable conflict presently flared to alarming dimensions. Sarah no longer made any effort to control her bitter hatred for young Hagar and her tempestuous son. "These imposters," she shouted, shrilly, "must go! Today! Now!"

With appropriate misgivings, Abraham conducted Hagar and their indignant boy to the rim of his claim, gave the bewildered girl a loaf of bread and a jug of water, and pointed south toward the mountains. Not a word was spoken. Abraham turned and plodded slowly toward his little colony of tents. Hagar did not look back.

When the vagabond minstrels sang the old story which, as the ages passed, lost nothing of the magical in the telling, they declared that Ish mael grew to full manhood that day. This may have been a slight exaggera tion, though enough had happened to hasten his maturity. He swore to his mother that from now and henceforth forever he and his seed would be at enmity with everyone else descended from his father's house.

Seeking refuge among the savage tribes of itinerant shepherds and camel-breeders in the southern mountains, Ishmael quickly became their acknowledged leader, fighting his way to power with an audacity and ruthlessness that commanded their admiration and obedience. It was no small matter to bind so many discordant elements into something resembling a nation, but before Hagar's forceful and fearless son was thirty the hard-riding, fierce-fighting savages of the desert were boasting that they were "Ishmaelites." The name was respected and feared, by rulers and robbers alike, all the way from the Jordan to the Mediterranean, all the way from Damascus to Gaza. As time went on, the wild new nation became known as "Arabia," meaning "Men in Ambush."

The descendants of Isaac, and his more resourceful but less scrupulous son Jacob, after many misfortunes and migrations—including a long, humiliating period of enslavement in Egypt—fought their way back into their "Promised Land," their western boundary on the world's busiest sea, their eastern rim within a sling-shot of the domain controlled by the Men in Ambush. If some stupid stranger inquired, "Why do the Jews and Arabs hate each other so bitterly?" he was told, "It is written in the sacred prophecies of both nations that they are destined to be at enmity forever."

It was commonly understood, therefore, that when the posterity of Father Abraham's two families met, they neither smiled nor saluted. They never broke bread together; never gave aid, no matter how serious the emergency. They conducted their necessary business briefly and gruffly; and, having brought it to a conclusion, turned away, and spat noisily on the ground. It was not often that they fought, but it was said that on such rare occasions the catamounts crept out into the open to learn new techniques of tooth and claw. Often the contentious children of Abraham quarreled; screaming, gesticulating and reviling; for both of their languages, stemming from a common origin, were rich with invective and ingenious in the contrivance of exquisite insults. Neither nation had ever sent an ambassador to the other's court. Officially, neither had ever acknowledged the other's existence.

Not meaning, however, that there was no commerce at all between these mutually contemptuous men. Racial antipathies had not deterred the ardent traders of both nations from venturing across the Jordan to engage in an undercover barter that would have amazed and enraged the ordinary rank-and-file of their respective kinsmen. Jewish merchants, far travelers by nature, quietly forded the river with pack-trains bearing imports from many distant lands, and did not lack for wealthy Arabian customers when they appeared with foreign fabrics of silk and velvet, fine linens, gold ornaments, precious stones, medicinal herbs, spices and other exotics. It was customary, on these occasions, for the negotiations to be conducted with all the sullen impoliteness that the everlasting feud demanded; but the expensive goods did change ownership, and the pack-asses skipped home, under a young moon, freed of their burdens. Had either the Jews or the Arabians been gifted with a sense of humor, all this might have seemed funny.

During the last score of years something resembling a commercial truce had permitted a group of Arabian camel-breeders to bring their incomparably beautiful and expensive animals to the celebrated stock-show and auction held annually on the disused drill-ground near Jerusalem during the Jewish Feast of Pentecost.

Indeed, it was the lure of the Arabians' superb camels that had lately made this Pentecostal stock-show notable throughout the East. Rich Romans, ever competing with one another in the lavishness of their gaudy turnouts in the proud processions of the Imperial City, would send their stewards to purchase the finest of these majestic creatures, regardless of cost. The Jews, well aware that this uniquely attractive camel-market was responsible for bringing desirable patrons from afar, tried to forget—for this one day of the year—that the coveted camels were Arabian. And the Arabs who owned the camels pretended they didn't realize—on this one day of the year—that they were doing business in the land of Israel. They growled and scowled and spat—but they brought the camels.

This camel business, profitable alike to the merchants of Jerusalem and the stock-breeders of Arabia, had come to a dramatic end, a year ago. A most unfortunate incident had occurred. The auction, last summer, had attracted an unusually large assembly of well-to-do foreigners. They had come from everywhere; Romans, Egyptians, Damascenes, Cyprians, Greeks from Petra and Askelon. The bidding was reckless and the Arabian camels were bringing unprecedented figures. By custom, the least valuable of the herd were offered first; and so it was that as the afternoon wore on, the excitement increased. In many of the later contests, the spellbound crowd—whose majority had long since been priced out of the market—held its breath in amazement.

The finest beast of the lot was not offered until all the others had been bought. This tall, tawny, pompous three-year-old was clearly the pick of the herd. When, at last, the haughty creature was led forward, two well-groomed men, who had taken no part in the previous sales, shouldered their way through the pack from different directions, and showed a serious interest. Not many men in the crowd recognized either of them; but Demos, the suave Greek auctioneer, knew who they were, and was suddenly weak in the knees. The clean-shaven, middle-aged Roman, with the cloth-of-gold bandeau on his brow and the black eagle on the breast of his tunic, was a purchasing agent for Legate Varus, Commander-in-Chief of the Empire's Armies in the West. The lean, austere, gray-bearded Jew, in the long, black robe, was Joel, the representative of the immensely wealthy Simeon Maccabee, whose political power in Jewry was responsible for Herod's strong position on the Judaean throne; for the Maccabee family paid the bulk of the tribute which Rome exacted of the province—and Herod was their man.

Commander Varus, who was distinguished chiefly for his high opinion of himself, had become accustomed to getting what he wanted. Simeon the Maccabee entertained a similar feeling about his own desires. It would be a very awkward situation if the representatives of these eminent men staged a battle in which one of them would be defeated. Wars had risen out of incidents more trivial.

Demos hastily consulted the Arabians, explaining the gravity of the impasse and suggested that they withdraw the camel from the sale. Disappointed but comprehending, they consented. The prize camel was led away, and Demos announced that the Arabs had decided, at the last moment, to keep the handsome king of their herd for the continued improvement of their own stock. This left the sons of Ishmael in a very bad spot indeed. The crowd jeered. There was some stone-throwing. The little party of unpopular Arabians were in no position to defend themselves, and they beat an inglorious retreat.

Upon their return home, the whole matter was laid before King Aretas who decided, promptly and firmly, that the Arabs were not again to participate in any of the Jews' affairs. That had been a year ago. This summer the camel-breeders had let it be known that they were marketing their valuable herd in Damascus. The announcement carried fast and far; and, as a result, the stock-show at Jerusalem, on the Day of Pentecost, was poorly attended by the people previously counted on to insure its prestige.

As King Aretas sat in counsel with wise old Ilderan, advising him of Herod's incredible request for a parley at Petra, the latter had said, after a considerable silence between them, "Perhaps he wishes to have our camels brought again to his Pentecostal fair."

Aretas shook his head slowly.

"No, my good Ilderan. It's something more important than camels."

The Arabian Horsemen at Herod's Bier

In the center of the room, on a bier, reposed
Herod, the King of the Jews. The military
guard, numbering a score, stood their ground.
Forming a circle about the corpse, the Arabians sat for a long moment in silence.

* * * * * *

There was no city anywhere quite like Petra. Nobody knew its origin or its age; a thousand years, perhaps. It was known to have sheltered at least four successive civilizations, and had borne as many names. For the past three centuries it had belonged to a wealthy colony of fugitive Greeks who had expensively bestowed upon it an incomparable beauty. It was Athens, minus the slums and the smells.

Petra was more than a city; for it embraced not only an exquisitely contrived municipality, distinguished for the architecture of its baths, theaters, forums, temples, and stately residences, but a broad, enveloping valley whose green meadows and fertile fields were nourished by innumerable gushing springs.

Nature had also made provision for the defense of this self-contained little city-state by encircling it with a ring of precipitous stone mountains, converting it into a natural fortress. Petra could be entered only through two gateways; on the west, where a deep-worn camel-trail began its ambling toward distant Gaza and the coast-road north to Damascus, and on the south, leading to the Red Sea. These approaches were made through narrow, high-walled defiles which a handful of guards could—and often did—defend against bands of reckless marauders. It had been a long time since the city had had to repulse a serious invasion; never, indeed, since its occupation by the Greeks.

Naturally, it had been, through the ages, a much coveted stronghold, populated and re-populated with rich traders, of various tints and tongues, whose dynasties successively fattened and fell, each of them leaving monuments and tombs which their victors wrecked to make room for the more extravagant memorials of their own.

According to what passed for history in Arabia, which had never gone to much bother about keeping records, the most recent invasion of this territory had been made by their own tribesmen, some five hundred years ago, who had thought it their turn to enter and sack the rich old city, then in the hands of a decadent generation of Nabataeans. At small cost to themselves, the Arabs had driven out all the inhabitants who were left from a ruthless slaughter, had carried off everything of any value, and then had wondered what to do with their new acquisition; for they were nomads and had no use for cities.

After an interval of a couple of centuries, during which only the bats and hyenas were in residence, one Andrakos, fleeing for refuge from a Roman invasion with a large company of well-to-do Athenians, offered King Retar of Arabia a great price for the deserted city. Much gratified to

have, as neighbors, a new kind of people, who had seen much too much
of warfare and might be expected to behave themselves, Retar promised
the Greeks that they would never be molested by the Arabians, and published a decree warning his own people that Petra was not to be violated.
This injunction they had scrupulously obeyed, not only because King
Retar was held in high regard but because the penalty for annoying Petra
was a public stoning. Arabia had kept the peace-pact; and, with this comforting guarantee of security, Petra had built the most beautiful city in
the world.

As for the current relations of Petra and Arabia it could hardly be said
that they had any at all. In the opinion of the Arabs, the Greeks were a
queer lot of people who spent their time carving figures out of stone, paint-
ing pictures, and reading old scrolls written long ago by men as idle as
themselves. Such preoccupations, however unprofitable, were harmless
enough, and if the citizens of Petra wanted to fritter away their lives in
this manner, it was agreeable with realistic and illiterate Arabia. All that
Petra knew about the Arabs was that they raised and rode the most
beautiful and high-spirited horses to be found anywhere on earth, that
their magnificent camels—too expensive for draught duty—were bred
for showy parades in which they marched accoutered with silver ornaments, that the long-fibered wool of the high mountains was eagerly
sought by the most famous weavers of Caesarea, Corinth, and Rome, and
that their interest in anything artistic was completely non-existent. Aside
from the fact that the bodily temperature of the Greeks and Arabs was
maintained at approximately the same level they had nothing in common
and regarded each other with a condescension not unmixed with pity.

Upon the accession of Aretas to the Arabian throne (a venerable cedar
chest covered with the spliced white pelts of two long-haired goats), a
richly caparisoned deputation from Petra had come to pay neighborly
respects. For all parties concerned it was a pleasant visit. The pundits from
Petra were shown every available hospitality. Their gift to the young King
was a richly illuminated scroll containing Thucydides' History of the
Peloponnesian War; and, to show his appreciation, Aretas sent the aged
Governor of Petra home on a tall, sleek, snobbish camel named Retar, in
honor of the Arabian King who had had such amicable dealings with the
Greeks in an earlier day. When, some weeks after the coronation, it was
amusingly reported to Aretas that Retar had proved unmanageable, he
replied, "That makes us even."

Chief Counsellor Ilderan, who had something of an instinct for statesmanship and was canny enough to take a long view of international relations, had sometimes urged Aretas to pay a visit to Petra.

"The time may come, sire," Ilderan had said, "when it might be to our advantage to have had a closer acquaintance with these people."

"Very well, Ilderan," Aretas had replied. "Sometime we will do that." But the young King had plenty of pressing problems on his hands. He had never found time to visit Petra, nor had he any inclination to place himself at a disadvantage in the company of men whose manner of life and thought was so foreign to his own. One day Ilderan, still nourishing the hope for a closer friendship with the Greeks, remarked that Herod and his sons were said to be frequent visitors in Petra.

"That makes me even less eager to go there," Aretas had replied, almost gruffly. "If the King of the Jews has found favor with the Governor of Petra—all the more reason why we should keep our distance."

*   *   *   *   *   *

It was high noon when the Arabian cavalcade by a circuitous route reached the southern gateway into Petra. A brightly uniformed detachment met the expected guests at the pass and conducted them through the fortified defile.

After a three-mile ride on a well-kept road, flanked by green pastures, orchards, and widely spaced villas of exquisite architecture, the visitors climbed a long hill, reining in at the summit to face a breath-taking view of the white marble city. There they dismounted to rest their horses. Aretas and Ilderan sauntered a little way apart and for some moments silently surveyed the beautiful panorama below them.

King Herod's encampment, easily identifiable, had already been set up in a spacious park at the center of the city. It monopolized at least three quarters of the park. The colorful tents and gay banners moved Aretas to mutter that it was a more gaudy show than he had expected of the ever dolorous Jews.

"That is the Roman touch, sire," observed Ilderan. "Herod does not forget how he came by his kingship."

"Aye," rumbled Aretas. "It was a lucky day for that Idumean upstart when his foolhardy father stopped the Egyptian arrow intended for Cassius."

"I have often wondered, sire," drawled old Ilderan, "whether Cassius might have been so generous with his gratitude had he known how much wealth these Idumeans would acquire in Judaea."

"It's never too late for the Empire to rectify a mistake of generosity," said Aretas.

"True—but there's no hurry. Herod took over a Jerusalem built of sun-baked brick and is refashioning it in granite and marble. Old Augustus

should be willing to let him do that, at the Jews' expense. Besides"—
continued Ilderan—"Judaea pays an exorbitant tribute. Why should the
Emperor send an army in to kill the goose that lays gold eggs?"

"Even so; Herod's nights must be troubled by bad dreams.... Shall we
proceed into the city, Ilderan?"

The old Counsellor did not assent promptly. His brow was furrowed.
Pointing toward the Jews' encampment with his riding-whip, he remarked, "Herod has occupied all but a corner of the park, sire. Doubtless
he expects us to content ourselves with what remains of it. Such an idea
would become him, I daresay."

"Let us not give him that satisfaction," growled Aretas. "We will pitch
our tents where we are—on this hill-top. Agreed?"

Ilderan nodded approval. Beckoning to Zendi, the popular young
Captain of the Royal Guard, Aretas gave the order. Noting the sudden
disappointment in Zendi's face, he added, "After our camp is in order, you
and your men are at liberty to ride down into the city."

There was a spontaneous murmur of pleasure from the tough young
cavalrymen, which prompted the King to announce, sternly, "You will
remember that we are guests here. Zendi, you are to hold your men strictly
to account for their behavior! . . . And—one thing more: There is to be
no quarreling with the Jews!"

Zendi raised his hand for permission to speak.

"Should the Jews attack us, Your Majesty, what shall I tell my men to
do?"

King Aretas swung into his saddle before replying.

"In that case, Zendi," he said, with a shrug of his shoulder, "your men
will know what to do—without being told." There was a concerted shout
of laughter. Even Aretas, who rarely smiled, pulled a reluctant grin as he
rode away in the lead of his amused Counsellors. Ilderan, riding beside
him now, resumed their conversation about Herod.

"Of course, sire, he cannot help realizing the instability of his provincial
throne. He proves his apprehension by the frequency of his journeys to
visit the Emperor—and the fact that his sons spend most of their time in
Rome."

"The Jews probably object to that," surmised Aretas.

"Naturally, sire; but Herod is in greater need of the Emperor's favor
than the good opinion of the Jews, who would despise him, no matter
what he did—or left undone. . . . All that flamboyant display of Roman
trinkets represents Herod's fear—rather than his admiration—of Augustus."

On the level now and four abreast, the Arabians quickened their speed and swept through the suburbs of Petra, presently drawing up before the stately palace of Sosthenes the Governor where Aretas and his Council were ceremoniously received. Sosthenes seemed flustered.

"I trust Your Majesty may find ample room in the park for your encampment," he said, with an apologetic smile which Aretas made no sign of interpreting. It was evident that the taciturn King of Arabia, whatever he might think of the King of the Jews, was not disposed to exhibit his feelings for the entertainment of this smooth-tongued Greek. "And if there is not sufficient camping-space in the park," continued Sosthenes, uneasily, "we will see to it that your retinue does not lack for hospitality."

"We have already encamped, my lord," said Aretas—"on the high plateau south of the city. Our people prefer the open spaces. Will you advise King Herod that Arabia is at his service?"

"He awaits you, Your Majesty." Sosthenes' tone indicated his relief that an awkward situation had been nicely disposed of. "If it is agreeable, your conference will be held here in our council-chamber." With a deep bow, he led the way to a high-domed, marble-walled room, luxuriously furnished with huge upholstered divans arranged in two semi-circles fronting a massive teakwood table, at either end of which stood a tall-backed, gold-covered, throne-like chair. The Arabians had not long to wait. Attended by a dozen venerable members of the Jewish Sanhedrin, Herod strutted in. Stiff bows and crisp amenities were exchanged. The Kings took their places in the tall chairs. The Counsellors and the Sanhedrin sat. Facing each other, with calm, steady-eyed curiosity, the rulers of Judaea and Arabia presented a striking contrast in costume, bearing, and physique.

Herod was urbane, suave, quite the man of large affairs. He was sixty and paunchy, and there were pendulous pouches under his experienced eyes. It was apparent that the paunch and the pouches were decorations won in courageous combat with nourishing food and rich beverages. His abundant thatch of graying hair—close-cropped after the Roman manner —glistened with scented unguents. His beard was short and well-groomed, a compromise between the patriarchal whiskers of Jerusalem and the cleanly shaved jowls of Rome. His robe was of fine-spun white linen, trimmed with purple at the throat, cuffs, and skirt-hem. Herod had the self-assured posture of a man who had been everywhere, and always with the right people; who had seen everything, and always from a reserved seat.

Aretas was carelessly dressed in a brown, travel-worn cashmere burnous, the skirt of which was parted revealing his brown goat-skin riding-breeches and thong-laced boots. The only touch of color on his clothing was the ancient crest of the Ishmaelites, an oval patch of blue silk appliquéd to the left breast of his burnous. In this field of blue were the well-known devices seen on Arabia's banners—a slim, gold-embroidered moon-crescent, half-circling a silver star—and pierced, in the form of an X, by a white sword and a shepherd's crook, the distinctive symbol of Arabian royalty. Aretas did not relax in his chair but sat rigidly erect with the air of a man accustomed to brief parleys, laconic statements, swift agreements, and an unceremonious adjournment.

In his early fifties, Arabia's King was lean as a leopard, tough as a bowstring, and as tanned as an old saddle. The hood of his burnous had been pushed back from his deep-seamed forehead, showing a tousled mop of grizzled hair. He, too, wore a short beard, but nobody had trimmed it that morning, much less anointed it with fragrant oils. There was nothing of smooth statesmanship in the face or bearing of this Arabian. Except for the royal crest, he was not accoutered like a king, nor did he have the manner of one accustomed to the adroit thrust and parry of diplomacy. Yet there were the deep-set black eyes to be reckoned with, eyes inured to long vistas and well-versed in the lore of the sky.

Having spent most of his life indoors, Herod—cannily competent in studying the minds and moods of similarly sheltered men, peered into the fathomless eyes of Aretas, and the carefully rehearsed speech he had obviously meant to make seemed to need revision.

"Your Excellency," began Herod, measuring his words, "we invited you here to discuss a matter of grave concern to both our nations." He paused for some response; at least a slight lifting of the Arabian's brows. But the face of Aretas was impassive, giving no sign of surprise or curiosity.

"We have recently returned from Rome with disturbing news," continued Herod. "Plans are rapidly taking shape for a Roman invasion into the northeast that will sweep this coast so bare of everything valuable that when it is ended the very vultures will die of starvation. Neither of us—and you may be sure that we will both be involved in this tragedy—can hope to withstand such an attack; but, firmly resolved to unite in a defense of our countries, we might exhibit enough force to dissuade Tiberius——"

"Tiberius!" broke in Aretas. "Is Tiberius not leading the Army in the West?"

"Not at present," replied Herod, pleased to be able to instruct his conferee from the hinterland. Tiberius had been recalled to Rome, some months ago, to be co-regent with Augustus. The Western Army in charge of the subjugation of the German tribes and the occupation of all Gaul, was given to Varus who had now been completely overwhelmed; put to utter rout; destroyed! "It is the worst defeat that the Empire has ever experienced. Never again will the Romans cross the Rhine. If they are to recover their lost prestige, at home and abroad, they must extend their power in the East—and the North. And our countries are on the highway to Damascus."

Aretas frowned studiously but made no reply, though the Jew gave him plenty of time for a rejoinder. Perhaps, mused Herod, the remote Arabian does not fully realize the predicament of the Romans, and their necessity to strike a blow—or invite disaster. He decided to post Aretas on some recent history that might have escaped him. The speech lasted for a full half hour, Aretas listening without comment.

Augustus—Herod went on—had made a great Emperor; no doubt of that. In spite of the fact that he never had had any health, at all, he had done much for Rome. But now he was old, and so ill that everybody knew about it. The reins of government had been slipping rapidly through his rheumatic fingers. He had lost his grip on the Senate. The rabble was restless. Of course the trouble was largely fiscal. Gone were the days when—in need of money to finance a fortnight's free feasting for Rome's improvident thousands—an expedition could be sent to raid Sicily, or Crete, or Cyprus, or Macedonia; returning with valuable slaves, grain, lumber, leather, and gold. True, the provinces could still be sacked and pillaged, again and again; but the Romans had less and less to show for it.

"You remember, don't you, Your Excellency, how Augustus was so hard up—a few years ago—that he required every man, in all of the provinces tributary to Rome, to pay a poll-tax?" Herod snorted with disgust. "It was a paltry thing to do, the act of a miser or a bankrupt. The provinces were already taxed to the limit of their endurance. And then this bewildered old Emperor childishly decides to screw a poll-tax out of the hungry provincials! He sought to clothe the ridiculous affair with dignity by pretending the main idea was to take a census; every man commanded to show up, on a certain day, in the place of his birth—wherever that was —and have himself enumerated. But that never fooled anybody. Augustus didn't care how many people were controlled from Rome. All he was interested in was their wretched little five farthings. Some of our poor people had to travel so much as a week's journey to obey the edict."

"I had forgotten," said Aretas. "It did not affect my people. The Emperor would hardly chase an Arabian through the mountains for five farthings."

"I'm not so sure that he wouldn't," remarked Herod, with a shrug. "He will—this time! Tiberius will want your sheep and cattle and camels; and your daughters, too. There is only one way out for us, Your Excellency. Let us make a treaty—and stand together. Tiberius will think twice before he risks another defeat."

"Do you imagine, sire," asked Aretas, "that Tiberius could be made to believe that the Jews and Arabs had concluded an alliance, after many centuries of hatred?"

"I had thought of that." Herod hitched at his big chair, which did not move an inch, and leaned forward, lowering his voice to a confidential tone. "I, too, had thought of that. Tiberius will need sound proof that our alliance is genuine."

"Have you something to suggest?" inquired Aretas.

"A tangible unity. I am told that you have a marriageable daughter. I have an unmarried son."

Aretas winced, and shook his head.

"My daughter," he muttered, "would not like that."

"Nor would my son," said Herod, with equal candor. "But for what reason are Princes and Princesses fêted and sheltered; for what reason are they fed ices cooled with snow brought from the mountains by swift runners with lungs on fire; and to what end do courtiers bow before them —if not that when the day comes on which they must subordinate their own desires for the good of their country, they shall pay their debt cheerfully and in full?"

"Perhaps this may apply to your son, my lord, but not to my daughter. She has lived simply, even frugally, as becomes an Arabian of whatever position. Arnon has had no ices in summer."

"Be that as it may," said Herod, crisply. "Ices or no ices, your daughter loves her country, I think. She would sacrifice much rather than see Arabia laid waste. Nor would she suffer hardship at the hands of my son, Antipas. He is a noble young fellow, gracious, kind, wealthy. They might even come to love each other, though that, of course, is unimportant."

"It would not be unimportant to my daughter," said Aretas. "Besides —she is already in love with a young man of our own people."

Herod stroked his chin with the backs of his plump fingers, and meditated.

"Has her betrothal been announced?"

"No," admitted Aretas.

"That is good," nodded Herod. He clapped his hands and an aide appeared. "We will dine," he said.

Aretas was not hungry, but it would have been impolitic to say so.

*   *   *   *   *   *

The Counsellors were in session all night. Aretas set forth their dilemma, expressing it as his opinion that Herod knew what he was talking about and had not exaggerated the threatened disaster.

Dumah made bold to say, "I had rather be enslaved by the Romans than allied to the Jews."

"As for you, yourself, yes," said Tema, "but how about your wife and daughters? The Romans are shameless butchers!"

"But how can we be certain that there is to be an invasion?" scoffed Dumah. "This fellow Sosthenes would be directly in the path of it—and he doesn't appear to be much upset."

"Well—he will be," muttered Tema, "when Herod tells him how much is expected of him—in gold!"

"Ah—so that's why we're meeting in Petra; is it?" queried Adbeel.

"It's a good enough reason," said Tema, wearily. "No—it's quite useless to debate this matter. We've been over all the ground—and there's no way out. An alliance of the Jews and Arabians is quite as distasteful to Herod as it is to us. He knows the danger, or he would never have made this proposal. We may be sure of that!"

"It is asking too much of our Princess," said Adbeel. "She will have a wretched life with this young Jewish scamp."

"Doubtless," agreed Naphish, "but at least she will live."

"I think she would prefer to die," muttered Adbeel.

"But that is not the point," said Mishma. "If the Princess marries Antipas she will be saving her country. When this is explained to her, she will consent."

There was a long interval of moody silence, broken by Jetur who ventured to raise the question that was on everyone's mind: What would young Zendi think of all this?

Ilderan was prompt with a reply.

"My son will be deeply grieved," he said, slowly, "but he, too, loves Arabia."

Aretas nodded his head, without looking up.

"Is there anything further to be said?" he asked; and when no one spoke, he rose, walked toward the door, and dispatched the fateful message to Herod. The Council adjourned, but not to sleep. Breakfast was disposed of shortly before dawn. The tents were quickly packed. By the time the Jews in the park were astir, the Arabian camp-site on the hill was deserted.

The journey home was swift; and, for the most part, silent. At dusk on the evening of the fourth day of hard travel they separated gloomily.

Arnon was anxiously waiting at the entrance to the encampment. Aretas dismounted slowly, heavily; a haggard old man.

"Father!" exclaimed Arnon. "What has happened to distress you so? Are you hurt?"

Aretas took her by the hand, as if she were a little child, and silently led her into the tent. When they were seated together on a divan, Arnon summoned a servant and ordered supper to be brought for her father, but Aretas shook his head. Drawing her close, he gazed sadly into her wide, frightened eyes and blurted out the story. Arabia had made an alliance with the Jews. It was the only way of escaping a Roman invasion that would utterly destroy both countries.

"But—if you have made the alliance, and have saved our country," said Arnon, hopefully, "why are you so downhearted?"

"Because—the alliance provides for a royal marriage of Arabia and Judaea."

Arnon gave a little gasp and her face paled.

"Does that mean—me?" she asked, weakly.

"Can you do this, my child, for Arabia?"

Closing her eyes, Arnon drew a long, shuddering breath, and slowly relaxed into her father's arms. After an agonizing moment, she straightened and looked up bravely into his deep-lined face.

"For Arabia—yes—my father," she said, barely above a whisper.

They sat in silence for a little while. Arnon patted him tenderly on the cheek. Swallowing convulsively in a dry throat, she murmured, "May I go now, Father?"

Aretas released her and she walked toward the door of her room with the short, groping steps of the blind. He watched her with brooding sorrow. He would gladly have given his life to save her this painful martyrdom.

*   *   *   *   *   *

If it was necessary for the Arabs and the Jews to guarantee the genuineness of their alliance by arranging an international marriage it was equally important that the wedding occur without delay, for Tiberius could not afford to wait very long after the catastrophe to Roman arms in the West before attempting elsewhere a recovery of the Empire's ailing prestige.

Nor was this royal wedding an event that might be conducted quietly. It must be distinguished for its pomp and flamboyant extravagance. The full military power of Judaea and Arabia was to be put on exhibition so that Tiberius, when apprized of it, would realize that these passionate little nations had resolved not only to stand together but had the strength to make their unity formidable.

Of course the responsibility for this impressive spectacle would fall more heavily upon Herod than Aretas, for the Arabians were inexperienced in showmanship. At this game, Herod was skilled. He had a natural talent for it and his long acquaintance with Roman pageantry had made him fully conversant with its tactics.

The big show would be held in Jerusalem immediately after the wedding in Arabia. With amazing speed Herod assembled his widely scattered troops, secured the financial backing of the wealthy guilds, and even won the timid support of Annas, the High Priest, who never liked to take sides in a political issue until sure which way the cat was going to jump.

The skeletonized "Legion" of Roman soldiers stationed in Jerusalem, ostensibly for police duty but really to keep the restless Jews in remembrance of their provincial status, merely joked about Herod's bombastic show until the habitually sequestered Jewish troops began mobilizing in surprising numbers on the unkempt and disused drill-grounds in the Kedron Valley. Fully accoutered, they were marching boldly through the city, en route from Joppa, Caesarea, Hebron, Jericho, and remote Capernaum in Galilee.

That, complained young Legate Julian to his Centurions, was what ailed the Jews: they never knew when they were whipped. The Sanhedrin made deep bows to the Empire's representatives, and retired to plot. Every evening at sunset the faithful appeared at the Wailing Wall to howl hopelessly over their subjugation, and strolled back to their cellars to sharpen their knives and spin tougher bow-strings.

Apprehensive of a dangerous incident, and anxious to head it off by polite appeasement—for he had been sent to Jerusalem to keep the peace at all costs—Julian went to Herod. Why all these military maneuvers? Herod smiled innocently. There was to be a wedding, he said. His son Antipas was marrying the young Princess of Arabia. Yes, yes, Julian knew all about that, and said it would be quite agreeable to the Empire, he thought, if a detachment of Jewish patrolmen marched in the wedding procession, but—

"A detachment!" broke in Herod, disappointedly.

"Well—a Legion, then," conceded Julian, "if that would better please Your Excellency; but we see no occasion for a parade of catapults weighing two thousand pounds! Is that customary—at a wedding?"

"It would be an interesting novelty," reflected Herod, in a tone of childish wistfulness. "Many of our people will be surprised to know that we have catapults."

"Our people will be surprised too!" exclaimed Julian. "And if a large display is made of such heavy weapons, Your Excellency may soon have a more serious use for them."

Herod smiled enigmatically, patted a yawn, and drummed absently on the table with his knuckles. Julian dourly accepted his dismissal and rose to go.

"In any case," pursued Herod, "they are good catapults, and they are ours, and they are here! It would be no easy matter to bring as large ones, or as many, from Rome."

Slightly stunned by this unexpected impudence, Julian stammered, "I am aware of that, sire."

"And so is Tiberius," added Herod, recklessly.

"Meaning that Your Excellency would like me to inform the Emperor?"

"As you please, Julian. You will anyway, you know."

This raw arrogance was something new to the Legate whom Herod had always treated with a suave, if insincere, deference. It was evident that the crafty Jew intended to gamble this time for very high stakes.

"The Emperor may suspect that this wedding is primarily a display of defensive armor!"

"How quick you are, Julian," drawled Herod, now candidly contemptuous. "You are wasted as a mere peace officer. You should be a Consul, at the very least." He rose and bowed ceremoniously. "Forgive us if we have to let you go now. We have another appointment; and you, doubtless, have business of your own."

As the troubled young Legate made his inglorious exit from the spacious gold and blue audience chamber, Prince Antipas lounged in through the King's private entrance. Herod glanced up, nodded amiably, and resumed his writing. His face expressed satisfaction with his favorite son; something of pride, too; for Antipas—not always so docile—was showing himself surprisingly co-operative in this affair of the Arabian nuptials. Not meaning that he was enthusiastic—which would have been too much to expect—but quietly acquiescent.

Of Herod's three sons by his much loved Mariamne, Antipas was his pet. Antipas was respectful, courteous, good to look upon, of better than average height, with a handsome face, an athletic figure, and the confident carriage of a soldier. The firm discipline of the Roman Military Academy was stamped on him. At twenty-five, his slow, agnostic smile gave more than a hint of the fashionable cynicism which characterized the indolent crew of rich men's sons who gambled all day at the baths and banqueted all night in the best possible places. Antipas was already an experienced man of the world.

As for his other sons by Mariamne, Herod had had but little occasion for pride in them. Archelaus, the eldest, was a contentious fellow, forever getting himself into embarrassing brawls. Philip, the youngest, whom the family invariably referred to as "Poor Philip," was so listless and impractical that he even had much difficulty in holding the government job his eminent father had found for him in Rome at the cost of much coaxing—and a bit of bribery. And, as if Poor Philip were not sufficiently weighted with handicaps, he had allowed himself to be led into an unhappy marriage by Herodias—a cousin twice removed—who was his senior by ten years, and a century older in experience. A widow, Herodias had brought along a pert young daughter, Salome, whose adventures were common talk. Herod could not be proud of Poor Philip. But Antipas! Here was a son worthy of all the costly investments that had been made in him!

Noting that his father was occupied, or pretended to be, the well-favored Prince strolled across to the high bank of cases which lined the eastern wall, drew out a new, heavily gilded scroll, read the title, and chuckled audibly. Herod regarded him with interest.

"Did the old man give you this?" inquired Antipas, amused.

"If you are referring to the aged Emperor Augustus," reproved Herod, "he did."

"Gave it to you—personally?" nagged Antipas.

Herod hitched uneasily in his chair, as to admit that the ostentatious scroll was one of a large number presented to Consuls, Prefects, Governors, Provincial Kings—and Senators, too, perhaps.

"I'll wager a hundred shekels that Your Majesty hasn't read a line of it!" taunted Antipas; and, when his father had shrugged, added, "You'd better, sire. This is Virgil's new eulogy to Augustus, extolling his brave deeds. He calls it *The Aeneid.*"

"We shall have to peruse it," consented Herod, absently.

"Indeed you will, sire!" Antipas made pretense of seriousness. "You may have to take an examination on it sometime." He flipped the gaudy scroll back into the case, sauntered to the King's dais, flung himself into a chair—and yawned. Herod put down his stylus and smiled benevolently.

"And how are you amusing yourself, my son? We hope the time does not hang too heavily on your hands while you wait for your marriage."

"Not heavily at all, sire. Your Majesty will recall that Salome, who is very good company, returned with us on our ship, for a visit."

"Specifically—she came to represent Poor Philip's family at the wedding," amended Herod. "Otherwise she would not have been tolerated— much less invited: you may be sure of that!" He lowered his voice, discarded his kingship, and impulsively became a father. "If I were in your place, Antipas, I should arrange not to be seen in public with the little trollop."

"My niece, sire!" Antipas feigned indignation, but his ironical smirk showed through.

"Niece? Nonsense!" growled Herod. "Since when did Poor Philip's notorious step-daughter become your niece?"

"Technically, she is my niece, sire; and Your Majesty's grand-daughter. Does that not entitle her to some courteous consideration?"

"Not from you! The women of the court can attend to Salome's wants. The Queen will arrange for her entertainment."

"But Mother does not care for her," said Antipas, sadly.

"Not much wonder!" muttered Herod. "But—however that may be— you are to have nothing further to do with her! The fact that your half-witted brother married her mother does not obligate you in the least. Your association with this Salome will do you no good; especially now that your heart is in Arabia."

"Is it?" Instantly Antipas realized that he had overtaxed his royal parent's patience. He had been sweetly wheedled into returning to wed the Arabian Princess. It had required a deal of coaxing. At first he had loudly protested, and his father had promised him an immediate cash payment of his patrimony. He had shaken his head sorrowfully, and his father had conferred on him the Tetrarchy of Galilee. Finally he had yielded to the King's importunate pressure. It had placed him in an advantageous position, and he had been trading on it sharply, with all the inconsiderate tyranny of a spoiled invalid. His father's dark frown warned him now that his impudence had reached a limit.

"It had better be!" rasped Herod, hotly. "This is a serious business! And you are a fool not to realize it!" He rose and paced to and fro, with mounting rage. "You should be in Arabia—at this moment—as I counselled you—making friends with these aliens! I tell you they are no more eager for this wedding than you are! And if you treat it too lightly you may get a dagger between your ribs! Blood-letting is a mere pastime with these Arabians! They never forget an injury or an insult!" The King was breathing heavily as he strode toward the door. "Don't say I did not warn you!" he shouted.

*   *   *   *   *   *

Arnon was given but little time to brood over coming events. Preparations for the marriage proceeded with breathtaking speed. Every day couriers arrived from Jerusalem to inquire of the Princess; or, more correctly, to report to the Princess what were her wishes in respect to details which, in the opinion of an Arabian, were childishly trivial, but apparently important enough to warrant a laborious journey from the Jewish capital.

The vanguard of servants and equipment began to appear in increasing numbers. Long caravans toiled up the tortuous trail from the valley floor, widening the bridle-path to a hard-beaten road. Skilled Arabian seamstresses and weavers worked in feverish haste on the wedding garments for the Princess and her attendants.

Tactfully, mercifully, Aretas had dispatched Zendi to far away Corinth on an errand no less important than the conclusion of a pending deal to lease another large parcel of land in the north to war-weary Greeks. It was a relief to Arnon when Zendi, pressed for time, called to say farewell; both of them glad that the leave-taking was done in the presence of their fathers. Arnon couldn't have borne it, she knew, if they had had their final moment in seclusion. Poor Zendi! He had been so determined to deal manfully with his sorrow that he had hardly raised his eyes to hers when they parted.

The thousand sheep were led to another pasture, and on their grazing-ground an awe-inspiring tented city rose. Soldiers in colorful uniforms made camp with such dexterity and precision that Arnon was forced to admire their skill. They did not squat in small huddles, an Arabian custom, to discuss what procedures were best. They knew exactly what to do. This, thought Arnon, was probably the way everything went in the outside world beyond her untamed but beloved mountains. Though firmly loyal to Arabia and its haphazard way of doing things, she felt a tug of excitement over being made a part of that competent society whose urbane representatives were now demonstrating their disciplined self-assurance.

Now delegations of wealthy Arabian sheiks swept by on their sleek horses, and entered the tents their servants had prepared on the broad plateau, each contingent accompanied by entertainers; minstrels, magicians, field athletes, acrobats, and comedians.

Then came the awaited day of King Herod's arrival with Prince Antipas, their tall camels resplendent with costly housings and trappings of gold and silver. Proudly, haughtily, the impressive caravan swung past the encampment of King Aretas and came to rest a few hundred yards away. With fluttering heart, Arnon watched her father and the Counsellors greet the party from Jerusalem. It was a dizzying spectacle. King Herod was undeniably a distinguished personage and the Prince was tall and handsome. And there was the High Priest, guessed Nephti, Arnon's lifetime nurse, who was holding the tent-panel open to see. Doubtless he had come, added Nephti, to conduct the wedding.

"I had not realized it was to be a Jewish wedding," said Arnon.

"The Jews like ceremonies," declared Nephti.

"And we don't?" asked Arnon, childishly.

"Ours is more simple. If you were marrying Zendi—"

"Don't, Nephti!" murmured Arnon. "You promised me."

"I am sorry, Princess. I only meant to explain that you would have taken his hand, in the presence of the Counsellors, and promised to obey and serve him, all the days of your life."

"And will I not be asked to obey and serve Prince Antipas?"

"Of course—but it will take longer, I suppose. The Jews are like that."

Nephti closed the leather panel as the girl turned aside, soberly. Her intuition read Arnon's thoughts. These strange people from afar were of immense interest, but they were of another world.

"I had hoped that Queen Mariamne might come," said Arnon. "You saw no women in the party, Nephti?"

No—the whole event was to be a man's affair; a political transaction, in which one woman would be included because she was necessary. Gladly would they have done without her, reflected Arnon, if that were possible. The wedding was a confirmation of an international alliance. The treaty had been formally written on a sheet of papyrus, duly signed, and now it must be ratified. Arnon was but so much sealing-wax stamped on an official document. Suddenly she was overwhelmed with a sense of heart-sickening loneliness.

That evening there was a banquet attended by the Kings, the Prince, the High Priest, several ranking members of the Sanhedrin, and the Arabian Counsellors. After an hour's feasting on the part of the men, Arnon was brought in to be introduced. She felt and looked very small and helpless.

Antipas stepped forward to greet her. He took both her hands in his and smiled down into her timidly upraised eyes. It was an experienced smile that skillfully appraised and evidently approved. For a moment the silence in the tent grew oppressive as they waited for an opinion from the beautiful young Princess. Presently she drew a shy, tremulous smile—and the suspense lifted. They all breathed freely again; and, with the exception of Aretas, exchanged glances of relief and satisfaction. Herod drained his goblet and smacked his lips. It was good wine. And—what was still better—by this time tomorrow the alliance would be an attested fact, and he would be ready—if need be—to confront Tiberius.

2

Now THAT the month of Tishri had come, and the trees were taking on rich colors, Arnon's homesickness became almost insupportable. Jerusalem was slowly strangling her. But for the understanding sympathy and tenderness of Queen Mariamne, she would have died or gone mad.

Nature had not intended that Arnon should be surrounded by walls. Because her own people were of necessity nomadic they had built no cities. Indeed the Arabians were contemptuous of cities, considering them pestilential prisons, stultifying to both body and spirit.

Every morning, in the far away and long ago, Arnon had risen at dawn to breathe deeply of the invigorating mountain breeze and rejoice in the peace of a silence broken only by the distant tinkle of camel bells. But here in Jerusalem she felt stifled, caged. Late in the morning she would struggle back to consciousness, finding herself hungry for clean, bracing air. The beautifully wrought antique tapestries which curtained her luxurious bed gave off a sickening odor of mold and the exquisite mosaics leaked the sour stench of disintegrating plaster.

Added to the tomblike atmosphere of her spacious bedchamber was a conglomeration of city smells seeping in from the outside, smells of old and decaying things, old walls, old towers, old markets, old stables, old cobbled streets. There were plenty of distasteful sights, sounds, and scents in this ancient city, but the worst thing of all was the stagnant, fetid air.

Every day now, Arnon woke nauseated, though the servants—who found nothing wrong with the air—graciously assured the foreign Princess that her morning sickness was due to her condition, always adding, piously, "For which the Lord God of Israel be praised!"

On this tenth day of Tishri, Arnon tugged herself loose from a nostalgic dream of riding swiftly beside her father in a noisy mountain storm, galloping, galloping hard, quite out of breath, with big splashes of warm rain pelting them. Half-suffocated and drenched with perspiration, she gazed up dully into the smiling eyes of the Queen.

Mariamne was the most beautiful woman Arnon had ever seen. She was in her early fifties but seemed much younger for by her abstemiousness she had retained a youthful figure. She had all the traditional dignity of a Queen but none of the arrogance. Arnon had known from the first moment of their meeting that she was going to like Mariamne. The Queen had no daughter and Arnon had never known a mother. Their friendship was instant and mutual.

But in spite of the affection she felt for her charming mother-in-law, Arnon had extended no confidences. Her father had warned her to guard her tongue in the presence of these people. "Spies are always friendly, and free to share their secrets with you." Sometimes it had been difficult to observe this reticence, her intuition assuring her that Mariamne's devotion to her was sincere.

"How are you, my child?" asked the Queen, gently.

"Very warm," mumbled Arnon—"and a bit sick, as usual. I shall feel better when I've had something cold to drink. You are up early, Your Majesty. Have you had your breakfast?"

Summoning a servant to bring the Princess a goblet of cold pomegranate juice, Mariamne sat down on the edge of the bed.

"I am not to have breakfast this morning, my dear. This is a fast day."

"All day?" Arnon's eyes widened incredulously.

"Until evening. Then there will be a bountiful feast. You are not expected to do any fasting, but we will want you to attend the banquet."

Arnon sat up in bed, pushed her tousled black hair out of her eyes, and inquired what this fast was about.

"It is the Day of Atonement," explained Mariamne. "Of all our special occasions this one means the most. It really begins the day before, with all the faithful Jews going about making things right with one another, doing neglected duties, paying their debts, returning things borrowed, and asking forgiveness for wrongs done and hot words spoken. Damaged friendships are mended, estrangements are cleared up. And then—today—with clean hands and a right spirit—everyone brings a gift to the Temple, and receives a blessing."

Arnon's eyes shone.

"It is very beautiful!" she whispered. "May I do it, too? It would be a relief—to go to the Temple—and be blessed." She bowed her head dejectedly. "My heart has been so bitter." Slowly she raised tear-filled eyes. "Your Majesty, I have been very unhappy."

Mariamne slipped an arm around her, compassionately.

"Arnon, dear, would you like to call me 'Mother' instead of 'Your Majesty'? Don't do it if—if it takes an effort," she added, "but it would please me."

With that, Arnon's tears overflowed and she sobbed like a little child. "I should like to," she murmured brokenly. "You have been so good to me. I want you to be my mother. That's the way I think of you."

Mariamne drew her closer.

"Tell me, Arnon," she said softly, "has the Prince been unkind to you?"

Arnon indecisively shook her head, but the pent-up tears ran unchecked. When she could speak she said, "No—he has not mistreated me—Mother. I see very little of him, you know. But the Prince is a busy man. He can't be spending all of his time entertaining me."

"Men are always busy, my dear." The Queen's usually placid voice showed a trace of asperity. "There are the games at Gath and a new Greek play at Askelon—and other important engagements." She paused for a moment. Dropping her tone of raillery, she went on, "Our Antipas is really a sweet boy. He wouldn't intentionally hurt a fly. But he is selfish and spoiled. How could it be otherwise? Too much money; too much leisure."

"And too many people wanting to win his favor," added Arnon.

"Sometimes I have thought," said Mariamne, soberly, "that a baby Prince should be left on the doorstep of an honest, frugal, hard-working family, and brought up as their son until he is about—"

"Twenty?" suggested Arnon, when the Queen had seemed at a loss for the right figure.

"Forty!" amended Mariamne. "Then he should be brought to the throne, knowing what his people need. As it stands, there is nobody in the Kingdom quite so ignorant of his duties as the ruler himself. He lives in a different world." After an interval of silence, she asked, abruptly, "Is anything else wrong, dear?"

"Almost everything," confessed Arnon. "Everything but you! It may be my own fault. I cannot be myself here. In my own country I am happy and free. I love to ride. The shepherds wave a hand and smile as I pass by and I wave my hand and smile too. We are friends. Their wives and daughters weave gay scarves for me and I visit them when they are sick. Often I stop at their tents and play with the little children."

"That is as it should be," approved Mariamne. "And they are not in awe of you, as the King's daughter?"

"They call me 'Princess,' but when we play they do not throw the game away to humor me. Maybe that is what ails a royal family: they are allowed to win all the games. . . . Here in Jerusalem, I am a Princess;

always, every hour, a Princess. I am unused to these stiff ceremonies; people bowing worshipfully—and backing out of the room. I have to change my costumes a half dozen times a day, and none of them is comfortable. Everything is strange—and I am becoming a stranger even to myself." Her voice broke completely. "Please—may I not go home—just for a little while?"

There was a long delay before Mariamne replied.

"I wish you might, Arnon. Doubtless the King would consent if it were not for this military alliance. If it should come to the ears of the Emperor—"

"I understand," said Arnon, weakly. "Let us think no more about it. . . . And—I should like to go with you to the Temple. Is the Prince going with us?"

Mariamne frowned and shook her head.

"Antipas set off early this morning for the north. You know he has been made the ruler of Galilee."

"Yes, Mother. He did not tell me, but I heard a friend congratulate him on it, at our wedding. Are we to live in Galilee?"

"Part of the time, perhaps," said Mariamne, uncertainly. "Antipas is a restless fellow. He does not like to stay long in one place. The King is building a Galilean embassy here in the city. Antipas will spend a couple of months every year in Jerusalem, attending to provincial business. He loves Rome, and I daresay he will want to be there occasionally. At the moment he is infatuated with the idea of building a beautiful villa on the western shore of the Lake Gennesaret in Galilee."

Arnon brightened.

"That would be lovely!" she exclaimed. "I have heard so much of that beautiful Sea of Galilee. Perhaps there would be sailing!"

Mariamne did not share Arnon's sudden enthusiasm.

"I doubt whether the Prince would be interested in sailing. There are some warm springs on the western shore. Antipas, who loves bathing, will build commodious bath houses in connection with his villa. I think he hopes to induce a few of his wealthy Roman friends to build villas there."

Arnon's interest gradually faded. Instinctively she gathered that the Queen had thought it time for her to know what manner of life she should anticipate. But perhaps Antipas had not included her in all—or any—of his plans. If he had expected her to live with him in Galilee, he might have inquired what sort of home she would like.

"Has the Prince planned the villa?" she asked.

Mariamne stirred uneasily, reluctant to discuss the matter.

"Perhaps," she said. "He spent all last week in Petra, inspecting a few of the beautiful marble villas built by wealthy Athenians. He may have told you."

"He tells me nothing," said Arnon.

Mariamne sighed deeply and rose to her feet.

"If you wish to go with us to the Temple, dear, you should be ready at noon. Your maid will tell you what you are to wear. His Majesty expects to leave the palace promptly at mid-day. It has been announced."

"I hope I shall be prepared for the blessing," said Arnon, wistfully. "I am much in need of it. Is there anything I should do? I'm afraid I do not owe anything that should be paid back, and I have spoken no hot words, though I have had them in my mind which is probably just as bad. Perhaps if my husband were here I might ask him to forgive me for all the unkind things I have thought about him."

The Queen drew a slow, sober smile, and shook her head.

"In that case," she said, quietly, "it is just as well that he isn't here."

*　　*　　*　　*　　*　　*

It was traditionally considered a misfortune in royal households if a titled infant was a girl. The father of the hapless child was expected to be grumpy and the mother was ashamed of herself. But nobody seemed much upset over the sex of Princess Arnon's baby; certainly not Arnon herself whose experience with one Prince had not made her eager to produce another.

Antipas was up in Galilee when it happened. But for a handful of servants, he had been spending his time alone. The new villa, on which more than two hundred skilled stone masons had been engaged for five months, has risen a few feet above the massive foundation. One could easily imagine its oncoming beauty, even in the bewildering clutter of construction. The great oval pool, to be related to the house by a series of graceful arcades, had been completed—all but the mosaic lining, a tedious business, to be postponed until the Prince should be absent for a season. The marble flagging that bounded the pool, the exquisitely sculptured balustrades, and the commodious dressing-rooms were quite finished. Antipas had given much attention to the architecture and appointments of these sumptuous rooms, furnishing them so lavishly that he was using them for his living quarters. The pool had every way surpassed his expectations. The warm water, reputed to be of invigorating quality, poured generously from stone lions' mouths in a steady flow that promised to be endless.

It was a great privilege, reflected Antipas, to be the ruler of the Province of Galilee. True, he had not yet become acquainted with any of his subjects, nor had he given a moment's thought to his executive duties, whatever they might be. He knew very little about the Galileans, except what everybody knew; that they were a stolid, inoffensive, pious people, who minded their own small business, and had no ambitions to make their country known abroad. They grew their own grain, wine, flax, and wool. They fished in the Lake Gennesaret. Their men were adept at fashioning articles of household furniture, sometimes showing themselves to be excellent craftsmen. Their women wove serviceable fabrics for domestic uses. Their lives were self-contained and, in consequence, narrowly circumscribed. They almost never traveled beyond their own communities, except on the occasion of the annual "Passover" when considerable numbers of them made a pilgrimage to Jerusalem where a week was spent in the performance of religious rites. Customarily they took along some of the products of their lathes and looms, which they offered for sale at the bazaars. They wore no distinctive costume, but were readily identified in the city by their accent and colloquialisms. They were a bit self-conscious and shy in the presence of urbane strangers, aware that they were considered outlanders.

Antipas felt that the task of governing these simple-hearted country folk would not be arduous. Doubtless their trivial disagreements would be quietly settled among themselves; and, as for possible entanglements with the other provinces, the Galileans, exporting and importing nothing of any value, would not be likely to invoke judicial aid. He had little or nothing to do, his wealth would enable him to live in luxury. Whenever he wearied of his lethargy, he could easily trek to Caesarea and sail for Rome.

Life in Galilee was still a novelty. Antipas had fallen in love with the entrancing view to be had from the eastern portico of the pool. At his command the servants habitually roused him early to see the dawn come in. It was a glorious pageant, with the steep banks of cumulus clouds transformed into symmetrical garlands of gold as the sun illumined them from behind the distant mountain range, while the beautiful Lake Gennesaret—which everybody, except the natives, called "The Sea of Galilee"—reflected the deep blue of a farther sky.

Then would come the dramatic moment when the sun itself would mount regally into the open, stripping the clouds of their gold and arraying them with silver. The slanting sails of the little fishing boats would flash brightly. The tall tower of the Roman fort, a mile to the north, and the squat dome of the Jewish synagogue, a mile farther in the heart of Capernaum, would be flatteringly high-lighted. The untidy clutter of fishermen's shacks and wharves on the lake-shore would seem less ugly than picturesque. And the ruler of Galilee, suffused with a sense of well-being, would send for his breakfast.

Only one thing was lacking; congenial company. And on this eighteenth day of Adar that want was supplied. The arrival of Mark Varus was not a surprise, though Antipas had not expected him so soon. He had promised to come in mid-summer. Attended by a half-dozen servants from home and a pack-train of baggage which had been disembarked at Caesarea, Mark had shown up in the late afternoon, warm, dusty, and noisy with his approval of all these impressive building operations. Antipas hugged him with fervor, then picked him up and threw him headlong into the pool where he wriggled himself out of most of his clothing, his host following along the ledge with a pike-staff, fishing out the discarded garments as they accumulated in the water.

Presently, refreshed and clad, Mark joined his friend who, sprawled at full length on an ornamented lectus, was in conversation with the butler concerning the arrival of a courier from Jerusalem.

"Make him comfortable," the Prince was saying, "and tell him we will see him in an hour or two."

"He says it is urgent, sire."

"Nothing is urgent—in Tiberias," drawled Antipas.

"'Tiberias'?" queried Mark lazily, from the adjacent loggia. "Name of your new villa?"

"Name of my new city!" declared Antipas. "One of the most beautiful cities in all the world. All of it—every building in it—great and small— to be of white marble. You're planning to build your villa of white marble, aren't you?"

"Apparently," chuckled Mark, "though I hadn't thought much about it."

"Are you ready now for a tankard of wine?"

"I've been ready this half-hour."

Antipas clapped his hands and the wine arrived. They drank earnestly, and their tongues were loosened. Mark was besought for the latest news of Rome. He shook his head dourly. Rome had quite lost her charm; many changes—and all of them for the worse. He did not bother to explain that his eminent father's disastrous defeat at the hands of the barbarous Germanic tribes had done the Varus family no good socially: Antipas could—and did—form his own conclusions about that. Mark would be glad enough, he went on, to change his residence. Rome was filling up with vulgar upstarts, rich nobodies busy with business; a strange crowd now at all court festivities. Old Augustus had his faults, to be sure, but he had some dignity. Tiberius had brought in an entirely new breed of favorites. He had made Rome the dullest place on earth. He hated games; considered them a waste of public funds. He was going in for all manner of economies, as if the Empire was on the verge of bankruptcy.

"Well—it is; isn't it?" mumbled Antipas.

Mark agreed that it was, and always had been, but it still contrived to carry on.

"This new Tiberian dynasty," he continued, "is going to strip the city of everything that made her name famous. All that we hear about now is the importance of making the land more productive and the common people more contented."

"Sounds sensible," said Antipas.

"That's what ails it," muttered Mark. "How can there be any pleasure in a country that has resolved to be—sensible?"

"Is Tiberius still thinking of a northern invasion?"

"He probably never entertained such a thought," scoffed Mark. "I'm surprised your father was ever taken in by that rumor. The Emperor is working night and day to rebuild his Western Army."

"Indeed! I had supposed there was nothing left of it," remarked Antipas, ineptly. To cover his unintentional rudeness he added, quickly, "So— we no longer have anything to fear? That is good—if you're sure you know."

"I've had it on the best of authority. You might have been spared that matrimonial alliance with Arabia. By the way"—Mark's eyes twinkled mischievously—"how has that little treaty worked out? Is she pretty?"

Antipas frowned slightly, shrugged the impertinence away, up-ended his goblet, sat up, blinked thoughtfully, and began slowly counting his fingers.

Beckoning to the butler he said, "Tell the courier we will see him now." Presently he was thrusting his jeweled dagger through the wax sheath of a heavily gilded scroll. In silence and without betraying any sign of interest—for he was aware of Mark's lively curiosity—he read the formal message from his mother. Signaling the courier, waiting at a little distance, he said, casually, "After you have rested, you may return to Jerusalem. Convey our regards to Their Majesties and our good wishes to the Princess Arnon, for her health and happiness. And you may say," he added, as an afterthought, "that the child's name is Esther."

"Why do you want her called Esther?" asked Mark, with childish impudence, when the courier had bowed himself away.

"Because she was born on the fifteenth of Adar, a feast-day in honor of Queen Esther."

"Never heard of her. What's she Queen of?"

"Persia—a century and a half ago."

"Jewess?"

"Of course."

"Why 'of course'? Persia is not a Jewish country."

Antipas dismissed this query with a negligent gesture, adding that he was not an authority on Persian history; but Esther, a very beautiful Jewess, had once been Queen of Persia, and did Mark want to bet anything on it?

"Is your baby a Jewess?" hectored Mark. "Half Arabian, isn't she?"

"That will not matter much," yawned Antipas. "She will be brought up as a Jewess."

"In my poor judgment," declared Mark, suddenly serious, "it's going to be an awkward situation for her, all her life. A very unfortunate combination—half Arab, half Jew."

"Not so bad as you think," said Antipas, reassuringly. "Both nations will want to claim her."

"You know better than that!" said Mark. "Neither nation will accept her, much less claim her! My guess is that your Esther is going to be a very unhappy little girl."

"Well"—muttered Antipas—"it's too late to fret about that now." He held up his goblet for refilling. "Of course, you've no idea how beautiful this pool will be when the lining is in. I'll show you the designs after dinner. They are absolutely incomparable!"

*   *   *   *   *   *

Again it was Tishri. The summer was over, and the grass was tipped with white in the mornings. Varus had left for Rome, gratified with the Prince's assurance that he would be joining him in a couple of months, after he had paid his respects to his family.

Arriving home, Antipas had spent a leisurely hour refreshing himself after the tedious journey. Strolling into the Queen's apartment, as casually as if he had taken leave of his mother an hour ago, he eased himself into a deeply cushioned chair and waited for her appearance.

"Antipas!" Mariamne threw her arms about him, hugging him hungrily. "You have stayed away so long! We wondered if we were ever to see you again!" She held him at arms' length. "You're brown as a peasant."

He patted her on the cheek.

"Beautiful as ever!" he declared. "How do you do it?"

They sat down together on the divan, Mariamne gently caressing his tanned forearm.

"You've seen Arnon?" she inquired, anxiously.

"Not yet." Noting his mother's frown, he added, "Naturally, I wanted to see you first."

Mariamne accepted the tribute with a wisp of a smile, but grew serious again, shaking her head slowly.

"I think I should tell you, my dear, that your neglect of Arnon has all but broken her heart. You might at least have written her a friendly letter—about the baby."

"Sorry," muttered Antipas. "I've been very busy. The villa, you know. I must tell you all about it. You see—when I first thought of it—"

"The villa can wait," said Mariamne, crisply. "In the name of common decency, you should go at once to see your Princess—and this beautiful child, Fara. Come—I shall go with you—if that will make it any easier." She rose, and tugged him to his feet.

"Why do you call the child Fara?" inquired Antipas, testily. "I named her Esther."

"You may call her Esther, if you like." Mariamne's tone was frankly indignant. "But Arnon has named her Fara!"

"Against my wishes?"

"Of course! Why should Arnon **pay any** heed to your wishes, after the way you have treated her?"

"She is my wife!"

"Oh—is she? I thought you had forgotten." Mariamne was angry now, and her words came hot and fast. "I don't want to upset you, my son, the first hour you are home, but not everyone has forgotten that you married the Princess of Arabia. King Aretas remembers! Your father has had a message from him. He will tell you."

Antipas searched his mother's eyes and swallowed noisily.

"You mean—the Arabian is hostile?"

"Your father will tell you," said Mariamne. "Come! Better do what you can to make amends to Arnon."

"No!" growled Antipas. "I shall not be applying for any Arabian's pardon; not even Arnon's! And if this sullen shepherd, who calls himself a King, has the effrontery to dictate to a Prince of Israel—"

Mariamne held up a hand, warningly.

"It is quite apparent," she decided, "that you are in no mood to visit Arnon. Go at once to your father, and learn where you stand—in this unfortunate business. I shall tell the Princess that you are here, and eager to see her, but that the King has summoned you to an urgent conference. And—let me say one thing more," she added, as Antipas moved toward the door, "it will be much to your advantage if you conduct yourself respectfully in your audience with your father. No strutting, no levity, no assumption that you are a petted favorite of the King!"

"Angry, is he?"

" 'Angry' is a very mild word for it! And—don't bother to tell him what all you have been building in Galilee. The King has other plans for Galilee!"

*　　*　　*　　*　　*　　*

It was not a happy interview. To begin with, Antipas was halted—politely enough, but definitely halted—at the door of his father's audience room, the Chamberlain announcing firmly that the King was engaged.

"But he will see me," rasped Antipas. "Go and tell him."

"His Majesty has been notified that you are here, Your Highness. He bids you wait until you are summoned."

Antipas turned to go.

"Say to His Majesty that I shall return when he is less busy," he said, indifferently.

"If I may venture a suggestion," murmured the obsequious Chamberlain, "the Prince would be well advised to remain here, until he is called."

Something of warning in the old man's tone checked Antipas' impulsive decision to leave. Indignantly he glanced about for a chair to fling himself into, but to his surprise and annoyance there were no chairs in the corridor. He was about to order one brought to him, but the Chamberlain had already slipped back into the room, closing the door behind him. Antipas paced up and down, fuming. He had never been treated like this before. Once he made up his mind to go, stalked as far as the great door that gave onto the terrace, but thought better of it—and returned. It was all of an hour before the Chamberlain reappeared to say that His Majesty would see His Highness now.

Forcing a filial smile, Antipas entered, bowed, and said:

"My greetings, sire! I hope I find you well."

"Sit down!" barked the King.

Antipas drew a sober face and sat, rigidly, at attention.

It was immediately evident that the King had carefully composed the speech upon which he launched with icy restraint. He had tried, he said quietly, to be an indulgent father. It was not easy for a King—hard pressed with cares of state—to give his children the firm discipline necessary to the production of a strong character. He had paid his sons the compliment of believing that—with their superb advantages—they would develop strength, dignity, integrity.

But he had been bitterly disappointed, he went on dejectedly. Where was there a father, in all this realm, who had less cause for satisfaction in his sons? There was Philip, the weakling, the cuckold! Herod's voice shook with contempt. And there was this insufferable braggart and brawler, Archelaus! What had he ever done, the King asked himself, to have deserved an affliction like Archelaus?

"Only last week," he went on, with rising heat, "your impudent brother came to advise us that we were too old to continue our rule; that we had toiled too long, too diligently; that we should retire, and confer on him the regency! Think of that! The regency—of all Judaea! To be conferred upon a loud-mouthed, contentious fellow who can't even get along harmoniously with his own lazy drinking-companions!"

Antipas smiled a little, reminiscently. Feeling himself to be presently in need of mercy, he thought it opportune to put in a defensive word for his elder brother. Herod, noting that the Prince wanted to speak, paused to listen.

"Archelaus was indeed over-reaching himself, sire, but is it so unthinkable that he should be made regent of Judaea? He is the heir to this throne! is he not?"

"That," snapped Herod, "is none of your business! We are just now about to come to your business!"

And so—after this considerable delay—they had come to the Prince's business—and a bad business it was, too. Antipas, had he the normal instinct of a six-year-old waif, would have known, declared the King, what a dangerous position he had accepted when he consented to be the son-in-law of an Arabian King.

Antipas feebly protested that the honor had been forced upon him, but Herod wasn't entertaining any mitigating circumstances.

"You have treated this Arabian girl shamefully! What a fool you are—to think that these savages in Arabia who, for all their uncouth manners, have their pride, would let you heap indignities upon the only child of their King! Now you have it to settle for! And in full, mind you! I have

had word from Aretas. His message is brief but clear! His daughter is to
be brought home to Arabia!"

Antipas raised his head and brightened perceptibly. He drew a long,
comforting sigh. His father, observing his relief, rose from his chair, and
stabbed a finger in the air.

"Mind you"—he shouted—"the Princess is to be taken home to Arabia;
not sent home. And you, Your Brightness, will accompany her. Aretas
insists upon that. His much cherished daughter, he says, has suffered
enough at the hands of this Court. She is not to be returned like some
article of rejected merchandise! Those were his words. Her husband is
to bring her home, in a manner befitting their station, and show her the
honors she—and her countrymen—have a right to expect."

"But"—spluttered Antipas—"why does he want me to play this farce?
He probably despises me."

"Indeed he does!" yelled Herod—"and not probably! And why
shouldn't he?"

"They will kill me—if I appear over there," muttered Antipas.

"They will kill you if you don't!"

"How long must I stay?"

"Until you have fully restored Arnon's damaged pride; until you have
satisfied Aretas and his Council that you respect their Princess as your
wife."

There was a long silence.

"I had expected to leave for Rome," protested Antipas. "I have business
there."

"That may be," snorted Herod. "But you have no business in Rome
that can compare, in urgency, with the business you have in Arabia."

"How about my obligations in Galilee?"

"You are to forget all about Galilee!"

"Meaning that you have deposed me, sire?"

"For the present, yes. We will take care of all Galilean matters.
Whether you ever find yourself in Galilee again is a question you may
answer for yourself. You may go now. Make peace with your Princess. And
prepare to take her home without delay."

Antipas noisily exhaled a self-piteous sigh, slapped his palms down hard
on the arms of his chair, and rose to his feet.

"This, sire," he muttered, "is the unhappiest day of my life."

"So far as you have gone," assisted the King. "See to it now that you
do not encounter unhappier days. Make things right with your Princess.

Tell her how you have longed to return to her, but that a revolt among the people of your Province—" He broke off, annoyed to find his son attentively listening for further light on this extemporaneous alibi. "Contrive your own lie," he went on, impatiently—"but make it good! Arnon will try to believe you, but she lacks a great deal of being such a fool as her husband."

"A revolt, eh?" reflected Antipas.

"A dangerous uprising; and you had to stay there—and deal with it." Herod grew thoughtful and continued, to himself, "I shall say that to Aretas. He may doubt the truth of it but a poor excuse, in a case so desperate, is better than none. When a man's pride is injured, almost any medicine is welcome."

"May I take my leave now, Your Majesty?" asked Antipas, with elaborate humility, hopeful that his father might relent and smile a little.

"Indeed you may, Your Highness," mocked Herod, with a profound bow. "What an ass you are!"

＊　＊　＊　＊　＊　＊

The return to Arabia was not as difficult as Antipas had feared. He was regarded with deference. It was obvious that his shameful neglect of the Princess had been a well-kept secret. On the surface, Arnon had been treated kindly in Jerusalem. King Aretas received his son-in-law graciously enough, though without any ostentatious amiability, an attitude readily explained by his habitual reticence.

The Counsellors, promptly assembling to pay their respects, were forced to concede to one another (for none of them knew how badly their Princess had fared but Ilderan and Tema) that if Antipas were not a Jew he would be almost likable.

"It isn't his fault that he's a Jew," remarked Adbeel.

"No," agreed Mishma, "but it is a great misfortune."

Arnon had wondered whether there might be some constraint in her meeting with Zendi, but when he called with his pretty wife Rennah, Dumah's daughter, the air was instantly cleared for them all by little Fara. Rennah, presently to bear a child, had taken Arnon's uncommonly beautiful baby into her arms, while the others, for various reasons, beamed happily over her unself-conscious display of maternal tenderness. They all laughed merrily when Fara laid a small pink palm against Rennah's cheek—and smiled. Antipas, who had a talent for making friends easily,

Fara Swears Vengeance

Fara did not smile or speak. Slowly leaving her place she walked with determined steps to the massive table. The audience leaned forward and held its breath, wondering what was about to happen. Moving around the table until she faced the King, Fara made a deep bow. Then, to the amazement of everyone, she whipped a little dagger from her belt and deftly drew a red streak diagonally across her left forearm. Bending over the long neglected, unsigned vow of vengeance, she took up the stylus, dipped it in her blood, and wrote FARA.

was delighted with his daughter's charming response to Rennah's caresses.

"What an adorable child!" declared Zendi.

"I never saw her make up with any one so quickly," said Arnon. "I'm quite jealous of you, Rennah."

"Beautiful women," commented Antipas, "do not have to be jealous of one another."

Arnon's eyes had brightened at that. There was no doubt now that the Prince was proving to be a good husband. Even Aretas, standing by, seemed gratified.

"They are beautiful," he put in, unexpectedly, for he was not given to compliments—"all three of them!"

And so—the return of Antipas to Arabia was made much easier for him than he had expected or deserved. The baby Fara had paved his way. The Arabians came from near and far to see this endearing child whose extraordinary beauty was on everybody's tongue. Grim old shepherds, who had bitterly resented Arnon's marriage to a Jew, came to see if her baby was really as lovely as the rumor, found the Prince so obviously devoted to his family that they went away to report favorably.

"He may be a Jew," they said, "but he is doing well by the Princess."

The ranking Arabians of his own age, suspicious and cold at first, gradually thawed toward Antipas. He was no match for them as an equestrian, but he was by no means inexperienced in the saddle. Respect for him increased almost to friendliness when, invited to join a party on a wolf hunt, he had appeared on a nervous, fidgety, unpredictable filly whose wet flanks showed that she had stoutly disputed his authority Aretas had told him to select his own horse, that morning. Old Kedar had been instructed to assist him. The Prince had looked them over carefully.

"I'll take this young bay mare, Kedar," said Antipas.

Kedar had drawn a long face.

"She needs quite a bit of handling, sire," he said.

"I dare say," drawled Antipas. "She probably wants exercise—and so do I."

Privileged by his age to speak his mind candidly, Kedar chuckled a little, deep in his throat, and replied, "Well—you'll both get it, I think."

When the young blades, waiting for him on a little knoll, saw him coming at an easy canter, they exchanged knowing grins. Approaching, Antipas dismounted.

"The girth is a bit tight," he remarked, loosening it with a practiced hand. "It annoys her, I think."

Everybody laughed companionably.

"It doesn't take much to annoy that filly," said Zendi. "Have any trouble with her, sir?"

"Nothing to speak of," said Antipas. He patted the perspiring mare on her neck and gently tousled her forelock. "You'll be a good girl now, won't you?" he murmured kindly. The filly tossed her head; but, apparently thinking better of it, rubbed her muzzle across his arm. They all laughed again. Antipas was getting along very nicely with the Arabians.

Winter closed in. It was rather hard to bear. The days were short and cold and uneventful. Sometimes Antipas would talk to Arnon about Rome, and she would listen with wide-eyed interest, thinking to please him. When the first hardy little edelweiss peeped through the melting snow, he suggested that they plan a trip to Rome; not to stay very long. He knew she would enjoy the voyage, he said, and she would be interested in seeing this greatest of all the cities in the world!

Arnon demurred at first. She would like to go—but there was little Fara. We will take her along, said Antipas. That would be difficult, said Arnon. Then leave her here, said Antipas. She has an excellent nurse. And we will soon be back. Do think it over, he implored, adding wistfully, "I am really a city-bred man, my dear—and it has been a long time since I have been on a paved street."

"He has done very well, Arnon," said her father, when she consulted him for advice. "Much better than we had thought. Perhaps you should humor him."

"I'm not very happy in a big city," said Arnon.

"And your husband is not very happy in the open country," said Aretas. "Better meet him halfway in this matter. Otherwise, he may grow restless here."

She nodded her head. It was good counsel. Antipas would grow restless here. She did not add that Antipas was already so restless that it was making him moody and detached.

*   *   *   *   *   *

No one could have been more graciously attentive than was Antipas on their long voyage from the port city of Gaza to Rome. The early summer weather was perfect for sailing, the little ship had better accommodations than most, and the ports of call were of fascinating interest.

Arnon could not be quite sure whether the Prince's good humor and high spirits represented his desire to make her contented, or could be accounted for by a boyish anticipation of a return to his enchanted city.

She gave him the benefit of the doubt and enjoyed the comfortable journey.

Antipas spent long hours, on lazy afternoons under the gay deck-canopy, discoursing of the life he had lived in Rome, and the friends to whom he would introduce her. But the more he talked, the less confidence she had in her capacity to find pleasure in the pursuits of such people as he described. Did they ride, she asked. No—there really was no safe and quiet place to ride unless one lived on an estate in the country. But—couldn't they do that, inquired Arnon. Antipas had whimsically wrinkled his nose: he had had quite enough of country life for the present. But—wouldn't it be frightfully noisy in the city? Doubtless; but Antipas didn't object to the sound of traffic; it made him feel alive.

One day she asked about the language of Rome. Latin, wasn't it? Perhaps Antipas would teach her. No, Antipas had replied, they did not speak Latin; that is, it was spoken only by the lower classes.

"Everybody who is anybody," he went on, "has had private tutors, and these men are invariably Greeks—Greek slaves."

"The better people are taught by slaves?"

"My dear, our Greek slaves are the most intelligent men in the world. We Romans do not pretend to match them in learning."

" 'We Romans'?" laughed Arnon. "You are not a Roman, are you?"

Antipas had glanced about, before replying in a guarded tone, "I am Jewish by race, but Rome is my city." Rearranging Arnon's pillows for her better comfort, he reverted to the language question. "You will pick up the Greek quickly, I think. You may speak with an odd accent at first. Most foreigners do. That is to be expected. But the Romans will find it charming. It always amuses them."

Arnon smiled uncertainly. Of course she knew that she would be considered a foreigner, but the word made her lonely. And she would speak queerly, and it would amuse them. Doubtless they would treat her as a child, learning to talk. She wouldn't like that. Some women were at their very best—playing they were six, prattling baby-talk, but Arnon had been taught to despise such silly affectations. Now she would be forced to do the baby-rôle, for which she felt temperamentally unfitted. She frowned thoughtfully. If she had been at a disadvantage in Jerusalem where at least she could talk like an adult, how would she feel in Rome? It worried her so much that she asked the question of Antipas who, summoned from his day-dreaming, replied absently, "You will not feel strange—after a day or two."

But she did. The great, garish, clamorous city bewildered her. The elaborate house to which Antipas brought her was conducted in a manner utterly unfamiliar. She had such difficulty in making the servants understand her wishes that she soon gave up trying to be the mistress of her home and allowed the score or more of slaves to run the establishment as they pleased. Often they were drunk, always they were lazy; it was suspected that the butler was dishonest. The meals were late and indifferently served. The rooms were untidy. Antipas coolly remarked that he had never lived less comfortably. He did not say it was Arnon's fault; but whose else could it be?

Their first social evening out was at the home of Mark Varus. Antipas had reminded Claudia that his Arabian Princess would be having language difficulties which might make her seem ill at ease, and would Claudia limit the number of her guests to a very small company who could be depended on to understand Arnon's predicament. So, Claudia had invited only twenty.

The first person to be introduced was Arnon's sister-in-law, Herodias, who spread a wide, red mouth, nodded gaily to her new relative—as if they had known each other since childhood—and threw her long, slim, jingling arms around Antipas' neck, drawing him to her in a daring embrace. Lagging behind Herodias was a sheepishly grinning, balding man whom Arnon readily guessed was Poor Philip. He advanced shyly and spoke in Aramaic.

"Thrice welcome, Princess Arnon, to this overestimated city. I am Philip, the pampered husband of that lady who is so firmly attached to my brother. We are, as you see, a devoted family."

Arnon smiled at this persiflage, but couldn't help feeling shocked over Philip's indifference to his wife's sluttish behavior.

"They must be very warm friends," she said, trying to be casual.

Claudia had turned away to greet arriving guests. Herodias had eased her grip on Antipas and was whispering earnestly into his ear. Mark Varus, flushed and lusty, approached to say—in Greek, "So—at last—we have the lovely Princess of Arabia with us!"

Arnon smiled, only half understanding.

"Her Greek isn't very nimble yet, Mark," said Philip. "Know any Aramaic?"

Mark said "Very little," and proceeded to prove it by discoursing, in extravagant terms, of the new villa in Galilee. Arnon, who knew less about the villa than Mark knew about Aramaic, could only say that she hoped to see it, some day. Mark's intuition suggested that this topic might profitably be dropped now, he offered her his arm and led her—

with a proprietorial swagger—among the groups of guests, introducing her to faces rather than names. Arnon had a feeling that no one knew who she was, or cared very much. They smirked, nodded, and continued their loud-pitched conversations in which three or four women seemed endeavoring to talk one another down. Arnon was stunned by the confusion. She had never been in a place so astoundingly noisy or so appallingly rude.

Mark Varus continued to drag her about in a manner that made it difficult to maintain any dignity at all, as if he were exhibiting a blooded colt, pinioning her arm tightly under his, while he gaily shouted greetings to new arrivals. Arnon turned about to look for Antipas, but he was lost in the crowd; probably had forgotten her.

Presently an elaborate dinner was served, the guests lounging languidly on an elbow in the deep upholstery of divans drawn close together about a long table. Mark, seated next to Arnon, was most attentive, embarrassingly attentive, finding frequent occasion to bend over her in an effort to serve her plate personally with some delicacy. She instinctively drew away from these intimate contacts; and Mark's ardor, after a few unmistakable rebuffs, suddenly cooled. Turning from her, he attempted to attract the attention of Herodias, on the other side, but finding her wholly preoccupied with Antipas, he laboriously resumed his attention to the Arabian Princess, scolding her gently for her abstinence. Arnon tried to explain that it was not a custom among her people to drink intoxicants. Sometimes, she said, their men had a glass of wine, but it was not considered suitable for an Arabian woman to drink, at all.

Philip, who was seated next to her, overheard the conversation and leaned forward to remark that one was expected to drink deeply at Roman banquets.

"It annoys half-drunken people," he went on, drolly, "to talk to anybody who remains sober. It embarrasses them. That's why Varus presses you to imbibe, Princess Arnon. He means it well enough. He is your host —and he wants you to be a social success."

Mark listened with a frown, but made no comment.

"And I won't be a success—unless I'm a little bit drunk?" inquired Arnon.

"Well—" drawled Philip, with a chuckle, "that's one way of saying it —but I never heard it put so briefly and clearly before."

He caught Mark's eye and was rewarded with a scowl and a shrug.

"I'm afraid I am not going to like it very well—in Rome," murmured Arnon. It was some time before Philip commented on that. Regarding her soberly, he said, "No—you couldn't. My brother should not have brought you here. You are of a texture much too fine to be soiled with this degradation."

For an instant, Arnon searched Philip's eyes, suspecting that he was taunting her, but found him seriously sincere.

"Perhaps you, too, would be happier—somewhere else," she said.

"Anywhere else," he replied.

*   *   *   *   *   *

After a few weeks of earnest but unsuccessful endeavors to accommodate herself to the mores of Rome, Arnon gave up trying and begged Antipas to excuse her from further attendance at banquets.

"And am I to spend my evenings at home, then?" he demanded, testily. "Is it your thought that I should live the life of a hermit in a cave?"

There was only one reasonable answer to that. Arnon assured him that he was quite free to go alone, whenever and wherever he pleased; which he did. It was not long before they were seeing very little of each other, making no effort to repair their estrangement.

One evening in early autumn when Arnon was about to sit down to a solitary dinner, Philip surprised her by calling. She insisted upon his dining with her, and he seemed glad to accept. She found it easy to talk with Philip, whose reticence everybody mistook for stupidity. It was not long until the conversation was becoming quite personal; by mutual consent, for they were both lonely. Arnon's life in Rome, Philip was saying, must have turned out to be very tiresome. Tiresome, said Arnon, wasn't the word she would have used, but it was at least that.

"Sometimes," declared Philip, dreamily, "I can hardly endure it. I have often thought of running away—to Sicily, perhaps, and live alone—" He seemed talking to himself now, with eyes half closed— "in the country, in a little house, on a green hillside, with fruits and flowers to cultivate, trees, grass, sunsets, and a friendly dog or two."

"But would you be happy—without your family?" asked Arnon, when he had ended.

"I have no family," he muttered. "Herodias is never at home. I do not ask where she spends her time."

"Why don't you?" ventured Arnon. "She is your wife."

"For the same reason that you do not ask Antipas where he spends his time," said Philip. He chuckled unpleasantly. "I daresay that if we inquired of their present whereabouts, we would find them in the same place."

"You mean—they are often together?"

"They are always together! And if I were you, Arnon, I should leave for Arabia at once—before this scandal humiliates you—and your people."

Arnon's heart beat hard and her throat hurt.

"I think that was why you came to see me tonight," she said, weakly. "You thought it was high time for me to know."

Philip nodded, without meeting her eyes.

"Everyone else knows," he said. "Why shouldn't you?"

Next morning, the unavoidable interview between Antipas and Arnon terminated their unhappy alliance. To his considerable relief, the Prince's scandalous behavior was not discussed. Arnon simply stated that Rome was no place for an Arabian Princess to hope for happiness, and Antipas cheerfully agreed that her return to her own people was the only solution to their problem. He would arrange for it without delay.

A well-appointed pleasure barge was chartered, stocked with everything that might make the long voyage comfortable. A score of trusted men, experienced in handling caravans, were engaged to safe-guard the overland journey from the port at Gaza.

On the day before the sailing, Antipas tried to slant the conversation toward the probable attitude of King Aretas. Reassuring Arnon on the wisdom of her decision to return home, he added, pleasantly, "And how pleased your father will be to have you come back to him. I am sure he has been lonely without you."

Arnon frowned, pursed her lips, and stared squarely into his uneasy eyes. He shifted his position and made a pretense of casualness. Slowly lowering her head, she continued to search his face from under her long lashes. She gave him a slow, enigmatic smile.

"My father will welcome his daughter's return to his tent," she said, measuring her words. "But Aretas, the King of Arabia, may not be pleased when he learns that the Princess of Arabia has been put to shame by an alien enemy."

"Meaning that he will seek revenge?" Antipas was serious now and his voice was unsteady.

"Prince Antipas is not well versed in Arabian history," replied Arnon, "if he thinks that this indignity might be easily overlooked."

The implied warning disposed of the Prince's suavity and self-assurance. He paced the floor, flushed and angry.

"Let the King of Arabia do what he will!" he shouted. "Doubtless the Princess will put the worst possible construction on her difficulties. She will not tell the King that she made no effort to fulfill her obligations to her husband." He paused in his march and regarded her sternly. "I have not injured you! On the contrary, you are abandoning me! And I may as well tell you now that when your ship has sailed tomorrow I shall execute a bill of divorcement—on the grounds of desertion!"

Arnon suddenly sat erect. Her eyes lighted.

"Do you really mean that?" she exclaimed. "Accept my thanks, Antipas, for this gracious favor!"

Stunned by this unexpected blow to his vanity, he studied her eyes soberly. No—she was not ironical. She meant it sincerely. He had hesitated to hand her this crushing news—and now it was evident that she was delighted to receive it. He bowed stiffly and walked toward the door where he turned for a final word.

"You will find on the barge a young, well-born Greek slave, whom I bought yesterday at considerable cost. She is your personal property. I hope you will take her with you. She reads, writes, and speaks Greek fluently. In addition to her other duties, perhaps she will teach my little daughter a more graceful language than the crude imitation of Aramaic that is spoken in Arabia."

Arnon flushed a little.

"Whether our language is crude or not," she retorted, "depends on who speaks it! And—I want no parting gift from you."

"As you like," said Antipas, indifferently. "The Greek slave will be on the barge, and she is your property. If you do not want her—pitch her overboard."

The Prince did not appear when the ship sailed. Arnon had not expected him, and was not disappointed. At the last minute before the hawsers were hauled ashore, Philip arrived in a surprisingly happy mood. He led her a little way apart on the afterdeck for a final word.

"This is a good day for you," he said, gaily—"and for me, too! You are going home to people who love you, freed from everything that has made your life unpleasant."

"And you?" queried Arnon.

"I, too, am free! Herodias has informed me that she and my brother want to be married; and would I divorce her. Would I? I do not often move with so much alacrity. And I am sailing, in a week, for Sicily."

"How fortunate you are, Philip," said Arnon. "I do hope you will be contented there. I shall often think of you—in your garden." She lowered her voice. "The Prince may have told you that he is divorcing me."

Philip nodded.

"I was gratified and a bit surprised that Antipas found the courage to tell you himself. My brother has always disliked to admit that he is a scoundrel."

After farewells were said and the ship had cast off, Arnon was conducted to her commodious cabin where an uncommonly bright and pretty young woman, of nearly her own age, was unpacking her boxes. She had quite forgotten about the slave. The girl made a deep curtsey, with eyes timidly averted, and continued with her task.

"I am told that you belong to me," said Arnon, kindly. "What is your name?"

"Ione, Your Highness," said the girl, with another obsequious curtsey.

"You may address me as 'Princess Arnon'—and you need not curtsey. Are you a good sailor?"

"I do not know, Princess Arnon."

"But this is not your first voyage."

"No, Princess Arnon. I was brought to Rome from Piraeus in a slave-ship when I was only ten, but we were crowded down deep in the hold where it was always dark and there was no air. I was very sick, all the time. Perhaps I may do better if—"

"—If you are allowed to breathe," assisted Arnon. "We will see to that." She smiled reassuringly and the girl's eyes softened. "It will be a long voyage," she added. "I am taking you to Arabia."

"I am glad, Princess Arnon," murmured Ione.

"You are not sorry to leave Rome? You will not be homesick?"

"I have no home, Princess Arnon. I am glad to leave Rome. I shall be happy in Arabia."

"But you were never in Arabia," said Arnon, amused.

"No, Princess Arnon," said Ione, "but I know I shall be happy—if you are there."

*   *   *   *   *   *

The caravan wearily drew up before the King's encampment at sunset. Old Kedar was much moved as he helped Arnon out of the cramped camel-housing, lifting her down as if she were still a little girl. Word spread rapidly that the Princess had come home. Nephti met her at the door and tenderly placed the baby Fara in her arms. Arnon's eyes were misty as she looked down into the child's smiling face. The servants gathered about, making soft little murmurs of fond delight. The Princess inquired for her father.

"The King should be here soon," said Kedar. "They buried the good Chief Ilderan, this afternoon."

As the twilight came on, Aretas arrived, sober and moody over the loss of his great friend. Arnon's presence comforted him, but he was impatient to learn why she had been brought back by strangers. She tried to spare him, tried to take most of the blame, tried to temper his rising anger; but he demanded the full truth, and she told him everything. Aretas did not eat or sleep that night.

Next morning, well mounted couriers were dispatched in all directions with messages to the Counsellors tersely telling the story. The Counsellors, in turn, sent word to their tribal sheiks that an expedition would move at once upon Jerusalem. A mobilization of cavalry was ordered, the concentration to occur on the east bank of the Jordan near the village of Jeshimoth. By the fifth day, two thousand armed horsemen were assembled.

The violent rage that had swept Aretas was not apparent now. That fire, still dangerously hot, had been banked. When the King spoke to his impatient troops he was composed. Arabia had suffered a great humiliation at the hands of the Jews. A swift and savage blow was to be struck at Herod, seeing that the despicable Prince Antipas was out of reach.

The Arabians needed no urging. They were so eager to proceed that the Counsellors postponed the election of a successor to Ilderan. Indeed, it was with much difficulty that Aretas detained the vanguard until the contingents from far distances had arrived. Young Zendi would have taken a score of his reckless neighbors on ahead of the others had not Aretas spoken to him sharply.

"You may be the ruler of these brave men, some day," he said, "and it is not too soon to let them know that you have not only a courageous heart but a cool head."

When the eagerly awaited order was shouted on that eventful morning they bounded away to the west, forded the river, scrambled up the bank into Judaea, galloped four abreast across the plain, through the startled villages, over the highways, into the palm-bordered avenue that bisected suburban Bethany. They dashed down the long hill from whose top the turrets and spires of Jerusalem shone brightly in the noonday sun. Still four abreast, they rode through the massive open gates, a score of bewildered guards and revenue officers scattering before them. They proceeded at full gallop through the narrow, winding, crowded streets, indifferent to the shouts and screams of the panic-driven crowds that scurried for safety in doorways and alleys. Now they had reached Herod's imposing palace, "The Insula," where they drew rein. Lining up in precise ranks that filled the spacious plaza fronting the huge marble Insula, they dismounted from their wet horses and stood waiting while Aretas and the

Counsellors rode up the broad white steps and across the stone-floored terrace and up another flight of steps toward the impressive bronze doors.

A thousand Roman legionaries stood guard, but had received no order to obstruct the mounted Arabians. Perhaps the Legate was stunned out of his wits by the sheer impudence of these grim horsemen who had dared to ride up to the very doors of the Insula.

It struck Aretas strangely that so large a force guarded the King's palace. Surely he had had no word that the Arabians were making an invasion; or, if he had ordered out his troops to repel an attack, why were they standing there motionless?

Aretas shouted to the Legate, who approached respectfully.

"Take me to Herod!" he demanded.

"King Herod is dead, sire."

"Have a care," shouted Zendi. "It is dangerous to lie to the King of Arabia!"

"I have told you the truth, sire," reiterated the Legate, calmly. "King Herod died of shock, early this morning." He gestured toward his troops. "This is a Guard of Honor."

"Open those doors!" commanded Aretas. "I came to see Herod—and I mean to see him—alive or dead!"

After a brief parley, Legate Julian gave the order. The great bronze doors slowly swung open. The mounted detachment moved forward.

"But, sire," protested the Legate, "I hope you are not going to ride your horses into the Insula! Surely you would show more respect for the King of the Jews!"

"Stand aside!" growled Aretas. "I am not here to show respect!"

They rode into the marble-lined palace, down the broad corridor, inquired of a frightened sentry where Herod's body was to be found; and, upon learning that it was in the Council Chamber, proceeded to ride into the high-domed, beautifully appointed room. In the center, on a bier, reposed the King of the Jews. The military guard, numbering a score, stood their ground. Forming a circle about the corpse, the Arabians sat for a long moment in silence. Aretas pointed his riding-whip toward the waxen face.

"It is clear we cannot take revenge on that!" he said, calmly. "And we have no cause to hew the Roman legion to pieces. And there is no Jewish army to fight." Aretas dismounted and the Counsellors followed his example. With bridle-reins in hand, they stood in a circle around the bier and held a conference. All were agreed that there was nothing further to do in Jerusalem. Dumah, dissatisfied, suggested that they hang Herod's body to a tree in the courtyard. Mishma—who was expected to be appointed Chief of the Counsellors—objected to this on the ground that it wouldn't be dignified.

"It would be as dignified," said Dumah, "as what we are doing now!" For Mishma's bay mare had taken a step forward and was inquisitively sniffing the gray feet of the late King. Everybody chuckled. Even Aretas grinned. They mounted their horses, rode out of the Council Chamber and down the corridor and out into the warm sunshine. A report was made to the cavalrymen. They were instructed to be at ease and do what they liked until sunset.

Disappointed and disgruntled, they rode back into the business zone; and, after the manner of idling soldiers, made a nuisance of themselves in the shops and markets. No serious damage was done. One indignant old goldsmith remarked, "Kindly leave your horses outside. You are welcome —but we have no accommodations for horses." The Arabians thought this was funny and laughed heartily at the joke as they rode about through his bazaar, examining the expensive merchandise. Pleased that the Arabs did not loot his store, the goldsmith cheerfully answered all their questions.

"How do you happen to be doing business today?" they asked.

"We've had no order to close up," replied the old merchant.

"You know that King Herod is dead, don't you?"

"Of course."

"Sick very long?"

"Hadn't you heard?"

"Heard he was dead; that's all."

"There's more to it than that! Prince Archelaus arrived from Rome, last night, and he and the King quarreled. Somehow the Prince was stabbed, accidentally, they say; and the King had a stroke—and died."

The Arabians stopped browsing about the shop and surrounded the goldsmith inquisitively. Was the Prince badly hurt? Yes—he was said to be dying.

As the afternoon wore on, some of the cavalrymen managed to find some wine which gave them renewed interest in their mission of vengeance. They rode their horses into the lobby of the Temple, tore down several exquisitely wrought tapestries from the walls, and set fire to the High Priest's palace. But—as for revenge—no one was satisfied. That could come later—when they had access to Antipas. He was the ruler of Galilee, and would eventually return to his domain. Some day, they declared, a few picked men of Arabia would pay him a visit.

At dusk they set off in the moonlight for their homeland. Next morning, as if the expedition had not already acquainted itself with a sufficient number of unusual incidents, the King's white stallion misjudged the width of a cross-country wall and pitched his rider violently to the ground. They hurriedly dismounted and gathered about him. Aretas was dead.

Improvising a litter made of young saplings, they slowly bore the body toward home. That evening they camped on the plain near Jeshimoth. After their supper, eaten in silence, the troops assembled to hear Mishma confer the Kingship of Arabia upon Zendi, the son of Ilderan.

3

To THE SATISFACTION of Arabia, young Zendi dealt quite generously with Princess Arnon. This he could well afford to do, for he had inherited from his father Ilderan large flocks of sheep, herds of cattle, and enough camels to outfit a dozen caravans on their regular journeys to the sea.

It was his right as the new King to take over the entire domain controlled by Aretas, but he immediately asked the Counsellors to cede a tract of the King's land to the Princess for the pasturage of livestock bequeathed by her father.

In view of the sympathy which the Arabians felt for their unhappy Princess, this warm-hearted display of kindness greatly advantaged the boyish monarch as he entered upon his duties. And it was clear that he would stand in need of his country's loyalty, for but little snow had fallen during the previous winter and the competition for grazing grounds would demand firm and wise control when the midsummer sun had made the problem serious. By this magnanimous act, Zendi had made a good beginning. Even Mishma, who had come so nearly being the new King himself, expressed his belief that Arabia was in competent hands, and gave the son of Ilderan his full support.

With the approval of the Counsellors, Arnon's establishment was set up on a broad plateau two miles south of the King's encampment, and it seemed very much like home, for she was entitled to all the furniture and household retainers belonging to her father. At Zendi's gracious suggestion, the royal ensign fluttered at her imposing entrance door, and its replica was embroidered on her apparel. "And Fara is to wear the royal crest on her clothing too," Zendi had added, much to Arnon's delight.

So many internal problems were distressing the King, the Counsellors, and the tribal chieftains, as this trying summer wore on, that the question of an immediate avenging of Arnon was abandoned. Affairs in Arabia were quite difficult enough without the added risk and responsibility of setting forth on a punitive errand requiring their best men and much valuable time. Word had drifted in that Prince Antipas and his disreputable wife had taken up permanent residence in Galilee. Very good, said Arabia. We will know where to find him. Let him be patient and wait our convenience.

A few of the more hot-headed young blades, still disgruntled over the recent fiasco in Jerusalem, demurred at this postponement, maintaining that the honor of Arabia was at stake and that any delay to deal out retribution might be interpreted by the Jews as a sign of indifference—or worse. To soothe the indignation of their reckless sons and nephews, the Counsellors prepared an imposing statement of intent to right this wrong, which any impatient young Arabian might sign—and act upon—whenever he wished.

In the King's main tent where all state business was conducted and Council meetings were held, there was a massive oak table elaborately carved with devices relating to the interests of herders and shepherds. This venerated table had long served as the equivalent of a throne. Nobody remembered the name of the craftsman who had built it, for he had been dead at least three centuries, but it had been in uninterrupted use as a symbol of executive authority ever since the reign of the fabulous Terah whose deeds of strength and skill had inspired the minstrels for many generations. On this table were laid documents of high importance; petitions to, and edicts of, the Counsellors and decrees of the King.

After much deliberation, the Counsellors drew up a formal vow, impressively lettered in colors, stating that the undersigned hereby pledged himself to avenge the Princess Arnon by destroying Antipas, the Tetrarch of Galilee and Peraea. The avenger was to choose his own time and manner of fulfilling his vow. It was his responsibility to decide whether he would perform it clandestinely and alone, or with the voluntary assistance of others. But once he had pledged to do it, the task was in his hands and Arabia would expect him to keep his promise, whatever the cost.

The heavy sheet of papyrus was ceremoniously placed upon the table, and the word went forth that it was there—with a stylus and inkhorn beside it—for any man to sign who felt urged to do so. But the blazing sun continued to scorch the grass, and every man was fully occupied with the desperate search for pasture to save what remained of his decimated flocks. Everybody agreed that the contemptible Antipas must be put to death, but he would have to wait for it until Arabia saw better times.

To Arnon, this tardiness to wreak vengeance upon Antipas was of small concern. It would be a dangerous business and whoever attempted it would almost certainly lose his life, for the stronghold in Galilee would be well guarded by the man who doubtless lived in fear of a reprisal. Quite enough unhappiness had already resulted from Arabia's pact with the Jews. She said that to Zendi, upon learning of the vow that the Counsellors had prepared. "I do not want to be responsible for any more trouble," protested Arnon. "Why not let the matter rest?" And Zendi had agreed that her suggestion was sensible enough, but added that all Arabia would sleep more comfortably when Antipas slept without prospect of waking.

There were some encouraging rains that autumn, much too late to benefit the burned pasture-lands, but giving promise of better fare next season. The winter however was bitterly cold and the snow alarmingly scanty.

The Arabian shepherd was not without his superstitions; nor was this fascination for the supernatural limited to the custody of lonely men who guarded their flocks in outlying regions where fears and dreads were personalized. Almost everybody felt that an unusual epidemic of misfortunes hinted at retribution. And while the more intelligent disclaimed any interest in such witcheries, even the best of them might be heard to remark —though pretending not to mean it—that Someone or Something must have laid a curse upon Arabia.

For the following summer was the worst season that the eldest could remember, and in the fall there were but few caravans carrying hides and wool to the Port of Gaza. The young camels they would have brought to market in Petra, Jericho, and Joppa were too lean and shabby for profitable sale. There was very little surplus of grain to see the livestock through the approaching winter.

The air was tense with complaint and constraint. Somebody was to blame. The trouble all seemed to stem from Arabia's alliance with the Jews. Everyone was able to recall now how he himself had predicted, at the time, that no good could come of it. Of course no one held it against Arnon, for clearly she had suffered from it far more than anybody. And it would be cruel foolishness to frown upon the hapless child who symbolized that unfortunate union. But—even so—the visits of Arnon's friends became less and less frequent. She did not fret about it at first, realizing that everyone was weighted with worries at home, and in no mood for sociability.

Curiously enough, there was better pasture on Arnon's land than anywhere else for many miles. Her neighbors did not openly begrudge the Princess this bit of prosperity, but it did seem strange. One day a sheik remarked half-humorously that wherever you found a Jew located you might expect to see fat sheep.

"A Jew?" queried the friend who rode beside him. "What Jew?"

"Had you not noticed Princess Arnon's pasture?"

"The Princess is not a Jew!" retorted his friend.

"No—but her child is."

It was all but incredible, the speed with which this idle quip raced across the browned face of Arabia until it was repeated in the coldest tents of the hungry highlands.

But there were a few whose unswerving loyalty to the Princess made them all the more eager to show her friendly attentions as this unfavorable sentiment developed. Zendi and Rennah rode over, every few days, to make sure of Arnon's welfare. Although she was now a Princess only by courtesy, Zendi endeavored to keep her informed of movements in the Kingdom, as if she still had a right to know. One day he talked of the unfortunate expedition to Jerusalem, and reported that Emperor Tiberius had decided not to appoint another Jew as a ruler of Judaea. Henceforth the chief executive would be a Roman. The new appointee was already located in Jerusalem. He had been elevated from the Prefecture of Crete. His name was Pontius Pilate. Doubtless he would get along with the Jews. He was said to be a tactful conciliator.

"Will this affect the position of Antipas—in Galilee?" Arnon wanted to know.

"Probably not," surmised Zendi. "The tribute Rome receives from poor little Galilee isn't worth what it costs to collect it. Antipas could afford to pay their taxes himself and doubtless would do so gladly enough, just to preserve the title of Tetrarch."

Sometimes Zendi and Rennah gave Arnon an opportunity to speak of the growing aloofness toward her, but she appeared not to be aware of it, and the painful subject was not discussed.

Frequently, Mishma's pretty daughter-in-law Kitra came to spend the afternoon, bringing her four-year-old son Voidi, who had promptly taken a fancy to little Fara.

The warm friendship of Kitra and Arnon, begun in childhood, had ripened to a comforting intimacy, nourished perhaps by the fact that Princess Arnon was no longer of the King's household while Kitra had missed being in that position by the mere accident of a delayed appointment of her father-in-law Mishma as Chief of the Counsellors and, as such, the immediate successor to Aretas. They spent long afternoons together, happily watching their children's absorption in one another, for

Fara had had no other playmates and Voldi had never taken such an interest in another child. Sometimes the two young mothers would wonder whether this tender little friendship might continue as their children grew up, though they admitted that it wasn't customary.

*   *   *   *   *   *

After three consecutive winters of such hardships as Arabia had never known, succeeded by scorched summers presaging further endurance of famine for both men and beasts, the snow fell in abundance. It fell endlessly and everywhere; on the mountains, in the valleys, covering great tracts of arid desert that had not seen any moisture for a score of years. It snowed and thawed and snowed again until the wadies were in flood. Spring came early, the sun was bright, all Arabia was a green pasture.

Men who had become so deeply depressed over their losses that they had actually debated whether, for the country's sake, it might not be advisable to carry Princess Arnon's child back to Jerusalem "where she belongs," were now glad that they had done no such thing, and some of them felt sheepish over having shared in these conversations.

It was hardly to be expected that such good fortune could happen again, but it did. Not only during the next winter, but the winter following, heavy snows blanketed the entire nation; and in the succeeding autumns long, heavily laden caravans trekked down the mountains, and rounded the southern shore of the Dead Sea, and slowly marched to the old "salt trail" from Engedi to Gaza.

Not infrequently some gratified shepherd, with silver jingling in his pouch, would remark that the young daughter of Princess Arnon, far from being a menace to Arabia, was bringing Jewish prosperity to the nation, to which his neighbor would reply, "I always said you were a lot of fools for hating that pretty child!"

"But—you said yourself that she ought to be put out of the country!"

"If I did, that doesn't make you any less a fool for saying so."

Everybody who had seen little Fara agreed now that she was the most beautiful child in Arabia, which was unquestionably true. She had the full, wide-set eyes and round face of a Jewess, and a much fairer complexion than her attractive mother. Her slim, lithe body was distinctly Arabian, as was her interest in outdoor life.

She had been lifted into a small saddle when she was barely five, the worshipful old Kedar walking alongside the pony. It was not long until she protested against such attendance. One morning when she was no more than six, she showed up alone at the King's encampment, to the consternation of the household. Zendi himself rode home beside her to make sure she arrived safely. Arnon, quite complacent, met them at the door.

"You shouldn't let her do that," reproved Zendi. "She isn't old enough."

"The pony is," said Arnon. "He wouldn't let her get into trouble. He follows her about like a dog."

"But ponies are treacherous, Arnon. I should much sooner trust a horse."

"That is true, sire. I shall let her ride one of the horses." She had spoken half-playfully, but added, in a suddenly serious tone, "Don't forget, Zendi, that my little daughter is every inch an Arabian! You were taught to ride almost as soon as you were able to walk—and so was I."

This incident, trivial enough in itself, was reported to the Counsellors who received it—and its implications—with smiles and nods of approval. The child was unfortunately afflicted with alien blood but it was clear that she was predominantly Arabian and deserved recognition as one of their own people. By the time the story was well circulated, losing nothing in its travels, little Fara was an accomplished rider, skillful and unafraid. And the rumor wasn't far from the truth.

But if Arabia had an imaginary picture of this growing child as a reckless rowdy, leaping half-broken race-horses over high hedges and deep wadies, with the firm hands and pliant knees of an experienced cavalry-man, there was another side of Fara's life which nobody saw but her own family—and King Zendi. Thanks to Ione, Fara was receiving a liberal education.

To all appearances, the beloved and indispensable Ione had fully adjusted herself to her Arabian environment, but it was a sorrow to her never to hear or speak a word of her native Greek. When little Fara was learning to talk, Ione amused herself by teaching her Greek words for familiar objects. When she handed the baby her porridge plate, she would say, "Pinakos." And Fara, ever eager to please Ione, would lisp, "Pinakos"; and because Ione seemed so delighted, she proudly repeated the word, over and over. The little porridge plate was always "pinakos" after that, and the little cup was always "poterion," and the napkin was "soudarion." Arnon, too, enjoyed the game. "Teach her to say 'I love you,' Ione."

Taking the child on her lap, Ione said softly, "Fara, I love you. Philo seh. Philo seh. I love you."

"Philo seh," repeated Fara, dutifully, happily.

"Say that to your mother, Fara."

Arnon reached out her arms and little Fara cuddled close to her.

"I love you," whispered Arnon.

"Philo seh," said Fara.

As the days went by, the intrusion of Greek words into their conversation was no longer a novelty that made them laugh merrily. Common nouns needed action. Words multiplied into sentences. Table-talk was conducted in Greek. After supper, on winter evenings, Ione taught Fara to write it. Happy to see her child profitably entertained, Arnon joined in these exercises, though she never acquired the effortless fluency with which Fara handled the strange language. By the time she was nine, the little girl spoke Greek by preference.

One day, King Zendi called to inquire about their welfare and overheard Fara in the adjoining room talking to Ione. He broke off what he was saying—and listened—and then grinned, incredulously.

"How long has this been going on?" he inquired.

"Ever since she was a tiny tot," said Arnon. "It's Ione's doing. I suppose there's no harm in it?"

"Harm? Of course not! I wish I knew some Greek myself."

"But—you do; don't you, Zendi?"

"A mere smatter—picked up on my journey to Corinth. I often have errands in Petra. It would be much to my advantage if I could speak their language."

Arnon laughed a little as she said, "Perhaps Fara could help you." To her surprise, Zendi did not see anything funny about this. He frowned thoughtfully.

"It just occurs to me," he said, "that we have, in our cabinet of curiosities, a scroll that the people of Petra presented to your father at his coronation. I shall bring it over. Maybe Fara might like to see it."

The next afternoon he brought the scroll. Ione was invited in to look at it. She gasped with happy surprise. What a treasure! Unconsciously ignoring the King, she breathlessly explained the subject of the scroll to Fara in a long sentence utterly incomprehensible to their important guest. And Fara clapped her hands with delight.

"I would give much for that knowledge," said Zendi, soberly.

"It's easy, sire," said Fara.

When he left, shortly afterward, Fara walked beside him to the paddock. He took her small hand. The old master of the stables led forward a beautiful roan gelding. Fara's eyes shone.

"How do you like my new horse, Fara?" asked the King, as he gathered up the reins.

"Prosphilay!" murmured Fara, reverentially, patting the gelding's glossy shoulder. "Prosphilay hippos!"

"What did you say?" demanded the King.

"Lovely!" said Fara. "Lovely horse!"

Zendi chuckled and swung himself into the saddle.

"Kai megaleios hippikos!" ventured Fara, coyly.

"And what does that mean?" the King wanted to know.

Fara shrugged a pretty shoulder, drew an enigmatic smile, and made a graceful curtsey. Zendi waved a hand and rode away. It was evident that Fara's final remark—whatever it meant—was complimentary.

After that, the tribesmen were often amused to see their King cantering alongside Princess Arnon's pretty child, evidently engaged in serious conversation. One day, after a visit to Petra, Zendi presented his young preceptress with an armful of scrolls which he had bought. Ione, on her knees, laid them out in a row on the rug, and caressed them with worshipful hands, murmuring, "Thaumasia! Thaumasia!" To have such a rich library—it was indeed wonderful! Marvellous!

As for Fara's early knowledge of her origin, she had been contented with the explanation that her father was a Prince who had been required to leave them that he might perform his duties as the ruler of a faraway country. Now that she was asking for a little more information, Arnon would talk of the great cities in which she had lived with Fara's father, carefully avoiding any mention of her unhappiness.

"Will my father ever visit us?" Fara had asked, wistfully.

"He would find it difficult," Arnon had replied; and this was the exact truth. "Great rulers," she went on, "have many cares."

"But—does he not care—at all—for us?"

"A ruler's life, my dear, is not his own. His only concern is for the welfare of his country." Arnon despised herself for what, in this case, was a ridiculous lie; but felt that it was an easy way out of a painful discussion. The time would come soon enough, she knew, when the whole matter would have to be faced; but she hoped to postpone it as long as possible.

Fara was beginning to be aware of her loneliness and singularity. She was nearing ten and growing very restless. She needed companions of her own age. It had been a long time since Kitra had brought Voldi along when she came to visit. One day Fara ventured to inquire how he was.

"Oh—that boy!" exclaimed Kitra, busying herself with her needlework. "He thinks he is quite a man now. Growing so fast; tall as I am. You know how boys of that age are, Fara. They don't want to play with girls. All they think about is their horses and hunting dogs—and archery —and fencing." Her eyes slid past Fara to Arnon. "You may be glad Fara is a girl. I never have a peaceful moment when Voldi is riding that un-ruly horse of his!"

"Fara rides too," said Arnon, quietly.

"Yes—I know," said Kitra. "And Fara rides very well indeed!"

Then the talk veered off to another topic and Fara strolled away to her own room. She languidly took up the little tapestry on which she had been investing oddments of unoccupied time. Ione joined her. They sat in silence for awhile, Ione exasperatingly tranquil, Fara recklessly stab-bing her needle into the stiff fabric.

"Don't you ever feel penned in, Ione?" The tapestry sailed across the room and landed on the bed. "How does it feel to be a slave?" Fara went on, savagely, as if she meant to offend. "If I were a slave, I'd run away! Why don't you?"

"Where would I run to?" asked Ione, blinking back the tears; for Fara's rudeness had hurt.

"You could go home," gruffly.

"But—this is my home, dear; same as it is yours."

"Nonsense!" muttered Fara. "You can't be contented here any more than I can! This place stifles me! Sometimes I think I'll jump out of my skin!"

"Your mother would be very sorry, Fara, if she heard you say such things," reproved Ione.

"Well—she won't," declared Fara. "But"—suddenly dejected—"I had to say it to somebody. Please forgive me."

"Of course," murmured Ione, quick to understand. "It's natural for children of your age to be restless. You're growing so fast that the encamp-ment isn't big enough to hold you. You will get over that when you are older."

Fara crossed the room, flung herself down on her bed; and, lacing her fingers behind her head, stared at the blue ceiling.

"Wouldn't you like to see something besides sheep?" she mumbled, mostly to herself. "And go someplace where they talked about other things than the price of camels—and how are we going to find enough grass? Wouldn't you like to live in a great house—in a great city?"

"No, dear," replied Ione, when some rejoinder seemed necessary. "I have done that. I'm quite satisfied to be here—where I am—in these beautiful mountains."

"Maybe I should be satisfied too," admitted Fara. "I wish I were like other people. There's something wrong with me, Ione," she exclaimed, impulsively. "I'm different! And I hate it!"

It was not until she was eleven that Fara learned how and why she was different. She came by accident upon the soul-sickening truth about her father's perfidy and her mother's incurable unhappiness and her own defenseless position as a half-breed. She had ridden with Arnon, that midsummer afternoon, to the King's encampment. Zendi was absent on a tour of the eastern tribes. Rennah and Arnon lounged in the Queen's suite while Fara and the spoiled young Prince Deran strolled about indifferently inspecting the kennels and stables.

Tiring of this entertainment and agreeing that the sun was too hot, the children returned to the spacious living quarters where Deran, eager to impress his guest, led the way into the huge, high-vaulted tent which was set apart for the exclusive use of the King and his Counsellors. With a boyish swagger, Deran stalked about, explaining the various appointments. Having casually seated himself in the King's massive chair, he invited Fara to do the same. He wouldn't think, he said, of letting anyone else sit there. Fara smiled prettily to show her appreciation. Thus encouraged, Deran led her around the ancient table, declaiming what he knew about the symbolic carvings, and—in a hushed voice—called her attention to the impressive documents which lay waiting official action.

Fara, who had come to have deep respect for ancient crafts and historical writings, gave full attention to the table and its important freight.

"You mustn't touch anything," cautioned Deran.

Fara shook her head and continued to survey the awesome documents with fascination. Presently she came upon a slightly faded, multi-colored sheet of papyrus which she read, with widening eyes and mounting comprehension. Deran, a little younger but much taller, stood at her shoulder, staring in bewilderment at her flushed cheek. She turned abruptly toward him, searching his face, but he gave no sign of knowing or caring what tiresome thing she had been reading.

When they arrived home shortly before sunset, Fara followed Arnon into her bedroom, impulsively reported what she had seen in the King's tent, and entreated her mother to tell her everything, which she did. Everything!—the alliance, the marriage, the lonely days in Jerusalem, the humiliating days in Rome! All the pent-up wretchedness of Arnon's ruined life poured forth, accompanied by a flood of tears. When the sad, sordid story was finished, the unhappy Princess dried her eyes and was surprised to find that Fara, instead of sharing her mother's grief, was standing there dry-eyed, with her childish mouth firmed into a straight line and her brows contracted into an expression of bitter hatred.

"And why has no one hunted him down—and punished him?" she demanded, indignantly.

"It's much too late for that," said Arnon. "When it happened, our country was in great distress. No one could be spared. And now that we have such great prosperity, no one remembers." She sighed deeply, and went on, "Perhaps it is just as well. Galilee is a long way off. The Prince is well protected. Let us try to forget all about it, dear."

Fara shook her head slowly.

"I shall remember—always!" she muttered.

That winter was long and severe. Arnon fell ill with a fever and relentless fits of coughing. Fara, through these anxious days, had no other concern but for her mother. Ione tried unsuccessfully to renew her interest in the classics, in her modeling, in her drawing.

"Do persuade the unhappy child to get out and take some exercise!" begged Arnon. "She is so unlike herself, Ione."

"It worries me too, Princess Arnon. Something has come over her."

"She is fretting because I am ill," said Arnon.

"Of course, Princess Arnon," agreed Ione, obligingly, "but you will be better when spring comes again."

And spring did come again, and Arnon improved enough to be able to sit in the sunshine and walk in the garden, but Fara's depression was unrelieved. All of her natural gaiety was gone.

One afternoon when Rennah came to call, she found Arnon and Fara together in the garden. Almost immediately, Fara excused herself and strolled away. Rennah followed her with troubled eyes.

"She is growing taller; but, Arnon, Fara does not look well. Is something worrying her?"

"Fara has been fretting all winter about me," said Arnon. "She is a most dutiful child."

"But now that you are getting well—"

"I have thought of that, Rennah. She should be happy again. I wish we could think of something that might divert her. She has no interest in anything."

"She will have a birthday soon," remembered Rennah. "How about having a party?" Her face lighted. "Would you let me have a party for Fara? I know Zendi would be glad. We will make quite a day of it—with the Counsellors and their wives and all the children and grandchildren—and races and games and plenty to eat."

"It is like you, dear Rennah, to want to do such a kindness," said Arnon. "I hope you will not go to too much trouble."

"Zendi will approve, I know," said Rennah. "It's high time we gave that sweet child some attention. We have neglected her too long. It should mean something to the people that Fara's grandfathers were Kings!"

So—on the fifteenth of Adar—which turned out to be the fairest day of that early summer, the King and Queen celebrated Fara's twelfth anniversary with a party that greatly exceeded Rennah's original plan, not only in the entertainment provided but in the number of guests; for, having decided to do it, Zendi included all of the sheiks and tribal leaders with their families.

Fara had been dismayed upon learning of the project in her honor and so seriously objected that she was all but in open revolt until Zendi himself explained that as a child of royal blood she was not only entitled to certain favors but was expected to receive them graciously. And when Fara continued to frown disapprovingly, Zendi's patience gave out and he informed her that whether she wanted it or not there was going to be a birthday party for her at the King's encampment on the fifteenth day of Adar; and that, whether she wanted to or not, she was going to be there, bright and early!

Late in the night, after the party was over and everyone had gone home, Zendi told Rennah what he had said, so impatiently, to Fara when she had begged him not to celebrate her birthday.

"If I had had the slightest idea of what was troubling the child," he confided, "I should have yielded to her wishes. As it stands now our celebration of her birthday has been of no advantage to her. Indeed it has done her harm. Everyone will think she is queer, if not definitely out of her mind."

The almost incredible thing that happened was reserved for the banquet in the evening, attended only by the royal household, the Counsellors and their wives, and a few distinguished guests from Petra where Zendi was becoming favorably known.

Nothing unusual had marked the happy events of the day. There had been exciting contests of strength and skill; acrobatic performances, wrestling, fencing, foot races. Magicians had done baffling tricks. Minstrels had sung. There were horse races that would have done credit to the famed elliptical track in Rome's mighty Colosseum. And there were equestrian exhibitions staged by various groups of reckless young Arabs, some of the contestants hardly more than children. As was to be expected, there were a few bad spills, some broken bones, and ruined horses. The final event was a breath-taking hurdle race ridden by youths in their middle teens. The hurdles were high and the race was dangerous. Of the twelve horses that started, three finished.

Obliged by the circumstances to sit with the dignitaries in the royal

stand, Fara turned to her mother as the perspiring young victor rode up
to salute the King, and whispered, "Who is that boy?"

Before Arnon could reply, Kitra, seated immediately behind them,
leaned forward to say, with a proud but nervous little laugh, "Why—
don't you remember him, Fara? That's Voldi! You used to play together."

Fara turned to her with a smile and a nod of remembrance.

"He is a wonderful rider," she murmured, in the husky-timbred tone
that her voice had acquired.

Queen Rennah, overhearing, said, "We will ask him to come up, Fara,
and renew acquaintance.

Fara bit her lip and flushed a little. Meeting Arnon's eyes, she frowned
and shook her head almost imperceptibly. Arnon smiled, pursed her lips,
and nodded, as to say, "We mustn't object to that: it's quite the thing
to do."

Presently Voldi, dismounting, came up into the royal enclosure, bowed
deeply to the King and Queen, and made his way toward his mother.
They gave him a seat beside Fara. She searched his brown, freckled face
with wide, sober eyes. Then her full lips parted in a smile of candid admiration. He colored a little through the tan, under this frank inspection,
and slowly met her smile with the bewildered expression of one who has
just come upon a valuable discovery.

Rennah, keenly observant, turned her head toward Kitra, and whispered, "Isn't that sweet?" Kitra nodded and smiled briefly, but there
was a trace of anxiety in her eyes. Rennah caught it, and thought she
understood.

"You grew up; didn't you?" murmured Fara, in her peculiarly low-
pitched voice that made everything she said sound confidential.

"So did you," stammered Voldi. "I shouldn't have known you."

"That was really great riding, Voldi!" said Fara, fervently.

"You ride too, don't you?"

"Not like that."

"Want to take a ride with me, some day?"

"If you think it wouldn't be tiresome—to ride very carefully."

Their mothers and the Queen, shamelessly eavesdropping, laughed at
Voldi's expense, but he was too fascinated to notice their amusement.

"Tomorrow afternoon?" he asked.

Fara nodded slowly, smiled a little; then suddenly retreated from the
enraptured eyes.

"You promised to spend the day with your grandfather, Voldi," put
in Kitra.

"I'll tell him." Voldi rose to go. "Tomorrow afternoon, Fara." They all—except Fara—followed the tall boy with their eyes and saw him pause to say something to his grandfather who soberly made a show of concealing his pride in the youngster's obvious affection for him.

"Happy days for good old Mishma," remarked the Queen.

"Yes," said Kitra, absently.

Noting the remote tone of Kitra's disinterested response, Arnon involuntarily turned her head to seek a reason for it, but Kitra did not meet her inquiring eyes. The little by-play was quite lost on Fara whose attention pursued Voldi as he strode down the steps and mounted his tired horse.

In the evening oxen were roasted over deep pits of glowing coals, and everybody feasted in the open but the royal hosts and their important guests. Fara was the only young person present at the King's banquet. There had been some debate whether to invite a few of the younger ones of Fara's age, but it was difficult to discriminate among them, and the room would not accommodate them all.

After the elaborate dinner was served, brief speeches were made in honor of Fara whom they all addressed as "Princess." No one of the eulogistic Counsellors made any reference to the royal blood contributed by Judaea, but memories were refreshed concerning the wisdom and courage of Grandsire Aretas who was already well on the way to an exalted rating among Arabia's legendary heroes.

Throughout the ordeal—for it was nothing less than that—Fara sat between her mother and King Zendi, attentive and sober-faced, as became a young girl unused to so much adult acclaim. She seemed to be listening to everything that was said, though close observers noticed that her expression remained unchanged when Chief Counsellor Mishma was reminded of an amusing incident and everyone else laughed. Apparently Fara had not heard it. It was evident that she had something on her mind.

When the speeches of felicitation were ended and nothing remained to be said except a word of adjournment, Zendi turned with a paternal smile toward his young honor guest.

"Now, Princess Fara," he said kindly, "it is your turn. You may make a bow—or make a speech—or sing a song."

They all applauded the King's half-playful suggestion, but stopped suddenly when Fara rose to her feet. Arnon, seated beside her, glanced up apprehensively as to inquire, "What is my child planning to do?"

Fara did not smile or speak. Slowly leaving her place she walked with determined steps to the massive table. The audience leaned forward and held its breath, wondering what was about to happen. Moving around the table until she faced the King, Fara made a deep bow. Then, to the amazement of everyone, she whipped a little dagger from her belt and deftly drew a red streak diagonally across her left forearm. Bending over the long neglected, unsigned vow of vengeance, she took up the stylus, dipped it in her blood, and wrote FARA.

For a moment they all sat stunned to silence. Then Rennah rose and hurried to Fara's side. Arnon, much shaken, quickly joined the Queen and together they led the bleeding Princess out to attend to her wound. Fara's face was pale but her eyes were bright and a proud little smile trembled on her lips.

Zendi rose, instantly claiming the full attention of his silent, bewildered guests.

"Some brave young blood has been shed here tonight," he said, solemnly. "You may be assured that Arabia will not permit this gallant child ever to risk her life in an attempt to keep her vow; but her courageous act, done in all sincerity, is proudly appreciated by her country."

"Aye!" rumbled old Mishma.

"Aye! Aye!" responded many voices.

There was a long moment of silence before Zendi signified with a gesture that they were now free to disperse. The people stirred, uneasily questing one another's baffled eyes. Mishma, standing at the King's elbow, suggested that the unprecedented event should be kept a secret.

"That would be most desirable, Mishma, if we could," agreed Zendi. "But it cannot be done. It is possible to pledge three people—or five—to keep a secret; but not fifty. Perhaps it is better to let them all talk until they have tired of it—and then it will be forgotten. After all—she is only a child."

And so it was told throughout the whole Kingdom of Arabia that Princess Arnon's young daughter had vowed to assassinate her Jewish father. The first reaction was that of sheer admiration mixed with amiable amusement. The little girl had shown great courage. She might be part Jew but she was all Arab! Of course her vow—considered practically—was ridiculous. When she grew a little older, her recollection of it would be embarrassing, no doubt. And after a few weeks of free discussion, the strange incident—as Zendi had predicted—was forgotten.

Young Voldi, completely infatuated and not caring who knew it, spent more and more time at Arnon's encampment, to the mounting anxiety of his parents; for he was a popular, well-favored youth, giving promise of a bright future. With his exceptional talents for making friends and the reputation he had already won as a fearless sportsman, it was not too much to hope that his country might some day confer honors upon him. He might easily win an appointment to the King's Council. But it seemed doubtful to Urson and Kitra that their idolized son could fulfill these high expectations if embarrassed by an alliance with a young woman of alien blood; especially Jewish blood. Whatever might be her beauty, courage and charm, Fara would be a heavy liability.

Nor was Voldi insensitive to his parents' uneasiness. He was deeply devoted to them and their anxiety distressed him. There were no stormy scenes. Perhaps it might have been easier for him to ignore their wishes if they had angered him with stern admonitions; if Urson had lashed out at him with bitter scorn, or if his mother had become noisily hysterical. The unhappy situation was hardly mentioned among them, but it was ever present in their thoughts. Urson seldom laughed now. And when Voldi, setting forth in the morning to spend the day with the adorable young daughter of Antipas the scoundrel, turned in his saddle to wave a hand to Kitra, standing before the doorway, trying to smile through her welling tears, he felt like an ingrate.

And he had other misgivings. He was seeing very little of his companions. Until recently he had spent most of his time with his hard-riding young cronies. Indeed he had been the acknowledged leader of this adventurous crew. What were they thinking about him? What were they saying about him, as they sat around their evening camp-fire in the mountains after a long day's chase for wild game? It would be a sore affliction if his friends were to chatter contemptuously of his demoralizing love-sickness. He resolved to free himself of this dread.

One morning, having had word of their plans for a three-day stag-hunt, Voldi arrived early at the accustomed rendezvous, fully equipped for the excursion. There was a bit of embarrassment at first but the constraint quickly lifted. Voldi was one of them again. Intent upon restoring himself to their good opinion, he led them for hours in the maddest ride they had ever taken; leaping deep gullies cut by mountain streams, hurdling fallen timber, plunging through tangled underbrush. Challenged by his recklessness, they did their utmost to follow. Young Museph, the elder son of Counsellor Tema, kept hard on his leader's heels, and brought down the largest stag of the three killed that day. Voldi accounted for the others. Most of the party were outdistanced and came straggling into camp in the late afternoon, weary beyond any words to tell of it.

A camp-fire was built beside a noisy mountain stream. The stags were hung up and dressed. Museph flung himself down on the aromatic pine-needles that carpeted the ground; and when Voldi sat down beside him, regarding him with a teasing grin, Museph opened one eye and muttered, "My brother, you have lost your mind."

The last to arrive in camp was young Prince Deran, King Zendi's arrogant son, attended by four members of the hunt who had reluctantly tarried with him when the pace had grown too hot. The Prince had bagged a little doe. No one ventured to rebuke him but the general silence expressed the party's opinion. Deran was quite aware of his companions' disfavor, aware too that had he been anyone else than the heir to the throne, he would have been appropriately chastised. He cared nothing for their unspoken disapproval. His manner said that if the King's son wished to kill a baby doe, who had a right to oppose him.

After supper there were some acrobatics, a wrestling match, and a fencing bout with wooden broadswords. It was proposed that they have a duel with daggers.

"How about you and Museph, Voldi?" a voice inquired.

"I'm too tired," said Museph. "Besides, I'm no match for Voldi."

"We will take him on!" shouted the Prince, getting to his feet.

All eyes—and they were sullen eyes—turned in his direction. They covertly scorned the pompous youngster, hated his poor sportsmanship, loathed his insolent "we."

"It wouldn't be fair, Prince," said Voldi, trying to make his tone sound respectful. "I am older than you—and I have had more practice."

"But not lately," sneered Deran—"or do you play with daggers when you visit your Jewish friend?"

All breathing around the campfire was suspended. Voldi flushed and frowned.

"I do not wish to fence with you, Prince Deran," he said.

"As we thought!" crowed Deran. "That's what comes of consorting with soft aliens." He took a step forward and drew his dagger. "Stand up and fight, fellow!"

Voldi slowly rose, and observed, as had several of the others, that the blade of Deran's dagger flashed brightly in the firelight.

"You're not intending to fight me with steel, I hope!" he said sharply. A concerted murmur of disapproval instantly backed him up. It was a shameful abuse of royal privilege. Every youth in the party knew that the Prince was not vulnerable to any injury. It would be worth any man's liberty, if not his life, to hurt this boy.

Bewildered by his predicament Voldi stood with his thumbs under his belt, making no move to defend himself. Young Deran, crouching, advanced with short steps.

"You'd better draw, Voldi," he growled—"or admit you're a coward."

Apparently it was the wrong word even for the King's son to use. Voldi lunged forward, drove his right elbow into the Prince's midriff, clutched the wildly flailing forearm in a vise-like grip, twisted the dagger out of Deran's hand, and tossed it into the fire. Panting with rage, the Prince again hurled himself at Voldi who, disregarding the impotent fists, slapped the youngster full in the face.

"You'll pay for that!" squeaked Deran.

Gentle if disgusted hands led the infuriated Prince to his tent for repairs to his royal pride and bleeding lips. Voldi resumed a seat on the ground, a little way apart from the others, and sat with bent head and slumped shoulders.

"I'm sorry," he mumbled, dejectedly, shaking his head.

It was a critical moment for all of them. No one cared to risk being quoted as having said, "Good work, Voldi! Just what he deserved! What else could you have done?" At length Museph scrambled to his feet, threw another pine stick on the fire, dusted his hands; and, sauntering over to Voldi, companionably sat down beside him. Young Raboth, the lean, hawk-nosed nephew of Counsellor Dumah, crossed from the other side of the silent circle, made a big business of poking the fire; and, as he passed Voldi, gave him a friendly pat on the shoulder. The rest of them breathed more freely, and exchanged grins. Deran did not reappear that night, and left for home early the next morning.

Voldi made no mention of the unpleasant affair at home, but for many days he waited, in considerable trepidation, a summons to present himself at the King's encampment; for it seemed almost certain that Deran would have made a bad report of the incident. But apparently the episode was to be overlooked. Either the Prince had decided to hold his tongue, or the King, having heard his son's story, had drawn his own conclusions and had thought it prudent to let the matter drop.

But the true story unquestionably had got to the ears of the Council; for, a week later, Voldi was invited to spend the day with his revered Grandfather Mishma. He went with anxiety pounding in his heart, for he was devoted to the old man and would be grieved at his displeasure. But it turned out to be a happy visit. Nothing was said about the unfortunate incident in the woods. When Voldi left for home, Mishma followed him out to the paddock and ceremoniously presented him with a beautiful, high-spirited, black gelding.

With one arm on the superb young animal's neck and the other hugging his grandfather, Voldi shouted his delight. The eminent Counsellor stroked his white beard complacently, and a twinkle shone in his eye.

The Rendezvous

Voldi and Fara rode together throughout the summer.

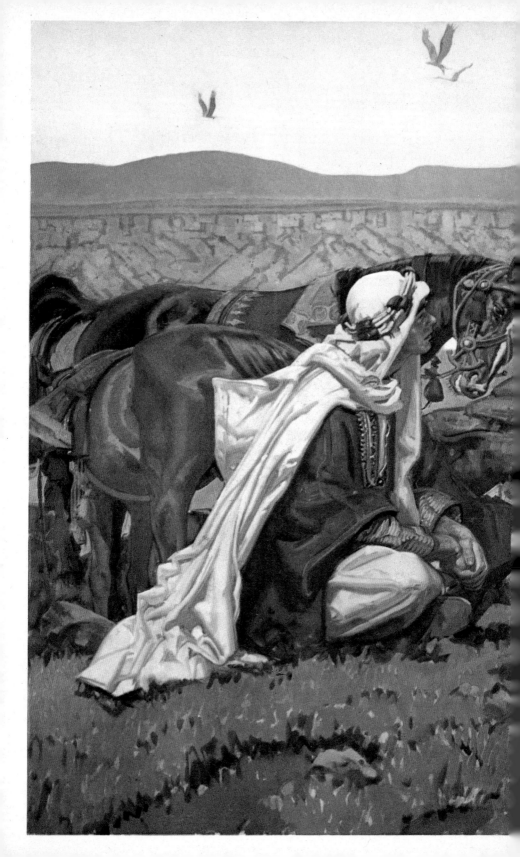

"This frisky colt's name," he said, "is Darik—after King Darik, of old."

"He was called 'Darik the Just,' was he not, sire?" asked Voldi.

"Right! Because he was always fair in his judgments," said Mishma. "It is told of him that King Darik was of a quick temper, and knew better than most men how to handle a blade; but he never drew his sword against a weaker adversary—no matter what the provocation." The old man laid his thin hand on the gelding's velvet muzzle. "This horse," he reflected, "will require some managing, but he is of good character. See to it, my son, that he behaves himself."

Voldi's visits to Fara continued. They rode together almost every day throughout the summer, and when the early winter came, with blustery weather driving them indoors, Arnon, observing their restlessness and lack of occupation, proposed that Voldi join them in their lately neglected studies. He consented to it with well-simulated interest. He had no particular ambition to learn, but any pastime was agreeable that would give him an excuse for hovering close to Fara. Ione was delighted with his progress. He had an aptitude for Greek, she declared; he had a feel for it; would soon be speaking it like a native! This was an exaggeration, but it encouraged Voldi to do his best. Moreover, he was able to tell his mother that the long winter afternoons in Princess Arnon's home were profitably spent. Kitra would smile indulgently—but it was plain to see that she was troubled.

And Fara, too, was troubled about Voldi's adoration, her intuition—and the widening intervals between Kitra's visits—informing her that he was getting into trouble at home because of her. Once she almost decided to tell Voldi frankly that he mustn't come to see her any more, but her courage failed, for she loved him devotedly. Sometime—no matter how severely it hurt—he must be told; but Fara postponed the day of their sorrow.

As the seasons came and went, Fara took on a maturity beyond her years. The circumstances of her life had made her thoughtful, even as a child; now, with her sixteenth birthday in sight, she had the mind of an adult. The conviction had grown within her that she was fated to be a person unwanted; viewed with suspicion; an alien. The Jews would spurn her for being an Arabian; the Arabians would ignore her for being a Jew. What ailed the world, that grown men and women should treat one another so? Once she had put the question to Ione who had replied, with a sigh, "It was always that way, my dear, from the beginning."

"It's a lonely world—for some people," said Fara.

"I know how you feel," sympathized Ione. "I have been lonely too."

"Yes—but you have a nationality, Ione! You are far away from your own country; but you do have a country. It isn't as if you were a mixture of two countries that hated each other. Me—I am nobody!"

"Do not be depressed, Fara," entreated Ione. "There are many who love you, who will always love you! No girl in the world ever had such a devoted lover as Voldi!"

"I know," murmured Fara, "but—he shouldn't!" Her voice trembled. "I mustn't let him! He can't marry me! It would ruin him! Ione—what am I going to do?"

*   *   *   *   *   *

Shortly before sunset the Princess Arnon, long ailing of infirmities associated with a broken heart, slipped away so quietly that for some little time they weren't quite sure.

It was Fara who first realized that it was all over. Since noon she had been crouching beside the bed with her forehead pressed against her mother's thin arm, now raising up tearfully to peer into the unresponsive face, then dejectedly slumping down again to wait.

At mid-afternoon old Kedar noisily rolled up the leather panels on the northern and eastern exposures of the octagonal tent, just as he would have done at this hour on any other fair summer day. Kedar had seen plenty of death in his four-score years, and it no longer upset him. Indeed he was almost too casual in its presence today, strutting his old bones about with something of a proprietorial swagger as if he and death had a private understanding.

All day long the female servants, a dozen or more, had tiptoed in by twos and threes to stand helplessly at a respectful distance from the bed, regarding their dying mistress with compassionate eyes, and had tiptoed out again as if remembering some neglected duty. Nothing remained to be done for Arnon; or, if so, there was old Nephti who had nursed both Princesses from babyhood, and the faithful Ione, hovering close—and a bit jealous of each other.

The whole mind of the household at present was concentrated on Fara and her probable plans for the future. Of course she would now marry Voldi whose constant attentions, during the past few years, had been unceasing and whose intentions were unmistakable. It was generally taken for granted that Fara had decided not to marry until her responsibility to her mother had ended. And that responsibility had increased as Arnon's strength declined; for the unhappy Princess had developed an immense capacity for absorbing all manner of trivial but incessant personal services. "Hand me the small pillow, please. No—the other one, dear, the blue one. Thanks, Fara, but I believe I'd rather have my shawl. It's out in the pergola, I think. Would you mind getting it, darling? I know I'm a dreadful bother." And so she was; but it had never seemed to annoy Fara who stayed on duty day and night. Obviously she couldn't bring much happiness to Voldi until she was free. It wouldn't be long now.

But where would they live? This was the question that troubled the servants; especially the older ones. Arnon's land had been ceded to her only for her lifetime. It was inconceivable that Voldi, as Fara's husband, would press a claim to it, or that the King could consent to such favoritism. Voldi would be as nomadic as all others of equal rating. The fact that his father Urson was the son of Mishma who, as Chief of the Counsellors, was the heir apparent to the throne, was of no immediate consequence. Arnon's land would revert to the King's domain. Voldi and Fara would follow the snow and the pasture. And the older servants, long accustomed to soft living, might be considered too frail for such a rigorous life.

Indeed, as they huddled in little groups, waiting, watching, they wondered whether Fara herself was likely to be happy as a nomad. She had never taken any interest in their herds and flocks. She had shown much friendly concern for the shepherds and their families, but cared nothing for the business that provided her own living. Of course, there was no use trying to understand Fara. They had never known what to make of this alien who had become more of an enigma as she matured. She was as mysterious as she was beautiful. Doubtless that could be explained by her racial heritages. It was an odd combination—Arab and Jew. True, it was an arrestingly lovely blend, viewed objectively. Arabian women were taller than Jewesses and more sinewy. At sixteen, Fara's figure was slim, supple, almost boyish: in short, Arabian. Her face was an interesting study in racial conflict. The old antipathy was written there, as on a map. The high, finely sculptured nose, with the slightly flaring, mobile, haughty nostrils, had been Arnon's gift. The childishly rounded chin and throat were Mariamne's. It was a readily responsive face, well disciplined in repose, but of swift reactions to any stirring event. She was capable of flashing Arabian rages, like sudden summer storms in the mountains, but it was well worth anyone's patience and forbearance to wait for the penitent smile Fara had inherited from long generations of highly emotional people who believed in atonements, and were never ashamed of their tears.

Arnon's last day wore on, and when the declining sun had been nicked by the glowing tip of Arcturus, twenty miles away, old Kedar rolled up the western tent-panels also, admitting a jasmine-scented breeze. Rousing, Fara lifted her eyes to the breath-taking panorama of rolling hills in the foreground descending to the green Valley of Aisne, with the majestic Arcturus in the far distance; and, beyond the southern slope of the mountain, the dazzling white shoreline of the Dead Sea.

Noting that Fara had been momentarily diverted from her vigil, Ione drew closer to whisper that Voldi had come. Did she want to see him? Fara shook her head.

"Tell Voldi not to wait," she murmured; and, as Ione moved away, she added, "Tell him I cannot come now. He will understand."

Fara's heavy eyes slowly returned to her mother's drawn face. She laid her cheek against Arnon's breast, and listened—and listened. Old Nephti took a step forward and help up an outspread hand for silence, though no place had ever been so quiet. At length Fara straightened and kissed her mother on the forehead, very gently, as not to waken her. Then she came slowly to her feet. Her eyes were tearless now and her proud face was composed. Lightly touching old Nephti's shoulder in a brief caress, and making a weary little gesture of appreciation toward the others, she left the tent.

Voldi was waiting in the garden. Rising, he held out his arms and Fara nestled her head against his breast. He could feel the silent, convulsive sobs, and drew her closer.

"She is gone?" he asked.

Fara nodded, wearily, dejectedly.

"I shall take care of you, dear," murmured Voldi.

"Let us not speak of that now," said Fara, gently releasing herself from his embrace. "There are many things to do, I suppose. Will you ride over to the King's encampment—and tell them?"

"Of course; and then may I come back?"

"Voldi, I am so very tired. Perhaps tomorrow—"

He took her in his arms again and kissed her, but her response was apathetic.

After Voldi had ridden away, Ione joined Fara who had remained in the garden, seated in her mother's favorite chair.

"What do we do now, Ione?" she asked, weakly. "I know so little about it."

"The men will come tonight, dear, and attend to the burial."

"And—am I to have anything to do with that?"

"No—you will not be expected to go along. Nephti and I will dress her for the burial." Ione reached out her hand. "Come now—and take some rest. You are quite exhausted. I shall bring you something nourishing to drink."

Late in the evening, King Zendi himself arrived, accompanied by a dozen neighbors. After a consoling word with Fara, he left her, saying that he and the Queen would see her tomorrow. Fara lay on her bed, with eyes closed and a pillow pressed hard over her head so that she might not hear the sounds of retiring hoofbeats. When she roused, everything was quiet. The full moon shone brightly through the tent-door. Ione slipped in very quietly. Fara sat up, patted the bed, and Ione obediently sat down beside her.

"I want you to do something for me, Ione," said Fara, hardly above a whisper, "and I want you to promise me you will never, never tell."

Ione's voice trembled a little as she promptly consented.

Fara faced her with sober eyes.

"I want you to hold up your hand, Ione, and swear by your gods that you will do for me what I ask of you—and never reveal it to anyone!"

Ione hesitated, and began to cry.

"I wish I knew, dear," she said, brokenly. "I hope this isn't something you shouldn't do!"

"Let me be the judge of that!" Fara's tone was severe. "Will you do as I say—and keep my secret?"

Ione protestingly put up a trembling hand and said, "Yes—Fara—I will do as you wish—and never tell."

Rising impetuously, Fara went to a small table where she kept her needlework, returning with a pair of scissors which she handed to the bewildered slave.

"You are to cut off my hair!" Fara wound her fingers about her heavy braid, at the back of her neck. "There! See, Ione? Just above my hand. I am to be a boy. Cut it like Voldi's."

Ione was whimpering like a child.

"You promised!" Fara shook her roughly by the shoulder. "Don't sit there crying! Do as I say—and do it quickly!"

Still gasping incoherent protests, Ione committed the crime. When it was accomplished, Fara retired to the alcove and presently returned to exhibit herself in the conventional garb of a well-to-do young Arabian, the burnous patterned after Voldi's best.

"How do I look?" she demanded.

"Where did you get it?" asked Ione, in a strained voice.

"Made it," said Fara, "a long time ago."

"But why? What are you going to do?"

"I am going very far away, Ione, to keep a vow," declared Fara. "Now—see to it that you keep yours!"

The alarming news broke early in the morning. Old Kedar rode to the King's encampment with the appalling report that Fara had disappeared during the night. The fractious bay filly that she had insisted on stabling in a separate paddock was gone. Zendi sent word to a score of young cavalrymen, informing them of what had happened. In his opinion, Fara, beside herself with grief and unable to sleep, had gone for a reckless ride in the moonlight. Perhaps she had met with an accident. They set off in all directions.

Voldi dashed away at a gallop along their favorite bridlepath skirting the rim of the plateau. At places where the trail was narrow and the descent precipitous, he dismounted and led his tired horse slowly, searching for ominous signs. When the late afternoon came, his hopes were fading. He was no longer meeting anxious friends engaged in the quest, for he was many miles beyond the farthest point he had ever traveled.

Slowly he retraced his course as the twilight settled down. At intervals, where the path was dangerous, he stopped and listened into the deep silence, and despairingly called "Fara! Fara!"

4

SAIDI, the bay filly, was independent and impertinent but sure-footed. Old Kedar, increasingly prudent at eighty, distrusted her; but Fara, better understanding the filly's caprices, knew that while Saidi was mischievous she was not malicious.

For the first five miles of gradual descent, Fara did not spare her. Time was precious. At any moment old Nephti, though strongly admonished to take her rest, might come in and find the bed empty. Immediately the household would be roused and a search would begin forthwith.

At first Saidi—in need of exercise—wanted to play, changing her gait without warning from canter to lope and pretending to be frightened at every huge white boulder and pale gray clump of sage standing in the bright moonlight, but Fara's spurs soon dissuaded her of the belief that this was a romp.

After a while the grade leveled off for a few miles before taking the sharp zigzags toward the valley floor. Here Fara dismounted and led Saidi until she began to toss her head impatiently, for she always objected to being led unless quite exhausted.

Occasionally they passed a weaver's hut; no lights visible, everyone asleep except the little huddle of goats that stirred and lifted a few heads inquisitively. The night was still. Fara thought it strange that she was not lonely. Even her bereavement, not yet of seven hours' duration, seemed to have occurred long ago, as indeed it had, for that incurable sorrow had set in when Arnon's waning strength presaged the inevitable end.

It was strange too, thought Fara, that she felt no apprehensions about the grim and hazardous mission on which she had set forth. She made the experiment of saying to herself that this was a very serious business, a man's business, that undoubtedly would cause her much trouble long before she reached her well-fortified objective in Galilee; in short, that

79

she was riding toward almost certain disaster as fast as Saidi's slim legs could carry her. But this re-examination of her purpose did nothing to discompose her, doubtless because she had so long and earnestly planned this audacious undertaking that it had become the sole aim of her life.

And there was dear Voldi! What a deal of anxiety she had caused him. How much more kind it would have been, reflected Fara, if she had told him firmly that she could never marry him; and, if pressed for the reason, she could have said that she did not love him. But Voldi would have known it wasn't true, for she had given him too many guarantees of her affection. However—Voldi would not fret very long. A girl might, in similar circumstances, but a man would quickly forget. How fortunate men were in their ability to pull their love up by the roots and transplant it so successfully that it grew again without the loss of a leaf or a petal. There was really no need for her to worry about Voldi.

Only one anxiety disturbed her: what success would she have in masquerading as a young man? Of course there was no other alternative. It was quite inconceivable that a sixteen-year-old girl could travel alone from southern Arabia to northern Galilee without risking some very unpleasant, if not positively dangerous, experiences; but this effort to pose as a young man would be very risky business.

A few facts were in Fara's favor. Her natural speaking voice was low-pitched and throaty; it might easily be mistaken by a stranger for the voice of a boy in his mid-teens. Too, the loose-fitting burnous ignored the curves of her girlish figure. But—even so—it would require much courage and self-confidence to maintain her rôle if suddenly projected into the company of men. It had not yet occurred to her that it would be quite as difficult to deceive another woman.

This dilemma had cost Fara many an anxious hour. She had privately practiced being a bold and bumptious youth, accustomed to rough talk and capable of serving a large helping of convincing profanity. She had stalked up and down her bed-chamber with long stiff-legged strides, jerking her head arrogantly from side to side as she scowled crossly into her mirrors, and growling gutturally. Once the absurdity of it had momentarily overcome her, and she had laughed at her reflection in the highly polished metal plate that hung by her door; but had instantly sobered at the sight of a pair of girlish dimples in this young man's cheeks, and resolved that she would do no more smiling.

At the first signs of dawn, Fara crossed the southern extremity of the fertile Valley of Aisne and moved on into the arid Valley of Zered that skirted the eastern shore of the Dead Sea. It was a desolate expanse of parched and blistered land, utterly without vegetation, birds, rodents, or reptiles. There were even no insects, with which most deserts abounded. The Dead Sea had been aptly named. Saidi clearly shared her rider's hope that they might soon be out of this forsaken country and quickened her pace, Fara straining her eyes for a glimpse of the ancient village of Akra which, she knew, maintained a precarious existence on a bit of oasis at the southernmost tip of the Dead Sea.

The sun was already hot when she sighted it, a clump of palms and cypress, a straggling group of shabby cottages surrounding a large brown tent. This would be the khan where travelers and their pack-trains were accommodated. At the door of the tent, Fara dismounted from the perspiring filly, handed the reins to a taciturn old Arabian, and with long steps and an experimental swagger followed along to the corral where she gruffly gave instructions how her mount was to be rubbed down and properly watered. And when the testy hostler growled that he knew how to take care of a horse, Fara shouted untruthfully that if he did he was the first old man she had ever seen who knew or cared whether a hot horse was safely watered, and that she proposed to stand by him until he had done it.

A wizened old woman glumly prepared a bad breakfast of stale eggs and staler bread. Feeling that she had need of practice in maleness, in the presence of women, Fara complained bitterly about the food and reviled the old woman in what she felt might be the customary terms for a man to use on such occasions. Then she demanded a bed, and denounced the old woman as a foul and dirty slattern when she saw the untidy cubicle provided for her. This execration she attempted in Greek, aware that her vocabulary of vituperation in that language—learned of the gentle Ione —would need some polishing.

After two hours of deep sleep, Fara was on her way again, after paying her hosts twice what they asked, and swearing manfully that the place wasn't fit for a goat to live in, to which contemptuous accusation the old man and his slovenly wife—grateful for their unexpected windfall—respectfully agreed. Fara smiled complacently as Saidi bounded away over the north-bound trail, her fears about her ability to be a man having been somewhat alleviated.

Late afternoon, after a sultry, monotonous ride along the blinding white seashore, she entered the town of Engedi, eastern terminus of the old salt trail from the Port of Gaza. It was an incredibly ugly place, its small, box-shaped houses built of sun-baked brick, suffocating a narrow, dusty street. At the principal inn, a little farther on, the stable-yard of which was crowded with camels, donkeys, and their grimy attendants,

Fara asked courteously for food and a bed for the night. Instantly she realized that she had made a mistake when the surly proprietor showed her a filthy pallet in a room containing a half dozen similar cots. Backing disgustedly out of the room, she opened her accumulated treasures of Arabian profanity and made it known to the master of the inn that she wasn't in the habit of sleeping in rabbit-hutches, dog-kennels, or pig-sties. Thus advised, the innkeeper deferentially led the way to a private room where the bed, if not comfortable, was less dirty than the one she had rejected.

Fara gave this incident much earnest thought. It was obviously a mistake to ask for anything politely. The public considered politeness a sign of weakness. It had a very low opinion of gentle speech. To wait patiently and take your turn, or to accept unprotestingly whatever was offered you, meant only that you were accustomed to being pushed aside; that you knew you could not defend your rights. It was a thoroughly abominable world, decided Fara; but if it was that kind of world she would try to meet it on its own terms. Contracting her brows into a sullen frown and puffing her lips arrogantly, she marched heavily up and down the bare creaking floor. In this belligerent mood she returned, with long steps, to the common room and flung herself into a dilapidated chair. Crossing her legs she sat impatiently flicking her high-laced boot with a finely crafted riding whip—a gift of Voldi's.

Well-dressed, good-looking men of affairs came and went, occasionally nodding to one another. Almost everybody knew everybody else. Fara honestly wished she were a man. They all seemed so effortlessly sure of themselves. She admired their self-sufficiency; tried to make herself think she was one of them. For the most part, her presence in the big, dingy room went unnoticed. Sometimes a young man, passing by, would toss an impersonal glance in her direction and move on without giving her a second look. This was ever so good, and Fara breathed more comfortably.

Immediately to the left of her, in the row of battered chairs backed against the wall, sat two men engaged in earnest conversation. They spoke in Greek, though it was evident that they were Romans. Fara had never seen one but she had been told how they looked.

The man in the nearest chair was probably forty. It was plain that he was a person of some consequence. Like his friend, who was many years his senior, he was smooth-faced and his graying hair was close-cropped. His face was deeply tanned, except for a narrow strip of white on his upper forehead which a bandeau had protected from the sun. His sand-colored tunic, trimmed in red, was of fine texture; his belt, dagger-sheath, and

tooled-leather sandals, strapped almost to the knee, showed expensive
workmanship. Fara surmised that they both were directors of caravans
probably belonging to the same company. Another survey of them revealed that the younger man had a small V-shaped notch in the top of his
ear. So—he was a slave. But apparently his servitude didn't bother him
much.

"I hope he is still there next week when we return," the distinguished
looking slave was saying. "I should like to hear him again. But it is doubtful whether he will be at large by that time. The legionaries will have
taken him in; for, as you have said, it was very inflammatory talk. But—by
the Gods, Aulus. it was all true—what he was saying."

"Yes, yes," agreed Aulus, "the world is bad enough to deserve a drub
bing, and it always was. But—the fellow is crazy as a beetle, Tim." The
older man turned his full face and Fara saw a long scar across his cheek;
relic of a savage fight long ago, she thought.

"That's where we differ, Aulus," countered Tim. "What the hermit
was preaching showed him to be indiscreet, foolhardy; but no merely
crazy man could collect a crowd like that, and keep them standing for
hours in the broiling sun listening with wide eyes and open mouths; and
they say he has been doing it day after day!"

"Oh—you know how people are," said Aulus, indifferently. "This half-
starved fanatic, living on dreams and desert bugs, climbs up on a big rock
and begins to yell that the world is due for punishment. Naturally the
rabble, with nothing better to do, gathers around to watch his antics and
shudder at his predictions." Aulus shifted his position in the creaking
chair and continued to extemporize. "People like to be scared, Tim. Their
empty lives are without stimulating sensations, and they enjoy feeling the
cold shivers run down their backs—especially when their instinct tells
them it's all a lot of damned nonsense."

There was quite a pause here; and Fara, who had been intently eavesdropping, leaned forward a little, hoping that Aulus hadn't said the last
word. Presently Tim remarked soberly, "I wonder if it is—just damned
nonsense."

"Poof!" scoffed Aulus. "The fellow is crazy as a beetle!" He rose,
stretched, yawned. "And so are you," he added. "I'll see you at supper. I
must have another look at that lame camel."

"Just a minute, Aulus." Tim patted the arm of the adjoining chair and
his scar-faced friend sat down again with an indulgent grin. "You have
been talking of that throng at Hebron as if it were composed entirely of
ignorant and lousy nobodies who would as gladly stand all day watching

a caged monkey scratch itself. But that doesn't account for it. There were at least a dozen well-dressed, intelligent men in the crowd giving serious attention to everything the hermit said."

Aulus dismissed this with a negligent flick of his hand.

"Local citizens, no doubt," he explained, "annoyed by the fellow's presence in their town, and waiting for him to start a brawl—so that they could lock him up—as a disturber of the peace."

"But some of them had come from afar, Aulus. I asked a bright-looking camel-boy if he wanted a job, and he loftily replied that he was in the employ of an eminent lawyer, Ben-Judah, a member of the Sanhedrin in Jerusalem."

"What's this Sanhedrin?" demanded Aulus, scornfully.

"The Jews' law-making body."

"I thought Rome made their laws."

"Just the laws on taxes. The Sanhedrin attends to the rest of it."

"You surely have a strange talent," observed Aulus, "for collecting useless information. What else do you know about Jewish laws?"

"Only that there are far too many of them. Why, a Jew can be arrested for dragging a chair across his dooryard on the Sabbath! It might dig a little furrow in the ground—and that would be plowing."

"I think you made that up, Timmie," chuckled Aulus. "But—be that as it may—perhaps this wise Ben-Judah, in the course of a journey, turned aside to listen to the prattle of this fool, just as we did—out of curiosity."

"Possibly; but it is much more likely that some influential people are spying on this hermit. He himself is a Jew, and he is talking to his own countrymen. Surely the Temple can't afford to let this fellow go on, gathering up a bigger crowd every day, shouting that the world is so bad it needs to be cleansed. That's the Temple's exclusive business; to see that the world—or at least the Jewish world, which is all that matters in this country—behaves itself. These learned lawyers and rabbis surely cannot permit a fiery prophet to march across Judaea informing thousands of people that their land is filthy with graft, greed, and injustice, all the way from top to bottom; and that his God—who is also theirs—means to take the whole job of renovation out of the hands of the recognized authorities, and attend to it personally!"

Aulus grinned at this long speech, and again rose to his feet.

"Perhaps you're right," he drawled. "In that case, they will probably toss the hermit into a dungeon—and forget about him. And so will the people. If a man dies a bloody death as a martyr to some new idea, the people remember, and build him a monument; but if he gets pitched into prison—Pouf! Let him rot!" Aulus dusted his hands, and sauntered away.

After a while the handsome man with the deep crows'-feet at the corners of his eyes and the notch on his ear turned his head slowly toward Fara and coolly looked her over.

"Which way are you headed, young man?" he inquired in Aramaic, signifying that he considered her a Jew.

"I am going west, sir," replied Fara in Greek—"as far as Gaza."

"Ever been there?" asked Tim; and when Fara had shaken her head, he remarked, "Very fine place—to lose your shirt—and have your throat cut. Let me warn you to ride straight down the middle of the street and have nothing to do with any of the inhabitants. Do not eat their food or drink their water or believe their lies."

"I gather that you do not care much for Gaza," commented Fara. "I shall take your advice. The first large city to the west is Hebron, is it not? Is that any better?"

"Much! Hebron has been sound asleep for two thousand years, so there's nothing very lively about it; but at least it won't rob you or poison your food or murder you in your bed." Tim recrossed his long legs and gave Fara a candid stare. "How do you happen to speak Greek, young man? You don't live in Greece, do you?"

"Nor do you, sir," said Fara, with equal bluntness, "yet you speak Greek."

"I am a Greek!" declared Tim, proudly. "You are a Jew, are you not?"

"I am not!" replied Fara. "I am an Arabian."

Tim studied her face with interest, pursed his lips, and nodded.

"My mistake," he muttered. "No offense, I hope."

"Not at all, sir. I have no quarrel with the Jewish people."

Tim laughed quietly, and said that he never thought he would hear an Arabian say that.

"But it is not so long, sir," Fara risked saying, "since the Jews and Arabians were in alliance."

"What an alliance!" scoffed Tim. "Of course you know all about that wretched marriage. One thing I never could understand: I know many Arabians; fine fellows who love nothing better than a good fight. Why haven't they ripped the bowels out of that Jewish rascal who humiliated your Princess? Surely it can't be that they have forgotten—or do not care!"

Unable to think of an appropriate answer to that, Fara abruptly changed the subject by saying:

"I could not help overhearing your talk about a prophet you met who said the world was to be punished for its misdeeds. Does he propose to attend to this chastisement?"

"No; not he," said Tim. "The fellow was careful to say that he himself was only a courier, announcing the early arrival of a divine person whom he depicted as a mighty avenger, a divinity to be sent from Heaven with an ax in his hand. The rotten old growth we have called Civilization was to be cut down, so that something healthy and fruitful might grow."

"Coming soon?" asked Fara.

"You would think, from his talk, that the prophet expected the avenger by next week—at the latest. If he had said it would occur a hundred years from now, his prediction would have been less risky."

"And less interesting," added Fara. "Do you think the prophet might be there—at Hebron—tomorrow?"

"Unless he has moved farther toward the hills. He was at least half a mile north of the road when we sighted the crowd. Apparently he does not study the people's convenience. They say he goes where he likes, and the multitude follows. If you are interested I suggest that you inquire along the way as you approach Hebron. Almost anyone will tell you. The air is full of him, over there." Tim rose to move away, and Fara also came to her feet.

"Am I right in surmising that you were inclined to believe what he said?" she asked, seriously.

Tim tugged at his lip, debating a reply.

"I don't know rightly what I do think about it," he answered, measuring his words. "The Jews are a singular people. They have always had their prophets, and many of their predictions have proved true, even to the dating of important events and the outcome of far distant wars. You'd better hear this man John for yourself. He may be greatly mistaken, but he is no fool!"

"Your friend says the man is crazy as a beetle," said Fara.

"My friend," drawled Tim, "is a typical Greek who became a typical Roman. He doesn't believe in anything he can't eat or wear or buy or sell or ride."

*   *   *   *   *   *

In spite of Saidi's strong objections to leaving the broad highway, Fara turned off at the unmistakable spot where an improvised road, fully fifty yards wide, led northward through a stubble-field. The tilled ground had been trampled soft, and the going was slow.

The deserted trail moved on across the field, across another less traveled highway, through another harvested field, over a bridge that spanned a little stream. It curved to miss a grove of cypress, climbed a hill, traversed a pasture, forded a creek, and went on—and on. After five miles of monotonous riding, Fara sighted a village. At the cross-roads a stone said the place was Tekoa. The trail had by-passed the little town but Fara rode into it. Perhaps someone could inform her how far she must go to find the prophet.

The village was quite abandoned. The small bazaars and markets on the principal street were closed. Farther on, in the residential section, a frail old woman bent over the ledge of a community well, tugging at the handle of the windlass. Fara drew up alongside, dismounted, and lent a hand. The dripping chain brought up a large wooden bucket which they pulled to anchorage on top of the low wall. The ragged old woman, breathing heavily, gave Fara a toothless smile and offered a rusty iron dipper.

"It is good!" said Fara. She filled the dipper for her hostess, emptied the bucket into the stone trough beside the well, and slipped off the filly's bridle. "Saidi is thirsty too," she added, lowering the bucket again.

"Never knew of a horse named Saidi," remarked the old woman. "Where do you come from, young master?"

"Arabia."

"But you are an Israelite, I think."

"No—we are both Arabians; Saidi and I."

The old woman tightened her shrunken lips and scowled.

"How do you happen to ask a drink of me?" she demanded crossly.

"Because you seemed friendly; and, besides, I was thirsty," replied Fara, unruffled by the woman's surliness. "I shall gladly pay you for the water."

"We don't sell water."

"Here is a little gift, then." Fara offered her a shekel.

The beady old eyes brightened at the sight of so much money, but the white head shook vigorously. Fara laid the shekel on the ledge of the well. The old woman turned and spat unprettily on the ground.

Suppressing her amusement, Fara said, "I am looking for a Jewish prophet. His name is John. Many people are following him, and I wish to hear him. I think he has passed this way. Do you know where he has gone?"

"He is a son of Satan!" shrilled the old woman. "A blasphemer! Cursed be all the infidels who listen to his revilings of Israel!"

Fara, who had been toying with her coin-pouch, unwound its thong and asked quietly, "Do you know where he is?"

For a moment the old woman maintained a sullen silence while Fara poured a few silver coins into her own palm. Pouring them back into the pouch, she vaulted into the saddle and gathered up the bridle-reins. The wrinkled old jaw was quivering. Obviously her poverty and her piety were in combat. Impetuously she pointed toward the northeast.

"They said he was heading for the river," she shouted—"and all Judaea is following him! Everybody in Tekoa has joined the infidels!" Tears ran down the leathery cheeks. "My own son—and my daughter—and her husband—and their children—they too have gone mad, like the others."

Honestly sorry for the pitiable old creature, who was now weeping aloud, Fara asked, quietly, "But what has this man been saying—to distress you so?"

"He scorns our ancient faith!" sobbed the old woman, scrubbing her cavernous eyes with the skirt of her faded apron. "He sits out there in the desert for years, doing no work, helping nobody, never attending the Synagogue, never bringing a gift to the altar; and now he come forth railing at the religion of his fathers!"

"He has a new religion then?" asked Fara.

"An angel is about to appear, he says, who will show us what to do—as if we were heathen who knew no God."

"Your priests are probably annoyed by such talk," surmised Fara.

"Annoyed!" The old woman slowly nodded her head and drew an unpleasant grin. "You wait! They will soon silence his blasphemies! God is not mocked!"

Fara opened her pouch and poured silver into the wrinkled hand. The old woman clutched the money, scowled, and made an unsuccessful effort to spit. Saidi, who had been pawing the ground impatiently, was pleased to be on their way at a brisk trot.

*   *   *   *   *   *

A half-hour before sunset she found them, acres of them it seemed, seated singly or in pairs or by families in a close-nibbled sheep pasture on the high-banked shore of the Jordan. They were busy with their supper which they had been forehanded enough to bring with them. Fara stopped a little way apart from the area where most of the pack-animals were tethered, hung Saidi's bridle on the pommel of the saddle, loosed the girths, adjusted a stout halter, buckled on a well-filled feed-bag, and staked out the tired filly for a hard-earned rest.

Strolling forward among the groups of people, she sat down near a good-looking family, father, mother, two half-grown boys and a pretty girl of her own age. The girl turned her head toward Fara and smiled shyly. Her father instantly muttered an inaudible command and his daughter, with some reluctance, left her place and wedged in between her parents. Fara was amused. She unwrapped her parcel of food and made a leisurely survey of the great multitude. It was a strangely quiet crowd. There was a low, inarticulate rumble of subdued conversation, but all faces were sober, pensive, and there was no laughter to be heard anywhere. A gentle but insistent, one-sided argument was in progress near by. The mother of the adjacent family was pleading earnestly with her husband. Yielding to her importunity he nodded, at length, and their well-favored daughter rose to resume the place where she had sat before. Her long black hair, unbound, was spread out covering her shoulders and back, and she seemed troubled about it. Turning to Fara with a smile she offered her a sweet roll which was accepted gratefully.

"My hair looks untidy," said the girl. "It's wet. I was baptized."

"It's beautiful," said Fara, galiantly. "How did you say it got wet?"

"The great prophet was baptizing, this afternoon."

"I'm afraid I don't know," confessed Fara. "What does that mean—baptizing? This is my first time here."

"The prophet leads us into the river and pushes us down under the water. That washes away our sins—and we are clean."

"And very wet, I suppose," remarked Fara, sympathetically.

The girl's full lips parted in a slow, reluctant smile that displayed the tips of beautiful teeth. Unable to think of an appropriate rejoinder to this dry drollery on a solemn occasion, she suddenly sobered and nodded her head.

Nothing further was said for a while, Fara regretting that she had spoken flippantly, the pretty Jewess, her face averted, apparently wishing she knew how to explain the cleansing she had had in the Jordan.

"I cannot think that you have been so very sinful," ventured Fara, gently.

"We are all sinful," murmured the girl, in a lugubrious imitation of experienced piety.

"Yes—I suppose so," admitted Fara with a companionable sigh. "Do you think the prophet is finished—for the day?"

"Oh no, he will speak again when the people have had their supper. It should not be long now." The young Jewess tipped her head toward the groups who were rising and stirring about.

The girl's plump mother, now that her family had been fed, wrapped up what was left; and, scrambling to her feet, came over and sat down beside her daughter. She and Fara exchanged amiable smiles.

"I am glad you made friends with our Ruth," she leaned forward to say. "There are so few young people here of her own age. Hundreds of us older ones, and swarms of small children; but it seems that our young people nowadays—" She broke off abruptly in response to an imploring look from her daughter, but immediately continued, "They don't seem to know that they have souls to save from the wrath to come!"

Ruth turned her head slowly toward Fara, with an expression that apologized for her zealous mother. Quite at a loss for a suitable comment, Fara mumbled, "Probably not," quickly aware that it was the wrong thing to have said for it showed a deplorable unconcern. The woman's eyes were alive with reproach.

"Young man," she said severely, "may I ask whether you have come here to seek salvation?"

"I came to see and hear the prophet," replied Fara.

"But not your own soul's salvation?" demanded the woman.

"The prophet is interested only in his own countrymen, I think," said Fara.

"Of course! But you are an Israelite, are you not?"

"I am an Arabian."

"Then you have no right to be here at all!"

"But—Mother!" pleaded Ruth.

"Never mind! You come with me!" Rising, the indignant Jewess drew her embarrassed daughter to her feet.

"Good-bye," Ruth turned to say softly.

Fara, who had risen, bowed and said with her lips rather than her voice, "I'm sorry." Striding through the milling crowd she observed that the people well forward were seating themselves compactly in rows. Finding an unoccupied spot, she sat down to wait. Presently a murmur of expectation swept the great audience. The prophet John, who had evidently been resting by the river's brink, appeared over the top of the embankment.

He was indeed a striking figure, tall, lean, lithe, bronzed. His heavy, tousled hair indicated an immense latent vitality. His massive head was held high above broad, bony shoulders. The craggy face was bearded, the forehead deep-lined, the dark eyes deep-set. He had the bearing of a man who had thought much and suffered. The crowd was very still. Stretching forth his long, brown arms, the prophet began to speak in a tone and mood of quiet entreaty. Fara found herself yielding at once to the strange compulsion of his vibrant voice. It was as one speaking from a great distance; from another age; from another world.

God had been patient—long—long. Of old He had planted a garden of delicious fruits and scented flowers for the delight of the human creatures He had made. It was a spacious garden, watered by cool springs and graceful rivers, along whose green banks were to be found much gold and many precious stones. On the hillsides jutted various metals which man's ingenuity might fashion into plows, pruning-hooks and other implements of husbandry. Great quarries bulged with enduring granite and delicately tinted marbles with which man might build temples and monuments. There were tall forests filled with all manner of trees from which might be hewn boats and shelters. Innumerable beasts pastured in the valleys, some to provide food, some to bear burdens. And had God's fortunate children been content to preserve and bequeath their rich heritage, their posterity might still be living comfortably and at peace in a garden.

Here the voice of the prophet rose to a little higher pitch as he proceeded to relate how this paradise was permitted to grow rank with weeds and brambles.

For, from the very beginning, God's children cared nothing about the garden. The first man flouted God's instructions. The elder of his two sons slew his brother and fled to the jungle. Restless and dissatisfied, humanity abandoned their paradise and began to roam, everywhere, without food, clothing. shelter, or destination, hoping only to escape the reproving eyes of their disappointed Father.

Sometimes, after long and aimless wandering, a group or tribe would settle in a fertile valley and till the soil. Another nomadic tribe, jealous of their neighbors' small prosperities, would come upon them with spears and swords and stones, killing the workers together with their old and helpless ones and their little children. Their Father had endowed them with inventive minds, so that they might make better and better tools, but their most ingenious inventions were not better tools but deadlier weapons. Stone was not quarried for the building of temples and monuments but for great fortifications. Iron was not molded into implements of husbandry but into instruments of war.

Everywhere there was fear, hardship, hunger. Pillage, rapine and slaughter spread over the face of the world until there was no peace at all, anywhere at all, and a man was not safe even in the home of his brother.

But—John was continuing with mounting heat—throughout all these dreadful ages of hatred and oppression, God had waited, waited patiently, anxiously, for the world's great ones to become aware of the poverty of their ill-gained wealth, and the empty sham of their vaunted power, and the shabbiness of their royal raiment, and the stink of starvation in their pilfered food. Now and again some brave voice would be raised in warning, but it would soon be stilled. Many were the messengers, sent of God, who were beaten, imprisoned and slain; fed to wild beasts, sawn asunder.

As a child, Fara had heard the legends about the world's creation, the disobedience of Adam, the wickedness of his posterity, and the great flood that had drowned them all—except one family. But the ancient tales, as John recited them, seemed fresh and frightening. For now his voice was at storm! God's patience was exhausted! He finally gave up hope of seeing His incorrigible children develop any beauty, any grace, any goodness, any peace. He determined to wash the world clean of them—thoroughly clean of them—and their filth and their spoor and the ravages of their hands until not a trace or a track or a trail of them remained! He told one peace-abiding old man to build a boat for his household; and the rain began to fall. The rain kept on coming—and coming—day after day after day. It poured as no rain had ever poured before!

Fara had listened, quite unmoved, when the wandering minstrels had sung of the fabled rain, but today the graphic picture of that appalling disaster made her draw her burnous tightly about her shoulders. The story made her flesh creep, as she heard the hoarse cries and strangled gasps of the doomed, clutching at one another in the swirl of rising waters, while the livid sky roared and the tempest screamed and the lightning stabbed relentlessly at the tossing debris.

And then—there was a sudden calm. The waters stilled and subsided. The sun was shining again; not upon a garden this time, but upon a stripped, deserted world of ruined cities leveled to the ground, and of empty thrones half-buried in the mud. Now men could begin anew and try to build a better world. But it was without any success—and without any promise.

John's voice took on a tone of deep sadness—and of shame too—as he reported how these men, wading out of the ooze and slime, began again to plot against one another as before. Prophets came and went, reminding the people of the great calamity that had befallen their fathers and predicting more trouble if they did not now obey God's command for peace. But the stronger ones ignored them, and those who sought the favor of the stronger ones laughed at them, and even the weak, who were set upon daily and robbed of their very rags—they too mocked the prophets and threw stones.

Here John paused for a long time—and bowed his head. The awed multitude sat transfixed, far eyed, holding its breath, though well it knew what was coming.

"So—now—in these latter days," he went on sadly, measuring his phrases, "it is our fate to witness another outpouring of God's wrath. It is not a flood this time, but a purge of the world's wickedness. You will ask, 'When is it coming?' And I shall answer, 'It is not coming: it is here!'

"And do I hear you say, 'It is not my fault that the world is wicked: it is the Empire that enslaves and robs and kills: am I to be punished for the crimes of Caesar?' Then I must answer you that everyone of us is guilty!" John's words came fast now, fast and scathing. "Do not blame all injustice, all cruelty, all meanness on Caesar's Empire! For each one of you is a little Empire filled with lust and greed and hate! It is easy enough to condemn the government which is, indeed, a rapacious thing that God will cleanse and cleanse until its bones show through! Easy enough to denounce the Temple for its well-fed lethargy: it deserves and will receive just punishment! But if any peace is to bless this sick world, salvation must first come to you; to you, the lonely shepherd in the hills; to you, the farmer at the plow; to you, the carpenter at the bench; to you, the housewife at the loom; to you, rabbi; to you, lawyer; to you, scribe; to you, magistrate. For —except you repent, you shall perish! It is so decreed! God has again spoken! There is One near at hand to rid the world of its iniquities! Indeed—He is now here!"

Suddenly a black-robed, distinguished-looking man of middle age, at the far end of the second row, arose from the small group of similarly well-groomed company surrounding him, and called out in a loud voice that turned all eyes his way:

"Meaning you, Baptizer? Are you, then, this avenger who will wreak God's wrath upon Caesar—and the High Priest—and upon us all?"

"No—I am not He," answered John, humbly. "I am but His courier, unworthy to stoop down and buckle His sandal-straps. I am but a voice, crying in the desert. I am commanded to say: make the way straight for the oncoming of the Anointed One. Level the road! Lift up the valleys where the poor despair! Pare down the mountain-tops where the powerful have sat in their arrogance and pride! Level the road for Him in your own hearts!"

Here the impassioned voice lashed out like the crack of a bull-whip.

"Do not be content with saying that the world might find justice and peace if the Greeks stopped hating the Egyptians, and the Romans stopped robbing the Greeks! Look to yourselves! Let the Macedonian merchant stop hating the Syrian camel-driver! Let the Jew stop hating the Arab! Let the Pharisees and Sadducees stop hating one another! Let the poor farmer, with two cows and an ass and twenty chickens, stop his sneering at the poor farmer with only two goats and ten chickens! Let the woman, with the fine cloak for Sabbath and the wedding-feast, stop her haughtiness toward the woman with only a week-day cloak and no wedding garment!"

Another man of the little company of critics now stood up in his place and said, "Does this avenger come with a sword—to make peace?"

"Not with a sword," said John, "but none the less with a power so mighty that the whole world will be shaken by it! He comes with an ax and a flail! The ax will be laid at the roots of all the trees. Every tree that bears fruit will be spared, but every tree that is barren and an encumbrance to the ground will be cut down and burned! His flail will thresh the harvest of your deeds. He will save the grain, but the chaff will be blown away!"

It was some moments before the crowd realized that the prophet had made an end of speaking, for he stood in silence before the people, with his head bowed in weariness; or perhaps, Fara thought, in silent prayer.

At length he lifted his head, turned slowly, and walked away toward the neighboring hill to the north. Their eyes followed him until he disappeared among the scraggy olive trees. Wordlessly, and without looking at one another, they rose and moved toward the camp-sites they had chosen in the broad pasture-field.

Dazed and bewildered, Fara followed the slow-moving crowd. She found herself abreast of the family she had met at supper. The pretty girl, Ruth, gave her a sidelong glance and smiled. Her mother, alert to her daughter's behavior, scowled and muttered, intentionally loud enough for Fara to hear, "Any more of that—and I shall tell your father!"

✻   ✻   ✻   ✻   ✻   ✻

Having brought no camping equipment except a pair of camel's-hair rugs, Fara slept for the first time in her life under the open sky. She retired early, for there was little else to do. A half-grown boy had been given a few pennies for bringing water to Saidi, after which Fara had removed the saddle and bridle, carrying them to a grassy spot near a cypress tree. During the slow twilight the people quietly pitched their simple camps and by the time the stars appeared in full splendor the pasture-field was still. Occasionally a tired baby cried, a dog barked, there was a brief argument among the pack-asses; but the people were quiet. Fara wondered whether they slept or reflected soberly on the strange words they had heard. The distinguished men from the city—what were they thinking? Ruth's mother—did she say to herself that at least she was innocent of any fault? And what would this peace-loving prophet think if he knew that one of his interested auditors was on her way to kill her own father? It was a long time before her mental confusion gave way to her bodily fatigue.

She went to sleep wondering whether Arabia, too, would be warned of what was coming. And would anyone speak to the Romans about it? Surely the world was larger than Judaea.

Even before dawn there was a stir of activity. Fara rubbed the sleep out of her eyes, sat up and combed her boyish hair, drew the red bandeau down over her forehead, rolled up her rugs, and set off to see how Saidi had fared. Saidi was gone! There was the stake to which she had been tethered, but Saidi was nowhere to be seen. Doubtless she had contrived to tug loose and wander away. She might even be well started for home. Intelligent horses were known to do that.

After fruitless inquiries of the men and boys who were attending to their beasts, Fara decided to climb the hill for a wider view. As she reached the summit, her heart beating hard with the exertion and alarm, she shaded her eyes and carefully surveyed the plain below, every rod of it, from the faraway north to the congested encampment; but there was no sight of Saidi. She suddenly felt so weak and faint that she laid a hand against the trunk of a tree for support against the westerly morning breeze. She started at the sound of a voice immediately behind her.

"What are you looking for, daughter?"

Fara turned slowly to confront the prophet, who was regarding her with sober eyes.

"My horse," she replied, unsteadily, returning to her search of the valley. "She must have wandered away in the night."

"May have been stolen," suggested John, advancing to stand beside her.

"Surely no one, among these people, would steal!" said Fara.

"There is no place in this greedy world, my daughter, where men do not steal."

There it was again—"my daughter." Fara hoped she had misunderstood, the first time; but there was no doubt about it now. Somehow he knew. But she must listen, for he was speaking, quietly, almost as to himself.

"They steal. They steal anything, everything, anywhere, everywhere; anything from a horse to a halter; anywhere, from a scroll in the Synagogue to a vase in the graveyard. They steal on the farm, in the marketplace, on the highway, at the inn, at the goldsmith's, at the rag-picker's, in the gambling-house, and in the Temple. There is no limit to it. They steal from babes and pennies from dead men's eyes. They steal from bankers and beggars. Where do you live, young woman, that you should be incredulous of theft?"

"I am from Arabia," said Fara.

John chuckled briefly, but without smiling.

"You must have lived a sheltered life," he said, dryly. "Your people have taken no prizes for honesty. Perhaps you are not very well acquainted with your countrymen. Have you always lived in Arabia? I detect an accent on your tongue, though I must say your Aramaic is correct. How do you happen to speak it? And you look Jewish—as much Jewish as Arabian. Tell me, daughter, why are you wearing a man's burnous; and why that shorn hair?"

Fara's knees were giving way now, and she sat down. The prophet seated himself on a small boulder near by. Slowly turning her face toward him, she encountered a searching gaze that compelled frankness.

"I am on an errand, sir, that could not be safely performed by a young woman. I told you that I am an Arabian, because I prefer to think of myself that way; but it is only half true. My mother was an Arabian. My father is a Jew."

"Your mother is dead?"

"Only three days ago." Fara turned her eyes toward the valley.

"And that sent you on your errand, I think; and your errand takes you to Judaea, and your father is a Jew. Perhaps you go to notify him of your mother's death."

"Ye-yes," stammered Fara, hoping the answer might suffice.

There was a considerable silence before John spoke.

"So it is something else besides telling your father. Has he not lived with your mother in Arabia?"

"Not for many years."

"How did they happen to marry?"

"It's quite a long story, sir. I have no wish to detain you." She looked again into his inquiring eyes. "Must I tell you?" she asked, in a voice that seemed a little frightened.

"Not if you don't want to," said John, kindly, "but perhaps it might help—if you confided in someone you could trust."

"I am on my way to find my father," said Fara. "He lives in Galilee—at the city of Tiberias."

"Then he must be in the employ of the Tetrarch," surmised John. "There is little else in Tiberias but the great establishment of Antipas."

Fara nodded and turned her eyes away. Tardily, and in a barely audible, reluctant voice she said, "Antipas is my father."

John seemed a person not easily surprised but he impulsively rose to his feet and exclaimed, "You don't mean it!" He searched her face, and apparently satisfied that she was telling the truth, he said, "Of course I know the story. Everyone does. You have no cause to be proud of your father."

"I am quite aware of that, sir," agreed Fara.

"But—surely—after the cruel and shameful treatment he gave the Princess of Arabia, you are not going to Tiberias to live with this—"

"I have vowed to avenge my mother," interrupted Fara, huskily.

"You mean—you would kill your father?"

"If I can."

"But you can't!" exclaimed John. "In the first place, it's quite impossible. The place is fortified like a besieged city. I was born a Galilean, and my friends have told me that the Tetrarch lives like a fugitive, heavily guarded by night and day. You would only lose your life to no purpose at all. And—even if you succeeded, which is inconceivable, your crime would haunt you all your days. No good ever comes of revenge."

"I heard you say yesterday that there was One arriving now to avenge God," said Fara. "Is no good to come of that?"

John did not have an answer ready. After some delay, he said, "That is a far different matter, my daughter. Vengeance is permitted only to God. He will repay!"

"But I mustn't!" Fara's tone was satirical. "It's all right for God to seek vengeance—but it is wrong for me to do it. I'm supposed to have a finer moral character?"

"That remark," reproved John, "does you small credit, daughter. It is irreverent."

"But practical," defended Fara.

"And excusable, I suppose," reflected John. "You probably had no religious training—in Arabia."

"Why not?" Fara demanded. "The Jews and Arabians worship the same God, do we not? Abraham is our common father; is that not so?"

Any further discussion of this matter seeming fraught with more heat than light, John nodded, absently.

"Perhaps you may see the Anointed One in Galilee," he said. "I wish you might be able to talk with Him. He lives in the town of Nazareth. He is a carpenter."

"Disguised as a carpenter?" wondered Fara. "Same as I am disguised as a boy?"

"No, He really is a carpenter, and a very good one, whereas you are only pretending to be a boy—"

"And not doing so well at it," she broke in, with a pensive smile. "However—" she added, "you are the first one to discover."

"You mean—I am the first one to tell you." John paced back and forth, frowning thoughtfully. "But this is no light matter," he went on. "You have vowed a vow. I shall not be the one to induce you to break it. A vow is a vow. You are intent upon going to Tiberias. Very well. Go first to Nazareth: it is not far from there. Tell your story to the Carpenter—Jesus. Abide by His counsel. You will make no mistake if you do as He tells you. . . . I must leave you now. Since your horse is gone, you will proceed on foot, I suppose. Follow the Jordan. It is much shorter than by the traveled roads and it will be safer for you." Pointing to an angling path down the northern slope of the hill, he said, "May God be with you, daughter, and keep you safe from any harm." He extended a big, bony hand, and she confidently gave him her small one. Turning it about for inspection, he smiled. "It is not a boy's hand. You must be very careful. I can't advise you, now that your hair is shorn, to dress as a girl should; but," he repeated, gently, "you must be careful. Those riding boots. That fine burnous. You should get into less conspicuous clothing—peasant's clothes—as soon as possible. You could be thrown into prison for this, you know."

"That would be unpleasant," said Fara. "They say that prisons are very uncomfortable."

"I have never been in one," said John, "but I expect to be—at almost any hour now. The authorities will arrest me as a disturber of the peace."

"But there is no peace," said Fara.

"No—there is no peace," agreed John, soberly.

"Is it the Temple that would silence you?"

"Yes—but the Temple has no authority to imprison me."

"Who, then?"

"The provincial government; and as I am a Galilean I shall be taken before Antipas."

"Then—we may meet again—in prison." Fara smiled grimly.

John shook his shaggy head in reproof of her ill-timed levity.

"It is quite clear that you do not realize the utter hopelessness of your undertaking, my child," he said sadly. "I do not expect ever to see you again. . . . Farewell."

"Until we meet," persisted Fara.

Halfway down the long hill, she turned and looked back. John was still standing where she had left him. She waved a hand and he extended his arm, as to give her his final blessing.

5

It was early morning on the western shore of the Sea of Galilee. Enough remained of an unusually hot summer to strip the fishermen to the waist, but intimations of autumn were in the smoky haze that overcast the distant mountains, obscured the dome of the new Synagogue in Capernaum, and dulled the sheen of the Tetrarch's marble palace.

The ugly huddle of weather-beaten shacks and wharves where the fishermen kept their tackle and dried their nets had come alive to the day's work. Browned, bushy, barefooted men and youths scampered about on the docks, loading flat-bottomed dories with equipment for the larger craft which rocked indolently in the quiet cove, tugging in unison at their anchor-chains.

Fully a score of these boats, of all shapes, sizes, ages, and degrees of dirtiness and disrepair, were congregated in the bay, waiting for their skippers and crews to haul up the much-mended sails and wallow forth to what they hoped might be promising fishing-grounds.

Haughtily apart from the clutter of nondescript old tubs, and conspicuous for their trimness, lay a fleet of three blue-hulled schooners moored side by side and so closely lashed together from midship to stern that their freshly painted gunwales would have chafed but for the heavy hempen pads that cushioned them. Built for stability, they were broad in the beam and sat low in the water; and they were of identical design, though the central ship, *The Abigail*, carried three masts and was somewhat larger than her two-masted companions, *The Sara* and *The Rachael*. Tethered loosely about their prows bobbed a half-dozen empty dories.

On the closely yoked afterdecks the combined crews, totaling thirty and ranging in age from sixteen to sixty, sat cross-legged, a few feet apart, forming a circle around a huge net that plainly needed extensive repairs.

Alone on the broad tiller-seat of *The Abigail*, a gigantic, hairy, deeply tanned Galilean of thirty-five—as busy with his awl as were his employees—occasionally looked up to survey their work, and sometimes they met his eyes as to inquire whether he was satisfied with what they were doing. They all worked skillfully, swiftly, and in silence, though their faces did not indicate that they were hard-driven. It was obvious that the relation of the master and his men was cordial; indeed it was better than cordial, for there was evident in their diligence a desire to please. Especially was this loyalty noticeable in the attitude of the younger ones who seemed proud of their employment, as they had reason to be, for it was a testimonial to a man's seamanship if he was signed on to sail under Simon the son of Jonas.

Among the Galileans the name of Simon was so common that it had to be tagged for better identification. Every Simon bore a special designation: Simon the tanner, Simon the weaver, Simon the clubfoot, Simon the juggler, Simon the little, Simon the scribe, Simon the sot, Simon the bald, Simon the son of Jonas. Doubtless if the skipper's sire had been less distinguished, an appellation appropriate to his characteristics would have been promptly contrived for him by the community. In that case he might have become known early in his youth as Simon the brawler, or Simon the scoffer. But to the neighbors and relatives who had known him since childhood he was Simon the son of Jonas; and—they were likely to add—not much of a credit to the good old man; for nobody was more fanatically devoted to the Synagogue than Jonas, and nobody had less use for it than his tough and burly son Simon.

It was inevitable, however, that the huge, noisy, quick-tempered, lamentably irreverent son of Jonas should become known by a more colorful name. All up and down the western shore, throughout Capernaum, Magdala, Bethsaida, and the hamlets between, and at the Roman fort, and among the servants in the great villa of the Tetrarch, and on the lake, and in the country round about, Simon the son of Jonas was referred to as the Big Fisherman.

From early boyhood the sacrilegious and belligerent Simon had been a growing affliction to his parents. True, he obeyed the laws, specializing in a scrupulous observance of the Fifth Commandment which, in this case, was not easy; for the religious duties of Jonas, his diligent attention to all the fasts and feasts, his frequent pilgrimages to Jerusalem, and his unctuous exhortations on the streets and in the market-place, left him but little time for any gainful employment; and had it not been for the industry of Simon and his elder brother Andrew, their parents would have lived on meager fare.

As for the docile bachelor Andrew, his idea of keeping the Fifth Commandment had required his regular attendance at the services of the Synagogue and a strict observance of the stated fasts, but it had laid no such burden on Simon whose conception of honoring his father and mother did not go any farther than being kind and respectful to them and seeing to it that they were well fed and clothed. By the time he was twelve Simon heartily despised the Synagogue and everything it represented because, he felt, it had made a loafer and a tiresome bore of an otherwise fine man.

By a practice of great restraint, he never disclosed his private contempt for his father's sanctimoniousness. Sometimes it was difficult to exhibit a proper respect when, on business in the markets, he would come upon Jonas parading the aisles, scroll in hand, solemnly haranguing the customers who rarely paused to give heed and more often grinned and winked at one another as he passed by. But if Simon's attitude toward his father was circumspect, he found a measure of relief for his pent-up feelings by a forthright excoriation of religion when in the company of his young contemporaries. He was still beardless when all the friends and acquaintances of the family referred to him as an infidel—and an uncommonly noisy one. Jonas knew it, and deplored it with tears, and prayed aloud in the public places for his wayward son; but ate with relish the provender that the incorrigible skeptic brought home.

Beginning as a mere roustabout and chore-boy on a dirty trawler, his wages paid in low-grade mud-suckers which he peddled from door to door among the very poor, Simon had gradually made himself useful enough to be in a bargaining position among the fleet-owners; for he was strong as an ox and fearless to the point of foolhardiness. In weather that tied up most of the ships in the cove at Tiberias—for the little sea could be dangerously rough on short notice—Simon would be eager to go out and do battle with the waves; and the catch—taken in such circumstances—fetched higher prices for lack of competition.

And so it was that before he was twenty-three Simon owned a half-share in a fairly good fishing-smack. At twenty-eight he owned it fully and had taken on a crew of four. And now he was master of the most prosperous and best known fleet on the lake.

As his self-made success increased, the Big Fisherman's character reflected both his earlier frustrations and his current achievements, not always to his credit. Conscious of having missed almost everything that lent enchantment to a normal childhood, he was inclined to be contemptuous of youngsters who wasted their time at play when they might be making themselves useful. He had never been to school; could hardly read and rarely tried to write anything more than his own name. In consequence of this illiteracy, he scoffed at education and considered the professional scrivener an object of ridicule. Physical weakness he viewed with smiling condescension.

As for his loyalties and enthusiasms, Simon, though stridently irreligious, possessed a passionate love of his race. Not to be a Jew was equivalent to not being anybody at all. In his regard, all nations—except Israel—were of one ignominious category. If they were in any way different, their distinctions were trivial. Never having traveled more than twenty-five miles from home—and privately sensitive about his provincialism—he had accumulated quite a lot of prejudices about the world beyond little Galilee. He spoke derisively of people who lived in cities, even Jewish cities. The Greeks foolishly pretended to be better scholars than the Romans, when the fact was that they were only lazier than the Romans and idled their time away on such fripperies as stone statues and the spinning of arguments concerning theories on which one man's guess was as good as another's; with nothing to come of it, no matter who was right. The Romans had proved themselves better fighters than their weaker neighbors, but so were dogs better fighters than conies, when it came to that. The Egyptians were in decay and thought only of building tombs to house their bones. And Arabia had never been anything but a murderous horde of liars, cheats and robbers. Israel was not only the Chosen Race but the Human Race. The rest of the people were no better than animals. Simon could and did discourse on this subject by the hour. He was an Israelite indeed!

And he was loyal to his comrades. From boyhood he had shown an extraordinary talent for making friends among all classes of people. He had an instinctive love of common justice and fair play, though he was not always himself a cheerful loser. He liked practical jokes but preferred not to be the object of them; and, sometimes, when finding himself at a momentary disadvantage, the Big Fisherman would display a childish petulance that seemed amusingly incongruous when exhibited by a man of his heroic stature.

In short, success had turned Simon's head a little. Having come up through many tribulations into a conspicuous prosperity, he was intolerant of other men's failures to achieve. He liked to be complimented upon his accomplishments and was not reluctant to speak pleasantly of them himself. But—for all his vanity, his intolerance, and his wide assortment of showy weaknesses, his employees idolized him, worked long hours for him, applauded his strength, laughed immoderately at his clumsy witticisms; and, when off duty, imitated his swagger.

By the time the Big Fisherman had won his prowess as a fleet-owner, saintly old Jonas and his mousey wife Rachael had been summoned from their cottage in Capernaum to an abode Elsewhere, leaving him free to marry young Abigail of Bethsaida who lived with her widowed mother Hannah. Andrew, who rarely offered any unsolicited advice to his more resourceful brother, perhaps because he was an employee, had gently cautioned Simon against this marriage; for Abigail, though winsome and pretty, had no health at all. Doubtless it was her very flower-like fragility that had attracted the big, brawny fellow whose latent talent for tenderness had never been given a chance to develop.

He had been very considerate of Abigail. As she slowly faded, the common solicitude and sorrow shared by Simon and Hannah greatly endeared them to one another, and when his girl-wife died he continued to live with his much-cherished mother-in-law in her commodious home on a quiet, shady corner in the northern suburbs of Bethsaida. Andrew joined them; though, unwilling to burn his bridges until satisfied that this arrangement was mutually agreeable, he kept the old family residence in Capernaum intact, and often went there to tend the flowers.

Now that the shadow was lifted from the small household in Bethsaida, it took on an unaccustomed brightness, for Hannah was gifted with a quiet drollery and an inexhaustible good humor refreshing to the brothers who had found so little to amuse them in their parental home. Andrew, sober and taciturn, allowed many a quip to pass unnoticed, though he could be depended upon to draw an amiable, bewildered smile. Simon's big, booming laugh, on an open-windowed summer evening, could be heard for a block. Near neighbors often wondered, rather testily, what manner of entertainment could produce such hilarity. It was the general opinion of the conservatives in that part of town that the Big Fisherman had added little to the gentility of Bethsaida.

But though they regarded Simon with scant respect, there was one thing about him that stirred their curiosity—and their envy too. He seemed to be on friendly terms with David, the wealthy, haughty Sadducee. Up the cross-street which bounded Hannah's property on the north side and rose gently for a quarter-mile to the east, lay the spacious grounds and imposing old mansion of the eminent Zadok family, now reduced in numbers to a pair of unmarried, middle-aged aristocrats and a score of elderly servants.

Old Zadok, the departed grandfather of David and Deborah, had held himself aloof from the town; nor had Bethsaida made any effort to intrude upon his lofty isolation, for he was a Sadducee, the only Sadducee in all that region, and if he wanted to live in seclusion Bethsaida was willing he should do so, the Sadducees being of a cynical, supercilious sect that affected a social superiority. Nor was that all that ailed old Zadok and the Sadducees, in the opinion of Bethsaida. It was a known fact that he hated the government of Galilee and had been heard to speak scornfully of Antipas the Tetrarch. It was a wonder he hadn't got into trouble about that. Of course he paid exorbitant taxes. Rich men who paid large taxes might be able to speak their minds more recklessly than poor people who, for the same indiscretion could be clapped in jail. Maybe it was better not to have much to do with the Zadoks, or any other Sadducee.

Just why David had retained his residence at the old palace on the hill was a mystery, for until his recent retirement he was seldom at home. Maybe it was the commanding view of the lake that had held him, and brought him back for his summers. Surely it was inconvenient for him to have lived there during his active life, for his law practice was in Caesarea and the only local client he served was Jairus whose large estate lay in the foothills above Capernaum.

Now David, it seemed, was home to stay; and on fair days it was his habit to stroll slowly down the hill, with bent head, apparently in deep meditation. Persons meeting him did not venture to speak, nor did he lift his eyes. Doubtless he was too busy with his own thoughts to take any account of them.

It was not surprising, therefore, that Hannah's neighbors should have been amazed the first time David stopped beside her white picket fence to engage the Big Fisherman in what seemed to be a serious, man-to-man conversation. And this happened again and again, usually of a late afternoon, when Simon had returned from his work. Sometimes Hannah joined them, presumably at David's suggestion. It was all very mysterious.

But while this friendship between Simon the uncouth and David the refined was incomprehensible to the Bethsaidans, whose social status was approximately level, it was not so unaccountable as it seemed; for though aristocracy might shudder at the thought of contamination with persons a notch or two lower in the social scale, it was willing to unbend pleasantly for those who, everybody knew, had no rating at all—and would not be expecting an invitation to dinner.

In this case, however, there was a still better reason for the friendship of the lawyer and the fisherman. The seed of it had been sown many years before when Simon, a self-conscious, ragged, immensely overgrown youngster, had regularly delivered fish at the Zadoks' kitchen door. David,

John Reports to Peter

Again John nodded, slowly lifted cloudy eyes, entreatingly shook his head, and tapped gently on the Big
Fisherman's knee, as if begging that his story might be
deferred until he could tell it in private. But this signal
for secrecy, now that the crew had become interested
in the pantomine, nettled Simon.

"And did you find this cracked Carpenter who has
turned vintner — and makes wine out of water?"

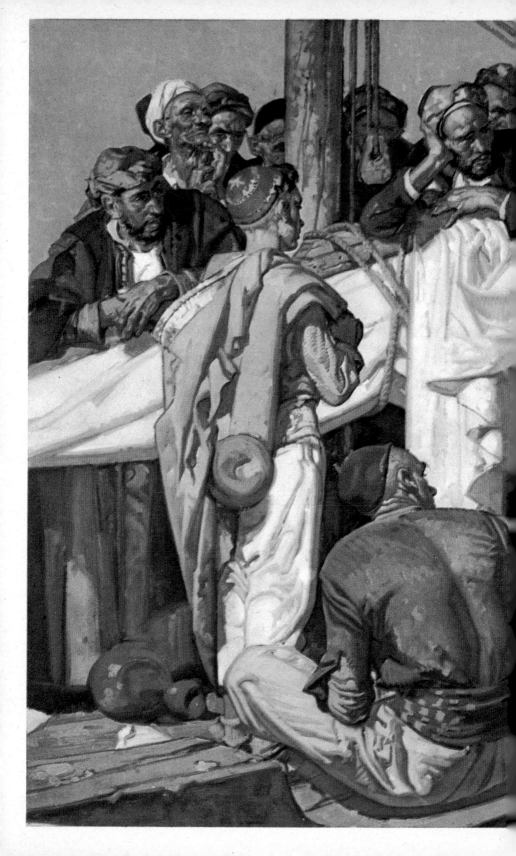

his senior by a decade, occasionally encountered him on a garden path and stopped to feel his bulging muscles in about the same careless manner with which he tousled the ears of his dog; and Simon would grin and mumble "Yes, sir" to David's playful comments on the astounding number of his freckles and the prodigious size of his bare feet. And then David had gone away to school in Athens; absent for five years. Returning, he had joined an eminent law firm in Caesarea, then rapidly becoming a metropolis, and was seen only rarely, briefly, in Bethsaida. At widespaced intervals Simon passed him. David would nod and smile, absently.

Even after arriving at something like dignity in his lowly occupation, Simon had continued personally to deliver choice fish to a few important patrons; to the Tetrarch's palace, of course, and to the Zadok mansion, and—for a while—to Jairus' beautiful villa, though latterly he had given that up: it was too far.

Now that David, slightly stooped and gray, had come home for good, Simon often saw him sauntering about on the grounds. One day they met. Without any preliminary greeting, David said, "Still peddling fish, eh? Surely you should have found a better job by now."

Simon was offended, but kept his temper.

"I do have a better job, sir. I do not peddle fish. True—I still select them carefully for you, and bring them myself to your house—and to the Tetrarch—but I could easily send them."

If Simon had thought to flatter his customer by mentioning that the House of Zadok and the Villa of the Tetrarch were somehow of the same standing in his esteem, he was quickly set right about that. David's lip curled unpleasantly.

"So—that abominable drunkard eats fish, eh?" he muttered. "I had supposed he lived exclusively on beverages."

Simon didn't care to risk a comment on this seditious speech, but he nodded, perfunctorily; and David, dismissing the subject with a flick of his fingers, said, "You're doing well, then. Perhaps you own a market."

Simon's lips twitched with a grin that hinted at something better than a market.

"No, sir. I am still a fisherman, but I own my ships and have a score and ten men in my employ."

"That is ever so good," commented David. "I am glad you have prospered. I daresay you have a home—and family."

Simon explained briefly about that, and David was respectfully sympathetic. After a little pause, he remarked, "Perhaps you have some office in the Synagogue, now that you have done so well in business."

"No, sir," replied Simon, almost bluntly. "I have no time for the Synagogue."

"You mean—you are not religious?" inquired David, surprised.

"Well, sir—" Simon shifted his weight, deliberating a reply. "I believe in the God of our fathers—who made the world—and gives us our life—and the sunshine, rain and harvests. I do not believe that He takes any notice of our small doings—or cares whether we roast calves and lambs in His honor."

"Very well spoken," said David, soberly. "You are thoughtful. . . . I bid you Good-day."

That brief conversation had marked the beginning of an acquaintance that was ripening to a friendship. There were frequent talks thereafter, Simon encouraged to speak his mind freely and David nodding his approval. Even when Simon had ventured quite beyond his depth, and it was obvious that he didn't know what he was talking about, David—in need of diversion—would slowly nod his head—and smile.

Then came the visits at the fence, which brought all that section of Bethsaida to the window. And one afternoon David consented to come into the yard, and sit down with Simon in the shade of the tall cypress, and Hannah brought them cups of pomegranate juice.

*   *   *   *   *   *

The early morning haze had lifted now. The sun had scented the old tarred ropes and softened the pitch in the deck-seams. The sailors worked in silence, deftly spreading open the frayed cords of the net and weaving into them the new twine.

Simon straightened his back, scratched his bushy head with his awl, and shaded his sweating brow for keener observation of the dory that was slowly approaching from the docks. His face lighted up. Other eyes followed his inquisitively.

"Who's that with John?" mumbled Andrew.

"I don't recognize him," said Simon. "Some youngster wanting a job, maybe."

"Looks like a tramp," thought James.

"That would be John—all over," remarked old Zebedee, from the adjacent deck of *The Rachael*—"always bringing home a lost dog to feed."

"Well—he might do worse," rumbled Simon, deep in his throat. "Go forward, Thad, and toss him a rope."

Work on the net was resumed without much enthusiasm, all of them curious to see what sort of passenger John had picked up. But, whoever the stranger was, the Big Fisherman would doubtless approve of his coming aboard. Anything that Johnny did was agreeable with Simon. Every member of the crew took that for granted.

Sometimes newcomers to the fleet were a bit annoyed over the skipper's partiality toward this absent-minded youth, but they soon accepted it without jealousy; for nobody could help liking him. Johnny was shamelessly lazy. On warm afternoons when everybody else was diligently fishing, Johnny could be found lying flat on his back, staring up into the sky. If Simon teasingly queried for a report on what he saw in the white clouds today he would raise his arm and dreamily finger a pattern of a dome, a tower, a bridge, a city; or perhaps a winged angel.

"You're not much good as a fisherman, Johnny," Simon would say, "but it's worth something to see pictures in the sky."

It is doubtful, however, whether Simon would have tolerated any such indolence had that been the boy's only distinction. In emergencies he was amazingly industrious, resourceful and courageous. In fair weather, when the sails were hoisted or reefed, the crew had to step over him while he indifferently viewed their labors through half-closed eyes. Let there be a storm, Johnny astonished them with his seamanship. If a raveled rope fouled a pulley high on the main-mast in the midst of a howling gale, everybody knew that the drenched sailor inching his way up the swaying ratlines was Johnny the dreamer.

Perhaps Simon loved the boy for his reckless bravery, perhaps for his visions in the white clouds, perhaps for both of these disparate talents; but, whatever may have been the grounds of his affection it was sincere and ever on display. Nor was it a one-sided devotion. Simon was Johnny's hero. It was a relationship that gave something of fragrance to an occupation much in need of it.

Now John and his unrecognized companion—a ragged youth of his own age—were climbing over the forward rail. Waving a hand, he led the diffident stranger into the little galley in the forecastle.

"Feeding him, no doubt," guessed Andrew. "He certainly looked hungry."

"Johnny missed his calling," said Simon. "He should have been a public almoner."

"It would have increased the taxes," remarked old Zebedee. "The boy has no regard for money."

"No—Johnny will never be rich," said Simon, "but he will always have friends."

"And they will have him to bury sometime," muttered Zebedee.

"You wouldn't expect him to bury himself," said Simon.

They all chuckled a little at this, but gave full attention as John appeared from the galley and came slowly aft, their curiosity about his movements whetted by the fact that he had been absent since noon yesterday. Stepping with the carefulness of a cat he walked across the big net and sat down beside Simon who edged over to make room. They all put down their work and waited for explanations.

"Camel-boy," said John, tipping his head toward the galley. "Hasn't had anything to eat for a couple of days; very tired. I found him sitting on the dock. He looked as if he had been crying; face all smeared and dirty. He said he had run away from a caravan bound for Damascus on the coast road, because they beat and starved him."

"You showed him where to wash—and gave him some food?" inquired Simon. He took up the net again as a hint to the crew, and they bent over their work. John nodded—and smiled.

"I never saw anyone eat before," he remarked to Simon "—not like this boy. The poor chap must be hollow all the way to his heels."

"Did you question him?" asked Simon.

"No—I thought I'd let you do that. He may be from the south. He speaks Aramaic; the Judaean kind; only down south farther, maybe."

"Well—we'll see," rumbled Simon, absently. Leaning closer he asked in a low voice, "Did you go out there, yesterday, as you intended?"

John nodded dreamily, averting his eyes; then shook his head.

"Well?" snapped Simon, with a sudden impatience that widened his audience—"did you go—or didn't you?"

Again John nodded, slowly lifted cloudy eyes, entreatingly shook his head, and tapped his hand gently on the Big Fisherman's knee, as if begging that his story might be deferred until he could tell it in private. But this signal for secrecy, now that the crew had become interested in the pantomime, nettled Simon.

"And did you find this cracked Carpenter who has turned vintner—and makes wine out of water?"

The crews of the three ships were leaning forward now, wide-eyed with curiosity, and frankly amused at the discomfiture of the skipper's pet. And when John still remained silent, crestfallen, Simon went on with his ridicule.

"I suppose the Carpenter urged all the poor farmers and shepherds to band together and storm the Roman fort with flails and pitchforks."

This brought a laugh. Everybody had heard Simon's savagely expressed opinions of the rumors afloat concerning the Carpenter from Nazareth, and it would be prudent to share his contempt. The Big Fisherman appreciated this loyal acceptance of his views, and gave his men another occasion for a guffaw. Turning toward John, he said:

"Perhaps you saw the Carpenter turn a field of rocks into a pasture full of fat sheep! Speak up, lad! You were bent on going out to see the Carpenter—and I gave you the day off. Tell us, now; what did you make of him?"

" I—I don't know," said John, thickly. He firmed his lips and shook his bent head. Presently he straightened, faced Simon with an expression of utter bafflement, and repeated, lamely, "I don't know, sir. It's all very strange."

"Hmm; so I gather," muttered Simon. "And what was so strange about it; the man, or his talk, or his tricks? Can't you tell us? Or are we too stupid to understand?"

"Please give me time, Simon." John seemed to be speaking from a distance. "The whole thing is mysterious. I can't think straight today. Let me tell you about it—a little later." He lowered his tone until it was inaudible to any but Simon, and added, "But I won't expect you to believe it."

"Humph!" grunted Simon.

At this juncture the tension was eased. The emaciated camel-boy—in a tattered and grimy brown tunic and trousers, easily recognized as the garb of a caravan lackey, ambled slowly toward them. Uncertain what to do with himself, he halted and leaned against a capstan. Simon beckoned to him and the net was relaxed for his crossing. Obedient to the master's invitation, he sat down on what was left of the tiller-seat. The crew looked him over without visible prejudice.

"Did you have something to eat, son?" The Big Fisherman's voice was friendly.

The newcomer nodded gratefully, and said, in a husky tone inaudible to any but the master and John, "You are very kind, sir."

"That was John's doing," chuckled Simon, apparently anxious to set himself right with his offended favorite who sat demurely reflecting on the ridicule he had suffered.

"Johnny attends to the feeding of visitors. . . . So—you're lost, maybe. Well—don't worry too much. You look as if you needed a rest. Where have you been sleeping lately—in hay-stacks?"

"No, sir; under the hedges, along the roadside. They don't want you sleeping in their hay-stacks."

"They can't be much blamed for that," commented Simon. "Tramps are always breaking down their berry-bushes and grapevines—and frightening the cattle. . . . What's your name, boy?"

"Joseph."

"I suppose they call you Joe."

"Y-yes, sir. That—and a lot of other things, lately."

Simon acknowledged this grim little pleasantry with an appreciative grin. Evidently the ragged waif was not stupid.

"Where are you from, Joe?" he asked, kindly.

"Far south, sir; near the Dead Sea."

"Idumea, maybe?"

The boy nodded, tardily, his reluctance being quite understandable; for no one had ever been heard to boast that he was a native of Idumea. Simon's lips tightened involuntarily, and he regarded the youngster with a frown, but instantly relented as he looked into the drooping eyes.

"I suppose you know, son, that we Jews don't have much to do with Idumeans."

"But Idumeans are Jews, sir," meekly protested the boy.

Simon sniffed and shrugged.

"Several centuries ago," he remarked, crisply. "Your people haven't been very good Jews—not for a long time."

"King Herod came from Idumea, sir," ventured the boy, softly.

"Well"—drawled Simon, "that doesn't improve Idumea's reputation very much."

The sailors laughed, a bit nervously. Old Zebedee cackled loudly.

"I always say," he shrilled, "it's cheaper to feed an Idumean and let him go on his way. Then—maybe—he won't steal from you." The old man grimaced for his immediate neighbors, feeling that he had scored a point.

"I never stole anything in my life," retorted the stranger, without turning to see where the insult had originated.

"I believe you, Joe!" declared John.

"Yaa!" railed his father, "you'd believe anything; anybody! That's your trouble. You're too easily taken in."

"I believe you too, my boy," said Simon, so pointedly that old Zebedee suddenly busied himself with his awl. Then, turning to John, the Big Fisherman inquired in a low tone, "Many people out there? Where was it?"

"Up on the hill—on the road to Cana." John's voice was guarded. It was apparent that he had no intention of explaining to the whole company if he could avoid it. "There were about a hundred people; perhaps more." It had grown very quiet. All work had stopped. Everyone was candidly eavesdropping. Simon observed it—and grinned.

"May as well speak out, Johnny. They're all interested. . . . We're talking about the Carpenter, boys. Johnny went out to see him, yesterday. . . . Go ahead, Johnny. Tell us all about it."

The men were pleased to be included in the conversation. They pocketed their awls. Some rested their elbows on their knees and cupped their chins in their hands. Even the weary young tramp showed a sudden interest at the mention of a carpenter whose doings had excited public curiosity. John was hesitant to begin; studied his slim, brown fingers as if he had never seen them before, and moistened his dry lips.

To fill in this awkward pause, Simon announced, "I gave John leave yesterday to go out into the country and see what this hullabaloo amounted to. There have been all manner of wild tales, and it's high time somebody came forward with the truth."

"Yaa!" yelled Zebedee. "That yarn about his turning water into wine, over at Cana! You can't find anybody who will stand up and say he saw it himself. It's always the cousin of a brother-in-law who saw it—and he lives over in Samaria some place."

Simon turned about and faced the old man with a scowl.

"If that is all you have to say for the present, Zebedee, we will give your son a chance to talk."

There was now no way out for John, except to tell the story. He lifted his head and began his strange narrative.

"Learning that he had left Cana and was headed in this direction, I went out, hoping to meet him. On the hill I came upon quite a multitude of people gathered about him. Many of them had followed him from Cana and apparently the others had joined the crowd along the way."

"What did he look like?" broke in James.

"It was late afternoon when I arrived," continued John, with a brief little gesture that postponed a reply to his brother's query. "I tried to question a few on the edge of the crowd but they gave no heed. They were all closely packed together, pushing in on him until he had hardly room to stand. I thought it was quite rude of them, though I soon found myself wanting to do the same thing." He paused reminiscently, shook his head, and muttered, "It was all very strange."

Simon hitched about, impatiently.

"Get on with it, Johnny! What was the fellow saying?"

"He wasn't what you'd call a big man," continued John, with a glance toward his brother. "Simon would overtop him by a good six inches."

The Big Fisherman squared his shoulders and listened more complacently.

"But not meaning that he was frail," amended John. "His skin was much whiter than ours, though he wore nothing on his head and the sun was hot enough to burn him. He seemed very warm—and tired. His brown hair was curly and the sweat had coiled some tight little rings of it on his forehead, softening his face until it might have looked boyish if it hadn't been for his short beard. Even with the beard he looked much younger than he talked. His eyes—"

John broke off here and fumbled with the old net while his audience waited in silence. Presently he drew a deep sigh, shook his head—and went on, in a monotone of reminiscence.

"He didn't talk in a loud voice; not like a teacher or a preacher. You know what I mean: the way the scribes talk to people—as if they were reciting something to the woods, or the moon; but not to anybody in particular. The Carpenter didn't seem to be speaking to the crowd—as a crowd, but to each person, as if they were alone together, apart. . . . That was the first thing I noticed about his talk. I couldn't help feeling that he had singled me out and was speaking directly to me. Maybe that was why I wanted to get closer. I suppose that was why everyone crowded in; wanting to get closer."

"Very well! Very well!" prodded Simon. "You wanted to get closer. Now—what did he say?"

"That's what we're all waiting for, John," shouted old Zebedee.

"He was talking about freedom—and happiness. Our country was never going to be free, he said. We should make up our minds to that. He said that if we were ever to have any happiness at all we must accept this bondage as something we couldn't alter, and plan to find our happiness within ourselves—seeing that our land would be subjugated—as long as we lived—and longer."

"Wants us to be contented with our slavery; does he?" called Alphaeus, from The Sara.

"No—it isn't that he approves of our slavery," John went on, unruffled by the interruption. "He said that all men everywhere are governed by conditions that curb their freedom, and—"

"Doesn't believe in government, eh?" commented Andrew, dryly. "The Tetrarch will soon cure him of that."

"What does he know about all men everywhere—this Carpenter from Nazareth?" scoffed Simon.

"He didn't say that he was against the government," answered John, weary but patient. "He said that every man could find freedom for himself, regardless of the laws. Freedom for his spirit. The richest gifts, he said, are beyond the control of any oppressor; property which nobody can carry away or withhold from us—"

"Such as what?" sniffed Simon, in a tone of raillery that made the sailors laugh.

"Dawn," said John, diffidently, knowing they would laugh again. "Dawn—and the sunset—the mountains—the songs of birds—and—" His voice fell to an almost inaudible murmur as he queried their grinning faces— "and the warm rain—and morning dew on the grass—and wild poppies growing on the hill-slopes—"

"Wild poppies!" broke in Thaddeus, from across the old net. "Wild poppies! Songs of birds! Dew on the grass! Why didn't someone ask him how to make these things up into a porridge to feed the family?"

This was so good, and they all enjoyed it so much that Thad, embarrassed by his own wit, yawned widely to show that his sally didn't really amount to anything and he could be funnier than that, if the occasion arose. It pleased him particularly to hear the Big Fisherman's roaring laugh. John accepted the general merriment with no sign of irritation. It was what he had expected.

"The Carpenter talked about that, Thad," he said, quietly, when the hilarity had subsided. "He thinks that most people spend too much time making things up into porridge, fretting about porridge, thinking that nothing is any good unless it can be made up into porridge; spending their lives worrying for fear they might be short of food next winter—and in their old age. Worrying—until they have no happiness at all. . . . He said the birds did not worry—and yet they were fed."

"Yaa!" yelled Zebedee—"but they've got to scratch for it!"

There was a gale of laughter. Old Zebedee was a pest, but this joke was excellent. The applause delighted him, and he repeated his witticism, again and again, for his nearest neighbors. "Yes, sir—they've got to scratch for it! . . . He! Ha! . . . Scratch for it!"

"That about the birds," said Simon, "sounds just like my old father. He never worried about where the next meal was coming from."

The men chuckled discreetly. Zebedee, to show that he knew more than any of the younger ones about the pious improvidence of Jonas, laughed himself into a noisy fit of coughing. Andrew effectively shut off this racket by scowling at him, as to say that if Simon wanted to jest a little about their righteous but unemployed father, that was his business; but there was no occasion for any comment from Zebedee, whose back always hurt him when there was anything to do.

Feeling now that his audience was neither sympathetic nor particularly interested in what he had been saying, John dug deep into his pocket, fetched up an awl, drew the edge of the old net across his knees, and set to work.

"Aren't you going to tell us anything more?" asked Simon.

"Not at present," said John, remotely. "I'd much rather not talk about it now. It's too serious. . . . It isn't at all a laughing matter."

"But—please, Johnny!" entreated James. "We will be quiet." Glancing about the circle, with his sober eyes coming to rest on his father's smirk, he added, "My brother has an important story to tell, if we will let him. I, for one, would like to hear it."

Slowly pocketing his awl, and giving James a grateful smile, John continued with his strange narrative—and the men listened.

How to find happiness: that was the thing. Few of us would ever be wealthy, no matter how hard we tried; no matter how greedily we grabbed things out of other people's hands. And the possessions we got, whether by fair means or foul, would turn out to be encumbrances. We would always have to be on the lookout for thieves. We would be afraid to leave home, even if we left a watchman, for he might be dishonest. We would sleep with one eye open, and we would be suspicious of strangers. And it was not only the threat of theft that would keep us disquieted. Our possessions would be menaced by moths—and rust.

"Surely he didn't object to our having a bed and a couple of stools to sit on and a roof over our heads," commented Alphaeus.

"First of all," John went on, undiverted, "we must stop fretting and complaining about our national servitude. Instead of flying into a rage when some gruff legionary imposes on us, we should quietly obey his orders, however unjust. If the soldier encounters one of us on the highway and hands us his pack to carry for a mile, let us take it and carry it for him—a mile—two miles."

There was some subdued grumbling here, but nobody spoke up. Old Zebedee vigorously shook his gray head and made a sour grimace. Simon clenched a big fist and waggled it experimentally. The dirty camel-boy yawned.

"This led him to talk about the bearing of burdens," pursued John. "That was the best way to find happiness—bearing burdens for others, whether they were friends or foes. If enemies, they regard you more mercifully; if friends, they love you for it."

"I don't believe that!" objected Thaddeus. "Toadying to enemies doesn't make them a bit easier on you. They get the idea that you are afraid—and then they do lay it on!"

Many of the fishermen nodded their agreement. John did not pause to take note of this general disapproval.

"He said the way to find your happiness and peace is in helping other people carry their heavy packs—whatever they are—" Here John paused so long that they thought he was through. They shifted their position for better comfort, and a few of them made as if to resume their work on the net. Simon stretched, yawned prodigiously, and rubbed his eyes with his big knuckles.

"And that was all there was to it?" he queried. "Nothing very exciting about such talk. You say the crowd listened?"

"Yes—we listened. We listened with our mouths open, so our breathing would not interfere with our hearing. As I told you—there is something peculiar about the Carpenter's voice. He doesn't talk as other men do. Nobody—ever—talked—like that!"

"But he didn't do anything—out of the ordinary?" James wanted to know.

"I had decided not to say anything about that; at least, not now," faltered John. "Because—I know you won't believe it."

They all came promptly to attention and were very quiet.

"It was while he was talking about our finding happiness by bearing burdens. There was a man standing only a few feet away from me who had a paralyzed arm; or something had ailed it so that it was much shorter and thinner than the other. But for this bad right arm, he was a pretty husky fellow. I had noticed him petting his short arm as if he was proud of it and wanted people to see it. All of a sudden, he broke into the Carpenter's speech, and held up this poor thing of an arm, hoisting it up by his good hand; and he shouted out, 'How about me, sir? You can see that I cannot bear burdens!'"

Here John stopped, closed his eyes, and shook his head like an emerging diver.

"No—no—I cannot tell you!" he muttered, thickly. "You will not believe it! If any one of you were to tell me this, I'm sure I wouldn't believe a word of it!"

"Say on, Johnny!" commanded Simon. "What happened?"

"The fellow's arm!" John's voice trembled. "It was well, I tell you! It was sound! It was as long as the other!"

The fishermen stiffened their backs and stared at young John as if he were a stranger. Simon broke the silence.

"No, John, no!" he muttered. "We can't have any of that, you know!"

Old Zebedee scrambled to his feet, pointed a shaky finger at his son, and shouted, "That's the first time I ever heard you lie!"

James, habitually tolerant of his father's incessant airing of his views, now surprised them all by rising to face the noisy old man with a stern rebuke.

"My brother is not a liar, sir!" he exclaimed. "Johnny may have misunderstood what he saw, but I shall not sit here silently and hear him reviled as a liar—not even by his father!"

"It's a long, hard climb—up that hill," put in Andrew—"and yesterday was a hot day."

"Aye," nodded Alphaeus, to his immediate neighbors, "the boy must have been a bit out of his head."

"No, Johnny," mumbled Simon, "that's much too much! Such things don't happen."

John hung his head, not as if he resented their disbelief, but regretful that he had consented to tell the story. Suddenly the murmurs ceased as Simon held up a hand for silence.

"Well, Johnny, you may as well go on with it," he said, roughly. "You can see that you've nothing to lose. Nobody believes you—but we'd better have the rest of it—if there is any more. Did this fortunate fellow, with the made-over arm, thank the Carpenter—and maybe hand him a shekel?"

"The people were stunned!" muttered John, without looking up. "A woman standing next to the man fainted and crumpled up on the ground. The man himself was panting hard, making queer little squeaks in his throat. You couldn't tell whether he was trying to laugh or cry. Everybody was quiet—and pale. I felt a little sick in my stomach, the way you feel at the sight of a bleeding wound—only—I think—the shock of seeing a deformed arm suddenly made well is worse than seeing a bad accident. . . . While we were all standing there, gaping at the arm, the Carpenter said, 'Now, my friend, you can bear burdens. See to it that you do—or a worse thing might come upon you.'" John's voice was unsteady as he finished his story. After an interval of silence, he rose slowly and faced the company with sober eyes. "I know that you do not believe what I have told you," he declared—"but may God strike me dead if it is not the truth!"

"Blasphemy!" yelled old Zebedee.

"I'm not saying you lied, Johnny," said Simon, "but I do think you have been seeing things—like the strange animals you find in the clouds. It's no harm to imagine things in the sky—but this is different! I only hope you aren't losing your mind! Tell us truly now: were you out there at all? Did you really see this Carpenter? I think you dreamed it—all of it—while you were asleep under a tree."

This brought on nervous laughter.

"Run along, Johnny," said Simon, as to a mere toddler. "You've done enough for one day. Go some place and rest your dizzy head."

Flushed with humiliation, John moved slowly across the net and walked with uncertain steps toward the bow. James watched him with troubled eyes.

"I think I shall go too," he said.

"Maybe you'd better ask permission," advised his father.

"You may go, James," growled Simon. "Talk your flighty brother out of this nonsense, and bring him back when he's cured of it."

"My brother may not want to come back," said James, "after the shameful treatment he has had!"

"He may do as he likes about that," snapped Simon, hotly. "The fleet can get along without him. . . . And you needn't come back, either, if you're so easily offended."

"Hear that?" shouted Zebedee. "You'll be losing your job—if you aren't careful!"

James made no reply, but followed his brother. A moment later the silent sailors heard the clatter of oars in a dory's locks. Craning their necks, they saw the little boat making toward the beach. Simon stood to watch it, frowning darkly. He turned about and faced Andrew.

"I'll not go out today," he said. "Finish with the net, and take the fleet over to the south shore where we fished yesterday."

Andrew followed him as he stalked forward, overtaking him at midship.

"What do you want done with this young tramp?" he inquired.

Simon drew a wry smile and stroked his jaw. Now that Johnny had turned out to be an ungrateful fool, he would teach him a lesson by giving his flouted friendship to this ragged waif. Johnny would come creeping back tomorrow to find that he had lost his place as the skipper's pet. He beckoned to Joe, who came promptly to his side.

"Come with me, son," he said, kindly. "You shall have a clean bed to sleep in tonight."

Old Zebedee had wriggled forward and stood by, rubbing his wrinkled hands.

"I'm sorry my boys acted that way," he whimpered.

"You'd do well to mind your own business," growled Simon.

*　*　*　*　*　*

There had been almost no conversation between them as they trudged along on the well-beaten highway to suburban Bethsaida. The sun was high now—and hot. A few steps in advance of his young companion, the Big Fisherman marched steadily with long strides, moodily preoccupied and quite oblivious of the sandal-patter behind him. These shorter footsteps were erratic, for the camel-boy frequently turned about to survey the huge marble palace of the Tetrarch, sometimes walking backwards for a dozen steps, and shading his eyes for better vision.

They were entering the residence district now where well-kept houses sat back from the dusty street, partly hidden by tall acacias, cypress, and olive trees. A corner was turned to the left. At the next corner Simon slowed, encouraging the camel-boy to come abreast of him. Opening a small wicket-gate, he led the way toward a commodious gray-brick cottage. The dooryard was shady. A pleasant-faced woman of middle age was raking leaves.

"What brings you home so early, Simon?" she inquired, with a side glance at the disheveled stranger. "Anything the matter?"

"You sit down here on the stoop, son," said Simon. "I want a word with you, Hannah."

The Idumean tramp was gratified by this tentative hospitality, and sank down wearily on the step; legs aching from trying to keep up with the long steps of the Galilean giant. The woman had put down the rake and they had entered the house. The skipper would confer with this Hannah, who was probably his mother—though she seemed too young for that—and she would shake her head and say, "No—please, Simon; not an Idumean! And he looks so terribly dirty! He's probably lousy too."

After what seemed a very long time, they came out on the little porch where Joe sat. It was a relief to see a cordial smile on the woman's face.

"My mother-in-law, Hannah, has consented to let you rest here with us for a day or two, seeing how very tired you are," said Simon. Turning to Hannah, he added, "I may not be home for supper."

"Perhaps you should have a bite to eat before you go."

"I'm not hungry." Without a farewell word Simon walked rapidly to the gate and down the street as if his errand might be of some urgency.

Hannah sat down on the step, a little way apart from her guest, caught up a wisp of graying hair that had fallen over her temple; and, after soberly searching the tired, long-lashed eyes, smiled a little.

"Your name is Joe," she said pleasantly. "And you are from away down in Idumea."

Joe nodded, but offered no further facts about himself.

"We do not see many Idumeans up here," said Hannah. "In fact, I never saw one before."

Joe drew a long sigh, but had nothing to say about Idumea.

"You would probably enjoy a bath," said Hannah.

"Ohhh!" breathed the dirty boy. "Would I!"

"Then—come with me." Hannah rose and led the way into the cool, well-furnished house. "That bedroom straight ahead of you, Joe. I shall bring you a tub of water. You will find towels in the room."

"Please let me do that!" insisted Joe. "Show me where it is—and I shall help myself."

Hannah darted an inquiring glance into the waif's eyes. She had not expected any graciousness on the part of this young vagabond. Showing him the large wooden tub in the store-room off the kitchen, and pointing to the cistern, she returned to her leaf-raking. Presently she retraced her steps and tapped at the bedroom door.

"If you will hand me your soiled clothes, I shall wash them, and hang them out in the sun to dry."

The splashing ceased and there was quite an interval of silence. At length the boy made a flustered reply.

"Oh—but I don't expect you to do that!"

"Surely you are not intending to put those dirty garments on again!" Hannah's voice rose in indignation. "They have got to be cleaned—for our sake—if not yours! Open that door now—a little way—and hand them to me?"

After some silence and delay the door was reluctantly opened wide enough to accommodate a small, brown, wet hand holding a shabby, dusty jacket and a pair of coarse trousers, clothing worn only by the poorest of peasants. Hannah took them gingerly with her finger-tips—and made a wry face.

"Didn't you have anything on under these dreadful rags?" she inquired.

"Y-yes," stammered Joe—"but, please, I can wash them myself."

"Don't be foolish!" snapped Hannah. "I won't have those filthy things in my house—not another minute! Let me have them!" And when there was no immediate response, she called sternly, "I'm waiting!"

Again the door opened slightly, grudgingly, and the damp hand delivered two badly rumpled under-garments which Hannah grabbed impatiently. Averting her face, she carried them to the back door and pitched them out on the grass. She was more than disgusted with the task she had set for herself. She had been foolish to take this dirty tramp into her house. Simon had no right to ask her to do it.

Then something attracted her attention. She stepped out on the ground and inspected the under-garments with wide-eyed curiosity. They were dainty and exquisitely made of the finest, sheerest linen she had ever seen. Unquestionably they were a woman's clothing. This Joe was a thief then! She might have known it.

She sat down on the grass and fingered the gauzy material. Where could this tramp have come upon such articles? What opportunity would he have had to steal clothing of this value? And—imagine a camel-boy wanting to wear a woman's clothes! Now an utterly preposterous idea arrived to confuse the problem. Could this Joe be a girl? Hannah recalled her wonderment at the extraordinarily long, curling lashes when she had looked into the boy's weary eyes. And the small, slim hand. But—even assuming that the youngster was masquerading, that didn't explain this expensive underwear.

She held up the shirt, woven of costly linen. On the left breast there was embroidered a peculiar device. Hannah studied it with mystification. The emblems in the blue oval meant something: she was sure of that. There was a new moon, done in gold thread, circling about a silver star; and crossing through the slim moon and the star, a white sword and a shepherd's crook.

Suddenly Hannah resolved to make an experiment that might solve the mystery. She returned to the bedroom door and listened. It was very quiet in there now.

"Joe," she called.

"Yes." The voice was sleepy. Or was it frightened?

"I've found out something about you."

There was no reply.

"Joe—you're a girl!"

"Y-yes," weakly, wearily, "I know."

"Well"—Hannah's voice was unsteady—"after you've rested, look in the closet for some clothing." Her tone had softened. "In the chest you will find under-garments—not nearly so fine as yours—but serviceable. They belonged to my daughter—who died." And when there was no reply, she added, "Or would you prefer to go on pretending you're a boy?"

The answer was muffled and inaudible.

"Perhaps you might enjoy being a girl again," persisted Hannah, gently

—"just for a day or two—while you are here. . . . I wouldn't tell on you."

"Yes—please," murmured the girl, brokenly. She was crying. . . . And so was Hannah.

After she had washed the clothes—and it had taken more time than such a task should have called for in any other circumstance—Hannah hung them out to dry. It had gratified her to find that while the rough outer garments were badly soiled, the dainty underwear, though wrinkled, was fairly clean. Apparently these garments had been recently washed, perhaps in some forest brook.

Although consumed by curiosity to learn the girl's story, Hannah had no thought of disturbing her now: she was utterly spent and would probably sleep for hours. There was still much leaf-raking to be done, and it seemed that the leaves which needed immediate attention were close to the north fence. Incidentally, David would be strolling by before long, as was his custom. David was learned and widely traveled. He would be almost sure to know what these strange symbols meant. Should she ask him?

More than an hour had passed, with Hannah becoming very warm and weary, before the eminent Sadducee appeared, sedately marching down the hill. He paused, laid a hand on the fence, and offered the usual greeting. The conversation did not flow freely. Yes, Hannah agreed, it was indeed a warm day for this time of the year. But she had enjoyed the exercise—and the leaves must be gathered up before it rained. No, Simon wasn't there, and might not be home until late.

When it appeared that nothing remained to be said, David bowed soberly and was taking his leave. Hannah advanced a step and halted him with a diffident query. She had come upon a bit of linen, she said, that bore some strange tokens. It was blue, and oval in shape, and in the center there was the figure of a new moon and a star.

David, smiling condescendingly, broke in with surprise that she did not recognize the well-known star and crescent of Arabia.

"But that wasn't quite all," continued Hannah. "Crossing through this moon and star there was a sword and a shepherd's crook."

"Impossible!" muttered David. "Where did you find this?"

Hannah was visibly embarrassed and her heart raced. She had not reckoned on a question that would demand fuller explanation and her expression showed that she now regretted having introduced the subject. Her confusion spurred the lawyer's curiosity. He stepped closer and soberly searched her eyes.

"This morning a hungry and ragged camel-boy appeared on one of

Simon's ships," began Hannah, nervously, "and Simon—you know, sir, how big-hearted he is—took pity on the young fellow and brought him home—to rest—and be properly fed—for a day or two. I had him take a bath; and, while he was doing that, I washed his clothing. These strange figures were embroidered on one of his garments."

"I should like to see it," said David.

"It's still wet, sir—from the washing," said Hannah.

David impatiently assured her that it wouldn't matter at all if the garment was wet. He wanted to see it, and he wanted to see it now! So Hannah brought it and handed it over.

"This is a woman's raiment!" said David.

Hannah dropped her eyes—and nodded.

"You will keep it a secret, sir, won't you?" she entreated. "I gave her my word I wouldn't tell."

"I should have no motive for betraying you, Hannah." He handed back the garment. "It is better that no one be told—about this insignia."

"Not even Simon? When he discovers that his waif is a girl, he will ask many questions. She has consented to wear my daughter's clothing while she is here."

"Let Simon think whatever he likes about the girl's having disguised herself. She may or may not confide. If I were you, I should not press her for her story." David was again on the point of moving away, but paused to inquire, "Is she Jewish in appearance?"

"Yes, sir. She told Simon she was from Idumea. That's Jewish; is it not?"

"Idumea? Nonsense!" snorted David. "Had she been from Idumea she wouldn't have wanted to bathe. No, indeed! That shirt did not originate in Idumea! . . . I shall see you again tomorrow. . . . I bid you good-day." He turned slowly and was retracing his steps toward home, with bent head, and hands clasped behind him. After he had gone a little way, he suddenly straightened, turned about, and came back.

"You say the girl looks Jewish. Think hard now! If someone were to tell you she is part Jewish—and part Arabian—what would you say?" David's eyes invaded Hannah's earnestly.

"I wouldn't know, sir," she replied, shaking her head. "I don't know how the Arabians look. The girl is a little taller than most Jewish women of her age—and more slender, too."

"What—would you say—is her age, Hannah?"

"Sixteen, perhaps; or seventeen, maybe "

David made no comment on that; but stood silently, thoughtfully, counting his fingers. Having finished the addition, he nodded to himself, drew an enigmatic smile, and withdrew. "I bid you good-day, Hannah," he said, absently.

For a long time the bewildered woman stood watching the venerable Sadducee's deliberate march up the hill. It was evident that David had been deeply impressed. Hannah hoped she wasn't getting into trouble. She wished she could feel free to confide the whole matter to Simon. But if the girl was—as David seemed to suspect—of Arabian blood, Simon would undoubtedly be angry and turn her out. He hated the Arabians. On the other hand, if he weren't told—and found out, later—he would have good cause for being enraged over the deception. Anyway you looked at it, the situation was disturbing. Hannah was not experienced in dissembling.

After standing there irresolutely until her legs were weary, she returned to the house. The door to the guest's bedroom was open now. The girl, in a simple white dress of Abigail's, was sitting on the edge of the bed, combing her cropped hair. Hannah smiled, but her eyes brimmed with tears. The girl instinctively guessed why.

"I'm afraid it makes you sad," she said, softly, "to see a stranger in this keep-sake dress. I am sorry."

Hannah brightened and dabbed at the tears.

"It was just for a moment, my dear. I am glad to see my Abigail's clothing put to some good use. She was a beautiful child. . . . And"—impulsively—"so are you! . . .What shall we call you—now that your name isn't Joe?"

There was a momentary pause before the girl replied.

"You may call me Esther."

"Though that is not your name—either," commented Hannah, disappointed—and hurt.

"I am told that Esther was the name my father chose for me," said the girl, eager to make amends.

"Shall I suppose, then," persisted Hannah, "that others in your family preferred another name for you, and that their wishes prevailed?"

Esther nodded, absently, diligently preoccupied with her combing.

Hannah waited uneasily in the doorway for a fuller confidence, and when the girl responded only with a childish little smile of entreaty, she turned away with an impatient gesture that said, Oh—very well, then— if it's such a secret. Presently the dishes clattered in the kitchen as if they too were annoyed. It was clear that Hannah was offended by her guest's reticence. Esther felt very uncomfortable. She had a momentary impulse to follow the friendly woman and make a full disclosure of everything. On second thought she decided that too much was at stake.

* * * * * *

Having inflicted upon Hannah the thankless job of looking after the ragged young Idumean—an impetuosity that had already caused him some appropriate misgivings—Simon hurried away as if late for an important engagement, though the fact was that he had no plans for the day. He had never been so restless in his life. As he neared the highway, his long strides shortened and slowed to an indecisive saunter; and, at the corner, he looked both ways, gnawing his bearded under-lip.

Daily habit suggested that he return to the fleet, but the idea was rejected. Simon had no relish for reappearing among his men so soon after the quarrel with Zebedee's boys, an affair which, he now felt, might easily have been avoided. Besides, Andrew would probably have sailed by this time. And, as for the Tetrarch's fish, doubtless one of the crew had been sent to deliver them, seeing the skipper had said he would not return today.

With no plausible errands in the direction of Tiberias, Simon turned the other way and walked slowly toward the sleepy little business zone of Bethsaida, for no reason at all except to keep in motion. He couldn't stand there on the corner any longer. Salutations were offered along the road to which he responded grumpily, in no mood for neighborly conversation.

Not for a long time had Simon been in this part of the town, but nothing had changed. Nothing ever changed in Bethsaida. Old Seth still sat where Simon had seen him last, on the stone flagging before the open door of his pottery-shop, hugging his thin knees tight against his bearded chin.

"Don't see you down this way very often," shrilled the old man, unexpectedly stirring from his torpor. It was an invitation to tarry and talk but Simon merely grunted and ambled on. At the wide doorway of the blacksmith's shop he paused only long enough to agree with sooty-faced, leather-aproned Ben-Abel that it was a hot day. Ben-Abel clanked down his hammer, advanced to the door, and further deposed that we needed rain. Simon nodded and moved away.

On the broad steps of the Synagogue lounged a beggar whom he distastefully recognized by the bulky and filthy bandage on a perennially sore arm. The loathsome creature straightened, grinned, and began to unwrap his odorous merchandise. Wrinkling his nose, Simon signed that he didn't want to see it, and dropped three copper pennies in the battered cup.

"No use going out there now," advised the beggar. "Everybody that's going today has gone a good two hours ago. Time you get there, it will be all over."

"What will be all over?" demanded Simon, gruffly.

"The Carpenter! That's where you're going, isn't it?"

"What gave you that foolish idea?"

"Oh—I can tell," snickered the beggar. "Some of them try to pretend they're going some place else, but I can spot 'em. Take yourself now. I know you. You're the Big Fisherman, that doesn't hold with the Synagogue and curses religion. But what business brings you out here, on your way up the hill? You're not carrying any fish, and there's none to be had where you're going. You want to have a look at this Carpenter, same as everybody else. Heh! Heh!"

"If you are so interested in this miracle-working Carpenter," growled Simon, "why don't you show him that stinking arm? Maybe he would heal it for you. But perhaps you don't want it healed."

"The fellow is a fraud—and a blasphemer!" The beggar rattled his cup and made a wry face. "Three pennies! And the Big Fisherman owns three ships! It isn't enough to buy a measure of leeks!"

Simon muttered a curse and strode angrily away, the beggar calling after him, "It won't do you any good to climb that long hill, I tell you! He'll be gone. You'll be meeting all the other fools on their way back."

The Big Fisherman had left the town behind him now and the highway was stiffly rising. He had been walking rapidly, stomping along still angry over his encounter with the impudent beggar. The dirty, insolent beast should be locked up as a public nuisance. However, he was a canny fellow; you had to say that much for him. He knew where Simon was bound for, even when Simon hadn't clearly decided on it himself. The impertinence of the filthy rascal! Simon had a notion to turn about and retrace his steps, just to show the beggar he had been wrong in his surmise; but then he might think that Simon had decided to take his advice. Simon wasn't in the habit of taking advice from beggars—or anyone else, for that matter.

The afternoon was hot and the Big Fisherman was not accustomed to climbing steep grades. He sat down in the shade of a wayside tree to rest and get his breath. He must be growing old. Sooner or later, men did grow old. Their muscles got flabby—and their lungs—and their hearts—yes, and their heads, too. An old man got more and more testy, surly, quarrelsome, cantankerous; like an old dog; like old Zebedee, who was always saying the wrong thing, making himself ridiculous. Fortunately for Simon, he wasn't that old yet. He didn't pick quarrels. No man should be blamed for defending his beliefs.

Well—what had happened had happened: it was too late to do anything about that now. Johnny had walked out in a huff, and wasn't likely
to make the first move toward a reconciliation; and, naturally, the willful
boy wouldn't expect his boss to hunt him up—and coax him to come back.
There'd be no living with the youngster after that: he'd think he was an
admiral—or something.

No—the only sure cure for Johnny's folly was the exposure of this
Carpenter as an unscrupulous mountebank. . . . Simon rose, wincing, and
plodded on, every step an effort. . . . The Carpenter must be pretty sure of
himself, expecting people to climb a mountain to find him.

The sun was all but setting when Simon's aching legs brought him over
the shoulder of the plateau. There he paused uncertainly, amazed at the
size of the crowd. Johnny had guessed there might have been so many as a
hundred out here yesterday. There were more than that today. He sauntered slowly forward toward the closely packed, silent, attentive multitude, wishing he might make himself invisible. It would be very annoying
if he were recognized, and a rumor spread that he had been seen there. It
would be useless to explain his reason for coming. What if Johnny should
see him? Simon walked slowly, softly, and stood at the rear of the crowd.
No one paid the slightest attention to him. He felt somewhat less uneasy.
And presently he left off thinking about himself at all.

Having come here to criticize; and, if possible, to discover some trickery,
the Big Fisherman had approached with a scowl. He was angry at this
Carpenter for creating so much hubbub and for trying to deceive a lot of
weak-minded people; but, in all honesty, the fellow did not look like an
itinerant showman. It wasn't the impudent face of a juggler, nor was it
the brazen voice of a street-hawker with some nostrum to sell. Johnny had
been right about the man's voice. It was calm, deliberate, conversational,
as if addressed to a single individual, a personal friend. You had to listen
closely or you wouldn't hear, certainly not from where Simon stood;
though it was to be observed that even the people in the forward rows
tipped up their good ear. It was not an harangue. And the man was not
exerting himself to compel attention. It was indeed a voice such as you
had never heard in a public address: it singled you out. You! Yes—Simon
—You!

He edged in closer against the backs of his neighbors. A head taller
than most, he had no trouble seeing the Carpenter clearly. The man was
tired. Surely the people should be able to see that. They had crowded in
on him until he had hardly standing-room, nor could he retreat for the
great rock immediately behind him. What the Carperter needed, reflected

Simon, was somebody to keep the crowd off him. This heedless pack of curiosity seekers were suffocating him; wearing him out. One would think he might have found at least one friend to stand by and protect him. Perhaps he didn't want any close friends. Maybe you couldn't get acquainted with him, even if you wanted to. But that conjecture was not in tune with the tone of the voice that appealed to your spirit of neighborliness—if not, indeed, to your comradeship. Johnny was right: there was something very strange about the man. Not much wonder the boy had stammered—and groped for words.

Simon's animosity had cooled now. He had come hopeful of hearing something revolutionary, something seditious; something that would get the Carpenter into trouble. He intended to be on the alert for it; and if he heard anything incriminating, he would be willing to testify when the matter came to court, as it surely would. The rabbis would see to that. They too were eager to show him up as a seditionist. Simon hadn't given any thought to this phase of the problem, and it now annoyed him to foresee that he might presently be on the side of the rabbis. No—he didn't want to have anything to do with it personally. Let the patrols and the priests attend to it.

The extreme weariness of the Carpenter made a bid for Simon's sympathy. If it weren't for making a spectacle of himself, he would like to get down into that front row and use his elbows. He wouldn't be above cracking a couple of heads together. Simon had often done that in a general brawl; suddenly grab two handfuls of hair, and whack! It was always effective. Yes, sir—he would enjoy nothing better than a chance to teach these yokels some better manners.

The soft voice was talking now about the Day of Atonement. Simon wouldn't be interested; wondered what the Carpenter could find to say on such a dull subject; surely the multitude wouldn't have climbed the long hill to listen to that. The farmer in front of him twisted his head around, looked up fretfully, and lifted a cramped shoulder. Simon had unwittingly crowded in on the fellow until he couldn't stand straight. The sour look suggested that some people should mind their manners—and stop pushing—even if they were big as Goliath—and knew they could impose on smaller folks. Simon moved back a step and tramped on a squirming toe.

He had quite forgotten that tomorrow was the Day of Atonement. And today, too, if you obeyed the Scriptures. It was a two-day affair. On the first day you went about paying debts, returning things borrowed, and making up with people you had injured; though almost nobody ever did anything about that. On the second day, if you were religious, you went to the Synagogue with such an offering as you could afford, ranging in value from a pair of pigeons to a fat steer; and received a blessing.

Time was when his father had talked of nothing else for a fortnight preceding the Day of Atonement, but it had been many a year since Simon had so much as made the motions of honoring it. He always dismissed the crews on the big day, the real day, the day of the Synagogue ceremonies. That was common practice. You gave your employees the day off: they could do what they pleased with it. It never had been customary to dismiss your help on the first day, the day you were to go about making things right with people you had defrauded or otherwise offended. As for himself, he usually spent the Day of Atonement mending ropes and oiling pulleys. Sometimes respectable people, marching soberly toward the Synagogue in their Sabbath garb, would regard him with reproach when they met him on the highway in his workaday clothes.

Now the Carpenter was going to flog the old straw; for surely there was nothing new to be said about the Day of Atonement. We would be told how important it was to go to the Synagogue and have our sins forgiven; not forgetting to take the yearling lamb along.

Simon came to attention. The Carpenter was talking about the first day of the Atonement event. That was the important day. That was today! What had you done about it? How about the quarrels you had had—since last Atonement Day? Were you and old Naaman still refusing to speak to one another because of that trouble over the line fence? Had you gone to see the old man today? If not—you would only be wasting your mutton tomorrow. How about that feud with the Ben-Gileads: you remember—the chickens that got into your garden—and caused such a rumpus that everybody in the neighborhood took sides. And cursed one another. And threw stones. Is that old quarrel still smouldering? Did you do anything about that today? The sun is setting. Are you going to do anything about that before you sleep tonight? If not—there's no sense in taking your pigeons to the Synagogue tomorrow; nor will the lamb do you any good; and you'd better sell the steer for whatever it will fetch; or slaughter it and eat it. Forgiveness and peace are to be had—but not bartered for beef.

Simon liked that. It was sensible. Not much use asking for pardon and peace if an old friend has something against you, especially if the quarrel was your own fault. The Carpenter was talking about peace of mind, considered as "property." You could toil all summer in the fields and fill your barn with grain. That was property, too; only the barn might take fire, or the rats destroy the wheat. Peace was the kind of property that wouldn't burn, and you didn't have to set a watchman over it to see that it wasn't stolen. . . . Make things right with your offended brother; then go to the Synagogue with your fat lamb—and be blessed.

There was some restlessness in the multitude now. What the Carpenter was saying was reasonable enough, thought Simon, but it would just go in one ear and out the other. You couldn't change human nature very much. . . . Take Johnny, for instance. He was probably in this crowd, and listening to this good counsel. But—do you suppose the stubborn youngster would take it to heart—and apologize? Of course he wouldn't! . . . It wasn't much wonder that the Carpenter looked lonely. If he really practiced what he taught, people would think him a queer one. Friendship with the man would be embarrassing.

The Carpenter had stopped speaking now and there was a perceptible stir in the crowd. It shifted its weight to the other leg, straightened its back, and stretched its neck for a better view.

A tall, broad-shouldered, bearded man stood forward from the pack and faced the Carpenter. He had a small boy in his arms. Whatever happened then, it was done so quickly that Simon could only guess that the child had received some attention; for the man who carried him turned away, apparently satisfied, and was making his escape through the craning multitude. There was much jostling, the crowd swarming about the man, blocking his way. The little boy was crying shrilly.

Simon impulsively went into action. Reviewing it later, on his way home, he couldn't decide whether he had elbowed his way savagely into the mob because of his indignation at the people's rudeness, and a desire to rush to the man's defense, or to satisfy his own curiosity; but, whatever inspired him to plunge through the crowd, he made a success of it, thrusting a shoulder and a knee, tugging at collars, elbowing ribs, pulling hair, tramping on feet, until he had mowed a swath to the defenseless man in the center of the congestion.

"Stand back!" he shouted. "Make way there!" Planting the heels of his open hands on the nearest chins, Simon cleared a path. Presently he and the rescued were out in the open, and almost alone; for the crowd seemed reluctant to follow. The child's frightened cries had subsided to convulsive sobs.

"Thank you, friend," murmured the exhausted man. He lowered the boy to the ground.

"No, no, Grandfather!" pleaded the little fellow. "It hurts! Lift me up!"

"What's the matter with him?" asked Simon.

"A crooked foot. Born that way. I heard of this Jesus and hoped he might heal the child. I carried him—all the way from Sepphoris."

"That's a long tramp." Simon peered down at the foot. "Apparently it hasn't done the lad any good."

"Are you a believer in this man?" inquired Justus, soberly.

"No—I'm not. We've been hearing many strange stories about him—over in Tiberias. I came out to see. My name is Simon."

"Mine is Justus, Barsabas Justus. . . . Now, Jonathan, see if you can't stand on the lame foot. Grandfather will not let you fall. Try it, my boy."

The child clung for a moment, but consented to be put down, whining with fear. He took an uncertain step.

"It hurts!" he whimpered. Justus gathered him up in his arms.

"Let's have a look at it," suggested Simon, kindly. They inspected the foot.

"It's hard to tell," muttered Justus. "It was bent over; like this. Seems straighter; don't you think, Simon?"

Simon felt of both feet.

"They're about alike, I should say. But why can't he stand on it?"

"Perhaps it's the rough ground," said Justus, still hopeful. "He never stood squarely on that foot before. It's tender as a baby's. Besides—the lad's frightened."

The crowd was dispersing now, many pausing to gape at the child. Simon glanced toward the rock where the Carpenter stood. He was gone.

"Well—I'll be on my way, friend Simon," Justus was saying. "I hope we may meet again."

"You've a long journey ahead of you, Justus, carrying the lad. Perhaps I should go with you, part way."

"You are kind; but there will be moonlight presently. The boy is not heavy. I shall stop for the night with friends in Cana."

Simon was reluctant to see Justus leave. He walked beside him to the southern brow of the hill where they paused.

"I wish I knew—about the boy's foot. What do you think, Justus? Has it been healed—or hasn't it?"

"I don't know," mumbled Justus. "Maybe it's too early to tell. I only hope so."

"Yes—so do I, Justus. It would be a great blessing to the child."

At that, Justus turned to face Simon with a sober stare.

"Do you—honestly—hope that?"

"Why—of course!" declared Simon. "What a question! Who could wish it otherwise?"

"Because"—muttered Justus—"if this village Carpenter can change the laws of nature, nothing will ever be the same again; not for any of us! Do you realize that, Simon? Nothing you ever thought—about anything —will be true; not any more—ever!"

Having no ready rejoinder for this surprising speech, Simon said he supposed it would affect one's views somewhat. They bade each other farewell; and Justus, shifting his burden to the other arm, made off down the road where he was promptly joined by many people who had tarried to wait his coming.

He was a peculiar fellow, thought Simon, as he walked away toward the other rim of the plateau; evidently had given a bit of careful thought to this business of miracles; not only was inclined to be skeptical about it, but wasn't sure he wanted to believe it. If it was true, nothing would ever be the same again; not for anybody! If a man could go about, straightening crooked feet and restoring paralyzed arms, everything would be topsy-turvy.

On his way down the hill the Big Fisherman's long legs and urgent thoughts overtook and passed everybody. He recognized no one, but as he moved aside to pass one group that had slowed to discuss whether they had seen a miracle or not, the voices were abruptly hushed, and he heard his name spoken in a half-whisper. It annoyed him more than a little. He had as good a right to be out here as anyone. What business was it of theirs? But—let them gabble! He didn't care. To hell with them! Simon was angry now; angry at himself; out here on this fool's errand! Miracles? Rubbish! He had seen quite enough of this Carpenter: it was high time to put all this nonsense out of his head.

Careless of his footing he stumbled along through the pale moonlight, finally reaching the valley. His legs were lame and his feet were hot and sore. He was exhausted in body and mind. It was to be hoped that Hannah had retired. Simon was in no mood for talking. Hannah, if awake, would be anxious to know where he had been. She wouldn't ask a direct question, but she would probably have it out of him somehow.

Bethsaida—at last! He sat down wearily on the stoop and took off his dusty sandals. Tiptoeing softly through the silent house and out through the kitchen door he found a basin by the cistern and washed his blistered feet. Hannah appeared and handed him a towel for which he thanked her briefly. In a tone of finality he bade her good-night and retraced his steps down the hall to his own room.

"I'll have a surprise for you—at breakfast," whispered Hannah.

"Honey cakes, I suppose," muttered Simon, apathetically. . . . Anything to detain him—and make him talk—he thought.

"Want to guess again?" pestered Hannah, sweetly.

"No—not tonight, Hannah. I am very tired." And because he didn't care to risk any further conversation with her, he closed his door, not noisily enough to give offense—he hoped—but with sufficient emphasis to accent his desire to be let alone.

It turned out to be a bad night for Simon. He tried to sleep, but his busy brain shuttled to and fro from one dilemma to another. Life had been suddenly stripped of all its brightness. Everything was in confusion. There was Johnny, to whom he was as devoted as he might have been to a son: Johnny had found another master, the Carpenter. If it hadn't been for this Carpenter, everything would have continued to be in order; the way it ought to be.

The more he thought about it, the more sure he was that his first impression of the rumors had been correct. The fellow—for all his gentle voice—was a deceiver; enticing people to follow him about and listen to his prattle; pretending to heal diseases; advising them to own nothing—and live like the birds. He deserved to be exposed.

This man Justus: he knew it was a fraud. Oh, yes—the poor man had pretended to be hopeful, but you could see he had lost faith in it.

Simon turned the pillow over, dug his big fist into it, buried his face in it, and returned to Johnny. The boy never had been worth anything as a fisherman. He was worse than no help at all, a bad influence on other lazy men. If Simon hadn't liked him so much, he wouldn't have signed him on; not even if he had worked for nothing—and brought his own dinner!

Rolling over on his back, Simon stared wide-eyed into the darkness and reviewed every unpleasant detail of yesterday's quarrel. The boy had behaved badly. Doubtless there was some weakness in his character that might account for it. Surely he hadn't inherited his disposition from old Zebedee, who couldn't see beyond the end of his leaky nose and talked so incessantly that he never had time to think. We might as well discharge the old bore; would have done it long ago if it hadn't been for the boys.

Of course Johnny hadn't inherited anything from his silly mother. Mothers didn't bequeath any of their traits to their children: everybody knew that. But Naomi could have had an unhealthy influence on him. She was forever nagging the lad to find a job where he could earn more pay; lamenting that he hadn't trained to be a scrivener which, she thought, would give the family a better social standing. Zebedee had been a fool to marry Naomi; almost old enough to be her grandfather. Well—he was getting paid off for wanting a young wife. Naomi had the old codger saddled and bridled; made him do most of the housework; beat him with a broom, according to reports. Maybe that was why Zebedee was such a nuisance on shipboard; had no chance to express himself at home. No— Johnny hadn't learned any star-gazing from Naomi. All she thought about was how to make her men-folks earn more money, the greedy little devil. More than once she had embarrassed the boys by waylaying Simon, in their presence, with a whimpering plea that they be paid better wages.

Johnny was a queer one; no doubt about that. He loved to look at the waves: the bigger they rolled the better he liked them. He saw pictures in the clouds, and a brilliant sunset would set him off into ecstasies. Maybe that was what had drawn him to this Carpenter.

Sunsets! Wild poppies! Bah! Lilies wear good clothes without having to spin and weave; better clothes than kings wear. Why should anybody work? The birds don't work. If you meet a soldier, carry his pack. Grin—and like it. Johnny would love that kind of talk. Simon wished he had said to Johnny, "How about making an arrangement for all of the people to work part of the time, so that everybody can get better acquainted with the poppies—and the birds—and the sunsets—and the dew on the grass?"

But there was that paralyzed arm. Johnny wouldn't lie. Why—if that tale were true, everything in your life goes overboard! If the Carpenter has enough wisdom—and power—to do a thing like that, then whatever he says must be true. If he tells you to take counsel of the poppies and the birds, you'd better do it. Yes—and if he tells you that the right way to walk is on your hands instead of your feet, you'll have to do it; for the Carpenter will know best. . . . But it was all nonsense! . . . In a few days the legionaries would have the fellow in jail—and the deluded people could get back to work. Then Johnny would want his job again. Well—if the boy came—in the right state of mind—admitting he had been a fool to go out and listen to the Carpenter—in the first place—Simon would be willing to forgive him.

6

AFTER a wretched night of tossing about, of laboriously taking the puzzle to pieces and reassembling it in patterns equally perplexing, and of fantastic dreams—in one of which Johnny, pretending lameness, limped up to the Carpenter and had himself healed—Simon roused dully and prepared for breakfast. His head ached and he was very much out of sorts.

His place alone was laid at the table, which meant that Andrew had eaten and gone and that Hannah too had breakfasted. As for the Idumean ragamuffin, Simon hadn't given him a thought since leaving him yesterday in Hannah's care. Doubtless the youngster was well on his way by this time.

Seating himself, Simon folded his huge, hairy arms and rested them on the table. He knew that Hannah was aware of his arrival in the little dining-room, for he could hear her gentle voice in the kitchen monotonously reciting The Shepherd's Psalm by which measure she habitually timed the boiling of his eggs precisely to his liking.

Presently he heard the door swing open behind him. That would be Hannah bringing him the eggs and a platter of wheaten bread and a large mug of spiced pomegranate juice. He did not look up. By that sign Hannah would know that he didn't want to talk and would slip quietly out again to wait until he summoned her. She already knew, of course, that he was disturbed about something. She was ever quick to perceive his moods; much too quick, indeed. Their close comradeship made it difficult for him to withhold confidences from her.

Now the bread and butter plate had been put down before him and the small earthenware bowl containing the eggs. Simon stared hard at the hand that served him. It was not Hannah's hand; it was younger and smaller. He slowly turned his head and gazed up into a stranger's face,

135

his mouth sagging open in bewilderment. Whoever she was, the girl was beautiful, the most beautiful he had ever seen.

She smiled down into the Big Fisherman's dumfounded eyes, a mischievous little smile that she seemed to be controlling with some difficulty.

"Are you surprised, sir?" she asked, in a throaty tone that he remembered having heard before.

For a moment Simon continued to stare at her, unsmiling and speechless. He shook his big, shaggy head. Something queer had happened to the world. Miracles could be had now for a penny a dozen. Cripples walked. Water became wine. Dirty and ragged camel-boys were transformed into comely young women. He lowered his eyes, blinked rapidly, and rubbed his fingers through his hair. Hannah came in from the kitchen, beaming.

"Joe turned out to be a girl," she said, unnecessarily.

Simon nodded, and gazed at his mother-in-law as if he had never seen her before.

"Her name is Esther," explained Hannah, rather wistfully, as if hoping that Simon might overlook the girl's deception; and, when he had offered no comment, she said, "The dress is Abigail's. You don't object to Esther's wearing it?"

"Sit down—both of you," commanded Simon, huskily—"and tell me whether I am losing my mind." This was said with such sober sincerity that Hannah laughed until she had to pat the tears from her eyes. Esther smiled shyly.

"There is a great deal about it, Simon, that Esther hasn't had time to tell me"—Hannah glanced at her encouragingly, as to say that we expected to have the full story out of her by nightfall, at the latest—"but this much she wants us to know: her home was broken up by the loss of her parents, and now she is on her way to find her uncle who lives somewhere in Galilee; not far from the lake, she thinks. It would have been unsafe for a young woman to travel alone in a strange country; so she cut off her hair, put on a boy's clothing; and—well—here she is."

"You were lucky not to have got into trouble," commented Simon, munching his bread. "Risky business, I'd say. Anybody would know at a glance that you're a girl."

"She fooled you," said Hannah.

"I didn't look at her closely," retorted Simon. "I had other things on my mind. . . . Haven't you any relatives, down there in Idumea, who might have objected? Maybe you ran away."

"Yes, sir," the girl admitted. "They would have detained me. I ran away."

Simon devoted himself to his breakfast, frowning thoughtfully.

"Her story sounds reasonable enough," said Hannah.

"So did her other story," muttered Simon, ungraciously. "You think this uncle of yours lives in this vicinity, eh? What's his name?"

"Joseph, sir."

"We have a number of Josephs hereabouts. What is your uncle's occupation?"

"He is a stone-cutter."

"Think he will be able to support you—on a stone-cutter's wages? They are not very well paid."

"My uncle is not a common laborer," ventured Esther. "He is skilled."

"In that case," said Simon, "he is probably in the employ of the Tetrarch. They are rebuilding the stables at the palace."

"Stables!" Esther's tone indicated that her Uncle Joseph was not likely to be at work on a stable; not even the Tetrarch's.

"Stone stables!" explained Simon. "White marble stables! The Tetrarch's Arabian horses live in mansions, while most of his subjects live in hovels; and they eat good food while the little children of Galilee often go to bed hungry. . . . The Tetrarch's stables are beautiful! Ornamented with statues! . . . But your uncle would not be found at work on such carvings."

"No?" Esther's uplifted brows wondered why her uncle wasn't competent enough to do sculpturing.

"He is a Jew; isn't he?" demanded Simon; and when Esther had nodded he said, gruffly, "You should know that the Children of Israel are not permitted to make graven images."

"I thought that rule applied to the carving of idols," said Esther.

"Apparently you Idumean Jews do not know the Commandments. High time you learned them! Hear the law: 'Thou shalt not make unto thee any graven image or any likeness—of anything! Anything—that is in heaven above—or in the earth beneath—or in the water that is under the earth!' " Simon pushed back his chair, still glowering over Uncle Joseph's defection and his attractive niece's ignorance. "However," he added, as he moved toward the door, "I have an errand at the palace this morning. I shall make inquiries. Perhaps you would like to go with me."

"Let her rest here today, Simon," urged Hannah. "Tomorrow will do as well."

The Big Fisherman paused in the doorway to remark testily that he wouldn't be going to the palace tomorrow; that if Esther wanted to find her uncle she might as well be about it without further delay; and Esther, thus advised that she had worn out her welcome so far as Simon was concerned, promptly consented to accompany him.

His frown cleared momentarily, but deepened again as he noted Hannah's expression of disapproval. For some reason, she didn't want the girl to go. Simon shrugged and petulantly mumbled something that meant he didn't care a damn whether she ever found her uncle. Embarrassed by his asperity, Esther was tardy with a reply; and Simon, tugging on his cap, left the house without a farewell word to either of them. After the outer door had banged, Hannah remarked gently that Simon seemed to be upset about something.

"Me—perhaps?" inquired Esther.

"I don't think so," said Hannah. "You have done nothing to annoy him, my dear. . . . I never saw him—quite like this—before. Perhaps it has something to do with the fleet. I feel sure that Andrew knows, but it's hard to get anything out of Andrew. I never knew anyone who could keep his mouth shut as long—and tight—as Andrew. He was unusually quiet this morning; didn't say where he was going; perhaps to potter about the old house in Capernaum; for the fleet won't be going out today. It's a holiday."

Esther offered no help in Hannah's dilemma. It occurred to her that Simon's quarrel with Johnny might account for his disaffection, but that was none of her business and she decided not to mention it. After a moment's indecision, she rose and announced that she would go—at once —and try to overtake Simon.

"He has been very kind—and I have offended him," she said.

"Let me go with you," said Hannah, "as far as the highway."

Even before they reached the gate it was evident that some unusual excitement had stirred the neighborhood. People were pouring out of their doorways and walking rapidly toward the corner where the quiet street met the broad thoroughfare. Already a sizable company had collected there, intent upon a procession approaching from the direction of Tiberias. They quickened their steps.

Observing David standing austerely apart from the others but apparently waiting for whatever had brought them out, Hannah moved toward him to inquire while Esther sauntered on into the swelling crowd.

"The Tetrarch," explained David, absently, his eyes following Esther with undisguised interest.

"Of course," remembered Hannah. "The days have been so like summer, I hadn't realized it was time for their voyage."

"So—that's the girl, eh?" rumbled David. "A most attractive young creature! Bring her here, Hannah: I want to meet her."

"You won't give me away, sir," pleaded Hannah; and when David had reassured her, she followed Esther into the craning pack and told her to come and meet a good friend of Simon's. The girl only half heard. She was standing on tiptoe, completely fascinated by the slowly advancing cavalcade. Hannah took her arm.

"I suppose you know what this is about. The Tetrarch and his household journey to Rome, every year at this season, to spend the winter." And when Esther had nodded abstractedly, without taking her eyes off the road, Hannah urged, "There will be plenty of time to see them. Come, please, and meet Master David."

Esther turned reluctantly and followed.

"I told him I would bring you," Hannah explained. "David is our friend —but he is an eminent man, a lawyer, very learned, widely traveled—" At that, Esther's steps lagged.

"But why should a man of such importance want to meet me?" she protested. "And why does he stare so?"

"All old men stare," said Hannah. "They can't see very well."

"They don't have to be old," retorted Esther, "to stare."

Hannah thought this amusing and they were both smiling when Esther was presented. She curtseyed but dodged the intrusive eyes. David bowed gravely, to Hannah's mystification and the girl's anxiety.

"Welcome to beautiful Galilee, my child," he said, in a tone of studied formality. "It would be a pleasure to see more of you if our good Hannah consents. We must not detain you now. You are eager to have a glimpse of our beloved ruler and his charming family." There was such forthright malice in his sneer that Esther darted an inquiry into his crafty eyes. Was he inviting her to share his contempt for the Tetrarch? Momentarily confused, she fought her way out of the little dilemma by asking to be excused, and drifted quickly away to merge into the waiting crowd. David turned to Hannah and lifted an inquisitive eyebrow.

"She has told me a little more," obliged Hannah. "Her mother died recently, leaving her without a home. She is searching for an uncle, a sculptor who, she thinks, lives near the lake."

"What has become of her father?"

"Dead, I suppose. She didn't say."

"Is this uncle presumed to be an Idumean?"

"I think so."

"Well—I don't," growled David. "They do not produce sculptors in Idumea. I'll wager there isn't a chisel to be found in all that country. Their favorite tool is the dagger. . . . Has she offered any information about the device you found on her clothing? No? I thought not. And you didn't inquire: that was right."

They moved closer to the highway where Esther was sighted in the front row of spectators, the tall Sadducee observing that the girl was utterly absorbed in the approaching cavalcade, the vanguard of which was now only a few yards distant. Hannah noted that David's interest was concentrated, not on the garish spectacle, but devoted entirely to her mysterious guest.

The procession was led by a company of gaudily uniformed cavalry from the Roman fort at Capernaum. They rode four abreast, their mounts jingling with polished trappings. After the military escort had passed, there was an open interval of a full hundred yards before the second unit came on, led by a distinguished figure on a superb white horse unmistakably of Arabian origin. The man was richly clad in a black tunic, trimmed in red, red riding breeches, and glossy black boots. He rode alone. His gray hair was close-cropped and circled with a silver fillet.

Esther gazed hard at the haughty, dissipated face, at the wide-set, bulging eyes that negligently drifted over the crowd with a bored unconcern. Now the roving eyes swept the upturned faces of the area where Esther stood, transfixed, with a dry throat and pounding heart. An instant later they returned to her, the finely sculptured brows lifted a little, and a mere wisp of a smile—compounded of surprise, insolence, admiration, and amusement—twitched the Tetrarch's lips. Esther's wide eyes gave no response. She was frightened.

There was a considerable interval before the luxurious litters were carried by. There were three of them, single-file, each borne by eight stalwart slaves, Greeks, Esther thought. The curtains of the first of the litters were tightly drawn. It bore Herodias, no doubt. The second was open, and the lounging occupant, a heavily jeweled woman of thirty, smirked impudently through her paint. This, Esther knew, would be Salome. However notorious, she was indeed a beautiful woman: even her awareness of her beauty did not mar it. The curtains of the third litter were closed. Esther hoped she might hear a name whispered by someone in the crowd, but the occupant remained unidentified.

There came now a score or more of camel-borne men and women, most of them in their twenties and thirties; household servants, no doubt. The majority of them were handsome. They were evidently in a carnival mood, exchanging banter that made them laugh. Whatever might be said of the

Tetrarch, it was plain that his retainers were well cared for and had no quarrel with their employment.

Trailing the camels, at a considerable distance, came a long pack-train laden with baggage.

Losing interest now, Esther was about to turn away when there was a sudden stir among her neighbors. A brilliantly uniformed cavalryman, leading his horse, had paused beside her. The people, with amazement and apprehension in their stares, drew hastily aside to make room.

"Your name, please," demanded the soldier, crisply but respectfully.

Esther's knees trembled. She felt sick and weak. Before she was able to stammer a reply, a hand was laid gently on her arm.

"I shall answer for this young woman," said David, calmly. "She is a member of my family. Who wants to know her name, Centurion?"

"His Highness, sir!" retorted the soldier. "And who are you?"

"I am David—of the House of Zadok. You may bear my compliments to His Highness and assure him that this young woman is not in need of his solicitude."

The Sadducee had spoken with such haughty self-confidence that the Roman seemed at a loss for an appropriate response.

"Well!" he barked. "We will see about that! You will wait here until I return!" Mounting his horse, he galloped forward. The crowd stood stunned, silent, gaping at Esther.

"Come," said David, quietly. "There is nothing more to see. We will go home."

"But—the man!" whispered Esther. "Are we not to wait?"

"He will not return." David laid a protecting hand on her shoulder and gently propelled her through the bewildered pack.

Hannah was pale with fright when they rejoined her. David smiled reassuringly as he walked between them.

"Have no fear, Hannah," he said. "No harm will come of this. Our Tetrarch is ever interested in a pretty face. He likes to have good-looking people about him. In this instance, he has made a mistake—and probably knows it by now. It is not to his advantage to accumulate any more enemies. You need not give it another thought."

"I do thank you, sir, for coming to my rescue!" Esther's voice was still shaken.

"It was my pleasure to serve you." David bowed. "I bid you both good-day." With lengthened steps, he strode majestically away and proceeded slowly up the street toward his home. The women faced each other with inquiring eyes, puzzled over Esther's predicament.

"You had better come back with me," advised Hannah. "Search for your uncle another day. The people will recognize you, and think it peculiar to see you alone on the highway after what David said."

"About my being a member of his household? I wonder why he did say it: he might have had to prove it."

"Evidently he had no fear of that, Esther. David is a man of great influence; greater, perhaps, than I had realized."

"Even so, he took the risk of offending the ruler. Why should he put himself in jeopardy—for me? I mean nothing to him."

Hannah's eyes were averted as she remarked, in a vague undertone, that it wasn't always easy to understand David. At that, Esther came to a stop, laid a hand on Hannah's arm, and asked, abruptly:

"How much have you told him—about me?"

"There wasn't much to tell, was there?" countered Hannah, with a reproachful little smile. "Look! He is waiting for us, beside our fence. He has thought of something more he wants to say."

"He will be wanting to talk to you alone, I think," said Esther, turning about. "I shall go now—and try to overtake Simon." And before Hannah had time to protest, she had hurried away.

*　　*　　*　　*　　*　　*

As he set off for Tiberias, after breakfast, the Big Fisherman was confused and unhappy. The mysterious girl's account of herself and her errand in Galilee—a much amended story—was anything but satisfactory. It was plain to see that Hannah was worried. He had been a fool to bring the waif home with him.

There was nothing to do today. The crews were off duty, supposedly at the Synagogue but more likely to be found loafing at the wine-shops. However, there were always some odd jobs to be done on shipboard. He would net a basket of fish from the live-box at the wharf and deliver them to the palace. The rest of the empty day he could spend alone, tinkering at trivial chores on *The Abigail*.

A quarter-mile down the road a procession was coming, led by a large contingent of cavalry, the sunshine flashing from their polished spears and the burnished bosses of their shields.

Still farther away a rising cloud of yellow dust, suspended over the rear of the parade, meant that a long train of heavily laden pack-asses was already scraping its hooves, though a laborious three-day journey lay ahead. Simon knew what it was all about: Antipas was setting forth, as was his custom, on the annual excursion to Rome. The party would travel to Caesarea and embark. Galilee would see no more of its Tetrarch until the flowers bloomed again.

Not that it mattered. He meant nothing to Galilee. The people's welfare did not concern him. He was more a Roman than a Jew. Nobody would care if he went to his precious Rome and stayed there. But he would be back, as usual. Returning, he would hold court for a month at the Galilean embassy in Jerusalem, at the time of the Passover fast and festivities; and then—with much pomp—he would come home to Tiberias, accompanied by a horde of other rich idlers, and sit half-naked in the sun—and swill his expensive wines—and splash in his celebrated pool—until it was time to go to Rome again. . . . But Galilee would be no better off under another ruler: provincial governors were all alike. Indeed, Antipas might be preferable to a more ambitious ruler: he was much too lazy to stir up trouble among the people. Perhaps the best ruler you could have—after all—was a drunken loafer who would let the province govern itself.

Ordinarily, when Simon sighted the Tetrarch's garish cavalcade making off toward Caesarea, he indifferently sneered and spat on the ground. Today—he was cross, anyhow—the pageant made him hot with indignation. This renegade, Romanized Jew had so little respect for the cherished traditions of Galilee that he thought nothing of setting out on his pleasure trip while the people were on their way to the Synagogue! The insolence of it! Fine way, indeed, to observe the Day of Atonement! It was little he cared about the feelings of the people! Antipas ought to be in the Synagogue today, at least going through the motions of honoring the religion of Israel. He was a disgrace to the province!

Simon wondered how many of the servants, and which ones, would be left behind, this time. He hoped Leah and Anna would remain at the palace. He always enjoyed their banter. Yes—and that impudent minx Claudia, too. It was impossible to have any respect for her; she was an outrageous flirt; and, besides, she was a Roman; but she was witty. And the Greek girl, Helen, who never had anything to say, but always smiled shyly as if she understood. Maybe she did. Sometimes he playfully winked at her, and she would show the tips of very pretty teeth. Helen often lingered for a while in Simon's thoughts, after he had discharged his errands at the service entrance, but he always put her out of his mind with a "Pouf!"—for, however winsome, she was a heathen. But—heathen or not—there was something very attractive about this Helen; her physical frailty, perhaps. Simon often asked himself why he had so much interest in fragile women when he was so contemptuous of any physical weakness in men.

Somberly dressed pedestrians along the road were withdrawing to the weeds and brambles where they waited, gaping. Some sat down on the low stone fences. Simon plodded doggedly on, resolved that he would not leave the highway until it was necessary; nor was he going to do Antipas the honor of staring at his damned parade. Entering the little hamlet of Magdala, he turned off into a lane to wait until the thing was over and the dust had settled. He eased himself down on the dry grass in the shade of an old olive tree with his back to the highway. The metallic clatter of the approaching cavalry was insisting that he should turn and look, but he scowled and closed his eyes.

Everything was going wrong for Simon, lately; everything! It had all stemmed from this mad Carpenter who had taken it into his head that the people would be better off if—if—they weren't quite so well off; that's what it came to: own nothing—and be happy.

And why did anyone in his right senses listen to it? Because they had heard a rumor that the fellow could cure diseases. Well—supposing he could: was that what we wanted; a man who went about defying Nature? Before the Carpenter had added this confusion to one's thoughts, life made some sense. To be sure, it had its difficulties, but you learned to accept them. Simon glanced back at his own complacency and wished he might recover it. He had never been one to bother himself about riddles. Such dizzying old problems as "What are we here for? What is the good of it? What is it all about?" had never cost him a moment's anxiety.

As a lad he had been forced to assume a man's responsibilities, requiring him to work early and late while other children were at play, but it had never occurred to him to complain that the world was mistreating him, or that Jehovah had singled him out for target practice. A lot of people were forever whimpering that God had "hidden His face" from them, when probably nothing much was the matter except that their cistern was low or a few of their chickens had died of the pip.

That's what you got for being so tangled up with religion; you were always in a dither about God. The new calf was a heifer, and God was on your side; your donkey went lame, and God was angry at you. Better not worry so much about God, Who was probably not worrying much about you.

Simon's religion—what little there was of it—had been quite simple. He assumed that there must be a Great Mind in charge of the stars and the sky and other large undertakings, but he couldn't believe that God ever stooped to such trivial engagements as willfully breaking the windlass-chain at the Abrams' well because the old man had walked a little too far on the Sabbath. Simon's God was a neat and trustworthy housekeeper Who put the sun out in the morning and took it in at night with a regularity you could count on, and He arranged that the seasons should come along in a dependable procession. Nothing ever got out of kilter.

Pursuant to this elementary creed, the Big Fisherman had not considered his childhood drudgeries as a visitation of God's displeasure. Indeed, he had taken pride in his ability to endure hard knocks and prosper in the face of obstacles. Never in his life had Simon looked up and cried "Why?" Not even when poor little Abigail died. It didn't occur to him that perhaps God was paying him off for his misdeeds. He knew he had made plenty of mistakes—mostly by letting his temper get the best of him, to other men's serious discomfort—and he had missed many a religious fast that he might have observed; but he couldn't think that God had decided to take an interest in his small indiscretions. And when the elderly Rabbi Ben-Sholem, visiting them the day Abigail died, had implied as much, Simon had retorted, bluntly:

"I don't believe that God would do a mean thing like that!"

Sounds from the highway indicated that the company of cavalry was passing now; the jingle of expensive harness, the clipped beats of well-shod hooves, the creak of new leather, the sharp bark of a military command, the crack of a whip. Simon listened to it, hated it, and returned to his reveries.

And—next morning after the burial, he had gone back to work, quiet and sad, but spending no time in useless brooding; for life was like that; people sickened and died; even young people like Abigail; even little babies who had had no chance to live at all. But why ask questions about it when you knew that nobody could give you an answer; not even the Rabbi, who should know if anyone did.

Now everything was in disorder. Now you couldn't count on anything! Johnny was not a liar; and that business about the little boy's foot, last night, was very peculiar—to say the least. Of course there was a possibility that the Carpenter had planned a hoax to deceive the people; but what could he expect to get out of it? He would be exposed; probably thrown into prison. There was nothing in it for him. He charged no money for his supposed healings; apparently had no money, and didn't want any; owned nothing; saw no value in anything—but birds and flowers. That didn't sound as if he hoped to fill his pockets by fraudulent practices.

It was quiet on the road now. But—Simon well knew—it was not because the Tetrarch's pompous parade had passed. No—this was just the gap in the procession. Presently Antipas himself would ride by on his mincing stallion. None of this belonged to Galilee: a Roman ruler on an Arabian horse! Surely poor little Galilee had enough to confuse it utterly without having the Carpenter on its hands!

Assuming that this Nazarene was entirely honest; that he really could change water into wine, and heal cripples—where did that leave you? The man must get his power from Heaven. If so—God did trouble Himself about a silly yokel with a short arm, and a small boy with a crooked foot. If you admitted that He did things like that, maybe it was true that the Abrams' water-bucket was lost in the bottom of their well because old man Abrams had absent-mindedly walked too far on God's dull and doleful Sabbath Day.

There was another interval of silence; and then the rhythmic lisp of sandal-straps. They would be carrying the hussy, Herodias. Simon had seen her once, in the palace garden: she had stared brazenly at him for a moment before shrugging a shoulder and tossing her head and turning away. Herodias was a hard one; anybody could see that; the most important woman in Galilee; the enormity of it! What had poor, pious little Galilee ever done to deserve such a humiliation? Perhaps God would wreck the Tetrarch's ship, this time, if He had determined to take a hand in the cure of afflictions. There was silence again on the road.

Now we had this mysterious Idumean girl to deal with. It was clear that Hannah didn't know what to make of her. Suppose she couldn't find her uncle: then what? Hannah wouldn't want to turn her out. Simon felt lonely; couldn't expect to be entirely comfortable anywhere; not on the fleet, where his men—some of them, anyway—would resentfully remember his quarrel; nor could he feel at ease in his own home with that deceitful Idumean at the table. What a fool he had been to take the dirty beggar home with him.

There were more whispers of sandal-straps. That would be Salome's tall slaves, bearing her costly litter. Simon had often seen Salome on the road, always with a detachment of mounted guards. She was a graceful rider; very pretty, too. It was common talk that she had no more chastity than a cat. It was also rumored that her mother hated her because the Tetrarch showed her too much attention. You couldn't believe everything you heard, but where there was so much smoke there must be some fire. You couldn't blame the Galileans for believing any evil tale about this young woman. They hated her: why, indeed, shouldn't they?

Simon shook away the contemptuous thoughts about Salome; and, for better comfort, shifted his position against the tree. He absently plucked a dry seed-pod, and slowly tore it apart. How wretchedly he had handled all that business with Johnny! It was Johnny's fault, of course, but he needn't have been so rough on the boy. After all—he had only reported what he imagined he had seen and heard; and they had all urged him to tell it. He said he had seen it with his own eyes, in broad daylight; had been standing beside the fellow; and a woman had seen it and fainted.

And the man had made funny little squeaks, though you couldn't tell whether he was laughing or crying. Simon tried unsuccessfully, a couple of times, to make a funny little squeak like that; for this detail had impressed him deeply.

Now there was much clamor on the highway. The air was full of dust, and the raucous shouts of the donkey-boys, and the thud of blows on the bony rumps of over-burdened beasts. The Romans were cruel to animals; seemed to enjoy beating anything or anybody who couldn't fight back. And they ruled the world! If God was going to concern Himself with the behavior of mankind, here would be a good place to lend a hand. Maybe we could have another flood; like the one that had drowned everybody but Noah and his family. Simon grew drowsy waiting for the donkeys to pass and the dust to clear. Noah had spent forty days in the big boat; along with all the animals; landed on a muddy mountaintop; nothing living but a grapevine. And Noah had made some wine—and got drunk. Well—you couldn't blame him much.

Of course, if Johnny had really seen what he reported, he wouldn't care whether he had a job or not. He would follow along after this Carpenter, and be content to live on bark and berries. Well—we would have to wait —and see. The boys might come creeping back in a day or two. They had to eat; didn't they? Nobody could nurse a grievance very long on an empty stomach. Simon came to his feet, stretched his long arms—and yawned mightily. Yes—they would be coming back. Their silly mother would see to that. Naomi would raise all hell until they returned to their jobs.

* * * * * *

The fleet rocked gently in the cove. A dory was tethered to the prow of *The Abigail.* That would be one of the boys doing his trick as watchman. The rest of them were on holiday, supposedly attending to their religious duties, though Simon surmised that they would be strolling idly about on the quiet streets of Capernaum, consorting with drunken legionaries from the neighboring fort, and guzzling raw, new wine. That was about all a religious holiday came to: the older folk would be huddled together in the Synagogue, praying for their wayward whelps who would show up an hour late in the morning with white tongues and red eyes. Simon had no patience with drunkenness, and was frequently heard to say that any wine at all was far too much wine. It had been a long time since he had tasted a fermented drink.

Pausing at his own wharf, he drew in the floating live-box and filled a basket with perch. The palace would not be needing so many, now that the number of residents had been greatly reduced, but the few who remained would see to it that they had enough to eat. Lysias, the steward who, during the family's absence, was always left behind in charge of the establishment, made no effort to economize and apparently gave but little attention to such trivial expenditures as the daily order of fish. Simon rarely saw the shrewd, stocky, swarthy Greek steward while the Tetrarch was in residence, but was always grimly amused at the swagger Lysias affected, once his master had departed. Evidently the fellow had a high opinion of his charms. Simon gathered that the servant-girls were more than a bit afraid of him.

Slipping his hairy arm under the handle of the dripping basket, the Big Fisherman trudged up the winding driveway to the rear courtyard, noting that all operations on the new stables had been suspended. That would be because of the religious holiday. Not that the Day of Atonement would mean anything to the stone-masons and sculptors who were all Greeks, but the hod-carriers and other unskilled workmen were Galileans. Their religion forbade them to do carving, but it was quite permissible for them to carry the hewn stones. Simon snorted, contemptuous of this hypocrisy. Nearing the kitchen entrance, he heard gay, bantering conversation. The servants were celebrating the family's departure.

At sight of him, the girls poured through the doorway, all talking at once, and fluttered about him with hilarious greetings. Murza, the tall, dark Arimathean, who had never before accorded him better regard than a nod and a sniff, relieved him of the basket and patted him on his arm. She was pungent with wine. The Roman, Claudia, seemed a little drunk. Simon tried to be jovial, but the pretense was not easy.

"Doesn't the Big Fisherman feel well today?" Murza contrived a condescending smile.

"Well enough," retorted Simon, unpleasantly. "Do I look frail?"

"You look sour," said Leah—"as if you'd eaten something."

"His own fish, maybe! No?" Claudia launched a shrill giggle.

Helen stood by, demurely studying Simon's glum indifference to the raillery which she couldn't understand very well. He gave her a brief smile.

"The Big Fisherman is in love!" shrieked Murza. "It has taken his appetite." She tossed a teasing glance toward the Greek girl who smiled childishly and shook her black curls, though whether she did not comprehend; or, comprehending, was showing a maidenly embarrassment, Simon could not tell. But it was an attractive little smile—whatever it meant—and his heavy frown cleared as he gave her a friendly look.

"See!—what I told you!" taunted Murza. "That's his ailment: he is lovesick!"

"I think you're right—for once," drawled Leah. "And he's always pretending to be so tough—and strong—and manly: no use for women; just a big man's man! And now he cannot eat—for love!"

"He should be put in the dungeon along with the other solemn owl who does not eat! No?" Claudia laughed gaily at her own drollery.

"She's talking about our new prisoner," explained Anna, with unexpected seriousness. "The legionaries brought him in the day before yesterday. They said he had been living on grasshoppers and other roasted bugs—in the desert."

"Well—you should be able to find some bugs for him," remarked Simon, relieved at this turn in the conversation. "It is late in the season for the larger bugs," he added, "but there should be plenty of the smaller ones in his bedding."

"Not at all!" protested Anna. "His cell is clean and comfortable. His Highness gave orders about that. He wants the man treated kindly: he thinks the poor fellow is crazy—but innocent of any crime."

"What is he charged with?" inquired Simon, unconcernedly.

"He is some sort of wandering prophet," said Anna. "Would you like to see him? He is a Galilean. And he is permitted to have visitors, though no one has come—so far."

"Perhaps his friends are afraid to venture that close to a prison," observed Leah. "I'm sure I would be."

Simon had straightened to his full height. He hitched manfully at his belt, and spat vehemently on the ground.

"I don't visit prophets!" he growled. "I hadn't supposed I looked that foolish."

"Well—as for me"—Anna enigmatically arched her eyebrows to signify that she knew more than she intended to divulge—"I don't believe the man is crazy. . . . Maybe he really is a prophet!"

"And how do you happen to know so much about this—this bug-eater?" grinned Simon. "Are you his keeper?"

"I'm supposed to feed him. He will not eat—but he will talk. He talks all the time! You should hear him! Brrr! It frightens me! He says that a Great One has been sent—from Heaven—to free the slaves and throw the mighty from their high seats!" Anna's frown showed genuine anxiety. "The whole world is to be shaken!" she added, soberly.

"As I live—it is true—what Anna's saying," confirmed Claudia, excitedly. "I was with her when he said it! The whole world is to be shaken! . . . Until its ears rattle!" she added, for good measure.

"You made that up," sneered Leah. "A prophet wouldn't say anything that funny."

"But—it isn't funny!" declared Claudia, grinning. "Not if it's true!

And Anna thinks it is; don't you, Anna?" She gave the sober-faced Jewess a thumb-jab in the ribs. "You do, too!" she went on, when Anna impatiently flinched—and shook her head. "You were scared—and you made off at once to your—what you call—Synagogue! No? . . . Your tiresome old god is much too hard on you poor Jews. We Romans now—we have many, many gods. All kinds of gods. One takes one's pick of them, and if he does not please—Pouf!" She airily kissed a rosette of fingertips and blew a negligent farewell to the incompetent deity.

If the half-drunken Claudia had expected a laugh, she was disappointed. Anna and Leah gave her a withering look. Murza scowled; she was not very religious but she was superstitious and disapproved of sacrilege. Helen, who didn't know what it was all about, and probably wouldn't have cared if she had known, turned to gaze complacently at the faraway blue mountains. Simon, who through Claudia's silly speech had remained staring at Anna's apprehensive face, took a step toward her.

"You say—this fellow said that a Great One is coming?" he demanded, so sternly that Anna blinked.

"He said the Great One has come," replied Anna. "He is here—now!"

"That's what he said!" put in Claudia, helpfully. "I heard him!"

"Shut up!" rasped Leah, as to a noisy terrier.

"Where?" demanded Simon, searching Anna's eyes.

"I know what you're thinking," replied Anna, after some hesitation. "There has been all this talk—about a Carpenter—who does strange things." She had lowered her voice to the tone of a confidence. "But—apparently the Carpenter is not our man. The Carpenter is said to heal diseases. This Great One isn't here to heal anybody: he's here to punish the rulers—and the rich!"

"I wonder if His Highness knows what sort of blabbing our prisoner can do," remarked Murza. "Perhaps he wouldn't have wanted the fellow handled so gently if he had heard some of his talk."

"But"—argued Simon, undiverted by Murza's comment—"if this Great One is down on the rich, maybe he will aid the poor: why don't you ask the bug-eater about that, Anna?"

"Ask him yourself, if you're so interested," snapped Anna, tiring of the Big Fisherman's queries.

"Interested!" he retorted, angrily. "And why should I be interested? Your prophet is a crazy dunce, who deserves to be locked up! And as for the Carpenter, he will soon turn out to be a fraud! They're both lunatics! Anybody who wants to believe in such nonsense is welcome to it!" Simon's voice was vibrant with indignation as he went on, "I don't believe in any of this rubbish! All religion is rubbish! I don't believe in any of it! . . . Not in any of it, I tell you!"

His puzzled audience gaped at him for a long moment as he stood glowering. At length Leah broke the silence by remarking, in a disgusted drawl:

"Well—who said you did?"

"I'll wager you do," yelled Claudia, "or you wouldn't be so hot and cross about it!"

The taunt rekindled Simon's anger and he muttered that all religious prattle should be prohibited—by law!—a suggestion that inspired Leah to remark, with a bitter, private smile, that he would probably go to hell when he died.

"And he will not like that!" laughed Claudia. "He detests big crowds: I heard him say so! No?"

"You're a fool, Claudia," said Anna, stifling a yawn.

"Perhaps—but I am a happy fool! You Jewish fools are much too sober and sad. No? What you need, on your holiday, is good cheer! Laughter! Singing! You should have a cup of wine to warm your cold bellies!" Claudia was whirling into a reckless dance. "I, myself, shall bring you wine!" she trilled, as she made off, pleased to have had such a happy thought.

"You needn't bring any to me," called Leah.

"Nor me," said Anna.

"Then—I shall bring some to the Big Fisherman!" shouted Claudia, gaily.

"Go—and stop her, Murza," said Leah. "She will listen to you. And see that she doesn't take any more herself. She's had too much already. If she gets any worse, Lysias will whip her."

"No fear of that," sniffed Murza, without moving. "Lysias has been warming his cold belly, too."

"I must go," mumbled Simon. "I have work to do. If you'll empty my basket—"

Claudia was returning now, staggering under the weight of a massive tray laden with a huge pitcher and wine-cups. She breathlessly put her burden down on the ledge of the sundial, and gave the company a bright smile.

"If Lysias catches you out here with that silver service—" warned Leah.

"Never mind my basket," muttered Simon, moving off. "I'll pick it up later."

"But—how rude!" protested Claudia. "Here I have gone to the trouble to bring you wine—in His Highness' beautiful silver—and you run away! And the Big Fisherman is said to be so strong and brave! Pouf!" She faced him with cool contempt. "Very well—hurry off to your Synagogue—Big Fisherman! And say your prayers!"

Simon flushed with anger. Claudia, noting that her insult had bitten him in a sensitive spot, poured a cup full of wine and held it out to him, with a wheedling smile.

"I shouldn't have teased you: it wasn't fair. We all know you are so very big—and brave—and manly!"

"I wonder—whether he is," sniffed Leah, negligently.

Stung by the indignities, Simon impetuously grabbed the cup and drained it. The heady wine warmed his throat and spread a pleasant glow through his vitals. Now that he had vindicated himself, he would furnish additional proof that he was no pious weakling. He handed back the cup and Claudia, giggling happily, refilled it.

"Better not lay it on too fast, Big Fellow," advised Anna, as Simon tipped back his head.

"That's enough now, Claudia," growled Murza. "You don't want to get him into trouble. You can see he doesn't know how to drink wine. He'll be tight as a drum, presently."

Simon wiped his bearded lips with the back of his big hand, sighed contentedly, grinned foolishly, and made a deep bow which amused them all except Helen whose tremulous smile showed anxiety.

They were relieved to see him go. With long, springing, military strides, the Big Fisherman made off toward the driveway—dizzy but exultant. He had never felt better in his life. He triumphantly swung his shaggy head from side to side, accenting his confident swagger with swinging arms and thrust shoulders.

What the Italian trollop had said was true: the Jews did take themselves too seriously; they made the business of living a sad and sorry undertaking. As for himself, Simon was now resolved to be more light-hearted in the future. Any Jew, so concerned over the world's wickedness that he would withdraw alone to the desert—and eat bugs—was entitled to all the pleasure he could find in it: Simon would have no part in such foolishness. Nor would he give another thought to the penniless Carpenter.

The well-kept driveway was rougher than usual—doubtless cut up by the hooves of the Tetrarch's pack-train—and Simon found himself slipping and stumbling over the loose gravel. He laughed aloud as he tried to mend his lurching gait, and hummed a little tune. He wanted to sing. It had been a long time since he had loosed his big, deep, roaring voice. An old chant came back to him out of his early childhood. In the well-remembered, low-pitched monotone of the Synagogue cantor, he began the plaintive recitative:

Have mercy upon me, O God, according to thy loving-kindness: according unto the multitude of thy tender mercies, blot out my transgressions. Wash me thoroughly from mine iniquity, and cleanse me from my sin. For I acknowledge—

He broke off abruptly and muttered a savage imprecation as he realized the meaning of the ancient Atonement Day hymn that, as a little boy, he had learned by rote; learned so thoroughly that the words had no significance at all; just an august procession of sonorous words intricately woven into a haunting tune. Simon cursed himself bitterly. Was he never to be delivered, then, from these dour broodings that flowed in the milk and the blood of the Jew? Was he—by nature—beyond the reach of any happiness? In a mood to sing, and to sing gaily, the only song he knew was a whimpering cry of guilt!

But now it occurred to Simon that he did know another song, a ribald sailors' ditty. Sometimes his men guardedly hummed it deep in their throats, knowing better than to articulate the dirty words; for the Big Fisherman, eloquently profane as he was, hated obscenities. Scornful now of all the self-flogging hymns wailed into his childhood by sanctimonious old Jonas, he sang the sailors' song as loudly as he could yell, defiantly bellowing the filthiest words as if he wanted God Himself to hear—and be hurt!

At the end of it, he laughed hysterically, laughed until his eyes were so wet he couldn't see the road, and found his sleeve caught in the shrubbery. It sobered him a little. The sound of his idiotic laughter resounded in his whirling head. He shambled back onto the road, hoarsely muttering that he was a fool; a damned, drunken fool!

He was nearing the highway now and its quietness warned him to cease his racket. There was a complete absence of the customary clank and clatter of vehicular traffic. Any man who pushed a barrow or drove a donkey-cart today would do so at the expense of his reputation for decency. The few pedestrians moved slowly, out of respect for the day. Meeting them, Simon bowed gravely, as if he too were mindful of the occasion. His recent sensation of reckless joy was completely dimmed out now.

At the wharf he stumbled awkwardly into a dory, sat down heavily, and began pulling toward the fleet. The vigorous exercise immediately fatigued him. His arms were heavy and the oars sliced splashes of water into the boat. Had he caught one of his boys pounding the lake as if flailing a threshing-floor, the Big Fisherman would have paid him off and kicked him out. He was weak with nausea and dripping with sweat when, at length, he pulled up under the prow of *The Abigail*.

Thad appeared at the rail and tossed the master a rope, calling out cheerily that it was a fine day. Apparently the boy had not yet noticed that anything was wrong with his hero. Simon wished the youngster was less attentive, and thought some of contriving an immediate errand for him in some other part of the ship, but decided to brazen it out the best he could. With a great effort he heaved himself aboard, produced a weak imitation of a smile, and said, with labored precision:

"I'll relieve you now, my boy. Perhaps you would like to go to the Synagogue."

"Hell, no!" scoffed Thad, expectant of an approving grin.

But Simon's face was sober and he made no comment. Walking slowly aft, he sat down on the sun-warmed tiller-seat and dully occupied himself with a pretense of mending some frayed odds and ends of old ratlines. After a while Thad strolled back and volunteered to help, but Simon shook his head absently. When an hour had passed, the loyal young fellow—showing some concern now—returned with a plate of smoked fish and a couple of hard biscuits in one hand and a mug of sweet cider in the other.

The skipper nodded his appreciation, gestured to Thad to put the plate down on the seat beside him, and reached out a hand for the mug. He raised it almost to his lips, sniffed it, blinked rapidly a few times—and shuddered.

"Not feeling very well today, my boy," mumbled Simon, truthfully.

Thad murmured something that sounded like sympathy and moved quietly away. It was evident that the master did not want to be disturbed. Doubtless, reflected Simon, as he gazed at the retreating figure, the boy had guessed why. And that was too bad; but at least Thad would know now what the trouble was, and not be fretting for fear he had somehow got himself into the boss's disfavor.

Simon continued thinking about young Thad. He was a good boy, a good sailor, a good fisherman; but a sore trial to his parents. It was said that they felt they had lost their son, and that it was Simon's fault. Well—maybe it was true, viewed from the angle of their fanatical piety. The youngster was completely devoted to him, even to the length of imitating the master's little tricks of speech and manner until the crew joked about it.

Bending forward, with his aching head in his hands, Simon retched disgustedly. Thad's parents were right: he was a bad influence. He wondered what Thad would say if he called to him and said, "See here, boy; why don't you wash your dirty face and comb your hair, and go to the Synagogue today? It would please your mother. Even if it didn't do you any good, it would be worth something to make your parents happy. . . ." But no—he couldn't do that: he had already bewildered young Thad with his extraordinary behavior. It was enough disillusionment for one day.

Glancing up dully, he saw Thad vaulting over the starboard rail onto the deck of *The Sara*. Something had attracted his attention. He was leaning far forward now at the taffrail, shading his eyes with both hands. Presently he turned about with a broad grin and called to Simon, excitedly:

"Damned if they haven't got her moving!"

Simon's curiosity brought him lumbering to his feet. He sluggishly climbed aboard *The Sara* and followed Thad's pointing finger. A full half-mile away, the discarded little fishing-smack that had been beached, all of three years ago, by poor old Japheth when he was no longer able to work, was making sail, a few hundred yards off shore.

"Somebody's going to get wet," rumbled Simon. "That old bucket must leak at every seam." He chuckled, disdainfully, remembering the sign that Japheth had nailed on her prow when abandoning her: "To Sell or Rent," under which announcement some clown had scrawled, "Or Rot." He turned to Thad. "Who—do you suppose—has been fool enough to float her?"

"Why—don't you know, sir? I thought you must have heard. The Zebedee boys have leased her." Thad's bright enthusiasm over the amazing project was quickly dimmed by the Big Fisherman's surly scowl.

"They're fools!" growled Simon. "That old vessel is not seaworthy. Even if she stays afloat, she's unmanageable. First little puff of wind— over she goes."

"Yes, sir," agreed Thad, obediently. "But Johnny is pretty good with the sticks. He'll ride out a gale if anyone can!"

"How much of a crew have they; or do you know?" queried Simon. "I suppose they have their old man with them."

"No, sir; they picked up three or four boys in Capernaum, but they didn't want to take Zebedee away from us." Thad risked a tongue-in-cheek grin, but Simon, not being in a jocular mood, only frowned bitterly and spat in the water, as he swung about and returned to his seat on *The Abigail*. Thad, bored and unhappy, tagged along.

"You may go now, my boy," said Simon. "I'll stand watch."

"But how about tonight, sir?"

"I expect to remain here."

"I don't like to leave you alone, sir."

Simon made no reply to that, and Thad lingered until the master called out, impatiently, "Go! Do as I tell you! I prefer to be alone!"

Crestfallen, the dismayed youngster slipped quietly away under this unearned rebuff, and dropped into one of the rocking dories. When he was safely gone, Simon—sick and wretched in body and spirit—plodded feebly forward to the little cabin, eased himself down on the bare bunk that nobody before had ever had occasion to use, and reeled dizzily off into a troubled sleep.

7

Once out of Hannah's sight, Esther abruptly slowed her scamper to match the aimless amble of the dissolving holiday crowd, and sauntered casually alongside the northbound groups of chattering women.

It was a relief to find herself unnoticed by her fellow pedestrians whose low-pitched voices seemed completely preoccupied with a review of the Tetrarch's cavalcade; or, at least, Esther surmised that this was the subject under discussion, though it was difficult to make out exactly what they were saying. The Galilean inflection of Aramaic had a tendency to slur a half dozen words into one, and when spoken rapidly took on a singular cadence that tipped every sentence up on end, making it sound like a query.

Inconspicuous in Abigail's simple country dress, Esther strolled along at the verge of the highway, busy with her own accumulation of problems. She had had no intention of trying to overtake Simon and make-believe she was searching for her fictitious Uncle Joseph. She was simply killing time until the eminent David, having concluded his conversation with Hannah, should have returned home. Then she would feel safe to retrace her steps to Bethsaida.

This deeply learned and widely traveled lawyer's almost reverential respect for her had been most disturbing. It was obvious that the shrewd old man had done some expert guessing about her identity. Her identity! —the thought produced a pensive, momentary smile. David wondered who she was. Well—who was she? Of late, she had been required to change her identity so often that she was a bit bewildered about it herself.

It was amazing, reflected Esther, what one could do to one's own mind if some emergency demanded the practice of a deceit that involved self-deception also. To masquerade successfully as a boy was a serious and

157

hazardous business. It wasn't enough to pretend she was a boy. To cut off her long hair and put on a man's clothing was the smallest part of it. The deception had required diligent, earnest, relentless concentration. Even when alone and unobserved, she had hardened her face, lengthened her stride, swaggered, scowled, growled and spat. Every little feminine trick of posture or gesture was critically examined and corrected. She practiced walking with her feet wide apart; was mindful to keep her fingers away from her throat, and make them into fists; kept her elbows away from her ribs, and swung her arms like a soldier.

John, the baptizer, had discovered her secret; that had been her own fault. The strong breeze on the hill-top, that morning, had molded her clothing tightly to her form. But for this carelessness of hers, the hermit might not have suspected. She had been lucky throughout the whole adventure.

When, however, it had become quite impossible to deceive Hannah, she had accomplished her reconversion to her own sex with a minimum of effort. She had dressed in Abigail's clothes from the skin out, tucking her own underclothing deep in the bottom of the old chest. Now she was Esther. But, curiously enough, the abandonment of her studied rôle as a boy had suddenly affected her memory of all the experiences she had had while playing that part. No—she hadn't forgotten them completely; but they were faded, distorted, as if viewed dimly through a clouded glass. It was a queer sensation, being Esther.

Nor was that all that had happened to her mind, now that she had taken on a new personality. This Esther had to account for herself. It wasn't sufficient to stop being a camel-boy, fugitive from a caravan. It was imperative that Esther should contrive—and on very short notice, too— a new explanation for her presence in Galilee. So, she had invented an uncle for whom she was searching. Aware that she mustn't take the risk of impromptu replies to the inevitable queries about this relative, she had elaborately created an Uncle Joseph whom almost anyone should be able to recognize from her detailed description. Uncle Joseph became as real to her as rain! He had a short, grizzled beard; his nearsightedness gave him the appearance of peering impudently into your face, though he really wasn't that sort of person, at all; rather shy and reticent, indeed. Uncle Joseph was bald and slightly stooped and walked with a limp. Yes— he had broken his leg when a boy and it had lamed him; not badly enough to interfere with his work. He had a friendly smile, though he never had much to say. All that—and plenty more—had Esther contrived about Uncle Joseph.

At the outskirts of unkempt little Magdala, she paused to take a leisurely look at the lake, shimmering in the summerish noon, turned slowly about, and began to saunter back toward Bethsaida.

No—it hadn't been difficult to become Esther, the orphaned niece of Joseph, the lame, near-sighted stone-cutter of Idumea; but the trouble was that in becoming Esther you were losing your hold on Fara! To be Esther you had to leave Fara far behind you; Fara—and everything that pertained to Fara!

She half-closed her eyes and a little shudder swept over her. Fara—and all that belonged to the Fara-personality—had dimmed to the vagueness of a dream. Arabia! Her mother! Ione! And Voldi! Voldi! She tried to recover the sensation of galloping alongside him on a narrow mountain-trail; tried to feel the tight grip of her knees hugging Saidi's hot, rippling withers; tried to smile up into Voldi's laughing eyes; and, failing of it, found herself blinded by sudden tears; tried—with a whimpering little sob—to feel again the caress of Ione's gentle fingers combing her hair. But it was all unreal now, as unreal as if it had happened to someone else and she was reading about it—or making it up. Esther was very lonely, and lost, and homesick for Fara—and frightened! She quickened her steps: she must get back to Hannah. Hannah was real!

It was the first time in her life that she had given any serious thought to the permanent effects of self-deception. Apparently you could deceive other people without suffering much damage, but once you entered upon a determined effort to lie to yourself—about yourself—you were in danger of losing your own personality!

A strict adherence to the truth had never seemed important. Lies were of no significance; unless, of course, they injured someone else. Certainly Arabia had never been scrupulous about truth-telling; nor had the Jews distinguished themselves for any sensitiveness on this subject. How indeed could one do any business at all if required to stick to the truth? Esther recalled that there was a Jewish commandment, written in their ancient law, making it a punishable crime to "bear false testimony against a neighbor," but that felony had very little relation, if any, to the casual untruth invented to implement a sale or save one from an embarrassing predicament. Today it had begun to appear that not only was the truth a form of property; but—what was still more important—it was possible to commit suicide by a long-continued course of self-deception.

Hannah was overjoyed at Esther's return, and deeply touched when the girl impulsively put her arm around her in a surprising display of sincere affection.

"I have good news for you, dear," she exclaimed. "Master David has invited us to come and see his garden; this afternoon, if we will."

To her relief and satisfaction, for Hannah had expected some reluctance, Esther promptly consented to go: indeed, she seemed pleased to go. An hour earlier she might have invented excuses.

*　*　*　*　*　*

Upon their arrival in David's extensive grounds, and after greetings had been exchanged, Deborah—a tall, gaunt spinster of fifty or more—abruptly suggested to Hannah that they stroll in the garden and see what was left of the autumn flowers, though her crisp tone hinted that it was much too late in the season and that the idea had certainly not originated with herself.

This laconic invitation, so pointedly addressed to Hannah, confirmed Esther's surmise that David had planned a private interview. His uneasy frown indicated that his forthright sister might have displayed a little more tact in this connivance; and Esther, unwilling to be thought too dumb to understand his annoyance, flashed a mischievous smile into his eyes. He accepted it with pursed lips and a shrug—and a slow, begrudged grin.

"My sister Deborah," he drawled, "has always believed—with Aristotle—that a straight line is the shortest journey between two points."

"And the safest," added Esther, suddenly sober, as if renouncing all devious ways.

He searched her eyes to make sure of her sincerity, and smiled his appreciation of her evident decision to disarm. They had been slowly following the women at a widening distance. Now David cupped his hand lightly under her elbow and they angled off into the well-kept grove containing a wide variety of trees, most of which Esther had never seen. For something to say, she remarked that it seemed strange to find them growing here.

"My father," replied David, "often traveled in foreign lands. He was greatly interested in trees. Not many of these are native to Galilee." He halted to give her time to look about, and asked, in a tone too craftily casual, "Do you recognize any of them—as of Idumea?"

She frowned impatiently.

"I know nothing whatsoever about Idumea, sir!" The unbridled asperity in her low-pitched voice reproached him for trying to trap her. Wasn't he going to play the game fairly?

Somewhat taken aback by the girl's irritation, David made the additional mistake of murmuring apologetically that he had been misinformed.

"I thought you were an Idumean," he said.

"You did not!" exclaimed Esther, hotly. Then, in a husky tone of entreaty, she asked, "Why can't we be honest with each other? That's why you asked me to come here, Master David. You hoped I might confide in you. You are making it difficult. I am much in need of your counsel—and your friendship. . . . I am lonely—and lost."

He pointed to a rustic seat beside the winding path and they sat down.

"Forgive me, my child," he said, softly. "Now—you tell me as much— or as little—as you want me to know. I shall respect your confidence."

"It may shorten my story, sir, if you tell me how much you already know of it."

David complied. Some eighteen years ago, while a student in Athens, chiefly concerned with contemporary political movements, he had been obliged to inform himself about the unprecedented alliance of the Jews and Arabians who hoped their united strength might discourage a Roman invasion. A royal wedding had been arranged to confirm this pact. Antipas had married the Arabian Princess—and shamefully mistreated her. There was a child, a little girl.

"I never learned her name," David was saying.

"It wouldn't be Esther," she ventured, without looking up.

"Not likely." He pretended to be debating the matter. "Esther is definitely Jewish, and by the time this baby was born her Arabian mother would hardly have wanted any more reminders of her unhappy life in Jewry."

"That is true, sir. My name is Fara." After a lengthy pause she added, "But perhaps you had better continue to call me Esther."

David nodded his approval of that decision. She was much safer in Galilee with a Jewish name, he said.

"By the way, " he continued, "do you want to tell me what brings you here? Surely you have no thought of restoring relations with your father."

She shook her head slowly; and, after some deliberation, said, "I shall tell you—everything, Master David."

And she did. It was a long story, but David did not often break into it with queries or comments. When she had told him about Ione's insistence that she learn Greek, his eyes lighted and he interrupted her to say:

"Excellent! It has been a long time since I have conversed in that beautiful language."

"It will please me, too," she replied; and David smiled happily at her evident relief in abandoning her imperfect Aramaic for the more musical tongue in which she felt at home. From there on, she proceeded with more self-confidence, David watching her lips with delight. The effortless shift to Greek had given the girl a new freedom that added much to her charm.

As she came to the end of her story, however, the old lawyer drew a long face and shook his head.

"No, no, my child!" he protested. "What you have set out to do is utterly impossible! You are very brave, but this is something that no amount of courage can accomplish!"

"Would you counsel me then to break my vow?" There was disappointment and reproach in her query.

"I hope you will not ask me to assist in sending you to certain death!" he muttered.

Esther's eyes widened. David didn't want to be asked to assist. Perhaps that meant that he could—if he wished.

"Please remember, Master David," she said, entreatingly, "I have burned all my bridges to Arabia: I have no home in Jewry: I have sworn to avenge my mother: and that I intend to do. If I should lose my life— well—is it not better for me to die with honor than to live to no purpose at all—unwanted anywhere—an embarrassment to those I love?"

The old man sat for a long time with half-closed eyes, stroking his gray beard. After a while he surprised her by what seemed an abrupt change in their conversation.

"My long-time friend and client, Jairus, informs me that the Tetrarch has recently acquired the entire private library of a bankrupt Corinthian. The scrolls—Greek classics, for the most part—have been long neglected, their owner having spent his recent years in a Roman prison."

Esther had come to attention and was listening with wide eyes and parted lips.

"Perhaps the Tetrarch will want someone to mend the broken scrolls," she said—"and put his library in order."

"Perhaps. We shall see," said David. "I shall inquire of Lysias, the steward."

Deborah and Hannah were approaching.

"Let me see you again," said David—"the day after tomorrow."

*   *   *   *   *   *

Simon had not been home for two whole days now and Hannah was beside herself with anxiety.

At breakfast on the first morning of his absence she had given his taci-

turn brother an opportunity to explain; but Andrew, whose only distinction was a talent for minding his own business, had not gone farther than
to say that Simon had slept on shipboard.

But on the morning of the third day the desperate woman decided to
learn the meaning of it even at the risk of a rebuff. Having brought in their
breakfast, she seated herself opposite Andrew and stared at him until he
reluctantly and briefly lifted his eyes.

"I cannot bear this any longer!" she exclaimed. "Andrew, you must tell
me now what has happened to him!"

Andrew, finishing his cakes and honey, waited until he had swallowed
the last mouthful. Glancing in her general direction, he made what was—
for him—quite an elaborate reply.

"I wish I knew," he said.

"Have I offended him, Andrew?"

"You would know if you had."

"Did Esther have anything to do with it?"

"Better ask her."

"I did."

Andrew grinned a little but exhibited no curiosity about the result
of this inquiry, his silence proclaiming that it was none of his business.
Hannah broke down now and cried. It distressed Andrew. He had never
seen her in tears since the day Abigail died. Pushing back his chair, he
faced her directly with sympathy in his eyes.

"I do not know what troubles him. The fleet goes out every day, same
as always. The fishing has been good, and the weather. There has been no
trouble among the men. My brother attends to his duties. He has little to
say to anyone. His mind is not in his work. He is worried about something."

"And you don't know what?" persisted Hannah, when Andrew seemed
to have ended his surprisingly long speech.

"No; he has not said, and I have not asked him."

"Why don't you?"

"It is not my habit to ask people what they are thinking about."

"But Simon is your brother!"

Simon's brother acknowledged this relationship with a slow nod, and
rose to go. At this, Hannah began weeping again, piteously, and Andrew
resumed his seat, fumbling awkwardly with his knitted cap. At length he
spoke.

"As you know, he has been very fond of old Zebedee's boy John, almost
as if the youngster was his son. A few days ago, Johnny went out into the

country to hear this Carpenter who, they say, has been performing miraculous deeds. You have probably heard strange tales about this man. He
is said to have been healing the sick."

"Pish!" commented Hannah, drying her eyes.

"Of course," agreed Andrew. "Well—Johnny came back and said, in
the presence of all of us, that he had seen the Carpenter heal a paralyzed
arm."

"But you didn't believe it, I hope!" protested Hannah.

"Me? No—I did not believe it; but Simon has not been himself since
Johnny told the story."

"But—surely—Simon wouldn't take any interest in a thing like that!"
Hannah's swollen eyes were wide with astonishment. "Simon—of all
people!"

"Maybe not," said Andrew. "Perhaps he has been fretting about
Johnny. The boy has quit the fleet. He and his brother James have rented
an old boat and are fishing for themselves."

"And Simon hasn't talked about it?"

"Not to me."

"But—what are we going to do, Andrew?"

"We? We aren't going to do anything. You may do whatever you like.
I intend to keep out of it. My brother is an adult, and of sound mind—far
as I know. If he wants any advice from me, he will ask for it." Andrew got
up to go, resolutely this time, and pulled on his fisherman's cap. Hannah
pursued him through the open door and out onto the stoop.

"He can't sleep comfortably on that ship," she said.

"In his present state," rejoined Andrew, "he might not sleep comfortably anywhere." He started down the path.

"Don't fret about it," he flung back. "Simon is big enough to look out
for himself—without anyone's help."

Hannah kept tagging along as far as the gate.

"Easy enough to say, 'Don't fret.' But that s all I have to do, now that
Esther's gone. She left yesterday—to work at the palace."

Andrew absently rattled the gate-latch—and frowned.

"I thought she was decent," he muttered.

"Couldn't she work at the palace—and be decent?"

"Perhaps—for the present," conceded Andrew, "—now that the
Tetrarch and his family are gone. They took most of the servants along."

"Maybe that's why Esther got a job," surmised Hannah. "I hope she
doesn't fall into trouble there. I didn't know it was such a wicked place,
Andrew. Simon delivers fish at the palace every day. Surely, he wouldn't
go there if—"

"My brother is not a rabbi or a policeman. He is a fisherman. Why should he concern himself with the Tetrarch's behavior—so long as he likes fish?" Andrew grinned with knowledge he would not be sharing with Hannah, and went on, "If Simon had to look into the private lives of his customers before selling them fish, he might soon be out of the fish business."

"Rather than have anything to do with such nasty people," snapped Hannah, "I should do just that; go out of the fish business!"

Chuckling a little at this impractical remark, Andrew inquired dryly, as he closed the gate behind him, "What other business would you go into?" And without waiting for a reply, he set off at a brisk walk, for he was starting later than usual and did not want to add the annoyance of his tardiness to his moody brother's frets.

*   *   *   *   *   *

Having given some last-minute instructions to young Samuel, who had been doing his turn as night watchman, Simon prepared to leave, though dawn was barely breaking.

"I expect to be gone all day," he had said. "You will tell Andrew, when he comes, to take over until I return. Tell him to see to it that the palace delivery is made, this afternoon; half the usual order, now that the family is gone."

As he climbed into a dory, he had called back to Samuel, "And tell Thad—or somebody—to go to my house and fetch another blanket for my bunk."

He had had the Cana highway almost to himself for a couple of hours. Nobody was awake in Bethsaida when he passed through. The long, winding hill beyond was deserted. At the broad summit, he paused to survey the landscape gaily dressed in autumn colors. In the area of the great white rock, which dominated the high plateau, the frost-touched grass had been trampled flat by innumerable feet.

The descending road began to veer toward the west. It had been many years since Simon had traversed this neighborhood of small farms and vineyards. He had never been lured by the soil. It was a common jest that men who followed the sea were always chattering about the ease and security of life in the country, declaring that they would some day rent a couple of acres and raise their own food. And often they seemed to be quite in earnest about it. This had always amused Simon, who couldn't imagine a less interesting tool than a hoe. But today the serenity of the countryside made a bid for his turbulent spirit.

Harvest was past, but the farmers were busy with the less urgent affairs of autumn, snugging themselves in for the winter, carrying well-laden baskets of root vegetables from the kitchen-garden to the sod-roofed cellar, the old women gathering herbs and tying them into bunches to be hung up and dried.

On the other side of the highway, a little farther on, three half-grown youngsters were lazily roping wheat-sheaves to the backs of as many shaggy pack-asses. Simon waved a hand to them, but they only stared back. That's the way it was in the country. Their ideas came slowly. Doubtless, if he stood there and waved at these boys for a half-hour, re-flected Simon, they might respond to his salute. It was a dull life; no mistake about that. He wondered how the country people took to the Carpenter's belief that food was less important than flowers.

At the far corner of the next farm, a larger one, father and the boys were on their threshing-floor, beating a knee-deep carpet of barley-sheaves. The mother of the family wielded a much-mended winnowing-fan. The two girls were sweeping the cleaned grain onto a hempen mat.

Simon paused here, turned off the highway, and approached them with a friendly greeting. They were early to work, he said. The women rested, sitting on the ground, and the boys—one of them as tall as his father—leaned on the long handles of their flails.

"We wanted to get as much done as we could," said the gray-thatched farmer, strolling toward Simon. "Not much work being done in these parts just now; everybody scurrying off to listen to this fellow from Naza-reth."

"Where is he today?" inquired Simon. "I should like to see him."

"There's no telling, exactly," said the farmer. "He moves around."

"Yesterday he was about six miles from here," said the oldest boy—"over beyond Hammath."

"Were you there?" asked Simon.

"The family went over in the afternoon," said the farmer. "I heard him talk, about a week ago, over here on the hill. Didn't think much of it. He was saying we should love our enemies. I don't hold with that kind of talk. Though I'm not saying he isn't a good speaker. You can hardly take your eyes off him."

"Big crowd yesterday?" Simon asked the young man.

"Bigger every day!" bragged the youth, as if he were part of the show. "Nothing ever like it in this country!"

"Tell me about it; won't you?" said Simon, squatting on his heels.

At this, they gathered about him, and sat, apparently eager to talk. It was plain on their faces that the subject was already well-worn—but by no means worn out. They all contributed to the conversation. Very strange doings. Very strange talk. They were agreed on that. As for the particulars, the testimony failed, in some respects, to add up.

"The trouble is," explained the woman, "the crowd is so big you can't get close enough to see rightly what's going on."

"I saw him cure an old man who couldn't hear," put in the youngest boy. "He danced up and down, he was so glad."

"But you didn't know whether the old man was deaf—or not," cautioned his father. "He might have been putting it on."

"He claimed he was deaf—and now he could hear," declared the lad, doggedly.

"All old people have more or less trouble with their hearing," commented his mother.

"And sometimes they can hear better than other times," added his little sister. "Father's like that."

"Never mind," mumbled her mother.

"But the sick woman on the cot," said the tall boy. "She really was sick. She wasn't putting it on: I'm sure of that!"

"Yes, sir," confirmed his brother, "she got up and walked away after Jesus spoke to her."

"But not very lively," demurred their mother. "She leaned on her son's arm; pretty heavily too."

That's the way it would be, thought the older girl—if she hadn't walked for a long time.

"Where do all these people come from?" Simon wanted to know.

"Everywhere; seems like," said the farmer. "A wool-buyer was telling me, last week, that he saw whole families he knew from as far away as Ramah and Shunem and Nain. Brought their tents along, and a couple of milch-goats."

"Plenty of people from Nazareth too, I suppose," said Simon, "if that's where he lives."

"No; funny thing about that," replied the farmer. "Very few from Nazareth, they say. If he's such a great one, you'd think—"

"Maybe his own folks got used to seeing him do strange things," suggested the youngest boy.

"Home folks never give much heed when their neighbors do something extra good, like fine wood-carving—or rug-weaving—or beautiful singing," said the mother. "They think that because they know a person, and grew up with him—he can't be very much."

"That's a fact," declared her husband. "Lots of country folks sneer at

what's going on around them, and praise what's going on in Bethsaida;
and the people in Bethsaida laugh at their own town, and envy the people
in Cana, and—"

Simon laughed a little and said he supposed the people in Cana thought
everything was livelier in Jericho—and that Jericho wanted to see the
more interesting sights in Jerusalem.

"I'd like to see Jerusalem myself," murmured the tall boy.

"Now you take our girl Judith here." Her mother laid a brown hand on
her elder daughter's arm.

Judith, apparently suspecting what was coming, lowered her eyes,
smiled shyly, and shook her head a little, as her mother went on:

"She plays the harp better than you'll hear it anywhere! And a poor old
harp it is, too, that's been in my family for three generations. But do you
suppose the people around here think anything of her playing? No, sir;
you have to go to the city—to hear a harp played."

"I should like to hear you play, Judith," said Simon, to which the girl's
cheeks flushed prettily.

"No time for that today," said her father, turning about toward the
threshing-floor.

"I told her to take her old harp along—and play for the people—when
the Carpenter isn't speaking," said her mother.

Simon politely approved of this as a good idea. They reluctantly ambled
back to their tasks. He waved a farewell and resumed his westward journey.
So—the people of Nazareth hadn't been very much impressed. This
wasn't a good sign. There must be something shaky about this business,
reflected Simon. The family he had just met was not of one mind in respect to these strange occurrences. It was still a matter of debate with
them whether the Carpenter of Nazareth was a healer or a fraud. Maybe
some light would be shed on that problem today. Simon hoped so. He
hoped the Nazarene would turn out to be merely a glib talker, with a
talent for making sick people feel encouraged; for surely the world was a
much more reliable institution if nobody was playing tricks with it, not
even for the benefit of a few. And—as he trudged along, moodily intent
on the road—Simon wondered whether the girl Judith, with the big,
solemn eyes and the wistful smile, was really a harpist. Not very likely, he
thought.

*   *   *   *   *   *

For the past hour the highway had been receiving more and more traffic
from the tributary roads and lanes; all manner of traffic; high-wheeled

Peter Watches the Conglomeration of Misery

For the past hour the highway had been receiving more
and more traffic from the tributary roads and lanes; all
manner of traffic; high-wheeled market-wagons filled
with people of all ages, elderly couples in donkey-carts,
here and there a garden-barrow occupied by a frail and
feeble old woman or a pale and wizened lad, pushed
by an earnest-faced young farmer. Occasionally a cot
joined the procession bearing the prone figure of an
emaciated, half-grown girl or a crippled old man with
pain in his eyes. Clumps of people on foot, by the
dozen, by the score, overtook and passed the sick ones.
Every path, every open gate, every cross-road fed them
into the highway.

market-wagons filled with people of all ages, elderly couples in donkey-carts, here and there a garden-barrow occupied by a frail and feeble old woman or a pale and wizened lad, pushed by an earnest-faced young farmer. Occasionally a cot joined the procession bearing the prone figure of an emaciated, half-grown girl or a crippled old man with pain in his eyes. Clumps of people on foot, by the dozen, by the score, overtook and passed the sick ones. Every path, every open gate, every cross-road fed them into the highway.

Simon had found himself wishing that the Carpenter would be soon exposed as an ordinary man who had nothing much to work with but a winning voice, a confident manner, and the ability to make people listen to him—and trust him. But as he surveyed these sorry crews of hopeful burden-bearers, he began to wish, with all his heart, that something could be done for them. If the Carpenter was a fraud, this conglomeration of misery was indeed a tragic spectacle. Maybe the Carpenter didn't realize what a responsibility he had taken on. If he didn't it was high time he found out!

It was a pitiful sight. Why couldn't this Nazarene have stayed in his carpenter-shop? What was the good of stirring up hope that couldn't have any outcome but a cruel disappointment? These wretched ones had learned to bear their galling loads. Most of them had done all their crying, and calluses had formed to ease the pain of their yokes. Now they would lay their burdens down at this Carpenter's feet! What monstrous cruelty if—after so great hope—they must strap on their heavy packs again and plod wearily home, broken-hearted!

A half-mile east of Hammath the highway divided, the road to the right proceeding to the village and on toward Cana, the left fork bearing southward through the Province of Samaria and onward to Jerusalem. In the triangle at the parting of the ways, a small encampment was breaking. The service tents were already down and being loaded onto the pack-train. The master tent, a beautiful thing of white and blue, was in process of dismantling. A half-dozen fine horses, expensively caparisoned, were restlessly waiting their riders who now emerged from the sagging tent.

Full of curiosity, Simon slowed his pace and candidly stared. The leader of the party was a mere youngster, certainly not more than eighteen, and his companions were youthful too, though not so young as he. They were extravagantly dressed. Simon drew off to the side of the highway, sat on the ledge of the stone-walled well, and studied this pageantry at his leisure. That it was a company of nobles he had no doubt. Presently, to his surprise, he saw the young master of the group point toward him and give an order to a servant, who made off at once to the well. Simon's brow furrowed as he saw the man coming. He was quite sure he was within his rights to rest at the well.

"Do you live in this neighborhood, sir?"

The servant, a tall, bearded man of Simon's age had bowed respectfully before asking the question in a quality of Aramaic that was spoken in Judaea.

Simon shook his head and replied, "Bethsaida."

"But that is not far away," continued the servant. "Would you perhaps know anything of this Carpenter who has stirred up so much excitement?" His arm swept the congested highway.

"Not much," said Simon. "I saw and heard him a few days ago, and I am hoping to see him again today."

"Would you object to having a word with my master, sir?"

"Who is your master?"

"Joseph—the Prince of Arimathaea," said the servant, proudly.

Simon rose now and followed. It was little enough he knew about the small but fertile Principality of Arimathaea, up north beyond Ramah, which had been ceded to the fabulous Hyrcanus and his descendants many generations ago, in consideration of some long-forgotten favor to northern Jews. Whenever Arimathaea was mentioned the word suggested wealth. "Rich as an Arimathaean" was a trite phrase which the Galileans used without examining it more closely than many another simile such as, "Tricky as an Arab," or "Wise as a serpent."

The beautiful tent was down now and the swarming servants were folding it with care. The vanguard of the pack-train was moving off down the Jerusalem road. The young Prince was standing by his white horse in evidently playful conversation with his friends. He was a handsome youth with a ready smile and a gracious manner. Simon was favorably impressed and doffed his forebodings about the interview.

Courteously requesting him to wait a moment, the servant approached his master and made a brief report in low tones, after which he beckoned to Simon who advanced rather diffidently and removed his cap.

"My friend," said the Prince, looking up at the big Galilean who towered over the lot of them, "we are curious about this great multitude and the man they are said to be seeking. They tell us that he speaks to great crowds and heals many sick ones. Noting your extraordinary height, it occurred to us that you might have been able to hear and see what has been going on."

"I would that I had more to tell you, sire," said Simon. "I heard the man speak.He has a strange voice. The people hang on his words as a sailor overboard in a storm clings to a rope."

"Good!" approved the Prince to his companions. "The fellow has some imagination." Returning to Simon, he said, "Perhaps you are a sailor yourself."

"A fisherman, sire." Simon smiled briefly, and went on, "No matter what he is saying, the people hardly breathe for fear of missing something; yet they are simple words."

"Such as what?" asked the Prince, interested now.

"He wants people to be kind to one another: that's about all," said Simon. "Everyone is to be kind and helpful, all the way up and down from the pauper to the—" He hesitated, and the Prince, frowning a little, crisply provided the obvious word. It was evident that he was annoyed His voice was challenging as he went on.

"So—this fellow is trying to make the people restless! Everybody is to be generous, eh? The pauper is as good as the Prince, eh? Is that it?"

"Not if I heard rightly, sire." There was a stiffening dignity in Simon's voice now. His frown deepened. He didn't like the arrogant tone of this spoiled youngster. After all—he hadn't arranged this interview; nor was he on trial. "Quite the contrary," he continued, courageously, "the Carpenter wants peace among the people. If a man is badly used by his oppressors, let him find his happiness inside himself."

"A good thought." There was a touch of mockery in the Prince's voice, though he had mended his temper somewhat. "And how does a man go about it—to find happiness inside himself?"

"He leaves off fretting about the things he does not have," explained Simon, "and he gives less heed to caring for the few things he does have. Thus he is freed from worry lest thieves should make off with his small possessions."

"And after the fellow says that," sneered the Prince, "he probably passes his cap through the crowd, inviting them to pay him for advising them to have nothing." They all chuckled a little at this cynical gibe—all but Simon who remarked quietly, "He has no cap, sire." There was a moment of silent embarrassment here, Simon having inadvertently flavored the talk with a bit of disconcerting sincerity.

"How about these strange deeds?" demanded the Prince.

"One hears differing opinions, sire," said Simon. "Some claim to have seen miracles performed, others try to explain them, still others doubt them."

"Our servant says you are now on your way to hear him again. Does that

mean that you yourself believe him honest? Surely you would not make
the journey if you considered him an out-and-out mountebank!"

"I am hoping to find out, sire," murmured Simon. Observing that the
Prince's friends were growing restless, he added respectfully, "May I go
now?"

The Prince shrugged and made a negligent gesture as to say it was of no
concern to him whether the big, burly fisherman ambled off at once or
remained here for the rest of his life. He laid a jeweled hand on the pommel of his saddle.

"Just a moment!" he said. "One thing more! We are advised that a
home-made, self-appointed prophet has recently been gathered in by our
good friend, your Tetrarch, for predicting the advent of an avenger who
is to upset thrones, strip the wealthy, free the slaves, and put all the
riffraff on horseback. Do the people hereabouts think that this wonder-
worker is out on such an errand?"

"It is quite impossible, sire!" declared Simon. "Surely no one who had
heard him speak could have that opinion. So far as I have learned, the
Carpenter has no quarrel with the rich; though I think he pities them."

"Pities them!" exclaimed the Prince, while the others grinned incredulously. "What impertinence! Who does this wandering beggar think he
is—to be pitying his betters?"

Simon ventured no immediate comment on this smug remark, but
his lip curled to match a frown that had a good deal of scorn in it. The
Prince was quick to notice this irritation, and prodded it.

"If you do not object to the question, my massive friend, how do you
yourself feel toward the rich? You are obviously not a man of property.
Tell me truly: do you too pity the rich?" The raw taunt was stirring Simon
to anger.

"No, sire," he answered, staring fearlessly into the young man's eyes,
"I do not pity the rich. I envy them, as they expect me to do. I peer
through their high fences and lament that I do not have their great
possessions, for this pleases them." Simon's voice rose and rasped as he
continued recklessly, "Whenever we poor cease envying the rich, we will
be punished for robbing them of their highest satisfaction!"

The Prince had mounted now. He rose in his stirrups to shout:

"That is the most impudent thing that was ever said in our presence!"

"Well"—growled Simon, sullenly—"you asked for it."

"In our country, Fisherman, you would get thirty-nine lashes for that!"

"Aye, sire—and in my country too," retorted Simon; and because he
now had nothing to lose by further frankness he added, "The great ones

are the same everywhere, I am told. They face the truth with a bull-whip."

"Be off with you!" shouted the Prince, raising his riding-crop.

"No—no—Joseph!" muttered the mounted friend at his side.

The Prince lashed his horse. They bounded away. Flushed with rage, Simon watched them galloping down the road. Never had he felt such bitter contempt for a fellow creature. Quite a courageous youngster, this Prince, when surrounded by his fine friends and a score of armed guards. Had he been alone, he would have been meek as a lamb. Simon wished he could have had the Prince all to himself for a few minutes. No—he would not have hurt the boy badly. He would have been satisfied to take the insolent brat by his beautifully curled hair—and fold him over the ledge of the old well—and spank him; a thorough spanking; a spanking to be remembered; one to make up for many a spanking he should have had earlier. Simon was sore. It had never been his habit to covet other men's property or privileges. He had nothing against the rich. Until now. Now he despised them! All of them! They were all alike! To hell with them! All of them!

He had trudged toward the Hammath highway now and had joined the pilgrimage. Looking across the field to the Jerusalem road, he observed that the Prince's party had halted for a parley. After a rather lengthy colloquy, they wheeled about, galloped back to the junction, and came bearing down upon the crowded highway. The people screamed and rushed to the sides of the road for safety as the gay riders ploughed a wide furrow through them. Everybody was for saving his own skin in this frantic rout. Old people were trampled. Carts were upset. Children were crying. Shouting with laughter, the princely cavalcade swept on.

Simon stood still and watched the shameless scene, his every muscle taut with impotent rage, his big fists clenched.

"Men on horses!" he shouted aloud. "Brave men on horses!"

*   *   *   *   *   *

The somnolent village of Hammath had swollen to a city of five thousand and was adding to its population. Every grass-grown path was as a sleepy stream that had suddenly become a river at flood.

The huge crowd had congregated on a harvested field some distance north of the main highway. On the outskirts of the densely packed multitude, venders pursued a busy trade with huge baskets of smoked fish, wheaten and barley rolls, sweetmeats and sun-cured figs swarming with flies, for which they found ready customers among the stragglers who were too far away from the point of interest to see what was happening.

The Prince and his party had ridden up close against the rear of the throng, apparently impatient to have been detained from proceeding through to the front where the Carpenter stood. The whole affair was a lark, a country circus, and the management should have been pleased to announce, "We are honored to have with us today His Highness Joseph, the Prince of Arimathaea. Clear the way for His Highness and his retinue! We welcome you, sire!"

The Carpenter continued speaking in a quiet voice, inaudible at this distance. Laughing loudly, the princely party urged their horses forward until the foam from their champed bits flecked the shoulders of men and women who were cupping their ears to listen.

"Make way!" shouted the mounted guards. "Way—for the Prince of Arimathaea."

The people turned their heads and scowled angrily, but did not budge.

"Hi! You! Fisherman!" yelled one of the Prince's friends, as Simon moved into the pack, "clear a road for the Prince!" But Simon did not reply, nor did he turn about to face them. Finding it impossible to hear anything, he circled the throng and discovered a spot nearer to the front where an amazingly large colony of cots and carts bearing the sick awaited the end of the Carpenter's address. A shaggy young farmer, standing by a bed on which an emaciated old woman lay shielding her sunken eyes against the sun with a bony hand, glanced up at Simon and grinned a rustic greeting.

"Your mother, maybe?" whispered Simon.

"Grandmother," replied the young farmer.

"Came to be healed?"

"She hopes so."

"Do you think there's anything in it?"

"There'd better be!" muttered the farmer, truculently, pointing to the quarter-acre of sick and crippled. "If he's a fake he'll he stoned!"

"Has he been speaking long?" asked Simon.

"Long enough. Granny is tired waiting."

"What's her trouble?"

The farmer guarded his voice as he replied, "Old age."

"Think the Carpenter can cure old age?"

"No—but Granny does. She's a little weak in the head."

Simon edged gradually into the rim of the crowd. By listening intently he could hear snatches of the Carpenter's talk. But it was difficult. What with the confusion of the people pushing in from the rear, the moans of the sick, and the crying of the babies, Simon had to be content with broken phrases. But it was a haunting voice, a magic voice that stilled and soothed and comforted you even though you couldn't hear all the words.

From what Simon could make of it, a man could have a secret life with God. Once he determined to find happiness within himself, he reached out for a strength greater than his own . . . Like a babe, creeping, he longed to rise and walk . . . lifts his small hand . . . is gripped by a stronger hand . . . having learned to walk with God . . . he wants to talk with God. Too often, men try to talk with God . . . only in the temple. . . . Talk with Him alone. . . . His voice more clear when you are alone with Him . . . a private league with God . . . a secret life with God . . . an understanding with Him . . . you and God alone . . . in your closet . . . closed door . . . He will listen . . . He will bless you.

Some short-statured person was digging a sharp elbow into Simon's back. He turned about and looked down into the contorted face of a woman with a little girl of five in her arms. The child was blind.

"Please!" entreated the woman in a whisper. "Help me to get closer! You are big and strong. You must help me!"

"Stay where you are—behind me," said Simon. "When the time comes, I'll do what I can."

The Carpenter was talking about doing things for others. That, too, was better done in secret. . . . When you make gifts . . . no trumpet. . . . A secret . . . so secret your own left hand does not know. Only God will see . . . only God will know . . . but He will bless you.

There was a general stirring in the great congregation when the Carpenter had stopped speaking. Now, according to his custom, he would receive the sick ones. The crowd pushed and shoved for a better view. The people were not very considerate of one another. The weak and timid were elbowed out of the way. Even among the very ill ones on their beds, the rivalry of the bearers was rude beyond belief. Simon wished he was up there in front to improve their manners. He expected and hoped that Jesus would rebuke the importunate. But, after all, they couldn't be much blamed, he thought. People couldn't be polite when it was a matter of life or death for a loved one.

The little woman behind him was growing desperate. She was crying hysterically. Bidding her follow him closely, Simon began edging his way forward, but it was quite impossible for her to make any use of his intervention. Other people crowded in behind the big man and pushed her roughly aside. There seemed only one practical thing to do now. Simon would have to carry the child himself. Turning, he held out his long arms, and the woman, tearfully grateful, relinquished her burden.

It was an arduous journey forward through the solid mass of seemingly immovable people. Simon entreated, pushed, scolded, shouldered, begged, shouted, as he pressed on.

"This child is blind!" he announced, in his big, booming voice. "Let me through! Please let me pass!"

And now—now—at last—he stood face to face with the strange man of Nazareth, close enough to have touched him. By comparison with Simon's height and bulk, the Carpenter was of slight physique; but something about him, emanating from him, made him a commanding figure. Simon sensed it, and felt inferior. In point of years, the man was his junior. Every other way considered, Simon felt himself a mere awkward, overgrown boy. He looked down into a pair of tranquil, steady, earnestly inquiring eyes. They held him fast; they brightened with a friendly smile, almost as if two long-time companions were meeting after a separation. The Carpenter's face was pale. Tiny beads of perspiration showed on his forehead, for he was tired, and the day was hot.

It was such a gentle gesture that it seemed like a caress when Jesus laid his hand lightly upon the little girl's eyes. The child had been frightened by all the confusion and had been holding herself rigidly, hugging her arms to her breast, as if to ward off a blow. At the touch of Jesus' hand, she relaxed and drew a babyish sigh of relief and reassurance. Simon's eyes suddenly swam blindingly as Jesus' forearm rested on his own. It was a strange sensation. He knew now what it was that had suddenly soothed the child and freed her of her fears.

Jesus was praying. He had closed his eyes, and was praying in a soft voice barely above a whisper. His prayer was made to his "Father," and it was as if they two were closeted together in some secret place. In a tone of intimate companionship and confidence he asked his Father to give this little one her sight, for it was through no fault of hers that she could not see. Then—and there was a note of sadness and longing in his voice—he prayed that all men everywhere, groping in the shadows, might be led into the bright sunshine of his Father's love. Then—and this stirred Simon deeply—he prayed for all those who, now and in days to come, would lead the blind into the presence of the Eternal Light.

Simon thought he couldn't bear it—when it happened. He gasped involuntarily and stifled a sob. The incredible thing had happened! It was impossible—but it had actually happened! Jesus had gently moved his hand from the child's eyes and his finger-tips touched the damp little ringlets on her forehead. Now she had slowly raised her wondering eyes to his—and smiled. Then, turning her head, she gazed bewilderedly into Simon's face; and, seeing his tears, her own little eyes overflowed.

Jesus was turning aside now to speak to a man on crutches. Simon tarried, trying hard to speak some word of gratitude. Glancing toward him, Jesus nodded his head and smiled companionably, as to say he understood.

A low murmur of astonishment swept the crowd as Simon turned about with the child hugged tightly in his arms. She was crying softly now, for she was frightened. Her mother, shrilly calling, "She is my child! Oh— let me go to my baby!" finally made herself heard, and was pulled, pushed, half-carried by the excited people around her. She was much too overwrought to thank Simon—even with a smile—when he gently placed the little girl in her hungry arms.

Suffocated by his emotion, and still half-blinded by his tears, Simon was forcing his way through the throng—now standing transfixed, breathless, and on tiptoe—in anticipation of another marvel, when a hand clutched his sleeve. He looked down into the sober, white face of the Prince of Arimathaea.

"Tell me, Fisherman," demanded the Prince, huskily, "was that child really blind?"

"Aye, sire," said Simon—"and now she can see!"

The Prince held tightly to the Big Fisherman's sleeve, his wide, baffled eyes questing more information, but Simon tugged away and pressed on toward the outer air. Circling the preoccupied multitude, he made for the rear—and the highway. He walked as a man in a dream, as one suddenly transported into a different world. A strange assurance of security possessed him—and a curious sense of peace that was quite beyond his understanding.

8

LYSIAS was flattered and bewildered to have so gracious a note from that haughty old Sadducee, David Ben-Zadok.

A bright young Jewess, well versed in the classics, orphaned and in need of employment (wrote David), might be available to make repairs on the dilapidated Corinthian library recently acquired by His Highness the Tetrarch. The letter was written in Greek, which still further pleased the steward with implications that he was a person of some culture.

But just why this crusty old lawyer, who had made no bones about his contempt for the Tetrarch, should show any concern about the reconditioning of these valuable but unsightly scrolls was not clear. One thing was sure: the old man hadn't bothered to offer the suggestion from any love of Antipas. Maybe he wanted an excuse to have a peek at that library himself: he was known to be something of an antiquarian. Lysias gently fingered the old scar on his ear, an involuntary aid to deep meditation, and reflected that there must be more in this situation than met the eye.

But—no matter what might be the crafty Sadducee's motive in proposing a remedy for these dreadful scrolls, it would be a great relief to the steward if, upon his master's return from Rome in the spring, he might be shown this costly collection in better dress; for it had been Lysias himself who had recommended and negotiated the purchase, and the Tetrarch had been noisily dissatisfied.

Much embarrassed by the shabbiness of the old books, Lysias had tried to impress His Highness with the importance of their great antiquity. Digging deep into the most ill-conditioned of the wicker hampers, he had brought up a mildewed scroll and held it toward Antipas who wrinkled his nose and put his hands behind him.

"This scroll, sire," Lysias had announced in a tone of reverence, "was written by Aristotle. It is titled, *The Directions and Names of the Winds.*

I do not mean, sire," continued Lysias, "that this is a scrivener's repro-
duction of the book. This is the original—done by the hand of the master, himself!"

"Well—whoever did it," grumbled Antipas, "it stinks. And I don't
want it put any place where I have to look at it." Then, noting the steward's chagrin, the Tetrarch had added, "I daresay some people would be
proud to have a mummified cat of Aristotle's—with a gold collar—set
with emeralds—perched on the mantel." Turning away, he had sauntered
toward the balcony window where, pausing, he had laughed aloud.

"And after they'd had Aristotle's cat on their mantel for a score of
years," he called back to Lysias, "some learned expert, with great knowledge of dead cats, would come along and say, 'Hell!—that cat never
belonged to Aristotle! Much more recent! Besides—Aristotle hated cats!
But he never so much as kicked this cat! It isn't a half-century old!' "

"What is my lord's pleasure, then, in regard to the scrolls?" Lysias had
inquired, meekly.

"Box them up again. Keep them in a dry place where they will suffer
no further decay. Some day, perhaps, we will have them repaired."

Lysias was going to feel more comfortable when the Corinthian scrolls
were restored. Quite aside from his responsibility for their extravagant
purchase he had a sentimental interest in them, for he too was a Corinthian and the same Roman raid that had despoiled his home and enslaved
him at twenty had likewise brought disaster to their neighbors of the
House of Timotheus, a wealthy ship-owner and generous patron of
the arts.

The Timotheus family and their rich possessions had been ruthlessly
disposed of. Timotheus himself had been put to death, his uncommonly
beautiful wife had committed suicide, their two elder sons, Leander and
Philetus, schoolmates of Lysias, had been taken to serve as scribes and
accountants in the office of the Prefect of Achaea. A younger son, Demetrius, who had already won some local renown as an athlete, was carried
off to Rome in chains, too savagely rebellious to be of much good to anybody looking for a servant. Lysias had often wondered what became of the
handsome, reckless Demetrius; beaten to death, perhaps, for insubordination.

The Roman looters hadn't known what to do with the books. There
was an enormous quantity of these scrolls, and not a man among the
invaders knew enough about literature to identify the extremely valuable
writings and give them special care. The books had been stored in a damp
cellar, and much of the writing on the rotted papyrus was presently in-

decipherable; but, regardless of their physical condition, many of these scrolls were historic treasures. Think of it!—to own a book written by Aristotle! In his own handwriting!

Of course, reflected Lysias, you couldn't expect Antipas to have much reverence for the old scrolls. Antipas was a Roman, and Rome had no veneration for the Past. Let the dreamy Greeks attend to the rotted scrolls—and the tombs—and the epitaphs.

The old Sadducee's note was answered forthwith, Lysias obsequiously thanking the eminent David Ben-Zadok for the great kindness tendered his master, the Tetrarch. And he would be glad to see the young person about the scrolls at her early convenience.

Lysias had spoken the truth. He was glad over the prospect of having some more attractive company than the kitchen afforded. The Tetrarch's palace could be a very lonely institution when the Family was abroad. By experience the steward had learned that the less he mingled with the servants the better account he could give of his stewardship upon his lord's return. On occasions he had shown himself friendly with the gardeners and vintners, only to encourage their laziness and disobedience. As for the kitchen crew, he had discovered that any playfulness in that department would certainly be paid off in impudence and disrespect.

The new employee would rate a higher classification on account of her learning. The servants themselves would understand that without being told. Lysias would invite this girl to have her meals with him. He hoped she would be comely, though that was almost too much to expect if she was—as old David said—well versed in the classics. Pretty girls didn't know anything. Indeed, the really beautiful ones were forthright fools; all but Salome, of course. Salome was a deep one. Lysias worshipped her. And he was afraid of her, too. Once, when Salome had had too much wine, she had encouraged Lysias to kiss her. She had managed the kiss and it had left Lysias dizzy and weak in the knees. Then she had savagely slapped him on the mouth with the back of her hand. The huge jewels in her rings had bloodied his lips. Salome had laughed. She enjoyed rough play. She wasn't punishing him for offending her. Quite to the contrary, she had been delighted with his caresses. But the sight of pain and the scent of warm blood gave her a queer little thrill, she said, while repairing his wounds.

Sometimes the Tetrarch, too, was confined to his rooms for a few days while the cuts on his face were healing. On these occasions, only old Glaucus, the ex-butler, was permitted to minister to His Highness. Lysias surmised that Glaucus was the repository for many a secret, his suspicion being based mostly on the animal-like ferocity of Herodias' hatred for him.

Too, there was a tell-tale quality to the old fellow's impudence. Herodias couldn't be blamed for despising him. Shamelessly trading on the strangle-hold he apparently had on the Tetrarch, Glaucus could be found on warm autumn afternoons in the most comfortable chair in the sunniest corner of the patio, with a tankard of wine at his elbow and a fat, elderly terrier asleep at his feet—as if he had every right to all the luxuries that the establishment afforded. This type of impertinence could mean only one thing, according to Lysias: Glaucus knew something about Antipas, and Herodias guessed what it was. And it was making a haggard, sharp-tongued, short-tempered old shrew of her. Sometimes a whole week would pass in which Herodias and Salome frankly avoided one another, though they both took pains to be polite in the presence of the servants.

Some day, reflected Lysias, as he sanded and sealed his letter to David, some day there was going to be quite a lot of trouble here at the palace; plenty—and plenty more—of trouble. . . . There would be an eruption of the Volcano Herodias—and somebody would get hurt.

*   *   *   *   *   *

Life at the palace was not only endurable; it was pleasant and interesting. Esther's relationships were quickly and comfortably defined. Lysias was disappointed, but not disgruntled, when she declined his special hospitality by explaining that it would make her unhappy if favors were extended to her which made the others envious. She also imputed to him a wealth of high-minded gallantry that was quite too nebulous for assessment; but made such a favorable impression that Lysias spent a whole afternoon conducting her through the palace; ordered the furniture unshrouded in the great banquet-hall, and invited her to sit in His Highness' tall, gold-plated, throne-like chair where she projected a brief, unspoken query to the King of Arabia: "Do you still think it's impossible?"

Her appearance in the kitchen, ready to make friends but not over-eager to the point of condescension, instantly gave her top rating. Claudia stated the situation neatly when she declared, after Esther—having carried her own dishes—had returned to her work, "I like her! If she was only a little better than me, we would probably hate each other; no? . . . But she is so very much better than me that we don't need to hate each other."

Work on the Corinthian scrolls was fascinating; like a game to play. Esther was not wholly unfamiliar with the task. The old books that Zendi had picked up in Petra had required repairs. You carefully unrolled the long, narrow strip of papyrus, detached it—whole or in pieces—from the spools, weighted it down on the library floor; and, wherever it was broken, pasted it together. If the text had been damaged badly, you copied as much as was legible and inserted the patch, with an editor's note explaining how much was missing. Then you sanded and scraped the moldy old spools, down to the bare wood, and redecorated them in black and gold.

Sometimes the girls came up from the kitchen and helped hold the strips of papyrus in place for splicing. Lysias frequently drifted in to express approval.

On the morning of Esther's third day at the palace, Claudia remarked, after the breakfast things had been cleared away, that she must now go out to the prison—"and feed my wild man."

"Wild man!" echoed Esther. "Are you not afraid?"

"No-no-no! That was what you call a joke! He is not wild: he just looks wild—with shaggy hair—and bony—like a starved cat. It is because he does not eat. And he is very sad. I fear he will die—if he does not eat."

"Why is he in prison?" inquired Esther.

"Ah—I don't know." Claudia waved a shapely armed salute to her own disinterest in the matter. "He talked too much, maybe; no?"

"He is a prophet," assisted Anna, without conviction. "He says the world is coming to an end."

"And for that he is locked up?" asked Esther, apparently unconcerned.

"There was more to it than that," explained Murza. "He sees the rulers overthrown, and the Empire smashed, and the poor made rich, and—"

"That's right," put in Claudia. "That's what he says. I've heard him! All hell's going to break loose! . . . How would you like to take him his breakfast, Esther? Then you could hear him for yourself. And perhaps he will eat for you: you are so very pretty. You need not be afraid of him. He will not harm you."

Esther pretended reluctance; hoped he was well guarded.

"Guarded?" laughed Claudia. "A tough legionary from the fort was in charge of him for a day, but he hasn't been seen since. He is on a big spree, no doubt. But the prisoner is well locked in, and there are no others in the jail to help him escape."

Assuming Esther's consent to feed the prisoner, Claudia had been preparing the breakfast-tray, making an appetizing arrangement of a plate of red apples, a dish of berries, a smoked perch and several small barley-loaves.

"Here you are," she said—"and here is the key to the prison door. You open the front door and there is a small corridor. The cell is the first one. There is a barred window in the door. You pass the food through the bars. Don't try to make love to him. It's no good. He is cold."

"For once," called Murza, from the pantry, "Claudia speaks the truth. "It's no use to make love to the man. It has been tried—by experts."

A startling "Hush!" broke in on Murza's malicious comment, presumably offered by the sober Jewess, Anna.

"Her Highness," explained Claudia, naïvely, "is restless and lonely. You never saw her; no? . . ." And when Esther had shaken her head, Claudia sighed and remarked in a confidential half-whisper, "Her Highness does not like to grow old. But—who does? . . . Come—let me show you the way."

Beyond the circular carriage-court a narrow path led through a trellised arbor toward a sturdy stone structure some two hundred yards distant. Having given minute directions, Claudia returned to the house and Esther proceeded on her errand. Her heart quickened as she reached the low wall that bounded the prison area. She wondered whether John, the Baptizer, would recognize her. There were broad stone seats inset in the wall, doubtless for the convenience of sentries. Depositing the tray on one of the seats nearest the entrance, Esther inserted the huge key and was trying unsuccessfully to turn it in the obstinate lock when a resonant voice deep in the prison startled her with the suggestion, "The key is crooked. Bear down on it—and a little to the left."

There was no mistaking the identity of that haunting voice. Laboring with the protesting key, she pressed her weight hard against the massive door and it grudgingly opened.

"Over here, my daughter," called the voice. "You are a stranger here."

They faced each other at the barred window and peered through the gloom.

"It's you!" she murmured.

"Did we not have an appointment to meet here?"

"It's so dark! You will be ill."

"I do miss the sunshine; that is true."

"You wouldn't try to run away if I gave you your breakfast outside?"

"That might get you into trouble."

"But—there's no one at the palace who would know—or care—provided you made no attempt to escape." Recovering the rusty key from the main door, Esther opened the cell and John came out shielding his cavernous eyes against the unaccustomed light. They sat down on the broad stone seat, with the tray between them.

"Tell me; where all have you been?" He ate hungrily, but listened intently while she talked of her experiences as a solitary tramp on the way to Tiberias.

"And have you seen him of whom I told you?" asked John, eagerly.

"No—but I have heard of him. On the day I arrived, a young fisherman who befriended me told his shipmates about a strange Carpenter who healed diseases and spoke words of comfort to the people, gently admonishing them to bear their own and others' burdens."

"Gently?"

"I could hardly believe, sir, that this Carpenter was the one of whom you spoke." She hesitated here, wishing she had not ventured so far upon a subject of which she knew so little. "Perhaps I misunderstood the young fisherman—or perhaps I had misunderstood you. I had thought of him as a frowning man with a stern voice—on an errand of vengeance. Apparently that is a mistake."

"Tell me more, daughter!" he demanded earnestly.

With that, Esther reviewed all she could remember of the report made by the dreamy young fisherman. The Carpenter had spoken with a strangely soothing voice, seemingly not of this world. No—there had been no talk of divine retribution, no threats of doom; indeed, no scolding at all. The man had urged the people to find their happiness within themselves, seeing they would never be free of their enslavement to foreign masters.

"And—no talk at all about the mighty being thrown from their seats—and the exaltation of the poor?"

Esther shook her head. After an uncertain moment, she said, "I shall go and hear him for myself. I am sure I can get permission to leave the palace for a day or two. If the man is not too far away—"

"Do that!" entreated John. "Find out what manner of man he is! Then —come and tell me." He rose and marched toward his cell. Esther turned the big key.

"It hurts me to do this," she said, softly.

*　　*　　*　　*　　*　　*

It was noon when she reached the cottage in Bethsaida. With a cry of happy surprise, Hannah ran to meet her at the gate. They embraced each other with tenderness.

"You came home!" exulted Hannah. "I hope they have not mistreated you."

No—they had not mistreated her, and she would be going back to her work tomorrow. But now—she was on a special errand; the strangest of errands.

Over the dining-table—for Hannah had insisted on preparing their luncheon—Esther told the story of the hermit and his gruesome predictions; and his queries about the Carpenter.

"Everyone seems to be excited about him," said Hannah. "Last night the neighbors were saying that he was leaving Hammath, and heading this way."

"I wonder you have not gone out to hear him yourself, Hannah," said Esther.

Hannah seemed confused and did not at once reply.

"I might have done so, dear. But—poor Simon, who for some reason has been living on his ship, might decide to come home, and I should be here. I should be much embarrassed—and I fear he would be very angry—if he came home to find that I had been away, listening to this Carpenter. That would be very offensive to Simon."

"Let us go, this afternoon, Hannah," begged Esther. "We would be home before supper-time. Simon is not likely to return earlier."

Presently they were in the stream of pedestrian traffic on the highway. All Bethsaida, it seemed, was on the march southward, the elderly stabbing their canes into the dusty road as they pegged along intent upon their singular quest, the younger men and women overtaking and passing them, sick people of all ages borne on litters, sightless people being led much too fast for their comfort.

There was very little talk. Apparently no words were suitable to this strange pilgrimage. The urge to hurry was contagious. Esther and Hannah immediately caught it and lengthened their steps. "Hurry!" the voiceless crowd said, "Hurry! Something is happening that never happened before and may never happen again! We must not miss this marvel! Hurry!" Esther and Hannah glanced into the strained faces of their companions, and then briefly sought each other's sober eyes, but exchanged no comments. Their throats were dry with the fast travel, the choking dust, the half-frightened anticipation. . . . Yes, this Carpenter—whether he was John's Carpenter or not—was bringing sleepy little Galilee to life, was turning stolid little Galilee upside down, was driving conservative little Galilee stark staring mad!

No need to inquire the way! A mile south of Bethsaida a freshly made highway veered off sharply toward the west; traversed a grove, riddled a vineyard, toppled a stone fence, muddied a creek, and fanned out into an open pasture swarming with thousands of people.

On a knoll, surrounded by a pressing throng, stood the man they had come to see. Apparently he had but now arrived, for he was not yet speaking. He was waiting, with folded hands and a faraway look in his eyes as if in calm contemplation of the distant mountains. There was no expression of surprise or gratification that so great a multitude had done him honor. Now he had slowly raised his arms. The people grew more quiet. He lowered his arms in a gesture that requested them to sit down. Nobody was willing to obey, for all wanted to see everything that might happen. The gesture was calmly repeated, and the people closest to the front sat down. Then, like a long, incoming, tidal wave, the impulse swept the throng until all were seated. The Carpenter held up an outspread hand, and there was silence. A peculiar silence. Not a mere cessation of sound and confusion, but a vital, unifying silence that made them kin. They did not shrug from the accidental touch of a neighbor's elbow, though the stranger had a ragged sleeve.

When he began to speak, Esther instantly remembered what young Johnny had said about this man's voice. He spoke effortlessly, but his words were clearly reaching to the outskirts of the great assembly. The uncanny thing about the voice was that it was speaking to You! To You alone! There was a tone of quiet entreaty in it. Come—let us talk it over together.

He was speaking about the blessed life, the abundant life. How few had been far-visioned enough to claim that perfect life for their own. A life freed of fear and foreboding, freed of frets and suspicions, freed of the sweating greed for perishable things. This was the life he offered, a life of enduring peace in the midst of the world's clamors and confusions.

Esther's senses yielded to it. All about her she could see and feel the people relax as she herself was relaxing in obedience to the voice. She had never realized before that her body and mind had been continually at tension. The Carpenter's peace invited her spirit. He was defining the terms of it now. Anyone could possess it. It was to be had for the asking, but one must seek for it, work for it; and, if need be, suffer for it. It was like living water, drawn from an ever-flowing spring. Once you had tasted of it, you would never again be satisfied without it. It might cost you many a sacrifice, but it would be worth the price. Esther, dreamily content, felt that any price would be reasonable. Maybe she wouldn't feel this way tomorrow, but it seemed reasonable and attainable now—here—today—under the spell of the quiet voice.

Personal peace, the Carpenter was saying, gave you personal power; not the kind of power that the world had to offer you for ambitious striving, but the peace-power of the Father's Kingdom. If you must let everything go to possess that peace-power, let it go! If an oppressor demands your cloak, give up your cloak—and your coat, too—but keep your peace-power. Do not insist upon justice. There had been much too much talk about justice—and not nearly enough talk about mercy.

"There is an old saying among us," he went on, "an old saying that our fathers believed and practiced, 'An eye for an eye, and a tooth for a tooth.'"

Esther had been brought up on that ancient adage. Whatever injury another person does to you, simple justice recommended that you repay it in kind. But the Carpenter was saying that we must have done with that eye-for-an-eye justice, in the interest of mercy and peace. Henceforth—if you would possess the blessed life—you must do unto others what you would like to have them do unto you. . . . The blessed life sounded very attractive. Esther was sensing an intimation of its richness. She sighed, shut her eyes, and involuntarily shook her head; for she had an eye-for-an-eye vow to keep.

The Carpenter had ended his speaking now and to the obvious surprise of the multitude he sat down on the grassy knoll, apparently very weary. The crowd shifted its posture a little, straightened its spine, re-crossed its cramped legs, but remained seated. Loosed from her deep reverie, Esther turned inquiring eyes toward Hannah who drew a long breath and shook her head mystifiedly.

"Esther," she whispered, "there never was anyone like him—never—never before—in this world!"

"There's something very queer about all this," agreed Esther.

Hannah leaned closer and was about to speak again when a stir and a murmur in the densely packed crowd fronting the knoll brought them to attention.

Two little children, a boy of six and a girl of four, had run up the slope and seated themselves on either side of the fatigued Carpenter. Perhaps he had beckoned to them. But no—for now their mothers were hurrying forward to bring them back. The Carpenter was shaking his head, apparently insisting that they let the children remain with him. Now—more little children broke loose from their parents and were clambering up the bank. They huddled closely about him. More and more children joined the party. They sat, blinking and squinting against the sun, seemingly intent upon what he was saying to them, in a low tone inaudible to the multitude.

From throughout the great assembly, scores of children, tugged by some irresistible invitation, were rushing forward, stumbling heedlessly over grown-up legs. One thin-faced little fellow was limping painfully up the slope, leaning his frail body against a crutch. The Carpenter, still speaking, had motioned to the children to open a path for the lame boy, and they edged over to give him room.

Now a spontaneous "Oh!" went up from the people close enough to see clearly what was happening. Without pausing in his gentle speech, the Carpenter had reached out his hand for the crutch. The boy had hesitated before giving it up, but now he stood on both feet, erect and confident. He took a few experimental steps. Now, apparently overcome by the amazing thing that had happened to him, he knelt down, pressed his face hard against the Carpenter's knee—and cried. And so did everybody else.

Raising his voice to embrace the multitude, the Carpenter spoke.

"These children come to me because, in their innocence, they are of the Father's Kingdom. And if you, too, would be of this Kingdom, you must enter it with the heart of a child."

He then spoke a final word to the little ones alone and they arose. The boy who had been lame marched down the slope with shining eyes. Intent upon his reunion with his parents, who had pressed forward to meet him, the crowd was not immediately aware of the Carpenter's retreat down the farther side of the knoll. The people remained seated, thinking that after he had rested—for he seemed quite spent with weariness—he might return and speak again. But it soon became evident that the day's events had ended. In groups, the multitude began to scramble to their feet. There was almost no conversation as the great crowd broke up and strolled back toward the highway.

Hannah and Esther, hand in hand, too deeply moved for any talk, trudged slowly along with the other awe-stricken people who had had a brief, mystifying glimpse into a Kingdom that was not of this world.

Far in advance of them, striding along alone, with slumped shoulders and bent head, was Simon. The women's eyes met, diffidently. Nothing was said for a long moment. Then Hannah murmured, "Now we know what ails him. It's this Jesus."

*　　*　　*　　*　　*　　*

A tall, handsome, self-assured, young sentry was pacing back and forth in front of the prison when Esther appeared, next morning, with John's breakfast-tray. He came briskly to attention as she approached, saluted gracefully, and made a candid inventory of her, with brightly approving eyes.

"You have come to feed the prisoner?" he inquired, unnecessarily; and when Esther had smiled an affirmative, he said, "He is a lucky fellow!"

"Yes—isn't he?" drawled Esther. "Such a nice place to spend these lovely autumn days."

"Let me have that tray," said the sentry, putting down his spear and extending his hands. "I'll give it to him, and while he is eating we will get acquainted. My name is Algerius."

"And my name is Esther." She smiled, but held on to the tray. "And the girl in the kitchen is Claudia, who is expecting you to come and have some of her honey-cakes while I am giving your prisoner his breakfast."

"I don't know about that," demurred the sentry, taking off his heavy helmet and mopping his brow. "If my captain were to hear of this, I should be flogged. And besides—" his voice lowered conspiratorially— "I'd much rather stay here and talk to you."

"What about?" she demanded, suddenly cool.

Algerius readjusted his helmet and picked up his spear.

"You say her name is Claudia?"

"Yes—and you needn't hurry back. I shall be responsible for the prisoner."

"Here's the key then."

"I have one."

"Sure you aren't afraid?"

"Of the prisoner?—No. He is very respectful." She put the tray down on the low stone wall.

"And I am not," grumbled the lingering sentry, with a grin.

"You could be, I think, with a little more practice—and quite a lot of encouragement."

Having given the sentry time to be well on his way, she unlocked the door and invited John to come out into the sunshine.

"I heard you tell the sentry your name, daughter," he said, when they had sat down together.

"Would you like to call me Esther?" She handed him a goblet of grape juice which he sniffed suspiciously. "It is not fermented," she said. "I pressed it only a few moments ago. Claudia told me you could not drink wine."

"I am a Nazarite." He touched the goblet with his lips, experimentally, and then sipped it with relish.

"Do the people of Nazareth not drink wine?"

"I do not mean that I am of Nazareth. I am a Nazarite, which is a different thing altogether. There is a monastic order among us known as the Nazarites. We take a vow—or, as in my own case—it is taken for us at our birth; chastity, poverty, abstinence."

Esther offered him the plate of wheaten bread. He put down the goblet and broke one of the small loaves.

"That doesn't seem quite fair," she ventured—"to have had a vow imposed upon you when you were only a baby."

"I have never regretted it," he said. "It is a good life." A shy, unexpected smile lighted his deep eyes. "And my name is John It would please me—after so long away from home—to hear my name spoken by a friend."

"What a lonely life you have had!"

"Not until recently. I have spent many years in solitude, pursuant to my Nazarite vow, but they have been spent under the open sky. I was not unhappy. But, here, in this dark prison, I am quite desolate, friendless, and strangely beset with forebodings." He turned toward her with anxious eyes. "Tell me, daughter, were you able to see him?"

She had hoped to postpone this query as long as possible, for she was unprepared to answer it to his satisfaction.

"Yes, sir—John—I saw and heard him yesterday afternoon. There was the greatest multitude I ever saw. It was gathered about him—in a pasture —not far from Bethsaida. I was amazed to see so many people. I wondered where they all came from. It was—"

He had been studying her face intently, as she laboriously put off the moment when she must tell him what manner of man she had seen. Divining her difficulty, he broke in upon her hesitations.

"You were disappointed, I think."

"No, John, I was not disappointed—but I fear you will be. This man does not seem to be an avenger. He speaks with the most gentle, entreating voice I ever heard, a soothing voice that makes you very quiet—inside. He did not talk about punishment in store for wrongdoers, nor did he say that the mighty would be dragged from their seats, nor that those of low degree would be exalted. But he spoke peace and courage to the poor.' She paused for a long moment. "And little children crowded about him—and he cured a small boy of his lameness."

John stared hard at his prison-door and drew a deep sigh.

"Begin at the beginning then," he said, huskily—"and tell me everything."

So—Esther began at the beginning, and told him everything she could remember; the wistful, hurrying pilgrimage on the road, the great mass of people in the field, the placid voice that reached far and tugged hard at your heart, the silent, breathless, yearning multitude, the uncanny sensation of peace.

"I can feel a little of it yet," she went on, dreamily. "While he spoke, this peculiar peace laid hold on me so fully that I wished—above all things —that I might possess it—forever." Conscious that John had come out of his moody reverie, and was giving her better attention, she turned toward him, and continued:

"I think that everyone in the vast crowd must have felt the same way. I found myself hoping that he would not stop, for while he spoke my heart grew still—and all the things that ever have troubled me were forgotten."

"Apparently his voice wrought a strange spell on the minds of the people," reflected John.

"Surely you should know, sir," said Esther, "for when I heard you speaking to a great crowd, everyone listened intently to your voice."

"But the Carpenter's voice was different, I think."   .

She nodded her head slowly, and groped for the words that might define that difference without hurting him.

"Your voice, John, stunned me—and made me afraid of the days to come. The Carpenter's voice stilled me—and gave me peace. I feel a little of it, today; but it is leaving me, and I am sorry." Again she was silent for a time. "Do you know," she went on, suddenly confident—"I believe that if a person could really get acquainted with him—and stay close beside him—for a while—one might learn how to keep it!"

"Perhaps there are others who feel the same way," wondered John. "Does he seem to have any close friends about him?"

She didn't know. She had not noticed any special companions with him, on the knoll, or when he departed.

"Why don't you try to meet him, face to face, Esther?" suggested John. "If he is so gentle and kindly disposed, might he not be willing to talk with you?"

"But what right would I have to intrude upon him when he is already so overburdened and weary?"

"Go to him with a message—from me!" said John, in a tone of command. "Say to him that I have given my life to foretell the coming of The Anointed One. Ask him if he knows anything about that—about me! Ask him—in my name—if he is the One I foretold—or are we to expect another!"

Esther drew a little smile and shook her head.

"I'm afraid I couldn't do that, John. He isn't the sort of person one walks up to with such a query."

"But I must know! Can't you see that my very life depends on my knowing? Will you not try?"

"Let me think about it," she said, soberly. "That's a very large assignment—for a girl."

"I agree," conceded John. "It is indeed a large assignment—for a girl—or for anybody; for a rabbi, or the High Priest, or the Tetrarch himself! But you have already undertaken a very serious and dangerous errand which shows the courage that is in you. Do this—for me!" He challenged her silent indecision with urgent eyes, and waited.

"I shall try," she whispered.

* * * * * *

It was on the same morning, but much earlier—the morning of the twenty-sixth day of Tishri—a date to be remembered—that Simon rose from his uncomfortable narrow bunk on shipboard, resolved that he would go again today into the country and hear Jesus speak.

And he was resolved also that if circumstances permitted he would try to stand close enough to the Carpenter to be of some aid in keeping the selfish, jostling multitude from wearing the man out with their thoughtless importunities. He had slept hardly at all, last night, for thinking about this, imagining himself standing protectingly at Jesus' side, keeping the crowd back, admonishing the cot-bearers to take their time, and remain in line, and not push in ahead of others who had got there first. Surely someone should be doing this for Jesus—and why not he? For he was tall and strong, and the people might listen to his demand that they keep in order.

He was quite alone on the ship, having sent young Thad home at nightfall. He had wanted to be alone, for his thoughts were incommunicable, and he did not want the boy to be bewildered and distressed by his moody silence.

A grayish-blue light was showing faintly in the east, presaging dawn. The autumn mist hung low on the water, obscuring the beach.

Simon walked forward, lowered a bucket, and carried the water into the little galley where he washed his face. Then he broke one of the barley loaves that Hannah had sent him and emerged from the galley, munching the bread dutifully but without relish, for he was wholly preoccupied with his thoughts about the day's possible adventures.

Strolling aft, he climbed over the side of *The Abigail*, boarded *The Sara*, and sauntered across to her starboard taffrail where he stood scanning the faraway eastern mountains. The whole range would show pink presently. His eyes drifted about to the northwesterly shore. If the fog lifted a little, he might be able to see whether Japheth's old boat was still afloat.

He thought he heard a voice on the shore, and turned about, narrowing his eyes in an effort to pierce the fog, but he could see nothing.

"Halloo!" he called, funneling his lips with his hands.

"Halloo!" came the voice—and Simon wondered if it might be an echo; but—no—it didn't sound like his voice. His heart was beating strangely. He waited—and listened—cupping his ear with his hand.

The dawn was coming now, coming fast, leaping over the mountains, pouring down upon the sea. Leaning far across the rail, Simon peered hard into the dissolving mist that enveloped the shore. He made out a dim figure standing on the beach, close to the water's edge.

The stranger waved his upraised arm, and Simon—after a moment of indecision—put up his hand—and waved it. The fog was lifting. Again the stranger waved his hand—and called:

"Simon!"

There was no mistaking that voice! For there was no other voice like it in the world—or ever had been!

"Coming!" shouted Simon, hoarse with excitement. His throat was dry and his big hands trembled as he vaulted over the rail and dropped into a rocking dory. He was an experienced oarsman, but no one observing would have thought so from the awkwardness of his nervous flailings and splashings. It seemed a long voyage but eventually he arrived, very much out of breath, and dragged the dory up on the sand.

Limp with emotion, his face twitching, he found himself staring mystifiedly into the calm, friendly eyes of Jesus. He dropped to his knees. He felt the wonder-working hands on his bent shoulders and experienced the same sensation that had thrilled him when their bare arms had touched—at Hammath.

Now Jesus was speaking, quietly but insistently.

"Simon, son of Jonas, I have need of you."

"But I am a very sinful man, Master," confessed Simon, thickly.

"I have come to save sinners, my son," said Jesus.

"How can I help you, Master? I am only a fisherman." Simon's voice was barely audible now, for his pent-up emotion was choking him.

"You are to remain a fisherman always, Simon," said Jesus. "But—from this day forward—you will fish for men!"

Humbly and penitently, Simon bowed himself far forward, his eyes overflowing. Now the invigorating hands were laid gently upon his shaggy head. It gave him a strange feeling of exultation.

"Come!" said Jesus, softly. "Arise, Simon, and follow me!"

And Simon arose—and followed Jesus.

*   *   *   *   *   *

But instead of leading the Big Fisherman to the highway, and south through Bethsaida, and on into the country near Hammath—as Simon had expected—Jesus walked northward, keeping close to the shore.

He had asked Simon to follow him, and Simon was obeying; trudging along through the sand, a few cubits behind him, and making no effort to come abreast, though Jesus was walking slowly.

In this manner they proceeded for half a mile, in silence.

It seemed strange to the Big Fisherman that he could so complacently consent to follow the Carpenter without asking him where they were going. It has been his intention to go out into the country today and volunteer his services as a strong-armed body-guard to help keep the jostling people from harassing Jesus with their importunities. He could do that, he thought, without making any alterations in his own beliefs or behavior. . . . Now, it seemed, he was expected to join cause with Jesus— and "fish for men." . . . Had anyone—the servant-girl Anna, for example —had Anna asked him, a week ago, whether he had a notion of following Jesus, he would have sworn a surly oath and spat on the ground!

Now he was following Jesus—and with a curious sense of peace; for the mysterious calmness that had briefly possessed him, yesterday afternoon, had returned.

Japheth's old boat was lazily rocking at anchor, some three hundred yards off shore, a dory bobbing at her stern. Doubtless the Zebedee boys were aboard preparing to sail early to a fishing-ground.

Jesus' steps slowed to a stop here. He turned about, silently regarded Simon with an inquiring smile, and then shifted his gaze seaward. For a long moment Simon stood beside him, indecisively stroking his chin. Then he moved toward one of the beached dories, pushed it into the water, climbed in, shipped the oars, and began to pull steadily toward the storm-battered fishing-smack.

Facing astern, he kept his eyes fixed on Jesus, who remined standing on the shore. After a while, as Simon neared the old boat, where James and John were awaiting him at the rail, Jesus waved a hand, turned about, and moved southward toward the highway.

9

AFTER a fortnight's diligent search for Fara, everyone but Voldi gave it up.

With tireless persistence, but waning hope, the loyal young fellow had continued his quest, investigating every square cubit of terrain which she might have covered in a reckless midnight ride.

He had even gone to the length of having himself lowered over precipices to the unexplored depths of bramble-choked chasms into which she might have fallen, and had vigorously queried shepherds in pasture-lands so far remote that the possiblity of their having any information for him was inconceivable. He had pestered the grief-stricken Ione with questions until she fled at the sight of him.

The plight of the once so well-balanced and self-contained Ione was indeed pitiable. Upon the death of Arnon and the disappearance of Fara, King Zendi had taken their helpless servants into his own household where the older of them fitted at once into the well-remembered routines of a King's establishment. But the inconsolable Greek slave seemed dazed. Everyone thought that she was going mad.

According to report, Ione sat all day alone in a far corner of the female servants' quarters, occasionally breaking into hysterical weeping; and, when anyone approached her, would shrink back terrified as if expecting a blow. Advised of her appalling condition, Voldi had left off hoping that she might be able to furnish a clue.

Of course there were many who recalled the fantastic vow that Fara had taken when hardly more than a child, but it seemed beyond all reason that she would have set off alone on a mission so palpably impossible.

To clear the air of these speculations; and, more particularly, to dissuade the now frantic Voldi from his half-formed decision to seek for her in faraway Galilee, the King and his Counsellors held a conference in which the matter was fully discussed. And when it was ready to adjourn, Voldi was invited in to learn the outcome of their parley.

Disheartened and ill, for his fatigue and sleepless anxiety had worn him thin, he listened dejectedly while King Zendi reported their unanimous opinion. It was their firm belief, solemnly declared Zendi, that no young woman in her right mind—as Fara had seemed to be—would attempt a solitary expedition into a hostile country with the intention of assassinating its well-fortified King. And it was the considered judgment of the Council that any effort to seek for her in that region would be an act of sheer lunacy.

Were the stronghold of Tetrarch Antipas situated twenty miles beyond the Jordan, continued Zendi, a thousand experienced cavalrymen might risk making a surprise attack; but that a seventeen-year-old girl would travel—unattended—over seventy leagues of bandit-infested territory—to wreak vengeance upon a King in his fortress—was too preposterous to be believed even by a courageous young man whose loyalty and love and sorrow had driven him to desperation.

After Zendi had spoken there was a long silence which suggested that Voldi might defend his foolish idea if he desired, but he did not speak. Old Dumah cleared his throat to add a word.

"Even if she had been mad enough to attempt it, she would have come to grief long before now."

Voldi suddenly raised his head.

"Do you mean, sir, that she may have been imprisoned?"

"Or worse," muttered Dumah.

At that, Voldi rose from his place, fell on his knees before the King, and cried, "I can no longer bear this anxiety, sire! I entreat you! Let me go and search for her in Jewry!"

Old Mishma, seated beside the King, whispered a suggestion. Zendi motioned Voldi to arise, and told him to wait outside. It was a full hour before they called him back. The Counsellors had risen from their seats and seemed restless to be off.

"At the request of your honored grandfather, Voldi, we are permitting you to go. We will give you a certificate of your Arabian citizenship, requesting safe passage through all Jewry. You realize that this document does not have the value which would be accorded it in Macedonia, Petra, Cyprus, or Rome. If you get into trouble over there in Judaea or Galilee, it will be your own affair. We wish you well, my son; but if you do not return, no one will search for you."

While Zendi was speaking, Voldi's grateful eyes drifted to his grandfather's sober face. What a grand old man was Mishma! When the King had finished, Voldi bowed deeply. Zendi laid a hand on his shoulder and wished him a safe journey.

"I shouldn't let you do it," he added.

"If His Majesty were in my place," ventured Voldi, "he would take the chance, I think."

"What weapons will you carry?" inquired Zendi.

"Only a dagger, sire."

"Very good. It is better not to bear conspicuous arms. And try to avoid controversies, however trivial. And don't draw your dagger unless you intend to use it. . . . Another thing: you should be well provided with money!"

Voldi's heart skipped a beat. He hadn't thought much about money. He had never carried money with him; never had had occasion to use money. Old Mishma instantly lifted that weight.

"He shall have ample funds, my lord."

Voldi impetuously reached for his grandfather's hand—and gripped it. Zendi stepped down from the dais, and was moving away.

"Arabia should be proud of you both!" he said.

At Mishma's request, Voldi rode home with him. It had been a long time since he had seen his grandfather in the saddle, and his heart swelled with admiration as he watched the effortless skill with which the old man handled the impatient bay stallion. Mishma's posture in the saddle was a score of years younger than his deep-lined face. They had little to say until they reached the old Counsellor's gate: there they drew their horses together.

"Shall we say good-bye, sire?"

"Presently. Come in."

Dismounting, they entered the luxurious living-quarters of Mishma's home. He disappeared into the adjacent bedroom and returned with a newly made money-belt. It was heavy with gold, so heavy that when Voldi took it he nearly dropped it.

"It is the amount you would have inherited, my boy."

"Was it not dangerous, sire, to have so much gold in your possession?"

"True—but I have not had it many days."

"Then—you had prepared it—for me?"

"I thought, at least a fortnight ago, that you would follow her. It is a great grief to me, Voldi. But I cannot detain you!"

It was a memorable moment. Their voices were low. They were both deeply stirred.

"I shall not expect to see you again. I am old." Mishma's words were barely audible. He was talking mostly to himself. "I had dreamed of you as a Counsellor. We must give that up now. Whether you find her or not—we have already lost that opportunity. . . . But—I cannot find it in my heart to rebuke you. . . . As I grow older my ideas of values change. The girl is courageous. Not much wonder if you love her enough to throw your life away for her. . . . You may not find her. I doubt whether you do. If she is lost, do not hurry to return. You will have sufficient funds for a considerable amount of foreign travel. . . . If you find her, you will marry her. Do not bring her back here. You would both be unhappy." . . . Mishma rose heavily and laid his hands on Voldi's shoulders. . . . "Go—now—my brave boy—and comfort your mother."

After the painful scene in his own home where Kitra, having made a valorous effort to control her feeling, finally gave way to a complete emotional breakdown, Voldi galloped away to pay his final respects to the King and receive his worthless passport.

At the last minute, it occurred to him to say farewell to Ione, but the servants couldn't find her. Mounting his tall black gelding he rode away at a brisk trot toward the trail that descended to the Valley of Aisne.

A few hundred yards ahead, a woman stepped out of the wild shrubbery and waved an arm. It was Ione, thin and haggard, but surprisingly animated. There was no accounting for the caprices of an ailing mind. Ione, who had sunk to the depths of melancholy, now seemed almost happy. Voldi reined in his horse—and stopped beside her.

"Good, Voldi!" she cried, excitedly. "Go and find her! Here is a little gift for you!"

She handed up a parcel. It was about the shape and size of a baby's pillow, and soft to the touch. A scarf that she had knitted for him, perhaps, encased in an envelope of fine linen securely stitched on all sides.

"Am I to open it now, Ione?" asked Voldi.

"No, no! You've no time for that! It's just a little present." She turned away, waving her hand and smiling. "May all the gods attend you, Voldi!" she shouted, as he put the spurs to Darik and rode on. But Ione's strange behavior stirred his curiosity. A few days ago, she was unapproachable, depressed, fear-harried, and clearly out of her head. Now that she had learned of his intention to search for Fara in Galilee, she was exultant! Perhaps she knew more than she had told about the events of that night when Fara had disappeared. He tried to reason it out. Ione had been sworn to secrecy! That was what had driven her crazy! In spite of all the opinions

Peter Sees the Figure on the Shore

Leaning far across the rail, Simon peered hard into the dissolving mist that enveloped the shore. He made out a dim figure standing on the beach, close to the water's edge.

to the contrary, Fara had unquestionably started for Galilee, intending to keep her vow! Voldi was on the right track: there could be no doubt of that. It made him impatient to press on. But when he considered the many possible misfortunes she might have encountered, he despaired of finding her alive, unharmed.

That night he stopped for food and shelter at an unpromising caravansary situated on a small oasis at the southernmost tip of the Dead Sea. After an abominable supper prepared by a sullen, wizened old woman, he inquired of the testy inn-keeper, presumably her husband, whether a well-favored young Arabian woman had ridden past that way on a bay filly—or perhaps rested there—some two weeks ago. And when the surly old fellow, with a frown and protruding lips, had shaken his head, Voldi prodded hard at his memory. Was he sure?

Of course he was sure! Would he be likely, he growled, to forget such a strange and pleasant sight? A young woman, traveling alone, in this country? No, sir; you could depend on him to remember seeing a well-favored young woman! He chuckled slyly, and his withered old spouse scowled at him, which made him laugh unpleasantly.

Then Voldi tried to probe the old woman's recollection, but she hadn't seen a pretty young woman, alone, on a horse, here or anywhere else, ever in her life, which seemed to dispose of her as a witness.

Though it was still early in the evening, there was little to do but retire. They lighted a candle for him and pointed out the wretched hovel where he was to lodge. Shouldering his saddle-bags, he groped his way into the filthy and meagerly furnished hut. Quite weary but not ready to sleep, he sat down on the edge of the dirty cot, and for lack of any other occupation decided to see what Ione had given him.

Taking the parcel from his pack, he attacked the fine stitches with the point of his dagger. It was a tedious and exasperating task, for Ione had done her work well. At length he laid the cover back, and his eyes widened with astonishment. The linen sheath contained a long, heavy braid of hair! Whose—but Fara's?

Voldi took it up and held it against his cheek. He pressed his lips to it. His eyes were misty. Gradually the implications of Ione's gift dawned upon him, and he muttered an ejaculation of sudden understanding. Fara was impersonating a young man! This was Ione's way of telling him that he should not make inquiries about a girl! He was to look for a man! How dared Fara take such a risk? But here was the incontrovertible evidence that she had done so! Poor Ione wasn't as crazy as they thought. Voldi

was exultant, but not for long. His apprehension soon cooled his joy.
How could Fara hope to preserve so difficult an incognito? Sooner or later
she must be discovered—and be worse off for her disguise.

He went to sleep, after hours of wakefulness, with the tender trophy on
his pillow. Awake at dawn, he found his taciturn host pottering about in
the stableyard.

"Let me ask you this question," said Voldi, sternly. "Did you see a
young man—an Arabian—in these parts—about a fortnight ago—riding a
bay filly?"

"That I did, sir," replied the old man—"a handsome young fellow he
was, and very well dressed, too. He stopped here; slept in the same room
you had last night."

"Uhh—what a room!" growled Voldi.

The old man chuckled shamelessly.

"That other young Arab didn't like the room, either. You should have
heard him! Upon my word, sir, that young fellow could swear like a
drunken sailor! I never heard such a mouthful of curses. Some of 'em
were new words that I didn't know."

Voldi looked puzzled for a minute—and then laughed.

"A pretty rough youngster, was he?"

"He was indeed, sir. He must be very rich; used to having his own way.
He ordered us about as if we were slaves; though I must say he was not
stingy."

"Why didn't you tell me about him last night, when I asked you?"

The old fellow's jaw sagged and a look of comprehension came into his
crafty eyes.

"But you inquired about a young woman!" he countered. "Might this
young man you're asking for be the young woman you thought you
wanted to know about, last night?" He threw back his grizzled head and
cackled shrilly. "We thought there was something queer about him! He!
He! Well—I still say that nobody ever cursed like that on this oasis—and
many's the camel-driver we've put up!"

                    *   *   *   *   *   *

Voldi broke out into loud laughter several times on his way to Engedi,
but he had his sober moments too. Fara was indeed playing for high stakes.
She might deceive the grumpy old pair at the filthy caravansary—but it
was a long way to Galilee.

At Engedi the young Arabian—of a fortnight ago—was promptly
remembered

"A proud, haughty, young fellow?" queried the innkeeper; and when

Voldi had nodded, he went on: "Do I remember him! Rich, he was! Rode a frisky bay mare with enough silver on her bridle—and enough jewels on his riding-whip—to have bought everything in my house!"

"Did you find him just a bit—disagreeable?" pressed Voldi.

"Just a bit!" grinned the inn-keeper, sourly. "He swore at me in three languages—Aramaic, Arabian, and Greek. He swore at the servants in Latin. Nothing pleased him."

Voldi tried to be serious, but he couldn't restrain a chuckle.

"That's the fellow I'm looking for," he said. "He's a tough one—and no mistake! Did you notice which way he went when he left?"

"The old Salt Trail. Said he was headed for the port—and if he wasn't robbed before he got there, they probably cleaned him out in Gaza. Any man's a fool to ride through that pest-hole alone—even in broad daylight!"

"Did you warn him of that?"

"No—I didn't!" snapped the inn-keeper. "He was so damned sure of himself. It wasn't any of my business if he got into trouble."

"I think my friend would be able to take care of himself," bragged Voldi, with much more confidence than he felt.

"He certainly could with his mouth," rejoined the inn-keeper.

"Yes—and with his dagger, too!" retorted Voldi, wishing he spoke the truth.

As he rode on, early the next morning, on the busy highway, his mind was troubled. So many misadventures might have confronted Fara. These lean, lazy, ragged fellows who led the camels in the long caravans, what might they not do to annoy and provoke a solitary rider who had taken no pains to conceal his wealth and rating? And the hawk-nosed, beady-eyed caravan-directors who looked Voldi over with such candid impudence, what would Fara's disguise amount to if they insisted on questioning her closely? Apparently she had felt that to be convincing in her new rôle she must be noisy and arrogant. Voldi hoped she wasn't overdoing it. She might meet someone who wouldn't be favorably impressed by her swagger and profanity. The poor dear wouldn't last very long in a fight.

At old Hebron he made inquiries at the two inns, but nobody remembered seeing a well-to-do young Arabian on a bay filly. After a couple of hours spent in asking questions, Voldi decided that Fara must have ridden directly on through the historic town without pausing. He fed and watered his horse, lunched briefly at the principal inn, and proceeded on his journey. It was a more fertile country now, and the donkey-carts were coming into the highway laden with melons, grapes, grain, and green forage.

A few miles west of Hebron, near a cross-road, Voldi saw a rider approaching who stirred his interest, for the beautiful bay mare he rode—far too good for the unkempt loutish fellow astride—bore a striking resemblance to Fara's Saidi. Slowing to a walk, as the distance between them lessened, Voldi's suspicions were confirmed. The stocky, shaggy fellow, with the ragged tunic and the uncombed beard, couldn't have afforded a mount of such value. His dark brown skin identified him as an Idumean, which was not to his credit. He was riding bareback. The disgraceful old bridle was a patchwork of straps and hempen cords, no fit equipment for a thoroughbred.

As they neared each other, the shifty-eyed Idumean, now aware that he was being carefully scrutinized, dug his heels savagely into the filly's ribs, apparently determined to pass quickly. Voldi instantly wheeled Darik across the road, blocking Saidi to an abrupt stop.

"What do you mean by that?" yelled the lout, in the thick guttural of half-civilized Idumea.

"How did you come by this filly?" demanded Voldi.

"Who wants to know?" retorted the Idumean.

"I do, fellow!" shouted Voldi. "She belongs to a friend of mine. . . . Here Saidi!" He held out his hand. Saidi's nostrils fluttered. She tipped up her ears and took an inquiring step forward, her rider jerking the reins to restrain her.

"This mare belongs to me!" growled the enraged Idumean. "I bought her many months ago! Hands off that bridle now—or it will be the worse for you!"

"No—the mare has been stolen! She does not belong to you. I see you have disposed of the saddle and bridle. Perhaps you can tell me what became of the young Arabian who owns her."

"What are you going to do about it, youngster?" sneered the Idumean, uncoiling a well-worn bull-whip. "Will you let me pass—or won't you?"

"Not until you answer my question!" said Voldi.

The Idumean replied by drawing back his arm and lashing hard at Voldi's face with the long whip. Voldi had defensively thrown up an arm, but the thong bit sharply into his neck. Again the whip descended, raising a welt across the gelding's withers. He reared—and backed away.

Neither the Arabian nor the Idumean seemed anxious to dismount and fight on the public highway. Already two market-carts had drawn up to view the altercation. A camel-train was bearing down on them from the west. Apparently apprehensive of trouble, the Idumean now wheeled the filly about, lashing cruelly at her flanks. Tearing loose from Voldi's grip, she bolted.

At the crossing, her rider tugged her to the left, onto the unfrequented road, little more than a lane, with Voldi in pursuit at full gallop. Both horses were experienced racers. More than a half-mile had been covered before Darik was abreast of Saidi. The country road had narrowed now, with dense thickets on either side. As Darik drew into the lead by a neck, the horses so close together that their shoulders grazed, Voldi, turning about, saw the Idumean leaning far forward with an upraised dagger poised for a stab in his back. He met the threat by striking the burly fellow full in the face with his riding-whip.

Urging his horse, he shouldered Saidi into the briers where—after a brief struggle to free herself—she stopped, and stood quivering. The Idumean made no effort to go farther. He dismounted now, as did Voldi. It was plain that he would be a very unsportsmanly antagonist, as he had already proved.

They threw off their coats, drew their daggers, and faced each other only a little way apart. The Idumean gingerly fingered the red welt on his cheek—and grinned.

"I am glad you followed, youngster," he snarled. "This is a safer place for what I intend to do to you." Crouching, like an angry bull, he began advancing, weaving slowly to and fro, slipping his ragged sandals forward with short, calculated steps. Voldi remained standing erect, making no effort to assume a defensive posture.

The stocky Idumean straightened and folded his arms, with an expression of bewilderment.

"Are you going to stand there—and let me kill you—without raising a finger? I thought you Arabians were fighters!"

Voldi seemed not to hear the taunt. He was staring, wide-eyed, down the road, past the Idumean's shoulder.

"Look!" he shouted in amazement.

His swarthy foe instantly jerked his head about to see what might be coming down on him from behind—and Voldi leaped on him, firmly clutching the wrist of his dagger-hand. The Idumean drew back the free arm and struck hard, sinking his big fist into the needlesharp point of the Arabian's dagger.

Now he had twisted his right hand loose; and, raising his weapon, drove it toward Voldi's heart, but the dextrous Arabian dagger parried the thrust with a blade that opened a long, deep gash in the Idumean's forearm. The blood was dripping from the fingers of both his hands. Again he struck, desperately, but his arm was too badly injured to deliver an effective blow. Voldi caught at the bleeding wrist and twisted the dagger out of his hand. Then he clutched the weary Idumean's beard, jerked his head back, and pressed the flat of his blade against the bared throat.

"Where did you get that filly?" shouted Voldi. "Answer me—quickly—or I shall kill you!"

The Idumean gritted his teeth and tried to tug loose, smearing his beard with his dripping hands. The Arabian's dagger-point moved slightly, pricking the dirty neck.

With that, the battle was over. The big fellow's knees buckled and he slumped to the ground where he lay noisily sick. Voldi opened one of his saddle-bags, tore up a towel, and bound it tightly above the spurting wound in the Idumean's arm.

"I have no interest in saving your life, horse-thief," he said, as he tied the bandage, "but I don't want you to die until you have told me where this filly was when you stole her."

Weakly, the Idumean confessed. It was a strange story; so strange that it could hardly have been invented. But why would Fara be a member of a great crowd—in a pasture-field beside the Jordan—assembled to hear an itinerant prophet? It didn't sound like anything that Fara would be likely to do!

No, mumbled the nauseated Idumean, he hadn't seen the man who owned the mare. He had followed the crowd; and, at nightfall, had found the filly tethered quite a little way apart from the other animals. No—he had seen nothing of a silver-mounted bridle or saddle. He had waited until the camp was asleep, and had led the mare away, after a struggle with her that threatened discovery.

"Very well," said Voldi, quietly. "When you think you are through vomiting, we will be on our way to the spot where you found the filly."

"I can't do it," muttered the Idumean. "I am too weak."

"You should have thought of that before you tried to stab me in the back, horse-thief! Come on! Get up—or I'll slit your bandage, and you can lie here and bleed to death!"

It was a tedious journey back to Hebron, and the riders drew many inquisitive stares from the people they passed on the highway. At the first public watering-trough, the Idumean was helped down to do a partial job of washing off the clotted blood. Fortunately for both of them, they encountered no patrols. East of Hebron, they turned off the highway toward the north. It was late in the afternoon before they reached the pasture on the bank of the Jordan. The dead grass still showed the hard trampling of a huge multitude.

"There!" pointed the ailing horse-thief. "That's where the mare had been staked out."

Dismounting, Voldi walked about, surveying the landscape. What, he wondered, would Fara be likely to do when she discovered that Saidi was gone? Did she have enough gold with her to buy another horse? Doubt-less; for she was on a long journey, and would not have started without funds. It was beyond belief that she would proceed on foot. Her con-templated trip would be hazardous enough without that added risk. No, he decided, Fara would have acquired a mount—of some sort.

And now—what should he do with Saidi? She was not his property. He could not sell her into better hands; nor could he conveniently take her along with him. His journey involved enough danger. It would be difficult to explain a led horse this far away from home territory. After some debate with himself, he mounted and drew up facing the slumped Idumean. He patted Fara's filly on her velvet muzzle.

"Good-bye, Saidi," he said, completely ignoring her rascally rider. "I am sorry to leave you—but it can't be helped."

Without a word to the bewildered Idumean, he galloped away, won-dering where, when—and whether—he would overtake Fara.

*   *   *   *   *   *

Having had enough excitement for one day, Voldi put back to old Hebron for the night. Early the next morning he was on his way west again, past the cross-roads where, yesterday, he had encountered the thieving Idumean, on through sleepy little Adoraim whose bloody his-tory, had he known it, might have stirred his interest. Frequently he paused to ask farmers, in their carts, and at work in their fields, whether they remembered seeing a young Arabian pass that way, a little more than a fortnight ago. Not only was there no information to be had, but the surly replies indicated that their concern for traveling Arabians was lack-ing in enthusiasm. Indeed they seemed very uncivil until Voldi speculated on the probable attitude of an Arabian shepherd if asked by a well-mounted Jew whether he had seen another Jew on the road some time ago. The shepherd would have seared him with comprehensive curses involving not only the Jew himself, but his parents, his uncle, his grand-father, and his heirs and assigns forever. A very pretty world, it was.

These occasional detainments, while brief, added up to a considerable delay in the travel-schedule he had planned, and it was late in the day when he arrived at the squalid old town of Lachish, with fifteen miles more to go before reaching Gaza. The moon was too young to be of much service for night riding. He drew up in the stable-yard of the only inn, finding it almost empty—a bad sign. He had already learned that where one found plenty of room there was always an easily discoverable reason.

A couple of loutish hostlers ambled forward to meet him, but he de-cided to attend personally to the comfort of his horse. While intent upon his task of rubbing down the faithful gelding—an operation that involved some quiet conversation between them, to which Darik contributed an occasional nod and a playful nibble—Voldi became aware of a silent on-looker standing behind him. Turning, he met the amused eyes of a quite good-looking, well-dressed man of forty, obviously a Roman. Voldi straightened and they exchanged amiable greetings.

"You are an Arabian, I think," said the Roman.

"Yes, sir. My name is Voldi."

Mine is Mencius. The caravan I am accompanying is camped up the road a mile. My horse is lame—or pretending. I had hoped to find a horse-leech here, but there is none; and these stable-boys hardly know the time c' day "

"Want me to take a look at him, sir?" asked Voldi.

"That would be very kind," Mencius said—"if it isn't asking too much. Your Arabians seem to know everything about horses."

"Not everything," protested Voldi. "But we do know that they get tired on a long journey, and go lame; and the more intelligent they are, the worse they limp."

"Right!" chuckled Mencius. "And sometimes they forget which leg it is and give themselves away. However—my horse may be telling the truth."

They sauntered across to the other side of the compound where a sleek white stallion was placidly munching his forage. Voldi stood silently watching him for so long that Mencius was moved to inquire whether he should lead the horse about for inspection.

"Not yet," said Voldi, absently, studying the animal's posture. Pres-ently the stallion raised his right forefoot and set it down gingerly. Voldi immediately approached, patted the horse's withers, ran his hand down the leg to the fetlock, and gently lifted the foot for inspection. Mencius hovered close.

"Badly shod," said Voldi. "The left wall of the hoof has been pared deeper than the right, throwing the pastern-joint off balance." He called to one of the roustabouts and inquired whether there was a farrier in the neighborhood. The oaf nodded.

"I'm afraid no farrier we're likely to find in this place will do us much good," observed Mencius.

"That's true—but his tools may," said Voldi. "If we can get into his shop, I'll reset the shoe myself."

"Do you mean to say you know how to shoe a horse?" Mencius' as-tonishment was so sincere that Voldi laughed. On the way to the farrier's shop. he went on to explain how every Arabian boy was a horse-doctor by instinct. "I never let a farrier touch my Darik's feet," he said—"and we have some skillful farriers, too." Again Voldi laughed boyishly as he noted the puzzled expression on the Roman's face, and added, "Our farriers are much better paid than our scribes. . . . Perhaps that's why Arabia rides more gracefully than she reads."

Mencius smiled a little at this drollery but apparently wasn't quite sure whether he approved of the handsome young Arab's careless disinterest in education; he had taken an instant liking to Voldi and didn't want to think of him as a shameless illiterate. Mencius—without meaning to be—was a bit of a snob when it came to the question of education.

Stripping off his tunic and handing it to Mencius—who couldn't help noting the fineness of its texture and workmanship—Voldi, with the consent of the bewildered farrier, sorted out a few rusty tools, dextrously removed and readjusted the badly balanced shoe, gripping the stallion's foreleg hard between his knees while driving the nails, to lessen the jar on the sensitive pastern-joint.

Hearing a subdued conversation—in Greek—he glanced up briefly to observe that Mencius had been joined by another urbane Roman, his junior and apparently his subordinate. Mencius was doing the talking, and it was obvious that Voldi was not expected to understand it.

"See how cleverly he does that, Pincus," Mencius was saying. "Loves horses; wants to spare them any unnecessary discomfort. Horses! That's all he lives for! . . . It's an odd thing about these Arabs! They're mentally keen; but they don't know anything but horses!"

Voldi was through with the nailing now; but, not wanting to disturb the Roman's disquisition on the Arabian mind, he held on to the stallion's leg, rubbing it gently—and listening.

"You take this fine-looking boy, Pincus; obviously well-to-do, undoubtedly from one of their better families, gracious, bright; I'll wager you five hundred sesterces he can't write his own name!"

"I wouldn't mind taking you up on that, your Excellency," said Pincus. "But how are you going to find out?"

"Why don't you ask him?" suggested Voldi, with a grin.

The awkward incident, which might so easily have given serious offense, really speeded their friendship. Mencius, experienced in diplomacy, humbly admitted that any attempt at apology would only add to their trouble, which prompted Voldi to say:

"You were right, sir, about Arabia. I should not have listened; but—well, sir, I couldn't get away. My knowing Greek was accidental; not intentional, I assure you!"

Pincus, who had been trying hard to maintain his composure, gave way to a whoop of laughter. The whole episode had been too ridiculous to be viewed soberly. Voldi, too, thought it was funny. Mencius recovered slowly from his embarrassment. It was with the dignity of refinement and respect that he formally presented Pincus as the manager of the caravan with which he was traveling.

When the younger Roman had gone, with instructions to take his caravan on to Gaza tomorrow and wait there at the port, Mencius and Voldi talked. They had supper together. It was late in the evening when they parted. Their acquaintance had ripened quickly into friendship. They both felt it.

Mencius, perhaps without realizing it, had opened some gates for the untraveled young Arabian. Voldi, utterly fascinated, had encouraged the Roman to talk of his far voyages. The better to explain the nature of his journeys, Mencius confided without reserve that he was an agent of the Emperor, engaged in various errands—of investigation, mostly, and organization, too. He had been on this present roundabout trip for many months; sailing from Brindisi to Crete in charge of a fleet of ten Empire ships, had hustled the procrastinating Cretans into their mines for iron which he had sent to Rome. He had kept one of the ships and had sailed to Cyprus where he had organized a caravan to bring copper from the mines of the interior; and, when his fleet had returned—in ballast—from Rome, he had accompanied the copper to Caesarea where it was to be used in building the extensive docks.

"You should spend a few days in Caesarea, Voldi, seeing you are intending to ride up the coast," advised Mencius. "The Empire is doing great things there! A two-mile-long stone breakwater; magnificent harbor; destined to be one of the greatest ports on our sea."

"I had not realized that the Jews had so much to export," remarked Voldi.

"Nor have they," agreed Mencius, lowering his voice—"but the day will come when the Empire will develop Jewry. Then there will be trade —in plenty."

"Meaning that Rome intends a complete subjugation of Judaea?"

"Well"—Mencius debated how best to say it—"when you've seen the new wharves at Caesarea, I think you will come to that conclusion. . . . However—I surmise that any calamity to the Jews would not inconvenience you Arabians very much."

"I don't know, sir," said Voldi, vaguely. "We were persuaded to think so, many years ago, and made a brief alliance, which we regretted."

Mencius nodded—and shrugged.

"Of course; I remember. Herod got scared. Married that cad, Antipas, to your sweet little Princess; broke her heart; sent her home. . . . I had a glimpse of her, once. Beautiful! It has always been a mystery to me, Voldi, why you Arabs didn't raise more hell about that!"

Voldi flushed a little and muttered that the Arabs were sometimes a bit tardy about paying their debts. After a pause, he added, "It's a long story, Mencius."

"I'd like to hear it," declared Mencius with an unexpected enthusiasm that proved somewhat disconcerting to the Arabian, who dismissed the matter with a careless flick of his hands.

"Tell me more about your trip," he said. "You unloaded the copper at Caesarea, and—"

"No—I did not unload the copper. As I told you, I had taken my stallion, Brutus, along. How the big fellow hated those voyages! I left the fleet in the hands of its commander, Fulvius, and rode south to Gaza. There, according to previous arrangement, I found my young fellow, Pincus, with a camel-train ready to start for Engedi. We had dropped Pincus off at Gaza on our north-bound trip to Caesarea. . . . I wanted to see how much of a working force we had in the salt-fields and whether our resources there were adequate."

"And now you're headed back to Rome?" asked Voldi.

"No—not quite yet. We load the salt and see it on its way. That will take a week, probably. Then I am riding back to Caesarea to join my friend Antonius who will be sailing The Augusta to Rome. I've had enough of these cargo ships: I'm going home in style. The Augusta is the Emperor's pleasure barge—and a beautiful ship she is, too."

When they separated, near midnight, they felt as if they had been friends for years. Mencius was leaving at dawn, anticipating that he might have to lead his horse most of the day. They parted reluctantly. Each man laid his right hand on the other's left shoulder in a comradely farewell.

"If ever you find yourself in Rome, Voldi—" Mencius was saying.

"Unlikely, sir, but you may be sure I should try to find you. . . . By the way—how would I do that?"

"Inquire at The Praetorium. They will direct you. Ask for Proconsul Nicator Mencius."

"And when you come to Arabia, Mencius, our home is yours. Go to the King's encampment for directions."

"Am I correct in surmising, Voldi, that your family is prominent in Arabia?"

"My grandfather, Mishma," replied Voldi, "is King Zendi's Chief Counsellor."

*   *   *   *   *   *

It was noon before Voldi resumed his journey. Fara would unquestionably have ridden through Lachish, and since it was clear that she had not tarried in Hebron, it was almost certain that she must have stopped here.

He had had no opportunity to speak to the inn-keeper on this subject, for Mencius had been standing by, but this morning Voldi pressed his inquiries.

The inn-keeper wanted to be obliging, though he professed to have no knowledge of the young Arabian who had passed this way. Certainly he had not stopped for accommodations at his house. It was possible, of course, he admitted, that the young man might have paused to ask questions at a private home and had been offered lodging for the night. That happened occasionally. He even volunteered to accompany his generous guest on a tour of the homes where travelers had been welcomed. But no helpful information was arrived at, though much valuable time was consumed. Voldi's heart was heavy as he gave up the quest in Lachish, and rode on.

It was a monotonous journey. A mile west he came upon evidences of the recent encampment of Pincus' caravan. Three miles farther on he came to the tumbledown village of Melissa where, without any hope at all, he stopped to ask the usual questions to which the replies were bucolic stares, scowls, and a spitting on the ground.

The sun was setting when a stone guide-post advised him that Gaza was still eight miles distant. Twilight came on rapidly. A quarter moon helped a little, but it would be a long way to Gaza. And Voldi had no relish for arriving in the night, seeing you could easily have your throat cut there in the daytime.

As he plodded along in the thickening gloom, he saw—on the highway, some two hundred yards ahead—a group of dim figures engaged in combat. There was an unmistakable sound of clashing swords, together with brief barks of warning and savage encouragements.

For an instant Voldi was undecided whether to ride into this mêlée, which might turn out to be a fight between rival groups of ruffians. He drew the gelding to a stop. Now he saw a white horse being tugged off the highway, and the reason for the commotion was clear. Spurring Darik to a gallop, he found himself within a few yards of a desperate fight in which Mencius was valiantly but hopelessly defending himself against three!

Flinging himself out of the saddle, he rushed into the fray. One of the stalwart robbers turned to meet him with a broadsword raised high. Voldi did not wait for it to descend on him, but leaped for it. Gripping the man's wrist with his left hand, he held the sword suspended for the instant required to drive his dagger deep into the shoulder of the sword-arm. With a scream of pain and rage, the bandit tried to strike. This time the dagger caught him in the left breast. It had found its mark. As the body sagged, Voldi flung it aside and dashed on into the battle which Mencius was plainly losing; for one of his two remaining assailants had moved to the rear of him and was preparing to strike.

"Behind you, Mencius!" he shouted. "I'll take this fellow!"

As Mencius wheeled about to parry the blow, the robber who had been facing him shifted his attention to the newcomer. Apparently satisfied that his fellow-bandit would deal successfully with the wearied Roman, he seemed disposed to take his time—and enjoy the slaughter of this youthful intruder.

"What have you there, youngster—only a dagger? What do you expect to do with it?"

Immediately Voldi showed him what he expected to do with the dagger. The savage thrust, with his full weight behind it, was so swift, so recklessly ruthless, that the older man had no chance to assume a defensive position. The young Arabian had come at him with a rush that upset his calculations. The big fellow who had planned to enjoy a murder was left no time to indulge in this luxury. It was only an eight-inch dagger-blade against a three-foot broadsword, but it was a bold and busy little dagger that laid open the sword-arm, pierced the hand that moved instinctively to clutch the wound, and drew a deep semi-circular furrow from forehead to chin; all this in one bewildering moment. Voldi stepped back quickly to avoid the last determined effort at defense, but the tip of the descending broadsword slashed his upper arm. He could feel the warm blood soaking his sleeve. He decided that the robber must pay hard for that cut; but as he moved in to finish him off the big fellow crumpled.

Meantime, Mencius had driven his antagonist off the highway and had him backed up against the low stone fence where he dropped his sword and shouted for mercy, a favor that the Roman was pleased to bestow, for he was thoroughly spent, and wounded. Voldi looked at the bleeding hand, and was happy to see that the cut was superficial.

"If you hadn't turned up—exactly when you did, Voldi—they would have killed me." Mencius, still breathing heavily, leaned against his friend for support.

"Have they got your money?" asked Voldi.

"Yes—and my horse."

"Here, you!" shouted Voldi, to the weary robber who had slumped down on the wall. "If you have the Roman's wallet, hand it over. If not— go through your friends' pockets, and find it. And be quick!"

Heaving himself to his feet, the bandit obeyed. Mencius' money was found in the blood-soaked tunic of the first robber Voldi had encountered. The recumbent man did not protest when they relieved him of the wallet. He lay very still. Mencius picked up his limp hand.

"The rascal's dead, Voldi!" he muttered.

Voldi was stooping over to peer into the gray face. Mencius interposed an arm and pushed him away.

"You don't want too clear a remembrance of him, Voldi," he explained. "It's easy to see you never killed a man before."

"You mean—he may haunt me?"

"Well—you haven't seen the last of him. They come back—in the night—and waken you. Sometimes they bring small children along, and weeping women."

"But, Mencius!" stammered Voldi. "The fellow had no right to live!"

"True! But it makes no difference. They return! . . . But come—let's see what is going on here!"

The ambulatory robber had half-led, half-dragged his injured friend to the roadside and across the stone fence into the pasture where the horses were tethered. The shadowy figure who had taken charge of the white stallion had abandoned him and was running through the field to join his companions. Brutus had made no attempt to leave, and was quickly taken in hand.

"Give me a lift, Mencius," said Voldi, after an unsuccessful effort to mount.

"You've been hurt, Voldi!" exclaimed Mencius. "Why didn't you tell me? Your sleeve is wet with blood."

"I know. Perhaps we had better bind it up."

"We will stop at the Fort of Minoa," said Mencius, as he applied a bandage to Voldi's dripping wound. "I know the Commandant, an old friend of mine, Legate Vitelius. I used always to stop there, on these trips; but—not lately. The Fort's badly run down, dirty, no discipline. Poor old Vitelius is a wine-bibber; never dead drunk, never cold sober; just stupid— all the day long."

It was midnight before they reached the huge, ugly, shabby, high-walled rectangle with the faded Roman banners suspended over the gates. Sleepy sentries admitted them without much questioning. Legate Vite-lius, shaky and dull but sober enough to be affable, was summoned from his bed; heard the travelers' story, routed out the regimental surgeon, and had the wounds cleansed and dressed.

Voldi and Mencius shared a commodious chamber. Neither seemed ready to sleep. The excitement of their encounter was still with them.

"I feel as if I had known you always, Voldi," murmured Mencius. "You saved my life tonight! I am deep in your debt! What can I ever do to repay your kindness, my friend?"

Somewhat to his own surprise, Voldi impulsively raised up on his elbows, and said, "I need your counsel. I am in a serious dilemma. I want to confide in you!"

Propping himself up on his pillows, Mencius gave full attention as Voldi told his almost incredible story—of Fara's childhood vow, and her disappearance, and his own desperate search for her.

"I don't know, Voldi," muttered Mencius, shaking his head, when the tale had been told. "I doubt whether she could make such a journey without being apprehended. But she's surely worth looking for; and if love and courage can find her, you will succeed!"

Before they slept, Voldi had promised to wait in Gaza until Mencius had dispatched his fleet, and together they would ride to Caesarea.

"But I must exact a promise of you, Voldi, if you are going with me to Caesarea." Mencius' tone was serious.

"Of course!" promised Voldi. "Anything!"

"*The Augusta's* errand in Caesarea is to pick up a royal family, on a pleasure excursion to Rome. You are to show no interest in any member of this royal household."

"But—why should I?" exclaimed Voldi.

"The man is the ruler of Galilee."

"Antipas!"

"Correct! Mind you keep your promise! Good-night!"

10

VOLDI had never met anyone with so wide a range of interests as his companionable new friend from Rome. Proconsul Nicator Mencius knew something about everything, classic and contemporary.

The Arabians were not very much concerned about history, not even about their own. Here and there in the high mountains massive sepulchers of their national heroes bore extravagant, weather-beaten epitaphs, but almost nobody tried to decipher them; for, in the opinion of Ishmael's tough posterity, it was as effeminate to be able to read as not to be able to ride. Literacy was left to the professional scriveners whose unenvied occupation was practiced mostly by men with crippled feet or weak chests.

There was no written history at all. Vagabond minstrels—rating no better than jugglers—toured the country, attending the auctions, fairs, and festal events where they chanted the ancient legends and mumbled interminable epic poems extolling the prowess of Arabia's distinguished kings and champions, but there was nothing resembling a comprehensive, sensible, sequential story of the Arabian people; and as for the average Arab's knowledge of the world outside, it was practically non-existent.

The Arab knew that he should hate and despise the Jews. That prejudice he had had in his milk. He never paused to examine it. It was as natural and necessary as breathing and heart-beats. He likewise loathed the Romans, though his attitude toward them was of distrust and suspicion rather than the forthright contempt he felt for the Children of Israel. As for other foreign nations—Egypt, Greece, Persia, Macedonia, Pamphylia, Cyprus, Crete—they were but outlandish names that were rarely on his tongue or in his thoughts. He knew nothing about them— and cared less.

As the grandson of a Counsellor, Voldi had been taught to read and write the language of his own people; but it was not much of an accom-

217

plishment, for there was almost no Arabian literature, nor did many occasions arise when it was of advantage to know how to write.

At Fara's gentle insistence—and because it gave him a reasonable excuse for spending longer evenings in her company—he had studied Greek under the competent supervision of Iona; and, spurred by their encouragement, he had done very well with the language. As for the contents of these venerable scrolls which they employed as text-books, he had very little interest in them. He was too polite to say so, but privately he considered Aeschylus a morbid old owl, Pindar a windy dreamer, Herodotus a tiresome bore, and Homer a shameless liar.

Mencius was now introducing Voldi to a new world. He did not parade his knowledge. Indeed he seemed honestly apologetic because he knew so little. But in the opinion of his young friend from Arabia, the Roman's wealth of information concerning past and present world affairs was related to Voldi's meager store as everything was related to nothing.

This morning, as they rode slowly toward Gaza, now only two miles distant, lagging far enough behind the shuffle-footed caravan to avoid the worst of its dust, Mencius found plenty of entertainment for himself and enlightenment for Voldi by calling attention to certain historic landmarks along the old highway.

"See that huge, tumbled pile of hewn stone over there in the field?" Mencius pointed with his riding-whip. "That was the great fort where the Philistines made their last stand against Alexander."

"When was that?" Voldi took no pride in his query.

"Of course you know about the various victories of Alexander, all over the world," said Mencius.

"Vaguely," mumbled Voldi, hoping he would not be required to bound or define the word.

"Well—as you undoubtedly recall—he died about three hundred years ago, and this was one of his later conquests. The Philistines made a gallant defense. It ended—over there."

They drew their horses to a stop and surveyed the ruins.

"Those rocks do not appear to have been there so long," commented Voldi.

"Granite does not deteriorate as rapidly as the people who quarry it," observed Mencius, half to himself. "To look about on the lousy cutthroats who now inhabit this region, one wouldn't suspect that they are descendants of the brave fellows who built that fort and defended it until the last man was dead."

"It's a wonder they haven't hauled that rock-pile away to use in other buildings," reflected Voldi.

"Oh—they will—sometime," soliloquized Mencius. "It is in the nature of nations," he went on, dreamily, "to rise—and toil—and suffer —and prosper—and fatten—and fall." After a long pause he continued, "Then they lie prone in the dust until some strong man appears among them—and commands the old stones and the old bones to rise again. All that these rascally beggars need—to put them on their feet—is a great leader. He will come—some day. It always happens—in time. Destiny is in no hurry."

"Mencius—you have the mind of a prophet," said Voldi, soberly. "Or, are you just guessing?"

They spoke to their horses and rode on a little way before Mencius replied.

"No, Voldi, I am not a prophet; nor am I guessing. The earth is a vast theater with many stages on which companies of actors present the same old play—a tragedy—in five acts. Sometimes the company puts it through to the end at breathtaking speed, if the man who enacts the principal rôle is very audacious and impetuous. You take Alexander, for example. That was a one-man show. He conquered the whole world, and when he died his Empire—as a military power—vanished over night. There wasn't enough left of his army to give police protection to his own town."

"I had thought that the Greeks held him in high honor," remarked Voldi.

"So they do," declared Mencius—"and very properly, too. They lost their rating as conquerors, but they gained something much more valuable—the world's respect. Everywhere they went, they carried their culture. They became known as the wise ones of the earth! Moreover— their wide acquaintance with the other nations opened their own eyes to the fact of their superiority as intellectuals. It made the Greeks conscious of their cultural supremacy, and more eager than ever to develop their talents." After a pause, he added, "Militarily, of course, Alexander's whirlwind campaigns accomplished little. His was a very brief dynasty."

"It usually takes much longer then—for the actors to finish the old play," surmised Voldi, anxious to hear more of this unfamiliar talk.

"Anywhere from three or four generations to half a dozen centuries," said Mencius. "Consider the case of these Philistines: they had been smashed before; eleven centuries ago. The end of that play was quite dramatic. . . . You've heard of Samson, I suppose."

Voldi shook his head and grinned; and Mencius, having found his polite supposition incorrect, proceeded to tell the story. The Philistines had had everything their own way for a handful of centuries. Then a powerful leader had developed in neighboring Jewry.

"It takes only one strong man, you know, to do the trick," continued Mencius. "If he is bold enough, successful enough, his people will follow him and fight for him. But he had better stay in the saddle! That's the only trouble with a one-man show. The great man becomes so infatuated with his personal conquests that he neglects to build up a few successors to take over in the event something happens to him. . . . The Philistines were quite unprepared to compete with a man of Samson's stature. They had grown rich, soft, overconfident—and, of course, corrupt. Samson bore down on them with the courage and voice of a mad bull! . . . There are plenty of legends about him; most of them lies, no doubt, but immensely entertaining. One old story has it that he single-handedly slaughtered three hundred Philistine braves with the jaw-bone of an ass."

"An odd weapon," commented Voldi.

"Yes—but not altogether inappropriate. The big fellow was a noisy braggart and buffoon, without a trace of dignity or commonsense. It delighted him to make monkeys of the haughty Philistines; loved to play pranks on them. His roars of laughter could be heard for a mile."

"What sort of pranks?" Voldi wanted to know.

"Oh—theatrical displays of his physical strength. One night he lifted the city gates of Gaza off their hinges and carried them away on his shoulders. . . . Then, when he had all Philistia beaten and shamed, he made the customary mistake of successful warriors, rested on his oars, enjoyed his fame, and strutted about the city with his head held high. Presently he became enamored of a beautiful and designing woman."

"Of Philistia?" inquired Voldi.

Mencius nodded—and scowled.

"It's strange," he went on, bitterly, "how many strong men have been taken in by women. It hasn't been so very long since our brave Marcus Antonius, with the applause of the Empire in his ears, traded his fame for the smiles of that scheming little Egyptian slut, Cleopatra! A great man he was—until he threw himself away."

"I gather that your admiration for Cleopatra is under control," drawled Voldi, for something to say.

Mencius growled—and went on with Samson.

"This Philistine girl, Delilah, soon had the big clown eating out of her hand. When the time was ripe she betrayed him to her fellow countrymen and they took him into camp. His cohorts made no effort to rescue him."

"So—that was the end of the Fifth Act?" asked Voldi.

"By no means!" declared Mencius. "It was only the end of the Fourth

Act! The Philistines went much too far in their vengeful celebration of victory over Samson. That, too, is customary. They made a thorough job of it; roped him and bore him away, burned out his eyes, harnessed him like a donkey, and made him grind corn in the King's mill. Day after day after week after month, the hapless fellow plodded round and round hauling the heavy beam until his big, bare feet wore a path three cubits wide and two cubits deep."

"Tiresome occupation—for a hero," observed Voldi.

"One day," pursued Mencius—"and this was the last act of the play— the sumptuously furnished balcony of Philistia's praetorium—or whatever they called their capitol—was crammed with banqueting royalty, generals, counsellors, and wealthy tax-payers, celebrating a religious festival—in honor of Dagon, I believe, or some one of their silly gods—"

"Were they so religious—the Philistines?" broke in Voldi.

"Just on feast-days. I think that's true of all religions—so far as the top layer is concerned. The influential people like to set a good example. It makes the common people more confident of their gods."

"And more contented with their rags and hunger," assisted Voldi.

"Up to a certain pitch of starvation—yes," agreed Mencius—"but that is another story. . . . The paunchy Philistines were hugely enjoying themselves at the banquet-table when some ingenious fool suggested that they parade poor old Samson in the plaza where everybody could see him— and have a good laugh. So—the flunkies in the mill haltered him and a small boy led him forth. Suddenly the blind giant felt a surge of his former strength, wrapped his long, bony arms around a couple of the marble pillars supporting the balcony—and pulled the whole house down."

"Incredible!" shouted Voldi. "You don't believe that, surely."

Mencius remained sober-faced and was tardy with his rejoinder.

"Maybe not all of it, Voldi; not the fantastic details. But the fact remains that blind old Samson wrecked Philistia so completely that she took orders from other nations for six hundred years!" Mencius appeared to have ended his speech. They rode on in silence for some time.

"That was indeed a strange story," mused Voldi, at length.

"No—not so strange—but a bit terrifying. Sometimes, Voldi, I wonder if the Roman Empire may not finish her play in much the same manner. We Romans may be nearing the end of the Fourth Act." Mencius was talking to himself now, and Voldi has to listen sharply. "We have gone about, almost everywhere, capturing and roping and blinding other

nations' giants, and making them grind our corn. Some day—unless
History is not to be trusted—they will pull our house down. I hope it
doesn't happen in my lifetime."

"Meaning that your enslaved provincials are growing restless?"

"Slaves are always restless, Voldi. At present, ours are helpless. But—
there will come a day—and a strong man! Then we will play the final act!
To predict how long that might take—or where the strong man is to come
from—is a job for a better prophet than I."

The noon sunshine bounced off the tarnished cupola of a distant tower.
Mencius pointed down the descending highway toward the city.

"Well—there she is, my friend, the famous old stronghold of Philistia!"

"Waiting for a strong man to appear—and put her in order again,"
said Voldi, after the manner of reciting a lesson.

"Not consciously waiting," amended Mencius. "Gaza is too stupid to be
aware that she is waiting for anything. Only when the strong man
shows up, will she know that she has been waiting. . . . And, meantime—
while she waits for Destiny to clean her up—we will not drink her stinking water or her wretched wine; nor will we touch her polluted food. We
will ride straight on through to the docks. The fleet will be there. We
will find plenty to eat and drink on shipboard."

"And it will be clean food and sound wine, I suppose, seeing it is
provided by the Romans," remarked Voldi, with a slow wink that made
his friend grin.

"Yes, sir!" declared Mencius, proudly. "It will be clean and sound! You
see—we Romans are still playing our Fourth Act—and doing a good job
of it!"

Suddenly, to Voldi's amazement, Mencius shed his quiet complacency
and assumed a new rôle. The tail-end of the long caravan was immediately
ahead.

"You are to keep close behind me now!" barked Mencius, over his
shoulder, as he spurred Brutus to a sharp trot.

With his spine stiffened to an arrogant posture, he rode past the
camel-train, looking neither to the right nor left. Arriving at the docks,
with Voldi trailing him, Mencius flung himself off his horse and shouted
a laconic order to Pincus. Then he marched with stiff-legged hauteur to
the wharf where the flag-ship of the fleet awaited him, Voldi trudging
along behind, feeling much like a convict on his way to prison. Sailors and
stevedores obsequiously saluted, but Mencius gave them no attention.

Reaching the ship's waist, the haughty Mencius marched aboard, passing between a double line of sailors and petty officers without seeing them, and stood stiffly before the graying Commander whose pose was as icily formal. Voldi was not introduced. Bowing, the Commander wheeled about and walked briskly aft, with Mencius striding beside him, and Voldi—at a disadvantage and a bit offended—tagging behind them.

When they had entered the Commander's spacious cabin and the door had been closed, the mood of the Romans instantly changed. They whacked each other on the shoulder, playfully.

"Fulvius, my lad," shouted Mencius. "It's a treat to see you again!"

"High time you turned up, you lazy tramp!" rumbled the Commander. "I've been rotting in this pest-hole for a week!"

"Serves you right! You have been spoiled with luxury!" Mencius peeled off his tunic and tossed it onto Fulvius' bunk. "Now I want you to greet an Arabian friend of mine. . . . Voldi, meet my good Fulvius."

The Commander, with candid disinterest, pursed his lips and nodded.

"Perhaps I should have added, Fulvius," continued Mencius, "that Voldi saved my life, at the risk of his own, in a bloody battle with highwaymen."

At that, Fulvius' eyes brightened—and he smiled amiably.

"Welcome to my ship, Voldi!" he said.

In gay spirits, Mencius became oratorical in his further introduction of his friends.

"Here's where two of the finest and bravest have found each other!" he exclaimed. "Here's where the high mountains and the deep sea clasp hands! Here's where a gallant Arabian who knows all about horses and daggers meets a Roman who knows all about ships and storms! Here's where—"

"If you're going to compose an ode, Mencius," broke in Fulvius, "let's have some wine to wash it down. Odes are hard enough to bear, in any case." He opened the door a little way and growled with all the irascibility of an old dog, presumably addressing a slave. They sat down, and presently the wine arrived.

"Was it really much of a fight?" inquired Fulvius, eager for some gory details.

"I was having it out with three bandits, alone, and in the dark," explained Mencius. "Suddenly, Voldi appeared and joined the battle. They would have finished me promptly—but for this foolhardy fellow."

Fulvius beamed toward Voldi and drawled, "Well—even if you do stick your nose into other people's business, you shall have a drink."

For all of three hours, over their dinner, the talk had been a recital of the Romans' recent experiences, spiced with persiflage; and, at length, Mencius and Voldi were shown to their bunks in an adjacent cabin.

"What are you thinking about so seriously?" inquired Mencius, tugging off a boot.

"You," replied Voldi, with a brief chuckle. "You astonished me today, Mencius. You play so many parts—and all of them so very well."

"Perhaps you are referring to our public formalities, as compared with our unconventional behavior in private?" asked Mencius, amused.

"I shouldn't have known you for the same man!" said Voldi.

"It's only good usage among us," said Mencius. "It's the Roman way of enforcing discipline. We officers have to be high-handed with our subordinates; and, in their presence, severely dignified in our attitude toward one another. It's a serious and dangerous business, Voldi—keeping slaves and mercenaries in control."

"Ever try the other way?" ventured Voldi—"getting acquainted with your men—and showing them that you trust them?"

"No—I never tried that, personally," admitted Mencius, "but it has been tried and it doesn't work. Give the average man an inch and he'll take a mile. Let the commanding officer show himself to be friendly and he is immediately suspected of being soft—if not scared."

"Our officials in Arabia do not strut and bark," said Voldi.

"Of course not!" agreed Mencius. "Why should they? Your King Zendi can eat with shepherds if he wants to, and they love him for it. But you're all Arabians; one big family! Look what we have to deal with, Voldi! In my caravan here are rascally Philistines, sullen Parthians, slit-eared Macedonians, and all manner of scheming hoodlums! And on this ship—why, if good old Fulvius relaxed his vigilance for a moment, the riffraff of a dozen nations would stick him in the back and toss him overboard! That's why we're cold—and haughty—and severe! It's the Roman method of government—all the way down the line from the Emperor to the overseer of my caravan!"

After a reflective moment, Voldi said, "What if all the riffraff in the Empire organized?"

"Slaves are hard to organize, Voldi. The Parthians would insist on having a Parthian as the great emancipator. The cut-throats of Sicily would follow only a Sicilian. It would take a very strong man to unite the Empire's provincials!"

"Like Alexander, maybe?" wondered Voldi.

"Much more powerful than Alexander! He would have to appeal to something that all these polyglots possess in common. I'm sure I don't know what that would be." Mencius leaned over toward the table and snuffed out the lamp. "Let's go to sleep, Voldi," he said, drowsily. "It's too big a problem to settle tonight."

After a quiet moment, he asked, "Have you your dagger in bed with you?"

"No," said Voldi.

"Better get it," advised Mencius.

"Is that a Roman custom?" asked Voldi, suppressing a chuckle.

"He is an impoverished and forsaken Roman," replied Mencius, soberly, "who dares go to sleep without a dagger strapped to his wrist."

*   *   *   *   *   *

Now they were riding north on the broad and busy coast highway, their horses frisky after a three-day rest at the port; eventful days for Voldi who had never seen a ship before and knew nothing of the ways of sea-faring men.

Seemingly endless files of slaves, each with a huge cake of Dead Sea salt on his shoulder, had plodded up the gangways and down the ladders into the dark holds of eleven sturdy ships. There was no haste, nor was there any rest for these empty-faced toilers. Overseers stood, small distances apart, along the wharf, occasionally flicking their bull-whips expertly, as if to keep in practice, but not often letting the lash bite into a slave's bare hide. It was enough for the burdened men to know that the whips were in experienced hands.

As each ship was loaded and the hatches battened down, she would move slowly away from her temporary berth and find a mooring half a mile away in the quiet harbor, and another vessel would be warped into the vacancy at the dock. Voldi spent most of his time alone at the stern of the flag-ship, listening dreamily to the lap of the waves against the barnacled piles, and the screams of careening gulls; more enjoyable entertainment than might be had where the work was in progress. Indeed Voldi was glad to find any distraction from the sight and sound of that slave-labor. With his belligerent Arabian background, he was anything but thin-skinned; but this monotonous scuff—scuff—scuff—scuff of spiritless sandals had taken on an ominous significance. Some day—according to Mencius' confidential forecast—this hopeless, helpless scuffing of enslaved sandals would suddenly attain a swifter tempo! It would spontaneously break into a run! It would be accompanied by savage shouts for vengeance! And the Empire's Fifth Act would open with a clash of angry metal!

For two hours, on that first day, Voldi had stood leaning against a forward capstan, watching and listening, until he became oppressed by an hallucination that the steady scuff—scuff—scuff—scuff—was, even now! this instant! accelerating to a threatening scuff!—scuff!—scuff!—scuff! that would raise the curtain for the final events of the old tragedy. He tried to comfort himself with the thought that—after all—the well-merited collapse of the Roman Empire need be of no concern to Arabia. But, on sober reflection, Voldi decided that the wreck of the Empire would be everybody's business; Arabia's too!

Bewildered and moody, he had moved away from the pattern and symbols of this threat, finding a measure of serenity in the blue sky and bluer sea. This sky and this sea had witnessed many an enactment of the inevitably recurrent drama and would doubtless witness many more repetitions of it in the ages to come. Nations would come and go, rise and fall, but the same sky would look down upon these mutations with calm detachment. The tide would roll in, twice a day, no matter if all the nations in the world destroyed one another—and themselves. It was comforting to let one's eyes rest upon something that would endure— forever and ever.

At high noon on the third day, the last laden vessel was ready to put out to sea. Mencius and Voldi stood together on the wharf as the flag-ship drew in her frowsy hawsers and drifted from the dock. Commander Fulvius, with a letter in his pocket for personal delivery to Mencius' wife explaining his delay, cupped his mouth to shout into a brisk seaward breeze, "What shall I say if she asks me when to expect you?"

"Tell her you don't know," yelled Mencius.

More canvas was slowly creeping up the foremast, sailors tugging in unison at the ropes. Pulleys squealed. Fulvius and Mencius, facing each other soberly, stood at attention, thrusting forward stiff right arms in a farewell salute. Voldi, less formally, waved a hand. A much mended sail was crawling up the mizzenmast. Out in the bay the other ships were winching up their anchors. The fleet was on its way to Rome.

In less than an hour, Voldi and Mencius were riding through an increasingly fertile and well-kept country, strikingly different from the unproductive and ill-conditioned lands eastward of Gaza. The vineyards showed good care. The houses and barns were larger. The cattle in the pastures were sleek and fat. Mencius swept the rich landscape with a panoramic gesture, and discoursed of its value.

"This is what Alexander wanted when he laid siege to Philistia. It has always been coveted by somebody, for it is truly a garden-spot. The owners of these farms and vineyards are temporarily unmolested—but it will not be for long. Voldi—if a man hopes to live at peace in this world he must pitch his tent in a desert so bare that even a bug would starve on it."

"How do you account for the peace that these prosperous people are enjoying at present?" inquired Voldi.

"That is an interesting and amusing story," replied Mencius. "For some time there has flourished in Jerusalem a politically powerful family—the Maccabees. They are rich as Midas and shrewd as Satan. Many years ago they took pains to ingratiate themselves with Herod, backed him solidly in his reign, flattered him with gifts and compliments. Remembering that the war-battered little town of Askelon was Herod's birthplace, they volunteered to rebuild it in splendor. You shall see, presently, what they made of it. The King, much gratified, donated a beautiful consulate. Then the Maccabees—with Herod's consent—encouraged a colony of wealthy fugitives from Athens to move in and redeem the neglected countryside."

"Now that it has been put in order," remarked Voldi, "it's a wonder you Romans haven't—"

"That's the amusing part of the story," broke in Mencius. "Tiberius would like to have it; but, to take it, he would instantly find himself at war with the Maccabees. He isn't quite ready for that—and the Maccabees know that he knows it. As the matter stands, the Emperor considers himself better off by levying heavy taxes on the Maccabees than risking a costly war with them. That will come—later."

"In our time?"

"You will think so when you see what is going on at the harbor in Caesarea."

"Don't the Jews realize what is in store for them?"

"Of course! But they are riven by sects and parties. It's the old story of internal feuds and factions, stubbornly refusing to co-operate with one another even in the emergency of saving their own skins!" Mencius was silently thoughtful for a while. "You may recall my saying, a few days ago, that the strength of a nation always depends upon the leadership of the one powerful man who has it in him to bind all the discordant elements together—and induce them to follow him! Let him be popular enough and they will share his glory or his shame! Well—the Jews have no such man among them. Each fanatical party has its chieftain, but no one of them can command the loyalty of the whole country. For ages the Jews have been expecting a great leader to appear and deliver them from their enemies. Their prophets have spoken of this fabulous person as the 'Messiah.' Now and again, the various sects have burst into revolutionary flames, incited by a 'Messiah,' but no one of these leaders has lasted very long, not even in the esteem of his own party. They have always ended up in some drab little martyrdom. And within the space of a generation or two nobody remembered what became of the great man's ashes."

"Apparently the real 'Messiah,' when he comes, if he comes, will have a big job on his hands," surmised Voldi.

"According to the Jewish prophets, he is to be something of a divine person. That might be greatly to his advantage." Mencius' tone was so ironical that Voldi laughed outright.

"I gather that you are not very religious, Mencius," he remarked dryly.

"As for the traditional host of deities, no: I have no interest in them, much less any faith in them. If they serve any useful purpose, it is only to frighten small children into behaving themselves."

A heavily laden caravan was bearing down on them from the north, and they drew aside into a cypress-shaded lane to let the long procession pass. Mencius guessed that it was a cargo of grain for embarkation at Gaza, but Voldi refused to be diverted from the serious discussion they had begun.

"Surely, Mencius, you do believe in the existence of some Higher Power," he said, soberly.

"Oh, yes!" admitted Mencius. "It is obvious that a Great Mind—or a group of Great Minds—created the world. Inconceivable that it could have created itself. Whether any High Power is still in control of the world is, in my opinion, doubtful. Humanity's antics do not indicate that any sensible Overseer is in command. . . . Sometimes, however, I find myself privately worshiping a god whom I think of as The Torchbearer."

Voldi's eyes widened with fresh interest. He urged Mencius to explain what he meant by a Torchbearer.

"He has been going about for ages, Voldi," said Mencius, slowly measuring his words. "Up and down—across the world—in every era—in every country—patiently searching for men with lamps in their hands—larger lamps than those of their neighbors or their fathers. And this light-giving god touches the wicks of these unusually capacious lamps with his divine torch."

"Go on, please!" insisted Voldi, when Mencius, having seemed to have made an end of his strange discourse, was counting the sullen, nodding camels as they passed.

"That's about as far as I've gone into it," confessed Mencius, vaguely. "My favorite god, The Torchbearer, wants the world to have more light—for men to see by—so he keeps on looking for lamps. It must be a very disappointing quest. I marvel at his perseverance. Only a few men—widely separated by leagues and centuries—have borne lamps worthy of the divine fire—and such light as they have kindled has brightened the way for a mere handful of adventurers. As for the multitudes, they still stumble along in the old darkness. Sometimes The Torchbearer lights a large lamp that attracts smaller lamps. Plato brings his lamp to Aristotle, and there is an unprecedented brightness on the path—for a few—for a while. For a little while."

"But—the mass of the people—they will keep on groping through the dark," mused Voldi. "Is that what you believe?"

"I'd much rather not, of course," sighed Mencius. "It would please me to hope that The Torchbearer might some day come upon the one great man—with the one powerful lamp—that would illumine the highway—for us all! But History does not encourage that hope."

The camel-train had passed now, and the dust was clearing. They rode, in thoughtful silence, onto the highway. Mencius pointed to a graceful tower in the distance.

"Askelon!" His tone was almost reverential. "Now you shall see what the Maccabee money made of a squalid, dilapidated, little town."

"The Maccabees must be a great-hearted family," remarked Voldi.

"That depends on one's point of view," drawled Mencius. "According to general opinion the Maccabees are tyrants. Wealthy patrons of the arts," he added, "are not necessarily great-hearted. The finest architecture and sculpture in the world may be found in Rome, but plenty of people could testify that we Romans are not benevolent."

*   *   *   *   *   *

Two days later, at sundown, the travelers arrived in the amazing city of Caesarea. If Voldi had been bewildered by the transitions from dirty and degraded Gaza, of the Philistines, to the marble splendor of beautiful Askelon, of the Greeks, and the frowsiness of decayed Joppa, of the Judaeans, he was now even more astonished by the feverish confusions of this rapidly rising metropolis which, according to Mencius, would one day be the focal point from which the Empire would move toward the utter subjugation of all Jewry.

Heretofore, the Emperors had insisted only upon tribute in cash. The Jews were sheep to be shorn annually but not converted into mutton. Presently the Romans would want more than Israel's fleece. They would march in and take everything, Mencius had declared; and when Voldi had inquired whether this threat was a secret, his friend had replied, airily, "Secret? Not at all! The Jews know the invasion is sure to come! Preparations for it are going on right under their noses!"

Too tired that night for sight-seeing, they had ridden through the congested streets to the principal inn, The Agrippa, recently built by the Romans to accommodate three hundred guests. It was situated in the very heart of the city, and crowded to capacity; but Mencius had a friend in the management, and a room was found for them.

After an excellent supper, they strolled through the spacious, newly furnished foyer where scores of opulently dressed Romans of self-assured and distinguished bearing stood in conversing groups or lounged in the richly upholstered chairs and divans. This unfamiliar view of flamboyant wealth dazzled Voldi's senses. He wasn't quite sure whether he was infatuated or infuriated. Every man in sight was extravagantly garbed and groomed. The air was heavy with pomades. Jewels flashed on well-kept hands. It was true then: the Romans were not only men of the world; they were the important, the impressive men of the world! It belonged to them! There could be no doubt of that!

Voldi's memory—which he suspected of something like disloyalty—rolled back for a glimpse of King Zendi and his Council, carelessly clad in their unadorned burnouses; grave, hard-muscled men who despised ostentation. How their thin; haughty nostrils would have flared in contempt of this gaudy show! But—wasn't it costing Arabia a pretty penny to maintain that attitude of scorn for prosperous people? Voldi wondered whether proud poverty wasn't—in the long run—more expensive property than ropes of pearls.

Suddenly a tall, handsome, close-cropped Roman—on the left breast of whose scarlet tunic the imperial black eagle was appliquéed—detached himself from a small party of friends and came forward beaming a welcome.

"Nick! You're here at last! The gods be praised for your safe arrival! I was getting anxious!"

They clapped their hands on each other's shoulders.

"Why anxious, Tony? I'm not late. This was the day."

"No—you're not late. But my distinguished passengers showed up this afternoon, hours before I expected them, and who knows when they might decide to sail? The wishes of Her Highness are never predictable. . . . I hope you've attended to all your business—and are ready to be off at a moment's notice."

Mencius nodded; and, reaching for Voldi's arm, drew him forward.

"Tony," he said, "I want you to meet a young Arabian friend of mine. . . . Voldi, greet my long-time-ago schoolmate, Antonius Lucan, Commander of the Emperor's ship, *The Augusta*."

Voldi bowed briefly. The Commander's eyes narrowed a little. He lifted his forearm perfunctorily and mumbled that any friend of Proconsul Nicator Mencius was his friend also; after which he turned toward his old crony with a quizzical arching of his grizzled brows, plainly inquiring how we happened to have an Arabian on our hands at this particular moment. Mencius was prompt to reply. Voldi had come upon him in the night, on the road alone, badly outnumbered by robbers, and had joined the fray. The reckless Arabian had saved his life; no less!

In response to this speech, the Commander of *The Augusta* bowed to Voldi in recognition of invaluable services rendered to a comrade, and Mencius supplemented his story of the fight with, "It's amazing—this young fellow's skill with a dagger! I think his parents must have given him a knife to play with when he was a baby."

Voldi drew a deprecating grin, shrugged slightly, and seemed eager for a change of topic. He was conscious of the old sailor's uneasiness about him. The tension was somewhat relaxed, at this juncture, by the appearance of another urbane, middle-aged Roman—more conservatively dressed than any of the others—who paused to greet Mencius with quiet affability, after nodding to Tony.

"What brings you here, this time, Mencius?" he inquired, lazily. "More copper?"

"At present, the fellow's not a peddler, Atrius," drawled Tony. "He's a tourist, absolutely empty-handed, sailing home with me on *The Augusta*. We're taking His Highness Antipas and his family on their annual excursion."

Atrius, taking pains to be extravagantly disrespectful, sniffed audibly and wrinkled his nose.

"I wish somebody would explain to me," he declaimed, "how the ruler of poor little Galilee rates a free voyage, every season, on the Emperor's pleasure-barge!"

"Psst!" warned Tony. "I mustn't be seen listening complacently to

such talk." Then, lowering his voice, he remarked, "You may be sure the
Tetrarch will eventually pay his passage. . . . And he is abundantly able to
do it—when Tiberius bills him for it."

Mencius broke in now to introduce Voldi with appropriate explanations of the circumstances accounting for their friendship. Then, to
Voldi, "Should you get into any trouble while in Caesarea, our excellent
Atrius—who is the best-known lawyer in the city—will befriend you, I
know."

Atrius, who had been gnawing at his bearded underlip and staring into
Voldi's face with undisguised curiosity, chuckled gruffly.

"Arabian, eh? And handy with a blade! Doesn't ask what the fight's
about, so long as he can get in there—and gut somebody!" He laughed
with evident relish, and poked Tony in the ribs with his thumb! "Hell of
a time for an Arabian gladiator to turn up, I must say! . . . What part of
Arabia do you hail from, my son?"

"The southern mountains, sir," replied Voldi, stiffly.

"Anywhere near the King's domain?"

"Not very far, sir; a few miles."

"Your King Zendi seems a popular man."

"Yes, sir."

"I daresay you know him," ventured Atrius. The others were growing
restless. The Commander was absently patting his be-ringed left fist with
his right palm. Mencius shifted his weight and frowned.

"Voldi's grandfather, Mishma, is the King's Chief Counsellor, Atrius."

"Ah?—So!" Atrius grinned. "Well—if there is anything we can do for
you while you are in Caesarea, Voldi, we will be happy to serve you. . . .
See you later, Tony. . . . You'll be glad to be home again, Mencius. Wish I
were going with you. You will be arriving in time for Saturnalia."

With the departure of Atrius, conversation lagged; and Voldi, surmising that the two Romans might wish to have some private talk, excused himself and sauntered through the lobbies to the loggia which half
circled a pool where a beautifully wrought fountain played. He sat down
on a deeply upholstered divan and reviewed the recent conversation. . . .
This Atrius might be a good man to know.

For some little time after Volid had strolled away from them, Mencius
and Tony found it difficult to sustain an interest in their talk about the
forthcoming voyage. Finally Tony blurted out:

"What's this boy doing in Caesarea, Mencius?"

"He is on his way north."

"Sight-seeing—or business?"

"A little of both, I think."

"Meaning that you aren't going to tell me." Tony's voice showed annoyance.

"He confided to me the nature of his errand," admitted Mencius. "It is nothing to cause you anxiety. He is looking for a fugitive. I shall be obliged if this much information contents you, Tony. I gave him my word."

"Very well," conceded Tony, grumpily. "But I'll expect you to see to it that your blood-letting Arab keeps his distance from my ship! If anybody sticks a knife into the Tetrarch while he is not in my custody, I shall make no protest; but—by Jove!—he's not going to be assassinated on *The Augusta!*"

"It's a wonder the fellow makes these voyages," observed Mencius.

"He can't rot up there in Galilee, all the year round! He'd go crazy! Nothing ever happens. He has no friends among his subjects. They all despise him. . . . However—he may be in for more excitement than he wants, presently. His Chief Scrivener was telling me, this afternoon, that something like a revolution is brewing—"

"In sleepy, stupid, little Galilee?" scoffed Mencius. "You're jesting!"

"According to this scribbler, Pamphylios, it's not an uprising against the government; at least not yet. It seems that a young carpenter has been haranguing great crowds. So far, he has said nothing to inflame the people. To the contrary, he has been urging them to be law-abiding and content with their poverty."

"And how could such soft words collect a crowd?" wondered Mencius.

"Pamphylios says the man has been healing the sick by laying his hands upon them," said Tony. "That, of course, is nonsense. Pamphylios admits he has no first-hand knowledge of it. But—the rumor is in the air, and all Galilee is buzzing with these stories."

"Bad time for the Tetrarch to absent himself," remarked Mencius.

"That's what Pamphylios thinks," assented Tony. "But Antipas couldn't be talked out of his customary excursion. Half the year, in Tiberias, he lives on his anticipation of the other half in Rome. The Scrivener says that a deputation of priests waited on His Highness, a few days ago, pleading with him to silence the carpenter; but Antipas made short work of them; told them they had better make their synagogues a little more attractive and useful—and maybe the people wouldn't be congregating in pasture-fields to listen to this carpenter."

"Not a bad suggestion," put in Mencius, with a chuckle.

"Any suggestion would be good enough, in the Tetrarch's opinion, so long as he wasn't hindered from going to Rome. He wouldn't miss the pageants and games of Saturnalia—not even if the Sea of Galilee went dry!"

Mencius was soberly meditative for a while.

"Ever hear of the Jewish 'Messiah,' Tony?" he asked, irrelevantly.

Tony shook his head and scowled; muttered that he had given up trying to understand the Jews. Mencius explained briefly; but his friend was disinterested. The Jews had always been too religious for their own good, he said.

"I'm surprised that you have so much concern for such rubbish," continued Tony, impatiently. "You read too much! You think too much! You know too much! It wouldn't surprise me to hear, some day, that you'd gone off to live in a cave—in the mountains—having it out with the gods—and the fleas."

"I'll admit," said Mencius, "a man can live a much happier life by not using his mind, at all. . . . I'm going to bed now. I have been all day in the saddle. Doubtless you will be turning in, too."

"Not quite yet," growled Tony. "I've an errand to do first. I must go down to the docks and notify my mate to be on the alert for an Arabian stowaway."

"You're putting yourself to unnecessary bother," said Mencius.

"I shall be satisfied if your new friend gives me no more bother than that," said Tony.

After Voldi had sat alone, staring absently at the fountain for a quarter hour, he was joined on the divan by the lawyer, who hoped he was not intruding.

"Expect to be with us for a while?" inquired Atrius, casually.

"I am leaving in the morning, sir," replied Voldi. It had occurred to him that if he showed an inclination to be frank, his explanations might be more readily believed. "I have an errand in Galilee," he went on. "I have been sent to look for a young Arabian who ran away from home and is believed to have gone up into the neighborhood of the Sea of Galilee. I am to persuade him to return—if I find him."

"Know anything about the city of Tiberias?"

"Not much. It's the seat of the Tetrarch. There is a Roman fort hard by."

"You will make inquiries at the fort?"

"Not at first; not until I have to. I'd much rather find my fugitive friend without calling so much attention to him. I shall not needlessly embarrass him. . . . Do you know that country, sir?"

"A little. If I may venture a suggestion, Voldi, there is a discreet man of my acquaintance living in the small town of Bethsaida, only a short distance from Tiberias. He is a lawyer, in retirement now; a man of broad sympathies and much prudence. You might give him your confidence."

Voldi was glad to accept the advice. He brought out a small slate tablet from his pocket and wrote the Bethsaidan's name and the directions for finding him. Atrius negligently allowed his eyes to follow the red chalk as the Arabian wrote.

"You've lived in Greece?" he inquired, when Voldi had pocketed the tablet.

"No, sir; I have never been in Greece."

"Do many Arabians understand Greek?"

"Probably not." Voldi rose, thanked Atrius for his kindness, and remarked that he must find Mencius before retiring.

"It would please me to learn how your mission succeeds," said Atrius, as they parted—"and please convey my greetings to my friend—and former colleague—David Ben-Zadok."

*   *   *   *   *   *

At the first intimation of dawn Voldi slipped out quietly so as not to waken Mencius, to whom he had said farewell at midnight after a lengthy but inconclusive discussion of the probability of his finding Fara in Galilee.

Mencius had then gone promptly to sleep, apparently undisturbed by the relentless racket of heavy traffic in the street below where enormous wagons, laden with building materials, ground their iron-shod wheels into the cobble-stones, and drivers screamed and lashed at their straining oxen. The hideous clamor had not annoyed Mencius. He was quite accustomed to it, he said. That was the way it sounded all night, every night, in Rome. The Emperor, wanting to keep the streets free of construction traffic in the daytime, had decreed that all heavy hauling must be done between sunset and sunrise. Caesarea, being now a Roman city, observed this rule. But Mencius didn't care. He was more than a bit homesick and the infernal din seemed to soothe him. Not so with Voldi, who had had no experience in big, bustling cities. The unceasing noise had kept him wide awake, and the dilemma confronting him had grown to appalling dimensions in the darkness.

At the well-kept stables, where he found Darik sleek and shining from the diligent grooming he had received (another attestation to the proficiency of Roman discipline), Voldi was not much surprised to encounter an armed legionary waiting courteously to escort him out of the city; for

Mencius had confided that Commander Antonius Lucan of *The Augusta* would feel more comfortable after being informed that the grudge-bearing young Arabian had ridden through Caesarea's east gate and had disappeared on the open road toward Galilee.

In a half hour he was alone on that road, after having received the legionary's deferential wishes for a safe and pleasant journey, though they were both fully aware of the reason why the honor of a Roman escort had been conferred upon a young citizen of Arabia. Voldi looked back over his shoulder, waved a hand, and laughed quietly over the little drama in which he had been invited to play. In spite of their reputation for insufferable egotism and bloody-handed ruthlessness, reflected Voldi, the Romans were—in many respects—to be admired. They were superbly organized. They were effective. They were cruel, yes; but not bcause they loved cruelty. They preferred your friendship to your enmity. They would rather lead than drive. They could even set a watch over your movements, and do it so graciously that you wanted to wave a friendly farewell to your keepei when he was done with you.

The road, angling to the northeast, was not so busy as the coast highway. It was therefore narrower. With a long day's journey ahead of him, Voldi encouraged Darik to settle down to a comfortable canter. They were in level country now, the broad Plain of Esdraelon, where the landscape was too monotonous to divert a stranger's attention from his own problems. . . . One fact brought a crumb of comfort: the Tetrarch was still alive. Of course, he didn't deserve to be alive; but at least Fara had not got herself into trouble by killing him. And it was unlikely that she had attempted to kill him, for surely Commander Antonius Lucan would have known of it; and having known of it, would have told of it.

Came now a plodding donkey-train, bearing small, greasy-looking casks, probably containing sesame and olive oil bound for Caesarea, in charge of shabby, shaggy, sullen men who frowned and spat as they passed.

But what would Fara be likely to do, now that her mission had failed of accomplishment? Assuming that she had arrived in the vicinity of Tiberias to await an opportunity for settling with her rascally father, would she await his return from Rome?

Here came a lone traveler, ambling along on an infirm, sore-eyed camel, followed—at a hundred yards—by a humpbacked old man with a scowl on his wrinkled face and an ax on his bony shoulder.

Voldi greeted each of them in turn with a cheery Good Morning. Neither replied. Was that because he was riding a good horse, and they were envious? Or was it because he was an Arabian? Or because he was a stranger—any stranger? Or because they were by nature impolite? He had to admit, though, as he rode on, that the Arabians would have shown no more courtesy to a traveling Jew.

Perhaps Fara would decide to return to Arabia, now that she had failed. But, having risked so much—to come so far—would she not persevere and wait for the Tetrarch's return? There really wasn't much in Arabia for her to go back to since her mother was gone. Himself, of course, but she may have put him out of her mind. Having left him without a word of farewell, she might assume that he would have given her up—and turned his attention elsewhere.

Now a family on foot, single-file, was overtaken. Reluctantly they sidled off the road and stood stolidly in the dusty weeds waiting for the rider to pass. Father, leading the procession, wore an impressive black beard and a ragged black robe, but bore no burden. Mother had a sleepy baby in the crook of one arm and a big basket of wheat in the other. The boy towed a white milch-goat. The half-grown girl carried a bulging bag of apples on her back. Voldi rode by slowly, yielding room. He nodded amiably. Father and the goat raised their chins and sneered with expressions so similar that Voldi grinned. Mother, imitating her lord, made an ugly face. The boy stared, without malice. The girl lifted pretty eyes and smiled shyly.

It was the older people's fault, thought Voldi, that the different races despised one another. He wondered whether the world might be more harmonious if all the old people were abolished; say, everyone over twenty. Luckily for himself, such a commendable decree would leave him to help establish the new order in which strangers—meeting on the road— would be more ready to smile than spit. But—they would all have to remain at twenty—and never grow old. Perhaps the project was impractical.

Well—it wouldn't be long now until he might know something more about Fara. An Arabian boy in his teens would be noticed in a small fishing village, where everybody knew everybody else. Someone would remember having seen this young Arab. Voldi wondered what success Fara might have had—posing as a boy. Risky business, that was!

At a cross-roads in sight of a village that the sign-post said was Megiddo, four legionaries, their spears and shields leaning against the stone fence, were sprawled on the ground intent upon a dice-game. Voldi expected them to challenge him. In that event he was going to say that the Tetrarch had bought the black gelding while in Caesarea and he was delivering it at Tiberias. But the soldiers barely glanced up as he passed. Apparently the discipline of the troops had been eased somewhat since the Tetrarch's departure. Or perhaps the attention of the officers had been diverted by the large assemblies that Mencius had spoken of, lately congregating in the vicinity of the Sea of Galilee. A carpenter had been addressing the people and was reputed to be healing all manner of diseases. This latter feat being clearly an incredible rumor, it was not likely that the carpenter would last very long as a popular leader, Mencius had said. There was nothing inflammatory about it, or the Tetrarch would not have left the country.

Voldi wondered how much interest Fara might have in such a movement. He could not conceive of her showing any curiosity about a thing like that, except for the fact that she had turned aside at Hebron to listen to another itinerant prophet. It had seemed quite unlike Fara to be attracted by a performance of that nature.

A bad lunch—smoked fish and stale barley-bread—was sullenly tossed onto a dirty table at Megiddo's only inn. Voldi nibbled at the unappetizing food and paid the pock-marked woman with a shekel. She threw down a handful of unfamiliar copper coins. He kept one of them, meaning to examine it later, and went out to water his horse at the public trough. A group of small boys, in soiled tatters, gathered about. A woman screamed from a near-by doorway and the oldest boy ambled off in that direction, turning to spit before leaving. There was another female screech from somewhere in the neighborhood and all the lads scurried away but two. The smaller boy's eyes were brimming with pus. Voldi reached in his pocket and brought up the copper he had been given in change at the inn. He offered it to the sore-eyed boy who did not reach for it.

"He's blind," explained his brother. "Give it to me!"

Voldi handed him the coin.

"Yaa! Yaa!" screamed the boy, flinging the copper down. "Bad money! No good! Yaa! Yaa!" He set off—dragging his little brother—doubtless to report the incident. Voldi mounted and rode on. A small group of indignant men and women was collecting about the outraged boy who had been offered a worthless coin. They reviled the Arabian as he passed. Megiddo was not an attractive village. Was it typical of Galilean communities? Voldi hoped not. Poor Fara!

As the afternoon wore on, the country became more fertile but it was plain to see that the inhabitants had not made the most of it. It was indeed a backward land. One day the Romans would come in and prosper. The Galileans would be virtually enslaved, but have more to eat, no doubt, than now.

At sundown Nazareth was sighted. At a distance, with the late afternoon glow on the squat dome of the synagogue and the houses whitely gleaming, the town promised to be picturesque. On closer acquaintance it was a disappointment. The residences were small, shabby and forlorn. As usual, the principal street widened at the center of the village, describing a circle around the inevitable community well. Apparently most of the mercantile business was concentrated here. Little bazaars and shops elbowed one another for standing-room. Beyond the circle was the inn. The proprietor made it obvious to Voldi that he was unwelcome, but grumblingly consented to give him lodging when he heard the clink of substantial money. After toying disgustedly with the worst food that had ever been set before him, Voldi strolled out onto the deserted street. Everyone was at supper.

He came upon a farrier's shop and found a graying man of fifty or more at his forge, mending a broken cistern-wheel, probably a matter of some urgency. Always interested in farriers' shops, he paused in the open doorway. The man looked up from his work and nodded amiably. It was a pleasant surprise to be greeted in this friendly manner, and Voldi sauntered in.

"Stranger in these parts?" The farrier gave the bellows-rope another tug and pointed to a seat on an old tool-chest.

"Yes—I am an Arabian." Voldi thought it better to have this awkward subject disposed of without delay.

"We don't see many," said the farrier. "Are you staying with us awhile, sir?"

"Tonight only. I am on my way from Caesarea to Tiberias."

"The Tetrarch came through here, a couple of days ago. Quite a procession. Going to Rome. Perhaps you know about it."

Voldi said he did.

"Ever been in Tiberias?" asked the farrier.

"No. I suppose you have been there, many a time."

"Never. But I mean to go—tomorrow. That's why I'm working late. Big doings over there, these days. Perhaps you've had wind of it, along the way. Our prophet, Jesus, has been talking to great multitudes."

"Your prophet? Meaning that you believe in him? Have you heard him?"

"I've known him since he was a baby! This is his home!" The farrier put his hammer down on the anvil and leaned comfortably against his work-bench, relishing the stranger's evident interest in him.

"Is it true that he performs miracles?" asked Voldi. "I've heard a rumor to that effect."

"That's what I want to know," said the farrier, soberly. "It wouldn't surprise me much; though he never did anything strange, here in Nazareth. He is a carpenter, a good one too." He pointed through the open window behind Voldi, who turned to look. "That's the shop, over there, across the road. It's his father's. And it was his father's before him. Jesus has worked there ever since he was a youngster—until a few months ago."

"Anything queer about him?" encouraged Voldi.

"He was a dreamy little fellow," remembered the farrier, averting his eyes. "The other children liked him though. As a lad he used to tell them stories."

"What kind of stories?" wondered Voldi.

"I never heard any of them myself. He seemed shy of grown-up people and didn't talk much when they were around. But my oldest brother Laban's boy Ephraim—my namesake—said the stories were mostly about some faraway country where there was no winter and no darkness—and the rivers never dried or overflowed—and nobody was ever sick—and nobody died—and nobody wept. And everyone loved the King."

Voldi waited in silence for the farrier to continue.

"It seemed strange for a small boy to have such fancies," soliloquized Ephraim. "According to my nephew, Jesus always talked about this distant land as if it was real; almost as if he had been there. The country was at peace. There were no soldiers, no forts, no prisons, no alms-houses. Everyone had some work to do, but not for money. There wasn't any money. No one was rich; no one was poor. And flowers grew everywhere and always—but nobody gathered them. . . . The child made much over flowers. From the time he was able to toddle, the little chap would carry water from the village well to his garden. We all thought he wouldn't amount to much, being so interested in flowers. But—as he grew up he turned out to be a skillful carpenter; better than Joseph, his father."

"But he never gathered up a crowd—and talked?" asked Voldi.

"No. As I say, he was not a one to talk much, except to the smaller children; and, after he came into his teens, he was very quiet and walked alone, most of the time. I think that was because—as he grew up—the older children laughed among themselves at the stories he had told. Once it was spread about that a half-grown boy, tormenting him about this faraway land, rudely accused him of being a liar, and Jesus replied that he had told them the truth; that there was such a country; that he knew more things about it than he had told them."

"And then the people thought he was crazy, I suppose," remarked Voldi.

"Well—we couldn't help feeling that he was different, and perhaps he guessed how we felt about him—for he spent most of his time alone, except when he was working in the shop."

"What did his family think about him?"

"They didn't know quite what to make of him. He used to go for long walks by himself, in the hills. His mother worried about him. Shortly before he left Nazareth, he was gone for a couple of months, and when he came back you would have thought he was walking in his sleep. He had something on his mind—and it weighted him. Nobody seemed to know where he had been. Maybe his folks did. But it was plain that he was much stirred up—inside. . . . On the morning of the day he left Nazareth—for good, I fear—he attended the service in the Synagogue, for it was the Sabbath Day. He sat with the family, as usual. Sometimes our good old Rabbi Ben-Naboth would ask some man in the congregation to read the Scripture Lesson; some one of the old men who were known for their piety. On this day the Rabbi called for Jesus to come forward. It was unusual to invite one so young. The place grew very quiet."

"You thought it would be something out of the ordinary?" asked Voldi.

"Wouldn't you?" countered Ephraim—"considering how out of the ordinary Jesus was? . . . Well—he walked forward and took up the scroll containing the writing of the Prophet Esaias. . . . I suppose you've heard of our famed Prophet Esaias—" he interrupted himself to say.

"No," admitted Voldi. "I have little knowledge of your great ones—since our Father Abraham." They both grinned.

"Nearly as I can recall the words," continued Ephraim, "what Jesus read went something like this: 'The Spirit of the Lord is upon me. He has appointed me to bring good news to the poor. He has sent me to release men in bondage, and open the eyes of the blind. I am to raise up those who have been beaten down, and I am to announce that the Lord will make this a blessed year. . . .' Then Jesus rolled up the scroll, handed it back to the Rabbi, and said, 'This prophecy is now to be fulfilled.' Then he returned to his seat. All eyes were fixed on him. Even the Rabbi seemed bewildered, and it was some little time before he went on with the devotions. . . . After the meeting, the congregation gathered about Jesus, as he came out, and asked him what he meant; and was someone coming—here—now—to Nazareth—to open the prison and free the slaves and give sight to the blind?"

"It hadn't occurred to any of you that Jesus might be referring to himself as the promised healer?"

"No: you see he had grown up with us. It was beyond our thought that one of our own neighbors might be gifted to do such things."

"What did Jesus say then?"

"He declared that it was to be his mission to spread the good news. And the people were silent and unbelieving—and slanted their eyes at one another with sulky faces. One old man shouted, crossly, 'You think you are going to open the eyes of the blind—here—in Nazareth?' "

"I'll wager they all listened to his reply!" said Voldi.

"They did indeed—and it made them angry. Jesus said, 'Not here—not in Nazareth. A prophet has no value in his own community.' At that, the people drifted away, grumbling; many of them turning to scowl or laugh scornfully."

"And—after that—they mistreated him?"

"No; he gave them no opportunity to mistreat him. He left Nazareth at once; not even tarrying to have dinner with his family. After the meeting at the Synagogue he wandered away—and he hasn't been back."

"Perhaps," surmised Voldi, "if he is really doing great things for people elsewhere, the people of your town will beseech him to return."

Ephraim shook his head and renewed his forge-fire.

"No," he replied. "It wouldn't be like Nazareth—to do that."

"Not even to have your blind ones see?" asked Voldi.

"No; not even to have our blind ones see!" Ephraim was now resuming his interrupted work with diligence. Voldi felt that the interview was over, and rose to go. At the door he turned to say with a smile:

"What will your fellow townsmen think of you for making a journey to see Jesus? Will they be annoyed?"

Ephraim tapped his anvil a couple of times, chuckling to himself.

"They can't be too much annoyed," he said. "I'm the only farrier in Nazareth. Perhaps if there were two, I shouldn't risk my neighbors' displeasure."

Voldi bade him farewell and returned to the inhospitable inn. Shortly after midnight he was awakened by a violent thunder-storm followed by a heavy rainfall that continued throughout the night and until mid-forenoon of the next day. When finally it cleared, he set off at the best speed he could make on a slippery road, hoping to arrive in Bethsaida before darkness fell.

11

I HAD RAINED steadily all night and was still hard at it when Jairus roused in the morning. He sat up in bed and frowned.

Ordinarily, Jairus would not have cared. Of complacent mind, it was his habit to accept all weathers without complaint. Besides, the country needed rain, for it had been the sunniest autumn that Galilee had seen for many years.

But, much as his cherished gardens and vineyards would benefit by a refreshing downpour, this was clearly an inconvenient day for it, and Jairus was annoyed; so very much annoyed that when Adiel, his uncommonly attractive wife, entered the room, she found him in a posture of dejection, with both hands in his tousled hair. He mumbled a gloomy acknowledgment of her presence without looking up. Seating herself on the edge of his bed, Adiel gently patted him on the shoulder. What was the trouble? Didn't he like the rain?

"Any other time," muttered Jairus, slipping his arm about her. "I was a fool to consent to that meeting here today. These tedious discussions always bore me, even when the day is fine and they can do their dull haranguing out in the pergola. Now we will have them on our hands—all day—indoors—with no chance of escape. . . . But one can't offend Rabbi Ben-Sholem. He is a good old man."

"Yes, dear; he is indeed—though a bit tiresome," murmured Adiel. "I had forgotten that you were having company today. What is this party to be: one of those dreadful, all-day meetings of the Synagogue Regents?"

"Worse than that," sighed Jairus. "This is a deputation of priests, scribes, legal counsellors, and such things, who are coming all the way from Jerusalem to decide what should be done with this preaching Carpenter."

243

"Maybe they won't come," said Adiel, hopefully—"now that it's such a bad day."

"Of course they'll come!" grumbled Jairus. "They will have been on the road for all of three days. We may as well prepare for them. They'll be here. You can depend on that!" He glanced up, brightened perceptibly, and waved his hand to a pair of smiling, twelve-year-old eyes that had appeared in the crack of the slowly opening door. His invitation brought the happy child dancing into the room. She snuggled down on the other side of her father.

"Breakfast's ready," she announced gaily. "And Rachael says we're to come directly and eat it, for there's to be a lot of company here for dinner. . . . What kind of company, father? Will they be jolly—and tell funny stories; or are they the other people?"

Jairus absently fondled his daughter's curls and replied sadly that they were—he regretted to say—the other people.

"No funny stories today, Sharon."

"Go and tell Rachael we will be there immediately, dear," said her mother; and when the child had scrambled out of the bed and was on her way, Adiel asked, "What are they planning to do to this strange person? You said he hadn't broken the laws. What charge will they bring against him?"

"That's what they are going to discuss today," replied Jairus. "They can't apprehend him as a disturber of the peace. If he has disturbed the peace by preaching to these big crowds, it is the business of the provincial police to arrest him. I had a talk with Antipas about this, a few days before he left. He had sent several of his men out into the country to see what the Carpenter was trying to do, and they reported that nothing seditious had been said. The Tetrarch seemed satisfied that the fellow was doing no harm with his admonitions to the people that they should try to be contented—and live at peace with all men."

"Surely the Rabbis can't object to that," reflected Adiel. "Perhaps they have been disturbed by all these tales of miracles." She grew suddenly serious, searching her husband's eyes. "You don't think there can be any truth in these stories; do you, Jairus? All the people on our estate are talking of nothing else! I've never known our house-servants to be so excited about anything!"

"Well"—drawled Jairus—"you know how servants are. They dote on such yarns. It's quite beyond belief that the Carpenter is really healing diseases. Have any of our people told you that they, themselves, have been cured of anything?"

"No—but they are convinced that the man has done some very remarkable things." Rising, Adiel held up Jairus' exquisitely quilted robe. Hoisting himself out of bed, he slipped his arms into it, and ambled off toward the spacious bath, pausing in the doorway to remark, "I think it's rather undignified for these pundits from Jerusalem to be making a big thing of this. If they pay no attention to the man, he will soon dispose of himself—and the people will forget all about him—and he can go back to his carpenter-shop. I'm ashamed to be serving as host to this foolish business, Adiel."

She loitered in the corridor for him, and when presently he rejoined her, Adiel tucked her hand under his arm and said, with some hesitation, "I wish you would have a talk with a few of our farmers; old Simeon, for one. You can trust him to tell the truth. He claims that he actually saw this Jesus give sight to a man who had been born blind!"

"Pouf!" scoffed Jairus, good-naturedly. "Don't be silly! There's some sensible explanation for these tales. You may be sure of that!"

They strolled toward the breakfast-room. It was on the east side of the villa, adjoining the large dining-room, and was usually flooded with sunshine. On fine summer days the servants rolled back the central panels of the roof, made of tightly woven goat-hair, and the family breakfasted under the blue sky. It was closed today and the room was dreary. Even the beautifully crafted mosaics on the walls were dingy and lifeless.

As they neared the high-arched doorway, Jairus slowed to say, before they entered, "If our people want this sort of entertainment, I've no objection. The crops are all in. The men have nothing much to do. Listening to the Carpenter is certainly better than loitering around the wine-cellars down in Capernaum. . . . Good morning, Rachael! We will make short work of our breakfast. You and the maids have a busy day before you, with the large party for dinner."

"Yes, sir," sniffed old Rachael, beckoning to her crew to proceed with their table-service. Then, with the bland impudence to which her seniority entitled her, she remarked, "And they will eat a lot!"

"What makes you think so?" inquired her master, anticipating some astringent drollery.

"We've had their like before, sir; men who speak big words. They always eat big dinners."

"I had never noticed that, Rachael," chuckled Jairus—"but, by Jove, I believe you're right! Well—make sure you have enough for them."

Sharon now came up out of her half-drained milk-goblet, with a gasp, and solemnly remarked, "Nurse says 'By Jove' is a Roman swear-word, father."

"Perhaps, if we must swear," commented her mother, "it is better to take the names of the heathen gods in vain."

"Is this By-Jove a heathen?" asked Sharon.

"Drink your milk, little one," admonished her father, gently. "We'll all have our fill of theology before the day is over, without beginning it now."

"I'm not expected to attend this dinner, am I?" asked Adiel.

"No, dear," said Jairus. "Not if you don't want to. It's a business affair. You needn't show up at all. It's Rabbi Ben-Sholem's party, really. We're just providing food and shelter."

*   *   *   *   *   *

By mid-forenoon it had cleared. Patches of blue sky were appearing and the sun was glinting on the puddles in the rose-garden as Jairus sauntered out to the pergola. Perhaps it would dry off sufficiently for the learned men—having fed well—to carry their weighty matters out of the house. That would be a relief. Jairus could see to it that they were comfortably seated—and then drift quietly away. The wise men would not miss him.

Upon examination, the vine-bowered pergola was still a-drip but giving off a promising steam, and the wicker chairs and divans were drying fast. Jairus was almost cheerful when Rabbi Ben-Sholem appeared, punching holes in the wet gravel with his cane. The Rabbi, habitually sedate, was almost animated.

"This promises to be an interesting day, my son," he said, in a tone that hinted at a treat in store.

"That's good," rejoined Jairus, without enthusiasm. "I have been hoping that the gardens and the pergola would be dry enough for your people to hold their meeting, this afternoon, out-of-doors."

"Well—as for that—this will not be a festive occasion," declared Ben-Sholem, soberly. "It is not a garden party. What we have to do today can better be done indoors!"

"Oh? So serious as that?"

"Yes. The Carpenter is to be here!"

Jairus, who had been shaking a dripping vine, straightened—and brightened a little.

"Indeed!" he said. "That's interesting!"

"Yes—a couple of our young students for the priesthood hunted the fellow down, yesterday, and—"

"Hunted him down, eh?" There was a trace of asperity in Jairus' tone. "That must have called for much shrewdness, seeing that the Carpenter has been openly speaking to great throngs. Had he hidden himself some-- where?"

"No—he was not in hiding," replied the old man, frostily. "He was shamelessly eating his supper in the home of Simon, the son of Jonas."

Jairus grinned, and the Rabbi scowled at his amusement.

"You don't mean to say, sir, that he was visiting the Big Fisherman! I thought this Carpenter was some sort of a religious teacher. Apparently he isn't very particular about the company he keeps. The Big Fisherman hasn't any more religion than our dog!"

"That is one of the things we will discuss with him," said the Rabbi. "He makes pretense of being a holy man; talks to the multitude about holy things; and then associates himself with all manner of profane and uncouth people. Some of our men saw him, a few days ago, sitting in the Revenue Office, chatting with Levi—that abominable Collector of Roman tribute!"

"Maybe he was trying to talk Levi into a reduction of his taxes," chuckled Jairus. "I must ask him how he got on with it."

"It is not a jesting matter, my son," said the Rabbi, sternly.

"Sorry," mumbled Jairus. After a moment of constrained silence, he asked, "Did your young men have any trouble getting the Carpenter's consent to come here today? Of course they couldn't command him to come."

"They did command him!" declared Ben-Sholem. "By the authority of the Synagogue!"

"Then he needn't come unless he wants to," said Jairus, brusquely. "He probably knows—as well as you do, sir—that the Synagogue has no power to arrest him—or subpoena him."

"Be that as it may," said Ben-Sholem, testily, "he is coming. He had the effrontery to say that he would be free to come because it was going to be too stormy this afternoon for the people to turn out."

Jairus' jaw sagged a little and his brows contracted.

"You say he made that forecast yesterday—when there wasn't a cloud in the sky? He must be a weather prophet."

"Not a very good one," remarked the Rabbi, with a brief smile. "It will be fair, this afternoon."

"Apparently," agreed Jairus. "By the way—did your bright young men invite the Carpenter to come early enough to have dinner with us?"

"Certainly not!" snorted Ben-Sholem. "He is not coming here as a guest! I must say, Jairus," the old man continued, hotly, "I am surprised at your attitude toward this matter. Here you are, a Regent of the Synagogue, the most influential man in this region, supposed to set a good example—but not caring what manner of doctrine is taught to the people. You even talk of having this blasphemer in your home as a guest, when it is clear that the fellow consorts with the ungodly, dines with Simon the brawler, who openly reviles the Synagogue—and hasn't attended its services for years!" The Rabbi's voice was trembling as he finished his impassioned speech, and Jairus reproached himself for permitting the unhappy episode to develop. Perhaps good old Ben-Sholem had some grounds for his indignation. As a Regent of the Synagogue, Jairus was expected to take more than a casual interest in the community's religious beliefs. To atone for his intimations of indifference, he drew a long face and showed concern for the reclamation of Simon's wayward soul.

"Rabbi, did you ever speak to the Big Fisherman, about his infidelity?" he inquired solemnly.

"It wouldn't have done any good," muttered Ben-Sholem. "I have known the headstrong fellow from his youth. There is no doubt but his apostasy hastened the death of his godly father. . . . Once, a few years ago, two of our young men of the Synagogue asked him respectfully why he did not pay his tithe, and he sneered at them. At that, they chided him —as indeed they should have done—and he grabbed them by the hair and whacked their heads together. Then, realizing the gravity of his offense, he added insult to the injury by presenting them with a basket of perch!"

Jairus frowned heavily at this outrage and seemed about to denounce such inexcusable conduct when, to the Rabbi's pained surprise, he broke forth with a loud cackle of involuntary laughter.

"I am amazed, Jairus!" murmured the old man.

"So am I, sir," confessed the culprit, suddenly sobering. "But I couldn't have helped that—if I had been on my death-bed. Please forgive me!"

"I sincerely hope, Jairus," entreated Ben-Sholem, "that you will regard this unfortunate affair of the Carpenter with the gravity it deserves. When he appears in your house today you must give him to understand that he is coming at the behest of the Synagogue!"

"Then you had better take him to the Synagogue!" retorted Jairus. "I do not like the part you are asking me to play. If I am to be this young man's host, there will be no rudeness, certainly not by me! I had surmised that you were inviting him here for a conference; now it appears that he is summoned for a condemnation! I shall not be a party to such procedure! Indeed, if he comes here friendless and alone, you may expect me to be on his side! Do you mean to say that all the Rabbis in the neighborhood are congregating here to judge the man without giving him the advantage of any defense? Are you all solidly against him?"

"The man must be silenced, Jairus!" declared Ben-Sholem, firmly. "We are all agreed on that, except—" he hesitated for a moment, and went on, reluctantly. "I cannot understand the attitude of Rabbi Elimelech of Bethsaida. He came to see me yesterday, to tell me not to expect him here today."

"Did he give his reasons?" inquired Jairus, with interest.

"Elimelech is getting old," explained the elderly Ben-Sholem. "He is in his second childhood. Indeed, it is said that he spends most of his time telling stories to the children. The substantial people of his congregation hardly know what to make of him."

"And he refuses to join you in rebuking the Carpenter?"

"Elimelech was imprudent enough to go out into the country himself —to hear this Jesus. His people do not approve of that: he admitted as much. He even took more than a score of their children with him. Elimelech needs to be careful or he will be retired."

"I must have a talk with the good old man," remarked Jairus. "It might be worth knowing what he really does think of this Nazarene. What did he say to you—about him?"

"He said the man might be The Messiah, for all we knew! We can't have that kind of talk, you know!"

"Of course not," mumbled Jairus, absently.

*   *   *   *   *   *

The dinner was a dull and difficult affair. Valiantly but vainly did Jairus endeavor to dispel the constraint of his taciturn guests. At first he had breezily introduced conversational topics which, he thought, might induce them to show some interest for sheer courtesy's sake, but they gave him no aid. They ate in silence.

Turning to Nathan, the High Priest's representative, Jairus inquired how Pilate was getting on, these days, with the Sanhedrin. After a lengthy interval, Nathan had stiffly replied, with his eyes on his plate, "As usual." It was implicit in Nathan's icy rejoinder that whatever might be the present relation of the Roman Procurator and the Jewish Court, it was certainly none of Jairus' business. The forthright rebuff nettled him, but he kept his temper.

Addressing Obadiah, the eldest of the scribes, at his left, Jairus asked whether the improvements to the Galilean Embassy had been completed. The old man shook his head. After a pause he elaborated on his response by mumbling that he did not know. He did not bother to add that he didn't care, but it was plain enough that Jairus was talking too much. He felt lonely and out of place. Perhaps he had been impudent in seating himself with these distinguished men. He had done better, he felt, to have donned an apron and helped serve the table. A few times he lifted his eyes hopefully in the direction of Rabbi Ben-Sholem, but the old man moodily munched his mutton, without glancing up.

Now it occurred to Jairus that Ben-Sholem, who had had time for a private word with the Jerusalem party before dinner, might have whispered that their host was not sympathetic with the inquisition to be held in his home. That was it! They were deliberately snubbing him! After that, Jairus—in the rôle of a mere inn-keeper—saw to it that their plates and cups were replenished, addressing himself only to the serving-maids. ". . . Another helping of chicken, Rachael," he murmured behind his hand, "for his Grace the High Priest's Emissary. . . . And bring more wine. . . . And open the windows. It is close in here. . . . And light the lamps."

Perhaps that was part of the trouble. The air had become oppressive and the room was growing dark. Jairus turned about toward the windows and faced a blackened sky. There was going to be a severe storm. Presently the very house shook under a crash of thunder. Vivid tongues of flame stabbed at the close horizon. Detached gusts of wind flung their weight at the awnings and thrust their shoulders against the straining doors. Spurts of rain splashed noisily on the tessellated pavement of the loggia, as if pitched from enormous buckets.

Jairus rose hastily and made for the high-domed atrium, now enveloped in gloom. That precariously supported ceiling had always worried him on stormy days, despite the architect's assurance that it was strong. He entered the huge room and looked up anxiously into the dome as another blast of thunder roared overhead.

Calmly seated, quite within the range of a catastrophe, were four men. Apparently Joseph the butler, having admitted them, had been too busy fastening doors and windows to announce their presence. They rose. A gigantic, bearded man, whom Jairus instantly recognized as the Big Fisherman, stepped forward, bowed, and deferentially tipped his head toward the evident leader of their party.

"Sir," said Simon, in a deep voice, "this is Jesus—of Nazareth."

On any other occasion, Jairus would have had at least a nod and a smile for the man who had so graciously introduced his friend, but there was something about the Nazarene that demanded his full attention. So —this was the Carpenter! Well—it was easy to see why the people were following him about. He was not an ordinary man. Jairus advanced toward him—and bowed respectfully.

"You and your friends are welcome to my house, sir," he said.

There was another crash of thunder and Jairus glanced up apprehensively.

"May I suggest, sir," he urged, "that you step back from underneath this dome? We are not safe here!"

"You need have no fear, Jairus," said Jesus quietly.

"But that roof is dangerous!" insisted Jairus.

"Perhaps," said Jesus—"but not for me, nor for you while you are beside me. My time has not yet come."

Jairus, rarely at a loss for an appropriate word, couldn't think of a suitable thing to say. He found himself held by the Carpenter's reassuring eyes; strange, searching eyes, they were, that asked, without impudence, what manner of man you were, as if they had a right to know. There was another savage blast of thunder, but this time Jairus did not look up. Apparently divining his host's relief, Jesus smiled, glanced aloft, and nodded his head. And Jairus smiled too, but shook his head a little as to say that something was going on here that he couldn't understand.

Now the face of the Carpenter sobered. He turned about and walked slowly toward the tall windows facing the highway, the others following him. Simon indicated his two young friends, who had not been presented. "James and John, sir," he said. "Brothers. Fishermen." Jairus nodded to them, absently. He was thinking of the men from Jerusalem who were waiting, probably with some impatience, to interrogate this mysterious Nazarene. Perhaps they were sitting with their heads together, organizing pedantic queries that no untutored carpenter could be expected to understand: hopeful of showing the fellow up as an ignoramus. . . . Well —he might surprise them!

Jairus joined the men at the window. Out along the roadside a great crowd stood huddled and hunched under the cypress and olive trees in the drenching rain. Simon, towering behind Jesus, turned to Jairus and murmured apologetically, "He entreated them not to follow him here, sir."

"Are these people friends of yours?" asked Jairus, moving to Jesus' side.

Jesus nodded his head and continued to gaze compassionately at the multitude. Then, as if talking to himself, he said, "They are sheep— without a shepherd."

"Well," said Jairus, "we can't have them out there in this storm!" He turned to the Big Fisherman. "Bid them come in!"

Striding quickly to the great doors opening upon the terrace, Simon waved a beckoning arm. The rain-soaked throng could not believe, at first, that they had been invited into the palatial home of Jairus. Simon continued to beckon to them. They raised a grateful shout and broke into a run across the terraced lawn. Jesus watched them coming, for a moment; then turned to give his host a comradely smile.

"You are bringing a blessing upon your house, Jairus," he said softly.

Gratified, but somewhat embarrassed by this tribute, Jairus replied that he hoped his wife would think so, a sally that briefly broadened Jesus' smile.

The crowd was literally pouring into the atrium now, wet to the skin. Simon, beside the open doors, was admonishing the people, in a strangely compulsive, resonant voice, to be orderly, not to push, and not to sit down anywhere in their soaked garments. Jairus thought it high time to conduct his strange guest away from this swarming pack. He touched Jesus' arm and signed for him to follow. They moved toward the corridor. As they came to the open door of the breakfast-room, Jairus observed that the party from Jerusalem had assembled there and were standing silently at the windows, apparently watching the advancing crowd. He signed to Jesus to enter the room, and invited him to sit down. The storm was abating. The rain still poured, but the thunder had subsided to mutterings in the mountains.

Approaching the preoccupied group at the windows, Jairus spoke to Rabbi Ben-Sholem.

"Your Carpenter is here," he said.

They all turned about and stared.

"I have the pleasure to present Jesus whom you have asked to meet," said Jairus.

Jesus rose and bowed respectfully. Jerusalem was glum. They all sat down. The crowd had got out of hand, apparently, the foremost inching along the broad corridor to the doorway of the room where the conference sat.

Ben-Sholem, flushed with annoyance, rose to say sternly, "Jairus, the public has not been invited to this meeting! I insist that the house be cleared of these people!"

"They came in out of the rain, sir," explained Jairus.

"But they have no business here!" expostulated Nathan.

Jairus was about to say that if they wanted to put the people out, they were at liberty to do so—if they could—when a sudden commotion overhead raised all eyes toward the roof. The portable roof-panels were being rolled back, letting in a downpour. Hurriedly dragging their chairs away from the opening, the men of Jerusalem were astounded at what they saw above them. A cot was being lowered into the room. It bore the rain-soaked, shivering, emaciated form of a young man. The roof was quickly replaced as the cot came to rest on the floor. Everyone in the room remained standing. Nobody spoke. Jairus tried to frown, without success.

The situation had become ludicrous. It was quite clear that the servants had connived with the sick man's friends to give him this extraordinary entrance to the crowded house. It had all the appearance of an atrocity that old Rachael might have conceived, probably in collusion with Joseph the butler who was reputed to be much interested in the Carpenter.

At this juncture, Jesus stepped forward and gazed down into the bewildered eyes of the invalid. Anybody could see at a glance what ailed the emaciated young fellow with the twisted, shrunken limbs. Every few years a dreaded epidemic of paralysis, to which children and youths were unaccountably vulnerable, would make helpless cripples of a dozen, a score, a hundred. No one knew the cause—or the cure.

Jairus edged in closer, full of curiosity to see what might happen. The silence in the room was tense. The Carpenter had quietly become the commanding figure in this company. All eyes were upon him.

"My son," he said, gently, "your sins are forgiven."

There was an impatient stir among the critics from Jerusalem, and a sullen rumble of indignation. Nathan, the High Priest's representative, growled angrily, "This is blasphemy!" Old Obadiah, Chief of the Temple Scribes, called out, "How does this man forgive sins?" Ben-Sholem snorted, "That is not what the sick man came for! He wants to be healed of his paralysis!" "Aye!" they all muttered. "Heal him!"

Jairus' heart was pounding hard now. He had found himself instantly attracted to the Nazarene, and had hoped that he might give a good account of himself before these surly pedants; but it was clear that he had got himself into an indefensible position. The wiseacres from Jerusalem were right. It was sheer blasphemy for any man to forgive another man's sins. The Carpenter was merely temporizing with his problem—and doing it in the worst possible way. How could he expect his enemies—or his friends, either—to endorse this stunning sacrilege? Jesus would have to do better than that if he hoped to combat the criticism of his detractors.

Now the room was suddenly hushed to silence again as the Nazarene, stretching forth an arm toward the sick man, calmly addressed the murmurers:

"You have questioned my authority to forgive sins. Let me ask you: is it easier to forgive sins, or to say to a paralytic, 'Arise and walk'? To assure you that I have been given this authority—" He broke off here to turn his full attention to the young man on the cot. Lowering his hand until it touched the thin arm, he commanded, "Rise up, my son, and walk!"

It was the craning crowd, massed in the open doorway, that broke the strained silence with a gasp and a cry of astonishment. The paralytic had reached up to take the proffered hand of Jesus, had pried himself up on his elbow, had sat erect, had struggled laboriously to his feet!

Jairus' throat was tight and dry, and he had a sickish feeling. Confusion broke loose now among the men from the Temple. "A fraud!" they shouted derisively. "Prearranged! . . ." "The man was not a cripple! . . ." "Away with this imposter!"

Out in the broad corridor the wide-eyed throng backed away to clear a path for the young man who advanced with short, experimental steps. His eyes were swimming and his lower lip twitched. The open-mouthed spectators stared into his contorted face as they lurched back to give him room, trampling their neighbors' toes. No one offered him a word or a smile as he passed. He was as one risen from the dead.

The rain had ceased while this strange event was in progress, and the sun was shining brightly. Slowly and silently the awe-stricken crowd was moving out of the house. The visitors from Jerusalem had circled into a compact, whispering group by the breakfast-room window that gave upon the front verandah, now congested with the departing multitude. Nathan was addressing them. Old Rabbi Ben-Sholem was solemnly nodding his head Jairus gave them a brief glance, and decided that his obligations as their host had been discharged. The venerable Ben-Sholem could attend to them from now on.

Jesus had slumped into a chair near the doorway, his posture denoting complete exhaustion. His elbows rested on the broad arms of the chair and his bowed head was supported by white, trembling hands. As Jairus neared he slowly lifted his head and smiled wanly. Tiny beads of perspiration dotted his pale brow.

"I shall go now," he said, huskily—'if there are to be no further questions."

"You are welcome to remain, Master," said Jairus. "You seem to be very tired. Tarry with us—and rest awhile. Come with me "

Wearily acquiescing with a nod, Jesus rose slowly and followed his host down the long corridor, and through the atrium, and on to the adjacent library. As they entered, Adiel and Sharon, who had been seated by the window, apparently in complete ignorance of the amazing thing that had happened, rose to go.

"My wife, Master," said Jairus. . . . "Adiel, this is Jesus—of Nazareth."

Sharon, hugging a small harp in her arms, stood staring up into the stranger's face as her mother murmured a response to the introduction. Jesus looked down into the child's wondering eyes with a smile.

"Our little daughter, Sharon," said Jairus.

Laying his hand lightly on her curly head, Jesus remarked that it was an appropriate name. "Name of a rose," he said. Sharon nodded soberly and continued to stare bewilderedly into his face.

"Come, dear," said Adiel, taking her hand.

"Let her remain, Adiel," said Jesus. "I shall tell her a story."

His calling her by name—a familiarity not to be taken by a stranger—warmed Adiel's heart. For an instant she felt as if they had been long-time friends, but this sensation was quickly succeeded by the feeling that he had addressed her as if she were a child, though she surmised that she was somewhat older than he. Jairus, taking note of her pleased bewilderment, remembered his own surprise and gratification when Jesus had spoken his name. It was not customary for village carpenters to address him as "Jairus."

"May I stay too?" asked Adiel.

Jairus pushed the luxurious leather chairs into a smaller circle and they sat down. For a little while Jesus' head drooped and his eyes were closed. It was apparent that he was utterly spent.

At the conference in the breakfast-room the question had risen whether it was easier to forgive a man's sins or to cure him of his paralysis. As Jairus sat sympathetically regarding the exhausted Nazarene he reflected that it must have taken a tremendous volume of energy to have done either of these mystifying deeds. According to the widespread but largely unsubstantiated tales of the Carpenter's marvels, one gathered that the self-confident magician had moved from one spectacular event to another with no diminution of strength. Now it appeared that these outgivings of vital force were made at great cost.

Sharon, who had a child's natural diffidence in the presence of adult strangers, now surprised her parents by drawing her low stool close beside Jesus. Becoming aware of her nearness, he opened his eyes, sighed, smiled, and took her small hand in his. Expectantly, Sharon drew her legs up under her and rested her dimpled elbows on the broad arms of his chair. Jairus and Adiel exchanged puzzled glances.

"This story," began Jesus, softly, as to the child alone, "is about a Kingdom in another land."

"A fairy story?" asked Sharon, hopefully.

"No—it is a true story, my child."

In a quiet voice and with simple words, Jesus talked of his Kingdom where all who wished to do so might live in happiness forever. Occasionally little Sharon interrupted with a query, somewhat to the embarrassment of her parents, though Jesus regarded her questions with interest and consideration.

As the colloquy proceeded, Jairus found himself yielding to the infatuation of an ideal life to come in a land where there were no storms, no
quarrels, no courts, no prisons, no slaves, no tears, no fears. And when
Sharon wanted to know whether we would all go there, Jesus had replied
that not everyone would want to go; for it was a brightly lighted city, and
many people, accustomed to performing their deeds in darkness, would
not like the perpetual light. And many people who had been proud of
their control over others' lives would not enjoy a land where everyone
was free.

The calm voice was interrupted now by a light tap on the door. Joseph's
face appeared. Jairus roused as from a dream, rose, crossed the room,
went out, and softly closed the door behind him.

"It is the Big Fisherman, sir," whispered Joseph. "He wonders how
the Master is feeling—and whether he is to wait."

"The Master is very tired," replied Jairus. "When he is rested I shall
give him conveyance to wherever he wishes to go. Tell the Big Fisherman
he need not tarry."

The butler made off with his instructions and Jairus laid his hand lightly
on the library door, but hesitated to re-enter. In some curious manner,
Joseph's intrusion had broken the strange spell that had stilled his mind,
and had brought Jairus back abruptly to familiar footing on solid ground.
His mind had resumed its normal process. There had been much too
much mystery that day. He had drifted along on the compelling tide of it,
offering no resistance, asking no questions. Now that he had been suddenly and roughly beached by this clutch of the commonplace, he began
—rather dazedly—to put his thoughts in order.

One thing was sure: his credulity had been severely overtaxed. He had
always been a practical fellow, with no talent for belief in things he could
not see, hear, taste, or handle. Today he had allowed himself to be in-
fluenced by a succession of mysterious events for which the strange
Carpenter was responsible.

To begin with, he had had a friendly interest in the Carpenter because
he had determined that the man should not be mistreated in his house. . . .
Then, in the excitement and confusion of the storm, there had been that
peculiar incident under the dome of the atrium. The Carpenter had
calmly assured him that it was safe, and Jairus had taken his word for it.
But—so had the architect assured him that the dome was safe. Doubtless
his fears had been groundless. Now that the storm was over, Jarius felt
ashamed of his apprehensions.

Then, there had been a miracle; or, so it had seemed, though until now he had had no opportunity to examine it calmly. The young man was ill and crippled; there was no doubt about that. Indeed, he had been far from well when he departed, as one could see by his pallor and weakness. Whether he had been helpless and quite unable to walk at all—well, there had been no testimony about that. The sullen critics from Jerusalem, whatever might be the unfairness of their hostility to the Carpenter, certainly had a right to raise that question. To what extent was the young fellow paralyzed?

Jairus had been willing—and was still willing—to give the Nazarene the benefit of the doubt concerning the validity of this miracle; though, with all respect for the Carpenter's obviously honest belief in his own power, it would be less disturbing if it could be shown that the young man had been able to walk; maybe not very well, or very far, but—able to walk.

But now another factor had been injected into the strange case of the Carpenter. He had been describing—and in a tone of deep sincerity—a Kingdom prepared for all who might be presumed to enjoy living in a land where it never stormed, where no one was ever sick or sorry, where no one owned anything for himself, and all were equal in the sight of the King.

Perhaps these were reassuring words when addressed to people who, in this lifetime, had never possessed anything. Jairus wished that Jesus had not ventured upon this story of his Kingdom. Let every man have his own hopes and illusions about a world to come. It distressed Jairus that Jesus had turned out to be a visionary. Apparently his imagination had been affected by his efforts to deal with the invisible.

Turning away from the library door, Jairus strolled through the atrium and out upon the trampled path that led to the rose-garden. He would return presently and resume his duties as Jesus' host, but he felt the need of this brief respite under the open sky. It had been his intention to invite the Nazarene Carpenter to stay for supper—and to spend the night if he wished. But now he felt that it would be a relief to see this Kingdom-to-come dreamer on his way. What would he do with Jesus in the event he remained as their guest? What would they talk about? What had they in common? No—the man's presence here was an embarrassment.

The rose-garden had taken quite a beating. In several places the splintered arbors hung limp over the drooping bushes they were intended to support. Jairus sauntered across to a damaged trellis where old Abner, the head gardener, was making repairs, bracing the arbor, cutting away the broken branches and re-tying those that remained unhurt. Life, reflected Jairus, was something like that. It had its misadventures and injuries; but, more often than not, you could tie up what was left and expect it to blossom and bear fruit again. For all its buffeting, our life here was worth all the worry and work it cost us. It had its frights, frustrations and storms, but it also offered many satisfactions—and these satisfactions were real—and they were to be had here and now. What folly!—to spend one's days in brooding anticipation of a Kingdom-to-come where it would always be fair weather! Jairus doubted whether he would enjoy such security even if it were to be had. He had accustomed himself to uncertainties; he knew how to deal with them. He was not so confident of his ability to deal with certainties. Even the promise of endless happiness threatened one with a manner of living for which one had had no training. Far better, mused Jairus, to content ourselves with come-what-may. Let the Carpenter dream of his fair-weather Kingdom: Jairus would feel more at home in a world beset by storms.

It occurred to him, as he slowly retraced his steps to the house, that he must presently have a serious talk with his architect about the dome of the atrium. It would be foolhardy to take any more chances there.

*   *   *   *   *   *

With heavy steps and a heavier heart, Simon slogged along over the muddy mile that slanted toward Capernaum. He was alone and lonely. This singular day of excitements and exultations had come to a drab ending.

Early in the afternoon Simon had been amazed and uplifted to find himself possessed of a peculiar talent that would make his service to Jesus of much value. At a difficult moment, he had taken full charge of an importunate multitude; and, if he did have to say so himself, it had been a good job. Tactfully but firmly he had kept that sopping wet, tatterdemalion pack in order and had successfully insisted upon an appropriate respect for the unusual privileges accorded the public by the eminent Jairus.

Their prompt and willing compliance had surprised him. He had not shouted or scolded or entreated. He had calmly commanded, as if he had a right to tell them what to do, and they—all of them, young and old—had acknowledged his authority. Scores of them he had recognized, finding in their sober, astonished eyes a bewilderment over the power he was exercising, doubtless wondering by what strange magic this huge, uncouth fisherman had achieved such leadership; for surely they knew that they were under no obligation to obey his voice.

It was the first time that Simon had ever issued orders to a crowd. Until now his commands had reached no farther than the decks of his fishing

smacks and had been obeyed only by his employees. Today he had
suddenly become aware of a hitherto unsuspected capacity for compelling
the attention and respect of a great throng. They had seemed mystified
by it, but no more than Simon himself.

Even Jairus had given him a grateful smile and an approving nod. And
Joseph, the butler, had sidled up to remark deferentially, "I don't see how
you do it, sir! I'm sure they wouldn't have listened to me."

When the densely packed crowd had finally come to a stand, Simon,
suffused with a new elation, had said to himself that this must be the
reason why Jesus had laid hands upon him. . . . Apparently the Master
had divined that Simon had been gifted by nature for the skillful handling
of great multitudes. Not much wonder that Jesus had asked his assistance.
"Simon—I have need of you," he had said. Or could it be that Jesus had
endowed him with this power? Well—however he had come by it, here
it was; and Simon was deeply stirred.

After the spectacular event of the day had occurred, and the rain had
ceased, and it was time for the house to be cleared of its dripping guests,
Simon had again assumed command, speaking calmly but confidently to
the people; and again they had obeyed him. His words still re-echoed in
his ears as he trudged through the mud on the way to Capernaum. He had
said, simply, "We are all leaving now." And they had left, without disorder and without tarrying.

When the last of them were out of the house, Simon had come upon
James and John who had lingered on the verandah, uncertain what was
expected of them.

"Jesus is with Jairus," Simon had explained. "He is resting. I shall wait
for him. . . . I think Andrew may be taking the fleet across to the south
shore for fishing at sundown, now that the weather has cleared. Perhaps
he would be glad to have your help."

Nodding briefly, the brothers had turned away to follow the departing
throng. They, too, had accepted Simon's quiet orders without a sign of
reluctance.

Hitching up his belt, he had leaned against one of the marble pillars in
a posture that might easily have been mistaken for an air of proprietorship,
and had absently watched the bobbing heads of the people as they
plodded doggedly down the sloping road. He had been moved to pity over
their bewilderment and their helplessness. They were like so many sheep.
Jesus had said so. Simon had straightened to his full height and had
drawn a sigh of satisfaction. "Sheep," he murmured.

While thus reflecting upon the very considerable—and gratifying –

difference between his present rating and theirs, his attention was diverted by the appearance of Joseph, attended by a crew of men-servants bearing mops, buckets, and brooms.

"I am waiting for the Master," said Simon, casually. "Do you happen to know how long he may be tarrying?"

"No, sir," said Joseph, respectfully.

"See if you can find out." Simon had spoken quietly, but authoritatively; and, after an instant of perplexed indecision, Joseph had set off on his errand, returning presently to say, with some embarrassment, that Simon was not to wait.

It seemed a rather cool and curt dismissal. Of course, Simon knew he had no right to expect that Jesus himself would come out and explain that he wasn't ready to go; nor was it likely that Jairus would appear with this message. As he tramped down the stone steps which descended from one terrace to another, he tried not to feel hurt. Jesus was indeed very weary. Jairus was taking good care of him. Perhaps it was an excellent opportunity for them to become acquainted. But—Simon was humiliated. After the singular service he had rendered, it was disquieting to be sent away by the butler.

Trudging along with his eyes on the road, Simon reviewed the events of the past few days. Not all of them had been entirely to his liking, or his understanding. To begin with: there was that deeply moving episode on the beach at dawn, when Jesus had laid his hands on Simon's bowed head and had commanded him to follow. It had been a high moment! And Simon had followed, gladly, proudly, blind with welling tears. But where had Jesus taken him? Not to some quiet spot for a conference or instructions in his new duties. No—he had silently led the way to the old boat leased by the Zebedee youngsters and had indicated that Simon had an errand there.

As he recollected it, this reconciliation with James and Johnny had given him some momentary pleasure. It was a relief to have their friendly relations restored. But now, flushed with disappointment, it occurred to him that if any apologies were due in patching up that estrangement, it might have been more fitting if Johnny had been invited to attend to it. Simon had not abandoned Johnny; it has been the other way about. It wasn't quite fair to make Simon do the apologizing; or, so it seemed, this afternoon, after the rebuff at Jairus' house.

And then, the next day, Simon had invited Jesus to come aboard The Abigail, and Jesus had seemed glad enough to say that he would do so. It had delighted Simon. Doubtless Jesus would be surprised to see what valuable ships he owned. Maybe Jesus would appreciate the sacrifice he had made when he consented to devote himself to the new cause.

"Master," Simon had said, "I am going to show you the finest fleet on the lake!"

And Jesus had suddenly changed his mind about visiting the ships. "Another day, Simon," he had said, absently, as if he didn't care whether he ever saw them.

Wholly preoccupied with his depressing meditations, Simon marched through the main thoroughfare of Capernaum, nodding soberly to those who hailed him, and proceeded toward Tiberias. His fleet, he observed, had put out to sea. He was glad that Andrew had decided to sail, though it would have pleased him to go along. It might have lifted his depression.

He slowed his steps to a stop and for a long moment gazed at his fleet with a feeling of pride. They were indeed beautiful vessels, even if Jesus had no interest in them, and didn't care to visit them. A homesick memory of carefree, sunny, happy days at sea swept through him, a vivid remembrance of restless sails overhead bending to a capricious breeze, wisps of sailors' songs drifting back from the little forecastle, the blended aromas of wet hemp, warm tar, fresh paint. Simon sighed deeply and wondered whether he would ever be really happy again.

Perhaps there would be some comfort in going home. Hannah would welcome him, he was sure of that. Hannah was dependable in all weathers. She could be sympathetic without being silly. He hoped she would not question him about his absence from home. Maybe she would chatter him out of his despondency. He brightened a little and lengthened his stride.

He found her near the front gate, mending a broken rose-trellis.

"Simon!" she cried, hurrying to meet him. "What a storm! And what a day you have had! How proud you should be!"

He laid a big hand on her shoulder affectionately.

"Proud?" he said, soberly. "What about?"

"Why—how you took charge of that crowd at Jairus' house! They're all talking about it! The neighbors have been here. Many of them were over there. How happy you must have been to be of so much help to Jesus! Do tell me more about him!"

"How much do you know about him, Hannah? Have you seen him?"

"Yes, Simon. I went out into the country to hear him. I would have done so sooner; but I feared you might be offended. Esther wanted me to go. He is indeed a wonderful man!"

They strolled toward the house.

"You were surprised, I think," said Simon, "that I should have anything to do with him."

"Yes—I was surprised." She waited for him to explain how it had happened, but Simon said no more until they had sat down in the little parlor. Hannah's eyes were bright with expectation.

Impulsively—for he had not planned to confide any of his recent experiences—Simon began, haltingly at first, to tell her how he had been forced to abandon his prejudices and admit the miraculous power of the strange young man from Nazareth. He told Hannah about the blind baby. He told her how Jesus had summoned him, in the early morning, to be his friend and helper. It was a moving story, and when he had ended it Hannah's eyes were full of tears. There was a long silence.

"But—it is not easy, Hannah," murmured Simon, shaking his head. "Following Jesus is not easy."

"Tell me," she entreated, softly.

With averted eyes, he slowly unburdened himself of the disappointments and humiliations he had suffered. No—following Jesus, he repeated, was not easy. He reviewed the events of the day at Jairus' mansion; the exaltation he had felt when Jesus had looked to him to control that dripping, selfish mob of curiosity-seekers; the strange sense of power that had come to him; and the dismaying rebuff that had sent him plodding off alone through the mud, plainly aware that—after all—he was nobody!

Hannah's eyes lighted with sudden understanding.

"Simon!" she exclaimed. "Has it not occurred to you that Jesus may be wanting you for some great service? Maybe he is training you for it! . . . You know!—the way they train soldiers—to endure hardship—and learn to obey—and ask no questions! The commander gives them heavy packs to carry—and long marches—and they are not told where they are going —or why!"

For a long time Simon sat moodily staring out at the window before attempting a reply.

"I should have been much happier, Hannah, if I had never met him. I was quite contented to be—just a fisherman. Now—I don't know who —or what—I am!"

"Why don't you go out with your fleet for a few days—and get this all off your mind?"

"I don't even want to do that!" rumbled Simon, dejectedly. "That's part of the trouble, Hannah. Even my ships mean nothing to me—any more. . . . I am this man's captive! . . . What is to become of me, I do not know."

"You are tired and hungry," said Hannah, gently. "I shall get your supper ready. You will feel better when you have eaten—and rested. . . . Come—and gather a few eggs for me."

Willing to be diverted, Simon followed her to the kitchen, caught up a small basket, and started out toward the chicken-yard, pausing at the little feed-room in the storage shed for a basin of corn. The hens fluttered about his feet, dabbing at the grain. They were unafraid, untroubled. Nothing ailed their world. Simon envied them.

Hannah stood in the kitchen doorway, watching him with brooding eyes. Her intuition told her that their quiet, uneventful life together had come to an end. Simon, she felt, would never be the same again.

12

CONSIDERING all the dangers she had faced and escaped on her audacious journey from the mountains of Southern Arabia to the Sea of Galilee, the young daughter of the Tetrarch felt that her expedition had been singularly successful.

However shabbily the gods had treated her in filling her veins with the incompatible blood of two mutually contemptuous nations, making it impossible for her to feel at home in either of their lands, it was clear that her quest of vengeance had not been disapproved on Mount Olympus where (according to Ione) these deities maintained their headquarters.

True, Fara's vow still lacked fulfillment; but perhaps the gods, having thus far blest her adventure, might be counted upon to help her see it through. Even if it should culminate in a swift tragedy for her, an untimely death would be preferable, she thought, to any length of life in a world that had made such poor provision for her happiness.

But, resolutely as she had schooled her mind to a stoical acceptance of her probable fate, there were occasional days when her courage ebbed, and for its renewal Fara would take counsel of their heroism who had lived dangerously—and, in many cases, briefly—for honor's sake. She was in need of such courage today.

Curled up childishly in a heavily upholstered leather chair that had been built expressly for the comfort of Tetrarch Antipas, and was therefore several sizes too large for his daughter, Fara had been trying to bolster her morale by reacquainting herself with her favorite hero. What a gallant youth was Demosthenes! No burden could weight him down; no obstacle could slow him up! He, too, had vowed a vow, pledging himself to prepare for a bold attack on the rapacious merchants and wicked politicians who had impoverished and debauched his beloved Athens. Like Fara, Demosthenes had had his bad days. Sometimes he felt that he was throwing his youth away on a hopeless undertaking, and only by the most rigorous self-discipline had he been able to adhere to his resolution.

The story about him that Fara liked best was of his shaving one side of his head so he wouldn't be tempted to abandon his hard studies and rejoin his gay companions in the baths and at the theater. Having herself done a bit of sacrificial barbering in the interest of keeping a vow, Fara felt that she and young Demosthenes had a great deal in common. Her admiration of him was unbounded. Of course this devotion took no toll of her maidenly modesty, for her hero had been dead these three hundred and fifty years, and would never know how tender was her sympathy.

But, this afternoon—it had been raining all day—not even Demosthenes was able to do much for Fara. As she riffled through the yellow old scrolls that eulogized his bravery, she wondered whether his famed career hadn't cost more than it was worth. True, he had stirred Greece to a noisy house-cleaning, but the evil-doers had survived him. Demosthenes had kept his vow—but lost his life. Fara pushed the scrolls off her lap and asked herself what was the good of it. Maybe she and Demosthenes were a couple of fools to have set their youthful, dancing feet on the rough and lonely road toward a guaranteed disaster.

The afternoon was wearing on and the somber, high-ceilinged library, never a bright and cheerful room even when the sun shone, was filled with depressing shadows. The gilded spool-ends of a pair of scrolls, high on a shelf in the corner, stared down at her through the gloom as if to inquire how long she thought she could sit there in the oppressive silence and ghostly shadows without losing her mind.

It had been her intention, yesterday, to leave the palace early this morning and spend the day with Hannah. She was homesick to see this motherly woman who had so tenderly befriended her. And perhaps Hannah could be persuaded to go with her into the country for another glimpse of the Nazarene Carpenter.

For a whole day, after her first experience of listening to Jesus, Fara had moved about, half dreamily, under the spell of his tranquilizing voice. Sitting there in that vast, stilled, yearning multitude, she had gradually yielded herself to the contagion of his calmness; and, retiring at length from his presence, she had carried with her a new possession. Indeed, it had so suffused her habitually unquiet spirit that for many hours thereafter nothing any longer mattered but the satisfaction of walking confidently under an almost tangible aureole of peace.

But she was not without misgivings, for she had never been really happy and carefree before, and something told her she had no right to this relief

from her anxieties. Ever since she was a small child, Fara had had something to worry about: her sweet mother's frailty, her rascally father's neglect of them; and, overshadowing all other frets, the feeling that she
wasn't wanted anywhere. She was the little Arabian who wasn't really
welcome in Arabia, the little Jew who would never be really welcome in
Jewry.

Now, by the magic of his persuasive voice, this Jesus had relaxed her
tension and lifted her burden. "Let not your heart be troubled," he had
said; and it was as if he spoke to her alone, with a full understanding of her
heart and its trouble.

But, after a day of this peculiar ecstasy, the sensation of peace gradually
gave way to the old anxieties. Again she strapped on her burden. Nor was
she disconsolate over the loss of her strange quietude of mind; for had not
Destiny ordained for her not only certain cares to be carried but responsibilities to be accounted for? It was all very well to possess an untroubled
heart if one's troubles were honestly disposable. Whether peace was a
virtue depended on how much duty-shirking was involved. What indeed
would have become of Demosthenes' moral character had he resolved not
to let his heart be troubled? Doubtless there were plenty of fortunate
people who could dismiss their cares; but Demosthenes couldn't—nor
could Fara. Returning that day from her curious experience in the presence
of Jesus, she found that she had lost all interest in her vow; and, that night,
her brightly polished dagger, with the jeweled handle, seemed an ugly,
loathsome thing!

And so it was that Fara, briefly experiencing this singular sense of peace,
gave it up for duty's sake. But the Carpenter's entreating voice continued
to haunt her, and she had a mounting desire to hear him speak again. Often
and often she found herself wondering about the nature of this strange
man. He was a Jew, a citizen of Galilee, a carpenter; but these facts about
him did not, Fara thought, explain him at all. He seemed to live outside
the bondage and security of his race and nationality. This wasn't his world.
Fara felt a strange kinship with him; for it wasn't her world either.

This morning, when she had wakened to find it raining, her disappointment had so depressed her that even Claudia's unfailing cheerfulness
brought no response.

"I shall myself take the bug-eater his breakfast," Claudia had volunteered. "The poor fellow is sad enough without having to look at you."

Soberly nodding her approval, Fara had made off to the gloomy library
where she had closeted herself throughout the whole wretched day, now
almost ended.

Because the great house had been for so many hours as quiet as a tomb, the shrill voice of Claudia, quite obviously excited, startled Fara out of her apathy. From the foot of the winding staircase, Claudia was shouting some unintelligible urgency. Perhaps the villa was on fire. Bounding out of her chair, Fara rushed to the doorway and ran into Voldi's open arms.

For a long moment their joy was too deep for any words of greeting. Utterly unnerved by her surprise, Fara leaned limply against him, snuggling her face into the folds of his tunic, while Voldi held her slim body tightly to him. After a time, she drew a long sigh, with something like a childish sob tugging at her throat, and softly patted his cheek. Voldi tightened his embrace, drawing her so close she was on tiptoe. Slowly raising her arms, she circled them around his neck and lifted her swimming eyes to meet his. He bent to kiss her parted lips and her instant response speeded his heart. It was not the first time that he had kissed Fara, but always before it had been Voldi's doing. She had received his kisses without reluctance; but they had been Voldi's kisses. Now Fara was sharing them, eagerly, hungrily! Voldi was ecstatic, shaken, suffocated by his emotion. Again and again he kissed her until, breathless and trembling, she relaxed in his arms.

"You are all mine now, darling!" he murmured, huskily. "We belong to each other—forever and ever!"

Pressing her cheek hard against his breast, Fara slowly nodded her head. Deeply stirred by her complete surrender, Voldi felt free to speak at once of their future.

"We will forget all about this dangerous business of revenge," he said, gently caressing the tight little curls on her forehead with his fingertips. "I shall take you home, sweetheart, and we will never be separated again."

Fara made no response to this, and he continued softy while she listened with her pale face uplifted and her eyes closed. Impetuously he poured out the story of his grief, the agony of his relentless search for her on the mountain trails, the lonely days and sleepless nights, his despairing descents into deep ravines, calling, calling.

"And now I have found you! We will go back to our beautiful mountains! Nothing can ever part us—ever—as long as we live!"

Suddenly, to Voldi's surprise, for he had never seen her weep—not even when Arnon died—Fara gave way to an uncontrollable seizure of crying, her whole body racked with convulsive sobs. Gently supporting her in his arms, Voldi waited in bewildered silence for the storm to subside. Gradually the sobs diminished to involuntary little spasms. Resolutely, she straightened, dashed the tears from her eyes, and released herself from his arms.

"Come, Voldi," she said, thickly. "Let us sit down—and talk calmly—if we can—and we must!" Taking him by the hand, she led him across the room to the huge leather chair, and signed to him to sit down. He made a brief effort to draw her with him, but she gently resisted, drew up a low footstool, and sat facing him, with her arms folded on his knees. There was a moment of silence, while her tears again ran unchecked. At length she spoke, barely above a whisper.

"Voldi—dearest—I cannot go back with you to Arabia. . . . No, no, darling"—she went on, insistently, when he made a murmur of protest—"you must hear me out! . . . Voldi—if I loved you only a little less than I do, perhaps I could obey my selfish heart—and you. Believe me, it is not easy for me to make this sacrifice. You see—it isn't as if you were a common shepherd, with no responsibilities beyond the care of your cottage and your flock. You are one of Arabia's most favored sons, destined to be one of the King's Counsellors—provided you are not encumbered with me."

"But I am willing, glad, to give all that up for you!" broke in Voldi, earnestly. "Nothing matters—but you!"

"That's the trouble, dear!" Fara went on. "You would give up your duty and your distinction for me. Do you think I could ever be happy, in the days to come, knowing it was my fault that you were unable to serve your King and your country?" And when Voldi mumbled impatiently that it meant more to him to have her love than any honor the King might bestow, Fara warned, "It may seem so now—but the time would come when we would realize that our love had been much too costly. . . . Voldi—think of your father and mother, and their pride of you!"

"They would understand."

"They might try to understand, but it would be a lasting grief to them. . . . And that wise and good old man, Counsellor Mishma! How he has counted on your future! . . . And there is another problem to be met." Fara lowered her voice almost to a whisper. "We would have children."

"Wouldn't that be wonderful, Fara!" exclaimed Voldi.

"Yes, dear, it would be wonderful—but not for them. They would soon learn that they were—somehow different from other children, and that they were different because of me! Voldi—they might even grow to hate me as the cause of their unhappiness."

They sat in silence for some time, Voldi having no answer for the problem Fara had proposed. At length, heartened by a new idea, he said, "Very well, then. We will not return to Arabia. We will make a home somewhere else. We will go to Rome."

Fara shook her head and sighed.

"Dear heart, you know you would be wretched there," she said. "You

hate cities, as I do. We would be exiles; we and our children; people without a country."

At this juncture, Claudia appeared at the door. Supper was ready, she
said. Would they come down, or should she bring it up? Fara murmured a
word of thanks and said they would come down. Claudia, divining that she
had arrived at an inopportune moment, disappeared.

"Sorry, darling," muttered Voldi—"but I can't eat this rascal's bread!"

"This is my father's house," said Fara. "Surely his daughter has a right
to invite a friend to supper."

Voldi leaned forward and searched her eyes for a twinkle, but found
them sober and sincere. The incongruity of the situation made him laugh.

"What's so funny?" demanded Fara, soberly.

"You came here to kill your father; didn't you?"

"Yes—but I haven't done it yet." Fara's tone was still serious, but a
little smile twitched her lips.

"And so long as you haven't yet had a chance to kill him," grinned
Voldi, "you feel free to extend his hospitality to your guest! Fara—this is
very amusing!"

She rose and reached for his hand.

"I'm glad to hear you laugh again, darling," she said, "even if you're
laughing at me. Come—let us see what Claudia has for us. By the way—did
she make eyes at you when you came?"

"Just a little, perhaps," admitted Voldi, obligingly.

"Well—don't let that turn your head," drawled Fara, as they moved,
arm in arm, toward the stairway. "Our Claudia is as friendly as a muddy
dog, and not very particular in her choice of friends." They both laughed.
It eased their tension.

*   *   *   *   *   *

The next morning dawned brilliantly bright but chilly. The two-month
season called winter in Northern Galilee was at hand, a dreary period of
searching winds and cold rains when the people were more comfortable
indoors. This might be the last day of autumn.

With Lysias' gracious co-operation, Fara had overcome Voldi's reluctance to spend the night at the palace. The steward had been given to
understand that Voldi was from Petra; and, as a student of the classics, had
wanted to see the famous library. Seeing that the personable young man
had been directed there by no less a prominent citizen than David, no
further explanations of Voldi's visit seemed necessary. Anyone from Petra

was welcome to the Tetrarch's hospitality. The beautiful, highly bred Darik had been properly stabled, groomed, admired.

After an early breakfast, Fara and Voldi had repaired to the library for a further discussion of their dilemma. It was soon made clear that the girl was adamant in her decision not to return to Arabia. She wasn't going to ruin Voldi's life and bring endless humiliation upon herself by being his wife and the mother of his children. No, she conceded, it was no fault of hers that her veins bore alien blood, but it was a misfortune that need not be bequeathed to others still unborn. In short, Fara had made up her mind and it was useless to argue with her.

"Let me give you a little more time to think it over, dear," pleaded Voldi; and when Fara had pointed out that there was no suitable place for him to lodge, either in Tiberias, Capernaum or Bethsaida, he said, "I shall ride back to Caesarea and tarry for a few weeks. Then may I return—and see you again?"

She tried to convince him that this would only be salting their wounds, that they would both be better off if he rode away to occupy himself with other interests; but, after his earnest entreaty to be allowed to come back in the springtime, she consented. Voldi saw that she was glad to have made this concession, and kissed her. Fara shook her head demurely, but shared the kiss, after murmuring helplessly that it wasn't fair to either of them. Voldi's failure to debate this point was an admission that she was right about that; but, drawing her closer into his arms, he kissed her again and again. "I shouldn't let you do this," she whispered; but she did. At length, reluctantly tugging herself loose from his embrace, she walked to the open window, Voldi slowly following. He put his arm around her gently.

"Let us get out into the sunshine," she said. "We will take a walk." Her eyes lighted with a happy thought. "We will visit Hannah!"

Voldi frowned thoughtfully, wondering whether it was discreet to add this emphasis to Fara's Arabian origin. Hannah might inadvertently say something to a neighbor that would expose Fara to the community's inquisitive conjectures. How does this Jewish girl happen, they would say, to be visited by a friend from Arabia? He voiced his anxiety.

"Hannah will not talk," said Fara. "My secret will be as safe with her as it is with David; and you have told me that you trust him fully."

"It is different with the Sadducee," said Voldi. "He knows who you are—and why you are here. Your friend Hannah is in the dark about you. If you trust her at all, you had better confide everything."

"If I promise to do that, will you come?"

They sauntered down the winding driveway, Voldi leading Darik, who tossed and shook his head impatiently, for he disliked to be led and made no bones about his annoyance. Presently they came out through the imposing gates and upon the broad road, joining the heavy southbound traffic.

"Where are all these people going?" Voldi wanted to know. "They're all headed in the same direction. What is it; a fair or a feast-day? Hardly a carnival: none of them seems to be very gay."

"Jews are never gay," observed Fara, avoiding his query.

"That's true enough," agreed Voldi. "They are a sober lot. But these people look troubled, frightened! Perhaps some calamity has occurred. Shall we inquire?"

She turned toward him momentarily, with indecision in her eyes as if debating whether to explain, but did not reply, which added to Voldi's bewilderment.

"You have more than your share of cripples in this country," he remarked. "And there goes a woman, leading a blind man." They drew aside to pass a party of four, carrying a half-grown girl on a cot. "What's all this about, Fara?" persisted Voldi.

"They are going out into the country, a little way beyond Bethsaida," said Fara, "where a village carpenter speaks nearly every day to great crowds. He has been creating quite a sensation. It is believed that he heals diseases."

"The Carpenter!" exclaimed Voldi. "The man from Nazareth!"

"You have heard of him then?" Fara searched his eyes.

"Indeed, yes! All along the way! There was talk of him as far down as Caesarea! It's a wonder you haven't tried to see him, what with your curious interest in religious prophets." He gave her a teasing smile: she had lost a valuable horse by showing too much concern about an itinerant preacher. Fara accepted his raillery with a wisp of a smile, but sobered to say that she had seen and heard the Carpenter. Voldi's steps slowed. Cupping his hand under her elbow, he drew her closer.

"But why are you so mysterious—and reticent—about it?" he queried. "It's nothing to be ashamed of. Didn't you want me to know?"

"I hesitated to tell you, Voldi," she confessed. "I know how you feel about magic—and miracles—and the weak-mindedness of superstitious people who believe in such things. . . . I didn't want you to think I had gone crazy."

"That sounds a little as if you had been impressed by this fellow. Did you see him do anything out of the ordinary?"

"If you like, we can go out and see him," suggested Fara. "Hannah may want to go with us. You will have a chance to form your own opinion."

"So—you would rather not tell me any more—until I have seen him?"

"I can tell you this much, Voldi," she replied, measuring her words deliberately—"his voice is not like that of any other man, and the things he says have not been spoken—just that way—ever before. He does not scold or condemn or threaten: he quietly takes possession of your whole mind. . . . You shall see for yourself, my dear. . . . The man does not belong to this world, at all." Fara's voice had lowered to a mere whisper as she added, "He is from somewhere else!"

There wasn't anything much to be said in response to that strange remark. Voldi studied her eyes with candid anxiety.

"I wonder," he murmured gently, "whether you realize what you are saying. Surely you don't think that this Carpenter is a god!"

"I don't know," she mumbled vaguely; and after a long interval, "It wouldn't surprise me—if that were true."

They had come now to the northern outskirts of Bethsaida and were turning off the busy highway into a quiet leaf-strewn street where Fara pointed to the cottage shared by Hannah and the fishermen, Simon and Andrew.

"The men will not be at home," she said. "I wish you might meet Simon, who is the master of his fleet; a gigantic fellow. He has no learning and knows nothing beyond his occupation, but one can't help feeling that if he had had any advantages at all he might be a very forceful person." Arriving in front of the cottage, Voldi said he would wait at the gate while Fara inquired whether her friend was prepared to receive them.

There was no response to her knock at the front door. She stepped into the hallway and called cheerily. A weak voice bade her come in. Hannah, fully clothed, was lying on her bed. She tried to smile a welcome.

"Hannah!" cried Fara. "You are ill!"

"It is nothing, dear," protested Hannah, feebly. "I am very tired; that is all." She made an effort to sit up, but slumped back upon the pillows. Her gray eyes were cloudy, her cheeks were flushed, and an agitated pulse pumped hard at her temple. "Give me you hand, Esther," she muttered, thickly. "Perhaps I can get up now." But a sudden seizure of faintness swept her and she made no further protest when entreated to lie still.

After what seemed like a long delay to Voldi—and Darik, too, whose restless capers were bringing elderly neighbors to their doors and windows —Fara reappeared at the gate, her serious face warning that something had gone amiss. Hannah, she reported soberly, was ill; perhaps very ill indeed.

Voldi had better go quickly down to the business district where, hard by the Synagogue, he would find the old physician, Gershon.

"When I have found the doctor and sent him here, I think I shall be on my way," said Voldi. "There is nothing I can do. Hannah will need your full attention. My tarrying here will be only an embarrassment to your friends—and you."

Fara's face showed mingled regret and relief. She nodded her approval of his decision. Promising to return with the spring flowers, he vaulted into the saddle; and Darik, apparently already late for some urgent engagement, clenched his teeth on the bit and bolted. At the corner of the street, Voldi was able to wave a farewell. It was not a satisfactory way to take leave of Fara, but—was there a better way? Perhaps this was less painful than a more deliberate parting.

To locate the physician's house was easy enough. The white-bearded, taciturn Gershon, having stiffened haughtily when approached by the young Arabian, listened, nodded, scrambled out of his chair; and, hastily stuffing an old leather bag with the various trinkets of his trade, tottered up the street in the direction of Hannah's house. He did not look back. Voldi watched him until he had disappeared around the corner.

The highway seemed even more congested with the unorganized procession moving southward. There were very few spectators along the edges of the road. This, thought Voldi, was in need of an explanation. Almost any parade, anywhere, however insignificant, was good for at least a scattered audience of loafers; but the main thoroughfare of Bethsaida was all but deserted, except for the passing throng. Voldi ventured to express his curiosity about this to a wizened, toothless, bent old man who stood near by sourly staring at the multitude.

"Where is everybody?" inquired Voldi, raising his voice as the old man bared his gums and cupped his ear with a trembling hand.

"Out yonder!" growled the ancient, pointing with his stick. "All Bethsaida is out there listening to the blasphemer from Nazareth, that dirty, thieving town from which no good thing could come!" He spat angrily but unskillfully, wiped his bearded chin with the back of a shaky hand, and dried the hand on the skirt of his faded robe. "You should laugh, Arabian, to see Israel renounce his proud heritage! This should be a day of rejoicing in the tents of Ishmael! Woe is come upon Bethsaida! Even our Rabbi Elimelech has joined the apostates!"

"How far do they go?" shouted Voldi, unimpressed by the tirade.

"To their destruction!" screamed the old man.

"I mean—is it a mile—or five?"

"Less than a mile. You had better go! It's just the place for you, Ishmael-ite! Then you can ride that fine horse back to Arabia and say that you saw the House of Israel fall!" The angry old eyes were dripping. Voldi could think of nothing to contribute to the conversation. Bowing, in respect to the Bethsaidan's years rather than his views, he mounted and joined the procession, keeping close to the rim of the road, Darik seeming to realize that no foolishness would be tolerated.

It was unlike any pilgrimage that Voldi had ever seen. Like a river at flood, with swift currents channeling the central stream and sluggish eddies eating into the weeds and bushes of its banks, the crowd pressed on in si-lent, sober, sweating, desperate haste. Crude, home-made crutches dug into the loose gravel, scraping dangling legs and crooked feet through the dust. Barrows and carts bore haggard old men and women, pale, dull-eyed, emaciated children, and on cots and litters helpless invalids lay supine, their sunken eyes tightly closed against the glare of the mounting sun and the callous stares of the passing pack; for, far outnumbering and outspeed-ing these hapless ones trudged a pushing, elbowing multitude apparently bent upon appeasing its curiosity. It was by no means a pleasing spectacle, this conglomeration of misery jostled by a heedless throng whose behavior too closely resembled the conduct of stampeded cattle.

The procession was moving faster now. Three hundred yards ahead, the more agile were breaking into a run as they reached the place where their ruthless predecessors had toppled the stone wall, and were racing across a flat-trampled stubble-field. Darik jumped easily over what was left of the wall. Voldi turned toward the old farmhouse and rode on to the stable-yard where a stocky, middle-aged, graying man was stirred to prompt in-terest in the sleek Arabian horse.

"You like horses, I think," remarked Voldi, pleasantly.

"I don't know much about them," replied the farmer. "Never owned one. That's the finest horse I ever saw."

"How would you like to take care of him for a little while?" Voldi dis-mounted, hopefully. Darik tossed his head and snorted.

"Is he dangerous?" inquired the farmer, dubiously.

"Tame as a kitten, after he's acquainted. I see you keep bees. Give him a little piece of honeycomb and he'll be one of your best friends. . . . Of course I shall want to pay you for your trouble."

"You're going over to hear the Carpenter?"

"Thought I would. Quite a crowd. I must see what it's all about. Some kind of religion, isn't it?"

"I haven't heard him," admitted the farmer. "I've got to stay on my place and see that the hoodlums don't carry anything off. If it's religion, it isn't doing them very much good. They trample down as many berry bushes on their way out as on their way in."

"You could have them all thrown out for trespassing, couldn't you?" suggested Voldi.

"I suppose so," nodded the farmer—"but that might cause trouble for the Carpenter. He stopped here, one day last week, for a drink of water."

"And you were favorably impressed?"

"Bring your horse into the paddock," said the farmer, ignoring Voldi's query. "Want him to have a basin of grain?"

"Oh—I'll not be gone that long."

"I wouldn't be too sure about that," chuckled the farmer. "If he gets to healing diseases you may want to stay awhile."

"You mean—the fellow really does heal the sick?"

"Well—my boy Jake—he's fourteen now; hadn't heard a word since he had the red fever when he was nine. I signed him to draw a bucket of water from the well and give the stranger a drink. The Carpenter took the cup and said, 'Thank you, son,' and Jake heard it. You should have seen the way his eyes popped open wide!"

"And—now he can hear?"

"Good as you can! Better than I can! Jake's over there now, listening to the Carpenter. He likes to tell about it when the neighbors ask him." The farmer laughed good-naturedly. "I can't get much work out of him, any more. The boy was quite a help to me before the Carpenter came along. In fact—nobody wants to work since the Carpenter showed up in this country. What time they're not out here listening to him, they're sitting around at home talking it over. I hear that the landowners are complaining about their laborers. Lots of corn still out in the weather. . . . There's going to be plenty of empty bellies this winter."

*   *   *   *   *   *

Upon Voldi's arrival at the luxurious new hostel in Caesarea, where he was immediately recognized, welcomed, and accommodated, he learned that an Empire ship, having disembarked a cargo of iron and other building materials, was sailing tomorrow for Rome; in ballast, which promised a speedy voyage. Having sought an introduction to the Commander he requested that a letter should be conveyed to Mencius. The Commander, a long-time friend of the Proconsul, gladly complied. Voldi finished the letter at midnight.

He had found Fara (he wrote) employed in the Tetrarch's palace!—if

Mencius would believe it. Their meeting had been 'ender, painful, disappointing. Fara was determined to keep her vow. It was inconceivable that she would succeed; or if, by some strange circumstance, she did succeed, it would be at the cost of her life; no question about that! Voldi had done his utmost to dissuade her, had begged her to come back with him to Arabia; but none of his arguments had availed. . . . He would return to her, in a few weeks, and try again.

Having ended his account of his unsuccessful visit with Fara, he proceeded to another subject that he felt would be of immense interest to Mencius.

"Yesterday I saw the Nazarene Carpenter in action. It was said that more than three thousand were present. The assembly had gathered in an open field. Many blind professed to have received their sight, most of them so joyful over their good fortune that it was difficult to disbelieve in the validity of their healing.

"When the crowd dissolved, after the meeting, the lucky ones were surrounded by astonished neighbors and friends whose amazement was too spontaneous to have been feigned. One bewildered fellow, a man of thirty, seemed annoyed when questioned. A circle of scribes and youngish priests blocked his way and asked questions which he was reluctant to answer. He was accompanied by his elderly parents who appeared to be embarrassed, if not frightened, by the attitude of the critics. When it was obvious that their son was in no mood to discuss the matter, the old people were asked for their opinion of what had happened, to which they replied, cautiously, 'We do not know. Our son is of age: ask him.' The inquisitors then renewed their attack on the young fellow. He tried to shake them off. At length he shouted, almost desperately, 'I cannot say what he did to me. All I know is that I was blind and now I can see! . . .' Things have come to a pretty pass in this wicked world when a country's religion denounces a citizen born blind for accepting the gift of sight!

"My own opinion of the mysterious Nazarene is difficult to define. On first sight of him I was a bit disappointed. He is not an heroic figure. I found myself wondering how he would look on a horse; probably not very impressive; but I believe my Darik would stand still while he mounted—a courtesy he does not often accord to his owner. The man has a compelling voice. I can't describe it or the effect of it. It's a unifying voice that converts a great crowd of mutually distrustful strangers into a tight little group of blood relatives.

"I never have had any respect for people who pretend to work wonders, but the things that happened out there yesterday—if not miraculous—

need quite a lot of explaining. . . . But it was what the Carpenter said, even more than what he did, that has disposed me to write you at such length of this strange business.

"After he had apparently given sight to a dozen or more blind ones, he went on to say that the entire population of the earth was groping in darkness; and that went for everybody, kings and peasants, philosophers and fools. He had been sent, he said, to give sight to these blind people. 'I am the light of the world!' he declared; and, strangely enough, nobody laughed, nobody sneered.

"Of course an assertion of this character sounds like the boasting of a crack-brained fanatic; and if I were to read of it in a letter, instead of hearing it from the man's own lips, I should marvel how the writer could have taken so much nonsense seriously.

"I confess I gasped a little when the Carpenter committed this outrageous audacity, but I couldn't help remembering what you said, one day, about your belief in a 'Torchbearer.'

"I was still further stirred to remembrance of your remarks on that matter when the Carpenter added that the light he carried would reflect from those who received it: they, too, would illumine the path for those who were lost in the dark, even as a lighted city on a hill-top.

"Whoever had his lamp lighted at the Nazarene's torch was in duty bound to let it shine. The lamp was not to be hidden where it would benefit only the possessor in his little corner. The lamp was the property of the man who held it, but the light belonged to the public! . . . (I hope I am doing the Carpenter's speech justice. You should have been there, Mencius. It was the sort of thing you would have enjoyed—and understood.)

"It is unlikely that the political and religious pundits will permit this Jesus to continue his present course very long. He has the whole province by the ears. Many well-to-do employers of farm and vineyard labor are protesting that their men have been absent, whole days, from their duties. Presently they will arrest the Carpenter, as a disturber of the peace— which, of course, he is—and if he gets a long term in prison he will be lucky. . . . He may be—as he says—the light of the world, but it is doubtful whether the world wants light. . . . I wish I might hear what you think about this.

"I remain in Caesarea until Spring. Then I shall return—without much hope, I admit—to Tiberias for further talk with Fara. If she still refuses to go back to Arabia, I may have no inclination to return alone. I cherish the memory of your kindness. . . .

"Voldi."

13

Now THAT the weather had become too inclement for outdoor assemblies, comfortable lodging was found for Jesus in the well-kept cottage that had belonged to the departed Jonas and Rachael.

It had been Andrew's suggestion. The snug little home in Capernaum, though jointly owned by the two brothers, had been the elder's special care, for Simon's chief concern was his fleet; and, besides, Andrew's memories of his childhood were more cherishable.

While privately agreeing with his prosperous brother that their good old father may have given too much of his time to the Synagogue, as between the overworked piety of Jonas and the noisy infidelity of Simon, Andrew had considered his saintly sire's attitude toward religion less objectionable.

For a couple of years after their parents' death, and while Simon's lovely but fragile Abigail still survived, Andrew had lived alone in the old house. When Abigail was gone, Simon had urged him to join Hannah and himself in Bethsaida, but he had continued his interest in the Capernaum home, visiting it every day or two, tending his mother's flowers and dusting the shabby but beloved furniture.

Various offers had been made to buy or lease the property. Simon had felt that this was a sensible thing to do, and had generously assured his less affluent brother that he might regard as his own whatever income was derived, but Andrew had been reluctant to let the place fall into the hands of strangers.

The general excitement stirred by the Nazarene Carpenter had not affected Andrew very much, one way or the other. He was not one to take up readily with new ideas. The old ones doubtless had their imperfections but it was to be noticed that the new ones never lasted very long. Occasionally dissenters created local confusions which put old friends at logger-

279

heads, but the hotter the fire the sooner it burned out, leaving everything much as it was before. True, the expanding tales of the Carpenter's sayings and doings were amazing, but Andrew's conservative intuition told him that it wouldn't be long until the whole thing blew over. The Carpenter would be silenced and the people who had been following him about would return, disillusioned, to their neglected duties.

Even when it had become common talk that Simon—of all people!—had been taking a serious interest in the Carpenter, Andrew had silently maintained his belief that there was something crazy about all this hubbub and resolved that he wouldn't have any part of it. He was privately amused, but not surprised, by his tempestuous brother's avoidance of the subject in his presence. Indeed it seemed that Simon was deliberately seeing to it that they were not left alone together; but that was easy enough to understand. Simon had been so blatant in his excoriations of the Nazarene and so contemptuous of all the half-wits who had been taken in by this hullabaloo, that it wasn't much wonder if he preferred not to discuss the matter. That, thought Andrew, was the trouble about uttering strongly spiced words of condemnation: they didn't taste very good if one had to eat them. Meditating on this, Andrew grinned, asked no questions, made no comments, and waited for the inevitable collapse of the new movement.

But when, one evening, Simon had brought this Jesus home with him for supper and lodging for the night, Andrew became aware that they were in the presence of a new kind of man. Although Andrew had never traveled farther than a day's journey from home, and had no notion how others than Galileans talked, as he sat there directly across the table from the Carpenter he felt sure that there could be no one else in the world like him.

Upon Jesus' unexpected arrival at supper-time, Hannah had been pretty badly flustered and was profuse with apologies for their poor little house which, she untruthfully declared, was untidy, and for the skimpy meal which, in fact, was more ample than usual because she had known that Simon—frequently absent from home in these days—intended to be here. Apparently Jesus had heard such talk before, it being customary for an excellent housekeeper to belittle her hospitality, but her remarks had given him an occasion to speak about the things that really mattered. He defined poverty by telling a brief story of a rich farmer who had prospered until his accumulations had become a serious problem. His fields had produced so abundantly that his barns were too small to house the corn: so he had torn down the barns and built bigger ones. And his harvests increased, requiring more barns, until all he thought about was larger barns. And when, one night, an Angel came for his soul, and inquired what he was worth, he had nothing to offer but huge barns bulging with corn. This was unfortunate; for there was no market for corn where the farmer was going, and there was nothing the Angel could do with a barn—no matter how big it was.

The story was told soberly enough but Andrew couldn't help smiling a little. It was so simple that a child could have understood it. The priests, who never talked that way, might have considered it trivial. But, when Jesus told it, in his quiet voice, it was more than a mere story: it seemed real! You could see the puzzled old rich man—whom everybody had envied for his wealth—sitting up in bed at midnight with his gray hair tousled and his silken nightcap askew, blinking into the disappointed eyes of the Angel who was shaking his head, and saying, "Corn? No; you can't bring the corn along—or the barns. You may bring only whatever you have given away."

When the story was ended, Simon, who had been eating industriously, made a little chuckle deep in his throat and glanced up to say:

"I'm afraid I wouldn't make a very good farmer, Master. If the Angel were to come for me, I wouldn't even be able to offer him corn-barns."

Andrew had wished, in the embarrassing silence following this speech, that his brother hadn't said it; for the attempted drollery sounded as if Simon was showing his family that he and Jesus were chummy enough to share a little jest. But, if that had been intended, the Master had quietly set Simon right by remarking:

"Ships—perhaps?"

Simon had not ventured to comment on that, and it was some time before anything else was said.

By nature shy and reticent, Andrew was accustomed, when guests (never of his own invitation) were present, to consider himself a mere boarder who had purchased his place at the table and whose sole interest in the party was his rightful share of the food. He always ate in silence, attentive to his plate, seeming not even to hear the conversation, much less to show any interest in it; and, by his long practice of such detachment, guests who did not know him very well but hoped to draw him into the talk for courtesy's sake, invariably raised their voices when looking his way, presuming him to be deaf.

But, that night, such was his uncontrollable fascination, he neglected his food and listened. Presently, finding himself staring hard into their guest's far-seeing eyes, he made an impulsive effort to avert his gaze—and

discovered that he couldn't do it. And the peculiar thing about this captivity was that—after the first bewildering moment—he didn't want to get
away; nor was he any longer self-conscious. Jesus had made him a member
of the party, in good and regular standing. It was really the first time in
his life that Andrew had felt like a member of any party; and when Jesus
asked him if he enjoyed his occupation as a fisherman he had surprised
himself and his relatives by replying, with a smile, that fishing was fun
only for people who had some other means of support. They all laughed
merrily; and Andrew, instead of being embarrassed, felt a previously unex-
perienced glow of pleasure.

Next morning, after Jesus and Simon, having finished their breakfast,
had left the house, Andrew had made a clumsy effort to define his im-
pressions. Hannah had said, when the silence between them had become
oppressive:

"Andrew, what is it—about this man—that makes him different from
everyone else?"

"Well"—Andrew had replied, after considerable deliberation—"everyone else is a body—with a soul. He is a soul—with a body."

"But—surely—Andrew—you don't think that Jesus is—is more than
human!" exclaimed Hannah.

"I don't know," mumbled Andrew, rising from the table—"but I think
he knows!"

*   *   *   *   *   *

So—it was arranged that Jesus was to have the use of the old home in
Capernaum. Simon had been delighted with Andrew's offer of it. Indeed
the proposal had drawn the brothers closer together than they had been
since early childhood. The truth was that while Simon had not willfully
patronized—and, by implications, belittled—his self-effacing elder
brother, their relationship, in the opinion of the fleet and everybody else
who saw them together, was no more intimate than that of any generous
employer and a trusted employee. No one had ever heard Simon speak a
harsh word to Andrew, but no stranger would have suspected that they
were of the same flesh and blood. Their acquaintance with Jesus had somehow made them kin, Simon showing a new affection and Andrew beaming
in the warmth of it.

When Jesus had been shown through the house, he inquired whether
there would be any objection to his doing some light carpentry. Both
brothers were prompt to approve. Indeed Simon was enthusiastic. There
had been criticism of Jesus. Plenty of substantial people had asked

whether the Nazarene intended to live off the country. And didn't he believe in work? And—it was easy enough for him to tell the people to live like the lilies that dressed better than kings, though they never spun or wove; or like the birds that God fed. That might be all very well for birds and flowers, but it was impractical for the father of a family to entertain any such delusions.

Even Jairus, who had shown a friendly attitude toward Jesus, had been heard to express this opinion. Jairus had said, further, that if the Nazarene wanted to live without working, it was his own business; but he shouldn't entice the people to leave their jobs and trail around the country after him. Jairus had been quite outspoken! Now Jesus was going to show them all that he did believe in work.

Surmising that old Ebenezer, a recently retired carpenter in the neighborhood, would not be needing his equipment any more, Andrew inquired whether they might rent it for the Master's use. When he returned to the cottage, well soaked by the rain, he was wheeling a barrow piled high with all manner of wood-working implements, most of them out of order. Except for the adze, the drawknife, and three variously sized planes, which were in fairly good condition, the heavier and more complicated instruments would have to be repaired or discarded. The old lathe, clumsy at its best, had been long in disuse because of Ebenezer's rheumatic feet, and the chisels which served it were dull and rusty. But Jesus was not dismayed. Ebenezer's lathe, he said, could be rebuilt.

The living-room, which fronted the street, was cleared and its furniture stored in the basement. In a day's time it was a carpenter-shop, and Jesus had already begun the repair of the tools. Andrew had put the small guest-room to rights for the Master's occupancy, and he himself had been sleeping at the cottage for several nights. The weather was cold, raw and wet.

In all this work of transforming the old house into a place of business, Simon had not participated. He had remained at home. Hannah was ill, had been ill for days; nor was she showing any signs of improvement; growing worse, if anything.

The testy old physician, Gershon, had been attentive, but his medicines were ineffective. Rabbi Elimelech had called and was astonished by Hannah's haggard appearance. The relentless fever had taken a heavy toll of her, as if she were gradually melting in its fire. Esther was doing her utmost to make the patient comfortable, but every hour increased her anxiety about Hannah who lay half-conscious, unresponsive, rousing only to accept a spoonful of cold water on a parched tongue. Simon clumsily tried to help Esther with the housework. Most of the time he wandered about from room to room, rubbing his bearded chin, and trying to make Esther say that Hannah was a little better.

Strangely enough, it had not occurred to the Big Fisherman that Jesus should be summoned. Somehow, Jesus' ministry of healing seemed to belong to great crowds of miserable people, strangers, the general public. Simon sincerely believed in the Master's power to heal diseases. Had he not seen it happen, again and again? Indeed he had become so accustomed to these breath-taking restorations that even while they were in progress he would calmly admonish the impatient cot-bearers, waiting their turn, to keep in line.

"No crowding, please!" Simon would say. "The Master will attend to you." Why—it was almost as if Simon owned the show and employed Jesus as an accomplished healer. Simon had enjoyed the sensation of seeing strangers tug their forelocks when they asked him, deferentially, if he would not speak to Jesus in their behalf.

And now, with such dire necessity for better help than old Gershon could offer, Simon had not called on Jesus. Looking back upon it afterwards he admitted to himself, with appropriate shame, that—without realizing the foolishness of his vanity—he had become a professional. Jesus could do, and had done, amazing things for the public; and Simon, as partner in—if not manager of—this awe-inspiring enterprise, had let his distinction go to his head. The public listened when Simon spoke—and obeyed him, too.

How long it might have taken him to become aware that he—Simon—desperately needed Jesus—in the privacy of his own house!—now!—was left undetermined by Esther's appearance in the open doorway of the living-room where Simon sat holding his shaggy head in his hands.

"I'm afraid Hannah is growing weaker, sir," she said.

He rose quickly, mumbling that he would go and notify Gershon. She laid a detaining hand on his huge, hairy forearm, and murmured:

"Had you thought of sending for Jesus?"

The girl's query resounded accusingly in his mind all the way to Capernaum. Having reached the highway his rapid strides had quickened to a run. He was too heavy for such exertion. His lungs hurt and his mouth was dry; and his soul cried out against him. Why hadn't he sent for Jesus? His mind was in tumult as he ran. What a weakling he was! . . . True—he had confessed to Jesus, that early morning on the lake-shore, that he was weak and sinful, and that Jesus had better not have anything to do with him. But he really hadn't meant that he was that bad. It had seemed the right thing to say, at the time. Within an hour, he had begun to feel that his self-abasement had been somewhat extravagant. Jesus had invited him to come and help him: Jesus knew what he was about: Jesus would not have asked him had Simon been as weak and wicked as he said. . . . Well —now we knew how weak and wicked we were!

Through the early part of the forenoon, Jesus had been diligently at work on Ebenezer's old lathe. It had rained all night, but had ceased now, and Andrew had been out in the dooryard bracing up some fallen vines. Passing the window, he observed that the Master had discontinued his labors and was sitting bolt upright on the battered tool-chest, staring straight ahead of him with troubled eyes. It worried Andrew; and, after awhile, he decided to go in and inquire. Entering, he was relieved to find Jesus busily at work again, his tension apparently eased. Presently, the Master walked to the door and stood, looking down the street, expectantly.

Simon was ready to drop when he arrived. Too breathless and exhausted to speak, he flung himself into a chair, panting.

"Whatever is the matter with you?" demanded Andrew, stooping over him. Jesus was slipping his arms into the sleeves of his robe.

"Come quickly, Andrew," he said, quietly. "Simon will follow us when he is rested."

*   *   *   *   *   *

There had been need of haste. Neighbor women filled the house and their men stood about, in low-voiced groups, under the dripping trees. Everybody made way for Jesus as he entered.

Gershon was ostentatiously packing his bag. He glanced up and frowned darkly when the Nazarene, whom he had often reviled as a conscienceless fraud, appeared in the doorway.

"And what might you be doing here?" he demanded, savagely.

Rabbi Elimelech moved forward, looking as if he wanted to intervene.

"I say the woman is dying!" Gershon faced the Rabbi indignantly. "Is she to be tormented by this—this Carpenter?" He glared scornfully at Jesus, who made no reply.

"But—if Hannah is dying, friend Gershon," ventured Elimelech, "she is beyond any harm. I beg you to let this young man see her."

"Very well!" rasped Gershon, making off with his kit. "You are all fools!" he shouted, as he elbowed roughly through the silent neighbors who had congregated in the hallway. "Fools!" he yelled back, angrily, from the open door. "All of you! Fools!"

"We must make allowances for Gershon, sir," explained the Rabbi gently. "He is getting old—and he isn't very well."

Jesus affectionately laid a hand on the Rabbi's thin shoulder and smiled into the old man's eyes.

"That," he said, softly, "is the right spirit. You are a blessing to these people, Rabboni!"

Elimelech's eyes filled as he turned away. The women stared into his contorted face as he passed. He seemed exalted! Something—they knew not what—had happened to their good old Rabbi!

Jesus now quickly and confidently assumed charge of the situation. Motioning the women to withdraw, he was closing the bedroom door. As Esther followed them out, he detained her.

"You will remain, daughter," he said.

For a time he stood gazing down into Hannah's waxen face, with sorrow and anxiety in his eyes. Then he drew up a chair close beside the bed and sat down. Glancing up at Esther he signed for her to kneel at the bedside; and, after some little hesitation—for she wasn't sure what was expected of her—she obeyed, resting her elbows on the edge of the bed and taking Hannah's hand in both of her own.

"It's so cold, sir," she said, in a half-whisper.

Jesus took Hannah's other hand in his and for a long moment there was complete silence.

"Do you know how to pray, Fara?" he asked, softly.

Startled, she looked up, wide-eyed, into his face; then put her head down on Hannah's arm.

"No, sir," she murmured, in a shaken voice.

"Do they not pray—in Arabia?" he asked.

"Some do, I think," she said. "We never did—in my home—except Ione." She did not explain Ione, implying that Jesus would know. "Ione prayed often. She had many Gods."

"There is only one God, Fara. Ione prayed for His many benefits thinking that there were as many Gods. . . . Shall I teach you how to pray?"

She nodded her head, without replying.

"Say, 'Our Father.' "

" 'Our Father,' " she mumbled, in a voice that was full of tears.

"Now—tell Him—in secret—that you love Hannah and want her to recover."

Fara was crying now. Shaking her head, despairingly, she looked up through blinding tears and said, thickly:

"It would do no good, Master; not from me. I am unworthy."

"Then—perhaps you had better ask Him, first, to cleanse your heart of evil. You are carrying a great weight, Fara. You, too, need to be healed."

Again she looked up into his compassionate eyes.

"You—you know about it, Master?"

Jesus drew a deep sigh.

"Ask our Father to set you free, Fara. Then ask Him to help Hannah."

She buried her face in Hannah's arm, her body trembling with convulsive sobs. Gradually her weeping ceased. At length, Jesus spoke, not in a tone of entreaty but command!

"Hannah!" he called. Rising to his feet, and grasping both of her hands, he called again: "Hannah! Come! Awake!"

With a long, shuddering sigh, Hannah opened her eyes, looked up dazedly into Jesus' face, smiled, and drifted off to sleep. Fara sat up, staring, in open-mouthed amazement.

"Prepare some porridge for her," said Jesus. "She will waken again, presently." The sweat was dripping from his face and his hands were trembling. As Fara reached the door, he spoke sternly. "If you have made a new promise, today, see that you keep it! God is not mocked!"

*   *   *   *   *   *

Having been house-bound for several days by the rains, David had decided to stretch his legs. It was still wet underfoot and dark overhead; not a pleasant day for a walk, but he couldn't stay cooped up any longer.

Slogging along through the mud he wondered why—when he didn't really have to—he remained in Galilee through the tedious and depressing weeks of the winter season. Of course there was his sister to consider. Deborah couldn't be budged from home, and David disliked the thought of leaving her alone with the servants.

Approaching the corner where Hannah lived, he was surprised to see the number of people who had gathered about the house. It was apparent from their attitude that something serious had happened. He paused and was about to beckon to one of the solemn-faced men when he saw the Big Fisherman toiling wearily up from the highway.

Sighting his eminent neighbor, Simon moved toward him and explained what the trouble was. Hannah was grievously ill; beyond recovery, maybe. David shook his head and murmured his sympathy.

"She may have taken a turn for the worse," added Simon, anxiously surveying the silent assembly of neighbors. "I have been gone for an hour. I went to summon Jesus."

"Ah? The Carpenter?" David was astonished. "I am surprised that you have any faith in the fellow." And when Simon made no reply, he went on, dryly, "And perhaps you haven't. . . . Any port in a storm; eh?"

Simon gnawed at his underlip, as if contemplating a response, but remained silent. It was evident that the cynical old Sadducee had not heard of his public association with Jesus. David had no reason to think that the Big Fisherman would take the slightest interest in this wandering preacher.

"Is the Carpenter in there now?" asked the lawyer.

"I suppose so," said Simon, almost indifferently. "If you will excuse me, sir"—turning away—"I shall go in—and see how she is." He walked rapidly around the corner and was unlatching the gate when the crowd on the stoop was plowed apart by old Gershon who, noisy with indignation, tottered down the path. Simon stood in his way.

"What is it, Gershon?" he demanded.

"Fools!" shrilled the old man.

"How is Hannah?" Simon clutched at Gershon's sleeve.

"Dying! Let go of me! You are all fools!" Gershon nearly upset himself by his angry tug to be free. At the gate he came face to face with David who had rounded the corner and stood waiting. Instantly the old physician's manner changed. Bowing deeply, he rubbed a shaky hand across his forehead, and tried to steady his voice as he explained his rage.

David listened impassively until Gershon had finished.

"How do you know he can't?" he inquired. "Apparently, all you know is—you can't! Perhaps you had better wait—and verify your opinion."

"But"—spluttered Gershon—"the fellow is not a physician! He is a carpenter!" He was moving sullenly away, disappointed over this interview with the most influential man in Bethsaida, when the sound of many voices came from the cottage; excited, astonished, happy voices! Amazing news circulated through the crowd that massed about the steps. Simon, his heart pounding hard, pushed his way into the house and down the hall toward Hannah's bedroom. Andrew was emerging with wet eyes and a queer little whimper that seemed oddly out of keeping with his radiant smile. It was true then! It had happened! . . . Hannah was sitting up. Esther, kneeling beside the bed, was feeding her from a bowl of broth. Simon stood there, silently, his eyes overflowing.

"Hannah!" he murmured.

"It was Jesus!" she said, hardly above a whisper.

"Where is he?" asked Simon.

Esther glanced up to say that he must be somewhere in the house; that he was here—only a moment ago. Simon withdrew to inquire. He met Andrew, and asked him.

"The Master has gone," replied Andrew.

"Did he say where he was going?"

"No. He may have gone back to Capernaum."

"You didn't see him leave?"

Andrew shook his head.

"He—the Master didn't inquire for me; did he?" asked Simon, after some hesitation.

Andrew shook his head.

"Did he have anything to eat?" asked Simon.

"Probably didn't want anything," said Andrew. "He was very tired."

"I shall try to overtake him—on the road," said Simon, moving away.

Walking rapidly to the highway, he shaded his eyes for better vision and searched the thoroughfare, far as he could see; but without sighting Jesus.

Troubled, lonely, ashamed, and sick at heart, he trudged slowly toward Capernaum. As he neared the old home, his steps lagged. The door was open. Jesus was at work on the old lathe. Simon went in and sat down on the tool-chest. He waited for Jesus to speak.

After a long silence, Jesus put down Ebenezer's broken contraption, and said, with a sigh:

"Simon, Satan has been beating you on his threshing-floor."

There was nothing that the remorseful Simon could say. He hung his head and tugged at his lip.

Leaning forward with a sigh, Jesus again took up the broken lathe and resumed his work. Presently he turned toward Simon with a compassionate smile and said gently, as to a chastised child:

"But I am still praying for you."

*   *   *   *   *   *

David had never been quite so confused. There were plenty of mysteries in life which nobody tried to understand, mysteries which everybody took for granted. But this one cried out for an explanation.

Previous rumors of the Carpenter's miracles had not bothered him too much. It was conceivable that a clever magician could talk a crowd of simple-minded, credulous people into a foolish interest in his charlatanry. Had he not seen it happen, again and again, on the streets of Athens? Even the Nazarene's alleged works of healing were understandable. It was a matter of record that bed-ridden paralytics, finding their house on fire and no one to help them, had risen and run to safety. Long-time lunatics had been briefly shocked into sanity. Doubtless the Carpenter's feats of healing could all be accounted for if anyone would go to the trouble of examining them.

But this thing that had obviously happened to Hannah seemed different. The behavior of the neighbors was puzzling. They were not all fools and the spontaneity of their amazement made it incredible that they had connived with the Nazarene to create the impression that a miracle had been performed.

For some time David remained standing, outside the fence, watching the people in the dooryard as they moved about with strained faces in which there was something of bewildered gratification combined with forthright terror, most of them mumbling questions which nobody tried to answer, groups of them falling apart and re-forming again, some crowding into the congested doorway, some struggling to get out, shaking their heads when queried. The thing that had happened in there might have a reasonable explanation, but the people didn't think so.

David felt at a disadvantage standing there, waiting. It certainly did not comport with his dignity to exhibit so much curiosity. He surveyed the crowd for a familiar face, someone he might beckon to him, but nobody glanced his way. . . . Now came the Big Fisherman, around from the rear of the house, walking hurriedly toward the gate, looking neither to right nor left. David hoped to attract his attention but Simon's errand was urgent and he gave no heed. It was evident that he didn't want to talk to anyone.

Rabbi Elimelech now appeared, the crowd on the stoop making way for him, and cautiously tottered down the two steps, leaning heavily on his cane. He glanced about at the staring faces, his own wearing a labored smile that intended to be amiable and paternal but an inner stress showed through. He laid a long, lean hand on his beard, perhaps to compose his chin which was trembling. David walked around the corner and waited for him at the gate.

"Ah—David! I am glad to see you. I hope you are well." The Rabbi was trying to be casual.

"Well?" David was brusque: he wasn't going to be put off with trivial amenities. "Not at all well! I'm quite upset! What has been going on here, Rabbi?"

"Walk with me, David," murmured the old man. "I cannot stand long. My legs, you know. I must go home. Take my arm, my friend."

David promptly complied and found that the lean arm was trembling. They moved slowly up the street together. For something to say, David remarked drolly, "I'm afraid your congregation will think you have fallen into bad company, Master."

"It won't matter," replied Elimelech, huskily. "Nothing matters now.

My people have objected to my interest in the Nazarene; but now—they don't know what to think—about anything!"

It wasn't as if they were strangers, the Rabbi and this Sadducee. David had no connections with the Synagogue, never attended its services, was presumed to hold it in contempt; but he was its chief financial support. Whenever he sent a contribution, he took pains to explain that the gift was not meant to imply the slightest interest in the Synagogue but only his appreciation of Rabbi Elimelech's kindness to the poor of Bethsaida. The Regents of the Synagogue always scowled when they got it, and indignantly talked of refusing it, which they never did.

Once the good old man had climbed the hill and spent the afternoon with the Sadducee. And they had enjoyed each other. On leaving, however, Elimelech had remarked, with some embarrassment:

"I wish we might do this—often—but—"

"I understand fully, Master," David had said. "You have enough to bear, without defending your friendship for a Sadducee."

Impatient as he was to inspect the old man's mind in regard to the alleged miracle of Hannah's healing, he refrained from pestering him with questions while they were on the way. They walked slowly, arm in arm, with short, shuffling steps, David acquiring the Rabbi's limp. It seemed a long journey to the commodious old house hard by the Synagogue. David tenderly boosted Elimelech up the steps and through the door. Courtesy demanded that the Rabbi invite his friend to sit down and curiosity compelled the Sadducee to accept.

When Elimelech's breathing was easier, David asked:

"What think you, Master? Was Hannah's recovery miraculous?"

"That word is often used loosely, David," replied the old man, apparently hoping that his candid evasiveness would preclude further questioning. Noting David's shrug, he elaborated on his irrelevant remark: "Frequently, a new experience is called miraculous."

"Let us not trouble ourselves about the careless use of big words, Master," said David, reproachfully. "This is a serious matter!"

Elimelech acknowledged his futile attempt to retreat from the main issue: he closed his eyes and slowly nodded his head.

"You know as much about it as I, David. Hannah was at the point of death. Gershon said so. Everybody said so. . . . Jesus spent a few minutes at her side, and she sat up, recognized those who stood by, and accepted food. . . . If that is a miracle—" The weary old voice faltered and finished lamely—"it was indeed a miracle."

"Then the man is divine!" persisted David. "Is that your opinion, sir?"

"How should I know?" Little beads of perspiration were dotting the Rabbi's pale forehead, but the Sadducee continued his inquisition.

"If he is divine, might he be the promised Messiah?"

"Many Messiahs have come and gone, my friend. None of them met the requirements of prophecy."

"Very true!" assented David. "And each of them had his loyal following, and most of them were honest and fearless men of good intent, like this Jesus. But they all failed of the one great task. According to the prophets, the Messiah would restore the Kingdom to Israel. No one of them could do that."

Elimelech made no comment, and David went on.

"Rabbi, how recently have you visited Caesarea?"

"Never was there in my life. Why do you ask?"

"Well—if this man has any thought of restoring the Kingdom to Israel he had better set about it with all speed. The Romans are preparing Caesarea as a port of invasion. It will not be long now. . . . Tell me, Rabbi; you have heard this Nazarene speak: has he talked about the Kingdom?"

"He talks of little else, David," said Elimelech, quietly.

"And what does he say?" David leaned forward, attentively. "Does this penniless Carpenter expect to withstand a Roman invasion?"

"The Romans will not invade his Kingdom, David."

"I'm afraid I don't understand, Master."

"No," sighed the old man, "you wouldn't understand. This man's Kingdom is his soul. He teaches that our Kingdom is our soul. The Romans cann t take it; nor can they destroy its peace. . . . You should hear him talk, David. Then you might understand."

With that, David rose to go: he had no mind for further discussion of this sort. Besides, he had tormented the good old man long enough. He moved toward the door.

"And come and tell me what you think of him, my friend," said Elimelech, over his shoulder. "The Carpenter may have a surprise in store for you."

*　　*　　*　　*　　*　　*

David, of the Sadducean House of Zadok, had been so stirred to curiosity about the Nazarene that he resolved to pocket his cynicism and pay the man a visit forthwith.

It was rumored that the Carpenter had opened a shop in Capernaum and during the season of rough weather would be available for employment. Would the Messiah be likely to do that? None of the other candidates for Messiahship had worked with his hands. However, reflected

David, it wasn't important that Jesus should pattern his career in imitation of men who had failed. Perhaps he was showing wisdom in making common cause with toilers: perhaps calluses on a prophet's hands were more to his credit than concealed callosities less comfortably achieved. . . . David chuckled a little at the possibilities of a detestable epigram dealing with this matter.

The crowd in Hannah's dooryard had thinned somewhat when he passed the house on his way home. He did not pause to ask questions. He walked more rapidly than usual, for he intended to visit the Carpenter this afternoon. In anticipation of the call it would be more seemly, he thought, to provide himself with a legitimate business errand. To do this he would first have to go home.

On his latest visit to Athens, six years ago, David had bought an exquisitely crafted curio-cabinet which, to his great disappointment, had been badly damaged in transportation. On various occasions he had invited experienced wood-workers to attempt repairs, but none of them wanted to undertake it. They hadn't the tools for it, they said. Now he would take it to the Nazarene.

The servants dusted it with care, loaded it on a cart, and followed their master to Capernaum; slowly, for the elderly lawyer was prudent about overtaxing his tired heart. It was mid-afternoon when they arrived at the old home of Jonas who, according to a local legend, had often prayed publicly for the Sadducees in a tone that poorly concealed his private disinterest in their welfare.

The Big Fisherman opened the door and showed surprise—and some embarrassment too, from which he quickly recovered. Ranged around the walls, sitting on stools and benches, several men silently surveyed the visitor. They came to their feet as Simon presented them to the eminent David, each of them bowing respectfully as his name was spoken; one Nathaniel Bartholomew, a man of apparent intelligence in his sixties, a light-complexioned, slender man of forty, whose name was Philip—

"A Greek?" inquired David.

"Quite a long time back, sir," Philip had replied. "My people fled from Macedonia a century ago."

Then Simon pointed out the young brothers, James and John.

"Are you carpenters?" asked David, addressing John in particular.

"Fishermen," said John, adding—"but not today."

A chuckle went around the circle.

"Johnny is not much of a fisherman, sir," put in Simon, "even in the best of weather. We take him along for ballast."

This was amusing, for Johnny was of slight build and didn't weigh very much. When the others laughed he smiled obligingly and rubbed a beard less chin.

Simon, they all felt, was doing very well: Simon had a way with him. Even the presence of the learned Sadducee had not disconcerted him.

"I think you have met my brother," said Simon, as Andrew came in trom an adjoining room carrying a comfortable chair obviously intended for the honored guest. David politely nodded toward Andrew and they all sat aown. After a little silence, David turned to Simon and said, "I came to see the Carpenter, Jesus. I have some work for him."

"The Master is resting, sir," said Simon.

David stiffened slightly and arched his eyebrows as to wonder how a carpenter could afford to be resting during working hours, but Simon offered no explanation. Philip, who sat by a front window observing the cart, inquired, "Is there anything we may do, sir?"

"Not unless you're a skilled carpenter," replied David, coolly; but he went to the door and told his servants to bring in the cabinet.

They all gathered in a circle around it, admiring its craftsmanship and deploring its injuries. Unobserved, Jesus joined the preoccupied group, standing beside and a little to the rear of David. Their sleeves lightly touched. Of ponderous dignity and deliberated movement, David was not one to act impulsively; but at this accidental contact, he suddenly re- treated, turned about, and found himself staring into the steady eyes of a young man who didn't seem to belong in this company at all.

Simon, observing, said, "Master, our guest is David, of the House of Zadok."

The Sadducee bowed deferentially, silently, and Jesus said, "You are welcome, friend. What may I do for you?"

David pointed toward the cabinet, but Jesus' eyes did not follow the gesture, as had been expected. His calm look of inquiry seemed friendly enough but it was apparent that he had no concern for the cabinet.

"I shall make no attempt to deceive you, sir," said David. "The cabinet aoes need mending; but, in truth, that was not the object of my call. I have heard many things of your words and deeds, and I desired to see you."

"You have spoken truthfully, David," said Jesus. "If that is your custom you should be able to understand my sayings. Men who love the truth are my friends. . . . Will you sit down?"

They all found their places and sat, with Jesus in the midst of them. Stooping over, he picked up a portion of the worn-out lathe, shook his head, and let it fall with a clatter to the floor.

"Let us talk of redemption," he said—"and of salvation." He pointed to the broken lathe, and then to the cabinet. In a low voice, almost as if he were talking to himself, he began to speak about the things that could, and could not, be reclaimed by mending. Some things were beyond repair. The life was gone out of them and nothing but newness of life could redeem them.

"It is useless," he went on, "to sew a new patch on an old garment. The worn-out fabric has no strength to support good cloth. It is of no profit to pour active new wine into an old, dried, inflexible wineskin." Turning toward David, he asked, "What say you, friend?"

"I fully agree with you, Master," said David. "And does it not apply as well to old systems of thought, old laws, old beliefs?"

A slow, sidelong glance of apprehensive inquiry slipped from man to man around the wall. Was this shrewd lawyer baiting the Master to some imprudent criticism of the Government or the Sanhedrin?

But apparently Jesus had no suspicions of the Sadducee's sincerity. He seemed eager to discuss David's pertinent query. . . . The tendency of any ancient establishment of laws or doctrines was the gradual accumulation of signs, symbols, tokens, amulets, sanctified vessels and enchanted words, until the life of the institution was smothered and its purposes forgotten. . . . Endless debates dealt with such trivialities of the law as how many cubits a man might walk on the Sabbath Day, whether a man might carry a stool across the room, whether a tailor was breaking the law of the Sabbath if he had a needle in his coat, but they never defined how much rent a landlord could exact of a poor tenant, or how much interest a money-lender could demand from a hard-pressed debtor. . . . Solemn conclaves dignifiedly wrangled over the proper compounding of herbs for incense—precisely how much mint, how much anise, how much rue—and days were spent in arguing about the breadth of a phylactery or the depth of a hem on a priest's robe, while the needy lay starving to death on rich men's doorsteps, and nobody cared! . . . The Master's voice rose indignantly as he pictured groups of hapless, hopeless men huddled together at the very lodgegates of well-fed pundits who spent their days splitting the hairs of ritual and ceremonial. And nobody noticed the plight of these wretched ones but the homeless dogs who paused to lick their sores. Nor was there any talk of mercy and brotherly kindness! . . . Any government so far gone toward utter futility could never be repaired. It would have to be reborn!

"Do you think then," asked David, respectfully, "that the old laws should be repealed?"

"No, David!" exclaimed Jesus. "Not repealed—but fulfilled!"

With that he rose and took leave of them, retiring to his bed-chamber. It was evident that he was very weary. After a moment of indecision, the Sadducee went to the front door to summon his servants. They had disappeared. He stood in the doorway, looking down the street; then impulsively beckoned to the men in the room, and set off with obvious agitation. They rose and followed quickly. Huge billows of black smoke puffed toward the sky in the vicinity of the Synagogue. Excited men were running down the middle of the road. Simon and the others soon overtook and passed David, all but old Nathaniel Bartholomew who had a weak leg and poor wind. The fire angrily spat and crackled and roared as they neared the Synagogue plaza. Rounding the corner they saw what it was, the residence of Rabbi Ben-Sholem.

There Simon's steps slowed to a walk. He was quite out of breath from all the excitement and unusual exertion. He let everybody pass him and stood for a long moment, panting hard. The acrid smoke stung his nostrils. Apparently there wasn't much to be done for the Rabbi's house. In any case, it was none of Simon's business. Rabbi Ben-Sholem had mistreated the Master. Perhaps the haughty old man was being punished for it. Maybe it was God's will that the Rabbi should lose his home. If so, who was Simon that he should have the impudence to interfere?

*　　*　　*　　*　　*　　*

Throughout those cheerless winter days the Big Fisherman learned that while it was highly exciting to be a friend and follower of Jesus when vast crowds of staring, sweating, importunate people trampled one another for better standing-ground to see and hear the Carpenter, it was very dull business when practiced privately in the rain.

It seemed that every circumstance of Simon's experience during this bleak period was part of a diabolical conspiracy to break down his faith and fortitude.

To begin with: nobody could remember such a protracted siege of bad weather. It rained relentlessly, a cold, marrow-chilling rain that soaked the heaviest garments and leaked through into the soul. The oldsters, who were not required to go out into it very much, counselled patience. "This abundance of rain," they said, "will bless our land next summer." And so it would—and did; but it was tiresome while it lasted.

As for the fishing, it was utterly profitless. Of course no one ever expected much of a catch on a stormy day, but it at least provided subsistence and kept the men out of mischief. Ordinarily the dismal weather had but little effect upon the spirits of Simon's fleet. The fishermen joked about their discomforts. This season it was different. The fishing wasn't worth doing. The men were restless, sullen and touchy.

Simon, who was never one to rush in ahead of everybody else to take the blame for something that had gone amiss, knew who was responsible for this unhappy state of affairs, and knew that his men knew that he knew.... No—it wasn't the Big Fisherman's fault if it rained all day and all night every day and every night, nor could it be held against him that the perch wouldn't rise; but the sour and surly attitude of his dispirited crews was because of the skipper's indifference. He had lost all interest in his business. And if he didn't care, why should they?

Simon sat alone and had little to say. His heart was heavy. Ever since he had met Jesus he had been increasingly inattentive to his trade. It was perhaps inevitable that this should have happened. Once he had taken his place beside the Master as his foremost friend and assistant, calmly directing an excitable throng of awe-stricken people and competently keeping order among frantic suppliants, the old routines of mending nets and splicing ropes and sluicing the slimy decks of his fishing-smacks had lost their hold on his imagination; and no longer had he any pride in his fleet, or any joy.

The worst thing about it was the quite apparent disaffection of the men and boys whose love and loyalty had meant so much to him. It was plain to see that their devotion to him was in serious disrepair. As the Big Fisherman, as the noisy, quick-tempered, profane, sacrilegious, hard-hitting Big Fisherman, they had idolized him. Now that he had been captivated by the soft-spoken Jesus, Simon was no longer their hero.

Nor was this the only cause of his dejection.

Nobody could have tortured this confession out of him, but Simon wished he were a little better satisfied with the Master's recent activities and attitudes. There was his carpentry, for example. Simon had thought it would be just the right thing for Jesus to engage in some gainful employment during the brief winter. The little carpenter-shop was indeed a happy thought. Maybe the influential Jairus would hear of it and approve. Jairus might even call, some day, and bring a chair to be mended; and remain to chat awhile.

But it hadn't turned out very well. Who could foresee that Jesus would consent to work on the interior of old Ben-Sholem's house? Not only was he giving his full time to it every day, but he seemed infatuated with the job of installing the fine-grained olive-wood paneling on the walls and ceiling of the Rabbi's library, paneling so perfectly matched and mortised that its symmetrical pattern appeared to have been chiseled from one great tree.

Simon hadn't wanted him to do it at all. Surely Jesus was under no obligation to do a favor for the Rabbi. Moreover the wages were niggardly. The contractor had had the impudence to say that any man should consider it a privilege to work on "a holy house," even if he were paid nothing at all. That's the way it was with the synagogues: they had a bad habit of imposing on people in this manner, asking skilled craftsmen to donate their time. Why was the Rabbi a mendicant? He had his share of the tithes; hadn't he?

And that wasn't the whole cause of Simon's petulance. There was Ben-Sholem's contemptuous attitude toward Jesus, even while the Master was working for him! One afternoon Simon had dropped in to watch the progress of Jesus' labors. Presently the Rabbi brought Jairus in to show him what was going on. Sighting Simon, he testily inquired of the contractor, "Is this man employed here?" And when the contractor shook his head, the Rabbi scowled and said,

"Then perhaps he should be on his way."

Flushed with humiliation, Simon had left the house. It seemed to him that Jesus might have said something in defense of his friend. Had Simon been in Jesus' place he would have thrown down his tools and walked off the job. And then let the detestable old man try to find another carpenter capable of finishing that beautiful room!

Simon earnestly wished that Jesus were made of tougher stuff! With all that miraculous power at his disposal, why didn't he use some of it to defend himself and his cause; yes, and his friends, too, who were giving up everything for his sake?

He recalled what the servants at the palace had said about a strange, bug-eating hermit who had been jailed for predicting the advent of an Avenger. There was one coming who would put down the mighty from their seats and exalt men of low degree. He would carry an ax and a flail! The unjust would be cut down! Threshed! Abolished! It was clear enough now that Jesus had no such intentions. Perhaps there was another Anointed One coming.

That night Simon stealthily approached the unguarded prison by a circuitous route through the Tetrarch's vineyards; and, at the window-bars, talked long and seriously with the emaciated prisoner. It was true, as the servant-girls had reported: this John was confident that stern judgment was at hand for evil-doers in high places. The whole world would be shaken! Not only High Priests and Prefects would be punished: Caesar himself would feel the sting of that lash!

Next morning, the questing eyes of Jesus brought forth a full confession from Simon of the interview he had had with John in prison. To his surprise and relief, the Master listened complacently. After a long silence between them, Jesus said:

"You were talking with one of the most courageous men this world has ever produced. But John—for all his bravery—does not understand the workings of the Kingdom—my Kingdom. He would see all evil uprooted by the punishment of evil-doers. To set things right by violence has been tried again and again by earnest men, ever since the world began, but to no avail. My kingdom will overcome evil with good. It is not an easy way, my friend, but it is the only way!"

"This saying is difficult to understand, Master," murmured Simon.

Jesus brightened, smiled reassuringly, and said:

"Go and talk with John again. Tell him what you yourself have seen; how the blind receive their sight, the deaf hear, cripples walk, and the poor are comforted with good news. . . . And tell him not to be disappointed in me."

That afternoon the sun shone and the sky was blue. It seemed that the long season of the rains was ended. Jesus had completed his work at Ben-Sholem's house. At his suggestion, Andrew loaded the borrowed tools onto a cart and returned them to Ebenezer, the Master walking alongside. At the old carpenter's house, he tarried for a friendly word and gave Ebenezer half the wages he had received from the Rabbi.

On their way back to the cottage, Andrew, who had been moved by Jesus' generosity and Ebenezer's tearful gratitude, found his voice and inquired:

"Will you soon be speaking again to the people, Master?"

"Tomorrow," said Jesus. "At Hammath. And then we are going on to Cana."

14

As HAD BEEN PREDICTED during the long season of the rains, spring—as if to atone for tardiness—now came forward fast, fragrant, beautiful.

Nobody could remember such an abundance or variety of wild-flowers along the roads and on the hillsides. Indeed gay blossoms bloomed in desert places and even the most arid areas on the Plains of Esdraelon offered pasturage.

Not much farm work had begun yet for the fields were still too wet for plowing, but everybody along the western shore of Lake Gennesaret, except the definitely bedridden, had come out-of-doors rejoicing; and of all who faced the spring with exultation there was no heart in Galilee more nearly ready to burst with happiness than Esther's.

So far she had not confided the nature of her ecstasy to anyone but David who had pressed her for an explanation. She had wanted to tell Hannah, and promised herself that some day she would, but it involved a long, almost incredible story; and, at the moment, Hannah's mind was wholly occupied with the mystery of her own miraculous recall from death. It was clear enough that Hannah wondered what had come over Esther: sometimes her soft, brown eyes, resting on the girl's radiant face, suddenly widened, narrowed, queried—and gave it up. Simon, too, meeting Esther's luminous eyes, would study them with a puzzled stare. Andrew suspected that her new radiance had something to do with Hannah's recovery, though he couldn't guess what the connection might be, and certainly had no notion of asking. If she wanted him to know her secret she would tell him. This much he was sure of: she had been an entirely different person ever since the day of Hannah's healing.

It had not immediately occurred to Esther that she no longer had any business detaining her in Galilee. Although her hazardous errand of vengeance had suddenly and conclusively arrived at an end, the new sensation of freedom had taken full possession of her mind. Nor had she any misgivings over her abandonment of the vow to which she had been so long in bondage. Jesus had commanded her to put down the intolerable weight she had borne, and Jesus was to be obeyed. Whatever he said was right.

But she was soon going to need some advice about the future. Obviously, Jesus himself was the person she should confide in, but she must wait for a suitable opportunity. Meantime, she could be helpful to Hannah who had not yet recovered her full strength.

On the first fair afternoon, when the rains had ended, Hannah insisted that Esther should take a walk in the sunshine. She gratefully complied, taking the road up the slope toward the Zadok mansion. It was not her intention to call; or, at least, that was what she told herself as she entered the grounds; but presently she found David sauntering along a garden path. He seemed very happy to see her, fell into step beside her, directed her to a rustic seat.

"I have been impatient to talk with you, my child," he said. "You were present, I think, when that strange thing happened to Hannah. I should be glad to hear your own opinion of it. The neighbors believe there was a miracle wrought. What say you, Esther?"

"Hannah was dying, sir," she replied, firmly. "Everybody knew it. No one who saw her has doubted it."

"And you think this Jesus, the Carpenter, healed her? Did you see that? What did he do? What did he say?"

"I am glad you asked me to tell you, sir!" Esther's throaty voice was vibrant with excitement. "I saw it. I was the only one he asked to remain in the room when he healed her. And he healed me, too," she added, impulsively.

"You!" exclaimed David. "And what ailed you?" Leaning forward, with knitted brows, he listened while Esther ventured upon her strange story. Presently he broke in to inquire, "You say he called you Fara?"

She nodded, slowly.

"He called me Fara, as if he had known me for a long time and was accustomed to addressing me so."

"I suppose you think, then, that he knows all about you—and your errand in Galilee."

Esther's reply was delayed, while David studied her eyes.

"I think, sir," she murmured, "that Jesus knows everything! Everything about me! Everything about everybody!"

"Proceed, please. I shall not interrupt any more."

With that encouragement, Esther continued; and, when she had ended, she searched the old lawyer's narrowed eyes and disappointedly shook her head.

"I'm afraid you don't believe me," she said, with a sigh.

"I'm afraid I do, daughter," confessed David. "My whole mind cried out against any credence in such things, but the evidence here is too strong. Whatever happened to Hannah, it is clear enough that something has happened to you! It is in your eyes, your voice, your smile! You are a new creature! Transformed!"

They had been speaking in Aramaic, Esther having wanted to quote the words of Jesus exactly as they were uttered. She now replied in Greek to David's unexpected comments on the change that had come over her. The old man watched her mobile lips with candid pleasure. It was not often, in these days, that he heard this musical language, and it not only delighted but amused him to note the new freedom and assurance in the girl's voice as she went on.

What to do now? That was the question. She confided in him as if he were a parent. Hannah would not need her much longer. She did not want to return to the palace. There was nothing for her to do in Galilee.

"But your friend Voldi will soon be returning for you," suggested David. "Perhaps you should go back with him to Arabia."

Her face clouded.

"I must not do that to Voldi!" she declared.

"Well—it needn't be settled today," said David, reassuringly. "When in doubt about what to do, it is usually wise to do nothing, and wait for more light. Perhaps you should talk with Jesus. . . . And stay where you are until Voldi comes. You have promised him you would do that."

*   *   *   *   *   *

But Voldi, unfortunately, would not be coming.

It had not occurred to him, so courteously had he been treated during his brief stop in Caesarea, when on his way to Tiberias in Galilee, that his association with Proconsul Mencius had accounted for the freedom he had enjoyed there.

Now that he had returned, alone, it was natural that the authorities should take a fresh interest in his movements. He was cordially welcomed at The Domus Agrippa and given the best of accommodations; but when, in reply to their query about the probable length of his stay, he informed them that he wanted to remain until spring, the management felt obliged to report; for the Prefect's office had an active curiosity to learn what manner of business in Caesarea required the attention of foreign visitors.

Routine inquiries would have been made into the affairs of any Arabian, however insignificant he might be. But Voldi was conspicuous. He had the air of a person of privilege, he was well-dressed, he rode a valuable horse and the horse's trappings were mounted with silver. He had plenty of money. But he had no business acquaintances—and no business.

And so it was that on the third day after his arrival, Voldi received a polite note requesting him to call at the Prefect's office in the Praetorium. The interview, with no less a personage than Prefect Sergius himself, began cordially enough but soon settled down to serious business. The Captain of the Praetorian Guard was called in as an observer, and a scholarly looking young amanuensis began taking notes. The Prefect's queries were courteous enough to befit an examination of a foreign nobleman, it having been already established that the guest was the grandson of Mishma, the King of Arabia's Chief Counsellor.

It would please the Prefect to know what errand had brought the young Arabian to Caesarea, and whom he had come to see, and anything else that he wanted to say about his purposes.

Not having expected this inquisition, Voldi had made no preparation for it, and the story he hastily contrived was not very convincing to the shrewd old Roman who had heard—and told—enough lies to be able to recognize one that had been so casually extemporized.

"So—you went to Tiberias to examine some ancient manuscripts belonging to the Tetrarch," said Sergius, dryly, "but you were already aware that the Tetrarch was not in residence. Now, what led you to believe that you might be welcome in His Grace's absence?"

Voldi, appropriately embarrassed, explained that he had come a very long way to see these scrolls, that they really belonged in a museum available to the general public; adding that Lysias, the steward, had shown him every courtesy.

The old Prefect sniffed cynically and drawled, "Your interest in ancient literature must be profound, sir. No one has ever confided to me that the men of your country have shown so much concern for learning. You say these scrolls you went to see are reputed to have belonged to Aristotle. How many Arabians are conversant with the writings of Aristotle? I'll wager that even your King Zendi doesn't know enough Greek to bid the time o' day to the Governor of Petra."

Voldi grinned and replied, "Just about that much, I think, sir."

Sergius chuckled a little at that, but soberly resumed his interrogations.

"Now, my young friend, the whole world knows that Arabia bears a grudge against Tetrarch Antipas, a very reasonable grudge, too, if I may say so. How do you happen to be so complacent about the indignity he wrought upon your Royal Family that you would accept the hospitality of his palace? Are you sure you weren't there to reconnoiter in preparation for a later visit? Tell me, please: where are you bound for—when you leave Caesarea?"

"I am going home, sir," lied Voldi.

"Very well, then," growled the Prefect. "See that nothing interferes with your plan. You have the freedom of the city. Should you decide to return to Tiberias, it will be an error of judgment." He pushed back his chair and rose. Turning to the Captain of the Guard, he said, gruffly, "You have your orders, Malus. When this young man leaves us, he is going back—directly—to his own country."

After that, while Voldi did not have the uncomfortable feeling that there were eyes at his keyhole, he found himself acknowledging the respectful salutes of the Municipal Police wherever he went. They smiled pleasantly and lifted their spears to their foreheads when he strolled along the docks. When he exercised Darik, which was almost every day, he invariably fell in with a mounted patrol.

One bleak morning when he was aimlessly sauntering through the public rooms of The Domus Agrippa, Voldi came face to face with a handsome, well-groomed Roman of his own age who bluntly confronted him with, "You're the Arabian; aren't you?"

"Well," drawled Voldi, "I may not be the Arabian—but I am an Arabian."

"My name is Felix," said the youth.

"Oh?" replied Voldi, casually. "Is there anything I can do for you? If so, I shall be glad to undertake it. I am not very busy."

"My father mentioned you to me. He said you were a stranger in Caesarea, and might welcome a little attention. Father is the Prefect."

Voldi grinned.

"It's good of you, Felix," he said. "I am a bit lonesome and restless here, though I must say your father has already provided me with plenty of attention. I can hardly turn around without stepping on a policeman."

It was the young Roman's turn to be amused.

"Don't let that bother you! Important aliens in Caesarea always come in for a lot of oversight. But I'm not a policeman; and, personally, I don't care a damn where you go or what you are up to. . . . I thought you might like to take a ride with me into the country, just to kill time."

"With pleasure!" Voldi brightened at the prospect. "Perhaps I should tell you that I'm not supposed to leave the city by any of the northerly routes."

Felix nodded in a manner indicating that he knew all about it.

"You're suspected of a hankering to make the acquaintance of the Tetrarch of Galilee. My pater wonders why—and so do I. Antipas is a cad, you know; a noisy, vain, arrogant old pretender. I'm sure you wouldn't like him." The Roman's eyes twinkled through this ironical speech, inviting the Arab to commit himself, but Voldi made no sign of understanding. The friendly son of the Prefect might not be a policeman but this was no time to risk a confidence.

"Perhaps not," replied Voldi, indifferently. "One can't be expected to like everybody."

Felix chuckled over this forthright evasion.

"You win!" he said. "Let's go for the ride. It's clearing off a little. I'll promise not to badger you about Antipas. . . . And when you meet him, you may slit his throat—with my blessing."

The Prefect's home was only a block away. Leading Darik, they walked to Sergius' commodious stables and a groom brought out a beautiful young sorrel mare. Felix ran his fingers under the saddle girths. Voldi liked that. It was commonly believed in Arabia that the Romans were careless about the comfort of their horses. Felix cared.

"I daresay you've noticed that this filly is an Arabian," he said.

"Yes," replied Voldi. "I know her family. You probably bought her in Damascus."

"My father did." They mounted and rode toward the avenue. "I'm told that you Arabians used to market your select stock, on a certain day, in Jerusalem; but—not any more."

"We have lately resumed attendance at the camel-auction in Jerusalem —on the Jewish Day of Pentecost," explained Voldi. "But the horses still go to Damascus."

"And why is that?" Felix wanted to know.

"Perhaps it's because the Jews aren't so much interested in horses," guessed Voldi. "The Syrians pay a better price."

They were proceeding southerly on the coast highway, at a leisurely canter.

"Tell me about this camel-auction," said Felix.

"I never attended it," said Voldi. "I never was in Jerusalem."

"What is this Pentecost business about?"

"I don't know," admitted Voldi. "It's a Jewish feast-day; fifty days after—after something; I forget what."

Felix counted on his fingers, and thought it might be fifty days after the Passover. Voldi nodded disinterestedly and said he supposed that might be correct. The horses, impatient over their mincing canter, changed their gait to a brisk trot. After an interval of silence, Felix slowed his filly to remark:

"The reason I happened to know about this annual Passover business: the Tetrarch always returns for it in the spring. He winters in Rome, and turns up with the sparrows about the Ides of March; makes much ado over his gaudy trip to Jerusalem. You'd think the Emperor had arrived. He has a toy Embassy over there; holds court for a couple of weeks; celebrates the Passover; and hurries back to Tiberias for the summer. . . . But—I suppose you know all about that."

Voldi showed no interest whatsoever in this discourse and abruptly changed the conversation by remarking that the stableboys at The Agrippa had been taking good care of Darik.

"See how his coat shines!"

"They're probably feeding him eggs," said Felix. "You'll be paying plenty for Darik's shine! . . . It won't be long now until Antipas appears. He will arrive on the Emperor's barge. You may have a chance to see him."

Voldi showed vexation.

"You're wasting all that on me, Felix," he declared, crossly. "My errand in this country does not concern old Herod Antipas. You surmise that because I am an Arabian I have designs on the Tetrarch. I am here on another matter."

"I see you don't want to tell me," said Felix, reproachfully. "Perhaps I could have helped you."

"Perhaps—but perhaps not," said Voldi. "We'll see. Meanwhile— let us have no more talk about Antipas. I have no business with him."

Felix pretended a childish pout.

"You wouldn't lie to me; would you, Voldi?" he asked, petulantly

"Don't be silly!" snapped Voldi. "Of course I'd lie to you if there was any reason for it."

"Well—you're candid, anyway," laughed Felix.

"Don't be too sure about that, my son," warned Voldi, dryly.

Felix knew now that he had employed the wrong tactics for the relief of his curiosity. The Arabian, albeit amiable enough, wasn't going to have any confidences pried out of him; and his determined reticence made the son of the Prefect feel years younger than his tight-lipped acquaintance from the eastern mountains.

Their friendship ripened slowly. Having begun with a verbal fencing-match in which the Roman youth was much too hasty with his queries, forcing Voldi to a stubborn defense, they found it difficult to be at ease with one another. Felix was encouraged to talk about himself. His father had been appointed to the Prefecture five years ago, after long service as Captain of the Praetorian Guard in Rome. Felix had been left behind to finish his course in the Military Academy, and had come to Caesarea only last summer. He was free to say that he hated the town and was bored to extinction. His father had promised that he might return to Rome—"in a year or two"—but wanted him to acquaint himself with conditions in Caesarea. He did not say why, but Voldi could guess. The Empire was preparing to complete the subjugation of Palestine, and Felix would probably be in line for participation in it.

For something to say, Voldi remarked that life in Caesarea must be rather dull, after living in the excitements of the Empire's capital.

"I'm slowly dying of it, Voldi!" confided Felix, adding, after a brooding silence, "That may account for my ruthless invasion of your private affairs. My instinct tells me that you're tangled up with an adventure of some sort; and—"

"And you want in it," assisted Voldi.

After that, they seemed to understand each other better. They sheathed their weapons. Felix continued his daily calls at The Agrippa, making himself at home in Voldi's apartment. On clear days they rode. It was an unusual comradeship, based mostly on their loneliness, boredom, and need of diversion. Felix frankly despised Aramaic and spoke it badly: he had been ecstatic when Voldi had aired his Greek.

"You're coming to Rome, some day," Felix said. "I'll show you the only city that really matters—in the whole world! Know anybody there?"

"Nicator Mencius," replied Voldi.

"Indeed! He's one of my father's closest friends! How did you make his acquaintance?"

Voldi told him briefly, and was privately pleased to learn of this connection between the Proconsul and the Prefect. It might be to his advantage, some time, if he got into a scrape.

The long and tiresome winter finally blew itself out and spring came on. Voldi was beside himself with impatience to contrive some way of seeing Fara. She would be expecting him now and if he did not soon appear she would surely conclude that he had given her up and returned to Arabia.

One sunny afternoon the news was circulated in the lobbies of The Agrippa that The Augusta had been sighted. Everybody not otherwise engaged had hurried to the docks to watch the Emperor's beautiful ship come in. The main point of interest would be the disembarkation of the Tetrarch and his retinue and the setting forth of their garish parade for Jerusalem.

Voldi felt that this was something worth seeing. When he joined the huge crowd at the wharf, The Augusta had already docked and the important passengers were leaving the ship, the Tetrarch surrounded by an unusually large company of fellow-travelers who—according to the low-voiced chatter of spectators—had come from Rome to spend the summer.

Felix had failed to put in an appearance at The Domus Agrippa today. Voldi saw him now, sauntering in his direction; but, when he approached, he gave no sign of recognition. As Felix passed, almost brushing sleeves with Voldi, he muttered, "This is no place for you. Better get out of here!"

The brusque command annoyed Voldi. He didn't like the idea of slinking away—like a dog that had been ordered home. He stood his ground. The Romans loved to boss people around: Felix, too, was learning to crow, the young cockerel! Voldi was sore; but so fascinated by the flamboyant pageantry on the wharf that he gave the spectacle his full attention. The Tetrarch's circus was moving away now and the crowd was disintegrating. As Voldi slowly advanced with the throng, two tall Praetorian Guards fell into step on either side of him, and the elder of them said, quietly, "Proceed, please, to your room at The Agrippa, and remain there until the Prefect gives you your freedom."

"May I ask what I have done?" demanded Voldi, testily.

"Nothing, sir," replied the Guard, "but the Prefect wants you to be kept under strict observation until Tetrarch Antipas has left the city."

Voldi shrugged and scowled but did as he was told, feeling like a warmly spanked little boy who had better swallow his indignation if he knew what was good for him. As he ambled toward the street, with the Guards trailing him at a respectful distance, he had to admit to himself that Sergius had not dealt too severely with him, considering the circumstances. It had been very indiscreet of him to come here, and he cursed himself for his impudence. Quickening his steps, he proceeded to the tavern and went at once to his suite. A few minutes afterward, a servant appeared and took his order for dinner.

"I understand you are to be served in your rooms, sir," he said. "Is that correct, sir? . . ." Voldi said it was correct. There were three whole days of this polite and luxurious incarceration. Felix did not appear; though whether he had been ordered to stay away or was disgusted by his friend's impertinence, could not be cleared up at the moment. On the morning of the fourth day, the dining-room servant who had been bringing his meals said, as he put down the breakfast tray, "I understand, sir, that you are dining downstairs at noon."

"Yes," said Voldi, as if he had been notified.

He was still eating his breakfast when Felix came in, glumly nodded, and flung himself into an easy chair.

"You certainly played hell with yourself by going down to the docks," he growled. "Now every move you make will be watched. And the Prefect will be annoyed if I am seen in your company. That's the worst part of it, as far as I am concerned."

Voldi flushed a little at this rebuke and was on the point of retorting angrily; but, aware that he had no case, replied, "It was a mistake, Felix. For your own protection, perhaps you'd do well to ignore me; at least until your father forgets about it."

"My father never forgets anything," said Felix. "He has the memory of an elephant. . . . I'll go now. And if I don't show up for a few days, you'll know why." He rose, and at the door, turned to remark, "I hope you will be discreet now, Voldi. I'm going to miss you."

Voldi nodded and smiled his understanding. After the door had closed slowly and reluctantly, he moodily contemplated the dismaying position into which he had so heedlessly placed himself. The companionship of young Felix had meant more to him than he had realized.

The fine spring days were interminably long and empty. Every morning early, sometimes at the break of dawn, Darik would be mounted for a fast ride on the coast highway to the south. By breakfast time, Voldi would have returned to The Agrippa. He began to study maps of the surrounding country. In his desperation to ease Fara's mind about him, and his interest in her, he began to consider a swift ride to Bethsaida. By getting away early, and urging Darik to his best speed, he might be able to make the round trip in three days. They would be out looking for him, no doubt, but he would be back at The Agrippa before they found him; he hoped!

With the plan for his reckless adventure well organized, he slipped past the sleepy night-watch while it was still dark, rode at a leisurely trot until he had passed through the southern outskirts of the city, pressed Darik to a gallop, and found an unfrequented road that angled easterly to Anti-

patris where he turned north on a weedy old donkey-trail. The day was hot
and Darik was not conditioned for such a journey, but Voldi did not spare
him. So far, so good. He had not been followed.

Late that night he applied for lodging at a filthy inn which befitted the
remembered squalor of Megiddo. After giving the exhausted Darik a rub-
down and a ration of grain, he tumbled down fully clothed in the straw,
and slept.

In the morning, two mounted patrols arrested him as he was leaving the
inn and conducted him back to Caesarea by the shortest route and put him
in prison to await trial for violating the Prefect's orders. He was not
manacled and his quarters were not too uncomfortable. The food was
coarse but edible. The stoutly barred window was too high for him to see
out. He had nothing to read.

When he inquired of the rotund jailor how long it might be until he
was brought to trial, the latter replied, "You picked a bad time to get yourself into trouble with the Prefect. He sailed for Rome, this morning, on
The Augusta. However," he added, wittily, "you're still young; and, besides, you may be better off where you are than where you might be later.
Prefect Sergius, my boy, is not a man to be trifled with! He has had men
beheaded for less than you did!"

15

THE ANNUAL WEEK of the Passover would begin tomorrow; and Antipas, who had always anticipated its games, processions and ceremonies with pleasure, was troubled by its arrival. His Roman house-guests at the Embassy, already bored to forthright rudeness toward their host, would find it a dull affair.

He now realized that it had been a mistake to invite so many of them. He might have managed comfortably with two or three, but—ignoring the warning of Herodias who was not particularly chummy with any of the women of the party—he had brought fifteen!

There were Mark and Aurelia Varus and their daughter Faustina, recently divorced by Consul Narro for spending too much time with Prince Gaius; Julius and Paula Fronto, lately recalled from the prefecture in Crete; Senator Manius Cotta; Nerius and Drusilla Hispo; the garrulous Valerie Flaccus, a friend of Salome's; Proconsul Fabius Tiro, his gossiping wife Amelia, and their restless and flighty young Flavia; Junius Manilius, a retired Legate and long-time crony of the Tetrarch; Tullius Fadilla, a wealthy, middle-aged bachelor; and the aging but kittenish Julia Drusus, who was driving Fadilla insane with her attentions. Deep in his cups at a banquet, Antipas had invited everybody within sound of his voice to accompany him home on *The Augusta*; and now he was paying for his indiscretion.

Usually the month of Nisan, spent in Jerusalem, was thoroughly enjoyed by the Tetrarch. The Galilean Embassy, by grace of the immense sums Antipas had spent upon it, was one of the most beautiful public edifices in the city and spacious far beyond its needs. It would have gratified the Tetrarch if more attention had been accorded it—and him. He craved popularity. He had even gone to the length of announcing that the night patrols were welcome to assemble, when off duty, in the huge

313

carriage-court, and had provided a wood-fire where, in chilly weather, they might warm themselves. As a further evidence of his hospitality, a midnight snack was served to the legionaries. But it couldn't be said that all this generosity ever did the foolish fellow any good. The soldiers nightly warmed their hands, enjoyed the Tetrarch's cakes and wine, and flirted with the servant-girls; but the Embassy was—for all that—a hissing and a byword, even in the opinion of its beneficiaries.

But the great man had pretended not to know where he stood in the public's estimation. For that one month, every spring, he conducted his Embassy as if it really mattered. He had always taken pride and pleasure in playing judge. The cases brought before him were rarely of any importance; and, when they were, the losing litigant always appealed to Pilate who, contemptuous of Antipas and his pompous little tribunal, customarily reversed the decision.

Undaunted by these embarrassments, the Tetrarch made a great thing of the trivial matters submitted to him, handling with ridiculous ostentation mere border brawls between the Samaritans and Galileans involving such issues as their joint responsibility for the repair of a wooden bridge on an unfrequented donkey-trail at a cost of fifty shekels. Indeed the Samaritans and Galileans had often gone to law for less. They had hated one another for at least five centuries and relished the occasional opportunity of exchanging elaborately contrived insults in this atmosphere of ponderous dignity, even if a favorable decision cost more than it was worth.

During his many winter seasons in Rome, Antipas, when queried about his official duties as Tetrarch of Galilee, candidly admitted that his executive responsibilities while in residence at Tiberias were not onerous. There was, of course, the month he spent annually at the Embassy. That, he implied, was quite another matter. When pressed for details he always closed his eyes, shook his head, and waggled his hand, as to say that it was too serious to be talked about. And he had foolishly allowed the growth of a legend to the effect that his court in Jerusalem dealt out horrible punishments to all manner of desperate criminals, seditionists and traitors.

Now the silly secret was out. There was no blood-letting to be had at the Embassy. The Romans had attended court, one morning, and had filed out presently, their shameless laughter echoing in the high-domed, mosaic-lined foyer. The Tetrarch's court, they said truthfully, was a poor show.

Antipas now had had three weeks of these insufferable people. He hated them all. There was nothing in Jerusalem that they wanted to do, nothing

they wanted to see. Most of them had visited Greece, all of them had been
in Egypt. As for architectural splendors and hoary antiquities, the Holy
City had little to offer to anybody who had seen the Acropolis or the ruins
at Karnak.

The Tetrarch was at his wits' end to find entertainment for his jaded
guests. He had wangled an invitation for them to luncheon at The Insula,
but it was a painful event, Pontius and Calpurnia Pilate making it plain
that their hospitality was an official duty, and no pleasure. Besides, the
very air was drugged with the long-festering animosity of Pilate and
Fronto; and Calpurnia had no use for Herodias whom she had publicly
snubbed on numerous occasions. The Procurator, brusque enough when
on his best behavior, went to no bother to brighten the hour. The most
interest he showed in any of them was when, after blinking solemnly into
Fadilla's baggy eyes for a long moment, he muttered, "Tullius, you're
getting paunchy; probably drinking too much. You'll have a stroke, one of
these days."

And now the Passover was at hand. These pagans couldn't be expected
to take much interest in that. Obviously the most prudent course now was
to get them all out of Jerusalem before they disgraced him with their flip-
pant comments concerning an ancient rite which—in the opinion of all
Jewry—was no joke. True, it would be an appalling display of indifference,
on his own part, to leave at this moment; but he would risk it. He tried the
idea out on Herodias, who approved it with the not very reassuring comment, "You may as well do it: you have nothing to lose."

Customarily, at the end of Passover Week, the Tetrarch's family and
retainers were escorted back to Tiberias by the Legion from Capernaum.
It would have been foolhardy to attempt this journey through the bandit-
infested mountains of Samaria without protection. Seeing that the gala
week in Jerusalem was in the nature of a vacation for Julian's legionaries,
it was doubtful whether the Legate would consent to leave the city on the
very eve of the festival, even if Procurator Pilate had permitted the withdrawal for no better reason than to accommodate a whim of the Tetrarch's.

However, it was worth trying. Antipas stated his case to Julian who, as
was to be expected, flatly refused. In desperation the Tetrarch told the
Legate that if he would release one company for this service every man
of them should be paid thirty shekels per day. This was tempting bait.
Julian said he would see. That afternoon he reported that a company of
one hundred legionaries, under the command of a trusted Centurion,
would be on hand early the next morning. And it was with a deep sigh of
relief that Antipas saw his long caravan through the Damascus Gate and

out into the open country. Now his malcontents, instead of fretting in the tiresome confinement of the Embassy, could amuse themselves as they liked. They could ride, bathe in the beautiful pool, tan their hides in the gardens; and, incidentally, relieve him of the responsibility to find entertainment for them.

But in a few days after their arrival it became apparent that the Romans were going to be as restless in Tiberias as they had been in Jerusalem. There were plenty of good horses in the Tetrarch's marble stables but the visitors petulantly remarked that there were no interesting rides to be taken; nowhere to go. The girls inquired why no use was made of the lovely lake; ideal water for a pleasure barge; moonlight, music, dancing. It was queer, they said, that the Tetrarch had never thought of that. Well— it was too late now.

By the end of Nisan everybody was at loggerheads with everybody else. Salome had had a falling out with Valerie who, to punish her, had transferred her attentions to the young Tiro girl, causing an estrangement between Salome and Flavia. At this juncture, Amelia Tiro, championing her child, remarked—in the presence of a half dozen loungers beside the famous pool—that Salome was no fit company for a young girl anyway; and although this comment did not come as a shock to anybody it did nothing to improve the climate of a house party already at storm.

Julia Drusus, savagely scorned by the exasperated Fadilla, belatedly showed a comradely interest in Herodias who, resentful of Julia's earlier aloofness, would have none of her.

Antipas made pretense of busying himself with the planting of a new vineyard, and coolly despised them all.

Salome, now left to her own devices, sought consolation in the companionship of her stepfather, making their mutual affection so flagrantly showy that everybody chattered evilly about them—and Herodias could have killed them both. Indeed so hard pressed for attention was the unhappy woman that she took to visiting John the hermit in his cell, plying him with fruits, flowers and flattery; and when it became evident that the grim prophet was too preoccupied with his own meditations to appraise hers correctly, Herodias threw away the last shred of her counterfeit decency and drove the hapless ascetic into a terrifying rage by attempting to caress him. Hot with such anger as she had never experienced, she slapped him on the mouth and slammed the cell-door behind her, screaming that he could stay there forever—and rot—for all she cared. Her eyes burned with self-piteous tears as she stumbled along toward the new vineyard muttering that things had come to a pretty pass when a shaggy.

penniless ragamuffin from nowhere would dare to yell into her face that she was a common slut. That the accusation was true did not mitigate the indignity. She would see to it that the bug-eater was punished.

By the time she reached Antipas, who was complacently viewing the building of rustic trellises at the far corner of the vineyard, Herodias had burned out her rage and was almost disposed to be companionable. Her husband nodded, smiled, and wondered what was on her mind.

"Really, my dear," she began, "something must be done about these unhappy people of yours."

Antipas nodded.

"I know," he said. "It's getting worse every day." Presently he brightened a little. "How about a dinner party? Something amusing. We will invite a few prominent citizens in to meet them."

"Who, for instance?"

"Well—there are Jairus and his pretty wife Adiel. Legate Julian, of course. Perhaps young Joseph of Arimathaea might come and bring his sister Tamar. Old David the Sadducee is learned and has been everywhere. His eminent friend Nicodemus Ben-Gorion, who is retired in Cana, would be glad to come, I think."

"It doesn't sound very lively," mumbled Herodias.

"We can attend to that," promised Antipas.

Within an hour he had dispatched messengers, bearing irresistible, cash-down invitations to several professional entertainers; a renowned magician of Caesarea, a troupe of harpists in Jericho, a famous family of Damascene acrobats, and a crippled girl of Cana who was reputed to have a remarkable voice. The date set was the twenty-second of Iyar, the Tetrarch's birthday, now three weeks distant.

Such was their host's enthusiasm over his project that even the Romans began to show a pallid interest. Fadilla said he would like to talk with this well-traveled old David the Sadducee. Julia Drusus, still incorrigibly romantic in spite of many rebuffs, cornered Herodias to ask eager questions about the rich young Joseph of Arimathaea, to which her hostess replied dryly, "Julia, of all the fools I ever met, you are the silliest."

When the couriers had returned from their errands it was found that all of the entertainers would be on hand except the singer from Cana who wasn't well enough to make the journey.

Replies from invited guests were less satisfactory. Joseph of Arimathaea and his sister Tamar were sorry (or said they were) that they could not come. The eminent Nicodemus Ben-Gorion was troubled with rheumatism, and couldn't travel.

Legate Julian, as was to be expected, sent word that he would be
honored, though Antipas knew this was a lie and that if he ever got into
any serious trouble Julian would let him stew. Jairus and Adiel were
pleased to accept, as was David the Sadducee, though his aged sister
Deborah was not well enough to accompany him. Antipas then dispatched
a surprisingly amiable note to David saying he had been advised that
there was a charming young woman, said to be a ward of the House of
Zadok, who would be warmly welcomed, to which the old lawyer replied
that there was no such person in his household. This brazen effrontery
annoyed the Tetrarch, but he decided not to make an issue of it. As the
time for the party drew near, the very thought of it wearied him. His
Roman pests would be bored by such tepid and dreary entertainment.
Harpists! Acrobats! Jugglers! Bah!

            *   *   *   *   *   *

Meantime—while Voldi fretted in prison, and Antipas was unwittingly
contriving an event that would make his name stink wherever and whenever it was uttered—all Galilee was astir with the news that the Carpenter
of Nazareth had come forth, with the spring flowers, to resume his public
ministry.

No such excitement had ever choked the highways of any Palestinian
province. Crowds! Confused and confusing crowds, immeasurably larger
than had followed the prophet and wonder-worker last summer. They
came from farther distances now, from the hinterlands of Northern
Galilee and Perea; yes, and from Samaria, too, though the Samaritans
abominated the Galileans and only the most urgent business could induce
them to cross the border.

They came on foot, on donkeys, in carts, on cots. Some prudently
brought tents and provisions, some carried only a blanket and slept on the
ground, buying, begging, or stealing their food. Thrifty hucksters made
the most of their opportunity to fleece the hungry, peddling stale bread,
rancid fish and fly-blown sweets at exorbitant prices. Vagabond minstrels
and shabby outlanders with tame bears and mangy monkeys set up booths
alongside the food vendors. And the crowds increased hourly.

Every foot-path, every lane, every grass-grown donkey-trail for miles and
leagues were tributaries to the highways that intersected at little Cana
where the resident population—as if ruthlessly shouted out of a peaceful
slumber—stared bewilderedly at the mounting horde of strangers, and
wondered whether the old well in the central plaza would survive. On
Jesus' earlier visits they had welcomed him. It was a bit different this time.

They were still friendly to him, but they wished they could have him all to themselves.

The amazing news had spread far and wide that the miracle-worker of Nazareth was healing lepers! This had added the spice of adventure to these strange doings. Last season, Jesus had healed the blind, the deaf, the crippled. Such disabilities were deplorable but they were not contagious. Leprosy was quite another matter! The leper was not only doomed; he was dangerous! The very word struck terror! Nobody was safe from the threat of it, not even the well-to-do, accustomed to clean living. By no means was it the exclusive monopoly of filthy ragamuffins. All you needed to do, to become infected, was to drink from a cup that a conscienceless leper had touched, or accidentally tread upon a discarded bandage.

Oh yes, there were laws, plenty of them, intended to protect the public. Once a man had contracted the disease, whatever his social rating, he was forever outcast, required to associate only with persons similarly afflicted. When he met anyone on the road he was expected to withdraw to the wayside bushes and shout "Unclean!" It was a living death, destroying the body piecemeal.

When the word went forth that Jesus was curing leprosy it was natural that he should have plenty of clients eager to avail themselves of his services. It was their custom, when traveling very far from the camps provided for them, to move in groups of ten or a dozen, and when a party of them would show up for healing there was an understandable consternation in the great throng. When the cry "Unclean!" was shouted, at the rear of the crowd, nobody tried to stop them. The legionaries, on hand to keep order, scampered out of their way; and at whatever sacrifice of dignity, the multitude cleared a wide path for the visitors. However bitterly the throng—comprised of all manner of discordant sects—might disagree about everything else, there was a complete unanimity in their sudden resolution to make way for a company of lepers.

The first time it happened, only two men stood their ground and calmly waited for the hapless crew to draw near. They were Jesus and Simon. Simon had his jaw set and his big fists clenched to tighten his courage but he stayed by Jesus' side. And when the Master had spoken the words that healed them, Simon grasped the leader of the party by the hand. After they had turned to go, their faces contorted so you couldn't rightly say whether they were laughing or weeping, Jesus gave Simon a comradely smile that made the Big Fisherman's eyes swim. Jesus hadn't said anything to him, but that approving smile had given him stature. Andrew, John, James, Philip, and Thaddeus, who had retreated to a safe distance, gathered about

Simon with admiration on their faces. There was no longer any doubt which one of them deserved to stand closest beside their Master.

It was a quiet, awe-stricken crowd that slowly closed its broken ranks and listened again to the interrupted message of Jesus. Making no reference to the dangerous miracle he had performed, he continued to speak about the security of a life that is lived by faith. There were, he said, two habitations from which one might choose one's place of spiritual residence. One of these houses was built upon the rock of faith: the rain might pour in torrents and the tempest might rage; but that house would stand firm, for it was founded upon a rock. . . . "Upon a petros," he had added, for the benefit of whatever Greeks might be in the audience. . . . The other house was built upon the sand; it might be good for fair weather but it could not survive a storm.

That evening, after the people had been dismissed to return to their homes or their encampments, Jesus and his small party of companions rested after supper in the shelter of a grove on a secluded hillside. The Master sat a little way apart from the others, for he was very tired. But he listened to the low voices as they reviewed the unprecedented events of the day.

Philip, always proud of his Greek ancestry and his own familiarity with the language, remarked, "I wonder where he picks up his Greek words. He uses them frequently. Did you notice how he said 'petros' when he talked about the rock?"

Nobody made any comment on that. They were tired of Philip's Greek.

Then they fell to discussing again the marvelous powers of the Master and their speculations as to how he had come by these amazing gifts.

"I was listening to one of these conversations in the crowd today," remarked Andrew. "One of the old men from Nain said he believed that Jesus is the great prophet Elisha, returned in the flesh."

"Why Elisha?" wondered the newest member of the group, one Judas, from the town of Kerioth.

"Perhaps because Elisha once healed a leper," explained Andrew. "Don't you remember? The Scriptures say that Elisha cured Naaman, a great one of Syria; made him bathe in the Jordan."

Alpheus chuckled softly at the recollection of this old legend, and remarked, "Naaman objected at first; willing to bathe—but not in the Jordan."

"You've a good memory, Alpheus," observed James.

"My father often told us the story," said Alpheus. "He thought it was quite funny."

"My father," drawled Andrew, "never thought that anything found in the Scriptures could be funny."

Apparently nobody cared to pursue that subject any farther and there was a long interval of silence before conversation was resumed.

"Almost everyone seems to think," said John, "that Jesus must be one of the ancient prophets, restored to life."

At this point in their conversation, held in subdued tones to avoid disturbing the Master's much needed rest, they were suddenly startled by his voice, inquiring, "And you! What do you think of me? Who am I?"

They all shifted their eyes to Simon whose courageous display of faith that afternoon had earned him the right to be their spokesman. After a long, thoughtful pause, the Big Fisherman came to his feet and declared, in a deep, impressive voice, "Master—I believe that you are the son of God!"

A hush fell upon them.

"Simon, son of Jonas," said Jesus, "henceforth your name shall be Peter—Peter the Rock! It is upon your faith that I shall build my Kingdom!"

*   *   *   *   *   *

At the close of the sixth eventful day in Cana, when the excitement over his words and deeds was at its height, Jesus astounded his companions by announcing that he must return to Capernaum tomorrow. He gave no reasons for his impulsive decision, nor did they press him for an explanation, though it seemed strange to them that he would now retire from so promising an opportunity for preaching his gospel.

At daybreak, the next morning, the little company took to the highway, leaving the Big Fisherman behind to tell the crowd when it assembled that the Master was unexpectedly required to go back to Capernaum, but would rejoin them here within a few days. They could remain or return to their homes, as they pleased. The disappointing news was variously received. Persons who had brought their sick from afar resolved to wait. Many disgruntled curiosity-seekers decided to go home. Hundreds of the younger and more agile members of the crowd, men mostly, started immediately for Capernaum. Something spectacular might happen there and they didn't propose to miss it. And throughout the morning scores more made up their minds to follow; so it was a long, straggling procession that made the hot and wearisome journey north to the western shore of Lake Gennesaret.

Peter, well spent by fast walking, overtook the Master and his company near Hammath. He had hoped that by this time Jesus might have confided his reasons for this journey, but apparently he had not done so. He was leading the way, at a swift pace, fully preoccupied by his own thoughts. The others were too tired to talk.

The farther they went, in a silence that seemed ominous, the more the Big Fisherman worried over the possibilities of trouble in Capernaum. Without doubt the Master would speak, and there was no telling what he might say. Already there were enemies awaiting an opportunity to discredit him. The priests, old and young, were almost unanimously against him; had held conferences about him; had appealed to the Sanhedrin; had sent a deputation to the Tetrarch. . . . There was Rabbi Ben-Sholem! Would he remember, with any gratitude, the skilled service Jesus had performed in his house? Of course not! Not that stiff-necked, vain old Pharisee! . . . And Jairus! The laborers on his estate had often dropped their hoes and scurried away to join the multitude that swarmed about the Master, whenever he spoke. Doubtless Jairus had been glad enough to see Jesus leave the Capernaum area, and would now be exasperated to find him returned. Jairus, if he wanted to, could have him silenced.

At the northern outskirts of Bethsaida, the Master's steps shortened and Peter quickly came abreast of him.

"I shall stop, for a little while, at Hannah's house," he said. "You may proceed with the others. I shall join you at Andrew's cottage." With that, he turned off the highway, and walked slowly up the shady street.

The vanguard of the pursuing crowd, now close on the heels of the little company, came to a stop and seemed bewildered. The Big Fisherman turned and shouted, not very pleasantly, that the Master had paused for a moment's rest at the home of a friend; and they were not to follow him. This appeared to satisfy most of them, but scores broke from the procession and ran in the direction Jesus had taken. Shortly afterward they drifted back, apparently mystified. Somehow they had lost track of their quarry, as if the ground had opened and swallowed him up. Men who had not joined them in the chase pressed queries upon them: what had become of the Carpenter? where did he go? But they could not say . . . And it was never explained. . . . Broad daylight! A clear view in all directions! It was very strange!

Andrew, frowning thoughtfully, turned to old Bartholomew, who was all but exhausted by the forced march, and said, in an awed undertone, "What do you make of that?"

Bartholomew shook his head, clumsily licked his dry lips, and croaked, huskily, "I guess he didn't want to be followed."

*   *   *   *   *   *

It was true, as Peter had learned, that Jesus had stopped to rest and
have a friendly word with Hannah whom he had not seen since the day he
had miraculously healed her; but this was not the main reason for his visit.
He wanted to see Esther; and said so, after brief inquiries of Hannah about
her health.

Sensing that her presence was not required or desired, Hannah excused
herself and left the two alone together.

"I have been anxious to talk with you, Master," said Esther. "There is
no reason for my remaining here any longer. What shall I do? Where
shall I go? I have no homeland now, no plans, no future."

He did not answer her importunate queries directly, but began to talk
about the great crowds that had followed him, and would be following
him, day by day, throughout the summer. It was, he went on, a multitude
that stirred one's compassion. So many grievously sick ones were brought
from long distances, through the heat, and into the confusion of a jostling
throng. Desperate young mothers from afar carried their blind and crippled babies in their arms, arriving hungry, dirty, and exhausted. Something
must be done for them . . . He paused and regarded the girl with entreating
eyes.

"You mean—me?" she faltered.

"Yes, Fara," he replied, quietly. "I offer you a mission—and a homeland
too."

"A homeland?" she queried.

"In my Kingdom."

There was a long moment before she spoke.

"I shall try to do what I can for them, Master; but I wish you had asked
me to do some service for you! I owe you so very much!"

"My child," said Jesus, softly, "whatever you do for the least of these
needy ones, you will have done it for me."

*   *   *   *   *   *

Within a few hours the swelling crowd had taken Capernaum. The
whole countryside hurried in from the fields and vineyards to double the
throng that knew something important was about to happen.

Early the next morning, Peter, James, and John appeared on the broad
stone steps in front of the Synagogue, and stood in an attitude of expectancy. Already the spacious plaza was half filled with restless people. At the
sight of these men, known to be associates of the Carpenter, the crowd

moved forward, and from the side streets and nearby lake-shore a multitude poured into the cobble-paved area.

At this juncture, Rabbi Ben-Sholem opened the imposing entrance-
door of the Synagogue, came out upon the highest step, and sternly commanded the crowd to disperse.

Nobody stirred. In some quarters there was impudent laughter. White
and shaken with anger, the Rabbi shouted that they had no right to be
there; that they were defiling a holy place.

A sullen growl of protest rose from the unruly crowd. Hecklers cupped
their mouths with their hands and yelled, "Since when was this plaza a
holy place?" . . . "The plaza belongs to the public." . . . One red-faced,
wine-soaked tramp (probably from Samaria, thought Peter), had the
audacity to shout, "Go to, Graybeard!"

Ben-Sholem impotently shook an outraged fist, gathered the skirts of
his robe tightly about his thin legs, and retreated, to the accompaniment
of more laughter; jeering laughter.

Peter was sorry and chagrined. He had no reason to be fond of the
Rabbi, but this indignity to the old man and his sacred office was much
too much! It was a pity, he thought, that Jesus could not pick his audience
and exclude all this rough element, this rude riff-raff from pagan Samaria,
these no-account émigrés from Macedonia, these dirty, half-civilized
Damascenes. The Master's message would be wasted on these hoodlums!
What was the good of talking to such people about a Kingdom of love—
and good will—and peace?

Now the enraged Ben-Sholem—and surely he had plenty to be angry
about—would call his Regents together and demand that something be
done. And Jairus would be forced to notify Julian, the Commander of the
Fort. And Jesus would be arrested; jailed, no doubt—and flogged, too. . . .
He should have been contented with his successes in Cana.

Presently the Master appeared on the steps of the Synagogue and began
to speak. It was immediately obvious that he had been aware of the rudeness of the crowd—and deplored it. He had been appointed, he said, to
offer a way of salvation to the world; and that meant everybody. In a task
so great as this, no prudent thought could be taken about the cost of it or
the waste of it. His mission, he said, was to sow the seed of good will
among men in the hope of an eventual harvest of peace. Much of this
seed would be squandered. Some of it would fall among weeds and brambles where it would have no chance at all to grow, but the sower could
not pause or look back to lament this extravagance. Some of the seed
would fall upon stony ground where there was very little soil to nourish

it and the tender plants would soon wither and die; but the sower must
not be dismayed. Some of the life-giving grain would grow! Some of
it would find friendly lodging in fertile ground!

The multitude had grown very quiet. Nobody was grinning now. Even
the toughest of them knew what the Carpenter meant when he added,
significantly, "Whoever among you has ears to hear, let him hear."

There was a sudden stir on the outskirts of the throng. A path through
the densely packed crowd was opening to admit a person of some importance who was forcing his way to the front. Peter, standing near Jesus, but
on the step immediately below him, craned his neck to identify if possible
the well-dressed, determined man who had assumed the right to intrude.
It was Jairus! Jairus was striding forward evidently intending to interrupt.
His face showed agitation. Peter's heart raced. Now the blow would fall!

Jesus stopped speaking—and waited. If he was apprehensive, he gave
no signs of anxiety. The crowd was silent, expectant, on tiptoe, holding
its breath. Jairus gazed up into the Carpenter's friendly eyes and drew so
close that when he spoke only those close by were able to hear what he
said.

"Master—my little daughter is grievously ill! We fear she is dying. I
implore you to help us!"

Before Jesus could reply, Joseph the butler, who had now arrived, quite
out of breath, huskily murmured into his master's ear, "She is gone, sir!"

Jairus' shaking head drooped and his tears were flowing as he turned
away. Jesus laid a hand on his arm and said, gently:

"I shall go with you, Jairus."

"It is too late, Master," said Jairus, brokenly. "She is dead!"

"Come!" said Jesus. "Let us go!"

*   *   *   *   *   *

The astounding restoration of Jairus' little daughter was a notable
triumph for Jesus. No one more keenly appreciated this than Peter who
had doubted the Master's prudence in returning to Capernaum where, he
feared, there might be serious trouble. Now it appeared that Capernaum,
instead of being a place of danger, was the safest spot in all Galilee for
Jesus to pursue his ministry without molestation.

As for the influential Jairus, his gratitude was boundless. He had made
it clear that he was on Jesus' side, and Jairus' opinion had weight. He was
known for his sagacity and his insistence on justice for all, and whatever
he believed in was good enough for Capernaum.

Ben-Sholem had got himself into an awkward predicament which had

eliminated him—at least for the present—as a hostile critic. Beside himself with rage over the indignities he had suffered at the hands of Jesus'
audience, he had retreated from the scene of his humiliation before Jairus
had arrived in the plaza, and had impetuously dispatched messengers to
each of the Synagogue Regents, summoning them to an immediate conference. With the exception of Jairus, they had all come at full speed,
learning on the way that Jesus had performed an amazing miracle in the
home of the Chief Regent.

By the time they were convened in Ben-Sholem's beautiful library, the
Rabbi himself had heard the strange tidings; but, so accustomed was the
old man to having his own will prevail in all matters, that he proceeded
with his demand to have Jesus tried as a heretic and a disturber of the
peace. The Regents, minus their potent spokesman, were embarrassed and
speechless.

Freshly indignant over their apparent disinterest in taking this drastic
action, the Rabbi impulsively resigned, his resignation to take effect forthwith. This, he well knew, would bring these dunces to terms; for it was
unthinkable that they would permit such as appalling disaster to fall upon
their Synagogue!

To his consternation, they all sat tongue-tied for a while; and then,
without debate, unhappily mumbled their acceptance. The old man wept
inconsolably while they tiptoed quietly away. After an hour of lugubrious
self-pity, Ben-Sholem dried his eyes in the warmth of his renewed anger
and decided to take his case to a higher tribunal. Summoning his servants,
he set off for Jerusalem.

Old Annas, who had recently retired as High Priest, to be succeeded
by his son-in-law Caiaphas, was one of Ben-Sholem's closest friends. In
the long ago they had been fellow-students in the Rabbinical College.
Indeed so intimate was their continuing comradeship that on the annual
occasion of Passover Week, Ben-Sholem was the house-guest of his eminent friend who, despite his retirement, kept his aging fingers on the pulse
of the Sanhedrin, composed of elderly men long accustomed to listening
attentively when he spoke.

Annas could be counted on to view Ben-Sholem's intolerable grievances
sympathetically; together they would tell the whole story to Caiaphas.
Then!—we would see whether a brazen young carpenter from obscure
little Nazareth had a right to ruin the Capernaum Synagogue and
incite all Galilee to flout the faith of their fathers! Yes, and it would take
more than the wealth and popularity of Jairus to save this charlatan
from the righteous wrath of the Sanhedrin!

Peter knew nothing about the abdication of the old Rabbi and his departure to avenge himself, nor would he have worried very much had he known, for Jesus' position was secure. He could take care of himself in any emergency.

Late that afternoon the small group of close friends waited in Andrew's cottage for Peter to return and report. Arriving at length, full of excitement over the day's events, the Big Fisherman flung himself into a chair, scrubbed a perspiring brow with the back of his hand, and declared, "You know I didn't want him to come back to Capernaum; but he knew what he was doing. Never again will I question his wisdom—about anything! Jesus knows best!"

"High time you found that out!" remarked his brother. "Now tell us exactly what happened. There are many stories afloat."

Peter began at the beginning. They would remember, he said, that Jesus had beckoned him to follow as Jairus and the butler led the way through the crowd. Three tall, racing camels, in the care of their drivers, waited on a side street.

"You mean to say you rode a camel!" exclaimed Johnny.

"Yes," nodded Peter, "but I shouldn't want to do it again."

"And the Master!" wondered Philip. "He rode a camel? How did he get along?"

"Very well, I think," grinned Peter. "I was too busy with my own excursion to notice. It was a rough voyage—but we got there. . . . At the house we heard the clamor of lamentations. A score of professional mourners who had been hanging about for hours, waiting to be hired, were huddled on the verandah, with their black hoods over their faces, howling like dogs. Jesus was vexed by the noise and commanded them to cease and begone."

"That's one advantage the poor have over the rich," put in James. "When there's death in the house, you aren't bothered with hired mourners."

"We went at once to the bed-chamber where the little girl lay," continued Peter. "Jesus led the way, with Jairus and his wife Adiel closely following. They asked me to come too. The Master sat down on the edge of the bed and gazed fixedly at the child for a long time. Her face had the whiteness of death. After a while, the Master said, softly, as if not to awaken her, 'She is sleeping.'"

"You mean—she wasn't dead?" exclaimed Thaddeus.

"That's in doubt," said Peter. "They all thought she was. She certainly seemed to be dead. He said she was asleep."

"Perhaps he meant the sleep of death," observed old Bartholomew.

"Perhaps," mumbled Peter, vaguely. "Whatever he meant, that was what he said. Adiel must have thought he believed the child was sleeping, for she burst out crying and shook her head. 'No, Master!' she sobbed. 'My precious Sharon is gone!' With that, he leaned forward, patted the little girl gently on the cheek, and said, 'Come, Sharon, awake!' "

The Big Fisherman's voice was unsteady: he noisily cleared his throat to control it.

"It was all very touching," he went on, huskily. "Little Sharon slowly opened her eyes; and as Adiel flung herself down by the bedside with a cry of joy, the child smiled sleepily and said, barely above a whisper, 'There were beautiful flowers, everywhere, just as he told us.' "

"It was a dream," thought Andrew.

"Who can say?" murmured Peter. After an interval of silence, he added, "As for me—I think the child was dead!"

They had sat transfixed through this recital. Now that the strange story was ended, they stirred.

"What are we supposed to do now?" inquired Philip. "Did the Master tell you?"

"He spends the night at the house of Jairus," said Peter. "Tomorrow he will rest here at the cottage. He is very tired. The next day we start back to Cana, though we are to make camp that night at Hammath."

"But why does he stop at Hammath," queried James, "when so many people are waiting for him in Cana?"

"Yes—and a great crowd will doubtless follow him from Capernaum, and along the way," said Philip. "He will be forced to speak at Hammath, and that will be wearisome."

"Well," said Peter, "be that as it may. We're stopping at Hammath."

"I think I shall go back to Bethsaida," announced Andrew, rising. "I should like to see Hannah before we leave."

"I shouldn't object to sleeping in a bed tonight, myself," said Peter. "Tell Hannah to expect me for supper. I shall be over there—in a couple of hours. I have promised old Manasseh that I would talk with him. He wants to lease one of the ships—just for the summer, of course."

"Not *The Abigail!*" protested Thaddeus.

The Big Fisherman patted Thad on the shoulder, but did not reply. The company was breaking up now. At the door, Thomas remarked, to no one in particular, "I can't understand why the Master wants to leave Capernaum, now that Jairus is solidly back of him—and the people are so anxious to have him stay."

"Don't forget," admonished Peter, "that we couldn't understand why he wanted to leave Cana, and come to Capernaum."

"That was different," mumbled Thomas. "He felt that he was urgently needed here."

"Maybe he feels that he is now needed elsewhere," observed Andrew, to which James added, "I don't believe he cares very much whether we understand him or not."

"You're quite right, Jimmie," rumbled old Bartholomew. "He's teaching us to have faith in him."

"But—can't a man have faith—and understanding, too?" argued Thomas.

"No!" declared Bartholomew, bluntly. "That's what faith is for, my son! It's for when we can't understand!"

"That's true!" approved Peter. "When a man understands, he doesn't need any faith."

"I don't like to be kept in the dark," put in Philip.

"If a man has enough faith," replied Peter, "he can find his way in the dark—with faith as his lamp."

16

THEY were finishing a leisurely breakfast. It was the first time the four of them had eaten a meal together for many weeks.

Peter's place at the square table faced the kitchen door: Hannah sat opposite him; Andrew was on his right; and, across from Andrew, Esther dropped down between her frequent excursions to the kitchen, for she had insisted on doing all the serving.

At appropriate intervals she had brought in the stewed figs, cups of milk for Hannah, Andrew, and herself, a tall mug of pomegranate juice for Peter, boiled eggs and wheaten loaves for all.

Every time Esther had risen, the Big Fisherman's eyes had followed her with such undisguised admiration that Hannah—ever alert to matters of fresh interest—was amazed and amused. She wondered if Andrew had noticed, and covertly aimed an inquiring glance in his direction, but the stolid bachelor did not come up from his plate to share her curiosity. She had never known anyone so exasperatingly indifferent to significant events transpiring under his very nose.

Esther, apparently oblivious of Peter's unusual awareness of her, was wearing a simple white linen house-dress that had belonged to his wife; but his fascinated expression as he frankly studied the uncontrived sinuosity of the girl's movements did not reflect a poignant memory of his all but forgotten bereavement. Indeed the dress, which had hung limp and shapeless on his frail and ailing Abigail, had so generously responded to Esther's figure that Peter marveled at its unsuspected beauty. The girl was superb! She was altogether lovely! It was as if he were seeing her for the first time!

He had never tried to get acquainted with her. Their relationship had got off to a bad start. On the very first day she had irritated him by coming onto his ship in the guise of "Joe," a half-starved, dirty, ragged camel-boy,

331

presently turning out to be "Esther," a mysterious young woman whose inconsistent accounts of herself seemed to have been recklessly made up while you waited.

The Big Fisherman had not known what to think about her, and had given it up. He had had many other things to bother him, in those days. He had thrown away Johnny's friendship; he had scornfully investigated the Nazarene Carpenter, only to be made captive by the strange man's unquestionable power. His orderly, uneventful, workaday world had been turned upside down. Not much wonder that he had had no time or mind for this Esther person.

If Hannah, alone all day and in dire need of companionship, wanted to mother this unexplained alien, Peter had no serious objections, but he had gone to no trouble to conceal his antipathy to the new member of their household. Whoever the girl was and wherever she had come from and whatever she was up to seemed to be a secret. Hannah appeared satisfied that the mysterious waif merited their hospitality; and, after all, it was Hannah's home. Perhaps the girl was helping Hannah to recover from the loss of Abigail. Moreover, Peter was obliged to admit that Esther was earning her keep, and that her presence in the household had never discommoded him in any way. But he rarely had anything to say to her beyond a perfunctory grunt at breakfast, nor had she made the slightest effort to improve their acquaintance.

This mutually cool attitude had been altered considerably at the time of Hannah's grave illness and miraculous recovery. Esther had taken charge of the house; she had become a member of the family. Too, it was evident that the Master had taken an interest in her. If Esther had a secret, he undoubtedly knew what it was; and, either in spite of it or because of it, had invited her to be the sole witness to Hannah's restoration. Exactly what had happened on that occasion had not been disclosed, but the event had wrought a change in the girl. Her new demeanor was difficult to define. It was as if she had been released from prison.

The Big Fisherman had been required to make a fresh appraisal of their increasingly interesting guest, even to the extent of bestowing on her a clumsy friendliness, though he was embarrassed somewhat by her indifference to his amiable condescensions.

This morning, every time she sat down beside him, Peter had turned toward her with a pleasant smile, for which she had given him no receipt, either of surprise or gratification. He had remarked, as she removed the empty bowl in which his figs were served, that they were very good, very

good indeed, and she had replied casually that Hannah had cooked them.
A few minutes later, he had said that the eggs were boiled just the way he
liked them, and Esther had nodded to Hannah as if inviting her to take a
bow.

Finishing his breakfast, and carefully folding his napkin, he had had
the audacity to tell Esther her hair had grown so rapidly that she could
never pass herself off for a boy any more, an observation accompanied by
a reminiscent chuckle. And to this impertinence he added that the little
fringe of curls on her forehead certainly did her no harm.

She gave him the merest wisp of a smile, as to a small boy who was
talking too much, and turned to Hannah with the irrelevant statement
that, if she might be excused, she would go out into the garden and gather
a basket of tulips, after which she left the table, Hannah following her as
far as the kitchen.

Peter fretfully rubbed his chin, and seemed out of sorts.

"What makes this girl thinks she's so superior to the rest of us?" he
testily inquired of his brother.

"Maybe she is," drawled Andrew.

"I'm afraid I treated her like a dog," admitted Peter, somewhat to the
surprise of both of them, for the Big Fisherman was not adroit in offering
apologies.

Andrew did not immediately abandon his meditations to refute this
statement; and Peter, anticipating something more comforting than his
brother's silence, went on to say, "But she needn't hold it against me—
forever!"

"If you're expecting her to come wagging up to lick your hand," remarked Andrew, "you'll have to give her a little more time."

"I should like to patch it up with her before we leave," mumbled Peter,
half to himself. "We will be gone all summer. She might be gone when we
return. There's no telling what she may do next. I might never see her
again."

"Oh, you'll be seeing her every day, Simon." Andrew hadn't yet got
his brother's new name firmly fixed in his mind. "Esther is coming along."

"What?" barked Peter. "With us? Impossible! Who told you that?"

"Hannah. Esther is to help look after the sick babies—and their
mothers."

"But"—spluttered Peter—"we can't permit that! This girl—well—she
isn't a girl any more, Andy. She is a young woman! A very beautiful and
desirable young woman! Much too attraetive to be exposed to all man-

ner of indignities! There are some very rough people in these big crowds! If it's anything like last summer, we will encounter plenty of unpleasant incidents—without having Esther on our hands!" After smouldering for a moment, he inquired, "Whoever put this foolish idea into her head?"

"The Master," said Andrew.

"She asked him if she might go along?"

"No—it was his own idea. He invited her."

Peter drew a deep, baffled breath that puffed his bearded lips when he let go of it. He shook his head, uncomprehendingly.

"Our Master does some strange things, Andy."

His brother nodded.

"We had all noticed that, Simon. But—so far—everything he has done—"

"I know! I know!" broke in Peter, with an impatient toss of his big hand. "Everything he does is right! . . . But—how is it going to look for this lovely creature to be camped all summer with a dozen men?"

Andrew drew a slow, sly grin, and remarked dryly that it would probably look better than if she were to be camped all summer with any one of them, a comment which his brother instantly resented with a scowl, a shrug, and an abrupt departure from the room.

The soft-spoken bachelor, who had intended no disrespect by his droll-ery, stared after the retreating figure, and chuckled a little. . . . "Ah—so that's what ails Simon," he mused. "Esther has become important to him. He is getting touchy on the subject. Well, well—who would have thought it?"

Hannah bustled in from the kitchen now. It had been very quiet out there for some time. She began clearing the table, and making quite an energetic task of it.

"I wonder if Simon isn't fond of Esther," she said, busily brushing crumbs.

"Why not?" rejoined Andrew, casually. "We all are."

Hannah's lips firmed in a little pout. Then, deciding on a more prom-ising strategy, she smiled, lowered her voice to a confidential whisper, and said, coaxingly, "Surely you know, Andy, that I wouldn't say any-thing."

Andrew soberly nodded his approval.

"That has always been my policy, too," he said. "It certainly keeps one out of trouble; doesn't it?"

Hannah did not pursue the subject any farther, though the kitchen door plainly said "Humph!" when she closed it behind her.

*   *   *   *   *   *

For many generations it had been customary for the reigning Prince of
Arimathaea to observe the fast and attend the festivities of Passover Week
in the Holy City.

This annual event, originally commemorative of the Jews' release from
their intolerable bondage in Egypt, had gradually evolved from a stark
and solemn re-enactment of that miraculous deliverance, and had acquired
many irrelevant but attractive characteristics. It was Homecoming Week
for all Jews who were able to return to their Holy City. Hundreds of them
came from great distances and from foreign countries, bringing with them
all manner of merchandise. Long caravans, laden with exotic foods, spices,
jewels, and costly textiles, encamped in the surrounding hills. Minstrels,
magicians, actors, acrobats, soothsayers, fortune-tellers, vendors of con-
fections and medicinal herbs swarmed the narrow streets. Passover Night
was still solemnly celebrated in the silence and seclusion of dimly lit Jewish homes, but Passover Week was a carnival for many more visitors than
viewed it as an austere ceremonial.

Young Prince Joseph of Arimathaea always looked forward with happy
expectancy to this pilgrimage. It belonged to springtime. The country was
beautiful. Had there been no pleasures in prospect at his destination,
Joseph would have felt repaid by the delights of the journey. He traveled
in a style befitting his wealth and position, attended by a gay group of his
young cronies and an impressive retinue of servants.

Jerusalem, in Joseph's opinion, was an enchanted city. Generations of
his forebears had been conspicuous in the making of its history, as the
inscriptions on their massive tombs in "The Garden of Sepulchers" eloquently testified. The day would come when Joseph himself would join
them there. His own tomb, elaborately planned, was even now under
construction and would be completed by the end of the summer. He was
in no hurry to occupy it, for life was good, but it was a comfort to know
that whenever he needed it the sepulcher would be ready to welcome him.

And he had many influential friends in Jerusalem who received him
cordially. Even the gruff and short-tempered Procurator, Pontius Pilate,
served him cakes and wine when he paid respects at the Roman Insula—
and called him Joe.

And he always paid a duty call at the Galilean Embassy, though this
was less to his taste. By custom, all inter-provincial affairs involving the
Principality of Arimathaea were adjudicated by the Tetrarch. Joseph was
glad that the services of Antipas were but rarely invoked; for he did not

like him and did not trust him. Another reason for not wanting to visit the Embassy: he invariably encountered the brazen, jingling, over-painted Salome, whom he detested. . . . And once he had been obliged to spend an unhappy hour with her mother whose reputation was in such appalling disrepair that to be on friendly terms with her was to invite a scandal.

Now he was on his way home from Jerusalem. Tonight they would break the trip, as usual, by camping at the road junction near the village of Hammath.

Early the next morning, the Prince's encampment was roused by the unexpected noise of traffic on the highways. A great crowd was converging on a meadow not more than five hundred yards away. Inquiries revealed that the Nazarene Carpenter was to appear.

Much annoyed by the intrusion of this rabble, Joseph's companions importuned him to break camp at once and defer their breakfast until they had arrived at some quiet spot farther down the road; but he saw no reason for scurrying away.

"Indeed, I should like to see him again, myself," declared the Prince. "He must be something more than a mountebank, or the people would not continue to follow him."

Remembering with embarrassment the cool reception they had had at the hands of the Carpenter's following, a few months earlier, Joseph's friends so strongly counselled him against risking another rebuff that he lost his patience and announced his intention of going into the crowd alone. And with that he set off by himself, on foot, to join the increasing multitude.

The throng had quieted as the Master mounted the little knoll where a space had been cleared for him. He began at once to speak in the effortless, intimate, far-reaching tone that always commanded complete silence and rapt attention.

Today, he said, he would talk with them about the eternal life. Citizens of his Kingdom did not have to wait until death to experience its happiness and its peace. If ever we were to be immortal, we were immortal now. "We are God's children," he went on—"and while it is not yet apparent what we may become, we can be sure that when we see Him, and know Him as He is, we shall find ourselves to be like Him. . . . But—if we are indeed the children of God we are His children today. To know this is to be of the Kingdom; for the Kingdom is now, it is here, it is yours! . . . Ask —and it shall be given you! Seek it—and you shall find it! What parent among you, if your child asks bread, will you give him a stone? And if you —heedless and selfish as you are—give good gifts to your children, how many more blessings shall our Father in Heaven bestow upon all who ask Him! . . ." This, then, was the life eternal; beginning now, beginning here; for you, for all!

He stepped down from the mound. Peter beckoned to the nearest cot-bearers. The day's miracles had begun.

Joseph gradually worked his way toward the front. For the most part, the people moved aside to let him through, perhaps because of his expensive clothing, his jewels, and his princely bearing. Now he was within a few feet of the strange business that the Nazarene was conducting. No—this was not trickery! It was conceivable that the emaciated fellow who had just risen from his cot, with tears of gratitude and incoherent little whimpers of amazement, had connived with the Carpenter to stage this dramatic scene; but it was absurd to suppose that the baby, in the arms of this disheveled young woman, had joined in a conspiracy to deceive the public.

Joseph's heart pounded hard and his mouth was dry. The hot bodies of his neighbors pressed close against him as they swayed for better vision, but he was heedless of these contacts which he would have found intolerable in any other circumstances. Indeed, far from resenting this intimacy with the common people, the Prince felt something almost like comradeship with them. The Carpenter had said that they were all children of God; and, for the moment, Joseph believed it!

The sweat was beading the Carpenter's pale forehead. It was evident that he was utterly spent. The gigantic Galilean who stood beside him had halted the approaching procession of suppliants with the announcement that the Master must rest. With this, the Master and his small coterie filed out toward the highway. Joseph followed close behind them.

Reaching the road, the Carpenter turned about and—to Joseph's surprise—waited for him to approach. His fatigue was such that his hands were trembling, but he greeted the Prince with a cordial smile.

"Master," said Joseph, in an unsteady voice, "what shall I do—to have this eternal life?"

Peter frowned. He had instantly recognized the Prince of Arimathaea. Ah, so? The Prince would be wanting eternal life on special terms; terms provided for Princes.

"You have been brought up to know the laws, my friend," said Jesus, kindly.

"True, Master," said Joseph, "and I have kept the laws since childhood, loving God with all my heart, mind and strength."

"Proceed, friend," urged Jesus; not smiling now. "There is another law;

to love your neighbors as you love yourself. . . . You have glimpsed the
Kingdom today, and you would share it. That will be more difficult for
you than for these poor. It is not easy for the rich to inherit the Kingdom.
Their lives are too crowded with Things!"

Joseph bowed his head, reluctantly nodded agreement, and remained
silent.

"If you would be of my Kingdom, friend, unburden yourself of your
great possessions. Dispose of them! Distribute them among the poor! . . .
And then come—and follow me!"

They all stood for a long moment waiting for the Prince to speak, but
he had nothing to say. With his head still bowed, he walked slowly up the
road. Jesus took a couple of steps, as if he might follow him; but halted and
watched the departing Prince with wistful, regretful eyes. No one in the
little group needed to be told that their Master was disappointed.

After a while, Jesus turned with a sigh and signed that they would proceed now to Cana. Peter walked beside him. He was not disappointed,
but he was hurt.

"Master," he said, pensively, "we have given up all to follow you."

"Yes, Peter," replied Jesus, wearily. "I know. And you will be rewarded."

Old Bartholomew, trudging along behind with Andrew, muttered,
"Andy—that's the first thing the Prince ever wanted that he couldn't
afford; a place in the Master's Kingdom!"

*   *   *   *   *   *

Contrary to Peter's expectation, Esther had not joined their company
when they passed through Bethsaida on the way to Hammath.

He had doubted the wisdom of her accompanying them at all; but,
now that she had been invited to do so, he was anxious to see her; and, as
they approached the corner nearest Hannah's house—followed by the
crowd that had assembled again in the plaza at Capernaum—his eyes
searched the street. He did not know that she had received instructions
not to proceed to Cana until the following day.

The next morning, after tenderly embracing Hannah, who had cried
a little at their parting, she started on her journey; but not alone, for the
procession that had filed through sleepy little Bethsaida, all day yesterday, continued to trudge along toward the south.

Arriving in the spacious field, a half-mile east of Cana, she made no effort to attach herself to the Master's company, but was content to be a
mere member of the multitude that increased hourly, and immediately
gave her attention to the weary and hungry women who had brought
their sick, blind and crippled children for healing.

It was not an easy assignment. Esther had often seen poverty in distress but never before at such close range; nor had she ever felt in any
way responsible for its alleviation. It had been her supposition that the
poor and needy were sympathetic toward one another; it seemed reasonable that this should be true. Her present experience quickly disillusioned
her. Whatever might be the traditional indifference of the rich to the
plight of the poor, it was becoming apparent that the poor had but
little respect for their unfortunate neighbors. The women she tried to
befriend were not disposed to co-operate. They wanted food and shelter
—and they wanted it now—and they wanted it ahead of the others. It
angered them to be asked to await their turn. Each footsore, dirty and disheveled mother thought her case deserved immediate attention.

At first the girl was indignant. When she asked a half-dozen of them to
accompany her into the town, where she told her story to not very sympathetic housewives and begged a few loaves of bread here and a coney-skin
of goat's milk there and a little basket of sun-cured figs somewhere else,
the women were reluctant to go. And the women who were asked to look
after the absentees' babies thought they were being imposed on. And when
she returned with provisions for them, most of them quarreled over the
distribution of food. It was quite discouraging.

With her patience exhausted, she silenced one bickering group by saying, "I'm not being paid for helping you, you know! I'm not doing this
because I think it's fun! . . . Stop quarreling now—and listen to what the
Master is saying!" They scowled, but turned their faces toward the Carpenter—and made pretense of listening.

Sometimes the sensitive girl marveled at the complacency of Jesus as
he pleaded for kindness and good will among men, and the mutual bearing of burdens and sharing of benefits, while the impatient audience that
had come to see the working of miracles trampled on toes and jabbed elbows into ribs and jostled for better vantage.

It was late afternoon on the fourth day of their mission in Cana when
the Big Fisherman unexpectedly came to her rescue, and none too soon,
for Esther was thoroughly disheartened and ready to admit that she had
failed of her task. Only the promise she had made to the Master kept
her from running away.

Peter had resolutely kept his distance from her, quite against his in-
clinations, for she was constantly on his mind. Indecisively he had lingered, today, as the great throng dispersed and the Master with the others
of his company proceeded up the slope toward their sequestered encampment under a clump of acacias. For a while he sauntered aimlessly among
the cots bearing the sick who had arrived late and would presently be car-

ried away to shelters for the night. He paused beside them to speak words
of encouragement. Doubtless the Master would take care of them tomorrow, he said. They must try to be patient.

His heart speeded a little as he neared the cluster of tents that had
been provided for mothers and their sick babies. Apparently they had had
their supper, for none of them was in sight, and Esther, having attended
to their wants, was seated on a camp stool apart from them, in a posture
of fatigue and dejection.

She raised her head as he approached and rose to welcome him with a
pensive smile that unsteadied his voice when he inquired, kindly, how
things were going—with her.

"Are these people wearing you out?" he asked.

She shook her head, as to say that there were no words to describe her
dilemma; and asked, "Have you time for a little talk with me, Simon?"

Never before had she addressed him by name, and the implied overture
of friendship stirred him deeply. It pleased him, too, that she called him
Simon. His new name had aged him somewhat, making him more sedate
and discreet, setting him apart from his fellows. At the moment he felt
more comfortable as Simon, temporarily freed from the rigorous responsibilities incumbent upon a Rock.

"Why not?" he had replied, quickly. "Or—I can take you to the Master, if you are troubled."

"The Master has enough to bear," she sighed. "Let me tell you about it,
Simon. Perhaps you can help me."

"Come then," he said, softly. "Let us go some place where we may talk
privately."

They took the winding path up the slope toward Jesus' encampment,
Esther leading the way, for the old, deep-worn foot-path was narrow. Simon, following with long, slow strides, was fascinated by the effortless
ease and grace of the girl's supple figure. No conversation was attempted
until they reached the flat, level limestone boulder that jutted from the
hillside, overlooking the teeming valley where every road and lane was
filled with plodding pilgrims returning to their bivouacs in the hills.

Now that he was seated beside this beautiful girl, who had unwittingly
preoccupied his thoughts and disturbed his sleep, the Big Fisherman was
not sure how—or whether—to break the silence. Esther promptly relieved
him of this responsibility.

Turning toward him, she declared, impetuously, "The trouble is, Simon—it all seems so hopeless; so pitiably hopeless! They are so rude, so
mean to one another."

"They are indeed," agreed Simon, "but I suppose some allowance must be made for them. A woman who has borne the grief of a blind or crippled child—and now has a chance to see him made well—is desperate. She will lie, steal and fight to be the first in line—for his food—and his healing. Their conduct is deplorable—but it is understandable."

"You have great patience, Simon," murmured Esther.

"No, my dear," he confessed. "If I seem to have patience, it is because of the Master's compassion on them. I'm learning—from him—to hold my tongue—and keep my temper. It isn't easy."

"Perhaps I, too, might learn to be more sympathetic, if there was anything—anything good—anything at all—to come of it!"

"He heals their sick, Esther. Surely that is something!"

"I know," she conceded, wearily. "He opens their babies' poor, little, blind eyes so that they can see; and what do they see but unfriendliness and greed!" The pent-up flood of her indignation was loosed now, and her passionate words came tumbling recklessly over one another while Simon, amazed at the outburst, watched the big tears gather and slowly trickle down her flushed cheeks. He tried to interject a gentle protest, but she went on, her husky voice breaking with emotion.

"There he stands," she cried, "day after day, entreating them to be kind, and to love one another, and live at peace with one another—"

"I think some of them try to do that," said Simon.

"A few, perhaps; but not enough," persisted Esther. "My heart bleeds for him, Simon! He is going to be so dreadfully disappointed! If he were just an ordinary man, deluded into thinking that he could save the whole world by teaching people to be merciful and generous, no attention need be paid to his dreaming; but—Jesus has the power of a God in his hands. He has proved it—over and over! I truly believe that he could save the world—or end it, if he chose; but not this way!"

"How then?" asked Simon, soberly.

"I heard John the Baptizer tell of a Great One who would come and wreck the world—and begin all over again—with better people in control. He would march across lands and seas, upsetting old temples and thrones, humbling the rich, freeing the poor, leveling the road for all the people. Maybe there's some hope for a plan like that! Jesus has the power to do it—if he wished. . . . But—how does he expect to save the world by pleading with these barefooted, half-starved country-people of Galilee! . . . Tell me, Simon! You have great faith. They are calling you 'Petros' now. Do you honestly believe that there is any hope for Jesus' Kingdom of Love?" Her long, wet lashes opened wide as she faced him with an expression of childlike confidence. "I shall try to believe—if you say you do!"

It had turned out to be one of the critical moments in the Big Fisherman's experience. He felt himself gaining stature and dignity as he gazed into the girl's questing eyes. Whatever had been his foolish thoughts of her, his infatuation, his desire, Esther had become as a trusting daughter now.

He laid his big hand over her small one, and said, tenderly, "I believe, dear child, that Jesus is the Saviour of the world!"

After a little pause, he went on, measuring his words.

"As for these poor—not many mighty will be called into the Master's service. He is not appealing to the mighty, for it is they who have made the world what it is. He does not expect to change the world into a garden today, but he is sowing the seed. We must be patient—and have faith in him."

Esther rose—and smiled into his eyes.

"Very well, Petros," she said, softly, "I shall be patient—and I shall have faith! . . . Shall we go now?"

They retraced their steps in silence. At her tent-door, she whispered, "You have done much for me, tonight, Petros."

"And you have strengthened me, my child," said Peter.

The next afternoon, as if to confirm what Peter had said about the Master's faith in the common people—and their value to him—he told a story of a king who had planned a wedding-feast for his son, the prince; and had invited all the great ones of his own and neighboring states to be his guests. The nobility offered flimsy excuses. So—the king sent his servants out into the highways and hedges to find guests for the banquet.

After the crowd had dispersed for the day, Peter paused at Esther's tent for a friendly word.

"Did you tell the Master about our conversation, last night?" she asked.

Peter shook his head and smiled.

"I think you have in mind his parable about the king's banquet—and the guests from the highways and hedges. . . . No—I had not told him about our talk. I didn't need to. He knew of it without being told."

"Do you mean to say that Jesus knows—without hearing—what we say—and think?" asked Esther, mystifiedly.

"I'm afraid so," said Peter. "There's abundant proof of it." He drew a slow grin, and added, "I always know when he disapproves of my thoughts. He does not chide me, but he calls me Simon."

Esther laughed a little and said she had never heard of anything so strange.

"And who are you today?" she asked. "Simon or Peter?"

"I'm Peter—today," he said, smiling.

*   *   *   *   *   *

It was the beginning of a comradeship which was to mean a great deal to both of them. The Big Fisherman's attitude toward the trusting girl was strictly paternal and protective, though at times uncomfortably possessive. He could be as jealous as a lover.

One afternoon—it was the day before they left Cana on their eastern journey—Philip surprised Esther by asking her to call on his aged mother. The lonely old lady was confined to her room, he said, and had few visitors.

"The trouble is," he explained, "my mother never learned to speak Aramaic with any confidence; and because she cannot talk with the neighbors, they do not come to see her. I think the sight of you would do her good, even if you find conversation difficult."

"What language does she speak, Philip?" Esther had inquired as they neared the cottage.

"We are Macedonians," he replied.

It appeared that Philip had promised his mother that he would try to bring Esther to see her, for her widowed daughter who opened the door for them seemed to be expecting their call. The aged woman, obviously made ready for company, was sitting up in bed. Esther took the proffered chair beside her, patted the thin hand, and was rewarded with welcoming smiles and vigorous noddings of the old gray head.

"I—do—not—speak—your—tongue," labored the frail voice.

"Then we will talk in your tongue, Mother," said Esther, in fluent Greek. "I'm never sure of myself in Aramaic, either."

Philip's mother took both of Esther's hands in hers, and cried, "Bless you, my child! Bless you!"

His sister laughed happily and drew her chair closer. Philip, dumbfounded, sat down on the other side of the bed and stared as Esther and his ecstatic mother chatted companionably.

At the first pause in their conversation, he broke in to ask, "Why haven't you told me that you know Greek?"

"You never asked me," said Esther, which made them all laugh.

"But you're not a Greek," said Philip, suddenly serious. "How did you learn to speak it so well?"

"It's a long story, Philip," she replied. "Much too long to tell; and, besides, we must be going now."

"Tell me this, Esther," he said, soberly. "Do you and the Master speak to each other in Greek? He seems to know the language."

At that, she rose, and again affectionately patted the wrinkled hand. Noting that Philip felt somewhat rebuffed, she murmured, as for him alone, "Our Master knows everything, Philip. Everything about everything!"

On their way back to the field, where hundreds of people, aware that the meetings were ended, were preparing to return to their homes, Philip was still questioning her, without results, about her origin. Preoccupied with their conversation as they moved through the throng, neither took notice that Peter was immediately behind them. Philip was finishing a remark as they turned to greet him. The Big Fisherman was frowning darkly.

"Esther speaks Greek!" explained Philip, in a tone that invited Peter to be pleasantly surprised; but it didn't have that effect on him. He was annoyed, and went to no pains to conceal it.

"Humph!" he grunted. "Now you should really enjoy yourself, Philip. Our own language is good enough for me!"

There wasn't much to be said in reply to that. Momentarily stunned by the Big Fisherman's unexpected rudeness, and looking as if they had been slapped for no reason at all, Philip and Esther, having exchanged a bewildered glance, turned to go.

Peter, angrily gnawing at his underlip, followed them for a little way, saw them separate at Esther's little tent, and slowly trudged up the hill. At the limestone rock he halted, sat down, ran his fingers through his shaggy hair and cursed himself bitterly.

Early the next morning they broke camp and took to the road, with Peter far in advance of the others. John said to James, "D'you suppose someone has hurt his feelings?" To which his brother replied, "More likely he has hurt somebody else."

"Let's catch up with him," suggested John, "and give him a chance to air his trouble."

"You may—if you like," said James. He turned about and called to Philip, who was strolling along behind them. "Phil—do you want to move on ahead with Johnny, and see what ails Peter?"

"Not me," growled Philip. "I don't want to know."

"Let him alone," advised Andrew. "He'll get over it, whatever it is. If he needed any help, the Master would have joined him."

Instinctively, they turned to face the rear. Far behind them they saw Jesus walking between Esther and old Bartholomew, with young Thaddeus, somewhat in advance of them pushing a high-wheeled cart containing Esther's tents and tackle.

"Where did she dig up those tents?" inquired Philip.

"Simon bought them," said Andrew, "with some of the money old Manasseh paid him for *The Rachael*. He gave most of it to Hannah." It was a long speech for Andrew and they listened attentively. "My brother has his odd moments," he added,—"but he is not mean."

"Come on, Johnny," said Philip, impulsively. "Let us overtake him."

"I'll go with you," said James.

They lengthened their steps and moved forward.

"They're good boys," said Andrew.

"Do you know how much he got for *The Rachael*?" asked Judas.

"Yes," said Andrew, crisply.

They walked along in silence for some time.

"I suppose old Manasseh got it for a song," said Judas.

"He used to be the cantor at the Synagogue when he was a young man," reflected Andrew. "Excellent voice, too."

*　　*　　*　　*　　*　　*

By the time the party reached Nain, where they were to tarry for a day, hundreds of people were following. That evening, a large crowd assembled on the village green intent upon hearing Jesus speak. As he rose to address them, a lean, middle-aged fellow raised his arm for recognition, and shouted, in a rasping tone:

"Good Master, I heard you speak a parable in Cana, about the king's banquet where the rich despised their invitations and the poor were brought in." His harsh voice had risen until it had gripped and silenced the restless crowd. "I believe you, sir!" he went on. "It is high time the poor, who outnumber the greedy rich, should sit at the banquet-table! I would that you repeat the story for these slaves in Nain who are toiling their lives away, working for beggarly wages, to keep old Simeon Ben-Edom in luxury."

There was a dissenting murmur in the crowd as the revolutionary diatribe came to an end. It was evident that the people of Nain considered the impudent fellow as a trouble-maker. They grew quiet now, wondering what Jesus would say. Peter had stepped forward, glowering at the self-appointed orator. The Master laid a gently detaining hand on the huge, flexed forearm; and, in a friendly tone, obliged his inquisitor by retelling the parable of the king's banquet, and how the poor were brought in from the highways and hedges to attend the party.

But the parable had taken on a new chapter since it had been told in Cana. Jesus continued.

The king, he said, was quite willing to welcome the ragamuffins into his beautiful banquet-hall, but he wanted them to look and feel and be

as respectable as possible. So he ordered his servants to offer each guest
a clean and suitable garment to wear at the dinner.

But one sulky fellow, wanting to show his contempt for the king—
and the palace—and the feast, refused to accept the robe they gave him
to cover his dirty tatters. "They asked me to come here, just as I was,"
he growled, "and now they can take me, just as I am—or throw me
out . . . ." So they threw him out.

The crowd was delighted. They laughed and cheered. When the meeting was over, Peter—who hadn't spoken to Esther since yesterday—turned
to her with a broad smile, and said, " 'The meek shall inherit the earth,'
—but they'd better be meek!"

*   *   *   *   *   *

The news that Jesus was coming to Jericho had raced on ahead of him
and a great audience was awaiting his arrival. It was the largest assembly
he had encountered. Within a fortnight, more than fifteen thousand
people—from all over Samaria and Judaea and the contingent following
from Galilee—had converted the open country north of ancient Jericho
into a city. Those were memorable days for the Master's companions.
Sometimes, when the day's trying work was done, Peter had sought
Esther for comfort and companionship. They had become very close
friends. One evening he had asked her, as they sat side by side on the
grass at her tent-door, whether Greek was a difficult language to learn.

"You shouldn't find it hard," she had replied. "Want me to teach you
a few words, Petros?"

He had smiled and nodded.

She patted the ground with the palm of her slim hand.

"Ge," she said. "The earth . . . Say it, Peter. Ge."

He repeated the word after her.

She patted her head. "Kephale . . . " She laid her hand upon her
heart. "Kardia." She touched her girdle. "Zone." She pointed aloft at
a brilliant star. "Astron. . . . Now what is the word for head?" she asked,
after the manner of a pedagogue. Peter couldn't remember—but he did
recall the Greek word for heart, and seemed happy over his progress. He
was learning Greek—and fast. . . . An inquisitive little lizard scampered
across his worn sandal. He pointed to it.

"Sauros," said Esther.

"What is the word for God?" he asked.

"Which one?" inquired Esther, innocently.

"The only one," he said, severely.

"Theos," she replied, after a little pause.

And that was the way they had spent most of their evenings during the strenuous weeks in the region round about Jericho. Peter, who had never known a word of any language save his own—and was far from being a master of that one—was infatuated with new interest and proud of his progress. Esther gave him every encouragement. It was not long until the Big Fisherman was piecing his Greek words into sentences. He had been jealous of Philip. Now he was cultivating the Macedonian and vaingloriously talking to him in his own language; though sometimes Philip laughed a little and offered an amendment.

The summer was advancing. There was an occasional whiff of autumn in the early morning breeze. Then came the day of Jesus', triumphal entry into the city of Jericho, the welcoming crowds that lined the streets, the memorable luncheon at the mansion where Zacchaeus lived in lonely splendor, despised and feared by his fellow-townsmen. And, as an outcome of that interview, the rascally Zacchaeus had publicly announced his intention of restoring, four-fold, the unjust taxes he had filched from the people.

That night, at their encampment in the hills, Jesus told them the summer's work was ended. Tomorrow, he said, they would start back to Capernaum. The twelve were glad, but somewhat surprised; for it might be all of a month before the rains came on. The Master seemed suddenly anxious to return to Capernaum. They did not ask him why: they knew better than to question him any more.

17

THE LONGEST WEEK that Voldi had ever spent elapsed before Felix called
at the prison. It seemed doubtful that their friendship would survive.

It was after supper when he came. Twilight was settling. The dim oil-
lamp had been lighted. Voldi was sitting apathetically on his bunk when
he heard an argument in the corridor.

"The Prefect isn't going to like this, you know," the fat jailor was
whimpering.

"Did you have orders that no one was to see the Arabian?" came the
irritated voice of Felix.

"N-not exactly, sir; no," admitted the jailor. "But if your father learns
of it, he'll punish me."

"Then you'd better not tell him. Open that door now, and run along.
I may be here for a couple of hours."

There was another whine of protest from the jailor, followed by the
screech of the key in the rusty old lock, and Felix entered. Voldi came to
his feet and they embraced each other in silence.

"I can't quite make you out," said Felix, soberly, when they were
seated. "It must have been something very urgent indeed that would
justify your excursion into forbidden territory. Obviously the Tetrarch
was not the object of it, for you knew he had gone to Jerusalem."

"You deserve to know, Felix," said Voldi, "and I'm ready to tell you.
My girl is up there, waiting to hear from me. I had to go, regardless of
consequences. I didn't succeed, but it was worth trying."

"Your girl, eh?" Felix brightened with interest. "It was a foolhardy
thing to do, though. She must be something very special. I never met a
girl I would risk going to jail for. . . . So—now—when it's too late for
anything to be done about it, you're going to tell me. . . . Very well: I'm
listening."

It took Voldi an hour to confide the story. At first he tried to explain—with many wide-open gaps in the tale—how and why Fara, the incomparable Jewish-Arabian, had got herself away up into Galilee; but when he saw that Felix was darkly frowning his dissatisfaction, Voldi backed up to the beginning of his narrative and told it all; every detail of it; Fara's shockingly rash vow of vengeance; her daring journey alone and in the flimsiest of disguises; the failure of her utterly impracticable mission; her refusal to return to Arabia. And when he had made an end of it, he searched the shrewd Roman eyes in an entreaty for his friend's sympathetic understanding.

Felix exhaled a deep breath, and said, as from a distance, "I wouldn't believe a word of it, Voldi, except that it's much too fantastic ever to have been made up! Nobody could invent a tale like that! The daughter of Antipas! Vowed to assassinate the Tetrarch of Galilee! Single-handedly! Sixteen-year-old girl! Still plans on doing it. . . . Well—she's either crazy as a hoot owl—or the bravest creature alive!"

"You wouldn't think she was crazy, if you met her," said Voldi. "As for her bravery, she doesn't value her life very highly. Fara is a woman without a country, you know. She cares little whether she lives or dies. The trouble is: she undoubtedly knows now that she cannot possibly succeed in her undertaking—and she has voluntarily cut herself off from Arabia. . . . I know she loves me, Felix, and I would gladly die for her . . . . Is it any wonder that I took a chance?"

Felix sat for some time with his elbows on his knees, digging his fingers into his close-cropped, curly hair; then he slowly raised his head to inquire:

"Well—what's to be done; if anything?"

"It's easily to be seen that there's nothing I can do," said Voldi, dejectedly. "If I could only get a letter to her, explaining why I cannot come; but a letter from me would certainly be intercepted, and lead to an investigation of Fara's business in Galilee."

"I have it!" declared Felix, impulsively. "You write the letter. I'll take it to her."

There was a quiet moment before Voldi replied. It was not natural for either the Arabian or the Roman to show any emotion. Laying a hand on Felix' knee, Voldi murmured, "You are indeed a loyal friend, Felix! I hope this doesn't get you into trouble."

"It's time I had some trouble. A bit of adventure will be good for me. . . . And this girl is well worth the risk."

"What will the Prefect think of you?"

"He will be annoyed, I daresay; but I feel sure that if he were in my place, he would do exactly what I intend to do. . . . The Prefect," added Felix, proudly, "is a very sound fellow!"

For the next half-hour they seriously discussed the ways and means. Felix wondered if some embarrassing curiosity might be stirred in little Bethsaida by the arrival of a stranger, easily identifiable as a Roman, to pay a visit to a young woman whose presence there had never been fully explained. It was finally decided that Felix should take the letter directly to the canny old Sadducee, David of the House of Zadok. Voldi confidently believed that David could be trusted to deliver the message to Fara.

*   *   *   *   *   *

A week later, Felix returned from his journey. Voldi searched his friend's face anxiously as he entered the cell, and was relieved to note that he bore no evidence of trouble.

Felix had taken the letter to David's house, as they had planned. He had been much impressed by the old man's sagacity, and wanted to talk about him, and the hospitality he had shown.

"But—what about Fara?" Voldi begged to know.

"She wasn't there," said Felix. "Fara is on a tour of the country with this wonder-working Carpenter and his companions."

"But—that's impossible!" protested Voldi. "She had been much impressed by this young prophet; but I cannot imagine her following him about. Fara is not a religious person, at all!"

"Maybe not," conceded Felix, "but she is infatuated with the Carpenter. When you were there, this woman, Hannah, with whom she lodged, was very ill. Some days later, when her life was despaired of, the Carpenter came and healed her. Fara believed it was a miracle; no less. She confided the whole story to old David; told him the Carpenter had healed her, also."

"Healed Fara? And what was her trouble?"

"A bit of a riddle turns up at that point," said Felix. "She told David that the Carpenter had healed her mind; lifted some intolerable burden. The good old fellow wouldn't say what the burden was. Perhaps he didn't know. More likely he knew—but wouldn't tell. . . . My own guess is that the Carpenter talked her out of her vow."

"That's probably it," thought Voldi. "I hope so!"

"She left a verbal message for you, with David, in the event you came while she was absent. Fara is very anxious for you to return to Arabia. She intends to stay in Galilee, and assist this Jesus, the Carpenter."

"Assist him? How?"

"David says she is helping to take care of the sick children who are brought to the Carpenter for healing. He thinks she is paying a debt of gratitude for the miracle he performed on herself."

After a long interval, Voldi said, "That ends it, I suppose. She will give her life to this Jesus. Well—it might be worse. She never could have done —the other thing."

"Oh—it might have been possible," reflected Felix. "Fara could have found employment in the Tetrarch's household easily enough; could have become a trusted servant; could have killed him. It would have been suicidal, of course; but—she could have done it."

"It's a disgrace to Arabia that this fellow is allowed to live!" muttered Voldi.

"I agree with you," nodded Felix.

"Perhaps you think it's my job now," wondered Voldi.

Felix made no reply to that. Rising, he said he would return tomorrow.

"You do think that; don't you?" insisted Voldi, clutching at his friend's sleeve.

Felix drew an enigmatic grin and dismissed the query with a shake of his head—which Voldi could interpret any way he liked.

"By the way," he said, at the door, "Darik is in fine condition. He is being exercised every day. When you get out of here, he'll take you— anywhere!"

*   *   *   *   *   *

As Herodias had predicted, the dinner-party was proving to be as dull as it was lavish and expensive. The Romans, beginning too early with the birthday celebration by drinking recklessly since mid-afternoon, were apathetic as they clumsily slumped down onto their couches around the banquet tables. The magician from Caesarea was half drunk and impudently vulgar. The acrobats worked furiously for their feeble applause. As for the harpists, they had not yet appeared. Upon their arrival, at noon, Salome had taken them in hand, after promising her stepfather that she— and the musicians—would have an interesting surprise for him.

There was a deplorable lull in the program as they waited for the entertainment to proceed. Senator Cotta yawned prodigiously and inquired, "What's next, Your Highness?" Tiro suggested, "Why doesn't somebody make a speech?" Mark Varus drawled, "How about that prophet you've had penned up, Antipas?"

"That's not a bad idea," approved Fadilla. "Bring him in! Let him talk!"

Antipas briefly demurred. He had been drinking more than was his custom, and was ready to agree with almost any proposal, but this suggestion, he felt, needed to be deliberated. Turning toward Fadilla, who sat some little distance away, he said, "There is an ancient legend among our people, Tullius, about a prisoner—one Samson—who was brought up from his dungeon to amuse a party of his captors; and he pulled the house down over their heads."

"The Tetrarch is superstitious," remarked Aurelia Varus.

Antipas frowned, beckoned to a uniformed guard who stood behind him, and muttered an order. Then raising his voice, as the guard left the room, he announced, "We have a prisoner in our jail, a demented fellow who thinks he is a prophet. We are having him brought in to make a few remarks. We have no notion what he is likely to say; but let us listen to him with a show of respect—or he may be unwilling to talk, at all."

The room grew suddenly quiet as the gaunt, unkempt prisoner was led in, blinking against the blinding light of the huge stone lamps that lined the walls. Two tall guards brought him to a stand before the Tetrarch's table.

"Prophet John," said Antipas, "a desire has been expressed to hear you speak. You may choose your own subject. It may interest you to know that this is our birthday. Should you wish to take that event as your text, we will be gratified. Perhaps—if we like your speech—we may set you free."

There was a tense hush as they waited for the shaggy hermit to begin. When he spoke, his deep voice betrayed no agitation or embarrassment, nor was there any evidence that he resented his role as an object of ridicule.

"Sire," he began, "on Your Majesty's birthday it is fitting to review Your Majesty's years and deeds. Doubtless this might be accomplished by any of the great and gifted ones in this presence more eloquently than by a humble captive; but perhaps no more truthfully.

"Not often, sire, in the history of this unhappy world, has it been given into the hand of one man to bring about the peace of two great nations, long at enmity. This task was entrusted to Your Majesty; the healing of the hatred between Ishmael and Israel."

The Tetrarch frowned darkly and drummed on the table with his finger-tips. Hispo whispered to Paula Fronto, "The man is crazy!"

"It is not for Your Majesty's prisoner," continued John, "to conjecture why our God, in His wisdom, should have called to this important task a man so vain and selfish as Your Majesty; but His ways are mysterious and past finding out. Who shall say when again—if ever—it may be one man's privilege and duty to heal the breach between the Arab and the Jew!"

"That will do, mad dog!" spluttered Antipas, lurching to his feet. "Get you back to your kennel!"

Seizing him, the guards pushed the prisoner roughly toward the door.

Throughout the room indignant murmurs rose, implying an attempt to reassure the Tetrarch that no attention need be paid to the hermit's ravings; but the damage had been done, and almost everyone present—certainly the older ones—knew that the truth had been spoken. Antipas unwittingly sought David's eyes to learn their view of the awkward situation, but the old Sadducee soberly stroked his beard and did not look up.

It was Salome who, quite unaware of what had been going on in the banquet-hall, now came to the temporary rescue of the stunned and embarrassed Tetrarch. Trailed by the score of well-rehearsed harpists, she sailed gracefully into the room, made a deep curtsey to her stepfather; and, snapping her castanets, pirouetted into a reckless gambado. She was light as a feather, and almost completely unencumbered by clothing of any sort. Except for a braided chaplet of rubies, an elaborate design of pearl necklaces, and a fringe of sapphire-strands across her loins, Salome was nude.

Antipas, suddenly tugged out of his helpless anger by the girl's beauty and grace, was beside himself with admiration and delight; and when she had finished, with a flashing smile for him alone, he shouted that she might ask what she would—and it should be hers! There was much applause! Salome had saved the day for the Tetrarch, and they were all glad for him.

Herodias had slipped out into the corridor and was awaiting her daughter when she emerged from the banquet-hall, beaming over her plaudits.

"You heard what he said?" queried Salome, still breathing rapidly from her exertions. "What shall I ask? A coronet of emeralds?" She had a better thought. "I know! I shall ask him for a beautiful pleasure barge on the lake!"

Herodias scowled.

"No!" she muttered. "I'll tell you what to ask." Drawing the girl close she whispered into her ear. Salome drew back, aghast.

"But—you're mad!" she breathed. "What pleasure could I have in the death of that poor fool?"

"This time, my daughter," stormed Herodias, "it's not going to be what you want—but what I want! You've been given enough! And what you haven't been given, you have stolen! Do now as I command you—or I shall punish you! I mean that! You say I am mad: well, perhaps I am! But that will not make your punishment lighter! . . . Go! . . . Now!"

She was hardly to be recognized as the same girl when she walked slowly into the room, with uncertain steps and downcast eyes. She stood before the Tetrarch, crestfallen. The place became suddenly quiet.

"Sire," began Salome, huskily, "I desire, as my gift, the silver serving-platter that the Empress Julia presented to you."

"But—of course!" replied Antipas, relieved but bewildered. "You might have asked more, my child."

"Sire—I do ask more." Salome's voice sank almost to a whisper. "I want the head of this John, the prisoner, served to me—on the silver platter."

All breathing was suspended. Pale and horrified, Antipas leaned far back against his cushions, his face contorted.

"But—we—we can't do that!"

"You promised!" declared Salome, with sober finality.

Like a tortured animal at bay, Antipas searched the faces about him, piteously seeking a way out of his dilemma, but finding no sympathy in the amused eyes of the cynical Romans. After a long moment of indecision, he beckoned to the Captain of the Guards and mumbled the revolting order.

Jairus scribbled a hasty note to be passed along to his host. Adiel, it said, had taken suddenly ill—and might they be pardoned for leaving? Without waiting for consent, they made a hurried exit.

Then there ensued a long, painful interval, the silence broken only by brief and brittle bits of labored conversation. Herodias had returned to her place between Manilius and Fadilla. Salome was not in sight. At length the doors opened. All eyes turned in that direction. The gruesome gift was carried in and deposited in front of the Tetrarch, who recoiled at the sight.

Young Flavia Tiro slowly collapsed into the arms of Senator Cotta and gave up her dinner. The Senator was wearing a scarlet tunic with a black spread-eagle embroidered on his left breast. He pushed the sick girl off him and left the room, savagely damning Mark Varus who had chuckled.

Small groups of guests began to file out, reassembling presently on the couches beside the pool. Now the banquet-hall was empty, except for the Tetrarch and the Sadducee who was rising to leave. Antipas called to him.

"Master David," he croaked, unsteadily, "you are a lawyer. Is it ever permissible for the Tetrarch to put a man to death?"

"I believe not, Your Highness," said David. "I bid you Goodnight."

*   *   *   *   *   *

Without an hour's delay, the shocking story fanned out across the country with incredible swiftness. The palace courtyard had been packed with servants and soldiers; Jairus' litter-bearers, David's attendants, and a score of legionaries who had escorted Julian. There were also the small party of armed guards who had accompanied the magician from Caesarea, the family of acrobats from Damascus, and the company of harpists from Jericho. It was a ghastly tale, and they all made the most of it. A southbound caravan, which had camped for the night near Capernaum, made off with the news at dawn. Within a week the sordid scandal had gone north through Perea, had crossed the Jordan in a half dozen fording places, and was common talk down deep in Judaea. It had even penetrated the thick walls of the old prison in Caesarea, conveyed by Felix.

Thousands who had listened apprehensively to the foolhardy hermit's reckless predictions of an oncoming doom that would blast a wicked world, toppling greedy temples and gaudy thrones—but had all but forgotten them, and him—were stirred to sullen anger by the monstrous crime.

Doubtless the shaggy preacher, who lived in a desert cave and ate roasted locusts, had been misled: the catastrophe he had so boldly threatened hadn't come off. But by what right had this pompous ruler of Galilee murdered his defenseless prisoner for no better reason than to entertain a handful of pampered Romans? Nobody knew what should or could be done about it. Pilate, with plenty of troubles on his hands, had merely shrugged and muttered, "It's no affair of mine. Let the Galileans attend to him."

And so they did, not with violence, which the Tetrarch could easily have overcome, but with a concerted campaign of inarticulate contempt for which he had no defensive weapons. A farmer could not be punished for having his back turned toward the highway when the Tetrarch rode by on his black stallion, nor could a whole village be tried because every door was shut, and not a soul in sight, when their ruler took his daily exercise.

Early the next morning after the disgraceful birthday banquet, when the vine-dressers and carpenters arrived for their day's work in the new vineyard, they learned what had happened; and, refusing to take up their tools, ominously gathered about the prison where the prophet's body lay. The Tetrarch made no move to quell this incipient rebellion. Instead, he voluntarily ordered the guards to be withdrawn and sent word that if any of the dead man's friends wished to claim his body they might do so without hindrance. This unexpected concession was obviously intended as a peace overture; but the outraged Galileans—by no means the fools Antipas thought them to be—interpreted this lenience as a sign that the great man was frightened, if not remorseful.

Jesus, who had just returned to the Capernaum cottage after ten labo-

rious and exciting weeks of speaking to vast multitudes in Cana, Ephraim,
Bethel, Jericho, and the region round about, was informed of the tragedy
late in the night. Andrew had wakened him with the bad news. At sunrise, Peter, hurrying in from Bethsaida, drew up a chair beside Jesus' cot,
and repeated the story.

"They are burying him this afternoon, Master, in the cemetery at
Bethsaida. The people are aroused. A great crowd will assemble there.
John thinks it would be well for you to speak some words of comfort at
the graveside."

After a moment's deliberation, Jesus slowly shook his head. That indignant throng in the Bethsaida burial-ground would be in no mood for
comforting words. Anything he might say to these angry people would
surely be misconstrued. If he deplored the Tetrarch's crime—and how
was the subject to be avoided?—it would amount to a sanction of public
rebellion against their government, in direct contradiction to his earnest
pleas for peaceful submission. Nor was it an occasion when the multitude
would listen, with any patience at all, to calm advice about loving your
enemies and praying for them who despitefully use you and persecute you.
John had indeed paid a high price for his courage in fearlessly speaking
the truth—but—

"But—Master!" broke in Peter, impulsively, "you have told us that the
truth will set men free!"

"Yes," said Jesus, softly,—"and John is free. . . . Come—let us cross the
lake to some quiet place—apart from these resentful people. Tell the
others to meet us at the shore. I have much to say to you."

Though it was still early in the morning, a great throng, noisily rebellious, had assembled in the Synagogue plaza. At the sight of Jesus, a shout
arose and the crowd surged about him, demanding that he speak to them,
but he proceeded to the lake-shore where Peter and the others—who had
been quietly summoned—awaited his coming.

Stunned to silence by this unexpected withdrawal of the Carpenter on
whom they had depended for counsel in this critical hour, they watched
the three borrowed dories moving out toward Peter's long-idle fleet where
their passengers boarded The Sara. The sails were quickly set and the little
ship slowly sidled away from her sister craft.

"I wonder why they took The Sara," remarked one of the puzzled on-
lookers, shading his eyes against the sun.

"They're bound for some shallow cove," surmised a bystander wearing
a sailor's cap. "See! They're heading northeast—toward the desert."

"Let us follow them!" shouted someone. The suggestion met favor. The crowd moved forward along the shore, unorganized and without leadership but bent on finding Jesus.

It was a hard-breathing, shuffling, straggling procession that labored through the reeds and weeds and sand for eight long miles. Many of the more provident ones, knowing what a difficult journey faced them and aware that no food was to be had in that desolate region, scurried to their near-by homes and the town's provision stores to stuff their pockets with smoked fish and wheaten loaves.

Weary, bedraggled, footsore, their sandals ripped and clothing torn by nettles and briers, five thousand exhausted people found Jesus and his company at mid-afternoon. There was no shouting now; they were too utterly spent for shouting; too tired to hate anybody.

The Big Fisherman immediately took command. In his self-confident, booming voice he directed them to sit as closely together as possible in semicircular rows facing the dune where the Master and his companions waited. Not until the last of the stragglers had arrived did Jesus rise to speak. A hush fell on the expectant multitude as his gentle voice began its ministry of comfort.

He beheld them, he said, as one great family of brothers and sisters who, weary and heavy-laden, had come to him for rest. Not strangers now, but men and women of one blood, all children of their Father in Heaven; not drawn together by any hot desire for revenge or redress but related by their mutual compassion. . . . And as the quiet voice continued a strange miracle was wrought that gave them a heart-warming sensation of kinship.

By the time his talk had ended, the shadows were lengthening on the eastern mountains. Released from the spell that had held them silent and motionless, the crowd straightened its relaxed spine, drew a long breath, and shifted its posture. What now? Should they go? They were hungry. On any other occasion, those who had been forehanded enough to bring their own food would have had no hesitation at all to eat it in the presence of others as hungry as themselves. But, though many a man silently inspected his neighbor out of the tail of his eye, nobody reached in his pocket.

There was a whispered colloquy among the Master's companions. They called him into conference with them, the expression on their sober faces indicating that they were troubled. Jesus did not seem worried over the situation.

"Feed them!" he said.

"With what?" they inquired. "Even if we had the money to buy that much food, there is no place out here where it could be had."

By now the crowd was craning its neck and listening sharply with its good ear. A small boy, overhearing the discussion, came forward and handed his small lunch-basket to the Master who thanked him; and, holding up the basket, addressed the people.

"We will now have our supper," he said.

Everybody laughed. It was the first time anyone had laughed today. But Jesus did not think it was funny. He held up his hand for silence, bowed his head, and prayed, thanking God for this food and for the kind heart of the generous child who wanted to share what he had with his neighbors. Then, breaking up the lad's five little loaves and his two fish into tiny morsels, he told his companions to distribute the food among the people.

With sheepish grins, the men and women who had provided for themselves tugged their parcels out of their pockets and passed them down the row. . . . It had turned out to be a day of marvels!

Presently the crowd began to thin out. The afternoon was far advanced and the northern sky was darkening. The people seemed anxious to be on their way.

Andrew, turning to Bartholomew, remarked confidentially, "I think I know now why the Master brought us over here."

"You're right, Andy," said the shrewd old man. "He knew the crowd would follow, and he wanted to give those hot-heads a chance to cool off."

"And think about something else besides their hatred of Antipas," added Andrew. "Well—they were cooled off by the time they got here; no doubt about that!"

"Yes"—Bartholomew pointed toward the menacing cloud—"and they'll be cooled off a little more before they reach Capernaum."

The old man's prediction was correct. It was hard traveling along the shore-line. And it was the roughest night that anybody could remember on the lake. *The Sara* all but capsized!

∗   ∗   ∗   ∗   ∗   ∗

And while all this strange business of feeding five thousand people out of a little boy's lunch-basket was taking place in the desert, a mere handful of Bethsaidans quietly buried John's body in the village cemetery beside his long-departed father and mother. Frail old Rabbi Elimelech quaveringly intoned an ancient prayer for the peace of the prophet's soul. Esther, who had returned only yesterday from her arduous labors in the hungry, thirsty, weary crowds that had followed Jesus during his eastern journey, tarried with Hannah until the grave was filled, and covered it with garden flowers.

So—there was no revolution in Galilee. But the public's attitude toward the Tetrarch and his household and his pagan guests, while lacking in any demonstration of hostility, became quite unendurable. Without waiting for The Augusta to come for him, a month hence, Antipas impetuously organized his retinue and made off early one morning for Caesarea, hoping to be lucky enough to find a vessel presently sailing for Rome. No spectators lined the streets to gape at the procession as it passed.

Fortunately for the harried Tetrarch, a dirty and dilapidated old freight-ship, The Ostia, was—at the moment of his impromptu departure from Tiberias—discharging the last shovelful of her cargo of Cyprian copper on one of the new wharves in Caesarea, and would sail home within a few days.

Among the small group of passengers who had disembarked from The Ostia was Sergius the Prefect. Captain Malus, half expecting him to arrive, was at the wharf and greeted his master with a warm welcome.

"And how is Felix?" the Prefect wanted to know, as they rode together toward the Praetorium.

"Very well, sir. He will be overjoyed to see you."

"Lonesome, I dare say," mused Sergius. "How has he been spending his time?"

"He rides, sir," reported the Captain. "And he often visits the young Arabian, Voldi, in prison."

Sergius scowled.

"I do not like that, Malus. You shouldn't have permitted it! I lock this fellow up for disobeying orders—and my son visits him. I won't have it! Suppose all this should reach the ear of the Tetrarch!"

Malus meekly protested that there had been no instructions to forbid callers at the prison.

"I had no authority, sir, to tell Felix where he might and might not go in your absence. I can't think that any harm's been done," he added. "The Arabian is still in prison. . . . And—by the way—Antipas has just arrived in town with his large party. They sail for Rome on The Ostia."

"That dirty old tub?" shouted Sergius. "The Tetrarch must be in a hurry."

"Yes, sir. Antipas made a mistake. All Galilee is buzzing with it; on the verge of revolt. Apparently it got too hot for him up there."

The Prefect demanded to know the story, and Malus told him of the Tetrarch's revolting crime; beheading a harmless fanatic to entertain a dinner party; having the bloody head brought to the table on a platter.

Sergius grew purple with indignation as the sordid tale unfolded. Never having had the slightest respect for this pompous Romanized Jew, the loathsome story disgusted him almost to the point of nausea. The Prefect had had men beheaded, but not to entertain anybody!

"Gossip has it," went on Malus, "that Herodias thought it up."

"She would!" growled Sergius. After smoldering in his anger for a while, he suddenly blurted out, "I've had quite enough of that low-lived Tetrarch! There'll be no pomp and ceremony wasted on him, this time! I don't intend to see him off! And you needn't make any ado about protecting him! If he asks to see me, tell him I'm sick abed—with leprosy! . . . And, Malus, go down to the prison and turn the Arabian loose. Take him his horse. Tell him he is free to go wherever he likes!"

They had drawn up before the Praetorium now, and were stepping out of the chariot. Felix came running up, and warmly embraced his father.

"Greetings, my son!" said Sergius. "I am glad to see you! Malus tells me you have been a good boy!"

"Thanks, Malus!" said Felix, so fervently that his shrewd old father grinned.

The three of them fell into step together and moved toward the marble steps leading to the bronze doors of the Praetorium. Sergius halted there and regarded his son so soberly that he winced. Good old Malus, he reflected, had done him dirt, after all.

"My boy—" said the Prefect; and Felix' face fell, for whenever his parent addressed him as "My boy," you wanted to look out. There would be bad news presently.

"My boy—I assume that in my absence you have continued your friendship with that rash young Arabian."

"Yes, father," admitted Felix, contritely. "I have been seeing him—almost every day."

"Quite right!" declared the Prefect. "Men should be loyal to their friends, especially when they are in trouble."

Felix gave a quick intake of breath and blinked a few times before he drew a tentative smile of relief.

"I have just ordered Captain Malus to set this chap free," continued Sergius. "But Malus is much too busy to attend to it today. Perhaps you would like to inform your friend that he is at liberty to go his way, in any direction that suits his fancy." He brought out a stylus, scribbled a note to the jailor, and handed it to his son.

"You are very kind, sir," stammered Felix. "Thank you, sir! . . . May I go now?"

"Why not?" The Prefect and the Captain of the Guard marched up the steps of the Praetorium. Felix thought he heard a chuckle but did not look back as he made off for his horse—and Darik.

At the prison, Voldi was astonished when his half-hysterical friend hugged the breath out of him. The good news was so incoherently sputtered that it was some minutes before the amazing tidings were made clear. They pounded each other on the back and shouted joyously. Soon the prisoner was out in the sunshine, squinting against the unaccustomed glare, and affectionately patting Darik on his glossy shoulder.

"Where to, now?" inquired Felix, suddenly sobering. "I have been so happy to see you freed that I've had no time to think about your leaving. I'm going to miss you, Voldi!"

"And I shall miss you, Felix," said Voldi, with deep feeling. "Something tells me I should return to Arabia and report to my King. He deserves to know what has become of Fara, and the faithful Ione should be told. And I must see my family."

"But—you will be coming back, I think," said Felix.

"Unquestionably," said Voldi. "King Zendi will doubtless consent to my return—on a special mission."

"Do I know what it is?"

"I'm sure you do."

"Ticklish job; eh?" reflected Felix.

"It could be that," agreed Voldi.

They mounted their horses to ride back to The Agrippa for personal belongings that Voldi had deposited.

"If there is ever anything that I can do—if you should get into trouble— if you should suddenly need a friend—" Felix was saying.

"There is no one I would rather trust, Felix," said Voldi. "But this is a one-man undertaking—and strictly an Arabian duty. . . . I shall try to be careful," he added.

"Careful!" scoffed Felix. "That sounds funny, coming from you!"

18

AGAIN the rains came on, earlier than usual this time but gentle and intermittent, in comforting contrast to the relentless ferocity of last winter's storms.

Sometimes there would be two or three consecutive days without showers, though the sky remained obdurately overcast and nobody ventured very far from home unless his errand was urgent.

Jesus seemed glad to retire to Andrew's cozy cottage in Capernaum and the old house resumed its service as headquarters for most of the devoted band that had left everything to follow their Master.

Of the absentees, Judas had returned to Kerioth to look after some neglected business; Philip had gone home to Cana to visit his aged mother; Thomas, lacking a lodging-place, had accepted a job carding flax for Jairus; and Thaddeus, unhappy over the deterioration of the fishing fleet, was living alone on *The Abigail*, diligently calking the deck-seams with pledgets of pitch and oakum.

The others, unemployed and restless, showed up every day at the cottage and watched the Carpenter at his work; for the decrepit tools belonging to Ebenezer, who had passed away in the summer, had been reborrowed and the improvised shop had all the business it could handle, though little of it was of any profit. Much discussion was had among them concerning tentative itineraries for the coming spring: some were for going back to Hammath or Cana and some thought they should revisit Jericho. Jesus was given every encouragement to express an opinion but he only shook his head and murmured, "Not now"—an enigmatic response that sobered them. It seemed clear that he had already determined what he would do. The fact that he was reluctant to confide caused them much anxiety. There was no telling what hazards might be in store for them all. . . . Following Jesus was not easy.

363

One morning when a yellowish sun was feebly attempting to shine through the ragged rents in a gray cloud-bank, John ventured the remark that a great many idle people might be willing to risk a wetting if it were announced that the Master would appear in the plaza and speak to them, but the suggestion was not approved. Noting his young friend's disappointment, Jesus explained briefly that he didn't care to be responsible for an epidemic of bad colds.

When, that afternoon, John reported this conversation to Bartholomew, adding, "But he could easily cure their colds," the old man said, "It would be much easier to prevent them." And then he went on to say, "These miracles of healing, son, make a heavy drain on his strength. Had you not noticed that?"

"I know," nodded John. "That's true. They make him sweat."

Bartholomew sat thoughtfully stroking his beard for a long moment: then he said, "Johnny—sometimes I have felt that every burden he lifts is taken upon himself. Don't misunderstand me: I do not mean that when he heals a leper he takes on the man's leprosy: I mean that whenever he lifts another man's burden he adds the weight of it to his own. Our Master is carrying a very heavy load. . . . I often think of Esaias' prophecy that the promised Messiah would be a man of sorrows and acquainted with grief."

The enforced inactivity of these inclement days, however irksome for the others, was especially disquieting to Peter who had been constantly in the forefront of the summer's excursions and excitements. And how he had looked forward to this period of rest and recuperation! Now—after a few days of idleness—he had begun to fret under the weight of little Bethsaida's apathy; and, much as he enjoyed the company of his Master, the long afternoons at the cottage in Capernaum where he sat with empty hands were increasingly depressing.

Sometimes, during those tumultuous days of sultry Sivan and Tammuz, the responsibility of directing the great multitudes of desperate and inconsiderate people had been almost beyond his endurance. Often when darkness fell and the throng had gone home or into improvised camps in the neighboring fields and hills, the Big Fisherman would fling himself down on the ground, with his shaggy head buried in his sun-browned arms, too utterly exhausted to eat his supper. Had it not been for Esther's gentle solicitude and the challenge of her amazing fortitude, Peter couldn't have borne his burden. And he had been honest enough to tell her so.

It was a most unusual friendship. A stranger, having made the acquaintance of both of them, but never having seen them together, would certainly have thought it incongruous, if not impossible that this huge, blustering, untraveled, uneducated fisherman and the sensitive girl who had been brought up in an environment of exceptional privileges could have anything in common. By training and temperament they were leagues apart. Simon Peter had had no use for Esther, nor she for him, until their boundless devotion and tireless service to Jesus had made them kin.

They had often talked about this frankly, agreeing that their peculiar relation was no less than a miracle, Peter declaring his belief that a close friendship with the Master could provide a bond for all the people who loved him, no matter how different they might be as to race, color, language, disposition or mode of living. If they loved him, they would love one another. Jesus had said so—and these two understood what he meant.

Their comradeship, that summer, had invited candid confidences. Esther had told Peter all about herself, and when they were alone together he had—at her request—called her Fara. One evening, as they sat for a little while on either side of the Master, Peter had inadvertently addressed her as Fara, and Jesus had smiled with pleasure, though he made no comment.

It was not, however, a selfish friendship. Often a little group formed about them. Esther was one of the family. She repaired old Bartholomew's tattered sandal-thongs, bandaged Johnny's thorn-torn hand, mended Andrew's jacket; even sewed on a button for Judas whom she intuitively distrusted and disliked. Thad was always at her heels, helping with the tents and carrying provisions, as devotedly as a friendly dog. And on their hurried trip back to Galilee, when Esther lagged a little, one afternoon, he wanted her to get into the high-wheeled cart, already heavily loaded with tents and tackle—and ride. She had declined the offer; but, walking alongside him, she said tenderly that if everybody were as kind to everyone else as Thad has been to her the world would soon be a beautiful place to live in.

A flush of pleasure, mixed with embarrassment, glowed through the shy young fellow's tan. After some deliberation he said that he thought the world was beautiful enough to suit him; and he ventured to give Esther a worshipful glance.

*   *   *   *   *   *

The winter days had dragged drearily. Peter, lodging at home in Bethsaida, would trudge through the mud every morning to Capernaum and return in the late afternoon, moody and taciturn. Andrew rarely came home; but last night he had accompanied his brother, for John and James had arranged to spend the night with Jesus.

This morning, Hannah's household had assembled about the breakfast table. It was something of an event, for they were having fried perch, the first they had had for a long time.

"I heard a meadow-lark a little while ago," remarked Hannah, cheerily, "and there's a patch of blue in the sky. We may be having some fair weather soon," she went on, "though I'm in no hurry to see it come, for it means you will all be leaving me again. . . . I do wish you wouldn't go this time, Esther. It's too hard on you."

"Well—as for me," said Peter, splitting open another fish, "I'll be glad when it's time to go. I've been penned up too long. And I want to see the Master get out of that shop. They've been imposing on him—dreadfully! . . . Don't you think so, Andy?"

Andy slowly agreed that that was "one way of looking at it"; and, turning to Hannah, irrelevantly remarked that he had seen a blue jay yesterday with a straw in its beak. Esther couldn't help smiling. Andrew certainly had a gift for rerouting a conversation. But Hannah wasn't interested in Andy's blue jay.

"How do you mean, they impose on him?" she inquired.

Peter was ready with the particulars. Apparently he had given the matter considerable thought. . . . Well—first there was all that work on old Becky's loom.

"It happened just after we had come home," he went on. "The people were all stirred up over the Tetrarch's crime, and the hot-heads were keen on punishing somebody. Antipas had broken the law; and, seeing they couldn't do anything to him, they decided to make everybody else obey the laws. This old Rebecca person lived alone in a mere hovel on the out-skirts of Magdala, and was generally disliked. Many people thought she was a witch—and she looked the part, a very ugly old woman. The children threw stones at her whenever she appeared on the highway. And she put a curse on the neighbors' cattle, so that their milk dried up."

"How ridiculous!" exclaimed Esther. "You don't believe that!"

"Of course not," said Peter, "but what I believe isn't important in this case. A lot of people did believe it—or said they did. . . . One charge they had against Becky was that she never attended the Synagogue. One Sabbath morning, they heard her rickety old loom clacking, and to show how righteous they were a dozen of them stormed into her hut and smashed the loom to kindling-wood. . . . And the next day she came to see Jesus about it."

"Were you there?" wondered Hannah.

"Johnny and I. Becky opened the door and came in, as if she lived there. She had on a dirty old dress. Her tangled white hair hadn't been combed, and her bare feet were muddy. She came directly to where Jesus sat, and dropped down in a chair beside him, without a word. Her wrinkled face was twitching and it was plain to see that she was badly upset. But if the Master saw anything peculiar about her conduct he gave no sign of it. He turned to her with a friendly smile and said, 'Good morning, daughter. What may I do for you?'

"Her leathery old face softened," continued Peter, "and she put her bony hands over her eyes, and cried. And Jesus said, 'What is the trouble, Rebecca?' "

"And then she did cry, in earnest, I'll wager!" put in Hannah, whose own eyes were misty.

"Little by little, he got the story out of her," said Peter; and when she had finished, he said, 'You should not have been working on the Sabbath Day—unless it was necessary to someone's welfare. If a man's ox should fall into a pit on the Sabbath, he should come to its rescue. . . . But you say you were weaving a rug—to sell. That was wrong, as you know. However, your punishment was much too severe. . . . I shall build you a new loom, Rebecca.' "

They listened attentively while Peter went on with his story. The Master had spent a fortnight making the loom, and when it was finished and the boys had hauled it to Rebecca's little house, he had gone along. Rebecca had cleaned up her room, and herself too. The neighbors had crowded in. The old woman didn't seem so ugly now. Jesus was her friend, and her manner suggested that they had better take notice.

"A few days ago," said Peter, "old Becky came and presented the Master with a robe she had woven for him."

"And that sweet soul will probably wear it," said Hannah, "no matter what it looks like!"

"It looks very well," said Andrew. "He likes it."

"Yes," nodded Peter. "He wears it constantly now. I think he's really proud of it. . . . But—after all—he shouldn't be burdened with hard labor; not for people like old Becky!"

"I think that is a beautiful story," said Esther, softly. "He did more for her than make her a new loom: he made her a new Becky!"

But now Peter had another tale to tell of the way people imposed on Jesus. . . . Last week, Zebedee's fretful and avaricious Naomi had called at the cottage to complain that John and James were spending most of their time at home doing nothing. Their little house was crowded. Poor old Zebedee hardly had a place to sit down!

"So—what did the Master do but promise Naomi that he would make a new chair for Zebedee, which he proceeded to do; a beautiful chair, too, that will make everything else in their house look cheap and shabby. It took him all week to finish it. Yesterday, Naomi came, we thought, to thank him; but she had come to complain. The boys, she whimpered, should have more attention paid to them. They were giving the Master all of their time, and what were they ever going to get out of it, she wanted to know!" Peter snorted his disgust.

"Did she say what sort of honors they should have?" queried Hannah.

"She did indeed!" growled Peter. "She wanted them to have the most prominent seats in the Master's Kingdom. . . . Yes—and the foolish creature got that off before the whole roomful of us. Didn't she, Andy? And the youngsters sat there, red-faced, making no attempt to stop her!"

"Maybe they didn't want to stop her," reflected Hannah. She glanced at Andrew, soliciting an opinion.

"I think they were embarrassed," he said.

"But they made no protest," Peter went on. "They just sat there, looking down their noses and counting their fingers while Naomi babbled. It was the first time the subject had ever come up, who was the most important man among us."

"And what did Jesus say to her?" asked Hannah.

"He said nothing, directly to Naomi," answered Andrew, "but he did say something to the rest of us."

"It must have made Naomi feel very small—and insignificant," said Peter. "Jesus paid no more attention to her than if she hadn't been there. He looked around the room, and seemed to gather us all into a confidential little group; and then he said, 'Whoever among you would be great, let him be your servant. And whoever would be the greatest of all, let him be the servant of all.' "

"And then what?" inquired Hannah.

"Well—Naomi left, and nobody could think of anything to say," replied Peter. "John and James looked ashamed, as they should have done. They were foolish to think that anything they had accomplished should give them prominence."

"It was an awkward moment," contributed Andrew. "Even my brother"—he gave Esther a slow wink—"was speechless."

"Somebody should have changed the subject," thought Hannah.

"That's what happened," said Peter. "The Master did it himself. He turned toward the Zebedee boys, with a smile, and remarked that it had been a long time since we had had any fresh fish. And they were quick enough to take the hint, for they surely wanted to get out of there. They got up—and left in a hurry. It was the best thing that could have happened to them—in the circumstances." Peter seemed about to go on with the story; but, apparently thinking he had said enough, he tossed his napkin aside and pushed back his chair.

"There's a little more to it," drawled Andrew. "As James and Johnny went out at the door, Jesus asked Simon if he didn't want to go along."

Peter gnawed at his bearded underlip, and nodded.

"I suppose that's the reason we have perch for breakfast," laughed Hannah.

"It's a good enough reason," said Andrew. "There isn't a better fisherman on the lake than my brother."

No one seemed inclined to add anything to that. The men rose, pulled on their caps and heavy jackets, and proceeded to Capernaum. The carpenter shop was well filled when they arrived, everyone in unusually high spirits over the signs of returning spring. The Master had finished the table he had been making as a gift for Lydia, the widow of Ebenezer, in appreciation of the tools he had borrowed. It was evident that he had planned no further work. Perhaps he would tell them now when and where they would go.

Peter ventured to bring up the subject.

"I suppose we will be leaving presently, Master," he said—"now that fair weather is in sight."

"Yes," replied Jesus, "we will start on the first day of the week, and attend the Passover in Jerusalem."

There was a heavy silence; and, for a long moment, all breathing was suspended.

"No, Master, no!" entreated Peter. "Anywhere but Jerusalem! You have dangerous enemies there! This must not be!"

Jesus gazed steadily and sternly into the Big Fisherman's eyes.

"I must ask you to stand aside, Simon," he said, firmly. "Your counsel is not that of a faithful and courageous friend. I am going to Jerusalem—on business for my Father!"

One by one, the dazed Galileans—all but the Big Fisherman, who sat stunned and disheartened with his shaggy head in his hands—slipped quietly out of the room and reassembled at the front gate.

Andrew broke the silence.

"Well—he apparently means it. There's no use trying to dissuade him. He is going to Jerusalem."

Old Bartholomew cleared his throat and murmured, huskily, "We too will go—and die with him."

* * * * * *

The oncoming winter season, so far, had not amounted to much in Caesarea; light, frequent showers, but no snow and no cold weather.

It had been Voldi's intention to visit Jerusalem on his way home; but, once started on the south-bound road, he decided to retrace the course he had pursued in the company of Mencius.

At Joppa he spent a day touring the docks, surprised at the extensive operations in progress there where the Romans were conducting harbor installations similar to those in Caesarea, though on a less lavish scale.

That the Empire contemplated an invasion had been plainly evident by the expensive works in Caesarea; now it appeared that the military strategists were not putting all their eggs in one basket. Frowsy old Joppa, too, was being converted into an available beach-head; and with such undisguised urgency and earnestness that it seemed the long-threatened Roman offensive might be imminent. All Palestine, preoccupied with her internal feuds, pretended not to notice. Perhaps Jehovah, who had fed the Children of Israel with manna in the Wilderness, would take care of this situation. He'd better, thought Voldi, or the Promised Land was doomed: yes, and Arabia too, if the Romans thought it worth the bother of conquest; though they might not want Arabia, for the Romans had no taste for a nomadic life. They might be content to levy a high tribute on the Arabs and let them remain unmolested with their flocks and herds. It was high time, though, that Arabia considered the danger she faced. Voldi felt that he would have much to report to his King.

And so on, day after day, with brief, begrudged pauses at night for rest, he followed the much-traveled highways, through beautiful Askelon, drowsing in charmingly unseasonable sunshine, to wretched old Gaza, whose squalor, plagues, stenches and wickedness no felicity of climate could forgive; and on and steadily on through ancient Hebron to parched Engedi and the Dead Sea. He made a half-circle of this dazzling white brine and turned east again over the blistered crust of the salt-flats into the Valley of Aisne.

Darik was so tired now that he didn't care who knew it. Instead of picking up his feet smartly, as was his custom, he was shuffling and stumbling along like a spiritless pack-ass; but after the Valley of Aisne had been traversed and the winding road up through the hills lay before him the tall, black gelding, recognizing his homeland, renewed his strength. As they gained altitude, snow was encountered on the northern slopes, and when the shoulder of the high plateau was reached Voldi was happy to find an endless, undulating blanket of white that covered the hillsides and valleys as far as he could see in all directions. This was good! Arabia had the sure promise of a prosperous spring and summer. There would be fat cattle and sheep. Well-fed camels would produce strong, sleek foals.

Voldi breathed deeply of the crisp, tonic, mountain air, inhaling it hungrily as if he ate of it. He rose in his stirrups and stirred echoes in the hilltops with boyish shouts. As never before, he realized how much Arabia meant to him. And Darik, noisily blowing his nose, tugged for an easement of the bridle-reins, tossed his head and stretched his long legs to a lope.

In the late afternoon King Zendi's encampment was sighted and a few minutes later Voldi dismounted at the main entrance to the extensive compound, warmly greeted by the amazed sentries. Soon he was surrounded by a score of excited household servants and hostlers, patting and stroking the streaming Darik who slobbered over all of them with cordial impartiality.

Wrinkled old Kedar now came limping up, elbowing his way through the pack to Voldi who affectionately laid a hand on the bent shoulder.

"You have ridden him hard, sir!" growled old Kedar, turning gruff to hide his emotion.

"It was his own idea, Kedar," laughed Voldi. "Once he was on a familiar road, there was no holding him in. . . . But tell me: how are their Majesties?"

"They are well, sir, but very sad today. You have come home none too soon. Counsellor Mishma is ill; very low. The King and Queen are over there now. You must go—without a moment's delay. I shall get you a fresh horse."

Ione, pale, thin and nervous, crept timidly into the circle. Voldi threw his arm around her and drew her closely to him. He bent and whispered into her ear.

"Fara is safe and well, Ione, and sends her best love to you. I shall tell you everything, when I return. I must go now—to my grandfather."

In a few minutes he had dashed away to Mishma's encampment, five miles distant. The commodious paddock was filled with beautiful horses, some of which Voldi recognized. His unannounced entrance into the Chief Counsellor's spacious bedchamber was greeted with gasps of surprise and relief by the sober-faced group of old retainers clustered within the doorway. The tall, dignified members of the King's Council stood in statuesque silence with Zendi in the midst of them, a distinguished figure, his hair prematurely graying. It was evident, by the posture and demeanor of all present, that they were waiting for the end to come.

Kitra gave a little cry of gladness in her grief and rushed forward to embrace her son. Taking him by the hand she led him to the bedside; and, raising her voice, called:

"See, Father! Here is Voldi!"

The frail old titan laboriously opened his eyes and drew a wan smile. Voldi dropped to his knees and slipped his arm tenderly around the thin, deep-lined neck. Mishma was trying to speak. With a great effort he managed to ask, huskily:

"Did you find her?"

Voldi's eyes were blind with tears. Unable to speak, he nodded.

"But—she could not do it," whispered Mishma, between labored breaths; and when Voldi had shaken his head, the old man drew a satisfied sigh, and murmured, "That is good."

There was a long interval of silence, after which the fading voice asked, "Is she with you?"

"No, sire," said Voldi, regretfully.

"But—you will bring her home—to Arabia," entreated Mishma.

"I hope to, sire, when I have completed the work she tried to do—for our country."

Old Mishma slowly nodded his approval and lapsed into sleep. Zendi had drawn closer, during this difficult conversation. Voldi, suddenly aware of the King's nearness, came to his feet—and saluted.

Bending over the bed, and raising his voice so that it startled the silent watchers, Zendi called:

"Mishma! Open your eyes, Mishma! Harken! Have you a final request to make of your King? Speak, Mishma!"

The dying statesman tugged himself back to partial consciousness, clumsily moistened his dry lips, and whispered:

"Voldi."

The weary old head slowly sank. There was an ineffectual reaching of the lips for one more breath. Mishma was dead.

Turning about to face the company, Zendi drew himself up to his full height, and announced:

"I hereby appoint Voldi to fill the vacancy in the King's Council!"

19

CAPTAIN FULVIUS, never given to rash predictions, had remarked at sunset to his most important passenger that if this brisk breeze continued through the night *The Vestris* might see Gaza at dawn.

"Good!" exclaimed the Proconsul. "I shall go down and tell poor old Brutus."

"Better take a handful of sugar along," advised the Captain. "Your poor old Brutus is getting mean. Yesterday, when I went down for a friendly word with the horses, he laid his ears back and bared his teeth. I'm afraid he is at the end of his patience."

"I don't blame him," grumbled Mencius. "So am I."

It had been seven weeks since the fleet had sailed from Brindisi, bound for Cyprus where a cargo of copper awaited transport to the new docks at Joppa. The winter had been so mild that Fulvius, hoping to make time, had risked a lighter ballast than the season justified; and, once they had rounded the peninsula and headed east, everybody was sick—and disgruntled, too, for the voyage was to be long and, in the opinion of the crew, inexplicably roundabout.

Their natural course, if they had business in old Gaza, would have taken their seven cargo-ships with the copper directly to Joppa, but *The Vestris* was under orders to sail first to Gaza where the Proconsul had an important errand at the Roman Fort of Minoa, a few miles inland. The rest of the fleet would proceed to Joppa, and stand by until rejoined by the flagship.

The capable Lieutenant Pincus, with a skeleton crew of experienced men, would also disembark at Gaza and engage a camel-caravan for the tedious trip to the salt-fields at Engedi on the Dead Sea.

Then *The Vestris*, having paid her brief call at Gaza, would sail to Joppa, join the fleet, dump the copper, and double back to Gaza to pick up Pincus and his salt. And nobody knew how long they might have to wait for the return of that plodding caravan. It was doubtful whether they would be back in Rome before mid-summer.

Mencius had paced the deck and counted the days like a jailbird. He had been required to make these long voyages to Palestinian ports so often that they had lost all interest for him. Of course he always enjoyed a shore-leave at Caesarea where he found many long-time friends at the luxurious Agrippa; but he wasn't going to Caesarea this time; only as far as Joppa which the Empire might make something of, eventually, though the moldy old city offered few attractions at present.

There was only one thing about this whole trip that had stirred the Proconsul's interest. He had been commissioned to deliver a letter to the young Legate recently appointed—for his sins—to command the Fort at Minoa. Mencius had not been informed about the contents of this letter, and his curiosity had nearly devoured him. All he knew about it was that the gaudily gilded scroll contained a message of considerable significance, for it had been written by the Emperor! What the half-crazy and wholly unpredictable old Tiberius might have to say to the incorrigible son of Senator Gallio was anybody's guess. The wayward young Legate, according to a freely circulated rumor, had been sent to this ill-conditioned outpost for publicly insulting the Regent, Prince Gaius. And now, the Emperor was sending the impudent Marcellus a letter!

Mencius, feeling that he had to talk this over with somebody, had discussed the probabilities with his canny old friend Fulvius.

"It's unlikely," he had remarked, "that these royal tidings are felicitous. Tiberius wouldn't put himself to much trouble to make anybody happy; certainly not the roistering son of Gallio, who is ever denouncing the Government for its extravagances."

"I'm not so sure about that," Fulvius had replied. "As for Senator Gallio's demand for economy, the Emperor himself is not a wastrel; and as for the youngster's ridicule of the Prince, the old man hates Gaius."

"Granted—all that! But can you picture Tiberius writing a pleasant letter?"

"No—I really can't," agreed Fulvius, "and if I were you I should just hand it to the boy—and run."

"Maybe the letter is a commission for Marcellus to some better command," speculated Mencius.

"Oh—it might be—anything!" rumbled Fulvius. "The old codger's crazy as a beetle! For all you know, it's a notification to young Gallio that you have been appointed his successor at Minoa!"

"That's a pleasant thought!" growled Mencius.

They had left it at that. It wouldn't be long now until they might know the answer to the riddle. Tomorrow they would warp up against the dock at Gaza.

The morning was bright and clear. The long wharf swarmed with the usual pack of filthy donkey-boys and villainous camel-drivers. Pincus and his men were the first to leave the ship and were promptly swallowed up in the noisy throng of competitive caravan-owners. More deliberately, the Proconsul and the Captain came ashore and mounted their stiff and clumsy horses. It was but a short ride to the Fort, and they decided to dispose of their errand without delay.

"Something seems to have happened here," remarked Mencius, as the heavy gates swung open to receive them. "Marcellus has taught these lazy louts to act like soldiers!"

"Perhaps the Emperor has heard of it," thought Fulvius, "and wants the Legate to come back and renovate Rome. She could do with a bit of grooming."

A bright young Centurion appeared, smartly saluted, and asked if he could be of service. The Proconsul introduced himself and Fulvius. They bore a letter for the Legate.

"Our Legate Marcellus, sir, left here yesterday with a company of cavalry to attend the Jewish Passover at Jerusalem."

"That's odd," muttered Mencius. "Since when has Minoa turned Jewish?"

The Centurion risked a dry grin.

"It is an annual custom, sir. All of our Palestinian Forts send deputations to the Holy City, during the Week of the Passover, to keep the peace."

"And rattle our armor," assisted the Proconsul. "I presume your Legate is to be found through the Procurator's Insula?"

"Yes, sir."

"We will have to proceed to Jerusalem, then, and deliver our message. It is urgent."

Mencius was turning Brutus about toward the gate when the Centurion invited them to tarry for such hospitality as the Fort could offer, but the Proconsul declined. They must be on their way. At the gate he turned to say, "This is a different place from the last time I saw it, Centurion. Apparently your new Legate believes in brooms and discipline."

"He does indeed, sir!"

"Tough taskmaster, eh?"

"He keeps the Legion on its toes, sir; but we like it better that way. The Legate is tough—but he's fair."

"Fine!" approved Mencius. "He must be enjoying his command at Minoa."

"Yes, sir. Probably not, sir. I don't see how he could, sir. Yes, sir! Thank you, sir!"

The heavy gates closed behind them, and they laughed all the way up the road.

"The fellow had humor, sir," chuckled Fulvius, with a fair imitation of the Centurion's stiff drollery. "He should go far, sir."

"Yes, sir," snapped Mencius. "Probably not, sir."

In an hour, the crew of *The Vestris*, unhappy over the brief shore-leave but with too much sense to protest, gave the old ship all the canvas she could carry and sailed for Joppa.

"Want to ride with me—to Jerusalem?" asked Mencius.

"Why not, sir?" said Fulvius.

* * * * * *

Esther had not been forbidden nor had she been invited to accompany the Master and his twelve close companions on their journey to Jerusalem.

No plans had been made for it and no advance announcement had been made of it. The portentous decision had come as a stunning surprise. Jesus, in his prescient wisdom, made no mistakes. How often they had all agreed that this was true! How often they had had occasion to chide themselves for questioning his actions! But this time, they all felt, he was headed— quite unnecessarily—for disaster.

Peter, deeply depressed, heart-sick with foreboding, had brought the distressing news to the supper table in Bethsaida on Sabbath evening. They were leaving early in the morning, he said, traveling fast and with light equipment.

"Dear old Bartholomew!" murmured Esther. "What will become of him?"

"He'll probably die of a heart attack," said Peter, "but he intends to come along."

"And you think I'd better not go?" queried Esther.

"There will be nothing for you to do," said Peter. "No meetings along the way, no healings; just a steady march to the city—and into who knows how much trouble."

For an hour they discussed the probabilities. Yes, Peter agreed, there would be hundreds, perhaps thousands of pilgrims in the city who had heard Jesus speak, scores and scores who had received marvelous benefits at his hands; but these friends of the Master were not organized; they could not be expected to defend him.

"They're country people, mostly," Peter went on, "people like Andy and me, and Johnny and James and Thad, people who lose their confidence and courage in the confusions of a great city."

"But—surely"—exclaimed Esther—"no one would dare to harm the Master when he is innocent of any wrongdoing!"

With a despairing sigh, the Big Fisherman tried to explain the dangers that threatened them. Jerusalem was the stronghold of all the mutually intolerant religious sects and political parties. They were ever on the alert to silence new voices that spoke the restlessness of the people.

Again and again, remembered Peter, deputations from Jerusalem had appeared in the Master's audiences, asking questions intended to betray him as a seditionist. The very fact that the populace hung on his words and found comfort in them was an indictment of his loyalty to the ancient institutions of Jewry.

On the occasions of the Passover, these stubborn men were particularly attentive to any indication of a movement among the people in defense of their common rights. Indeed, it was said that during Passover Week when the city swarmed with home-coming Jews from the provinces—habitually ignored and neglected by all officials save only the tax-collector—the Roman patrols were under orders to disperse even the little groups that gathered on the street to hear a blind beggar sing! . . . Now—Jesus would appear in Jerusalem. There would be hundreds, perhaps thousands of people in the city who would crowd about him and entreat him to speak to them; and undoubtedly he would do so. . . . "Oh—why does he put himself in this danger?"

Soon after supper, Peter had retired to his room, and when the women awoke in the morning he had already gone. They ate their simple breakfast in moody silence; and, after the household chores had been disposed of, Esther slipped out of the house and walked briskly up the hill to talk with David the Sadducee.

By some means, the old lawyer had already learned of Jesus' decision to attend the Passover in Jerusalem. He greeted Esther soberly and his replies to her anxious queries were anything but reassuring. David, of the ancient House of Zadok, knew more than the Big Fisherman about the conditions to be faced—by any popular prophet who might appear on the streets of the Holy City at the time of the Passover.

"Yes, my dear," said David, "our friend Simon has good reasons to be apprehensive. The most influential men in Jerusalem, the bankers, the lawyers, the rich merchants, cannot take the risk of a scramble on the part of the people. This Carpenter has talked quite freely, to great multitudes, about fair dealing, good measure, just weights and balances in the market-place. He has had much to say about exorbitant rents and usurious rates of interest. He has told stories of poor men who died of starvation on rich men's doorsteps."

"That is true, sire," put in Esther, "but he has been equally critical of the greed and ill-will among the poor themselves! He has not tried to set the poor against the rich! He only wants everyone to be kind and charitable to everyone else!"

"Yes, yes, dear child, but the thing that Jerusalem will remember best is his bold denunciation of fraud and wickedness in high places. Even the Temple has not escaped his criticism!"

At that, Esther wanted to know how much influence the Temple was able to exercise, seeing the city was governed by the Romans. David proceeded to explain. It was a long and involved story.

Yes, he said, the Romans governed all Palestine, and their will was supreme. In any clash with the Sanhedrin, the Insula would have the last word; that was true, theoretically.

"But the Romans," he went on, "want no clash with Jewry now. They are deliberately preparing for the day when they will take full possession of this country, looting it and enslaving it. They could do it tomorrow if their armies were not engaged in the recovery of their losses in Gaul. When they are ready, they will strike. Until then, they want no friction. Pontius Pilate makes a gaudy show of authority but he is under strict instructions to keep the peace of Jerusalem, whatever the cost to his personal pride. When Caiaphas, the High Priest, speaks, Pilate listens!"

David seemed to be talking to himself now. After a long, silent interval, he mumbled, "Pilate scowls and squirms—but he listens. When there's any sign of unrest among the people, the merchants confer with the bankers, and the bankers confer with the Sanhedrin, and the Sanhedrin confers with the Procurator."

Esther had many questions she wanted to ask, but hesitated to interrupt the wise old man's monologue. Turning about to face her he asked, "Did they tell you about Rabbi Ben-Sholem of Capernaum?" Without waiting for her response, David continued. "It seems that some months ago a great crowd was waiting in the plaza for the Carpenter to speak. The Rabbi, beside himself with indignation, appeared on the porch of the Synagogue to denounce the throng, and he was reviled and ridiculed. His Regents failed to support him, and he has retired to Jerusalem. Ben-Sholem and the old High Priest were schoolmates. . . . You may draw your own conclusions, Esther. The Rabbi is not a man to forget or forgive an affront to his dignity."

"But that unhappy affair wasn't the Master's fault, sire!" declared Esther. "He rebuked the crowd for its discourtesy."

"Yes—I know, dear child," said David, "but that didn't restore Ben-Sholem's wounded pride. He wanted no favors from the Carpenter."

The old lawyer sighed deeply and drew his robe about him. It was chilly in the shade of the trees. Esther rose, and they strolled toward the gates.

"I feel that I should go to Jerusalem," she said.

"I shouldn't if I were you," advised David. "You have had enough trouble—and there is nothing that you can do." He bade her Good-day and slowly retraced his steps through the grove.

As Esther neared Hannah's house, she paused to note the little companies of pilgrims on the highway, setting forth on their annual journey to the Holy City. In each family group one of the younger men pushed a cart containing tents and provisions. Some of the larger carts were drawn by donkeys. The people moved along slowly, for it was a long trip on foot, and they must conserve their strength.

Hannah was cutting an armful of roses. She wept inconsolably when Esther said she had resolved to go to Jerusalem. Silently they packed a rucksack with the necessities of the journey; and, that afternoon, they parted tearfully at the shady corner where the quiet street met the broad highway.

"Something tells me," sobbed Hannah, "that I shall never see you again! Never!"

Esther was too moved to make a reply. She kissed Hannah tenderly— and joined the plodding pilgrims. A friendly young woman told her it was a beautiful day, and she agreed; but her heart was heavy.

"Are you alone?" asked her new friend.

"Yes," said Esther. It was true. She had never felt more alone in her life.

*   *   *   *   *   *

It had been Peter's hope, rather than his belief, as they set forth from Capernaum in the early morning of the first day of Nisan, that they might enter Jerusalem unobtrusively.

The city would be crowded with thousands of pilgrims, all of them scrambling desperately for a lodging-house within the walls or a tent-site in the suburbs. They might be so preoccupied with their own affairs that the arrival of Jesus would attract little attention. After the first half-hour on the highway, Peter wondered why he had tried to comfort himself with such a foolish delusion. He might have known better.

Everybody on the road—and they were all bound for the same destination—instantly recognized the Master, hailing him with joyous shouts, crowding about him, begging him to speak to them. It was not long until he was at the head of a procession that increased by the hour, by the mile.

James, stepping to the edge of the highway, looked backward and returned to his place between his brother and Andrew, and said, "Remember the day in Bethsaida when he suddenly disappeared from the people who followed him? I wish he would do that now!"

But he didn't disappear, and the pilgrimage grew. Every side road that met the highway contributed. At night, when Jesus stopped, they all stopped, and the heavy-laden carts and the older people caught up. In the morning, when he resumed the journey, they were all ready to follow. Dozens of the well-to-do, who could afford tall camels, paid their respects and preceded the pedestrian parade. They would arrive many hours earlier than Jesus, and would have an amazing story to tell, no doubt.

When the Master's company broke camp at Ramah, on the morning of the third day, Peter—who hadn't wanted a crowd along—began to take pride in this astounding display of public interest. . . . Could it be possible, he exclaimed to Philip, that Jesus intended to enter Jerusalem in triumph?

"From the size and temper of this crowd, he could do it!" said Philip.

"Perhaps that has been his plan—from the first!" said Peter, in an awed voice. "Do you suppose he means to restore the Kingdom to Israel?"

"I don't think he wants to be the King of Israel," put in Andrew.

"Why not?" demanded Judas, sharply. "Has it not been foretold by the prophets? Is not the Kingdom to be restored to Israel? Who else has the power to do it?"

Throughout the Sabbath Day they remained quietly in camp at Bethphage, with only three miles further to go on the morrow, the day the Romans called "Sunday." The village was suffocated with the enormous concentration of excited pilgrims. All manner of rumors and conjectures were in circulation through the camps. It was generally believed that Jesus of Nazareth was about to proclaim himself the King of the Jews, the Messiah, the Restorer of Israel!

Some of the older and more pious men remembered that an ancient prophet had predicted such an event. The King would ride into the city on an ass. A group of zealots set forth to find one. By good fortune they discovered a young ass, a beautiful, white beast, tied at the gate of a paddock. He bore no saddle-scars or marks of harness. That was good; for the old men had said it should be an ass that had never been ridden. They besought the owner to lend them the beast, and told him why. Jesus, the wonder-worker of Galilee, would ride into the city as Israel's King! The man laughed coarsely.

"You may have him—and welcome!" he said. "And I'll go along with you. This is something I want to see! Jasper has never been broken to ride."

"Good!" they exclaimed. "You say no one has ever tried to ride him before?"

"Oh yes, indeed!" guffawed the owner. "It's just that Jasper doesn't like the idea. You'll see! . . . No—I don't want any money for the use of him. I just want to go along!"

Next morning, shortly after dawn, the great multitude swarmed about the house where Jesus was stopping. It was a noisy, half-hysterical crowd whose leaders shouted, "Hail to the King! Hail to the King!" The turbulent throng took up the chant!

Peter was experienced in handling great masses of people but this demonstration was already quite out of anyone's control. The little band stood close about the Master and tried to protect him from the fanatical pilgrims. A small company of men pushed through the jostling pack leading a shaggy white ass. Jesus mounted and the frantic procession moved forward with his close friends walking on either side of him, awed and anxious—but ecstatic.

They had left Bethphage now and were entering Bethany, the richest of the city's suburbs. The street was beautified with stately palms which the advance contingents of the crowd ruthlessly pillaged of their branches, carpeting the highway for the King.

Jerusalem's towers and domes were plainly visible now across the deep valley that marked the course of the shallow Kedron. A huge multitude of pilgrims, lodged in the city, had been shouted into action by couriers from the main body of celebrants; and here they came, hundreds of them, racing up the long slope of the Mount of Olives. At the brow of the hill, the procession halted, and gradually the triumphal shouts subsided. A strange silence fell upon them. The King was about to make an announcement. This was the moment for which they had been waiting!

For a long while, he sat in a posture of dejection, gazing down upon the ancient stronghold of his people. Then the transfixed thousands who stood silently waiting witnessed an incredible sight. The King was in tears. He extended both arms in an embracing gesture, and cried, "Oh—Jerusalem! Jerusalem! How often would I have gathered you—as a hen gathers her chickens under her wings—but you would not!"

For a moment the people were stunned and unbelieving. The Nazarene had thrown away a Kingdom! The crowd began to disintegrate. Everyone was scurrying down the hill. The pilgrims had lost their King, but they still had Jerusalem. The man who owned Jasper came and led him away. Jesus' companions were speechless. Peter gnawed his underlip. Andrew looked sober. John and James consulted each other's clouded eyes and shook their heads. Philip's face was pale. Old Bartholomew had edged to the side of the street and was sitting on the curb, mopping his forehead. Thad was standing beside him, holding the old man's pack. . . . Judas had gone on down the hill.

*   *   *   *   *   *

The little company, with Jesus in the midst of them, proceeded slowly toward the city. Straggling groups of pilgrims overtook and passed them, staring into the Master's face with various expressions of sympathy, entreaty, disappointment and reproach. Many were in tears.

Little was said, for there was little to say, as they trudged along, each man busy with his own thoughts. Although it was dismayingly certain now that the spontaneous public clamor to recognize Jesus as the promised Messiah had been silenced beyond any possibility of its renewal, the disciples—albeit distressed over the whole affair—were breathing easier than on yesterday. Then they had feared that a great crowd of Jesus' admirers, surging about him in the streets of Jerusalem, would evoke the attention of the patrols; and the Master would be arrested—and punished as a disturber of the peace.

As it had turned out, Jesus had dealt with that situation before it had become acute. He was safer now than he might have been if this demonstration had not occurred. It was unlikely, they thought, that the authorities would take action against a movement which the Master himself had dissolved.

When they came to the East Gate and were about to enter the city, Jesus turned to say that they would go at once to the Temple. Peter smiled his gratification. Surely the authorities could find no fault with that. Had Jesus decided to ignore the Temple it might have aroused criticism. But, like any other pious pilgrim, he would pay his respects to the hallowed shrine of Jewry. The moody silence that had gripped them was eased somewhat and they conversed in voices that tried to sound casual. "There's the Pool of Siloam, Johnny," remarked James. "That's where Nehemiah began the rebuilding of the wall." "See—there's Herod's Tower," said Andrew. "Looks new," observed Philip, "compared to the rest of these buildings."

The Temple was having a busy day. Everybody had brought a sacrificial offering, each according to his means. The beautiful court of the Temple, lined and walled with exquisite designs in mosaic, was crammed with the gifts of pilgrims: fat calves and lambs, and large, slatted pens full of doves. The air was heavy with animal stench and raucous with the bellowings of the cattle and the bleating of the sheep; and over all this racket shrilled the strident voices of the money-exchangers who were there to serve the donors. For, very frequently, a lamb was found to be blemished, and the astonished pilgrim, who had thought his offering was entirely sound, would be told that they could provide him with an unblemished lamb in exchange for a small cash difference. The pilgrim would glumly produce the money; but, in many cases, it was coinage of the provinces, and countries even more remote. He had to present himself at the desks of the exchangers who could ill afford to conduct this service free of charge. It was a sordid scene, especially to anyone from the open country, unused to such dickering within consecrated walls. Even if it had been entirely honest, which it wasn't, this was not the place for it!

The Master's indignation suddenly flared! Above the babel of voices and bellows, he shouted, "My Father's House is a place of worship! You have made it a place of merchandise!"

Seizing a drover's whip, he began to drive the animals out of the Temple Court. They stampeded toward the street, the crowd scurrying to give them room. The cages of the doves were thrown open and the birds were soon all over the building. Then the unscrupulous exchangers came in for their share of the rebuke. Jesus charged on them, upsetting their tables and money-tills.

The grim-faced companions of the Master retreated to the outer wall, astounded by his action. "This," muttered Peter, "will settle it! They will never forgive him!"

Nor did they.

*   *   *   *   *   *

Esther's journey to Jerusalem was much more pleasant than she had had any right to expect. After her sad leave-taking of Hannah, whose intuition informed her—and quite correctly, too—that they would never meet again, she immediately realized her good fortune in falling in with this friendly party from Capernaum.

There were a dozen of them, all related, and they seemed eager to welcome her into their company. The pretty girl Myra, instantly divining that the stranger was facing the trip unhappily, had been quick to confide that she herself hadn't wanted to come along because all the others were so much older "and so tiresomely pious." And now that she had found a friend of her own age she was going to have a good time, after all.

This warm-hearted proffer of comradeship was irresistible, and Esther surprised herself by the promptness with which she accepted it. The peculiar circumstances which had surrounded her—and almost suffocated her—ever since her early childhood had permitted but few youthful acquaintances. Since leaving Arabia she had had no girl-friends at all. Myra was charming.

Having nothing to conceal, the girl from Capernaum opened the way for mutual confidences by chatting freely about her family. Wizened and wiry Grandfather Asher, with the patriarchal beard, no teeth and two canes, was, by right of seniority, the leader and mentor of the party. Myra's father, Gideon, lean, sober and untalkative, walked beside the old man. Her mother, with a timid smile, followed with the other older women.

"My grandfather," she said, "is a great one for religion. He thinks of nothing but the Synagogue—and the Temple at the Holy City. He will be talking to you presently, and you'd better show him you're interested, or he'll be annoyed."

They agreed that old people were funny, and should be humored. With her family accounted for, Myra talked about herself, her friends, her harp, her weaving, her sheep-dog, and—demurely, with lowered voice—about handsome young Joel, Jairus' chief vintner, adding in a whisper that her parents, and particularly her grandfather, did not approve of him.

"But you do, I think," said Esther, which brought a pink flush to the girl's cheeks.

"Now let's talk about you, Esther," she said.

This wasn't going to be so easy as it had been for Myra. Esther was an orphan, vaguely related to a family in Bethsaida with whom she had been living recently; but she was so indefinite about her origin that she soon began to seem somewhat illegitimate. Myra came to her rescue by asking if she lived with the woman who had accompanied her to the highway.

"Yes," replied Esther. "Her name is Hannah."

"There was a Bethsaidan woman named Hannah who was supposed to have been healed by that Carpenter when she was at death's door," said Myra, in a tone of incredulity.

Esther nodded. "That was my Hannah," she said. "And it was a miracle. I was there. I saw it."

Myra laid her hand lightly on Esther's arm, and murmured, "Don't let my grandfather hear you say that. He gets very angry. That's what he has against Joel."

They gradually improved their pace, putting a little distance between themselves and the others. Myra wanted to pursue their talk about the Carpenter.

"I never heard him speak; never saw him," she went on. "I wasn't allowed to. But I don't like him because he has come between me and Joel."

"Joel believes in him, then," said Esther.

"He not only believes in him," said Myra. "He has left his job, for days on end, to follow him about! He was gone so often that Jairus discharged him. And my grandfather was glad of it and said it served him right. . . . And then, when it was told that the Carpenter had cured the sickness of little Sharon, Jairus' child, Joel was taken back and his wages were raised. We all thought my grandfather would have a fit."

"Did your grandfather ever see Jesus?" Esther inquired.

"Not he!" rasped Myra. "Grandfather's got it into his head that this Jesus person is down on the Synagogue, and encourages people to break the Sabbath, and consorts with publicans and sinners. You should hear him! . . . I hate religion," she added, angrily. "Any kind of religion!"

"I don't believe you would hate Jesus, if you knew him," said Esther, quietly.

"Well—I'll never know him," snapped Myra. "My family will see to that. . . . Come—let us talk about something pleasant."

So they talked about Joel.

That night they camped at Hammath. The next morning they passed through Cana. Grandfather Asher, learning that this was Esther's first trip to Jerusalem, took her in hand and pointed out memorable landmarks. She listened attentively, but asked no questions that might betray her ignorance of Jewish history. As they passed through Samaria, the old man gathered his flock around Jacob's Well, and told them all about it. It was the first time Esther had ever heard of the hallowed well—or of Jacob; but she managed to show a becoming reverence. Indeed she was much more deeply affected by the story than Myra who patted a yawn and gazed at an excited dog that had chased a cat up a tree.

That afternoon, Asher hobbled forward, grasped Esther's arm and pointed to a distant mountain-peak.

"It was up there," he declaimed, impressively, "that the great prophet Elijah lived! Right up there where you see that notch!"

"Indeed!" murmured Esther.

The old man fell back to inform the others and Myra moved in close beside her friend.

"Tell me more about this wonderful man Elijah," said Esther.

"He lived centuries ago," drawled Myra, "lived alone, and important people came to him for advice. He was very poor. Once he was so hard up that the ravens brought food to him."

"How did they know he was hungry?" inquired Esther.

Myra chuckled, a bit irreverently.

"Because he ate what they thought was good, I suppose. A man would have to be pretty hungry to enjoy a raven's choice of victuals."

"You're incorrigible, Myra!" laughed Esther. "It's a good thing your grandfather didn't hear you say that."

"Yes," agreed Myra. "He wouldn't like it. He dotes on all these old miracle-yarns, handed down from long ago. . . . And Joel can talk of little else than the miracles of his wonderful Carpenter. . . . Me?—I don't believe in any of it! I hate the whole business of miracles!"

At noon on the days the Romans called "Monday," they entered the Holy City through the ancient Damascus Gate and proceeded directly to the Temple, as was the custom of pilgrims to the Passover. Having paid their respects there, the party from Capernaum would go, as usual, to the home of wealthy Uncle Boaz in Bethany. Myra, with the full approval of the family, had invited Esther to be their guest. That would be quite agreeable, they all said, to their hospitable Uncle Boaz.

Jerusalem was very old and showed many battle-scars. The thoroughfare they traveled was a bewildering hodge-podge of dilapidated antiquities built of sun-baked brick, dwarfed by magnificent modern structures in marble. The cobbled street was crowded with all manner of traffic, on foot and on wheels. Camel-caravans and heavily laden donkey-trains pushed the pedestrians to the narrow sidewalks. Beggars whined and thrust out their basins. "Make way there!" barked the mounted patrols in their gaudy Roman uniforms as they cleared a corridor for some haughty procession of black robes. It was very confusing to people from the country.

Myra, who had been here several times before and was able to identify the most prominent buildings, walked arm-in-arm with Esther. . . . There was the Procurator's Insula, a breath-taking achievement in Roman architecture. . . . A little farther on, Myra pointed out the palace of the High Priest, Caiaphas, a massive old weather-beaten pile of marble. It was grim as a fort. The shutters at the high windows were tightly closed. A dozen sentries strutted slowly to and fro on the broad terrace.

"Not very homelike," commented Esther, for something to say.

"It has quite an interesting history," said Myra. "It was formerly the palace of King Herod the Great."

Esther tugged them to a stop for a longer look, wondering what Myra might say if she told her that this was her birthplace.

At length they sighted the Temple. It was the most beautiful building that Esther had ever seen. She stood fascinated, slowly shaking her head in wonderment. Their further progress was at a snail's pace for the street was packed to suffocation. After many long delays they reached the exquisitely sculptured entrance to the Temple Court. Old Asher had found an acquaintance of his own years with whom he was exchanging affectionate hugs and excited greetings. Presently the other old man was whispering some important news into Asher's ear. His eyes widened as he listened. He nodded vigorously. His friend moved on.

It was easily to be seen that old Asher was bursting to tell what he had heard. Gathering his family about him he announced dramatically:

"Galilee will be troubled no more by this Carpenter who has scorned the faith of our fathers! He came to the Temple yesterday and created a disturbance; drove the people's sacrificial offerings into the street; upset the tables of the exchangers who were here to assist the pilgrims! Now the authorities intend to deal with him as he deserves!" Asher scrubbed his thin hands together and grinned happily. "This time," he shouted, "the Carpenter will pay for his disrespect to Israel!"

Esther leaned heavily on Myra's arm and felt her knees giving way.

"You're ill!" muttered Myra, supporting her. "Hold on tight—and we'll get out of here!"

"What's the matter with her?" demanded old Asher, crossly.

"She is fainting," said Myra. "It's so stuffy and hot in here. I'll take her outside. . . . Help me, Father!"

Gideon obediently took the other arm and they half-carried Esther through the jostling pack and out onto the pavement where she revived enough to murmur that she was ashamed to have caused them so much bother.

"We must find a place where you can sit down," said Myra. "I shall take care of her, Father. You go back and join the others. We will meet you in Bethany. I know the way."

Gideon hesitated.

"Your grandfather will be put out, Myra, by your leaving."

"You tell him I'm sorry," she said. "Esther can't go back in there, the way she feels! And I don't want to, myself! It's stifling! It stinks!"

"That," said Gideon, reproachfully, "is not the way to speak about the House of God."

"Forgive me, Father," said Myra, contritely. "I didn't mean to hurt your feelings."

Gideon clumsily patted her arm.

"It is rather close in there," he conceded, as he turned away. "Don't get lost. We will see you at Uncle Boaz' house."

"Your father is so gentle—and kind," said Esther.

"Yes," said Myra, "when my grandfather isn't looking, my father can be quite a darling. Sometimes I wish I knew what he really thinks—about our religion."

They were walking slowly south in the direction of the old Sheep Gate. Although the whole Temple area for many blocks was densely packed, it was so much more quiet here that by comparison the street seemed almost deserted. Esther had recovered from her sudden weakness, but was silent and depressed.

"Tell me, Esther," said Myra, confidentially, "was it really the bad air in the Temple that affected you—or what my grandfather said about the Carpenter getting into trouble?"

"It was a shock, Myra. We were all afraid to have him come here. I hope they don't hurt him."

"If he can do miracles, as they say, maybe he can defend himself."

"I'm sure he could, if he wanted to; but he seems unconcerned about his own safety. He will go to any lengths to help other people, but—"

"Perhaps he has left the city," thought Myra; but Esther doubted it.

"He wouldn't run away," she declared.

They were nearing the twin-towered Sheep Gate now. Hard by, at the end of the street, loomed a grimy old edifice, bearing a peculiar star-shaped roof supported by massive stone columns. On all of its five façades it was open, without walls. Esther inquired what it was and Myra obliged with an amazing story.

The queer old pavilion sheltered a pool. It was commonly believed that an eccentric angel occasionally touched the water, and whoever dived in immediately was cured of whatever disease he had.

"Surely you don't believe that!" said Esther.

"Me? Of course not! But plenty of sick people do; and they lie here all day on the flagging, waiting for this angel. It's quite pitiful! What an angel! Swooping in here, once in a while, to help just one person, and letting the rest suffer!"

They paused on the well-worn steps that led into the cavernous old structure, Esther remarking that apparently the institution wasn't operating today.

"It's usually crowded," said Myra. "I suppose they're all up around the Temple, begging. . . . I see one man over there."

Suddenly Esther clutched Myra's arm and uttered a little cry of surprise. A small group of men sauntered into the building through an opposite entrance.

"Look, Myra!" she whispered excitedly. "There is Jesus! It seems so strange to see him without a great crowd following."

"It's not strange, at all," said Myra, "if he's in trouble. People aren't going to risk being seen with him."

"Come!" said Esther. "I must speak to him!" She took Myra by the hand and tugged her forward. Jesus, somewhat in advance of his little company, was strolling beside the pool, gazing down into the water. He halted now before an emaciated invalid, lying motionless on a mat, and engaged him in conversation. The disciples had gathered around to listen. Esther and Myra, unnoticed, crept in close behind them.

"The trouble is, sir," the sick man was saying, feebly, "whenever the angel comes, those who have very little ailing them, and are more nimble, leap into the pool. . . . My people have been bringing me here, sir, day after day, for many years, to be healed of the palsy; but always another reaches the water before me."

"Come, friend," said Jesus, gently. "You have waited long enough. You may get up now—and go home."

Myra suddenly tightened her grasp on Esther's hand and drew a quick, audible breath like a child's sob. The paralytic was slowly rising to his feet! He was weeping, and incoherently mumbling his thanks.

Peter, turning aside with wet eyes, recognized Esther and came to greet her.

"This is Myra," she said. "I came to Jerusalem with her family. Her father is Gideon, of Capernaum."

"I used to know him well," said Peter. "Your father is an upright man. . . . And your grandfather is Asher," he went on, a little frown creasing his forehead. "Did he come with you?" And when Myra had nodded, rather diffidently, he said, "You have just witnessed a miracle, Myra. Is that not true?"

"Yes, sir!" declared Myra. "That is true!"

"Your grandfather, Asher, is hostile to our Master," said Peter. "Will you tell him what you have seen here today?"

"He would not believe me," said Myra.

"But you will tell him?" entreated Peter.

"I—I don't know, sir," stammered Myra. "It would only make him angry at me."

While this colloquy was in progress, Jesus had sauntered on through the pavilion and was descending into the street, his company following at a little distance.

"I'm sorry we weren't able to speak to him," said Esther, as they moved out into the sunshine. Myra made no reply.

At the corner of the street, they came face to face with him. He smiled and extended his hands to them, saying, "Peace to you, my daughters." Esther warmly clasped one of his outstretched hands and murmured, "Master!"

Myra, visibly perturbed and with eyes averted, nervously toyed with the fringes of her cape. Then, tentatively, her eyes ventured to meet his. They widened and swam with tears. Impulsively she reached for his hand with both of hers, and whispered brokenly, "Will you be my Master, too?"

20

FULLY AN HOUR before sunset on the fourteenth day of Nisan Jerusalem began to go into retirement. It was as if the shadow of some spectral hand had moved across the Holy City invoking silence.

The bazaars and food-markets, seemingly responsive to a prearranged signal, were closing their shutters. Vehicular traffic was rapidly clearing from the streets. The pedestrian throngs were melting away. Only the Roman patrols remained.

Residents and their Jewish relatives and guests from afar were quietly assembling behind closed doors. Even the Gentiles, who had come to Jerusalem on business and were under no obligation to do honor to Jewry's solemn observance, had tethered their camels and were lounging in their tents.

On such a springtime night as this, fifteen centuries ago, the Israelites had escaped from their intolerable bondage in Egypt. On that occasion, according to their sacred Scriptures, the Angel of Death had passed over Land of the Pharaohs, striking down the first-born son of every Egyptian home; and that the avenging Angel might identify the houses to be spared, the Children of Israel had been instructed to sprinkle the blood of a lamb upon their door posts. And while they waited for the summons to depart they stood in silence around their tables, equipped for their adventure, and solemnly ate the sacrificial lamb.

That was "The Passover," and it was still annually commemorated. Perhaps the dramatic event might have been long since forgotten—such is the inconsistency of human nature—had the daring flight to freedom led the fugitives to a permanant peace and prosperity in their "Promised Land." They had not found peace and prosperity. Through the ages they had worn the yokes and chains of many oppressors; but, in spite of their enslavements, or because of them, they dutifully ate the paschal lamb, emblematic of a freedom unachieved but still to come. The Jew was a melancholy optimist. He shed tears over a tragic past, but he had never lost his faith in a triumphant future.

Tonight he was farther from freedom than he had been for at least a century. Even while he devoutly ate the lamb he could hear the ominous jangling of the Roman Empire's armor on the street outside his blood-smeared door.

Grandfather, at the head of the family table, bent with the burden of his years, piously read from the well-worn scroll in his trembling hands, "O Jerusalem, that bringest good tidings, lift up thy voice! Say to the cities of Judah, 'The Lord will come with a strong hand.' "

And while Grandfather read the comforting words, the young Centurion on the street was harshly measuring, in clipped syllables, the well-disciplined foot-beats of his marching legionaries.

"Thine eyes shall see Jerusalem a quiet habitation; a tabernacle that shall never be taken down!" intoned Grandfather.

"Un'! . . . Du'! . . . Tres! . . . Quat'!" barked the Centurion.

*　　*　　*　　*　　*　　*

On a hillside in the country, halfway between Bethphage and Bethany, with no shelter but the spreading branches of an ancient cypress, a company of forlorn men from Galilee sat silently watching the sun go down.

They had made no preparations for a celebration of The Passover, and it was too late now to do anything about it, even if the facilities had been available. They had no lamb, no house, no doorposts to anoint with blood, no roasting-oven, no table.

It wouldn't have mattered—certainly not to the Big Fisherman—had they faced this predicament at home in Capernaum. The Passover had meant nothing to him for many years; not since he was a youngster in his pious father's home; and even then he had regarded the depressing ceremonies with glum indifference. But here, on the outskirts of the Holy City, where the commemoration was so universally and reverently observed, the Jew in Simon, the son of Jonas, felt lonely, lost, expatriated.

"Andy," he remarked to his sober-faced brother, seated on the ground beside him, "Andy, down there in the city are hundreds, perhaps thousands, from all the provinces, who would feel honored to have the Master eat The Passover with them; but are afraid to admit that they are his friends."

Andrew nodded, slowly, but made no reply, and Peter continued, reminiscently.

"Last summer, when they brought their sick ones to him for healing, and were deeply moved by his words of comfort, they wished they might invite him home with them to be their guest. Now that he is in danger—"

Peter's low-voiced soliloquy was interrupted by a little stir immediately behind them. Jesus, who had been sitting quite apart from the silent men, had come forward and reseated himself between John and James. All eyes slowly drifted in that direction.

"We will observe The Passover," he said. "You two brothers will arrange for it. Go now to the highway and proceed through Bethany until you overtake a man who will be entering his home with a pitcher of water on his shoulder. There is an unused upper room in his house. Tell him to prepare it for your Master and his company."

They rose to do his bidding.

"Shall we try to find a sacrificial lamb?" asked John.

Jesus closed his eyes and shook his head.

"The master of the house will provide you with wheaten bread and a flagon of wine," he said. "That will suffice."

"Will we be returning here for the night, Master?" asked James.

"No. Take your blankets with you. After supper we will rest in the Garden of Gethsemane."

"Have you money to pay this man for the use of his room?" inquired Judas, jingling the coin-pouch.

The brothers turned inquiring eyes toward Jesus and he waved them on their way, making no reply to Judas who, realizing that he had spoken out of turn, shrugged and resumed his seat. Young Thad, sitting nearest him, presently came to his feet and strolled over to drape his jacket about old Bartholomew's shoulders; for the sun was setting and the air was chilly.

✲   ✲   ✲   ✲   ✲   ✲

It was a most depressing feast. The fear that had haunted them for many days was now confirmed. The Master told them that the end was near. This, he said, would be their last supper together.

He had preceded them on the road, and when their intuition told them he preferred to walk alone they slowed their steps as he retraced last Sunday morning's journey when he had been attended by the shouting thousands who thought they wanted him to be their King. Under the bright moonlight could be seen the withered palm-branches which the disappointed crowd had flung into the gutters. Peter was blind with tears, and when Philip pointed to the palms, he could only shake his head. There were no words for his grief.

When they arrived at the house where John and James were standing at the gate they found that Jesus had already entered and was waiting for them at the doorway of the upper room. He had provided himself with towels and a basin of water. It was customary, when guests were expected, to station a servant at the door to wash the visitors' dusty feet. The disciples were appalled to find that the Master intended to perform this menial service. Peter, when his turn came, stoutly refused to consent; but yielded reluctantly when Jesus insisted.

They quietly took their places about the table. The supper was not after the manner of the traditional Passover feast. This, Jesus explained, was the inauguration of a new festival. In the days to come, he said, whenever they—and the others who would believe in him—sat together, and the cup was passed among them, they were to remember him as the sacrifice for men's salvation. He would die that all those who believed in him might live.

The words were spoken softly. The disciples were heartsick. Judas slipped quietly out of the room. They were all relieved to see him go. Johnny, sitting beside the Master, now broke completely and cried like a lost child. Jesus put his arm around him tenderly and drew him close. They were all weeping.

"Let not your heart be troubled," the Master was saying. "In my Father's house are many mansions. I go to prepare a place for you, that where I am you may be also."

*   *   *   *   *   *

It was close to midnight when Jesus rose from the table and announced that they would now depart. The evening, despite its sadness, had passed quickly; for the disciples, now awake to the fact that they were presently to be left without his guidance, had many questions to ask of their Master.

And the questions were of a surprising nature. Even in the face of all the instructions they had received concerning a Kingdom-to-come, their last-minute entreaties for reassurance showed how vaguely they had understood. So long as they had had him by their side, walking and talking with him, the future seemed far off, something to be dealt with when they got to it. Now that they had got to it, the future demanded a fresh examination.

Jesus had just finished saying, "You all know where I am going. Though you cannot come with me now, you know the way."

Thomas had spoken up promptly: "But, Master, we do not know where you are going: how can we know the way?"

"I am the way," said Jesus, patiently. "I go to our Father."

"Tell us about the Father," begged Philip, as if he had never heard a word on the subject.

"The Father is in me," said Jesus. "The words that I have spoken are His words. The deeds that I have done are His deeds."

They all nodded their belief that this was true, but their apparent understanding did so little to assuage their feeling of utter desolation that the Master continued, tenderly:

"I shall not leave you comfortless. I shall come to you."

At length they descended the stairs and came out into the moonlight, Jesus pausing to offer a gracious word of thanks to their host who followed them to the gate as if reluctant to see them leave his house.

It was only a short distance to the brow of the hill that overlooked the silent city. Jesus tarried there for a long moment before turning off the highway to the hard-beaten path that wound through the grove of aged olive-trees.

Peter, James and John had followed closely, the others trailing at some distance, not sure what was expected of them. Deep in the shadows of the grove, Jesus turned to the three and asked them to wait there. He went on a little way and knelt in the shadow of a rock. After a while the watchers' eyes grew heavy. For the past few nights they had been too gravely troubled to take their accustomed rest, and this evening's drain on their emotions had left them exhausted. Soon they were stretched on the ground with their heads pillowed in the crooks of their arms, fast asleep.

After an hour of anguished prayer, Jesus returned to them. The little group of men who had known him best and loved him most were unprepared to support him with assurances of their sympathy and affection. He was alone now, without a friend in the world.

*   *   *   *   *   *

The arrest was quite obviously unauthorized and singularly lacking in dignity. It was not conducted by the Roman patrols but by an unofficial rabble under the leadership of the High Priest's butler, Malchus, a Roman.

Malchus, with an ear accustomed to lingering at keyholes, had learned of his eminent employer's decision to hale the Galilean into court; and, thinking to improve his rating in the esteem of Caiaphas, had taken it upon himself to make the capture, which was the last thing that the High Priest desired on the solemn night of The Passover.

There was quite a crowd of them, armed with sticks and stones, as if they were out to hunt down a mad dog and beat it to death. Judas had been shameless enough to come along with the riffraff that comprised the mob. Malchus needed him to identify the victim.

Peter lunged forward and surprised the butler with a savage blow on the head, but Jesus cautioned him against further resistance. He would go with them quietly. Seeing that their captive intended no defense, the crowd became boldly courageous, bound his hands, tugged him roughly down the long hill and through the darkened streets to the palace of the High Priest.

Although it was long past old Annas' bedtime, he was still up. With a dozen or more dignitaries of the Rabbinical College and the Sanhedrin, he had accepted the invitation of Caiaphas to celebrate The Passover with him in his council-chamber. Deep in a discussion of the most feasible procedure to dispose of the Nazarene with a minimum of protest from his adherents, the pundits were suddenly startled by an unseemly clamor in the corridor.

Malchus, exuberant over his conquest and confident of a warm welcome, burst in upon the conclave with his quarry, pushing his disheveled prisoner into the midst of them and presenting him with a proud flourish. "Ecce homo!" announced Malchus, dramatically.

The wise men were stunned to speechlessness. This was not the place, and certainly not the time, to prefer charges against this man; but here he was, and they must do something about him.

"So—you are this Jesus of Nazareth!" snarled Caiaphas, contemptuously.

Jesus said he was; and, after an awkward pause, Caiaphas asked, "What have you been teaching?"

"You might inquire of those who have heard me," said Jesus.

Malchus, standing close beside him, slapped him in the face and shouted, "You should not speak so to the High Priest!"

Ignoring the blow, Jesus continued, "I have not taught in secret, but openly." His eyes swept the group and came to rest on the face of Rabbi Ben-Sholem who seemed annoyed by this searching scrutiny. "Many people," Jesus went on, "could testify as to my sayings."

"The rabble!" squeaked Ben-Sholem, shrilly. "Outlanders! Damascenes! Samaritans! Camel-boys!"

Jesus made no reply to that. A few more questions were asked, but the inquisition lacked spirit. They were all aware that there wasn't much that they could do, and they surmised that Jesus knew it. It had been their intention to bring him to trial before the regularly constituted authorities. This present company could badger him and insult him as long as they liked, and nothing would come of it except damage to their own dignity. It was difficult to decide what to do with him.

Caiaphas ordered Malchus to take the prisoner outside and await further instructions. The command was growled so crossly that the butler,
disappointed over the apparent failure of his effort to ingratiate himself
with these learned men, jostled and jerked the capitve out of the room
to make him share his own inglorious exit. A servant slipped quietly into
the room and upended the tall hourglass on the table at the High Priest's
elbow. It was two o'clock.

After a considerable silence, each man hoping that someone else
might come forward with a promising idea, Obadiah, Chief of the Scribes,
cleared his throat.

"Why not send him directly to Pilate?"

"What?" snorted Caiaphas. "At this hour?"

"He'll still be up," muttered old Nathan, the High Priest's legal ad-
viser. "He'll be drinking and telling bawdy stories all night with the
visiting Legates."

"He might even be pleased with some diversion," chortled old Annas.
"Write him a note, Caiaphas. Tell him we want him to try this fellow—
forthwith!"

"Good!" exclaimed Ben-Sholem. "The whole thing might be over and
done with before the city awakes in the morning!"

"No—it's not that good!" grumbled Caiaphas. "All this business on
Passover night! What will he think of us? If such a note is to go to Pilate,
Father Annas, you may write it!"

"I'm not the High Priest," rumbled the old man. "And what does that
Roman know or care about The Passover!"

"And why should we care what he thinks?" added Nathan. "He will
do what he's told to do."

They all seemed agreed on this. Nathan got out his stylus and wrote
the note, Caiaphas signed it, and Malchus was given his orders. The mob
hurried their prisoner to the Insula.

The Procurator was not only awake but, as Nathan had predicted, was
having a party for the visiting Legates and a Prefect or two who had
accompanied the legions from forts related to their cities.

It was a beautiful night, warm enough to be comfortable out-of-doors,
and the Procurator was entertaining his long-time friends on the spacious
porch of the Insula.

"What now?" he growled, as the mob swarmed up the marble steps.
He scowled at the note that Malchus handed him and stared hard at the
prisoner.

"What evil have you been up to," he demanded, "on a night when you're supposed to be attending to your religious duties? You are a Jew; aren't you?"

It was not a question that could be answered in a word, and Jesus was tardy with a reply. The butler jabbed him in the ribs with his elbow and shouted, "Speak up, fellow!"

Pilate's lip curled.

"And who are you?" he demanded, scornfully.

"My name is Malchus. I am of the High Priest's household."

"Well—you're no credit to it, I must say. Malchus, eh? That doesn't sound Jewish."

"I'm a Roman, sir!" said the butler, with a little more confidence.

"That's unfortunate," snapped Pilate. "Take your hands off the prisoner, and stand aside!" He held the note at arms' length and squinted at it distastefully. "Now, then, Jesus; what's all this about? You're said to be a disturber of the peace. In the name of all the Gods, where—in this quarrelsome country—have you found any peace to disturb?"

The crowd was getting restless, a few of them suspecting—and not without warrant—that the Procurator was more interested in amusing his grinning guests than attending to his business as judge. The muttering in the rear of the pack grew urgent. Somebody shouted, "Away with the Galilean!"

Pilate caught at it.

"Are you a Galilean?" he inquired, and slowly turning his head toward Legate Julian of Capernaum, he winked impishly.

Jesus said that he was a Galilean.

"Then you don't belong here at all," declared Pilate . . . "You—Malchus—or whatever your name is. Take him to the Galilean Embassy —and tell your troubles to Herod Antipas."

There were many angry shouts of "No!" But the Procurator hurled an overhand gesture of dismissal at the crowd—and ordered some more wine. The Chief of the city patrols stepped forward and whispered, "Shall I send a deputation over there to keep order, sire?" To which Pilate replied, indifferently, "No—let the Tetrarch attend to that; unless," he added, "there is disorderly conduct in the streets."

And so—bitterly disappointed and noisily disgruntled—they led Jesus to the Embassy, the crowd increasing as they proceeded. The disciples had fallen far behind the shouting mob, and trudged along, silent, helpless, frightened.

They hammered at the imposing bronze doors of the Embassy until they were admitted, and stormed into the beautiful, high-domed courtroom, yelling impudently for Antipas. All of the disciples edged themselves into the lobby, all but Peter. For a while he stood irresolute and alone on the pavement outside, tugging nervously at his underlip. Then he ambled over to the wide-open gate to the carriage-court and looked in.

There was a pleasant fire burning in the middle of it and a few tall, gaudily uniformed patrols were warming their hands. Peter felt chilly, and advanced toward the fire. The urbane legionaries saw him coming—and grinned. He knew they were amused at his provincial garb. For a moment he had a notion to retreat; but, presuming that the soldiers would laugh scornfully if he did so, he shambled on, feeling himself very much out of place; for the first time in his life an object of derision.

*   *   *   *   *   *

The Vestris had done very well on the voyage up from Gaza; had berthed at one of the new wharves in Joppa shortly after dawn on Thursday. The sister-ships of the fleet had discharged their cargo and were swinging lazily at anchor in the roadstead waiting orders to sail.

Proconsul Mencius and Captain Fulvius limbered up their horses and started on their thirty-mile journey to Jerusalem, intending to break the trip at Ashnah; but after a bad supper and a glance at the guest-rooms of the only inn, they decided to press on. Their horses were fresh and the moon was bright and the highway, all but deserted of traffic, was free of dust. It was half past two when they reached the city.

They were going to put up at Levi's Inn, known to be the best tavern in Jerusalem. It was a little way outside the east gate, on the slope leading up the long hill toward Bethany. As they passed the front of the large, high-walled compound adjacent to the Insula, Mencius wondered whether they might not find better accommodations for the horses in the barracks-stables. It might be worth inquiring about.

Fulvius was too tired to take any interest in this suggestion. He had no taste for a long walk. He wanted to get to bed. Mencius decided to stop at the Insula's stables. Fulvius, with the Proconsul's saddlebags, was to go on and make a reservation for him at the tavern. He would be up later, and see him at breakfast.

They were quite deferential at the military stables; but, "As you can see for yourself, sir, we haven't a stall. Everything full up. But I feel sure there is room in the stables at the Galilean Embassy. It's only a little way; just around the next corner to the right. You can't miss it, sir. Some kind of a brawl going on over there."

"I don't want to get into a brawl," said Mencius.

"It isn't among the horses, sir. Everything will be quiet in the stables."

"What's the racket about?" asked Mencius.

"Oh—they're trying some country preacher for teaching the wrong doctrine," drawled the old hostler. "The horses aren't in it. They've too much sense to get mixed up with a thing like that, sir."

The Proconsul handed the old fellow a couple of shekels, remounted Brutus, and followed directions.

There stood the costly and superfluous Embassy that Herod's rich and worthless son had built to satisfy his vanity. The main part of the imposing structure, fronting the street, was brightly lighted and noisily doing business. From the tone of the excited voices that shrilled through the open windows the litigants were angry. The Proconsul chuckled. You'd never hear such a bedlam as that in a Roman court. No, sir! A Roman court wasn't always fair but it was always orderly . . . A country preacher —being tried for his heresies—at three o'clock in the morning—when everybody was supposed to be sequestered because of The Passover. It was incredible! . . . A country preacher, eh? . . . Could it be possible that this was Voldi's "Torchbearer?" . . . Mencius rode on a block further and found the stables. They were of an architecture consistent with the Embassy, ostentatious to the point of absurdity if not vulgarity; quite appropriate for the official seat of an Ambassador, but too foolishly grand for his horses.

The white marble stables were scrupulously clean, but Brutus had a sharp nose and he was very tired. He needed no urging to turn in. A middle-aged man, whose tunic bore the Embassy's crest, came to the door. The Proconsul dismounted, identified himself, and made his request, which was cheerfully granted.

"My name is Aulus, sir. You've a fine horse there! He deserves the best. The Tetrarch will be pleased to have him here. His Highness is a great one for beautiful horses." Aulus had tugged off Brutus' trappings and was leading him into a roomy box-stall, Mencius following along. "You see that tall, black Arabian in the next box, sir?" chattered Aulus. "He's the latest one. The Tetrarch bought him—for a song—only the day before yesterday."

Brutus had stretched his neck and was nuzzling the oak stanchions that separated the stalls. The black horse moved closer to the partition and nickered softly.

"By Jupiter!" laughed Aulus. "They act as if they were acquainted!"

Mencius walked over to the waist-high door to the adjacent box. Darik turned his head in that direction; and, sauntering to the door, sniffed the visitor's extended hand.

"He's making up with you, sir, better than he has with me," remarked Aulus. "He's not a friendly horse; sort of a one-man horse, as we say."

"The Tetrarch bought him cheap, eh?" Mencius tried to sound casual. "How did that come about? He is a very valuable animal."

Aulus became confidential.

"If you ask me, sir, I think he was stolen. The young Arab who brought him here was in rags and tatters; had no business owning a horse like this. Wanted only three hundred shekels for him. His Highness was quick enough to take him."

"It's a wonder the Tetrarch did not suspect that he was buying a stolen horse."

"Maybe he did." Aulus' crafty chuckle did not improve his royal employer's reputation. "The ragged young Arab is still hanging around. We gave him a job. He's handy with horses. All Arabs are, I guess. That's about all they know; horses. It's a funny thing now about this gelding. He follows the fellow around like a dog. Maybe he did belong to him, though it doesn't sound reasonable."

"Is the Arabian on duty?"

"Just daytime, sir. . . . Thank you, sir. We'll take good care of your horse. Yes, sir!"

The Proconsul was turning toward the door. Aulus, happy over the half-dozen sesterces clinking in his hand, called after him:

"If you stop in the carriage-court, sir, the kitchen-girls will gladly bring you a bowl of hot broth. Might taste good after your long ride."

Mencius told him he was going directly to Levi's Inn and would have his breakfast there. . . . He walked north and halted before the open doors of the noisy Embassy. In the street a score of Roman patrols leaned casually against their long lances, apparently under orders to give no attention to the clamor within the building.

Mencius ascended the steps. The spacious foyer was filled with unpleasantly scented men who apparently had been unable to gain entrance to the courtroom. Mencius joined them. They seemed to be inquisitive spectators rather than partisans, all of them shabbily dressed, probably roustabouts. The Proconsul wore no distinctive uniform; his credentials were in his pocket; but the loafers inferred from his bearing that he was accustomed to being treated with deference, and made way for him as he moved toward the door into the high-ceilinged auditorium.

The place was full of restless, clamorous civilians who seemed to have little in common but their exasperation over the proceedings of the court. A pompous, distinguished-looking man of fifty, in a black robe, presided; or, more correctly, was seated behind the massive table up front where the magistrate would naturally be found. This puzzled man, with the frozen grin, was obviously the Tetrarch, and it was equally obvious that the trial had got completely out of hand. The affair had degenerated into a repulsive travesty.

The defendant was seated in a high-armed, tall-backed, thronelike chair, facing the audience, clad in a scarlet robe absurdly inappropriate to the man's pale, dejected face and slumped posture. A thorn-bush, wound to imitate a crown, had been so roughly forced upon his head that slender streams of blood were coursing his cheeks and spattering the embroidered collar of his royal robe.

It was not difficult to guess what this undignified play-acting was about. The hapless captive was being mocked as a pretender to the throne. But what throne? Mencius could hardly believe his own eyes. Surely this supine young man, with the bearing of a teacher, and the long, slim hands of an artist, could have no kingly ambitions. Apparently he had no following. Nobody championed his cause. Whose throne would he attempt to usurp, even if he had ten thousand troops behind him? Caesar's? Nonsense! Could he have been plotting to supplant Pilate? Ridiculous!

But now the light broke for Mencius! The noisy persecutors who passed before the prisoner, with exaggerated bows of reverence, were satirically hailing him as The King of the Jews! That was it! The young prophet must have identified himself as "The Messiah" who would restore the Kingdom to Israel.

The unhappy Tetrarch appeared now to have had more than enough of the farce. He rose and demanded order. Gradually the racket died down. The crowd seemed expectant of a judicial decision. It was high time, they grumbled.

"Whip him—and let him go!" shouted Antipas.

A storm of protest rose. One enraged zealot mounted a chair and screamed, "To death with him! Nothing less!" The crowd yelled its approval. Antipas held up a hand for silence, and the place grew suddenly quiet again.

"It is not in the province of this court," he declaimed, "to put any man to death."

"Yaa!" shouted the man on the chair. "You sentenced the Baptizer to death—for no reason at all!" The noise was deafening now. . . . The Tetrarch, clearly frightened, wheeled about and disappeared through the small door behind him. The prisoner was roughly jerked from his mimic throne and a thick-set hoodlum with a bull-whip began lashing him cruelly.

The Proconsul's impulse was to leave the disgusting spectacle, but the exit was already blocked and he stood aside to wait. Pandemonium had broken loose in the vicinity of the magistrate's elaborately carved bar. The august tribunal was being wrecked. The Tetrarch would presently learn his rating in the opinion of Jerusalem's unwashed and irresponsible. Costly tapestries were being torn down, broadswords were thrust through the upholstery of the furniture, pikes were gouged into the exquisite mosaic portraits. Even the haughty face of Emperor Tiberius had lost an eye (not that the Proconsul cared a damn).

Pressing into the rioting pack that funneled through the door, Mencius struggled out into the street. A score of the more audacious were attempting to tear down the hoarding and scaffolding from a building under repair across the street; and the legionaries, feeling that enough was enough, were cracking heads and making arrests. The rioters had been free to do what they liked to the inside of the Embassy, but they were not at liberty to set the building on fire.

With no taste for getting himself involved in the brawl, Mencius walked hurriedly north to the avenue of the Insula and turned to the right. Once away from the sight and sound of the frenzied mob, his thoughts turned toward the doomed Galilean. He wished he might have heard the man speak. He had never seen anyone quite like him. Not much wonder that Voldi had been impressed. It was a face that puzzled you; difficult to assign to any category. A profound student? A dreamer? What manner of man was he? A "Torchbearer"? No; Voldi had been clearly mistaken about that. A Torchbearer, with the mind and will of a Plato, a Socrates, or an Aristotle, would never have got himself into such an appalling predicament. He might be a teacher, but that didn't mean that he was a Torchbearer. Whatever light he had thrown upon the path of a few people of the Palestinian provinces would be snuffed out before another sunset. Whose lamp—in backward little Galilee—would shed a reflected glow beyond the borders of his own community?

Anyhow—mused Mencius, bitterly, as he moved wearily up the long slope toward Levi's Inn—the human race didn't want any light; it didn't deserve any light; and it would never be granted any light—certainly not in his time! . . . The world was a disgrace to its maker, whoever he was; or to its makers, whoever they were! It was a wonder it had survived so long in its brutalities. Brutalities? That was not the right word for it. The brutes carried themselves with some dignity!

21

As PETER NEARED the glowing fire he walked more slowly and diffidently, realizing that he had made a mistake to enter the courtyard.

The half dozen tall patrols, self-confident in their brightly polished helmets and scarlet-and-black uniforms, were awaiting his approach with an embarrassing interest. Yet, when he stood among them, taller and heavier than they, he was relieved to see something of friendliness in their faces.

"A chilly morning," remarked the eldest, stepping aside to make room for the massive stranger. Peter agreed that it was, and warmed his hands. "The kitchen-girls will be bringing some mulled wine, presently," said another. "Here they come—now."

And here they came, the girls he had joked with when delivering fish at the Tetrarch's palace in Tiberias on the almost forgotten days before he had left all to follow Jesus. He recognized them instantly, with a sinking heart; the tough little Roman, Claudia; Murza, the cynical Arimathaean; Anna and Leah, the Jewesses.

While still at some distance, Claudia, tripping along with a loaded tray, shouted to the others:

"But look! Murza! Leah! Do you see what I see? It is the Big Fisherman; no less!" They put down their flagons and mugs and honey-cakes on the serving table and swarmed about him with excited little cries. "The Big Fisherman!" Claudia tried to span both hands around his heavily muscled arm, as she had been accustomed to do. The patrols gathered closely about, enjoying the reunion.

"You girls seem to know this Hercules," chaffed the gray-haired soldier.

"Know him!" echoed Claudia. "But of course! And a bad influence he was, too, what with his making sport of all the gods! A quite terrible fellow; no?"

"And what brings you to Jerusalem?" inquired Anna. "I'll warrant it wasn't to eat The Passover!"

Peter hadn't had a chance to put in a word. He stood there grinning foolishly; tugging at his underlip.

"Maybe he's here with this Carpenter," teased Leah—"this man who thinks he's the Messiah."

"That's it!" shrilled Claudia. "The Big Fisherman's gone religious!" They all laughed.

"You know better than that!" growled Peter. "I don't hold with such nonsense!"

"Well—seriously—" said Anna. "What do you think of this Jesus?"

"I have no opinion at all," answered Peter, huskily. "Never met him!"

"They're trying him over there—for blasphemy—and treason!" said Murza.

"Indeed?" grunted Peter. "Well—he's no friend of mine."

The patrols were tiring of this conversation and had edged toward the serving-table, the girls following along. Peter suddenly turned to leave.

"Wait!" cried Claudia. "Have some wine!"

But the Big Fisherman did not wait, and he did not reply. Unsteadily, for he felt sick and his legs were shaky, he made for the gate. Outside, he leaned against the wall, panting and swallowing hard. He walked with uncertain steps, bracing a hand on the wall for support, toward the entrance of the Embassy. Now he could hear the clamor of angry voices. He stopped. The noise subsided. Now came the sound of lashes. They were whipping his Master! He turned about and staggered down the street, still with a groping hand on the wall. His legs were weak and his knees buckled under him at every step. Now he began to cry, the whimpering, retching cry of a badly hurt little boy.

22

NOTWITHSTANDING his weariness, Mencius was unable to sleep. Obsequious old Levi had waited up to conduct the Proconsul to what he asserted was the most comfortable bed in the house; the tavern was quiet, nobody astir; there was no vehicular traffic on the cobbled street. But Mencius lay wide awake, still listening to the bull-whip cutting into the bleeding shoulders of the defenseless Galilean.

It was not because he was unused to the sight and sound of cruel floggings. Roman discipline was harsh and punishments were severe. Three quarters of the Empire's population were slaves. To treat their infractions of the law with any lenience at all was to invite conspiracy and rebellion. Every free-born Roman lived dangerously, alert to the merest hint of insubordination. Corporal punishment, administered in public, was the best medicine for disobedience, far more effective than imprisonment. The brutal scourging of the young Galilean, therefore, would have been— for the Proconsul—just another brutal scourging added to all the brutal scourgings he had witnessed on land and sea throughout the Empire but for the fact that the victim was a man of mystery, a man to be treated with dignity; imprisoned, perhaps; beheaded, perhaps; but not flogged.

Mencius readjusted his pillow and resolved to stop thinking about it. It wasn't his problem, he told himself. It was none of his business. He would go to sleep now. But that whole affair at the Galilean Embassy needed explanation. The noisy prosecution was in the hands of a mob that had no respect for the court although the baffled Judge had utterly disgraced himself to humor the screaming riffraff who apparently had no warrant for the captive's arrest, no formal charges preferred by any recognized authority, and, in short, represented nobody but themselves, which was the same as saying that they represented nobody at all.

It was evident that Pilate, who couldn't help knowing of this shocking abrogation of justice, had decided to keep out of it. But that didn't tally with what Mencius had heard of Pontius Pilate's reputation as a self-respecting Prefect. No Provincial Governor could afford to ignore such an impudent flouting of the law. It would require some very potent behind-the-scenes pressure to persuade the gruff Procurator of Judaea that he must keep his hands off and let the riot run wild. That course, for any Roman ruler, was a direct road to ruin.

Pre-dawn light was breaking now. With an exasperated apostrophe to all the gods, for none of whom he had more than an antiquarian's respect, Mencius rose, dressed, and went softly downstairs to the small patio hedged at the rear of the quadrangle by a rose-garden which extended almost to the high wall that enclosed the area. The roses were softly lighted by the oncoming sun. Mencius strolled toward the garden. A few yards ahead of him, and moving slowly with a furtive glance over his shoulder, was a tall, lean, ragged young fellow who, instead of stepping aside, turned and waited at the wall, thrusting out a dirty hand for alms. Mencius chuckled.

"You might have fooled me with your tatters," he said—"but I knew you were in the city. What's all this about, Voldi, selling your horse to the Tetrarch, and working as a hostler in his stables?"

"Let's step behind these rose-bushes," said Voldi, soberly. "We mustn't be seen together. I've only a moment to stay."

"Very well. Talk fast. I'll listen. What's up?"

Voldi proceeded rapidly with his story.

"Aulus told me where you were, Mencius."

"I was expecting you."

"You know what happened in the night at the Embassy. The mob all but wrecked the building. Antipas is badly frightened, as he need be, and expects to leave within the hour for Tiberias. He has engaged a small detachment of cavalry from the Capernaum Fort to accompany the caravan. He will ride his own horse. I am to ride Darik."

"But you aren't going all the way to Tiberias, I think," put in Mencius, with a knowing grin.

"Probably not. There are bandits in the Samaritan mountains. They may attack us. Our force is small. Someone may get hurt . . . I may be looking for some place to go—in a hurry. . . . What are your travel-plans, Mencius?"

"I'm here to deliver an important letter to one of the visiting Legates. I shall do that this morning. Then I ride to Joppa where my ship is ready to sail. We will wait there until you come."

"Have you room in your hold for Darik?"

"Of course! . . . But I thought you had sold Darik to the Tetrarch?"

"He may not need a horse—after tomorrow night." Voldi was getting restless to be on his way.

"Good luck!" said Mencius, earnestly. "We'll be on the lookout for you. It's The Vestris. New pier number seven."

"If I'm not there by noon Sunday, don't wait any longer; for I'll not be coming. . . . By the way: what's your next port?"

"Gaza—and then home, Will you come with us, all the way?"

"It depends. I don't know. I must go now!"

Mencius clutched his sleeve.

"Your 'Torchbearer' seems to be doomed. Any news about that?"

"Aulus says they carried him off to the Sanhedrin, hoping for authority to try him before Pilate. If they succeed, the trial may be held this morning. . . . Did you see him?"

"Yes—but I didn't hear him speak. I saw him scourged. It's a strange case. I'm full of curiosity about the man. Perhaps I'll go down to the Insula—and see what happens."

"It's all up with him, I'm afraid."

"Doubtless. If Pilate consents to hear the case at all, he will probably accommodate them with a decision. If the Sanhedrin's back of it—"

"That's the trouble. They're in the driver's seat."

"Still think he's 'The Torchbearer'?"

"Perhaps; I don't know."

"Think a Torchbearer would let himself be condemned to death?"

"It's possible! Socrates did! I'll see you on Sunday—I hope."

*   *   *   *   *   *

After a brief breakfast alone, Mencius left a note for Fulvius, before setting forth to the Insula.

"I am leaving early," he wrote, "to attend a trial of peculiar interest in Pilate's Court, the case of that young Galilean who has had the whole country by the ears and is now indicted for blasphemy, treason, and the Gods only know what else. I must see it. You have the Emperor's letter in your baggage and I do not wish to disturb you. Keep it locked. I shall probably return within a couple of hours."

The broad, marble-paved terraces leading to the imposing portico of the Insula were already packed with a scurrying crowd when Mencius arrived. Way was made for him as he advanced to the highest level where the prosecutors waited impatiently with their haggard prisoner, still ar-

rayed in the scarlet finery that had mocked his phantom kingship last
night at the Embassy.

Apparently it was the Procurator's custom to hold open-air court from
the spacious porch, for it seemed to be the focus of interest although still
unoccupied. A huge desk served as the bar of justice; behind it stood a
tall, thronelike chair, flanked on either side with orderly rows of less
conspicuous seats.

On any ordinary occasion Mencius would have felt free—indeed he
would have felt obliged—to enter the Insula and present himself. It would
have been no presumption for a Proconsul to express fraternal greetings to
a Prefect with the assurance of a cordial welcome. In terms of protocol
they were of much the same rating. And should Pontius Pilate learn that
Nicator Mencius had attended a session of his court without making himself known, he could consider it a breach of etiquette. But the extraordinary affair confronting the Procurator of Judaea would be sufficiently
embarrassing, thought Mencius, without adding any more witnesses to
Pilate's discomfiture than were already available.

He surveyed the group of principals that clustered closely about the
captive. There was quite a delegation of scribes, ostentatiously busying
themselves with their papyrus rolls; a detestable breed of prigs and snobs
wherever you found them, in any country. There was a sprinkling of
priests, young ones, mostly, none of them distinguished in appearance.
Evidently the real prosecutors were represented only by proxies. Perhaps
they had conveyed their wishes—and demands—by letter.

Presently a shout went up as the great bronze doors swung open and
the impressive procession of dignitaries filed out into the portico, Pilate
leading in his official robes, followed by a dozen Legates, Prefects, and
other bigwigs. Mencius recognized only a few: there was Julian, who
had been his instructor in tactics at the Military Academy in Rome; Julian
was getting to be an old man, cropped hair white as a rat, wrinkled face
brown as a boot: yes—and there was dapper old Menelaus, Governor of
Petra; Mencius had sailed with him once. . . . And of all things—there was
Prefect Sergius of Caesarea, though why, in the name of every unpredictable God, Sergius would be in Jerusalem at Passover time, was beyond
imagination. Mencius searched the faces for a youngish Legate who might
pass for the obstreperous son of Senator Gallio, but couldn't find anybody
with the probable measurements. . . . The court sat. The crowd quieted.
Pilate, frowning darkly, puffed his lips as he studied the document which
bragged of its importance with a clatter of dangling waxen seals. He
pounded on the massive desk and looked down sternly at the prisoner. At

length he spoke, in a tone so low that it was obvious he didn't care whether the crowd heard him or not.

"It says here that you have made pretense of being a King," and then he added, with fine irony, for the benefit of his Roman guests, "though the Sanhedrin"—Pilate tapped the ornate document with his finger—"assures this court that it will recognize no King but Caesar. Doubtless Emperor Tiberius, when he learns of this, will be pleasantly surprised." The distinguished guests grinned appreciatively. "Now, young man," continued the Procurator, "you do not look much like a King, in spite of your royal garb. Has it been your custom to go about in this ridiculous costume?"

The prisoner shook his head without looking up.

"Has the prosecution anything to say about that?" demanded Pilate.

After some hesitation a young priest admitted sheepishly, "It was put on him at the Embassy, sire."

"Then you will restore his clothing to him immediately," growled Pilate. "This court, probably lacking in humor, is in no mood for buffoonery."

There was some delay before the defendant's brown homespun robe was found. His back, when they bared it, bore deep lash-wounds, still bleeding. Pilate's sharp eye may have seen the prisoner wince, may have seen the people stare, for he commanded the Galilean to turn around.

"It would appear," he said, "that the prisoner has been already tried, convicted, and punished. By what process of law has he now been brought into this court? Has he then committed some fresh crime since his case was judged?"

Nobody volunteered to answer this question, but an ominous rumble of dissatisfaction rose from the densely packed throng. Pilate glanced again, with distaste but something of anxiety, at the indictment. Mencius, studying the Procurator's expression, gathered that the document worried him. Putting down the papyrus on the desk, and leaning forward on his folded arms, Pilate asked:

"Are you, then, a King?"

"I am!"

It was the first time that Mencius had heard the Galilean speak and the tone of his voice produced a peculiar sensation. The words were crazy enough but the man who spoke them was not crazy. The voice was calm, respectful but self-confident. Evidently Pilate had been similarly affected, for his face remained soberly attentive. The murmuring in the crowd had ceased.

"Tell us about your Kingdom," said Pilate. "Where is it?"

"My Kingdom," replied the Galilean, "is not of this world."

He paused. Pilate listened. The multitude was silent.

"Proceed," said Pilate. "Your Kingdom is not in this world, you say. Where then is it?"

"My Kindgom is not of this world, but it is in this world for all who seek truth. They who love truth hear my voice—and understand what I say."

The words were not spoken in the strident tone of a demagogue. Mencius had a feeling that the Galilean was talking to him personally. Perhaps Pilate felt the same way. The Romans who sat on either side of the Procurator were leaning forward. Nobody was smiling.

"Truth," mused Pilate, half to himself. "What is truth?"

There was no reply to that. The Galilean faced the Procurator squarely for a moment and then averted his eyes, closed them, smiled briefly, and shook his head, as to say that this was not the time or the place to explain truth.

The spell that had gripped the crowd suddenly lifted now, and impatient voices rose in angry demand for a decision. Pilate pounded for order and didn't get it. He rose and shouted for silence in the court and there was a momentary cessation of the tumult.

The defendant, he said, was apparently innocent of any wrongdoing. There was no evidence that he had committed a crime. He had already been severely punished. . . . But the crowd would have none of it. "Away with him!" they yelled. "To death with him! Crucify him!" The frantic shouting rose to a concerted roar! "Crucify! Crucify!"

Pilate sat down heavily. His hand shook as he beckoned to one of the guards, and flung an order over his shoulder. Presently the guard returned with a silver basin of water. Pilate turned back his sleeves. . . . That settles it, thought Mencius. The Procurator is helpless—and has given in. He will wash his hands of the whole affair. After all—Pilate wasn't there to quarrel with Jewry but to keep the peace, or at least the semblance of it. He could save the Galilean only at the risk of his position, already precarious enough. Pilate dipped his hands in the water, and the crowd cheered. . . . Mencius had seen enough now, and wanted out of the snarling pack. He turned about and worked his way to the street, intending to return at once to Levi's Inn and deliver the Emperor's message to the Legate from Minoa.

On the corner, across the street, stood a little group of forlorn and frightened men, garbed in simple, country dress. Mencius guessed that these despairing people might be the helpless friends of the doomed man from Galilee. He crossed over and joined them. They were too preoccupied with their grief to notice his presence among them. One huge, middle-aged man, towering over the others, with streaming eyes and a contorted face, stood beating an open palm with a clenched fist, breathing in audible gasps like an exhausted runner.

There were a few weeping women in the company, two of them quite young and attractive in spite of their red and swollen eyes.

Now the crowd at the Insula was breaking up, coming apart, and a platoon of Roman legionaries marched through and down the terraced steps. The Commander, with the insignia of a Legate, was a handsome young fellow with an exaggerated military bearing which Mencius surmised was not quite natural for him. No—he was tipsy; that was the trouble; and doing his best to walk straight. A few paces in advance of him strutted a grizzled veteran bearing a banner. Mencius recognized it as a duplicate of the old rag that used to hang limp and listless over the big gate at the Fort at Minoa. So—it was young Gallio, then, who had been given this disgraceful job. . . . Now came the prisoner, towed by a rope, and not gently, for the legionaries were marching with long strides. The rabble pressed closely. There was very little shouting now. They had got what the Sanhedrin wanted. Everybody would be satisfied now; the money lenders, the landlords, the grafters; yes, and the Temple that couldn't afford to offend anybody with property.

As the captive was tugged past his weeping friends, he turned his face toward them compassionately. They slowly followed the crowd with irresolute steps as if they were uncertain what to do; all but the gigantic fellow who turned the other way and began to walk rapidly, lurchingly, toward the west. Apparently he had no mind for attending the execution. Mencius followed him with his eyes, trying to contrive a story that might explain the man's conduct. Was he, for all his physical strength, a coward? Or had the condemnation of his hero driven him to utter stampede? . .
Now a youngish chap, who had been in the company of the Galilean's friends, hurried past in the direction taken by the big man. Mencius expected the young fellow to overtake him, but he made no effort to do so. He continued to follow at a distance.

There was no occasion now for any hurry in the delivery of the Emperor's message to Marcellus Gallio, whose day's work had been cut out for him. It would take hours to complete it. Mencius had never seen a crucifixion, and didn't intend to see one.

He walked the short distance to the Embassy stables. The place was practically deserted. A hostler saddled Brutus and led him out. Mencius mounted and started for the inn. The usual traffic clattered in the street. Jerusalem had resumed her customary activities. The food-markets were crowded with shrilly bargaining shoppers. Somewhere, in an out-of-the-way place, nails were being driven through the hands and feet of a man whose only offense was his confessed devotion to the truth. The quarreling markets, with their short measures, short weights, short change, and short tempers, were still doing business in the old way, the merchants trying to sell bad produce and the customers trying to pay for it with bad coinage; and had any one of them adhered to the truth—either as a buyer or seller—he would soon have nothing left but his impractical idea. The truth was a luxury that nobody could afford. Mencius himself—he had to admit—couldn't afford it: a Proconsul must be diplomatic. Pontius Pilate couldn't afford it: a resolve on his part to abide by the truth would have meant his prompt recall from his Prefecture. And had old Tiberius decided to tell the truth he would have lost his Empire. It was that kind of a world.

The brave Galilean, reflected Mencius, had accomplished nothing. He had thrown away his life to no purpose at all. The world wasn't ready to hear his voice. There never had been a time, in human history, when the world would have listened to his voice. And—there never would be such a time. It was too much to expect. Humanity had no capacity for moral grandeur. This Jesus had misjudged the world. By sunset, this evening, he would be dead and buried. And by next week he would have been forgotten, except by a little handful of little people in a poverty-cursed little hinterland.

*   *   *   *   *   *

It was mid-forenoon. The sun was hot. Esther and Myra were slowly plodding up the long hill to Bethany. They walked in silence, for they were physically and emotionally exhausted: they had wept until they could weep no more.

As for Myra, however deeply she grieved over the soul-sickening tragedy, she still had her family to go back to—and Joel. She was definitely on Joel's side now, whatever her grandfather might say. . . . For Esther, everything was lost. The Master, for all his superhuman power, had been led away to die. He had saved others but he had been unable to save himself. Not a friend had come to his aid. Even Peter had run away.

In a day or two, Myra would return to her home and friends in Galilee. Esther had no home. There would be no reason for her returning to Galilee. Hannah didn't need her. And she wasn't sure that she wanted ever to see Peter again.

As a guest in suburban Bethany, Esther might have known nothing of the dreadful night and tragic morning that had befallen Jesus until it was all over, had not an expected friend of Myra's Uncle Boaz—who had met with a delaying misadventure on his long journey from Askelon—arrived at daybreak with the appalling news.

Grandfather Asher's high-pitched voice had roused the house. Habitually an early riser, Asher had been the first to hear the report. The Sanhedrin was sending the Nazarene blasphemer to Pilate's court this morning to be tried for treason. And that, shouted the old man, would finish him! And it was about time!

Uncle Boaz hadn't been much stirred by the announcement, and when his excited father declared he was going to the Insula to hear the trial he had cautioned him against it. "It's a long trip. It will be a hot day. There will be much confusion."

"But I cannot miss this, my son! I want to see this troublemaker finally disposed of! A day to remember! An historic occasion!"

Esther listened with a sinking heart. She felt she must go. Myra had tried to dissuade her; and, failing of it, decided reluctantly to go along. They did not wait for Grandfather Asher, but left the house through the patio and the garden gate. They sped through Bethany, down the hill, into the awakening city—and on to the Insula. A great crowd of clamorous men had massed there at the entrance. The girls did not venture into the angry throng, but crossed the street and waited. Huddled together at the corner were the disciples. But why were they not beside the Master? There was Peter, wide-eyed, haggard, gnawing at his lip. Surely Peter could have been depended on to stand by the Master, even at the risk of his life! Esther could not believe her own eyes.

Terrible things, incredible things were happening now. A savage voice had screamed, "Crucify him!" The mob instantly echoed it, "Crucify him! Crucify him!" The words mounted into a horrifying chant, "Crucify! Crucify! Crucify! . . . ." There was a sudden silence; then a wild cry of victory! The mob spilled over the terraces and cascaded into the street. A company of Roman soldiers marched rapidly down the steps, tugging Jesus by a rope. The crowd closed in behind them. Now the bewildered disciples followed; all but Peter who was running away! Young Thad had taken after him.

Myra cried that she could bear no more, and entreated Esther to return with her to Bethany. There was nothing they could do. But Esther caught her by the hand and pulled her along into the procession. At the next corner, a dozen men came in from a side street bearing a heavy piece of timber about twelve feet long with a cross-bar dissecting it near the top.

The parade halted. Esther, still dragging Myra by the hand, forced her way toward the front. The roughhewn cross had been laid on the Master's shoulder. He staggered under its weight and sank to his knees.

A burly lieutenant, sighting a tall, heavily-built man standing among the spectators, shouted, "You, there! Put a shoulder under this cross, and help the man carry it!"

"That I will not!" boldly boomed the big man. "I am a free-born Roman citizen! And this is no affair of mine!"

"We'll see about that!" shouted the young Commander. "What's your name, fellow? And where do you come from?"

By this time the crowd had grown quiet, expectant. It was not customary to talk back to a Roman officer.

"My name, sir, is Simon. I live in Cyrene, a ten days' fast journey from here, in North Africa. I am in Jerusalem on business, with a caravan of herbs and spices. I protest that you have no right to impress me into this degrading service."

In spite of his tragic predicament, Jesus was listening sympathetically to the Cyrenian's courageous self-defense. He gave the big man a friendly look of compassion. . . . Then, to the surprise of the soldiers, the bluster-ing Cyrenian stepped forward and shouldered the cross. Jesus smiled his gratitude, and made a feeble attempt to help.

"No," said Simon, kindly. "I shall carry it. You have quite enough to bear today."

The procession moved on. Esther and Myra stood, for a little while, watching. Then they turned and silently went their way. Near the top of the long hill they sat down to rest under an ancient olive tree.

"I have just now decided what I shall do, Myra," said Esther. "I am going back to find my old nurse, Ione. She is in the southern mountains of Arabia. If she still lives, perhaps I can do something for her."

"You mean—you would go alone—all that long way?"

"It would be safe enough, I think. I would keep to the main high-ways—and stop at night in the homes of farmers." Esther elaborated her plan. She would provide herself with some inexpensive trinkets—and be a peddler. . . . Yes—and she would try to find a tame little donkey to carry her pack. Proceeding from village to village, in the daytime, no harm would befall her.

"You will need money," cautioned Myra.

"I have money," said Esther. "Not much—but enough."

Myra remembered having seen a sign on a paddock gate, a little further up the road, announcing a donkey for sale. Esther came to her feet, eager to find the place. They stopped before the gate and a middle-aged man came toward them. Was it true, Esther inquired, that he had a donkey for sale.

"What do you want with a donkey?" he asked, suspiciously. "Do you live hereabouts?"

"No," said Esther, "I want a donkey to carry a light pack for me—on a journey—many miles away."

"When are you going?"

"Early tomorrow morning."

"Very well, you may have him—for ten shekels—if you take him at once!" The man went into the stable and led out a little white donkey.

"What's the matter with him," asked Esther, "that you are selling him for ten shekels?"

"There's nothing the matter with him," said the man—"except that I don't want to be involved in any trouble. If you're going away, you won't be bothered. But I lent him to a man, a few days ago, who is accused of treason; and I don't care to be mixed up in it. And you'd better not go through the city when you leave!"

Esther produced the money and the man handed her the halterstrap. The little donkey sniffed at her hands.

"His name is Jasper," said the man, as he turned toward the house.

*   *   *   *   *   *

Mencius tied Brutus to a hitching-rack in the stable-yard of Levi's Inn and found Captain Fulvius lounging in his room. Briefly he recounted the events of the morning, Fulvius listening attentively. When he had made an end of it, the Captain, who had been fascinated by the story of Voldi's dangerous errand, inquired, "But suppose the youngster sees a chance to do his work while they are in camp tonight? In that case he would flee at once, and arrive in Joppa many hours before the time he had set. They would have no authority to take him aboard *The Vestris*; and there he would be, without protection; possibly pursued."

"You are right!" said Mencius. "I had not thought of that. Perhaps I had better leave at once for Joppa, and make sure he doesn't get into trouble."

"How about the Emperor's message?" queried Fulvius. "This young Legate Marcellus will be occupied most of the day."

"Do me a great favor, Captain," entreated Mencius. "Take charge of the letter. See that it gets into the Legate's hands as soon as he has returned to the Insula."

Fulvius consented, without enthusiasm, and the Proconsul set out on his journey. Once out of the city's congested streets, Brutus was encouraged to a brisk canter. At the village of Emmaus, twelve miles to the west, he drew up before a tidy-looking inn for something to eat. The place was doing a thriving business today. In the paddock a dozen or more beautiful horses were tied, all of them a glossy black, their saddle-blankets bearing the familiar Roman device, the fasces.

In the center of the dining-room there was a long table surrounded by a dozen fine-looking patrols, impressive in their black-and-scarlet tunics. By a front window Prefect Sergius sat alone. He rose with a welcoming smile, an action that brought his stalwart guards instantly to their feet.

"By all the Gods, Mencius!" he exclaimed. "So it was you then, and not your ghost, that I saw in Pilate's loathsome congregation this morning! . . . Do sit down and we will find you something to eat."

The old inn-keeper shuffled up and put a bowl of steaming lentil soup and a plate of small barley loaves before the new guest.

"Yes, I was there, Sergius," said Mencius, soberly. "It was a disgraceful affair; was it not?"

"Shocking!" agreed Sergius. "A sad tragedy for the young fellow from Galilee, but worse for the Procurator. By this time the hapless Galilean will be dead and out of his trouble, while Pilate's disaster is still to come. The canny old men of the Sanhedrin now know that they have him saddled, bridled, and ready to ride whenever they like."

. "Didn't they know that before?"

"Not so definitely. Pilate has been walking his tight-rope with something like dignity. Today he lost his balance. They had no case at all against that inoffensive young dreamer, and they knew it. And they knew that Pilate knew it. Everybody knew it. They demanded the Procurator to commit a murder, and he did it. . . . What I can't understand, Mencius, is the terrific volume of malice hurled at that defenseless Galilean. . . . A King? Absurd! Imagine that supine young philosopher—or fool—or whatever you like—attempting to lead a revolution! Imagine him on a horse! Imagine him directing a charge of ten thousand bowmen!" The Prefect waved it all away with his spoon. "The Sanhedrin has too much sense to believe that this country preacher threatened their prestige."

"Better not be too sure about that," cautioned Mencius. "All you saw of the Galilean, this morning, was an utterly exhausted, blood-smeared young idealist on his way to execution. The fact is: this man has demonstrated supernormal power. Thousands have followed him about through the provinces. There is plenty of good evidence that he has healed the sick, the blind, the crippled."

"Pouf!" railed the Prefect. "I don't believe these tales, and neither do you! Such things don't happen. . . . Who told you?"

"I was informed by the last man in the world who could be taken in by a trickster. . . . Do you remember that rich young Arabian who came with me to Caesarea, after he had saved my life in a fight?"

"Do I?" Serguis laughed aloud. "I had to lock the youngster up to make sure he wouldn't murder our precious Tetrarch."

"And turned him loose, later, to go wherever he pleased, and do what he liked, with your blessing," grinned Mencius.

"Well—Antipas isn't fit to live," mumbled Sergius, defensively, "but I couldn't have him assassinated while under my protection. When he was out of my custody, I didn't care what happened to him. . . By the way, what became of your handsome cut-throat? Did he return to Arabia?"

Mencius nodded, and for a moment Sergius thought there might be further information on that subject, but the Proconsul was attentive to his food.

"I'm rather surprised that your Voldi hasn't tried to settle Arabia's claim on Antipas. The boy seemed not lacking in courage. My Felix became greatly attached to him."

"What's Felix doing?" inquired Mencius.

"He's in Rome, attending the Military Academy."

"Good! I'll look him up when I get home. . . . Reverting to this mysterious Galilean, Sergius, I'm no more gullible on the subject of miracles than you are—or my cynical young Arab who isn't interested in anything but fine horses, sharp steel, and good sportsmanship. But there can be no doubt that this Jesus performed some remarkable deeds, quite beyond human understanding."

"Very well! Very well!" barked the Prefect impatiently. "Have it your own way! For sake of argument, let us say that these wonder-tales were true. Let's concede that the Galilean gave sight to the blind, ears to the deaf, new legs to the cripples. Let's say he cured leprosy—and raised the dead! Where does that leave you? Why didn't he try to help himself to-day? Either he had superhuman power, or he didn't! If he had it, he could have exercised it! Instead of standing there, helpless, roped like an animal on the way to slaughter, he could have pointed a finger at Pilate and stiffened him into a cataleptic fit!"

"There you are!" Mencius brought his fist down hard on the table. "That's where the mystery mounts! Let us say that the man was no ordinary creature; that he did possess superhuman power: that he had a commission to improve the world's way of living. Let us conjecture that he performed these miracles of healing solely to attract an audience, and give the public a valid reason for believing that he spoke with divine authority! All he asked of them was that they treat one another with kindness. That, he said, would cure the world of its afflictions." Mencius paused.

"Well—go on!" prodded Sergius. "You haven't answered my question yet."

"We're coming to that—now. Let us say that it finally dawned on this Torchbearer that the world wasn't ready to receive the light. Men were too selfish and greedy to make the experiment. Everybody wanted peace and prosperity; nobody would do anything to earn it. Next-door neighbors quarreled and fought, blood-relatives hated one another, the religious sects were contemptuous of other beliefs.

"He looked about him and found that every institution in the world was at enmity to his proposed Kingdom of truth and good will, and peace. No government wants peace, Sergius! Which one of us would have a job if good will became popular? Can you imagine the Empire taking steps toward peace? . . . Why, a wave of decency among men would wreck the Empire! . . . What would become of the temples, the shrines, and the Gods themselves, if humanity suddenly decided to be honest and merciful? No man would need to howl for somebody to save his soul from hell if he lived a life of rectitude! . . . But—it was a lost cause! . . . And so," concluded Mencius, "the messenger gave it up as a hopeless job!"

"That's certainly a fantastic theory," commented Sergius.

"It's better than none," said Mencius.

"Let me ask you—" The Prefect regarded the Proconsul with a sly grin. "Would you, yourself, have adopted this soft and silly program of patting everybody on the back—slaves and all—and being kind?"

"Of course not!" declared Mencius. "I couldn't afford it. I'd soon be on the street in rags, begging my bread."

"Then—the Galilean's theory is no good?"

"Apparently not. And that's why he gave it up. You wondered why he didn't stand up for himself, this morning. My solution is that he saw it was no use. The world wasn't ready for it."

"Do you think it ever will be, Mencius?" The Prefect was pushing back his chair.

"Frankly, no! One would think that whoever devised the world might have something better in store for it than hunger, slavery, and bloodshed, but—"

"But—meantime," grinned Sergius, "you will continue to bring copper for our invasion wharves, so that we may raise all hell with these poor Jews. . . . You're quietly losing your mind, Mencius. You think too much.

You'd better accept things as they are. The world's a pretty grim show, but it's the only world we've got. . . . Shall we go now?"

They preceded the patrols to the paddock, mounted their horses, and rode for some distance in silence.

"You haven't told me what brought you to Jerusalem," said Sergius.

Mencius told him briefly about the Emperor's message to Marcellus which Captain Fulvius would deliver before the day was over.

"What do you suppose it was about?" wondered Sergius.

Mencius had no idea, but surmised it might be a recall to Rome.

"The old man probably wouldn't order Marcellus to go hang himself," he said.

"He's crazy enough to do that," remarked Sergius. "It was a dirty assignment that Pilate gave the boy," he added, wincing. "But it's doubtful if the Legate will have much to do with it, personally. Those tough rascals from Minoa will know how. Marcellus was tight as a drum. . . . I was to have stayed for the banquet tonight, but begged off. Pilate will not have a very happy time, I'm thinking. He'll have a load on his mind."

They were nearing the fork in the highway, the road to the right leading to Caesarea, straight ahead to Joppa. Their horses were slowed to a walk.

"Give my regards to my boy," said Sergius.

"I shall do that—with pleasure," said Mencius.

"When do you expect to be home?"

"In seven weeks, if all goes well."

"Well—good luck—and fair weather."

They rose in their stirrups and exchanged a formal salute, for the benefi. of the observant patrols. Spurs were put to the horses and the distance between them rapidly widened. Mencius was glad to be on his way. He had had a most distressing experience in Jerusalem and hoped he would never have an occasion to visit the Holy City again. In seven weeks he would be at home with his family. . . . It would have appalled him if he had known that in seven weeks he would be back in Jerusalem again, on an errand of such mystery that even he himself did not know who had summoned him—or why.

*   *   *   *   *   *

All that forenoon, Thad had followed Peter, making no effort to catch up with him, but keeping him in sight. It wasn't like Peter to be running away. Perhaps his grief over the Master's plight had gone to his head.

Well—whatever it was that ailed Peter, he needed someone to look after him. There was nothing more that could be done for Jesus.

Peter had walked fast, with long, lurching strides, until the Damascus
Gate was reached. Then he began to run. It was not easy for Thad to keep
up with him. Sometimes Peter would fling himself down by the roadside,
with his head buried in his arms; then he would wearily drag himself to
his feet, and hurry on.

At the village of Lebonah, Thad bought a half dozen small wheaten
loaves and a few smoked perch. Peter was out of sight when he took to
the road again, and it was all of a mile further before he overtook him. It
was mid-afternoon now. Peter was lying, face downward, under a cypress
tree. Thad approached quietly and sat down on the ground a few feet
away.

After a long time, the Big Fisherman sat up. His eyes were swollen
and bloodshot. Thad silently opened his knapsack and offered the food
he had brought. Peter shook his head.

"You shouldn't have followed me, Thad," he said, hoarsely. "Don't
touch me! I am unclean!"

"You mean—you're—a—leper?" mumbled Thad.

"Oh—my boy—if that were all!" moaned Peter.

"What's the trouble, sir?" begged Thad.

Tears were streaming down Peter's cheeks.

"I denied my Master!" he cried. "They asked me if I was his friend—
and I said, No! . . . Go back, Thad! Join the others! I'm no fit company
for you! Go back, I tell you!" And, with that, Peter rose, and staggered on
toward Galilee.

And Thad, bewildered, heartbroken, continued to follow him.

                    *   *   *   *   *   *

Shortly after noon, Joseph of Arimathaea called at the Insula and asked
to see Pilate. He was informed that the Procurator was resting and must
not be disturbed. Joseph insisted that the matter was urgent. After a
considerable delay, he was shown into the council-chamber where Pilate
sat at his desk, blear-eyed and sullen.

"Well, Joe," muttered the unhappy Procurator, gruffly, "what is it?"

"I want permission, sire, to bury the Galilean—when he is dead."

"Friend of yours, Joe?"

Joseph nodded, slowly.

"At a distance, sire," he said. "I was not a follower. I did not have the
courage. But—I want to put him away—in my own tomb."

"Perhaps you think the Galilean was unjustly convicted," rasped Pilate,
crossly.

"I am not here to criticize," murmured Joseph.

"But you think the man was innocent," said Pilate. After a pause, he added, impulsively, "So do I, Joe! . . . But—what could I do?"

"May I have his body, sire?"

The Procurator picked up his stylus and wrote a brief order.

"Give that to the Legate from Minoa."

The door was quietly opened, and the Captain of the Insula Guard approached the desk.

"A small delegation is here, sire, sent by the Sanhedrin," he said.

"Very well," muttered Pilate, wearily, "bring them in."

The spokesman, a youngish priest, bowed deeply, and said:

"The writing, sire, that we requested, is misleading."

"What writing?" demanded Pilate, irascibly.

"That we nailed at the top of the cross, sire. You wrote, 'This is the King of the Jews.' It is misunderstood. We would like you to write, 'He said he was the King of the Jews.'"

"Do your own writing!" shouted Pilate, angrily. "I have written enough! Quite enough! Let me hear no more of it!" He beat the desk with both fists. "No more of it—I tell you!"

The delegation bowed itself out. Joseph rose to go.

"Farewell, sire," he said, "and thank you!"

Pilate, glumly preoccupied, nodded, but made no reply.

The Angel

"You're not being summoned by a mere Emperor, Simon. You might defy Caesar: you might hide from him. But you will obey my Master. He wants you in Jerusalem on the Day of Pentecost — and you will be there!"

"And who is your Master?" demanded Simon.

"You know him," said the youth. "You carried his cross."

23

HARD ON THE HEELS of the shocking news that Jesus had been crucified bounded the incredible story that he was alive again.

The provinces couldn't believe their ears. In areas where he had spoken and healed the sick all work was suspended. Nothing else was talked about; nothing else mattered.

Nor was this excitement contained within the confines of Jewry. The mysterious Galilean had for so long been a popular topic of conversation that his fame had filtered into all the surrounding countries. His sayings and doings had been discussed not only all the way from Damascus to Petra and from the Jordan to the Sea, but up in far-away Cappadocia and down in farther-away Ethiopia.

It was not true, as Proconsul Mencius had surmised, that the extraordinary career of the wonder-working Carpenter was a localized phenomenon observed only by the farmers, vine-dressers and fishermen of Israel's hinterland. Mencius was to discover presently that the slaves who tugged at the heavy oars in his cargo-ships had heard of Jesus and his forecast of a Kingdom in which all men of good will would be free.

The stunning news of Jesus' death and restoration to life had got off to a swift start. Ordinarily the long caravans that regularly plodded to and fro between the interior and the ports were the common carriers of current doings. They were notorious gossips, in a class with the wandering minstrels in respect to their reliability. And had the astounding story of Jesus' resurrection been caravan-borne, it may be doubted whether many sensible people would have believed it. But this news had outsped the caravans. At the end of Passover Week all the highways and their tributaries were full of travelers and all the travelers were full of talk.

First on the roads were the Gentile merchants from distant places who

425

had no compunctions about beginning a journey on the Sabbath Day. They told of the crucifixion. Next came the Jewish pilgrims who had set off for home at daylight on Sunday. They sadly confirmed the earlier reports of the Gentiles. Then, later in the forenoon, the confounding stories of the resurrection started on their journeys, moving forward at various speeds, hour by hour and day by day, on foot, on horseback, on camelback, in donkey-carts, in litters, in chariots, in ferry-boats and deepwater ships, until everybody for a thousand miles in all directions had heard that the crucified Galilean wonder-worker had come alive!

It was the first time in anyone's experience that good news was startling; the first time that good news was news at all. Life was uncertain for every man, but Death was not. When men died they were permanently dead. Nobody was exempt; not even the Caesars, who claimed to be divine. Now it appeared that a penniless carpenter had overcome Death. He had more power than the Emperor. Not everyone believed the story, but everyone talked about it. Even those who shook their heads wished they could believe it; hoped it was true.

There were various versions of the story. Reduced to its simplest form: certain women, devoted followers of the Master, had gone out at dawn on Sunday to the beautiful Garden of Sepulchers to anoint the mangled body with myrrh. They had found the tomb open and empty. Then they had seen him, strolling among the flowers. After a tender moment of ecstatic recognition the women were told to notify "my disciples—and Peter."

* * * * * *

Proconsul Mencius was restlessly pacing the wharf when Captain Fulvius arrived at twilight on Saturday evening accompanied by the Legate from Minoa, his slave, and a half dozen cavalrymen.

"We are taking Legate Marcellus Gallio with us to Rome," explained Fulvius as he wearily dismounted. Lowering his voice, he added, "Don't expect too much of this boy. He's out of his head."

Introductions were attempted unsuccessfully. Young Gallio, pale, haggard and bewildered, made no effort to be gracious.

"The Legate is ill, sir," interposed Fulvius. "I shall show him to his quarters at once." He beckoned to the slave who collected their luggage and followed his badly befuddled master. Mencius reflected that he had never seen a more perfect specimen of physical manhood than this handsome Greek. In a few moments Fulvius reappeared on deck and took the Proconsul aside.

"What a day!" The Captain mopped his perspiring brow. "First chance

I had to deliver the Emperor's letter was at Pilate's banquet, last night, for the visiting officers."

"And Marcellus read it—and lost his balance?" wondered Mencius.

"He had already lost his balance. He was dazed, dead on his feet, utterly indifferent to the Emperor's message ordering his return to Rome. He inquired when we were sailing and asked if he might go along." Fulvius shook his head. "It's beyond me. I tried to talk to him today. All he would say was, 'Were you out there?'"

"Maybe the crucifixion was too much for him," suggested Mencius.

"He's used to the sight of bloodshed."

"The slave seems intelligent. Think he knows what ails the Legate?"

"Perhaps. He is worried about him. I told the Greek we weren't sailing directly to Rome and he replied, 'There's no hurry.'"

"He probably wants the Legate to have time to recover his senses before he meets the Emperor," thought Mencius.

Fulvius chuckled.

"Old Tiberius may like him better if he is a bit crazy. . . . By the way, you haven't heard anything from your Arab?"

"It's hardly time yet."

"Looks like an interesting voyage," drawled Fulvius, "with a crazy man in one cabin and a fugitive in another."

* * * * * *

Late in the forenoon on Sunday, Voldi cantered up the wharf to the ship's side. Somewhere along the line he had abandoned his rags and tatters, and was well clad in riding clothes and boots. He was in good spirits.

"It was just as I expected," he explained. "At dusk, last night, our caravan was set upon by bandits. There was some hard fighting, but we drove them off. We lost a few men, among them the Tetrarch himself. Somebody killed him with his own dagger."

"Perhaps you'd better go aboard," advised Mencius, soberly.

"It's a good idea," agreed Fulvius.

In a few minutes The Vestris was inching away from the dock and her sails were creeping up the tall masts. Darik and Brutus, in adjoining stalls, were rubbing noses. The other ships of the fleet were winching up their anchors and hauling up canvas.

Voldi rejoined his Roman friends on deck. A slave brought them their luncheon. Mencius grinned mischievously and remarked, "You stole the Tetrarch's horse."

"Not at all!" protested Voldi. "I stuffed the coin-pouch, containing the three hundred shekels, into the Tetrarch's pocket."

"And so—" said Fulvius, solemnly, "you and the Tetrarch are square."

"Right!" declared Voldi. "And the Tetrarch and Arabia are square!"

*   *   *   *   *   *

It was Wednesday morning. For the past hour, the Big Fisherman had been down on his knees, industriously calking the open seams on the deck of *The Abigail*. He had found that this monotonous manual labor, if he gave himself to it with diligence, temporarily eased his wounded spirit. There was something, too, about being on one's knees. That helped a little.

Thad had gone ashore for some provisions. The loyal youngster had hardly left Simon's side since their abrupt departure from Jerusalem until their arrival Sunday evening. As they hurried through Capernaum, Thad had entreated the unhappy skipper to go home and get some proper food and a good night's rest, but Simon wasn't ready to face Hannah. No; he would wait until Andrew had had time to come home. Andrew could tell her.

"I'll sleep on *The Abigail*," he had said. "But I want you to go home tonight, Thad. It's no more than fair to your parents. You row me out—and then you go home."

"But that would leave you without a boat, sir."

"That's the way I want it," Simon had declared, grimly. "If there's a dory tied up to the ship, it will mean that somebody's aboard. And I want to be alone."

Thad had remonstrated but Simon had been obdurate; and after the little boat had pulled away into the thickening gloom, *The Abigail*, instead of offering a welcome, seemed aloof and reproachful. The long-unused blankets in the little forecastle were damp and moldy. Simon had dipped up a bucket of water and washed his dusty feet, trying to pretend that he was back again on familiar ground and repeating accustomed habits, but nothing was quite real. He flung himself down on the cot, hoping his exhaustion would compel sleep; and presently he dozed only to waken with a start, and the awful thing that had happened to him would engulf him, bringing out the sweat on his forehead. The silence was profound, terrifying. It had been a mistake to let Thad go.

The long, wretched night had eventually ended and a pink dawn came up rapidly from behind the eastern mountains, giving promise of a beautiful early summer day. It was an hour that had always stirred Simon deeply, but this morning his spirit did not rise to sense the oncoming glory. He strolled aft and stood at the rail, dully facing the pageant, and there recurred to his mind a remark of the Master's—not fully understood at the time, "You are the salt of the earth; but if the salt lose its savor—" That was the trouble. From now on, as long as he lived, Simon's life, he felt, would be tasteless.

To his immeasurable relief, he saw the dory coming now. Thad pulled up under The Abigail's bow. Simon lowered a basket and drew it up, well filled with supplies, bread, smoked perch, and sun-cured figs. He leaned far over the rail and grasped one end of the cot that Thad had brought from home, and hauled in a great roll of bedding. It was a comfort to know that he would have company now.

All that day they had worked side by side, and mostly in silence, on the long neglected deck. Occasionally Thad ventured some brief comment but received little cooperation. Once, when he addressed the taciturn skipper as "Peter," the Big Fisherman had said, sadly, "My name is Simon. Please remember that." On Tuesday, Thad rowed in for one of the tents Esther had used last summer. If it should rain in the night he would be protected. His eyes were bright with excitement when he returned.

"They're saying in the village," he reported, "that the Tetrarch's caravan was set upon—and he was killed!"

But even this shocking news failed to lift Simon's apathy. He was silent for a while and then remarked, "That will close the palace." After another interval, he added, "They will not need any more fish."

And now it was Wednesday morning. Thad had gone ashore on an errand. Simon's knees were lame from his unaccustomed exercise, and after an hour of it he came wearily to his feet and walked the length of the deck, wondering what had detained the boy. Three dories were on the water, and moving rapidly, their oars flashing in the sun. With narrowed eyes, shaded by his cupped hands, Simon identified the occupants of the boats. Thad was bringing Andrew. James and John were in the second dory which had overtaken and was now passing Thad's. Lagging behind came Philip with Thomas and old Bartholomew.

Simon's heart was in his throat. How could he face these men? They were drawing closer now, near enough for him to see their animation. They seemed happy! Whatever could have happened? He tossed a rope to the first dory and Johnny scrambled up, flung a leg over the rail and threw his arms around the bewildered skipper.

"You haven't heard!" he shouted, exultantly. "You don't know! Listen! Jesus lives! . . . I tell you—he is alive again!"

James had grasped Simon's arm.

"We have seen him, Peter! He came to us—Sunday night—at Ben-yosef's house!"

They had all swarmed over the rail now, all but Bartholomew who was being tugged on board by Thad. Simon stood there dazed, his lips quivering, the tears running down his cheeks.

"He told us to make haste, and go home," said Philip. "He was anxious for you to know."

"That's what he said," put in Johnny. "He said, 'Go and tell Peter!' "

"Are you sure he said 'Peter'?" asked the Big Fisherman, huskily.

"Aye! That he did!" declared Bartholomew. " 'Go—quickly—and tell Peter!' "

"Where is he now?" entreated Peter. "I must go to him!"

"We're to wait here," said Andrew. "He is coming to us."

They slowly drifted to the afterdeck and sat in a circle around Peter. If anyone remembered his unaccountable apostasy and flight on the morning of the great tragedy, it was not apparent. They were too full of joy to remember anything but their Master's conquest. They were all talking at once. Peter's brightened eyes darted from one to another as he tried to follow their fragmentary narratives. Then he began asking questions: "Was Jesus the same; with the same body?"

"Absolutely the same," declared Thomas. "A bit pale, perhaps. There were deep black thorn-cuts on his forehead, and purple nail-wounds in his hands and feet, and the gash of a sword-thrust in his side; but he was real!"

"Not just a spirit, then," concluded Peter, "but flesh and blood."

At that, they suddenly fell silent. Old Bartholomew cleared his throat.

"There was a little difference, Peter," he admitted. "It is true, as Thomas says, that he appeared in his real body—"

"And he ate, too, a bit of fish and some honey in the comb," interposed Philip.

"We don't know that—for sure," put in James. "The only light in there was a small candle, for we were in hiding."

"Well—he took the plate," persisted Philip. "He could have eaten."

Peter turned his attention to the old man.

"What was it you started to say, Bartholomew?"

They all listened, their eyes lowered as if they knew what was coming.

"Only this, Peter," replied Bartholomew. "There was a little difference. When he came into the room, he didn't bother to open the door."

Peter's eyes widened. The others did not look up.

"You mean—he walked through it!"

"I suppose so," said Bartholomew, lamely. "The door did not open; and then—he was standing there."

"And when he left you," pursued Peter—"did he open the door? And do you know where he went?"

"That was mysterious, too," rejoined Bartholomew. "He was standing there among us, as I say, talking earnestly with us; and, as James has told you, the room was but dimly lighted; and, presently, he was gone."

"Didn't go out through the door?"

"Didn't go near the door! Didn't move! . . . He just vanished!"

Johnny broke the ensuing silence to say, "It was reported that two men met him on the highway near Emmaus, that evening at suppertime. Both of them were firm believers in the Master; had often seen him and had heard him talk. They were discussing the report of the resurrection when he overtook them and joined in the conversation. They invited him to have supper with them at the Emmaus inn. He sat with them for a time at the table—"

"But ate nothing," put in James.

"And vanished!" ended John.

"The queer thing about it was that he talked with these men at Emmaus about the same time that he appeared to us at Benyosef's house," contributed Thomas.

"And it's a good three-hour walk from Emmaus to Jerusalem," said Philip.

Nothing more was said for a while. Peter sat thoughtfully stroking his jaw. Andrew observed that there was a mixture of white in his brother's black beard. Yes—and there was a patch of silver in his forelock that had not been there before. It must have taken a deal of suffering to do that to Peter.

Thad had now caught Johnny's eye and wiggled a beckoning finger. The two arose quietly and strolled arm in arm toward the little galley, presumably to prepare food for the party.

"What it all comes to, Peter," summed up old Bartholomew, soberly, "is that our Master, having overcome death, is set free to go wherever he pleases, whenever he pleases! He is independent of miles—and hours!"

"He might even be here—on The Abigail—now!" mused Andrew.

Peter gave a startled look over his shoulder, and then stared into his brother's eyes.

"Does that affright you, Andy?" he asked.

"No—it does not affright me," replied Andrew. "But—from now on

—so long as I live—I'm going to be more careful—about what I say—
and do. . . . One never knows when he may be standing there."

* * * * * *

Early the next morning—it was the twentieth day of Nisan—they were
all reassembled on *The Abigail*. There was plenty of work to be done in
reconditioning the neglected ship and her sister craft, *The Sara*, but no
one had any keen interest in it. They were restless, inattentive and preoccupied by their expectancy of a visitation. Every little while some one
of them would make a tour of the deck, scanning the horizon. The animated discussions of yesterday had reviewed the story, over and over again,
until nothing was left to be said.

"Think he will come today?" one would ask, aware that the question
had no answer. The strain of waiting was beginning to tell: waiting and
watching and listening was hard work. Late in the afternoon Andrew,
customarily so frugal with suggestions, startled them by calling out to his
brother who for the past hour had been sitting on the tiller-seat, gazing
across the shimmering water, "Let us go fishing tomorrow! I think he
would rather find us working—when he comes." The proposal brought
general relief. The rest of the day was spent in putting the nets and sailing tackle in order. The tension was relaxed. A frayed rope at the end of
the mainmast's boom broke with Johnny and dumped him into the
lake. They hauled him out dripping and everybody laughed. How good it
seemed to be able to laugh again, especially at Johnny whose agility in
scampering all over the rigging had made him amiably envied.

Next day they fished off a cove on the north shore and with considerable success; came back to anchorage in the evening, stocked the big
live-box, half submerged at their wharf and carried home well-filled baskets
of perch. Peter thought some of returning that night to Bethsaida, but
when the time came to leave the ship he decided to remain. All the others
went home, including Thad, who was ordered to take some fish home to
his family. At twilight the dories were all gone and Peter was alone, but
with a tranquil mind. And that night he slept.

At the first gray-blue light before dawn, the Big Fisherman rose and
walked forward. It was still too early to indentify the familiar landmarks.
On such a morning, he had stood here gazing toward the shore in the
pre-dawn haze and had heard a voice calling "Simon!" With what heart-
racing haste had he scrambled into the little boat and flailed the lake with
excited oars! And then he had received his commission as the fisherman
who would now "fish for men."

The sky was brightening a little and the fog was dissolving. Dimly the outlines of the wharves and huts became visible. The Big Fisherman's narrowed eyes slowly swept the shoreline. A tall, slender column of blue smoke was rising from a small, bright fire at the water's edge. Beside the fire, warming his hands, stood the Master. He raised his arm, waved a hand, and called:

"Peter!"

*   *   *   *   *   *

A half-hour later the disciples began to arrive, by twos and threes, for the day's work. They hurried to the spot where Jesus and Peter sat side by side before the fire, and were greeted by the Master's welcoming smile. The Big Fisherman's shaggy head was wet; he was bare to the waist; his shirt lay near by on the sand, drying. His eyes were red and swollen with weeping, but strangely luminous. It was plain to see what had happened. Peter had tearfully repented his weakness and had been fully restored to the Master's comradeship.

Thad and John ran to the live-box and returned with fish for breakfast which they broiled over the fire, and produced wheaten bread from their well-filled baskets. The hour that followed was memorable. In a few days, the Master said, he would return home to his Father's House, and leave them to continue his work.

Eventually he would revisit the world. In the meantime, they who believed in him—"and they who will believe in me through your testimony" —would receive many indubitable evidences of his spiritual presence.

"Can you tell us when to expect your return, Master?" asked Philip.

"No one knows the day, nor the hour, Philip," replied Jesus. "What I say unto you, you may say unto all—Watch!"

In a quiet voice he gave them instructions for their movements in the days immediately before them. No more fishing now: their fishing days were over. They were to return to Jerusalem and await further orders. With that, he rose, held his outstreched hands over them in blessing, and said, tenderly, "My peace be with you." They had all bowed their heads while the touching words were spoken; and when, at length, they lifted their eyes, he was gone.

For a long moment they sat stunned to silence. Peter was the first to rise. They all came to their feet and gathered about him, their questing eyes fixed on his sober face. No one needed to inquire which, among them, was appointed to be their leader. Peter had suddenly acquired maturity. His resonant voice, when he spoke, had a tone of authority. There was no trace of pride or arrogance in it: indeed, it had something of the tenderness and compassion that had distinguished the voice of the Master. It quietly entreated, but with full confidence that it would be heard with respect. He remembered the strange sensation of power that he had experienced on the day, long ago, in the palatial home of Jairus when he had been in complete command of the crowd that had swarmed in out of the storm. It had been a heady potion, that consciousness of ability to command. . . . Today, he had no pride of power: instead, he felt weighted with respon-sibility. Jesus had privately said to him, "You are a shepherd now! Feed my sheep!"

"We will proceed to Jerusalem," said Peter. "James, John, and Thad-deus, you will row out to the ships, stow the nets, and secure the hatches. Then you will return home and prepare for your journey. The rest of us will go to our homes and say farewell to our families. We will all meet in Bethsaida an hour after noon."

The Big Fisherman picked up his shirt and tugged it on over his mas-sive shoulders.

"And bid farewell to the lake," he added, as he turned away with An-drew. "It is unlikely that we will ever see it again."

"What will you do with the ships?" asked Andrew, as they moved toward the highway.

"I shall give them to Hannah," said Peter. "She can dispose of them—and use the money for her support. . . . And your house in Capernaum, Andy?"

"That shall be Hannah's, too."

*   *   *   *   *   *

Making their headquarters at the shop of the old weaver Benyosef, the disciples restlessly awaited their summons. At length it was announced that they were to assemble on a near-by hill-top in the early morning of the twenty-fourth day of Iyar.

In obedience, they went singly up the long hill where the Master met them; and, after a few enheartening words, instructed them to remain in Jerusalem until they received further tidings.

Then they all knelt while he prayed for them; and when they arose from their knees, he was gone. Nor did they ever see him again, though—to the end of their days—they were constantly on the alert for his return.

24

FOR MORE than a dozen centuries the fifth of Sivan, fiftieth day after Passover, had been celebrated as the harvest festival. It was the gayest occasion of the Jewish year.

Many an oldster, with the ancient traditions as his hobby, would tell you that Pentecost was originally intended to commemorate the giving of the law to Moses on Mount Sinai; but little if anything was made of that now. This carefree day was singularly detached from historic events.

Whereas the Passover enjoined a period when the houses were shuttered and prayers were offered for the recovery of a long-lost freedom, and the Day of Atonement implored on bended knees the forgiveness of the people's sins, Pentecost was observed with joyful music, colorful processions and dancing in the streets.

The gala-day marked the end of the barley harvest, Palestine's largest and most reliable crop. For a little while, and until the grapes and other early autumn fruits were ripe, rural Jewry was at leisure with a few well-earned shekels in its pocket. It was an appropriate time for a pleasure trip to the city.

And Jerusalem always did her best to accommodate the merrymakers. Her open gates were adorned with bright bunting and banners. The booths and bazaars were decorated with garlands of mid-summer flowers. Merchants put away their expensive jewels, rugs and furniture to give display to gaudier items within the reach of a reckless holiday wallet. Trinkets and baubles and gimcracks, anything that glittered on a necklace or jingled on a bracelet, could be had at what seemed a bargain. The narrow old streets swarmed with crowds in a state of happy confusion. Vendors with trays of sweetmeats shouted their wares. Confectioners, busy over hot braziers, filled the air with tantalizing aromas of mint and anise. Harpists and pipers discordantly competed with mendicant minstrels for

435

the attention of hilarious groups that paused to listen, laugh, drop a penny on the rug, and press on into the pack. The youth of Israel were serious—but not on Pentecost.

It was not to be expected that everybody would behave. There was plenty of rowdiness and drunkenness which the Roman patrols pretended not to notice; for, in the opinion of the tough and seasoned Roman soldier, inebriation was not a capital offense. Tipsy country boys who embraced and harangued strangers on the street were casually admonished by the legionaries to take it easy, but nobody was arrested. It was the one day of the year when the Holy City unbent a little. If the solemn graybeards didn't like it, they could stay at home.

But there were many people who visited Jerusalem on Pentecost who did not come to play. These men were mostly from the larger cities of the Mediterranean countries who came to attend the celebrated camel-auction conducted by Arabians. Anybody could tell you that the Jews and Arabs hated each other so consistently that neither would set foot on the other's land, but it was a long-established custom for the Arabs to forget, on Pentecost, that Jerusalem was Jewish; and the Jews, on that one day, forgot that the camel-breeders were Arabs and permitted their use of the old drill-field for the exhibition and sale of their incomparable camels.

And so it was that the annual day of Pentecost not only brought to Jerusalem the youngster from the country, with a handful of coppers to spend, but an assembly of the wealthy and urbane who came, from far distances, on business; big business transacted in gold and precious stones. They stayed sober and were closely attended by body-guards. When the day was over, they set off for home with the tall, sleek, haughty camels they had bought at breath-taking prices; and the Arabs leaped astride their beautiful horses and galloped home with a king's ransom in their pockets.

Such was the nature of the Pentecostal celebration which annually brought to Jerusalem not only a crowd of provincial pleasure-seekers but scores of serious-minded, wealthy and influential men representing every land and language of their turbulent world, whether barbarian, bond or free.

This year, the festival of Pentecost was considered an appropriate occasion for the dramatic demonstration of God's Holy Spirit in the presence of a selected company mysteriously assembled for this purpose by an irresistible compulsion. In all the world's history, nothing like this had ever happened before. At certain critical moments, young men had seen visions and old men had dreamed dreams, but nothing like this had ever happened in the world before!

*   *   *   *   *   *

Because he was the farthest away and needed more time than any of the others for the unexpected journey to Jerusalem, Simon of Cyrene was the first of the one hundred and twenty men to receive an invitation.

It was anything but welcome. Simon had left the old city at daybreak next morning after the soul-sickening tragedy in which he had unwittingly become involved and he had promised himself that he would never set foot in Jerusalem again. Never!

It had been his custom, and his father's before him, to attend the Pass-over Week in the Jewish capital where he had always found a ready market for his merchandise: tropical spices, aromatic and medicinal herbs and the bulbs of exotic plants.

This season, business had not been good. His potential customers were preoccupied and uneasy. They bought the spices as usual but had no interest in tulip-bulbs or flowering shrubbery. It was almost as if they expected an early invasion demanding flight, though anybody could see that the Romans weren't ready for their long-threatened offensive. Simon's sales hadn't been worth the bother and expense of the trip and he was half minded not to do it again.

Then, on that dreadful Friday morning, he had become accidentally entangled in the crucifixion of the young Galilean. It had done something to Simon. He was not a man given to meditation on the mysteries of human existence. Whenever some thoughtful friend had expressed an interest in such old riddles as: Why are we here? What is the good of it? Who is in charge of it? What will be the outcome of it? Simon would chuckle and shake his head and say that he was willing to leave all that to the unemployed wiseacres who had time to worry over these matters. Now Simon himself had joined the worriers. The shameless abrogation of justice in the case of the innocent young preacher—a crime sponsored and legalized by both the Insula and the Temple in a country proud of its piety—indicated that humanity was not moving forward toward the achievement of a better world: it was not even standing still! It was losing ground, by the hour! The Cyrenian was a very unhappy man as he departed from the Holy City firmly resolved that he would never return.

The homeward trek had been tedious. Although habitually light-hearted, Simon had become taciturn and glum. The men of his caravan, customarily full of laughter and song, lost their gaiety. And as if the journey were not long enough and dull enough, they had been required to detour almost to Memphis for a river crossing, the lower Nile being at flood later than usual. This had added many wearisome miles to an already intolerable journey.

Now—at last—the jaded caravan was within one day's tramp of its destination. Tonight's encampment would be the last. By late afternoon tomorrow they would all be back on the beautiful and beloved plantation within sight of the sea where even the oldest of them had been born.

Simon, weary and dispirited, retired early and fell at once into a deep sleep, a sleep so profound that he was quite defenseless when the handsome young courier rode boldly into his tent and, dismounting gracefully, approached the cot and stood in silence for a long moment looking down upon the inert figure of the man he had come to see. Strangely enough, Simon was not affrighted by this unbidden visitation. The messenger was obviously intending him no harm. Indeed he seemed a friendly youth, probably in his later teens. There were tight little ringlets on his fair brow and at his temples that had escaped from the gold bandeau circling his head. He was exquisitely dressed in white silk, and on the left breast of his tunic was a device appliquéed in gold which Simon could not identify. The beautiful white horse stood quietly waiting. It, too, was equipped with trappings of great value, the bridle and saddle heavily ornamented with silver.

Simon felt now that he was expected to acknowledge the presence of his incredible guest.

"That's quite a turnout you have there, my son," he found himself saying.

"It befits my errand," said the courier. "I come on business for my King."

"Say on, then, friend," said Simon, "if this business concerns me."

"I bear a summons to you, Simon. Early in the morning you will send your caravan home. You are not going home. You are required to be in Jerusalem on the Day of Pentecost."

Simon was instantly stirred to anger.

"I'll not go!" he growled. "I've seen quite enough of Jerusalem! I do not know by what authority you command me, but I tell you I shall not go! Not even if the Emperor summoned me!"

The courier smiled and shrugged indifferently.

"You're not being summoned by a mere Emperor, Simon. You might defy Caesar: you might hide from him. But you will obey my Master. He wants you in Jerusalem on the Day of Pentecost—and you will be there!"

"And who is your Master?" demanded Simon.

"You know him," said the youth. "You carried his cross."

"But he is dead! I saw him die!"

"True; he was dead. But he came alive again!"

"Nonsense! This is only a dream!"

"It is not a dream, Simon."

"Give me a token, then; some sign that shall remain when I awake."

The young courier obligingly thrust his hand into his tunic and brought forth a long, rough, blood-rusted nail and laid it into Simon's open hand.

"Ever see that before?" he asked, soberly.

"Yes—but it could be part of my dream. I'm sure you'll not be leaving it here for me to find in the morning."

"No—I shall not leave it here. I may need it again." The courier retrieved the heavy nail, restored it to an inner pocket of his tunic, and seemed ready to depart.

"Farewell, friend Simon," he said, gently. "Tomorrow you will ride your horse to Alexandria where you will find a ship embarking for Joppa. This will shorten your trip. I shall see you on the Day of Pentecost. . . . Mid-forenoon—at the Coppersmiths' Guildhall."

Simon chuckled a little.

"This is the strangest dream I ever had," he mumbled. "It seems impossible that I could have invented so many things I never saw before. . . . I'm sure I never saw anybody like you! . . . By the way—what is that golden device on your tunic?"

"It is the crest of the Master's Kingdom."

"Come closer," said Simon. "Let me see it plainly."

"What does it resemble?" asked the courier, bending over the cot.

Simon frowned and shuddered.

"I should never have chosen that ugly, cruel thing as an ornament!" he muttered.

"Simon," murmured the courier, impressively, "that device is destined to become the most beautiful emblem in the world!" And with that, he mounted and rode out of the Cyrenian's fantastic dream.

Again Simon slept, a sleep so deep as to be deathlike. It was broad daylight when he awoke, dazed by the recollection of having had an eventful dream. He heard the cheerful voices of his men as they dismantled and packed their tents for the final journey home. He wondered if they would notice, in his face, any evidences of his bewilderment. He must pull himself together—and try to forget about it.

Throwing open the door of his tent, he beckoned to his body-servant who came running with a basin of water and an armful of towels. Simon plunged his bearded face into the basin and splashed the sleep out of his eyes.

"How did you hurt your hand, sir?" asked the servant. "There's blood on it."

Simon gazed intently into his right hand. A broad bloodstain diagonally transversed his palm. He dipped it into the basin and scrubbed it vigorously, but the stain was indelible. The servant stared hard but ventured no comment when he observed that his master's hands were trembling. . . . The butler now appeared with a breakfast tray and stood ready to serve.

"Take it away," ordered Simon, huskily, "and bid Enos come to me."

It was obvious that the butler had been disturbed by his master's strange manner; for when the steward arrived his wide eyes showed concern.

"Enos," said Simon, "I find that I must return at once to Jerusalem. You will take the caravan home. I shall ride to Alexandria and take passage on a ship."

"Are—are you well, sir?" stammered Enos. "Perhaps I should go with you."

"I am quite well, Enos. Notify my family that when my errand in Jerusalem has been accomplished I shall return. . . . Order my horse. I shall leave directly."

The loyal steward reluctantly turned to do as he was bidden. At the tent-door he paused to say, "But you have been injured, sir! There is blood on your hand!"

"Be at ease, my good Enos," said Simon, quietly. "I have not been injured. That is not my blood."

*   *   *   *   *   *

Although the virile young Prince of Arimathaea was customarily an early riser in summer, and this was an exceptionally beautiful day, he was finding it difficult this morning to shake off his lethargy and regain full consciousness.

For a long time he sat on the edge of his bed, with a bare foot in one hand and a silk stocking in the other, staring dully out through the open window, unable to proceed with his dressing. He was still under the spell of an extraordinarily vivid dream.

At length he tugged himself loose from his captivity, drew on a robe, and made his way out to the patio where his pretty sister awaited him at the breakfast-table.

"Whatever has been keeping you, Joe?" she inquired. "Hassan is in a great dither; says they have been ready to start for an hour."

"Start?" mumbled her bewildered brother. "Start where?"

"Maybe good old Hassan is going crazy—or perhaps you are. I thought it queer that you had said nothing to me about this sudden trip to Jerusalem. But—weren't you intending to go?"

Now the sleepy Prince came awake with a start. Leaning forward on his elbows he studied his sister's eyes. Then he slowly rubbed the back of his shaky hand across his forehead, and huskily ordered the serving-maid to send for Hassan.

"This is the most unbelievable thing that ever happened," he muttered, half to himself. "Tamar, just what did Hassan say?"

"Here he comes," she said. "He'll tell you."

The dignified steward, tall, graying, dressed for travel, approached the table and stood at attention with anxiety in his eyes.

"Hassan," said the Prince, "who told you we were going to Jerusalem?"

The steward's voice was unsteady as he apologized for his mistake.

"I am very sorry, sire! I had a most peculiar dream, last night; something more than a dream. It seemed real!"

The Prince impulsively turned his chair about to face his steward directly.

"Proceed, Hassan," he said, soberly. "Tell me about this dream."

"I fear it will sound very foolish, sire. I know you do not believe in dreams."

"Don't be too sure about that!" said the Prince. "Let's have it!"

"Well, sire, to begin with: do you remember the well-favored youth who assisted us that night when we took the body of Jesus down from the cross? And how he helped us at the tomb? And we couldn't understand his behavior, at all; the way he held the Master's body caressingly, as one might carry a sleeping child; with a tender smile—and showing no grief; no grief, at all!"

The Prince nodded his full remembrance, and Hassan went on.

"The handsome youth was garbed in a workingman's clothing; but, after his exertions and while we rested at the tomb, he slipped off his brown jacket and revealed a white silk tunic of exquisite texture—"

"That sounds like a dream, too, Hassan," interposed Tamar.

"What Hassan says is true, my sister. I was about to pay the handsome youth for his service to us; but when I saw that tunic it seemed inappropriate to offer him anything. . . . Continue, Hassan."

"This strange young man has been much in my thoughts, sire. There was one story, you will remember, about the women seeing an angel, clad in white, when they went to the tomb that Sunday morning."

"Perhaps you have thought about it so much that it has gone to your head, Hassan," put in Tamar.

"No, no, sister!" cautioned the Prince. "Hassan is not crazy! Let him tell his story!"

"He came to my bedside last night, sire, saying that we were wanted in Jerusalem, mid-morning of the Day of Pentecost, at the Coppersmiths' Guildhall; an important meeting, to which Your Grace and his humble servant Hassan were both invited. . . . He said you had been notified, sire. It was all so real that I believed it, and prepared for the journey. I see that I was mistaken—and I crave Your Grace's pardon!"

There was a lengthy silence before the Prince spoke. In an unsteady voice, he said, "Hassan, you were not mistaken. I was notified. He came to me. I dismissed it as a dream. We will go to Jerusalem, as he commanded."

Hassan's gloomy face instantly cleared. He drew himself up to his full height, saluted, and withdrew. Tamar broke the silence.

"Joe, dear," she said, solicitously, "you know you don't believe in such things! . . . They just don't happen!"

"I wish you could have seen him, Tamar! Wherever he came from, they practice no economy. You never saw such clothing! White silk; satin, maybe, with a luminous sheen! On the breast of his tunic was some sort of insignia done in gold. I didn't recognize it." He beckoned to the maid. "Bring me a slate and a stylus. . . . See, Tamar; it looked like this! What is it?"

She rose, came around to his side of the table, studied the drawing, and shook her head.

"Have you any idea what it means?" she asked.

"Yes," said Joseph. "It is the cross on which they crucified the Master! . . . Tamar—that was a greater event than we knew!"

*   *   *   *   *   *

Every able-bodied employee on Jairus' vast estate, whatever his specific occupation, was annually drafted for a week to assist in the barley harvest.

By virtue of his recent appointment to the position of Overseer of the vineyards, Joel could have claimed exemption from this hard work in the harvest-fields; but had not done so. From dawn to dusk, every day that week, he had cheerfully toiled beside the common laborers, adding much to their diligence and his own popularity. Nor had this evidence of his sincere concern for his master's welfare escaped the attention of Jairus himself; and when the last load of yellow sheaves had been stored and the harvesters were wearily trudging home with Joel bringing up the rear, he dismounted from his horse to express his appreciation.

"You are entitled to a few days' rest, my boy," said Jairus. "Perhaps you would like to go fishing."

"If you would be so kind, sir," said Joel, "I should like to go to Jeru-salem and see the celebration of Pentecost. I have never been there, and, sir"—he hesitated, flushing a little through his tan—"I have a particulai reason for wanting to go."

Jairus' face had suddenly become so sober that it seemed stern; and Joel, rather crestfallen, feared a rebuke.

"What is this particular reason, Joel?" demanded Jairus.

"I'm afraid I can't rightly explain, sir," murmured Joel, much embar-rassed. "If you prefer not to let me go, I shall think no more about it."

"No! No!" barked Jairus, impatiently. "I did not say you couldn't go! I asked you what is your reason for wanting to go to Jerusalem—on the Day of Pentecost!"

Joel sheepishly dug the toe of his worn sandal into the ground and avoided his rich employer's eyes. After a long moment, he confessed, "I dreamed that I was expected to be there."

"My God!" ejaculated Jairus, in a shaken voice. "So you dreamed! Tell me about it!"

Joel was frightened now. Jairus had thought better of him than that he would turn out to be a superstitious dunce. He shook his head and grinned foolishly.

"It was nothing, sir," he mumbled. "I can't remember."

"Perhaps I can refresh your memory, Joel," said Jairus. "You dreamed that a fine-looking young man came to you—By the way, was he riding?"

Joel was staring up into Jairus' face now, with wide eyes.

"Yes, sir; on a white horse."

"Silver-mounted bridle?"

"Yes, sir." Joel swallowed noisily. "And a silver saddle! How did you know, sir? Did you see him?"

"He rode into my bedroom last night," admitted Jairus. "He told me to come to Pentecost. It seemed very real. But, this morning when I awoke, I decided to give it no further thought; though, I must say, I have thought of nothing else all day. . . . It's a strange business, Joel!"

"Yes, sir! It is that!" And it was also a strange business, reflected Joel, to be having this man-to-man talk with his eminent employer.

"Well, Joel—" Jairus turned to mount his horse. "We are summoned. Go home now and make ready for the journey. We will try to get off at daybreak."

*　　*　　*　　*　　*　　*

Ephraim, the good-natured farrier and general blacksmith of Nazareth, lounged at full-length on his tool-scarred workbench and waited for a cessation of the pelting summer shower that was detaining him long past suppertime.

Since early morning he had been toiling on a broken plowshare, hoping to complete his task by the end of the day, but the sudden storm had darkened the shop, already at dusk, and he had given it up, complacently however for the gardens needed the rain more than Joseph needed his plow. Wearied by the day's work, and drowsy in the darkness—for he had banked his forge-fire in preparation for leaving—Ephraim stretched out comfortably and fell asleep so soundly that he was quite unaware of the opening and closing of the double doors facing the street.

A brightening glow from the suddenly revived fire on the forge attracted his attention, though he did not stir. In his dream he saw a well-favored youth tugging at the bellows-rope with what seemed an experienced hand. Every fresh blast from the old leather bellows quickened the fire. It was possible to see more clearly now. The tall white horse—a superb animal— was attempting to take a drink from the grimy water-tub beside the anvil, just as any other horse would have done, and his young master was forbidding him to do it, just as any other man would have done; but Ephraim knew it was only a dream because neither the horse nor the man was wet.

With his curiosity considerably stirred, Ephraim turned on his side, elevated his head into the crook of his arm, and had a better view of his remarkable visitors. The handsome youth was gorgeously clad in white, with a broad fillet of gleaming gold circling his head, and the horse's trappings were heavily ornamented with silver.

"How does it happen, young master," Ephraim heard himself inquiring, "that your clothing and your horse's coat are dry, after coming through that rain-storm?"

"We came another way," replied the youth, casually, still pumping the bellows.

"But you're cold," remarked Ephraim, "or you wouldn't be firing the forge."

"That's for light," said the youth, raking the coals toward the center.

"A young fellow as queer as you are," chuckled Ephraim, "should be able to see in the dark."

"Perhaps I can—but you can't." The strange visitor let go of the bellows-rope now and approached the work-bench. "I wanted you to see me plainly enough to remember what I came to say. I have an important message for you, Ephraim. You are expected in Jerusalem on the Day of Pentecost."

Ephraim heard himself laughing softly in his sleep. What a dream this had turned out to be!

"What's the idea of my going to Pentecost?" he inquired. "I don't need a camel. I can't even afford a good donkey."

At this juncture the young messenger seriously proceeded to explain. A large number of the friends and followers of Jesus were being called together in Jerusalem on the morning of the Day of Pentecost. The meeting would convene in the Coppersmiths' Guildhall, in the middle of the forenoon.

"And you are entitled to be there, Ephraim," he went on. "You always showed kindness to Jesus, from his childhood. Nobody in Nazareth, except his family—and you—had any sympathy for him because he was different from other children. And when he was grown to manhood, the Nazarenes—all but you—openly scoffed at his singular powers. So he went away and talked to people who believed in him and loved him. And you left your shop—and followed him."

"Aye, sir; that I did!" said Ephraim. "I heard him speak, for many days, in Cana and Hammath and Capernaum. And I saw him heal the sick. . . . But how did you know?"

"And when you returned to Nazareth," continued the young messenger, ignoring Ephraim's query, "you told all Nazareth what you had heard and seen, and they said you were a blasphemer. . . . Doubtless it injured your business."

"Not very much," replied Ephraim, cheerfully. "When the chain to the well-bucket is broken, Nazareth is willing to have it mended by a blasphemer. . . . But I must say for Nazareth that the people were sorry when they heard that Jesus had been crucified."

"What did they say when the word came that he had returned to life?"

"Well —of course they didn't believe that!"

"How about you, Ephraim? Do you believe it?"

"I don't know," replied Ephraim, vaguely, after some delay. "It's not easy to believe, especially in a town where the people are sure it can't be true. . . . I ponder on it—every day."

"Would you be glad to have firm proof that it is so?"

"Indeed I would, sir!"

"Then come to Jerusalem on Pentecost."

"I might do that if I knew that this message was real."

The youthful messenger made no reply to that. The leaky old bellows wheezed a few times, so loudly that it brought Ephraim wide awake. He sat up, rubbing his eyes. His visitor was gone. But the coals on the forge glowed brightly. . . . Ephraim knew now that he would be in Jerusalem on the Day of Pentecost.

*   *   *   *   *   *

The strong and steady northerly breeze that had shortened the voyage of *The Vestris* from Gaza to Joppa continued unabated to the considerable delay of the return trip.

Captain Fulvius, whose detestation of all labor that wasn't strictly necessary, had sailed in light ballast, and *The Vestris* had frisked about in a manner unsuitable to her age and decrepitude. The voyage had been tiresome beyond description for everybody but Voldi who was in no hurry to make port anywhere though the Captain and the Proconsul were of the opinion that only a perfunctory investigation, if any, would be made into the assassination of Herod Antipas.

To make sure, however, that Voldi was not apprehended, an action that might disturb the ever delicate political relations of Jewry and Arabia, it had been decided that Voldi was to remain under cover during the stop at Gaza and proceed on *The Vestris* to Rome. He could return to Arabia when the sensation caused by the Tetrarch's death had ceased to be of interest.

It had been the hope of Mencius and Fulvius that the salt-caravan from Engedi might have arrived by the time *The Vestris* tardily waddled to her berth in the dirty old city but they were disappointed. Of course almost anything might have happened to delay that slow-plodding, heavily laden procession. The weather was cruelly hot, requiring longer and more frequent periods of rest for the camels. You couldn't hustle a camel, either by appealing to his moral obligation to serve the Empire with all his heart, mind and strength, or even by the more practical method of beating his rump with a club. When a camel decided that he had done his day's work he sat down, right where he was, and no amount of flattering cajolery or forthright brutality would alter his resolution to adjourn. Mencius and Fulvius knew, from experience, that they might have to wait another fortnight.

As for Voldi, his confinement on the ship, as the empty days and hot nights dragged out their length in the suffocating stench of Gaza's waterfront, was almost more than he could bear. He had promised to remain on board at the insistence of men who had befriended him at no little risk. It was not only that they didn't want him to get into trouble; they didn't want to get into trouble themselves for harboring a fugitive.

But after a week had passed, the Arabian's impatience boiled over. He had had time to do much thinking and most of it concerned Fara. Now that Jesus was dead, and there was nothing more that she could do for him, where would she go? Surely not to Galilee to be dependent upon the fisherfolk. In her loneliness, was it not likely that she would want to return to Ione? Now that she was adrift, perhaps Fara would listen to reason. Voldi felt confident that she loved him. This might be the time to present his case with some hope of success.

Mencius sympathetically heard him out and Fulvius too agreed that if the authorities had suspected he was sailing in *The Vestris* they would have had ample time to pursue the ship by land and arrest him. After some debate it was decided that Voldi might leave without much risk to any of them, which he did, forthwith, it being then two hours past midday when all Gaza had crept into the shade to sleep. At the last minute, Mencius impulsively announced that he would accompany him for a few miles. Brutus needed exercise.

They stopped at the old fort of Minoa for water. The sentry at the gate immediately recognized the Proconsul and deferentially volunteered to notify Centurion Paulus who, he said, was in temporary command. Paulus cordially extended such hospitality as was to be had, and while they lounged in the shade their conversation promptly turned to the singular case of the young Legate, Marcellus, who had been unexpectedly summoned to Rome.

"And half out of his wits, too," put in Paulus. "That crucifixion was too much for him."

"The whole affair," growled Mencius, "was a disgrace to the Empire! The dead man is better off than the people who condemned him."

"So you think the Galilean is dead," remarked Paulus.

"What else should I think?" demanded Mencius. "You crucified him; didn't you?"

Then the strange story came out. The contingent from Minoa had not left Jerusalem until Monday morning. By that time the city was buzzing with rumors that the crucified Galilean had left his tomb and had been seen by many credible witnesses. The Sanhedrin was making every effort to have the report officially denied and the rumor-spreaders punished, but Pilate was doing nothing about it.

"Of course, sir, it can't be true," added Paulus, unwilling to be suspected of half-believing it himself.

"Why not?" barked the Proconsul, to the Centurion's amazement.

"This Galilean was no ordinary man. There is no doubt at all that he healed the sick and gave sight to the blind! Why shouldn't he have the power to come to life?"

"Well, sir, the way I look at it, if he had the power to recover his life after death, why did he permit himself to be killed? It cost him great suffering." Paulus waited for further comment from the grizzled Roman who outranked him, and when it was not forthcoming he ventured to ask, "Do you think it makes sense, sir?"

"No," muttered Mencius. "It doesn't make sense. And opening the eyes of the blind doesn't make sense, either. . . . I should give a great deal, Paulus, to know whether there is any truth in this story. . . . How does it strike you, Voldi?"

"I have no opinions, Mencius. It's difficult to believe."

"But you saw him in action, and were deeply impressed. You even suggested that he might be humanity's 'Torchbearer.' "

"That is true," admitted Voldi, "but it hadn't occurred to me that he would live forever. Couldn't he give the world all the light it needed— and then depart? What more can he do, now that he has returned from his tomb? Will he continue to admonish the new generations as they arrive?"

It was a long speech, coming from Voldi who was habitually laconic, and Mencius regarded him with fresh interest.

"That raises an important question," he said. "If this generation paid no attention to his panacea for the world's agonies, what hope is there for better success with the next generation?"

"In other words," interposed Paulus, "what's the good of his resurrection—assuming it to have happened? The world doesn't want him; didn't want him last week; won't want him next week!"

"You're a cynic, Paulus," drawled Mencius.

Paulus grinned, shrugged, toyed absently with the handle of his dagger, and mumbled that his occupation was not calculated to make a man sentimental or optimistic.

Apparently having had his fill of this inconclusive discussion, Voldi said he would be on his way. Paulus suggested that he spend the night at the fort and leave in the cool of early morning. Mencius, too, thought this was sensible. Paulus extended the invitation to the Proconsul, but he declined. Fulvius might think he had got into trouble. After an early supper under the trees, farewells were said, and Mencius departed for Gaza at sunset.

The air grew cooler as twilight came on; and Brutus, seeming anxious to stretch his long legs, quickened his canter to a brisk trot. After a half-mile, he suddenly threw up his head, laid back his ears, and increased his speed, Mencius wondering why a horse so intelligent as Brutus would be eager to get back to his sweltering stall in the hold of *The Vestris*.

Now Mencius himself heard the distant hoof-beats to the rear. Brutus had remembered an unpleasant incident on this road and wanted no repetition of it. The sound of hoof-beats was increasing. Mencius turned in his saddle and saw, through the gloom, a rider rapidly overtaking them on a tall white horse. Brutus, who had no intention of being outrun, leaped to a greyhound gallop, putting everything he had into it, but his pursuer presently drew alongside, making no effort to pass.

Mencius stared hard into the face of the stranger and was amazed to see a mere youth, clad in white, whose disarming expression of good will caused the Proconsul to check his speed, an action immediately followed by his unexplained companion. After some effort they tugged their panting horses to a walk. Mencius spoke.

"That's a very indiscreet thing to do, my boy, overtaking a man in the dark, on a bandit-infested road, without giving a sign of your intentions."

"I shouldn't have done it," admitted the handsome youngster, "but you have a very fast horse, Proconsul Mencius, and it's so rarely that Israfel has a chance to let himself out; and he was enjoying himself so much, sir."

"So were you, I think," commented Mencius, dryly. "I see that you know my name. And who are you? Where do you hail from? I'm sure you don't belong in this poverty-cursed neighborhood. What's that insignia on your tunic? I don't recognize it."

"It's the cross on which they crucified my King."

They halted their horses now, and Mencius turned Brutus about so that they faced each other directly.

"There are tales in circulation," said the Proconsul in an unsteady voice, "that he returned to life. Have you any information on that?"

"That is what I came to tell you, sir."

For the next few minutes the young courier talked earnestly, the bewildered Proconsul listening in silence.

"It all seems very strange," said Mencius—"but I'll be there."

"The Coppersmiths' Guildhall," said the messenger, gathering up his reins. He spoke quietly to "Israfel," who bounded away into the darkness. And by the time Mencius had turned Brutus about in the direction of Gaza the sound of the hoof-beats was faint in the distance.

* * * * * *

And so it was that in strangely convincing dreams, and by intuitive, compelling impulses, and many other indubitable signs, one hundred and twenty men, having no consultation with one another, turned their faces toward Jerusalem, arriving mid-morning of the Day of Pentecost, to receive tidings concerning the future of The Kingdom. Nothing like this had ever happened in the world before.

25

Not until they were halfway up the tortuous trail that ascended sharply from the Valley of Aisne did Darik give signs of recognizing his own country by jerking impatiently at the bridle-reins, noisily blowing his nose, and picking up his tired feet with fresh interest.

Last night Voldi had put in early at the tavern in Engedi and had been on the road before dawn. Within an hour the sun was hot and its reflection on the white salt of the seashore was blinding, but there was no shade to rest in and Darik had been advised to get it over with as soon as possible.

It was two hours past noon now, and they were climbing the narrow, well-worn road that clung to the mountain-side. At intervals on the zig-zag trail there were evidences that travelers had paused to rest, for it was a rugged ascent. The foliage was becoming more abundant as the increased altitude tempered the midsummer heat.

Darik, sniffing the cool, blossom-scented air, was so improvidently over-doing his efforts to reach home that Voldi—unwilling to see him wear himself out—dismounted and led him off the trail into a heavily shaded dell where a narrow little stream, edged with wildflowers, tumbled lazily over an eroded niche in a flat ledge of limestone. Loosening the hot saddle-girths, and tossing the reins over a low-hanging willow-branch, Voldi strolled farther into the sequestered bower. A shaggy white donkey was munching the fresh grass that grew luxuriantly near the water. Deeper into the thicket a young woman, quite unaware of his presence, was in-dustriously gathering blackberries and devouring them hungrily. Evi-dently she was not far from her home, for her simple country dress was hardly appropriate for travel. Her head was bare and her curly black hair, unbound, had been tousled by the clinging vines.

Voldi sat quietly on the moss-grown limestone ledge, regarding her with interest; hesitant to speak for fear of startling her.

Presently her intuition seemed to warn her that she was not alone. For a little while she stood motionless in an attitude of listening; then turned her head slowly to glance backward over her shoulder. Suddenly her eyes widened and she threw up her berry-stained hands in surprise.

Leaping to his feet, Voldi dashed across the little stream and clasped her in his arms with ecstatic little murmurs of rapturous relief, kissing her sun-browned forehead and her sun-warmed hair, her cheeks, her half-closed eyes, while she hung limp in his embrace. Then, lifting her face, she offered him her parted lips and twined her arms around his neck, holding him so tightly to her that he could feel the racing of her heart. After a long, blissful moment, she slowly relaxed with a happy sigh, gazed up tenderly into his eyes and pressed her face hard against his breast.

"I was afraid I had lost you, Fara." Voldi's shaken voice sounded as if he had just finished a grueling foot-race.

She slowly nodded her head without looking up.

"We shall never be parted again!" he declared.

Fara made no reply, but clutched his arms tightly and snuggled her cheek against his heart.

"Say it, darling!" he entreated. "You are mine now—for always!"

She did not answer, but raised her face to his and impetuously returned his kisses without reserve.

"So—that is settled!" he exclaimed. "You have made me very happy, dear!"

Gently releasing herself from his arms, Fara steadied her voice to say, "Let us sit down—and talk, Voldi!"

Gathering her up in his arms, he carried her back to the stone ledge and sat close beside her. They were both bursting with queries about each other's recent movements. . . . Oddly enough, they had left Jerusalem by different routes on the same morning. . . . Voldi explained briefly that he had accompanied a caravan bound for Tiberias in Galilee. Fara's eyes widened.

"And then what?" she asked.

Well—then Voldi had left the caravan—in the night—in the Samaritan mountains—and had ridden to Joppa—and boarded a ship.

She did not press him for further details. After a little silence, Voldi insisted on knowing her story and she told him about her journey to Jerusalem, the wicked trial and conviction of her Master, and wept pitiably as she remembered her last sight of him on the way to his execution. Voldi held her close and tried to comfort her.

"You heard nothing more—about his death?" he asked, gently.

"Was there more—to hear?" She raised her tearful eyes to search his face.

"Much more," said Voldi. "It sounds incredible, but—well—it is firmly believed by his disciples that Jesus left his sepulcher on Sunday morning and is alive again!"

Fara sat bolt upright and stared soberly into his eyes. Could such a thing be possible?—she wanted to know. Did Voldi believe it? . . . Voldi didn't know; didn't know whether it was possible; didn't know whether he believed it.

"But he was a man of singular powers," he admitted.

"I saw him bring Hannah back from death," pondered Fara. "How faithless of us—to think that his power would die with him! . . . Voldi—I believe the story! I am sure he is alive!"

"If it is true," reflected Voldi, soberly, "it will not be a local secret very long. A great many people, besides the farmers and fishermen of Galilee, are interested in life after death. It is no small matter that a dead man—any dead man—should return to life and walk the streets in broad daylight—and sit at supper with his friends."

"Jesus did that?" Fara's eyes were radiant.

"That's what they're saying, dear."

"I must go back—and find him!" she cried, impetuously.

"That can wait," admonished Voldi. "If he is alive, he will stay alive. . . . You must see Ione now—and the King and Queen." He glanced up at the sun. "And we should be on our way, if we expect to get there before nightfall."

Fara slipped her hand under his arm and searched his face thoughtfully.

"Think they will be glad to see us, Voldi?"

He hesitated a little before replying.

"Ione will: you may be sure of that."

Thinking she detected some evasiveness in the tone and manner of his reply, she asked, "But not the King and Queen?"

Voldi was leading the way toward Darik now. Turning about, he said, with a labored casualness that only increased Fara's curiosity, "Don't expect too much—and you will not be disappointed."

She patted Darik on the muzzle and they imagined that he recognized her. Voldi picked her up lightly and tossed her into the saddle.

"You ride on to the King's encampment," he said, "and send a horse back for me. I'll be trudging along with your silly little donkey."

" 'Trudging' is what you will be doing," laughed Fara, "if you walk with Jasper. He never hurries."

Voldi's face was sober as she gathered up the reins to depart.

"One more thing, dear," he said. "If Deran should be there, keep your temper."

Her bewilderment showed in her reluctance to go, but Voldi waved her on. Digging her heels into Darik's ribs, she set out on the last lap of her home-bound journey.

After she had disappeared, Voldi wondered whether he should have been more explicit—or, better, should have said nothing at all about conditions in the royal household. Perhaps Fara's intuition might provide a partial explanation. She couldn't help remembering that Deran had shown himself to be unfriendly. Maybe she would guess that the jealous Prince would resent his return. It was difficult for Voldi to tell her that Deran was bitterly envious of him: she would presently discover this without being told.

It had often occurred to Voldi that the King had unwittingly done him a disservice in appointing him to succeed his eminent grandfather as a member of the King's Council. Deran had been noisily resentful and derisive. Voldi's long-time comrades, approving his appointment, were treated to the Prince's scorn.

Before he left again, on the grim errand from which he was now returning, a dozen of Voldi's boyhood cronies, all of them sons or grandsons of distinguished Arabians, had invited him to join them on a stag-hunt deep in the wooded mountains. And that night around the camp-fire they had confided their bitter opposition to the Prince who, they said, had become so arrogant and so thoroughly detested by the people that his accession to the throne would amount to a national disaster. Voldi had tried to temper their anger. . . . "He's young yet. Be patient. His attitude may change as he grows older."

"The trouble is," they told him—"the Queen, who is passionately devoted to the Prince, encourages him in his folly."

"And the King?" Voldi had asked.

Well—the gentle-spirited, peace-loving Zendi, whatever he might think of the situation, had done nothing about it.

"The fact is—" Museph had blurted out, recklessly, "Arabia needs a King with a loud voice and a savage temper; somebody like rough old Aretas who could outyell and outcurse the toughest sheik in the land!"

At this juncture, Voldi had said, quietly, "Let us forget now that this matter has been discussed. Such talk is treasonable—and we all know it."

"Someone ought to tell Deran," rumbled Raboth, "just how thin the ice is where he walks!"

And Voldi had brought a laugh—and a conclusion to the talk—by reminding Raboth of the convention of mice that resolved to put a bell on the cat, and found that no mouse would volunteer to perform this service.

*   *   *   *   *   *

All the way up the mountain-side Fara's thoughts were busy with Voldi's enigmatic warning of a cool reception. It was not like Voldi to imagine a feeling of animosity on the part of young Deran. The Prince had been overindulged and badly spoiled. Even as a child he had been rude and impudent. Doubtless Voldi, on his recent return to Arabia, had been given fresh evidence of Deran's unfriendliness.

Arriving at the King's encampment, Fara was instantly surrounded by a devoted company of servants who swarmed out of the service tents and stables and paddocks. Ione, a mere shadow of her former self, was tearful and speechless with joy. Old Kedar dispatched a rider, with a led horse, to meet Voldi. So far, it was a happy reunion.

But an hour later, when the home-comers sat at supper with the royal family, their welcome lacked enthusiasm.

Fara was shocked to see how King Zendi had aged in the past three years. The hair at his temples was white. His face was thin and haggard. His smile was feeble and fleeting, and he had little to say. But what Zendi had lost in forcefulness Rennah had gained. Arabia had never been governed by a Queen: Arabia was distinctly a man's land. But as Fara glanced from the Queen's imperious face into Zendi's unresponsive eyes, it was clear enough that the peace-loving King had abdicated.

Deran strutted in late when their supper was nearly finished, and sprawled in his seat, nodding carelessly to their guests as if he had seen them within the hour. His face was flushed. It was easy to see that he had been drinking.

"It's going about, Counsellor Voldi," he remarked, with a patronizing grin, "that you finally paid off that frail old rascal in Galilee. How did you do it? Stick him in the back while he slept?"

Voldi made no reply to the raw insult; seemed not to have heard it. Presently he glanced across the table and confronted Fara's indignant eyes. His look repeated the warning that she must control her temper. Quickly masking her sudden anger, she darted a wordless inquiry. "Counsellor?" Voldi knew she was inquiring about that. He had not told her.

There was a brief, awkward silence which Rennah now broke with a dry trill of mirthless laughter.

"Perhaps Counsellor Voldi doesn't think your remark is very amusing, Deran," she cooed, softly. . . . Then, turning to Voldi with a contrived smile to which he did not respond, she added, "The Prince is such a tease." . . . And turning to Fara, "One never can tell when he's joking."

"But it's easy to tell when he is not joking!" retorted Fara, crisply. Voldi gently rebuked her with an almost imperceptible shake of his head.

Deran was having a good time now. If Voldi wouldn't quarrel, perhaps he could bedevil the girl into some reckless disregard of his princely rank. He turned on her with a sardonic chuckle.

"We observe that Princess Fara returns to us as sharp-tongued as ever. We had hoped that her long sojourn with her meek Jewish relatives—"

"Now, Deran," interrupted his mother, impatiently. "There has been quite enough teasing, please."

Voldi now surprised them by addressing the King, who had sat demurely through these indignities, occasionally shaking his graying head, but saying nothing.

"Sire, if I may be excused now, I shall go home and see my parents."

"Of course, Voldi," said the King, with obvious relief. "You should go while there is still moonlight. We will see you tomorrow."

Voldi promptly came to his feet, bowed deeply to Their Majesties, smiled for Fara, ignored the Prince, and straightway made his exit.

"And may I go now, please?" entreated Fara, in a half-whisper to the Queen. "I have had only a glimpse of poor Ione—and she is waiting to see me."

Rennah drew a pursed smile and nodded. Fara, bowing to the King, quickly left the room.

Deran leaned back in his chair, stretched his arms, yawned, and chuckled, "That was fun."

"You're a fool!" muttered his father.

"I'm sure Deran meant no harm, Zendi," put in Rennah.

"Deran is a fool!" shouted Zendi.

*　　*　　*　　*　　*　　*

But now a more acute problem than the foolishness of Prince Deran was monopolizing the mind and conversation of Arabia.

At widespread intervals, usually in midsummer, there had been many cases of a sudden, crippling paralysis, affecting children mostly, though occasionally striking down an adult, too. This season the mysterious affliction, for which there had been found no cure, was rapidly mounting to epidemic proportions. Alarmed mothers were keeping their children at home, but with no assurance of their safety. The dreaded disease struck at random, and struck hard! Nor was it a respecter of persons, in testimony whereof the Thing laid its hand on Prince Deran. The news traveled fast, and the sorrow of Arabia was under excellent control. The sheiks and the shepherds did not risk saying, "Served him right!" But they scowled and lifted an indifferent shoulder, which came to the same thing—and couldn't be quoted.

26

NEVER HAD THERE BEEN a fairer morning in Jerusalem than on this Day of Pentecost.

Since dawn, every road leading into the city had been filling with merry-makers on foot from the provinces, and within an hour the highways were crowded.

Frequently the country people scampered to the hedges, good-naturedly conceding the right of way to impressive caravans from distant lands, unannoyed by the haughty stares of the urbane strangers.

Once within the gaily decorated gates, the festive throng jostled toward the bazaars and food-markets while the sober-faced men of consequence, indifferent to the city's gaiety, proceeded on through to the Sheep Gate and up the steepening Bethany boulevard to Levi's Inn where, after a comforting bath and a change of linen, they would rest until it was time to attend the famous camel-auction in the early afternoon.

Half a block down the hill from Levi's stood a massive old stone structure which had long served as headquarters for the Coppersmiths' Guild. It was an undeniably ugly building but no discredit to the street, for the organization that it housed was one of the most honorable institutions in Jerusalem. The Coppersmiths' Guild had been the first society to volunteer substantial aid to Nehemiah when he rebuilt the city's walls more than four centuries ago.

The high-ceilinged, rectangular second story of the Guildhall, accessible by an outside staircase, was used as an auditorium. It had seating for approximately two hundred and served not only the general conclaves of the Guild but was frequently rented to business conventions with a large non-resident membership.

The hall was open this morning and gradually filling with men of all sorts whose only observable relation to one another was their apparent

459

uncertainty as to the nature of their errand. For the most part they came singly. The majority of them were of middle age, plainly dressed in country garb, and obviously from the provinces. They slowly mounted the stone staircase, diffidently entered the dingy old auditorium, and stood awkwardly for a long moment wondering what was expected of them, for there were no ushers, nor was there anyone in sight who had the appearance of being responsible for the mysterious meeting. After tarrying awhile at the door, the bewildered men from the country found seats and sat down to wait. A sprinkling of well-dressed men of affairs stalked in, one by one; but, for all their urbanity, they seemed quite as confused as the unsophisticated provincials.

Jairus turned to young Joel, as they lingered in the doorway to survey the half-filled room, and asked, "Do you see anyone you ever saw before?" And Joel, craning about, shook his head; but immediately amended his reply to whisper, "Over there is a man I recognize. His name is Micah. He was a laborer in the Tetrarch's vineyard."

"I wonder what brings him here," mumbled Jairus.

"His little girl was blind," said Joel. "Jesus opened her eyes. I saw him do it, sir. Last summer. But I heard, a few days ago, that the child had just died. Of a fever. . . . Maybe that's what brings him here, sir."

"You mean—perhaps Micah thinks that Jesus—now that he is alive again—may give his little girl back to him?"

"I wouldn't know, sir," murmured Joel.

"Do you suppose that all these people knew Jesus?" wondered Jairus.

"It could be, sir."

They found seats near the rear of the hall. Presently a distinguished-looking, smooth-shaven Roman with close-cropped, grizzled hair came in, glanced about, and strode directly to the rear, seating himself at the end of the row but one vacant chair apart from Jairus. They gave each other a brief appraisal without speaking.

For a full quarter-hour there had been no new arrivals. Apparently the company was complete. Now the heavy oaken door began to complain of its rusted hinges. All heads were turned in that direction and mystified eyes watched the massive door slowly close, though no one had touched it. Jairus darted an inquiring glance at the Roman at the same instant that Mencius arched an eyebrow toward Jairus; but neither spoke. The baffled audience again faced forward. The room grew strangely quiet.

Then a giant of a man, seated in the front row, rose and walked confidently to the rostrum. Only a few in the transfixed audience failed to recognize him; but even those who had seen him, again and again, as he stood at the Master's side, protecting him in the crush of great throngs, observed instantly that something had happened to the Big Fisherman.

They hadn't always liked his attitude on those eventful summer days. He had kept the great crowds in order, yes; and he had made the bearers of the sick ones take their turn. But sometimes his manner had annoyed them. It was almost as if he owned the show—and Jesus was his exhibit. Not infrequently some offended man, who had been unceremoniously pushed back into line, would grumble, "Who does that big fellow think he is, anyhow?"

Now it appeared that some sort of miracle had been wrought upon Peter.

For one thing, he had a different face. The former face had been more than a bit bumptious, the darting eyes audacious, the lips inclined to purse protrudingly. The Big Fisherman's new face was refined. All the old deep-chiseled lines carved by habitual brashness and bluster were gone; ironed out as by fire. There were still plenty of lines but they had not been engraved by self-pride: Peter had evidently suffered to earn his new countenance.

Maybe the changed color of his hair had had something to do with the softening and refinement of his face. His heavy thatch, previously black as a raven's wing, had turned gray—in patches. It was sprinkled with gray throughout, but at his temples and where the hair grew low on the middle of his forehead, there were broad strips of white; snow-white! His formerly unkempt black beard had been shortened: it too glistened with white. Peter's face had lost its austerity and had taken on dignity. . . . Mencius, who once had had a fleeting glimpse of the gigantic man running down the street, recognized nothing about him but his extraordinary height, and told Captain Fulvius, when he rejoined The Vestris, that the massive Galilean, who directed the meeting on the Day of Pentecost, was the most august and majestic figure he had ever seen.

But perhaps the chief distinction of the transformed disciple was his arresting voice; deep, resonant, commanding. It had the tone of authority. When he began by saying that he was speaking on behalf of the Living Christ to a selected company of men reverently awaiting tidings of him, it was evident in the faces and postures of the audience that Peter's commission was, in their opinion, authentic.

It had been the hope of God from the beginning, he said, that His children would inherit the Kingdom. He had not compelled them to accept its benefits. He had endowed them with free will to claim or refuse their heritage.

But God had not left them in darkness concerning the results of their decisions. Every generation had had its inspired prophets who had entreated men to receive and enjoy their heavenly legacy. Only a few had heeded these messages. The lonely prophets had been imprisoned, flogged, and stoned by the forces of greed and the lust for power.

God had been patient with the evil-doers. Again and again, through the ages, humanity had reaped such appalling harvests of its own misdeeds that even the kings and warriors had stood aghast at the tragedies they had contrived. And always, in the midst of ruin and the fear that had chastened both the just and the unjust, the prophets had shouted, "Now we shall begin anew! We shall rebuild the wastes! We shall repair the world's desolations!"

But when a brief day of peace had brought prosperity, new tyrants rose up and another era of rapine, slavery and slaughter would bring distrust and terror to the children of men. The scepter had passed from one bloody hand to another as the nations clamored for power, and yet more power, over the lives of the helpless.

Here the Big Fisherman, after pausing for a moment, continued in an ominous tone that deepened the silence. He had done with his calm review of mankind's unfortunate history. It was time now for the world to be shaken wide awake. God had sent forth His Son with power to heal the sick, bind up broken hearts, open blind eyes, and proclaim a new era of good will among men.

But the world would not receive him. He had been scorned, whipped, and put to a shameful death! But he had come alive again—and had been seen of many. Now he had returned to his Father's House.

"Think you then," demanded Peter, "that the will of God has been set at naught? Think you that His Spirit will no longer strive with men? I declare to you that our Christ is King! He has begun to reign! And he shall reign until all the kingdoms of this world shall have become his Kingdom!"

For a moment the one hundred and twenty men thought the Big Fisherman's speech had ended, for he stood silent with his head bowed as in prayer. Then he faced them to say impressively:

"We, who confidently believe in him, have been summoned here to receive unmistakable proofs that his Holy Spirit abides with us. And from this day forward we are commissioned to spread the good news of his conquering Kingdom!"

Suddenly Peter drew himself up to his full height and glanced upward as if he had been struck. His auditors straightened and stared. Immediately above the Big Fisherman's head, and touching it, was a shimmering crimson flame—in shape like the flame of a torch! All breathing in the spacious room was suspended.

Then the massive oaken door flew open and banged hard against the wall. There was the deafening road of a mighty tempest that swept through the hall. The startled men held to their seats and clung to one another as the rushing wind lashed to and fro. It was as if the world had come to an end! Now tongues of flame stabbed through the storm, coming to rest—torch-like—upon the heads of all present! The glow of the fire possessed exhilarating properties. Some of the men shouted ecstatically. Some wept for joy. Strangers grasped the hands of strangers and gazed at one another in wonderment. Jairus put his arm around Joel who was weeping. Mencius put both hands over his eyes and shook his head. Joseph of Arimathaea clutched Hassan's arm.

Now the torch-like flames departed and the tempest roared out as suddenly as it had come. Every man was on his feet, all talking at once, loudly, as if the tempest still raged. Mencius, not one to be easily discomposed, was so utterly stampeded that he turned to Jairus and shouted —in Greek, "This is a most amazing thing, sir!" And Jairus, who didn't know a word of Greek, instantly replied, in that language, "Surely the Lord has visited us!" Young Joel, listening intently, nodded his head; and when Jairus asked him if he had understood what they were saying he said he had, and added, in his own Aramaic, "It is true, sir! God Himself has been in this place!"

But the pandemonium in the Coppersmiths' Guildhall was no secret. The roar of the storm had been heard throughout the city. The urbane guests at Levi's Inn had rushed out into the street to see what was happening. It was evident that the fury of the tempest was confined to the Guildhall. They ran up the stairway, arriving when the tornado had spent itself and all the men in the auditorium were shouting joyfully. Crowding into the room they stared at the strange scene.

A tall, haughty man from Crete remarked sourly to his bodyguard, in the outlandish dialect of that country—a curious composite of Greek and Egyptian, "Bah! They're all drunk!"

Peter, striding toward the door, answered him in Crete's guttural patois, "These men are not drunk! They are rejoicing because the Kingdom of God is at hand! The world shall have peace! The slaves shall be freed! The Lord has proclaimed a new day!"

"How do you happen to be speaking our language?" demanded the stranger. "You are not a citizen of Crete!"

"I am a citizen of the Kingdom of God!" declared Peter. "And from henceforth that Kingdom includes Crete!"

"You say—all the slaves are to be set free?"

"Yes—and their masters, too. No men can be free while other men are slaves!"

"You should be locked up!" growled the Cretan. "You are speaking treason!"

The controversy was attracting attention. A dozen of the illumined men gathered close and joined in supporting Peter, all of them speaking the barbarous jargon of far-away Crete. The man from that country, with baffled eyes, raised his elbow as if to ward off a blow, and slowly backed toward the door, muttering, "No! No!"

The Guildhall rapidly emptied. The street was packed with a huge crowd of bewildered people. The newly commissioned men, radiant, confident, infiltrated the throng, shouting, "The Kingdom of God has come for all who believe in Him!" They scattered through the city, spreading the news. They were unafraid. They stopped Roman legionaries on the street to announce the new Kingdom; and the legionaries, stunned by their audacity, did not detain them.

That day, three thousand men in Jerusalem said they believed it and would join the disciples in preparing for the reign of peace.

*   *   *   *   *   *

Late in the evening, as the little company of Jesus' Galileans sat together in Benyosef's house, exhausted to the point of speechlessness by the amazing events of the day, Philip, who had spread the tidings to incredulous groups at the camel-auction, remarked, "It is said that the Prince of Arabia has been smitten with paralysis."

Peter made no comment but seemed deeply impressed by this tragedy that had befallen the royal house of Israel's long-time enemy. Presently he arose and seated himself in a far corner of the dimly lighted room, with his elbows on his knees and his head in his hands, apparently wrestling with a difficult problem.

After a half-hour of silent meditation he took leave of them and trudged slowly up the long hill to the Garden of Gethsemane where he knelt beside a great rock and prayed earnestly for guidance. Could it be possible that God might use him as a messenger of good will to hostile Arabia?

27

FOR A WHILE the authorities in Jerusalem were so stunned by the fearless activities of the new movement that they took no action at all.

Within a week after Pentecost the number of determined men who saw the promise of peace in a divinely sponsored Kingdom that would overwhelm all tyrannies had risen to five thousand.

Many of the converts were sincere believers in the miraculous power of the inspired Galilean. Many more, who had neither heard nor seen him, were ready to cast their lot with any party that guaranteed liberty from oppression. With the rapacious Roman Empire preparing to close in on them they had little to lose by joining in this quest for freedom. Some wanted to save their souls and others their necks. The threat of disaster was urgent. Any port was good enough in this storm.

It was futile for the city fathers to dispose of this Kingdom-movement by declaring that the men of the Pentecostal experience had conspired to fabricate a fantastic lie; and, at the risk of their lives, proclaim it on crowded street-corners and in the Temple. Three men might have been foolhardy enough to do that, but not one hundred and twenty! And ten credulous men might have been taken in by such a fanciful tale, but not five thousand!

The Sanhedrin met in day-long sessions, stroking its beard, successively suggesting and rejecting remedies ranging in tactics and temper all the way from the conciliatory to the admonitory to the punitive; and adjourned until tomorrow.

The venerable and highly respected Gamaliel, Chief Legal Counsel to the lawgivers of Israel, when besought for advice, reminded them that on several occasions revolutions had collected a few hundreds, made reckless by their discontentments, but all such little tempests had quickly blown out and away. "Give these infatuated Galileans time. If their cause is

465

unworthy of regard it will perish. If it is inspired of God, as they insist, you will not be able to thwart it, even if you would."

This sensible deliverance offered a measure of temporary relief. The Sanhedrin would wait—and see. . . . But it didn't have to wait very long. That same afternoon the news broke that Peter, the leader of the new party, had picked up a helpless paralytic on the terrace in front of the Temple; and, setting him on his feet, had told him to walk—and he had walked! And this was no trumped-up tale. A hundred people had witnessed it. The paralyzed man had sat on the Temple steps every fair day for years, waving his alms-basin under the public's nose. Now he had leaped up, shouting for joy! However he might feel about it tomorrow when he realized that his occupation was gone, he was spry enough now; and if the Sanhedrin was to offer a plausible explanation of this event it would have to think fast and hard!

As for Pilate, he gave little credence to these stories of miracles. The whole movement, in his opinion, was but the natural aftermath of Jerusalem's blunder in crucifying a harmless prophet. The victim's friends were belatedly showing their colors. Perhaps it were better to keep hands off and not dignify the new party by opposing it. If the Sanhedrin demanded action, Pilate would act. In the meantime the Insula would pretend not to notice. The jaded Procurator felt under no obligation to relieve the embarrassment of the Sanhedrin.

And so, with no opposition at all, the Kingdom-movement in Jerusalem became increasingly confident, proving its courage by the organization of a "Christian Ecclesia." Regional meetings were held throughout the city and mass meetings met in a huge vacant warehouse.

So amazing had been the unexpected triumph of the new cause that the little group of original disciples became convinced of the early reappearance of their Lord to fulfill his promise of "peace on earth and good will among men." It would be well to prepare for his coming by binding together in harmony all the disparate elements comprising the Ecclesia.

It occurred to Peter that if these people could live together they might provide Jerusalem with an object lesson in tolerance and generosity. He proposed the establishment of a commune. No one would be compelled to join it, but those who desired to experience its benefits should convert their realty into money and bring it, with their household goods, into the new communal home where the well-to-do's and the ne'er-do-well's might share alike.

The people who had next to nothing thought it was a grand idea. The more fortunate, who had something to contribute, weren't so sure, but

Peter had already demonstrated supernormal power, and perhaps—under his administration—the experiment might succeed.

But the thing never worked. Peter's theory that the more closely acquainted the people were the more they would love one another turned out to be erroneous. He had declared that if men understood one another, regardless of their training or temperament, they could enjoy a pleasant and profitable fellowship. The facts were that as their mutual understanding increased their mutual distrust mounted from dispassionate contempt to forthright animosity.

In vain did the Big Fisherman plead for harmony. Often and often he used the arresting phrase, "these latter times," in his warnings that the Lord might come at any moment, and that when he came he would expect to find his faithful followers ready to receive him. But this ominous admonition, albeit listened to with respect—for they all idolized Peter— failed to cure the quarreling. The Greeks complained that the Jews, who outnumbered them, were unfair in their distribution of the necessities. This could easily have been true, though the Greeks in Jerusalem, even in the minority, may have been too keenly apprehensive of discrimination. But, whatever may have been the merits of these mounting controversies, the commune was becoming a burdensome disillusionment to Peter. How indeed was the world ever to realize universal peace if a hundred devoted followers of Christ, in the most religious city on earth, couldn't get along with one another?

The problem having now become too hot to handle, Peter appointed a board of seven representative men to administer the benefits of the commune while he himself gave most of his time to visitation of the needy throughout the city. And the commune, now lacking his direct oversight, quickly deteriorated into a public nuisance. Now the Sanhedrin really did have a case against the phantom Kingdom, and pressed it with vigor. Pilate ordered a few companies of legionaries to exterminate the unhappy commune and forbid any Kingdom-talk either in public or private. Peter tried to salvage what was left of his branch of the Kingdom, and was tossed into prison. That same night he walked out of jail, barred doors quietly opening before him. Considerately stepping over the big feet of recumbent guards in the prison corridors, he went to his lodgings; and, next day, no effort was made to recapture him. The authorities in control of the prison were appropriately embarrassed over the incident and Pilate sneered at their shame, advising them not to risk a repetition of their chagrin.

So Peter went free and continued to walk fearlessly and unmolested in

the city, his spiritual power gaining such prestige that invalids—whether
Christian believers or not—were carried on their cots into the streets so
that the great man's shadow, as he passed, might fall across their wasted
form and heal them of their diseases.

As for the hapless adherents of the Christian Ecclesia, they had been
dispersed, silenced, scared, jailed, and stoned. Peter viewed the wreck of
his local project without dismay. Considering the enormous weight of the
forces aligned against it, it was a wonder that it had been permitted even
a brief existence. Its disintegration did not mean that the Kingdom was a
failure. Christ's Kingdom would prevail—but not today—not tomorrow
—and not easily.

*   *   *   *   *   *

And perhaps it was just as well that the Jerusalem experiment in communal living had come to a prompt and decisive termination.

Had it shown any promise of recovery by careful nursing, the disciples
might have felt obliged to stay with it for better or worse; but its collapse
had been so complete, so far beyond the reach of repair, that the disciples
immediately set forth on other missions: Philip to Antioch, Andrew to
Damascus, Thaddeus to the fisher-folk on the Sea of Galilee, Matthew to
Capernaum and Bethsaida, John and James to Askelon, Gaza, and
Idumea, Thomas to the Parthians in India, the aged Nathaniel Bartholomew to Jericho—and then on home to die.

Learning that a little company of Christians were meeting secretly in
Joppa, Peter decided to visit them. The shabby old city had lately come
awake, shaken out of its torpor by the Empire's activities on the waterfront. Reconstruction of the wharves and reconditioning of the harbor
had tripled the population. The newcomers were slaves, for the most part,
many of them quite unused to pick-and-shovel labor, paying with their
sweat and calluses for futile efforts to defend themselves and their communities against the engulfing tyranny of Rome. Obviously the Christian
movement in Joppa was a good thing to keep away from, especially for a
distinguished-looking man whose unusual height and bulk made it
difficult for him to remain inconspicuous.

Peter was deeply touched by the welcome he received at the lame and
blistered hands of these despairing men. He had gone to Joppa with no
acquaintances to vouch for him. It was a wonder to him—once he had
learned in what danger they stood—that the wary slaves should have accepted his overtures of friendship without distrust; for the Romans were
taking no chances of insurrection on the part of these intelligent men,

enslaved for political reasons; nor were the slaves risking exposure by confiding in strangers. But the Big Fisherman instantly disarmed suspicion.

Taking lodgings in the humble home of a tanner who lived near the docks, Peter quickly won his taciturn host's confidence and discovered, to his delight, that the quiet old man was a believer in the promised Kingdom of justice and peace. It soon became evident that the house of Simon the Tanner was a secret meeting-place of lonely men. In the night they would arrive in small groups of twos and threes and sit together in dim candle-light, listening to the Tanner's reassurances that all would be well —sometime—somewhere.

Now that Peter had come, they could learn about the divine Nazarene from one who had walked daily by his side. The lean and haggard men hungrily heard the intimate details of the Master's ministry; his comforting words, his marvelous deeds, his courageous death, his return to life; and—most heartening of all—the amazing disclosures of his abiding presence and power on the Day of Pentecost.

Very few of the wistful listeners understood Aramaic but all of them knew Greek, and although Peter's Greek was anything but fluent it served its purpose. Indeed, the thoughtful old Tanner told him that his groping for the right words, which his sympathetic—and sometimes amused—audience supplied, had but deepened their interest in what he was saying.

"They help you tell the story," said Simon. "It means more to them that way. Don't ever try to improve your Greek, Peter," he added. "It's much better when it's not so good."

Those were blessed days—at Joppa. Not only had they brought fresh courage to the hard-pressed slaves who, to all outward appearance, were irretrievably doomed, but they had renewed Peter's faith in the inevitable victory of the Kingdom. . . . Perhaps it wasn't going to be so difficult, after all! Perhaps the world would accept it sooner than he had thought! The unhappy people of every nation needed only to be told that peace and freedom were about to come—and with faith in that promise their yokes would be easy and their burdens light.

"Surely," Peter had remarked to the old Tanner, "if these enslaved men of Joppa, who live such wretched lives, can believe in the world's liberation and look forward with confidence to the future, it shouldn't be so difficult for the more fortunate to accept the promise."

"I think you are in error there, my friend," Simon had replied. "It is the faith of the beaten men in chains, for whom all human reliances have failed, that will hasten the coming of the Kingdom."

Late one afternoon—it turned out to be Peter's last day in Joppa—he climbed the narrow stairs to the flat roof of the Tanner's house to meditate in private. It was not yet suppertime, but he was hungry; very hungry. Simon was a frail old man who didn't require much food. Peter's appetite was robust. He found himself thinking about Hannah's table. There was always more than enough to eat. Sometimes he and Andy would buy a fat lamb and roast it over a glowing fire in their back yard. He wished he were at home in Bethsaida now! . . . While he daydreamed, he grew drowsy, stretched out comfortably in the big chair—and slept. The well-pastured sheep and sleek calves of Galilee strolled into his dream. Here came a spring lamb that he might buy. But now the coveted lamb moved on and all the sheep and calves were gone. Presently some other animals appeared: strange, misshapen, repulsive beasts. Peter scowled with disgust.

Someone in the chair opposite chuckled a little.

"If you are so hungry, Peter," remarked the visitor, "how about slaughtering one of these?"

"Ugh!" Peter heard himself muttering.

His dream companion laughed softly and Peter gazed in that direction to see what manner of man he was. The newcomer was a well-favored youth, elegantly clad in white, with a broad band of gold encircling his head, and a gold cross on the breast of his tunic.

"You should make the acquaintance of these animals," said the youth, with a smile. "They're not to be found in Galilee or Judaea, but you will encounter them. This is a big world, Peter, and it all belongs to our Father. . . . That tall, ungainly beast is a giraffe—and the short, not-very-pretty one behind it is a wart hog. The next one is an ant eater and beside it is a rhinoceros—"

"They're loathsome!" mumbled Peter.

"And the one on this side of the wart hog," continued the Angel, undisturbed by Peter's interruption, "is a chimpanzee. Looks a little like a man; does he not? And the creature shuffling along behind him really is a man, even if lacking somewhat in refinement."

"What's all this about?" demanded Peter, crossly.

The mysterious visitor drew his chair nearer and when he spoke his tone was serious.

"Peter—I have been sent to say that you have been entrusted with a very important mission. It will take you to far places and you will meet all manner of God's creatures. You must learn to say to yourself, 'God either created all of us—or none of us!' The Master intends his Kingdom to serve the whole world. If it is not open to everybody, it is not open to any-body! I was sent to tell you this."

Peter came wide awake now and found himself alone. Good old Si-mon's white head appeared at the top of the stairs.

"There are three strangers here to see you," he said. "They are from Caesarea."

"What can men of Caesarea want of me?" muttered Peter, crossly.

"Perhaps they will tell you," said Simon, retreating down the stairs.

*   *   *   *   *   *

How he had hated the Romans! Ever since he was a little boy, the very word angered him! Their cavalry from the Capernaum fort had galloped, four abreast, on the Galilean highways, frightening poor people half out of their wits, sending women and children scurrying into the hedges. Their drunken foot-soldiers had reeled into the little shops shouting for attention. They had grossly insulted women of all ages on the streets. They had helped themselves to the defenseless farmers' grapes and melons. Peter had despised the Romans with a bitter loathing!

And now, here he was in Caesarea, the honored guest of "The Italians," a social club composed entirely of Roman civilians in the employ of the Prefect's government.

The three mounted men who had called for him in Joppa had defer-entially explained that Cornelius, the Senior Regent of "The Italians," urgently desired him to come at once to Caesarea for an important confer-ence. Very much bewildered, Peter had awkwardly climbed onto the tall black horse they had brought for him; and there he was, riding along under the bright moonlight, in the company of Romans; to all appear-ances the same kind of Romans he had learned to hate! Sleek, well-fed, well-accoutered Romans, with the despised black eagle insignia on their scarlet tunics, with the clean-shaven faces and close-cropped hair, and the inevitable black bandeaux on their heads. The journey was made mostly in silence. The couriers had told him little about his summons to Cae-sarea. Cornelius wanted to see him. That was about all. The name of Cornelius meant nothing to Peter, but evidently it meant a great deal to these men. They spoke his name almost reverently. Peter was to learn later that Cornelius was the treasurer of the Roman government in Caes-area and high in the esteem of Prefect Sergius.

It was a fast trip. Peter had had almost no experience in riding. When they arrived in Caesarea, he was weary and lame. They took him directly to their well-appointed clubhouse, showed him to a beautifully furnished guest-room, and told him to rest until Cornelius came. He bathed, slept, and wolfed the food a servant brought him. And now—in the early afternoon—he was invited to see the mysterious man who had summoned him from Joppa.

Cornelius was seated behind a large desk in a sumptuous office. As Peter entered, he rose, bowed deeply, and pointed to a heavily upholstered chair opposite his own. Peter sat and regarded the Regent with interest. He was a handsome old man of seventy, with snow-white hair and a benign countenance. When he spoke, his voice was low and gentle.

"You may think it strange, sir," he began, in labored Aramaic, "to be summoned here with so little information concerning your errand. . . . By the way," he interrupted himself to ask, "do you converse in Greek?"

"Not too well," admitted Peter.

"Is your Greek as good as my Aramaic?"

"Yes, sir; not meaning any offense." They both grinned.

"We will speak Greek, then," said Cornelius, softly. "What I have to say to you could not be confided to those fine fellows who brought you here. They would not have understood. I have had a mysterious dream, and I am informed that you can interpret it."

Peter leaned forward and listened attentively.

"On the night before last I was visited by an Angel," continued Cornelius. "Let me say that it is not my habit to dream of Angels. This one seemed very real. He was a handsome young fellow, clad in white satin, and wearing a golden fillet. On the left breast of his tunic—" Cornelius laid his hand over the black eagle on his breast.

"There was a gold cross, I think," assisted Peter.

Cornelius' deep-set eyes widened. He nodded his head.

"You, too, have seen him, then?" he asked.

"Yes, sir. He is a courier, representing the Kingdom."

"Precisely!" said Cornelius. "That is what he told me! And when I asked him to tell me about this Kingdom, he told me to send for you! . . . Proceed, please! What manner of Kingdom is this?"

"It is a long story, sir," said Peter, wondering where to begin. "Doubtless you have heard of Jesus, the Galilean, who went about the Jewish provinces, healing the sick, encouraging the downtrodden—and was crucified by Pontius Pilate—and, on the third day, left his tomb, to be seen alive by many witnesses."

Cornelius nodded, indifferently, almost impatiently. Yes—he had heard all that—but these were tall tales—and who were these witnesses? And what was this Kingdom?

Peter recrossed his legs and began at the beginning. He himself had been a witness. He hadn't wanted to believe in this Carpenter. He had been a rough, profane, skeptical, roistering fisherman. He had gone out into the country to scoff at this young upstart and prove to the deluded men of his fishing crew that the wonder-working prophet was a fraud.

Cornelius listened with mounting interest.

Peter told him of the day when he had been forced to carry a blind child to Jesus, and had seen the bewildered eyes open; told him of the vast throngs that followed, day by day, hungry, footsore, fascinated by tidings of a Kingdom to come where all men would be free of oppression; told him of the healing of cripples; yes, and lepers!

The afternoon wore on. The story continued.

The authorities had tried to silence the Carpenter, but feared an up-rising by the people. The crowds increased. The highways were crowded with frantic relatives bringing their sick to be healed.

Dusk came down. A servant slipped quietly into the room and lighted the lamps. Cornelius told him to serve supper here on the desk. The servant retired and Peter went on.

Now it was Passover Week in Jerusalem. Jesus had rebuked the Temple as a place of merchandise. He had been arrested, tried for blasphemy and treason, convicted, whipped, reviled, crucified. And then he had come alive again.

"And you say you saw all this?" demanded Cornelius, sharply.

"I saw it all, sir; yes, sir, all but—" Peter's voice broke. He bowed his head and covered his distorted face with his huge, trembling hands. Cornelius waited silently. Recovering his voice with an effort, Peter went on. "I saw him after he had returned to life, sir; but I must confess, in shame, that I was not present at his trials, nor was I at his side when he went to his death. At the last, when everything seemed lost, I denied—in the presence of strangers—that I had ever known him—and I ran away!"

There was a long silence. At length, the old Roman huskily cleared his throat and said, gently, "You are a brave man, my friend! And your testimony is believable! Your confession proves your integrity! You would not have told me this if you were not speaking the truth. I believe you, Peter! I believe everything you have told me!"

Servants came in to serve supper, but Cornelius shook his head and motioned them to leave.

"Do you want to tell me now about this Kingdom?" he asked, softly. "Or would you prefer to wait until tomorrow?"

"Tomorrow," murmured Peter.

"Come," said Cornelius, rising, and laying a hand on Peter's bowed shoulder. "You shall go to your room; and when you are ready for your supper they will bring it to you. . . . I know you are weary. It was a heavy task. Only a very strong man could do that!"

Taking his arm Cornelius accompanied him back to his room and quietly close the door. Utterly spent, Peter flung himself at full length upon his bed. It seemed very strange that his shameful confession of cowardice and disloyalty should have made him an accredited ambassador of the Master's Kingdom!

*   *   *   *   *   *

The following afternoon, closeted with Cornelius, was a memorable occasion. Peter had never met anyone like him. The gentle-spirited old Roman had given much serious thought to the future of mankind. Indeed he disclosed a far deeper invasion of this subject than had ever been undertaken by Peter who knew next to nothing about the history of nations.

"Now, as for this universal peace and freedom which your Kingdom expects in the near future," Cornelius was saying, "I fear that you—and all who share your hope—are letting yourselves in for a great disappointment."

"But, does not every sane man desire peace?" queried Peter.

"As an individual, yes," agreed Cornelius, "but men are not permitted to exercise their own private desires. They are in captivity to their nation, and nations have neither the talent nor the training for the achievement of peace."

"But every man can claim the peace of the Kingdom in his own heart," argued Peter.

"Certainly!" said Cornelius, "as an individual, he may acquire peace of mind, or, as you say, peace in his heart; but why call that a Kingdom? . . . You have been talking about a triumphant King whose reign will supersede the authority and power of all regularly constituted governments. You have been too discreet—or too polite—to tell me that the coming Kingdom of your Christos will destroy the Roman Empire; but that's what it comes to, does it not?"

Peter had shifted uneasily in his chair.

"I shouldn't want to put it that way, sir," he said. "The Christos will not destroy the Empire. The Empire will destroy itself! As men see the advantages of living in good will toward one another—"

"They will not need the Empire," broke in Cornelius. "But it isn't that simple! Your man of good will is not at liberty to choose how he may treat other men. His nation decides that for him."

'But you, yourself, my good Cornelius, believe in kindness and friendship toward all men," said Peter, softly, "and you practice it, too. You are not far from the Kingdom."

"Farther than you think, my friend," insisted Cornelius. "It is true that I do not bear arms. I do not slaughter or enslave other men. I have not the physique to be a soldier. The Empire has given me the more decent task of keeping the accounts and disbursing the funds for the building of these great wharves which will be used some day in an attack on you unhappy Jews."

"If it hurts your conscience, why do you do it?" ventured Peter.

"What would you have me do?" countered the old man. "Shall I live in solitude, despised by my friends, unable to support my dependents? ... What I am saying is: your Kingdom presupposes that every man is free to determine what manner of life he shall live. In that it is hopelessly impractical."

Peter was no match for the old Roman in debate. His faith in the victory of the Master's Kingdom was undimmed, but he had no answer for the problems that Cornelius presented. He had never confronted them.

"Is it your belief then," he asked, "that men are forever to be the victims of greed—and their rulers' lust for power?"

"It has been so from the beginning," sighed Cornelius. "Have we any way to judge the future, save by the past?"

The afternoon slipped away quickly, Cornelius doing most of the talking today. ... It was, he reflected, a strangely constructed world. All that it knew about heroism it had learned on the battlefield. All that it knew about the navigation of the seas it had learned in naval warfare. Its sculpture, its architecture, its monuments, its songs, its poetry; was there any art-form that found its theme elsewhere than in the valor of armed men? ... It was unfortunate that this should be true; but wasn't it true?

The pity of it, admitted Cornelius, was that whole nations so often were obliged to follow mad rulers, wicked men recklessly gambling with the blood and property of their subjects.

The sun was sinking.

"I hope I have not wearied you, Peter," said the old man. "And I hope I have not discouraged you. ... Good luck to your Kingdom of love. ... I can say that much without committing an act of treason; for the Roman Empire will not regard your Kingdom seriously. If it really constituted a threat to the Empire, you would be tossed into prison—and so would I, for entertaining you as my guest."

"But—do you expect the Empire to endure forever?" asked Peter.

"I have no opinion, my friend, about the Empire's ultimate future. It is customary for the scepter to pass from one hand to another. A nation may be in the saddle today, and on foot—and barefoot—tomorrow. Perhaps that, too, is God's will." The old Roman sat in meditative silence for a while; then said, "I have been wondering today about the fate of your neighbors in Arabia. Their Crown Prince lies hopelessly paralyzed. Word came last night that their King Zendi is dead. The Arabs have known what to expect of their royal house. What becomes of them now will depend upon a new ruler. Will he reach out for territory that he does not need? Will he be content with what he has? Will he let the shepherds tend their flocks, or will they have to leave them to the wolves and the weather while they gallop off to war?"

"War? With whom?" asked Peter.

"With Judaea, perhaps. It is possible."

"The Empire might not like that," observed Peter, naïvely.

Cornelius smiled dryly and said no, the Empire might be annoyed.

It was suppertime now, and they proceeded to the club's spacious dining-room where two hundred of The Italians were assembled. Peter sat at Cornelius' right and was formally presented. After supper he was asked to speak, and he told the story of the divine Galilean who had laid down his life in the cause of world-friendship. The Romans listened respectfully. Peter did not raise his voice or his hand. His audience, from the first moment, was held completely captive. He confidently promised peace and freedom for all men in the name of his risen Lord. He even dared to tell his fascinated audience of the torch-like flames of Pentecost. And nobody stirred. And nobody smiled.

Next morning, after bidding farewell to Cornelius, Peter left Caesarea on foot; his destination, Arabia.

28

Had any doubt lingered in Fara's mind about the unwisdom of making Arabia her permanent home, it would have been dispelled on the evening of her return.

The fact that she wasn't wanted there had been ruthlessly demonstrated by the Queen and Prince Deran, and when she retired that night to lie wide-awake for hours beside the happily sleeping Ione, she was firmly resolved to leave at the earliest possible moment.

It was not the shocking conduct of Rennah and her detestable son that had wounded her most deeply, though that intentional rudeness had been as painful as a physical blow. King Zendi's utter indifference to the distressing incident was beyond understanding.

From her earliest childhood Zendi had been as tender as a father. Fara had all but worshipped him. Sometimes, during the loneliest days of her self-exile in Galilee, when her deep devotion to Voldi and her desire to share his life had momentarily shaken her resolve to sacrifice her love rather than jeopardize his career, it was the remembrance of Zendi's unfailing kindness that had abetted the temptation. The King's affectionate attitude toward her would go far in making her future life in Arabia pleasant and his undisguised loyalty to Voldi would silence all criticism. . . . Now it appeared that Zendi didn't care.

At dawn after a sleepless night, the unhappy girl slipped quietly out of Ione's humble quarters in the midst of the servants' tents—hardly an appropriate lodging for the daughter of an Arabian Princess—and strolled out toward the well-remembered paddocks, feeling that the sight of good old Kedar might be comforting. As she had hoped, Kedar was already going about his morning duties. At the moment he was brushing the glossy coat of a beautiful bay filly. He straightened his rheumatic back with an effort.

"Did you do much riding while you were gone?" he asked.

"None. Saidi was stolen, and where I lived in Galilee we had no horses."

"That was too bad—about Saidi. Voldi told me." Kedar patted the filly's satin shoulder. "This girl is Saidi's niece," he said. "Her name is Hagar."

Fara stepped forward and laid her hand gently on the young mare's velvety muzzle, murmuring, "She's lovely!"

"She hasn't been ridden much," said Kedar. "I hope this isn't a secret but the King intends to give her to you."

Fara's eyes widened in surprise.

"How long ago did he tell you that, Kedar?"

"Oh—three years ago, when she was foaled, shortly after you disappeared."

"The King may have changed his mind in the meantime," said Fara, soberly. "Has he ever spoken of it since then?"

"Last night," said Kedar. "After you had gone to bed. Want to take a little canter, Princess? Nobody will be up for an hour. Why don't you ride over to your old home?"

Fara shook her head. It would be quite too painful. They would not have left those valuable tents and equipment unattended. Nothing would be there to see but the sad ghost of a garden and old paths overgrown with weeds. Kedar had left her now to her pensive memories. In a moment he returned with a saddle and bridle. Tossing the saddle across Hagar's back, he fastened the girths; then turning to give Fara a candid head-to-foot survey, he adjusted the stirrup straps, mumbling, "Guess your legs aren't much longer than when you left. A little, maybe. . . . There you are! Up you go. . . . She's got a tender mouth—or pretends she has," still gripping the reins close against the filly's chin. "Let her show you how she can pace. She's very proud of it. She makes believe she is scared of anything white, same as her Aunt Saidi. . . . That mare was an awful liar!" he added, as he opened the paddock gate and released his hold on the reins. Fara gathered them up, gently but firmly, with practiced hands and Hagar made off at a mincing rack. She was as beautiful as the legendary woman whose name she bore, and as vain as a peacock.

Fara laughed merrily and waved a hand to old Kedar who stood beaming. How good it was to feel and watch again the ripple of a horse's muscles! It had been so long! And Zendi had planned for her to have this incomparable filly! It was very confusing. Zendi was her friend, after all.

Perhaps his conduct, last night, could be explained: it certainly needed an explanation!

"Come out of it, Hagar!" called Fara, digging her heels into the filly's ribs. Hagar tossed her head and broke into an easy lope. . . . It was an intoxicating sensation! The early morning breeze tousled Fara's hair. She was ecstatic. In spite of her decision not to visit the site of her old home, she found herself on the familiar trail.

As she had anticipated, nothing remained but the sturdily built paddocks. In the one nearest the vacant area where the tents had stood, a beautiful black horse was tied. His saddleblanket bore the Arabian royal insignia. Dismounting at a little distance, Fara tied the filly and strolled to the dilapidated garden. On the weather-beaten rustic bench, where she had so often sat beside her mother during those anxious days of her illness, King Zendi smilingly watched her approach. She paused for a moment, slowly proceeded to the bench, and sat down beside him. He took her hand.

"I have been waiting for you, dear child," he said, gently.

"What made you think I might come?" she asked.

"I surmised you might be up early. You would want to talk to old Kedar, everyone else being unfriendly. You knew you could count on Kedar. He didn't tell you I was here?"

She shook her head.

"That's good," said Zendi. "I told him not to tell you. You might not have come had you known. I hurt you badly last night."

Fara made no comment. Tears stood in her eyes.

"It is not easy for me to tell you," said Zendi, hesitantly, "but you deserve to know. My life, at present, is difficult. Rennah is ill. It is a sickness of the mind. She has become madly obsessed by the idea that—that —" He broke off here and sat moodily tracing lines in the sand with his riding-whip; then he faced her to ask, entreatingly, "You can't guess what I'm trying to say, can you?"

"I'm afraid not, sir," murmured Fara.

"Then I must begin at the beginning. Did you ever hear that your mother and I were deeply in love when her marriage was forced upon her as a patriotic duty?"

"I knew you were devoted friends," admitted Fara.

"All of that!" said Zendi. "After your dear mother had been carried away into bondage, and it became expedient for me to marry, Rennah seemed contented with her belief that she had taken Arnon's place in my heart. But after your mother returned alone to Arabia, the Queen became uneasy. She tried hard, I think, to treat your mother kindly; but her suspicion grew. . . . Perhaps I was at fault."

The unhappy King paused so long here that Fara wished she could think of something appropriate to say.

"Yes," he continued in a barely audible tone of soliloquy, "I was clearly at fault. Your mother had been used cruelly. She had come home in humiliating circumstances. I tried to show my friendship. Then, realizing that my attitude would be misunderstood, I went to special pains to allay Rennah's jealousy; and so successfully that the Queen began to take an interest in Arnon. I must give her full credit for that."

It was a long story, and Zendi insisted on telling it all. Fara listened pensively, her heart aching for him.

"Of course," he was saying now, "Rennah had always humored our son in many things that were to his disadvantage. The boy was willful, and his over-indulgence had made him arrogant; but I hoped that as he grew older his disposition might improve. Any Crown Prince is an object of pity, Fara. No one dares tell him how to treat his fellows. No other boy dares slap him for his impudence. Deran never had any discipline, at all.

"When your mother died," continued Zendi, "and you disappeared, I was sorely grieved. I tried not to show how deeply I had been wounded; but Rennah knew. I had no appetite: I was moody: I wanted to be alone. Rennah turned to Deran for companionship. Anything Deran did or said was exactly right. She made believe he was witty and laughed at his impudences. He insulted my Counsellors: he ridiculed me in the presence of our servants. Nothing short of divorcing Rennah and disowning Deran could have relieved my intolerable predicament."

Again Zendi reached for Fara's hand.

"Now, my child, you know why you were so shamefully used, last night, at our own table."

"I am glad you wanted to tell me," said Fara. "It does relieve my mind to know that you are still my friend. It would be unfair for me to remain here and add to your burden. I shall take Ione—and go. She will be happy to return to her own country. And as I have no country, I think I should prefer to live in Greece. May I have your permission to do that?"

"What about Voldi?"

"Voldi knows I can't marry him."

"But you do love him, I think."

"Dearly! Far too dearly to risk ruining his life!"

"You two will be unhappy as long as you live."

"But I cannot live happily in Arabia, and Voldi will not be happy any-where else. Our choice is limited to two kinds of unhappiness."

"Well—you're making the wrong choice! How many thousands of times I have wished that your mother and I had had the courage to run away. I don't know where we could have gone; but any hardship would have been preferable to what we endured." It suddenly occurred to Zendi that he had unwittingly drawn a picture without Fara in it, and he mumbled an apology that didn't help very much.

"Don't mind me!" said Fara, with a half-bitter chuckle. "I've never thought it was any fun to be alive."

King Zendi now sighted something on the trail that won his interest. He stood up and surveyed with apparent satisfaction an approaching train of camels. Fara rose and stood beside him. He took her arm.

"Your tents and furniture," he said, "Everything will be put in place today, just as you left it. Your servants will be here soon."

"Oh—but you mustn't! I cannot stay here!" pleaded Fara.

Then Zendi explained. He had supposed, he said, that she might not want to remain. When the news arrived of her father's assassination, he had assumed that she would return for her beloved Ione, and plan to re-side in some other country; possibly Greece, for she had often expressed admiration for that historic land. In view of this probable decision, he had been converting her property into money.

"Your sheep and cattle were sent to Damascus," he said, "and the caravan will return shortly with the proceeds. Your estate should be ample to take care of you wherever you may decide to live."

All through the forenoon the King watched as the experienced men pitched Fara's tents on their former site and installed the familiar equipment. The old servants came and set about their accustomed tasks. Ione, directing them, was dizzy with joy. Lunch was served in the garden and Voldi arrived in time for it. The King declined an invitation to stay. Deran had been taken ill in the night, he said, with what appeared to be an unusually bad cold, accompanied by a fever. The Queen was greatly worried about him.

＊　　＊　　＊　　＊　　＊　　＊

During the next three days the servants went to and fro between the King's encampment and Fara's compound, bringing forgotten articles of household gear from the storage. They brought also disturbing news of the Prince's illness. His fever had mounted dangerously and he was de-lirious much of the time. In the morning of the fourth day of his sickness,

Voldi rode over to tell Fara that the fever was subsiding but Deran was unable to move his legs. The Queen, he said, was hysterical with grief, noisily upbraiding the physician for his failure to propose a remedy.

But there was no remedy for Deran's disease. He had fallen victim to the dreaded epidemic that had wrought such havoc this summer. Within a week all Arabia had learned that the Crown Prince was a helpless, hopeless paralytic.

Rennah's lamentations were so appalling that even Deran was disgusted by her emotional collapse and bitterly complained that he had enough to bear without being tortured by her outcries—and would she have the decency to shut up and let him die in peace. His surly comment was of no consolation to her. Still in need of some outlet for her distress, Rennah turned to accusations, reviling the baffled old physician, badgering the servants, and making life wretched for the King.

For relief from this tumult, Zendi rode alone for hours and leagues in weather that was becoming increasingly inclement as the chill winds of autumn began to lash the mountain trails.

One snowy morning he brought Fara's money, six heavy pouches loaded with gold, stowed in huge saddle-bags. He handed down the precious freight to the stable-boys, but did not dismount.

Late one afternoon, he arrived home, wet to the skin, his teeth chattering, his face flushed with fever. They helped him off his horse and asked him what was the matter. He was too hoarse to make an audible reply. They put him to bed with hot bricks at his feet and plied him with the usual remedies for severe exposure. The Counsellors were summoned. The physician tried everything he knew. The hours of the night dragged wearily through, and at dawn Zendi died.

*   *   *   *   *   *

A fortnight had passed since the death of the King. Much snow had fallen, earlier than usual, but the sun shone brightly at midday, melting the drifts. Old men who remembered freely predicted a mild, open winter which meant that Arabia faced the heartening prospect of ample pasturage and prosperity. This was ever so good, especially in view of the fact that the nation was without a ruler. It was in seasons when the grass was scarce that the tribesmen quarreled and fought, and the country needed the control of a firm hand. When the traditional thirty days of mourning passed, the Council would meet and consider the appointment of a new King, it being quite obvious that Prince Deran was unable to succeed to the throne, a fact which the wise men discreetly deplored in their demeanor and conversation but to which they bravely reconciled themselves in their hearts.

At dusk one afternoon, Ione came into Fara's bed-chamber to say that an old man whom she had never seen before was asking to see her.

"A huge man!" she said. "Very tall and very tired and very wet; someone important, I think," she added. "I brought him in out of the snow."

Fara followed her quickly. At the sight of the visitor, who stood waiting, she stared incredulously for an instant, and then rushed into his arms.

"Petros!" she cried. "Is it possible? Is it really you?"

"Have I changed so much?" he asked.

She led him to the glowing fireplace and began tugging off his snow-covered robe. He sat down wearily and Ione knelt to unfasten the soaked sandal-thongs.

"Your hair!" exclaimed Fara. "Your beard! Even your voice is different, Peter! I'm afraid you have suffered deeply. But—" She studied him candidly, intuitively. "But—whatever has happened to you, it has made you great!" Her husky voice lowered to a tone of reverence. "Did the Master leave you in charge of his earthly Kingdom?"

Ione stood before them, wide-eyed with bewilderment, apparently unable to decide whether to listen or leave. Fara said, in Greek, "Petros, this is my dear Ione, of whom I have often spoken. . . . And Ione, this is the Big Fisherman whom Jesus named Petros."

"A rock?" murmured Ione. "Yes," she added, quickly. "That is so! A rock! Yes—it is true!" Impulsively she knelt at his feet; and Peter, taking both her hands in his, raised her up gently.

"I am not to be worshiped, Ione," he said, in her own tongue. "I am only a man who has walked humbly beside a King. I give you his blessing."

Ione supervised the preparation of a nourishing supper; and, after they had eaten, Peter and Fara sat by the fire talking earnestly until far in the night. Fara listened with increasing perplexity as Peter confided the nature of his errand in Arabia. A strange power had been bestowed upon him, he said. The Holy Spirit had enabled him to perform miracles of healing. He had made cripples walk!

Fara's heart raced as her intuition informed her of the amazing experiment he had in mind. He was going to try to heal Deran!

"No direct command has come to me," Peter was saying, "but surely it would please God, and advance the Master's Kingdom of peace and good will among men, if some act of kindness might cure the ancient enmity between the Arab and the Jew. Perhaps it is my task, by God's help, to do this thing."

Fara made no comment; did not lift her eyes. After a moment's waiting, Peter continued:

"Would it not soften the heart of Arabia if a Jew should be the means
of restoring the heir to their throne?"

"I do not know," murmured Fara; adding, when Peter's searching look
called for an explanation of her doubt, "It has been a bitter enmity for
ages." She could not bring herself to tell him that it would be no great
favor to Arabia to put Deran on his feet. Who was Fara—to discourage
the healing of any man's paralysis? And how dared she pit her judgment
against that of the man whom God had invested with superhuman power?

"Think you, Fara, that the Queen will let me see the Prince?" wondered
Peter.

"I do not know," she replied. "The Queen is much overwrought by the
recent afflictions. There's no telling what attitude she might take."

"Will you go with me tomorrow," entreated Peter, "and tell her why
I have come?"

"Queen Rennah is not friendly to me," said Fara.

"Your Voldi is a Counsellor," said Peter. "Could you persuade him to
present me?"

"No! No!" exclaimed Fara. "I couldn't ask Voldi to do that!"

There was a long, tense silence. Peter sat gnawing his bearded underlip
in perplexity. At length he spoke, almost sternly.

"Something tells me that you do not want the Prince to be healed! Is
this true?"

There was no use trying to evade this query. Fara straightened for her
task.

"The Arabians do not like Prince Deran, Peter," she said, firmly. "From
his childhood he has been detested for his selfishness and arrogance. They
will want—and they deserve—another kind of King."

"But if, by a miracle, the Prince should be healed, might he not change
his ways and become acceptable?" argued Peter.

"It is not for me to say," replied Fara.

"You remember what happened to the rich Zacchaeus? How the people's hatred of him was changed to loyalty and affection when Jesus re-
deemed him?"

Fara slowly nodded her head, without looking up.

"I'll go with you, Peter, in the morning," she said.

*　　*　　*　　*　　*　　*

"A Jew, you say?" sneered Rennah. "The Prince would not tolerate the sight of him!" She sat up indignantly. "How like you Jews to mock us in our distress!"

Fara had experienced no difficulty in gaining an audience with the Queen who was curious to learn what had induced the girl to visit her. Supine on her couch she had stared crossly without speaking when Fara was shown in. Wasting no time on insincere amenities, Fara had briefly stated her errand. A friend of hers, a man possessed of divine power to heal, had come from a great distance to see the Prince. The man waited without. He hoped he could help the Prince as he had helped other men. He wanted no money.

"And where did you become acquainted with this—this God?"

"In Galilee, Your Majesty. He is a Jew."

That had brought Rennah up in a towering rage. With fine scorn she had voiced her opinion of Fara's impudence, and was pointing a trembling finger toward the door.

"There is a legend among the Syrians," said Fara, undisturbed by the Queen's anger, "about their famous warrior-king, Naaman, who contracted leprosy. Learning of a Jewish prophet, who had been endowed with the power to heal diseases, Naaman reluctantly besought this Jew to cure him, and was told to bathe in the Jordan River. This was an unthinkable humiliation to the celebrated Syrian, and he started home enraged beyond any words to tell of it. But—he was a leper and there was no help or hope for him, at all. So he turned back and bathed in the Jordan—and was healed."

"Nonsense!" screamed Rennah. "Get out of here! You and your holy Jew! Go—I say—go!"

Fara bowed and moved toward the door. Rennah suddenly came to her feet and followed her, clutching her arm.

"No!" she muttered, hoarsely. "You shall not go! I forbid you to go!" She burst out crying. "Bring him in!" With that, the hysterical woman rushed to the door of the Prince's bed-chamber and entered. There was the sound of voices, Rennah's softly wheedling, Deran's shrill with scorn. Fara stepped out into the entry and beckoned to Peter who followed her through to the Prince's room where the Queen nervously admitted them.

"Deran," she said, steadying her voice, "here is the Jewish healer who has come all this way from his own country to help you."

Peter moved toward the bed.

"And since when," stormed Deran, "has Arabia sought favors from the Jews?"

"My son, I am not here as a Jew." Peter's calm, resonant voice seemed to drive the anger from the Prince's sunken eyes. "Nor have I come," he went on, quietly, "to minister to an Arabian. We are two fellow men, both of us God's children. Let us forget our nationality now, and treat each other as brothers." He reached out his hand to take Deran's. Instinctively, the Prince recoiled, withdrawing his hand; but, on second thought, slowly and reluctantly offering it.

Rennah drew in closer. She was weeping quietly.

"You are in great trouble, Deran," continued Peter. "There is no earthly cure for your disease. If you are to regain your health and strength the remedy must come from our Father. I have no power of my own. Whether it is the will of God that you should be restored to rule your country, I do not know. Perhaps that decision rests with you."

"What do you want him to do?" broke in Rennah.

"A King should desire and deserve the respect of his people," declared Peter, ignoring the Queen's query and searching the Prince's eyes. "As a Prince, you have been vain and froward of heart. My Master taught that whoever would become great among men should be as a servant, and whoever would be the greatest of all should be servant of all. You, Deran, have served no one but yourself."

"Sir!" interrupted Rennah, "That is no way to speak to a Prince!"

Deran made an impatient gesture in her direction.

"Say on!" he mumbled.

"Now if it should please God to heal you," continued Peter, "it will be a miracle, and if you should win the devotion and obedience of your people, that too will be a miracle. Are you willing to accept both of these benefits? If it is the will of God, you may have both—or neither. Will you promise that if your strength is restored you will serve your country unselfishly?"

Deran soberly nodded his head. There was an impressive silence.

"Be well aware," cautioned Peter, "that if, in the days to come, you forget your vow, and turn again to your unseemly ways, a worse affliction may befall you."

Again the Prince solemnly nodded his head. Instantly Peter startled them by stretching forth both of his huge hands. Clutching Deran's arms, he sat him up in bed; and, raising his voice to a tone of command, he shouted, "In the name of God, stand up on your feet—and walk!"

No place had ever been so quiet during the brief moment that followed. Slowly, bewilderingly, Deran put his feet out on the floor, and stood erect. Rennah threw her arms around him, and sobbed. Fara's eyes were wet. The Prince pushed his mother aside and walked slowly across the room. Peter sank heavily into a chair. His face was pale and great beads of sweat stood on his forehead. Fara moved to his side and laid her hand on his shoulder. Rennah, with tears of joy running down her cheeks, fell on her knees before him, and cried, "We shall repay you! Whatever you ask, we will give it! What will you have?"

"A drink of water, please," murmured Peter, huskily.

Little was said after that. Deran was pacing about, his face alight. Rennah was bringing his clothing and boots. They were too preoccupied with their good fortune to notice that Peter and Fara had slipped quietly away.

*　　*　　*　　*　　*　　*

He was visibly annoyed by the servants' stares when they came to serve luncheon to him and his mother. When the maids offered him dishes, at arm's length, he growled, "One would think you were serving a ghost!"

"Please don't be impatient with them, son," begged Rennah. "It is no small matter that you are walking again."

"I would have recovered—in time," said Deran, airily. "I was feeling better. I lacked confidence; that was all. The old Jew pulled me up—and I found I could walk. That's about all there is to it."

"Even so—if I were you I shouldn't resent it if the people are surprised to see you out again," admonished Rennah.

"Why should I care what they think!" muttered Deran.

After he had eaten, the Prince swaggered out to the paddocks to be greeted by the silent, open-mouthed awe of the stable-boys.

"This is amazing, sire!" exclaimed old Kedar, limping forward.

"Saddle my sorrel mare!" commanded Deran.

Rennah had followed him out. She stood soberly watching as he bounded into the saddle and rode away at a gallop. Then she turned and slowly retraced her steps, with bent head and drooping shoulders.

Back in her own room, she sat motionless, leaning far forward with her knuckles pressed hard against her teeth. Deran had no intention of keeping his vow to the Jewish healer. It wasn't in Deran to change his nature. It was too much to expect of him. He was a high-spirited, proud young Prince. It was his destiny to rule his people. Any sign of sympathy or friendship on his part would be mistaken for weakness. The Arabians needed a firm hand to govern them; not an outstretched hand, but a closed fist!

Yes—but the mysterious Jew was still to be reckoned with. In a few hours he would learn that Deran had repudiated his promise. Then what? If this miracle-worker had the power to put Deran on his feet he probably had the power to put him to bed again. He had solemnly declared that the Prince must keep his pledge—or a worse affliction might befall him. In God's name—what could be worse?

Rennah's mind was in tumult. Something must be done promptly or the potent Jew might put a curse on Deran! He must be got out of the country! Now!

She walked determinedly to her desk, drew out a sheet of papyrus, and wrote in large, sprawling letters:

"Fara: Much as the Prince appreciates the kindness of your Jewish prophet, we are aware, as you doubtless are, yourself, that there is bitter enmity between the Jews and the Arabians. Already there is muttering among our people that our Prince shall not be beholden to a Jew for his recovery. For the old prophet's protection—for Deran does not want anything to happen to him—it is important that he leave the country forthwith! Let there be no delay! I am sending, with this note, a purse of gold. Give it to this man—and tell him to go! Perhaps it would be well if you accompanied him. You may not be safe here when it is learned that you brought the Jew to Arabia."

*   *   *   *   *   *

Less than two hours after the return of Peter and Fara to her home Rennah's letter, accompanied by the bag of gold coins, arrived. Shortly afterward Voldi came. His face was serious. He had stopped at the royal encampment and old Kedar had told him everything. The three of them studied the letter. Peter's only comment was, "God will not be mocked!"

"It is obvious," said Voldi, "that the Queen made this up. However, her advice should be taken. Peter is in danger, not because he is a Jew but because he miraculously restored the Prince after Arabia was assured that he had been disqualified to accede to the throne."

"You are right, Voldi," agreed Fara. "And I shall go with him. It is quite impossible for me to remain here any longer."

So it was decided that Peter and Fara should start early the next morning for Gaza and take passage on a ship. It was now at the height of the season for grain shipments to Rome and they might be lucky enough to sail without much delay on some craft that called at Piraeus, the port of Athens. Voldi impulsively resolved to go along.

"In his present mood," explained Voldi, "the Prince will not object to my absence."

All through the night, preparations went forward for departure in the morning. Voldi rode to the royal encampment and confided their intentions to Kedar who took it upon himself to organize a pack-train to

Peter Leaves Athens

Fara had pleaded with him.

"Dear Petros, you have had trouble enough. You deserve some rest, free of danger. Let us take care of you."

carry Fara's and Ione's belongings to the port. Assured that the Queen had commanded them to clear out, Kedar felt himself on safe ground to give his full aid to their departure.

In the gray light that announced the coming dawn, the caravan started down the tortuous trail toward the Valley of Aisne. In two hours they had left the snow behind them and the men were taking off their leather jackets. Peter preferred to walk—and he walked alone, his gray head bent in serious meditation. He had made a mistake, it seemed. He had wanted to do a great favor to a foe, but his good intentions had only widened the breach and fanned the smoldering fire of hatred.

* * * * * *

The astounding and unwelcome news of Prince Deran's miraculous recovery, after the country had thought itself well rid of him, traveled fast and far. The Counsellors met informally in the venerable Dumah's encampment but found no cure for their dilemma. Only one opinion was unanimously agreed upon: the Jews should mind their own business.

But if the Counsellors had no plan to alleviate the tragic situation, the "Sons of Ishmael" thought they might give aid. This exclusive and secretive organization was composed of the sons and adult grandsons and nephews of influential tribal chiefs who ran the caravans from Arabia to the port cities. These long and dangerous journeys conducting flocks and herds, hides and wool, to far-away Damascus and Caesarea and Gaza, menaced by well-equipped bands of robbers, demanded the safeguarding of fearless men. It was an honor to be chosen for this perilous business, and the young fellows who undertook it were indeed a tough aggregation.

Now that winter was coming, most of the caravans had returned from their expeditions, and the "Sons of Ishmael" were having some free time. On the second day after the Prince was restored, word was passed from camp to camp announcing a secret meeting for the following night in the tent of Jeshri, their leader. After an hour's conference, Jeshri, in their presence, filled a quiver with thirty arrows, which was the number of men present. All of the arrows, but one, were made for target-practice. The exception was tipped with a long, slim finger of steel, sharpened to a needle-point.

Jeshri walked out of the tent and into the moonlight, and mounted his horse. A half-mile up the trail he halted beside a large oak tree; and, still mounted, drove a nail at the height of his shoulder, hung up the quiver, and returned to camp. One by one, at intervals of a few minutes, the silent men mounted their horses and set out for home. As each man passed the quiver, he paused to take an arrow.

Late in the afternoon of the following day, Prince Deran's sorrel mare arrived at her paddock, riderless.

* * * * * *

The Antonia would sail within the hour. Grizzled old Captain Polemus was happy to make this announcement, for his passengers had been on board nearly a week and were growing restless.

With plenty of time to reflect on his dilemma, Voldi had decided that the course he was taking was the right one. As a Counsellor he would be completely at odds with Deran, and it would be of small service to Arabia if a Counsellor and the King were in constant conflict. Besides, once he and Fara were in a strange country, relying more and more upon each other for companionship, he might persuade her to marry him. He faced the voyage and their new adventures with increasing interest.

Fara stood by his side at the rail as the sailors made ready to cast off. She slipped her arm under his and Voldi felt her trembling with excitement.

"It will not be long now," she said, softly.

Voldi did not hear her. His eyes were fixed on two horsemen, riding on the wharf. He identified them now. Museph and Raboth! Their horses were wet.

Leaving Fara abruptly, he ran down the gangway as his friends dismounted. He faced them with apprehensive eyes.

What could have happened to bring them here? They straightened—and formally saluted him.

"That was a close thing, sire!" muttered Museph. "We weren't a minute too soon."

Voldi grinned at the "sire," and wondered why. It was a strange time to be teasing him.

"Deran is dead," said Raboth, in a half-whisper.

"Dead!" echoed Voldi. "How?"

"He was found beside a mountain trail with an arrow in his back," said Museph.

"And I suppose you have come to ask me to return," said Voldi. "But I can't now! I have gone too far with my other plans!"

"But the King's Council insists that you return—forthwith, sire!" entreated Raboth in an unsteady voice.

"And why is my presence in Arabia of such urgent importance?" demanded Voldi. "And why—in God's name—are you fellows 'sire'-ing me?"

"Because"—said Museph—"you are the King of Arabia!"

29

PETER HAD NOT BEEN too uncomfortable here. For one thing, the cell was dry, a welcome change from the perpetual dampness of the Catacombs. Perhaps when winter came—it was August now—the prison would be damp too; but Peter did not expect to be here when winter came, so there was no need to worry about that.

The cot was narrow but there were two folded blankets on it, kindly provided by Glaucus, the jailor. There was also a bare wooden chair. Throughout the daytime hours a little strip of sunshine penetrated the mere slit of a window near the ceiling; not enough light to read by, but better than the Catacombs where there was no sunlight at all.

True, it was wearisome, sitting here all day with nothing to do, and the nights were still more tedious; for, with no physical exercise to tire him, he did not require much sleep. Indeed it was the long nights that had made his prison-life so hard to bear. His mistakes asked to be reviewed as he lay awake for hours in the darkness. Every painful detail of his quarrel with Johnny that day on *The Abigail* was re-experienced. There was no use saying to himself that he had been fully forgiven for his treatment of Johnny: he had to go through it again, night after night. When the torturing memory of his denial of Jesus' friendship threatened to invade his mind, he would sit up and make an effort to drive it away by sheer will-power; and sometimes he succeeded, but not always.

Occasionally through the day a guard would pause briefly at his barred door and inquire how he was feeling today, and Peter would say that he was very well, thank you. A slave brought food and a pitcher of water in the morning and again in the late afternoon, but without tarrying to talk. Perhaps he was not permitted to speak to prisoners. Twice, during the past month of his incarceration, Glaucus himself had come in to call. On these occasions, Peter sat on the cot; and Glaucus, turning the chair

491

about, bestrode it, facing him. It was not easy to talk with Glaucus, who spoke some outlandish variant of the vulgaris. By exerting his imagination, Peter gathered that the badly scarred jailor was a veteran of the wars. Once he had understood Glaucus to inquire why these foolish Christians were throwing their lives away, and he had tried to explain; but Glaucus didn't get it. He had shaken his head and yawned and left.

For several days now Peter had been expecting a visit from Mencius who was making an effort to have the sentence commuted. He had worried more than a little about Mencius' intervention in his behalf. It was risky business, even for an influential Proconsul, to be showing such concern for the welfare of any Christian, especially for the known leader of the movement. It was of no great importance to Peter whether he himself lived or died, but he didn't want to see Mencius punished; and that might easily be, for young Caligula was fiercely determined to stamp out this indomitable underground party that seemed to thrive on persecution.

As he had sat there alone in his cell day after day, Peter had passed the dragging hours by re-living his experiences of recent years. During the first days of his imprisonment, his reminiscences would speed from one event to another. A couple of hours would cover the significant episodes of the past quadrennium. Next day he would do it all over again. So—he had contrived a better plan. He would give a whole half-day to the recovery of one event.

On one morning after breakfast he would project himself back to Gaza. . . . After a tedious delay, *The Antonia* was making ready to sail. Peter felt himself standing at the rail, watching the last bales and boxes of cargo come on board. Voldi and Fara stood very close together, only a few feet from him. What a handsome, well-matched pair they were! Voldi had made a wise decision to get out of Arabia. He and Fara were made for each other.

Suddenly two young horsemen had appeared on the wharf. Voldi had run down the gangway to greet them. The three friends had held a brief parley. Then Voldi had slowly returned, followed by the visitors who explained to Fara why Voldi could not leave the country. His fellow Counsellors had just appointed him King of Arabia. She had taken Voldi's hands in hers and had tried to smile. Then Voldi had put his arms around her, had kissed her tenderly, before them all, and had whispered something into her ear; and she had nodded her head. And he had whispered to her again, and she had shaken her head. Then he had followed his friends down the gangway. His horse had been brought up from the hold. Fara had disappeared, probably to her cabin. Captain Polemus had shouted an order. The mainsail was creeping up. *The Antonia* edged away from the wharf.

It would take Peter all forenoon to remember that scene in its every detail. In the afternoon, he would decide to review the voyage, the long talks with Captain Polemus and with Fara who tried to be cheerful but the sight of whose eyes made his heart ache.

Peter had made no secret of his devotion to his Master and his firm belief in the early victory of the Kingdom. Weather-beaten old Polemus had listened respectfully but shook his gray head. It was a pleasant dream, he would admit. It would be a happy day for the world when all men were brothers but Polemus didn't expect to live that long.

"You'd better be careful who you talk to about this," he cautioned. "You're safe enough with me, of course. I like to hear you tell of this Jesus. He must have been a great man. But—this idea of a new Kingdom— you'd do better to keep that to yourself. . . . Of course, in Athens, you won't be in much danger. The Empire doesn't care what they talk about in Athens."

"And why is that?" Peter had wanted to know.

"Oh—Athens is full of windy old philosophers who spend their time sitting in the park on Mars' Hill, talking all manner of nonsense. Not meaning"—Polemus was quick to add—"that what you believe is non-sense; but you can say almost anything you like in Athens, and nobody will take you seriously. . . . I'll wager you could make a public speech predicting that the Empire would collapse tomorrow, and even the Roman patrols wouldn't bother you."

"But—isn't there a Christian Ecclesia in Athens?" Peter had inquired.

"I suppose so," drawled Polemus. "Almost every place now there is an organization of these Christians. And some of them have to be cautious; but not in Athens. I'm glad you are going there. Now if it was Rome, I'd advise you to stay away. They're making it mighty tough for these poor people in Rome."

Peter hadn't felt much complimented by the Captain's friendly counsel to avoid all danger.

"Perhaps that's where I'm needed, Polemus," he had said.

"You wouldn't last very long, sir!" the Captain had declared. "Some ordinary fellow, average height, dragging his heels, looking like ten thou-sand other men of no importance, might not be taken in for a long time. You, sir, would be a marked man! You take my advice—and make your home in Athens!"

So—Peter had gone on to Rome. He hadn't even got off the ship at

Piraeus. Fara and Ione didn't need him. In fact, they might be better off without him. He might get them into trouble. It had been a sad parting, though. Fara had pleaded with him.

"Dear Petros, you have had trouble enough. You deserve some rest, free of danger. Let us take care of you."

And that would have been very pleasant, Peter knew. Good old Polemus had overheard the conversation. "You'd better do as she says," he advised.

Then *The Antonia* had swung about to resume the long voyage. One chilly morning, for it was mid-winter now, they had arrived at Ostia's busy roadstead; and, after brief formalities of clearance, proceeded up the river. It was late in the evening when they tied up at the wharf that served the huge granaries. Peter had expected to find the streets deserted but they were noisy with heavy vehicular traffic and crowded with pedestrians. Did these Romans never sleep? . . . He had walked the streets all night, bewildered by the throngs. The food-shops were open. Hawkers shouted their wares. Mendicant musicians added to the din. Blind men whined.

He found himself in an area of magnificent public buildings; The Praetorium, the forums, the stupendous Colosseum. In the gray light of morning he had come upon the broad Via Appia and had followed it out of the city. Polemus had told him how to find the Catacombs. . . . It always stirred him when he remembered the welcome he had received. He was amazed that these forlorn fugitives had heard of him, and the miracles he had wrought in the Master's name. They had gathered about him and knelt at his feet; and he had prayed that they might all be given faith to watch and wait for the coming of the Kingdom.

*   *   *   *   *   *

And then there was that first visit from Mencius. Peter loved to recall it. One morning, late in the autumn, Mencius had come. He hadn't said how he had discovered Peter's whereabouts, but here he was, in the Catacombs; a Roman Proconsul! The frightened refugees had scurried away in the darkness. But Peter had had no fear. He had heard all about Mencius: Voldi had told him.

"Let us go outside," Mencius had suggested. "It will do you good to breathe some fresh air."

"Will it not endanger you, sir," Peter had inquired, "if you should be seen talking with a Christian?"

"No," Mencius had declared. "The patrols are not interested in my goings and comings. I talk with whom I please. The Emperor might not approve of my being here in friendly converse with you, Peter; but he cannot dispose of me. I know how to deal with the copper-miners in

Cyprus. I know the ruffians who run the salt-caravans from Engedi to Gaza. I know what is going on in Joppa and Caesarea. . . . Come—we have much to talk about."

So—they had gone up the narrow ladder and had sat down under the locust trees.

"How do you find it possible to live down there in those caverns?" Mencius had wanted to know.

"Because I must!" Peter had replied. "It is not so difficult to do what one must do." And then he had told the Proconsul about the little groups of Christians who met secretly in their own houses until the patrols suspected them, and they would flee to these labyrinthian caverns for safety, frightened, beaten, sick, and hungry; and of the secret exits from which the more fearless ones emerged to procure food from the peasant farmers and cheap fish from the smaller markets along the waterfront. "I pray with them and minister to their sick ones, Mencius. I offer words of comfort when they die—and beside their graves. . . . And I bid them be of good cheer, for the Kingdom is coming!"

"It must take great faith, Peter," mused Mencius, "to believe that the Kingdom of the Christos is coming when everything they had is lost."

"That's when our faith is strongest, Mencius," Peter had replied— "when there is nothing else to lean upon. The Spirit of God is very real— and near—to these distressed ones. . . . You remember how you felt on the Day of Pentecost? We have Pentecost every day in the Catacombs!"

After a little silence, Peter had asked Mencius to tell him about himself —and his recent journeys; and the Proconsul had had quite a story to tell. He had just returned from the usual round; Cyprus, Caesarea, Joppa, Gaza, Engedi; and had ridden up into Arabia to see Voldi.

"Is he making a good King?" Peter had wanted to know.

"The best ever!" Mencius had declared. "The Arabians love him."

"Married?"

"No—and perhaps it's for the best. Voldi rarely shows up at the King's Encampment. He spends his time visiting the tribesmen. Arabia has never been so completely unified. . . . By the way, he told me a good story. I know he would want you to hear it, for you were on the ship when the word came that Prince Deran had been assassinated. The secret band of young caravan-guards, who called themselves the 'Sons of Ishmael,' drew lots to see which one should attend to the Prince. Old Jeshri, their leader, filled a quiver with thirty arrows, the exact number of all men present at the meeting. Only one arrow was armed with steel. Jeshri hung the quiver on a tree and each man as he rode past took an arrow."

"So no one of them knew which man was appointed to kill the Prince?"

"Right. . . . But, afterwards, one of the men who had aspired to be their leader, remembered that old Jeshri himself had not taken an arrow from the quiver, and he talked about it to Jeshri's disparagement. . . . Voldi told me that when the old man lay sick unto death he asked them all to leave his bedside but the King, and to him he said, 'I have been maligned for refusing to take one of the arrows. I want you to know, sire, that I did take one of the arrows before I hung the quiver on the tree. It was the steel-tipped arrow. When I am gone, sire, will you tell my brave lads?' "

* * * * * *

It had been very wearisome, sitting here, day after day, in his prison cell, with nothing to do but remember. Often he spent a whole afternoon recalling that eventful night when Marcellus and Marcipor had brought him out of the secret passage into the old quarry, and had taken him swiftly to the Gallio mansion where the gallant Greek slave lay dying of his wounds. . . . The Spirit of God had empowered him, that night, to heal Demetrius. . . . And, after that, many agitated fugitives came with reports that the Gallios' physician, one Sarpedon, was seeking in high quarters for his arrest. . . . But God had withheld the hands of his enemies.

Perhaps God would save him this time, too; though Peter was not sure he wanted to be saved, this time. Life in the Catacombs had taken a heavy toll of him. He was gaunt, weak in the legs; hollow-eyed. Maybe his work was done. If there was anything further for him to do, he would try to do it. But if it should be his Father's will to take him home now—to the House of Many Mansions—it would be a relief.

* * * * * *

One morning he fell to thinking about the day when Marcipor brought him the Master's robe. Marcellus had sent it to him. Noble fellow, that Marcellus! And his bride! They had been very brave! . . . Only a little while, perhaps, and he would see them. . . . Marcipor had brought the robe. Peter remembered its comforting softness when he had taken it in his arms. He had not tried to put it on over his huge shoulders. Somehow he didn't want to put it on, anyhow. It was too sacred for that. They had laid it reverently upon the altar in the taper-lit chapel. . . . It was there now. Every day the people knelt before it. He had tried to counsel them not to worship it, but they probably did. . . . Well—he couldn't blame them much. After all, it was the Master's robe. If they needed something tangible to fix their eyes upon while they prayed for courage, what token of his presence could serve so well?

"I have often knelt there beside them," Peter had admitted.

"And worshiped the robe?" wondered Mencius.

"It stirred cherished memories, Mencius, and brought the Master very near. If that is idolatry, I think I shall be forgiven."

*   *   *   *   *   *

For the past few days, Peter had meditated deeply upon the incident that had brought him to prison.

Mencius, returning from another long voyage, had come out one morning, very much agitated, to say that the son of his longtime friend, Prefect Sergius of Caesarea, who had just finished his course in the Military Academy, was dangerously ill.

"This splendid young fellow, Felix, is the apple of his father's eye," Mencius had said. "He is very near death, I fear. He is burning up with a fever. Since yesterday he has been unconscious. The physicians admit they are helpless. . . . Now I cannot ask you to go to him, Peter. You would certainly be arrested. Sarpedon, who has charge of the case, would see to that. You must not be seen there."

"What would you have me do?" Peter had inquired.

"Can't you pray for his recovery?" entreated Mencius.

For a long moment Peter had wrestled with his problem. Then he had said, "I shall go with you, Mencius."

"It is too great a risk! You would be seen by many. Doubtless Sarpedon himself will be there. He would leave no stone unturned to have you brought to trial."

"But if, by the Holy Spirit, I should heal the boy—"

"No; that would make no difference to Sarpedon. His professional pride is more important than the life of young Felix."

"Be that as it may, Mencius, I am going with you!"

"Come, then," said Mencius, in a shaken voice. "Perhaps an Angel will stand guard over you."

*   *   *   *   *   *

But no Angel had intervened. Nor had Peter been permitted to see the dying Felix. He had been arrested in the courtyard of the Academy, upon arrival there; and, after a hasty trial on the charge of conspiracy to overthrow the Government, he was thrown into prison.

"Is it true, then," the Judge had demanded, "that you believe, and have taught others to believe, in the coming of a King who will rule the world?"

"Yes," Peter had replied, boldly, "that is true!"

"You are a fool!" the Judge had growled, adding, "but an honest and fearless fool. You do not have the manner and speech of a seditionist. If you will renounce this idiotic theory and promise not to speak of it again, this court will let you off with a prison sentence. Otherwise you are condemned of treason by the words of your own mouth, and the penalty is death. Which will you have?"

The courtroom had been very quiet.

Mencius had dared to rise and ask permission to speak. The Judge showed surprise, but replied, deferentially, "It will be our pleasure, Proconsul Mencius, to hear anything you wish to say."

"Your Grace," began Mencius, "this man Peter is well known to me. He has no designs on the Empire. He has incited no one to rebellion. He has healed the sick and comforted the down-trodden and distressed. This Kingdom in which he believes is not a temporal but a spiritual Kingdom. It has naught to do with Caesar!"

Then Mencius had sat down and the Judge had faced Peter, inquiring: "Is this true?"

It had been a trying moment. It was not an easy question. Mencius had done his best to find a way out for him. After some delay, Peter had found his voice.

"Sir," he said, "the Proconsul has told you truly that the Kingdom of the Christos is a spiritual Kingdom. But when it rules the hearts of men everywhere it will be their highest allegiance. Peace will reign throughout the earth. And when it comes, there will be no need of armies; no, nor of magistrates."

"And what becomes of Caesar?" demanded the Judge, sternly.

"Our Christos, sir," declared Peter, "will rule the world, and every knee shall bow before him!"

The heavy silence now had been broken only by the rattling of the papyrus sheet as the Judge recorded his decision on the indictment. Then he arose and said:

"You have left this court no alternative, Peter. The law is the law. It is not in our province to amend it, not even to save the life of a misguided fanatic. You will be taken hence to prison and in thirty days you will be put to death!"

*   *   *   *   *   *

The next day, Mencius had come to see him. Glaucus, admitting him, had waited. The court order, he said, required him to remain. The Proconsul had sat silent for a while before speaking.

"Peter," he began, gently reproachful, "why did you do it? Fabius was doing his best to save you."

"I had to tell the truth," Peter had replied. "I disowned my Master once. I think he depends on me not to do it again."

"But—did you have to say that the Master's Kingdom would rule the world? Judge Fabius is really quite a decent fellow. He did not want to inflict the sentence of death upon you. It was your prediction of the fall of the Empire that left him helpless. Had he been lenient with you, the Emperor would have punished him."

"And you have risked too much, Mencius," said Peter in Greek. "Much as I value your aid—"

"None of that, Peter!" broke in Glaucus. "You will speak in our tongue!"

"I am having another session with Fabius," said Mencius, ignoring the interruption. "Perhaps the sentence may be commuted. . . . This makes me sick at heart, Peter."

*   *   *   *   *   *

And so the days had dragged on. The day after tomorrow would mark the expiration of Peter's month in prison.

Late that afternoon, Mencius had come. His haggard face made his report unnecessary. He laid his hand on Peter's arm and sadly shook his head.

"I am permitted to be with you for only a moment," he said. "But on Friday morning, I shall be here for a farewell word. Is there anything I can do for you, Peter?"

"Pray for me, good Mencius, that my faith fail not."

"I have prayed for you, Peter," murmured Mencius, "but it hasn't done you any good."

"I'm sure it has!" said Peter. "I haven't been afraid. Your prayers may have helped me. You have been a loyal friend, Mencius. We will meet, one day, in our Father's House!"

30

PETER HAD RISEN early and was calmly waiting. His mind was at rest. The only question that had troubled him had been answered in the night. An Angel had visited him in a dream.

On the Day of Pentecost the stirring demonstration of the Holy Spirit's power had led him to believe that the establishment of the Master's Kingdom throughout the world was imminent. It was not easy to conceive of such an event, but neither was Pentecost easy to accept as an actual experience. All things were possible with God and His ways were beyond understanding. God had waited long and patiently for His children to acknowledge His fatherhood and their brotherhood. Now the time had come for the cleansing of the nations, and the reign of peace. Now!

He had expected it to begin in Jerusalem where thousands of fear-ridden men had hung upon his words. Jerusalem was the right place for the new Kingdom to manifest itself first. A society would be formed for the demonstration of friendship and good will. The news of it would quickly spread. But the Jerusalem experiment had been unsuccessful. Perhaps Jerusalem was not the right place to begin.

He had declared the early coming of the Kingdom to the harassed slaves in Joppa. They had listened wistfully, but without comment. He had repeated his message to "The Italians" in Caesarea: they had received him politely and had left the dinner tables in silence. No one had paused to ask a question or express an opinion. Wise old Cornelius, quite dissatisfied with things as they were, had no expectation of a remedy for the world's sorry predicament, and had shaken his gray head at any mention of an early triumph of the Master's Kingdom.

Undaunted, Peter had journeyed to Arabia in the hope of effecting peace and friendship between the Arabs and the Jews. Perhaps the Kingdom would begin its work here. It would be a great day for the Kingdom

501

when the tidings spread that two hostile nations, at enmity for fifteen centuries, had resolved their difficulties. But his efforts had been in vain. The relations between the sons of Israel and Ishmael had not been improved. Indeed they had been worsened.

Fara was a firm believer in the Master's power; but, when the Kingdom of peace on earth was mentioned, she had nothing to say. Captain Polemus thought the idea fantastic. Mencius, although deeply impressed at Pentecost, was silent when Peter talked of the coming Kingdom. In the opinion of Judge Fabius, clearly a man of good intent, Peter was a fool; a brave and honest fool—but a fool.

In the days of his solitude, he had wondered whether he might be mistaken. He still clung to his belief, but he wished more people shared it. Was the Kingdom coming now? And, if not now, was the Kingdom coming at all?

Last night an Angel had cleared his mind.

Yes, Peter, the Master's Kingdom is coming, but not by some spectacular miracle whereby thrones would topple in a day and all men everywhere would cast aside their weapons and clasp hands.

"From the beginning of the world, Peter," the Angel had said, "the rulers of the nations have striven for power over other men's lives. The ablest minds among their subjects always spent their genius on contriving instruments of destruction.

"The kings of the earth, for their own pride and glory, have laid waste their neighbors' lands and enslaved their children. . . . You, Peter, have daily talked about 'these latter times.' But—these are not 'latter times.' The world has suffered grievously, but it must suffer more and more. Again and again, in desperate hours, men have come to a parting of the ways, and they have always chosen the road to national pomp and glory; never the road to peace and friendship.

"The kingdom of the Christos will come, but not now, not soon. Empires will rise and fall. Slavery and slaughter will prevail and increase in horror until the sight of it will sicken the heart of God! Terror will reign until the hungry and homeless will cry to the rocks to cover them! And when all seems lost—then the Kingdom will come.

"Remember how the Master said that the Kingdom would grow as a mustard tree, from the smallest of seeds. Always there will be some who hear his voice. In the midst of their distresses, they will watch and wait and hope for the coming of the King! And he will come, at length, to keep his covenant, and set men free.

"Meantime, he offers the benefits of the Kingdom to every man who yearns to see the Kingdom come. For them the Kingdom has come! You, Peter, have earned that peace. For you, the Kingdom is here; it is now; it is yours!"

* * * * * *

The time had passed quickly. Peter was roused from his reverie by the sound of many footsteps in the corridor. There was the heavy tread of hobnailed boots.

Glaucus rattled his keys and drew the cell-door open. Surrounding him were prison guards and two tall legionaries in battle dress, their polished helmets gleaming.

Mencius edged past them and entered.

"You have only a moment, Proconsul!" muttered Glaucus. "Let there be no tarrying!"

"Is it well with you, Peter?" asked Mencius, in a half-whisper.

"Yes, good Mencius," said Peter, "I am quite ready."

"Have you a final request? Is there anything I can do?"

"I wish you would go to the home of Senator Gallio," said Peter in a steady voice, "and ask to see the old steward, Marcipor. Give Marcipor my abiding love and tell him to be a shepherd to my little flock. Tell him to say to them that the Kingdom will come, but they must not expect it to reign now—except in their hearts; for the world is not yet ready to receive the King."

"Come now!" commanded Glaucus. "Time is up."

Peter moved slowly toward the door. There he paused for another word with Mencius.

"Last night in a dream I saw the King. He was standing on a high hill, gazing entreatingly into the far distance, across the mountains, plains and seas. And I heard him saying, in sorrow:

" 'You would not come unto me that you might have life!' "